About the Author

Rich Newman (Tennessee) has been investigating the paranormal for over ten years and is the founder of the group Paranormal Inc. He is also a filmmaker whose first feature film, a documentary called *Ghosts of War*, will be released in 2011. His articles have appeared in *Haunted Times* and *Paranormal Underground*. Learn more about his investigations at www.paranormal incorporated.com.

To Write to the Author

If you wish to contact the author or would like more information about this book, please write to the author in care of Llewellyn Worldwide and we will forward your request. Both the author and publisher appreciate hearing from you and learning of your enjoyment of this book and how it has helped you. Llewellyn Worldwide cannot guarantee that every letter written to the author can be answered, but all will be forwarded. Please write to:

Rich Newman
ᶜ/o Llewellyn Worldwide
2143 Wooddale Drive
Woodbury, MN 55125-2989

Please enclose a self-addressed stamped envelope for reply,
or $1.00 to cover costs. If outside the U.S.A., enclose
an international postal reply coupon.

Many of Llewellyn's authors have websites with additional information and resources. For more information, please visit our website at:

www.llewellyn.com

THE GHOST HUNTER'S FIELD GUIDE

OVER 1000 HAUNTED PLACES YOU CAN EXPERIENCE

RICH NEWMAN

Llewellyn Publications
Woodbury, Minnesota

First Edition, 2011
First Printing, 2011

Book design and layout by Joanna Willis
Cover design by Kevin R. Brown
Cover images: house on hill © iStockphoto.com/Jarek Szymanski;
    road sign © iStockphoto.com/Julien Grondin
Interior illustrations of the states © Art Explosion Image Library

Llewellyn is a registered trademark of Llewellyn Worldwide Ltd.

Library of Congress Cataloging-in-Publication Data
Newman, Rich.
  The ghost hunter's field guide : over 1000 haunted places you can experience / Rich Newman.
      p. cm.
  Includes bibliographical references and index.
  ISBN 978-0-7387-2088-3
  1. Haunted places. 2. Ghosts. I. Title.
  BF1461.N49 2011
  133.10973—dc22
                              2010042499

Llewellyn Publications
A Division of Llewellyn Worldwide Ltd.
2143 Wooddale Drive
Woodbury, MN 55125-2989
www.llewellyn.com

Printed in the United States of America

33090014601811

CONTENTS

INTRODUCTION:
HOW TO USE THIS GUIDE

Everywhere you look nowadays there are ghost hunters. They're on television, in the movies and storming the net in greater force day by day. We watch the shows, read the books, and listen to the legends, but what is it that we really want to do?

We want to experience a haunting for ourselves.

I personally have been investigating the paranormal for over a decade (I have a paranormal investigations group in Memphis, Tennessee, called Paranormal Inc.), and I have captured audio, visual, and photographic evidence of a haunting many times. Since I have been in Paranormal Inc., getting to the locations has not been that difficult—oftentimes we are directly contacted by places to come out and visit them. As an individual/amateur ghost hunter, though, this is not usually the case. It's often quite difficult for the beginning investigator to get out into the field to begin researching and investigating the paranormal.

That's where this guide comes in. This book you are holding in your hands contains over 1,100 haunted locations all across the United States—and every one of them can be visited by you. There are no locations in this book that

will pan out to be ruins, or end up on closed, private property—or that's simply too dangerous for you to visit. These are all locations you can actually go to. Sometimes it's as easy as simply driving there. At other times, it may mean buying a meal or checking into a hotel to see the site. Either way, they are accessible to you and you can visit and experience them all.

You will also notice as you read about the individual haunted locations in this book that there are no cemeteries listed here. This is because I do not encourage ghost hunters to go to cemeteries; a cemetery is a place for family and friends to honor the memories of their loved ones, not a place for strangers to desecrate. Yes, I know, you are a responsible paranormal investigator. Unfortunately, though, there are many "ghost hunters" out there who are actually thrill seekers, so sending them to cemeteries is always a bad idea.

The listings in this book are alphabetized by state and city and contain specific information and history about each haunted location, as well as the paranormal activity that occurs there. I have verified each haunting through at least two separate sources (listed in the back of the book) to make sure of the validity of the tales. There is also a "legend" featured after each listing that you can use to interpret the specifics of that haunting, such as the type of spirit there (residual hauntings are marked as such) and the experiences associated with the site (this is helpful when determining the equipment you may want to take along with you).

All of us at Paranormal Inc. are staunch "anti-orb" folks. Ghost lights (actual, visible glowing balls of light) we document. Dust, bugs, water condensation, etc. that show up as "orbs" in photos/video we do not. They are not indicators of haunted activity. That said, I have "orbs" listed as an activity type in this book. But when I list a location as having orbs, I mean REAL orbs (ghost lights). The same is also true of "mists" that have been documented at haunted sites; these are true, paranormal mists, not the product of condensation, smoke or anything else that can be explained away as a natural occurrence.

I have also included Web addresses and directions when necessary for finding the places within this book—as well as specific rooms and areas within the sites to concentrate your investigation on. All of this will be helpful when planning your trip.

There are a few things to keep in mind, though, before traveling to any of these locations:

1. Plan ahead. If you are visiting a restaurant, B&B/hotel, or museum, you should call and make reservations to visit there if possible. These are places of business and with haunted tourism at an all time high, you don't want to drive all that way and not be able to get in! Not to mention the fact that places do go out of business. Also consider that a lot of these locations are quite historic and frequently undergo renovations, so check out their website or contact them to make sure they are open before visiting.

2. Dress appropriately. Some of these sites are outside locations (such as battlefield parks); so check on the weather before going there. Plan for rain/inclement

weather as well—not only for yourself, but for any gear you may take along.

3. State and national parks are not usually open at night. If you're going to investigate a park after hours, you need permission either from the park itself or local authorities. Going into a park at night without permission is trespassing, and this practice gives all ghost hunters a bad name. That said, a lot of these same parks offer camping.

4. Consider a day investigation. Despite popular belief, ghosts do not just come out at night. Investigating in the daytime is safer, involves fewer logistics, and can be done with relative ease. It also offers opportunities that you would not otherwise get—such as taking a tour within a haunted museum.

5. Respect the location. Leave everything as you found it and don't ruin a good haunted place for future visitors. If you're at a haunted B&B or hotel, limit your investigation to your room (try to reserve one of the most haunted—they are usually designated in the individual listings) and the hallways/common areas of the hotel once everyone is asleep. If there are more areas you'd like to explore within the location, ask the manager for permission first—you'd be surprised what you can get when you ask. And, never, ever trespass!

6. Keep your group small—but make sure you're not alone. The more people you take with you, the more noise you make. This pollutes your evidence/data and limits your chances of experiencing anything at the site. You do want to take one person with you, though, if for no other reason than safety.

7. Be safe. Don't take unnecessary chances. Watch your step in the dark, stay in

safe areas, and keep your partner close at hand. It will keep you from panicking when you experience something paranormal and will supply you with another set of ears/eyes that will help you separate what's going on around you from your mind playing tricks on you.

If you follow these guidelines you will have a pleasurable and exciting experience in the field. Have fun, be a responsible investigator, and let me know how you did. If you have a haunted location that's not listed in this book, send it along to me at the e-mail address below—maybe it'll turn up in the next edition!

RICH NEWMAN
Paranormal Inc
www.paranormalincorporated.com
info@paranormalincorporated.com

ACTIVITY KEY

A–**Apparition.** The visible spirit of a former living being. They are sometimes said to glow or emanate a single color (most often white). Most often they are "see-through," though they can also appear as a solid living person who usually disappears in front of the observer.

C–**Cold Spots.** This is a commonly reported phenomenon. It's said that when a ghost draws near, he or she will need energy in order to manifest itself or to perform any actions. As a result, they draw the ambient heat from an area to this end. That spot is then said to feel cold.

E–**Audio or EVP (Electronic Voice Phenomena).** Sometimes the actual disembodied voice of an entity can be heard—or even music. This is an actual audio experience. At other times, the voices of spirits are only heard after reviewing an audio recorder. This is called an EVP. These are usually collected because the microphone of the recorder is more sensitive than our actual ears are.

M–**Mists.** Sometimes when an entity is trying to manifest, there is not enough energy to fully form an apparition. This can appear as a "misty" person or a mist.

N–**Phantom Scents or Aromas.** Self-explanatory. Usually the scent of tobacco, perfume, or food.

O–**Orbs/Ghost Lights.** This is the most commonly overused classification of paranormal activity. Orbs are not the small bits of dust or moisture that are commonly captured using flash photography, but actual glowing balls of light that are visible to the human eye.

R–**Residual Haunting.** Rather than actually being the soul or spirit of the former living, this type of haunting is the simple recording of an event in time that seems to replay over and over again. When a listing does not have this type of haunting noted, the activity at the site is considered to be of an "Intelligent" nature. This means the spirit has the ability to interact with his or her environment and was once alive.

S–**Shadow Shapes.** When an entity lacks enough energy to manifest in detail, he or she will often simply appear as a large black mass—sometimes in the actual shape of a living person.

T–**Telekinetic or PK Activity.** In simple terms, this is when a ghost has the ability to physically move something. This usually requires an inordinate amount of energy, so this phenomenon is usually accompanied either by cold spots or in the area of a large electromagnetic field.

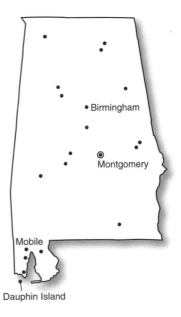

Mobile

Dauphin Island

ALABAMA

Albertville Albertville Public Library

Built in 1963, the first stand-alone library of Albertville, Alabama, is known for the Winston Walker Jr. Civil War Collection, a top-notch rare book room, and for being haunted! Some say the spirit(s) there are the product of a place that existed on the property prior to the construction of the library. Unfortunately, the exact identities of those that haunt the building have yet to be discovered. Activity occurs during the night and early mornings of the library—usually the kind of activity associated with an intelligent haunt—and includes faucets and lights that turn on/off and the opening/closing of doors (to include the elevator). Employees of the library have also heard the sounds of footsteps and banging in areas where nobody is present at the time. The library is, of course, open to the public, so plan your visit today.

Address: 200 Jackson Street
Website: www.albertvillelibrary.org
Activity: T, E

Anniston The Victoria

A Victorian mansion built in 1888, The Victoria is now owned and operated by Jacksonville State University. The home is listed on the National Register of Historic Places and has housed several prominent Anniston family members over the years. Today, the place is a bed and breakfast and has been the site of many strange occurrences. The spirit of a female in period dress (Victorian, of course) has been seen many times within the home. Usually she is spotted on the stairs or at the top of the staircase on the second floor, though she is also known for hanging around the downstairs piano as well. On occasion, the piano can be heard playing throughout the house. Other activity centers on the downstairs bar where glasses have been known to move and be heard hitting one another. The B&B is still open, and as mentioned above, is operated by the university.

Address: 1604 Quintard Avenue
Website: www.thevictoria.com
Activity: A, E

Auburn Auburn University Chapel

Known as the oldest original building at Auburn University (the chapel was built in 1851), this old Greek Revival property has existed as many different things over the years: a Presbyterian church, a Civil War hospital, and a theater, to name a few. It was after the building was renovated in a Gothic style, though, that things began to happen at the old chapel. Visitors to the site have reported a male ghost that has been seen throughout the place—as well as heard! Known as "Sydney Grimlett," the spirit is said to have been one of the Confederate soldiers who passed away in the place during the hospital period. He is said to be an Englishman who fought for the Southern forces, and he is most known for his activity during the years the building operated as a theater. During productions, he would open and close doors (and lock them as well), move props that were needed, and could be heard generally making a racket throughout the place. Today, the chapel is open to the public and can even be rented for events.

Address: 139 South College Street
Website: www.auburn.edu
Activity: T, E, A

Bay Minette Bay Minette Public Library

Opened in December of 1930, the Bay Minette Public Library has seen many hardships over the years—not the least of which was the Depression, which caused a constant struggle for the library to keep books in serviceable condition. Today, of course, this is no problem. The library is said to have a fine collection of reading material—as well as several ghosts known for staring out the library's windows at night! Local legend has it that the library was built on the site of a turn-of-the-century morgue, but this has never been confirmed. What has been confirmed, though, is the many visitors to the location that have witnessed the strange faces peering from dark windows at night. People have also been known to see books moving of their own volition and "dark shadow shapes" that seem to dart between the rows of books. You can visit the library Monday through Saturday to see for yourself.

Address: 205 West Second Street
Website: www.cityofbayminette.org
Activity: A, S, T

Bayou La Batre/Coden Gwodz Road

Though it smacks of an urban legend, Gwodz Road (located just east of the Alabama towns of Bayou La Batre and Coden) has been known for decades as an extremely haunted area of the state. Legend—and history—states that the area was well known for illegal hangings held by racist individuals and groups there (such as the Ku Klux Klan). Most of the hauntings that occur up and down this road seem to occur around old trees that locals state were used for the hangings. Several paranormal groups have investigated this area and have gotten great results: strange mists and shadow shapes have been photographed around the trees and EVPs (Electronic Voice Phenomena) have also been captured that seem to suggest the presence of at least one entity. Gwodz Road is a safe place, but you may want to let the local sheriff know about your visit beforehand if you decide to investigate this location.

Address: South Intersection of Patruski Road
Activity: S, M, E

Birmingham Sloss Furnaces

Founded by Colonel James Withers Sloss in 1882, the Sloss Furnaces has been well known as a haunted location for many years. Being an ironworks, a few workers did perish on the job, usually from poisonous gases coming from the furnace before the factory was mechanized in 1920. However, men also died from exposure to sudden blasts of steam while working with or repairing the equipment. Their skin would literally be cooked off. Sloss Furnaces was recognized as a National Historic Landmark in 1981 and now operates as an industrial museum that offers tours, educational programs, and metal arts classes to the public on a regular basis. The paranormal activity seems to take place both inside and outside the main building. Theophilus Jowers, an actual blast furnace foreman who suffered a fiery death when he fell into the top of the Little Alice Furnace, is reputed to walk the stairs, catwalks, and dark hallways of the place and is often seen as a black mass darting about the property. There is also a music venue on the site that is known for the entity appearing above the stage area. Catch a concert here or take a tour to experience the place at its best.

Address: 20 32nd Street North
Website: www.slossfurnaces.com
Activity: S, A

Birmingham The Tutwiler Hotel

Known to locals as the second coming of the infamous Tutwiler (the first was imploded by the city in 1973), the first incarnation of this hotel was built in 1914 by Major E. M. Tutwiler. It was later known as the Ridgley Apartments over the years prior to the construction of the second hotel. The Tutwiler is listed on the National Register of Historic Places and is known by the employees as the stalking grounds of a spirit called "The Knocker." People who stay in the hotel have reported hearing a strange knocking on their door in the middle of the night (especially on the sixth floor of the hotel) and, after investigation, found nobody in the hall. Other paranormal occurrences in the hotel have been witnessed in the kitchen area of the hotel where employees have had lights and stoves turn themselves on. Reservations for the hotel can be made online at the hotel's website.

Address: 2021 Park Place North
Website: www.thetutwilerhotel.com
Activity: E, T

Camden Gaines Ridge Dinner Club

The Gaines Ridge Dinner Club, formerly known as the Hearn Place, was built in 1827 and is known throughout the Camden area as a haunted location—mostly because the "history" of the haunt there is written right on the restaurant menu! Visitors to the eatery have seen a white form on the stairs and in windows, and have heard the sounds of a spirit that often imitates others within the establishment. The owner of the club was even once fooled into thinking a cook was screaming for her—but, of course, it was not the cook making the sounds. The sources of the haunting seem to center around two events—the first of which involves a baby that was accidentally smothered by her mother while the two were sleeping in the same bed. The second event involves a downstairs restroom where the sounds of someone falling have often been heard. One customer even reported finding the bathroom door unmovable, as if a person were lying on the floor behind it. Sounds of the baby crying have been heard in the upstairs area of the house and the smells of a pipe being smoked have been experienced in the place as well.

Address: 933 Highway 10 East
Website: www.wilcoxwebworks.com/gr/
Activity: A, E, N, R

Dauphin Island Fort Gaines

Constructed between 1853 and 1861—and named after General Edmund Pendleton Gaines—this old fort on Dauphin Island has had its fair share of history…both normal and paranormal. The battlement was involved in the Civil War (Battle of Mobile Bay being the most prominent warfare there) and the Spanish American War. Spirits from both battles have been seen at this place over the years, not only at the fort, but all over the surrounding area to include a campground. The most common apparition seen is a male soldier dressed in a Confederate uniform. He is often spotted standing beside one of the cannons overlooking the bay. This apparition is also known to have followed visitors as they are leaving the fort.

Address: 51 Bienville Boulevard
Website: www.dauphinisland.org
Activity: A

Enterprise The Rawls Hotel

Originally named the McGee Hotel, Japheth and Elizabeth Rawls built the hotel in 1903 to serve as a place for travelers along the railroad to stay. Just after the end of World War I, the Rawls Hotel became known for something altogether different, though—ghosts. Hot spots in the hotel include the basement, the entire third floor, and most areas in the original 1903 section. (The hotel had an addition built in the 1920s.) The basement (now a wine cellar) is said to be haunted by Mr. Rawls himself, with his apparition often being seen there. The third floor seems to be the roaming area of the spirit of a female child that has often been heard laughing. Her spirit has been seen in several rooms—and she has been known to move items placed within them. In addition to these spirits, guests and employees have reported seeing a young boy standing on the stairs of hotel between the cellar and first floor.

Address: 116 South Main Street
Website: www.rawlsbandb.com
Activity: A, E, T

Guntersville The Whole Backstage Theatre

More than just a theatre, the WBT is known as a community gathering place in Guntersville. Children and adults who are interested in learning about the arts, acting, and even just enjoying the occasional production have been frequenting the local establishment for more than 30 years. The theatre is also known for possessing a very unique ghost—a pyromaniac. Throughout the years, reports of spontaneous fires breaking out in strange places have taken place in the building—including a mattress that burst into flames unexpectedly one day. Folks who have regularly spent time in the theatre say the spirit is that of an old man who was a pyromaniac. Interestingly, the only sounds of spirit activity in the place have been attributed to a small boy who is often heard in the backstage area of the building. Purchase a ticket to one of their wonderful productions—a trip worthy in and of itself—to see if something paranormal happens to you there.

Address: 1120 Rayburn Avenue
Website: www.wholebackstage.com
Activity: E, T

Jasper Camax Mill Bridge

Located north of the town of Jasper, Alabama, on Country Club Road, the Camax Mill Bridge is certainly not an intimidating structure. It's a small, one-lane bridge perched over the Black Water Creek that could easily be passed by without a second look—unless that second look involved seeing a ghost! For decades, the Camax Mill Bridge outside Jasper has been a spot for paranormal investigators to get their feet wet. Sightings there have included apparitions, strange sounds, and black shadow shapes all along the bridge, as well as under the bridge and along the banks of the creek. Locals have dubbed the spirit as "Moon Mullins" (a nickname that has been used many times over the years in this area of Alabama), though no history of this person has actually emerged—much less the association of the entity with the bridge. One thing is certain though—there have been consistent reports of activity on this bridge for almost 50 years!

Address: Country Club Road
Website: www.jaspercity.com
Activity: A, S, E

Mobile Seaman's Bethel Theater

The Seaman's Bethel Theater, located on the campus of the University of Southern Alabama, is also called the Honor's Center. Having existed long before the creation of the university, the place was just sort of swallowed up by the school over the years. It is in the basement of this theater that the paranormal activity is said to occur. The area is said to be haunted by a female child that is often heard playing there. Actors/production personnel have also reported costumes being moved around during productions. Other visitors to the place have stated that there is a second entity—known to those there as a "seaman"—who reputedly haunts the upper area above the stage.

Address: On Campus on USA Drive South
Website: www.southalabama.edu
Activity: E, T

Mobile USS Alabama

After being decommissioned following World War II, the USS Alabama has been perched in the Mobile Bay, pleasing tourists and history buffs from all over the world since 1965. Dubbed the "Mighty A" during the war, the battleship saw its fair share of warfare and disaster. Today, the ship is the centerpiece of a wonderful state park and offers daily tours to visitors. Though you will get no official opinion about the haunting of the ship, visitors over the years have consistently reported hearing the sounds of people walking in the sleeping quarters of the ship while nobody else was present. There have also been reports of a spirit who likes to tug at people's clothing as they visit the cooks' galley and officers' quarters. If you are interested, you can visit the USS Alabama every day of the year except Christmas.

Address: 2703 Battleship Parkway
Website: www.ussalabama.com
Activity: E, T

Montevallo University of Montevallo

The university in Montevallo dates back to 1896 and has had ghost stories circulating about it since its creation. The first, and most well known, spirit is said to be that of Henry Clay Reynolds, a captain during the Civil War. He is often seen in different spots on the campus grounds, but always outside. The second entity on campus is said to be that of Condie Cunningham, a girl who lived in the Old Residence Hall in 1908 (when the school was called the Alabama Girls Industrial School). Condie is said to have burned to death in her bed one night and now roams the fourth floor of the residence hall to this day. Students who stay there have heard female screams, cries for help, and the sounds of footsteps running down the hallway. A third ghost is also said to haunt the historic King House on campus. This spirit is thought to be Edmund King (a past resident of the house) and is often seen peering from windows there—presumably guarding a treasure that was rumored to be buried in the area.

Address: Visitor Center is at Oak and Middle
   Streets
Website: www.montevallo.edu
Activity: A, E

Montgomery Lucas Tavern

This old tavern and stagecoach stop was originally located east of Montgomery in an area now known as Waugh. It served as an overnight stop for travelers to get a meal and bed before continuing on their journey. Today, the place is part of the Old Alabama Town exhibit. It's said that the spirit of one Eliza Lucas—a previous owner of the tavern during the 1830s—now haunts this old building. People have witnessed her apparition within the tavern, as well as peering through windows and doors. Other activity in the tavern includes footsteps and, occasionally, the voice of Eliza. Old Alabama Town offers tours of the site, as well as the tavern, so visiting this location is a must if you are in the area.

Address: 301 Columbus Street
Website: www.oldalabamatown.com
Activity: A, E

Montgomery State Capitol Building

After the original Capitol of Alabama burned down in 1849, the state decided to build a second capitol building on top of the ruins of the first. It was completed in 1851 and designed in a Greek Revival style that was very popular at the time. Today, in addition to serving as the capitol, the building is a museum to Alabama politics and history—including the spot where Jefferson Davis took the oath as President of the Confederate States of America. Paranormal activity in the building seems to happen mostly on the second floor of building where employees have seen what they describe as a "Confederate woman" roaming the halls and offices. Others have reported faucets turning on and off by themselves as well. The capitol building is open to the public Monday through Friday.

Address: 600 Dexter Avenue
Website: www.preserveala.org
Activity: A, T

Opelika Spring Villa Plantation

When you think of the South and haunted homes, you think of plantations. That said, the Spring Villa Plantation in Opelika, Alabama, is probably one of the most haunted antebellum homes in the state. Built in 1850 by William Penn Yonge, Spring Villa has been reputedly a haunted place since the late 1800s. The entity that is said to roam the halls is none other than Yonge himself. He was known by locals to be cruel to the slaves that resided on the plantation, and it is said that one of these slaves hid in a small niche just above the thirteenth step of the home's spiral staircase. When Yonge passed by, the slave leaped out and stabbed his owner to death on the stairs. Today, this stair is avoided by those who don't wish to anger the spirit of Yonge. His apparition has been seen peering through upstairs windows, on the stairs, and roaming the upstairs halls of the house. Visiting the plantation is easy since it is now located within a park in Opelika. The park grounds also contain picnic shelters, a swimming pool, and even a campground.

Address: On Spring Villa Road
Website: www.opelika.org
Activity: A

Parrish Jack's Family Restaurant

Jack's is a chain of restaurants that has locations throughout the state of Alabama. But only one of them is known for paranormal activity—the Jack's located in the city of Parrish! Visitors to this eatery have reported seeing doors open and close by themselves, as well as feeling unnatural "cold spots" in the bathrooms. Over the years, most of the activity there has been reported by employees. They have experienced equipment in the kitchen turning itself on and off, strange voices speaking from the drive-through speaker, and objects being knocked off the shelves throughout the cooking area.

Address: 6258 Highway 269
Website: www.eatatjacks.com
Activity: T, E, C

Saraland Kali Oka Road

With names like "Deadman's Curve" and "Cry Baby Bridge," the Kali Oka Road in Saraland, Alabama, can be quite an intimidating locale. Add in the fact that locals have been telling strange tales about this area for many years and you've got a trip worthy of taking. Besides being home to a foreboding plantation house that has been used in several horror movies, the road itself, and a bridge located on it, is said to be haunted. Visitors down Kali Oka have often seen the ghost of a large black man—thought to be a vengeful ex-slave—walking the route to and from the plantation house. The sounds of a small baby crying have also been reported in the area of the bridge along the road. Though all the stories involving the entity are just that—stories—one thing is certain: there are strange sounds and sights along the Kali Oka Road.

Address: Kali Oka Road
Website: www.saraland.org
Activity: A, E

Selma St. James Hotel

Built in 1837, this hotel was originally known as the Brantley Hotel—named after General John Brantley. Over the course of its existence, the building has served as a trade center, a Confederate army distribution center, and a hideout for Jesse James and his gang. The latter event is the main reason the place is known to be haunted. It is said that in 1881, Jesse James spent a great deal of time at the hotel due to a woman there named "Lucinda" that soon became James's mistress. Current visitors to the site have reported seeing both of them still residing and walking the halls of the St. James Hotel. James himself has been seen sitting at the bar, as well as at a corner table in the dining room. Both spirits have also been witnessed in Rooms 214, 314, and 315 of the hotel. Room 305 is known for bright balls of light—or orbs—that float through the room. In addition to these tales, it is also said that the spirit of a dog is often heard throughout the hotel, including the courtyard.

Address: 1200 Water Avenue
Website: www.historichotels.org/hotel/
    St_James_Hotel_Selma
Activity: A, E, O

Selma Sturdivant Hall

This mansion, which was erected in 1853, has been known as a haunted location in Alabama for over a century. It is said to be haunted by John McGee Parkman, the second owner of the house, who drowned in a river while trying to escape prison. (He was imprisoned for using bank funds for unauthorized investments.) Visitors to the mansion have spotted Parkman in various locations throughout the house: the parlor, upstairs bedrooms, and the staircase, just to name a few. His presence is usually accompanied by the movement of objects—usually a door—though sometimes his apparition is simply seen gazing out a window. The home is now a historic site that can be toured. Get the current times for these—as well as a listing of other events at this location—on their website.

Address: 713 Mabry Street
Website: www.sturdivanthall.com
Activity: A, T

Thomasville White Lion Inn

Though there isn't a lot to be said about the White Lion Inn itself—a simple home-turned-B&B—there are plenty of people talking about the paranormal activity happening there! People who have stayed in the place—particularly the upstairs guest rooms—have reported feeling uneasy, as if somebody or something is constantly watching them. Many have even said the place gave them severe nightmares, or night terrors, as they are sometimes called. Misty apparitions have been seen shooting through walls and down the hallways, as well as in the bathrooms on the upper floor. Many have also experienced intense cold spots mysteriously appearing in odd locations. Rooms in this B&B are limited, so be sure to book in advance if visiting (Since they have no website, you may want to call information for a phone number.)

Address: 230 West 3rd Street South
Website: www.thomasvilleal.com
Activity: A, C, M

Tuscumbia/Hillsboro Belle Mont Mansion

Known as one of the best examples of a Palladian-style house in the American South, the Belle Mont is a mansion with direct links to Thomas Jefferson, as well as famed architect Andrea Palladio. The haunting of the Belle Mont, however, is associated with yet another part of the home's history that is not so glorious. During the years prior to the Civil War, the mansion was the home to many slaves, and it is said that the place is still haunted by several of them. Throughout the house and the grounds, the apparitions of former slaves are seen roaming—especially in the basement where the shackles that once held them are still present. Today, Belle Mont is being renovated, but is open to the public by for tours. Check out their website in advance for times and dates.

Address: Cook Lane, three miles south of intersection US 43 and US 72
Website: www.preserveala.org
Activity: A, S

Tuscumbia Winston House

Currently a part of Deshler High School, the Winston House (sometimes called the Winston Plantation) is said to be haunted by the original owner, William Winston—though it is also thought that he may not be the only spirit located within the place. A room within the house that's called the Maude Lindsay Room has been the site of several eyewitness accounts of an apparition (thought to be Winston), as well as the usual sounds of footsteps and voices. As mentioned above, the place is part of a current high school, so visit or call the office to find out tour/visitor information prior to traveling there.

Address: 200 East Commons Street North
Website: http://deshler.tch.schoolinsites.com
Activity: A, E

ALASKA

Anchorage Chilkoot Charlie's

As one of the more happening joints in Alaska, Chilkoot Charlie's is already quite popular with the local crowd. Besides featuring great drinks and a stage that hosts national acts, the place is also the home to a frisky male ghost. Female visitors to the bar have felt a male presence—sometimes literally, as he enjoys grabbing women by the arm—in the restrooms as well as in the main bar area. A male voice has also been heard on occasion in the same areas. Employees of the bar have reported beers that seem to move down the bar on their own as well.

Address: 1071 West 25th Avenue
Website: www.koots.com
Activity: T, E

Anchorage Courtyard by Marriott

Ghosts don't always just frequent old homes—sometimes they linger at modern, chain establishments as well. Such is the case of the Marriott hotel in Anchorage. The hotel is known for several haunted rooms, though only one has any real weight to it. Room 201 of this hotel apparently had a guest who stayed beyond the normal checkout time; he passed away in this room and apparently was not found for a while. According to some sources, there is also a spirit that the hotel has named "Ken" who is known for haunting the courtyard along with rooms 103 and 107. Reports vary on this site, but no activity has been reported other than seeing the occasional glimpse of Ken or the gentleman in Room 201.

Address: 4901 Spenard Road
Website: www.marriott.com
Activity: A

Anchorage Diamond Center Mall

Local rumors/legend says that this mall was built upon a burial site for a local tribe of Alaskan Native Americans. Because of the age of the graves—and the fact that there were only a few of them—construction was permitted to continue. Though no construction crew involved with the building of the mall can verify this, local paranormal groups say the story is true. Paranormal activity in the mall seems to center around the bathrooms, where investigators say voices are heard and photographs containing true orbs and mists have been captured over the years.

Address: 800 East Diamond Boulevard
Website: www.diamondcenter.com
Activity: E, M, O

Anchorage The Historic Anchorage Hotel

Built in 1916, the Anchorage is known as the only hotel listed on the National Register of Historic Places in Anchorage. The hotel is also known locally for its paranormal activity. With characteristics of both residual and intelligent haunts, the Anchorage is said to be inhabited by a young girl who frequents the second floor of the hotel. Notably, rooms 215 and 217 are most often the site of her appearance—though she also has been witnessed many times in the hallway. She makes her presence known in the rooms by turning faucets and the television on and off. The residual part of the haunt seems to center around "crowd noises" that seem to emanate from the stairway. Employees of the hotel have reported hearing them many times. There are no entities seen on the stairs, though—they're just heard.

Address: 330 East Street
Website: www.historicanchoragehotel.com
Activity: E, A, T

Anchorage Inlet Towers

Paranormal activity at the Inlet Towers has been reported for many years. According to guests and employees alike, there are several entities that seem to wander the place. The most common is that of a little girl who is known for playing on the ground floor. She is often seen in the hallways—and the sound of her laughter has also been reported on occasion. Another ghost—that of an adult male—has also been witnessed in the hotel's elevator. It is rumored that he is the spirit of a man that was killed while repairing the elevator. Finally, there is another male spirit that is

often seen entering the hotel from the street. This particular entity doesn't speak or notice anyone around him—leading investigators to believe that it is probably a residual spirit left behind from times past.

Address: 1200 L Street
Website: www.inlettower.com
Activity: E, A, R

Anchorage University of Alaska, Wendy Williamson Auditorium

Like most theaters, the WWA has had its fair share of ghost stories—some credible, some pretty far-fetched. In the far-fetched realm, there is reputedly a male entity that likes to manipulate the light switches for the stage and gets a kick out of pushing people around—literally. Students of UAA say the spirit has pushed female students down the stairs in the facility before. But nobody can actually name a student! In the credible arena, there have been reports for many years of a woman dressed all in white who has been seen in various locations throughout the theater. Local sources in Anchorage say reports of this particular apparition have been making their rounds with paranormal groups for quite a while—and the stories have weight because witnesses have stepped forward to report the occurrences. Visit the campus and take a tour there for yourself.

Address: Corner of Lake Otis Parkway and
  Providence Drive
Website: www.uaa.alaska.edu
Activity: A, T

Chugiak Birchwood Saloon

The haunting of the Birchwood Saloon in Chugiak, Alaska, is a pretty recent affair. Workers at the watering hole credit the death of a local for the haunting; it seems he was shoveling snow off the roof of a neighboring building when he accidentally hit a hot power line. Rather than spend an eternity wallowing in despair on said rooftop, he opted instead to haunt the bar next door. Employees of the bar say the spirit is fond of typical Poltergeist-like activity: he often turns the jukebox on/off without warning, plays with the lights, and likes to entertain the folks there by moving various items around the bar. In addition to this activity, patrons have reported seeing an apparition of the man at times and hearing an odd voice in areas of the bar where nobody is currently hanging out. Head up to Chugiak, grab a drink, and see if you can catch a glimpse of the ghost there.

Address: 20145 Pilots Road
Activity: A, T

Chugiak Native Village of Eklutna

When Russian settlers introduced the Russian Orthodox Christian religion to the local Native Americans in the 1700s, the result was a strange belief system concerning death and the afterlife. Once a member of the tribe passed away, it was believed that he/she would walk the earth for a period of time, looking for their possessions before moving on to the otherworld. Rather than allow these spirits to bother the living, the members of the local tribes would instead build a tiny house over the grave of the deceased with some of their possessions—essentially giving him/her a place to inhabit during the "walk the earth" period. Over the years, many people have witnessed spirits moving throughout this park, which has made it a great place for beginning ghost hunters to get their feet wet.

Address: 26339 Eklutna Village Road
Website: www.eklutna-nsn.gov
Activity: M, A, E

Fairbanks Captain Bartlett Inn

Though this small hotel is relatively new compared to most other haunted hotels, the feel of this cabin-style lodge is that of the pioneer days of Alaska. In addition to the standard lodgings, the inn offers a top-notch bar/restaurant called the Dogsled Saloon & Roadhouse. Employees of this inn have been reporting paranormal activity

there for quite some time. It's said that barware has been witnessed moving, strange orbs have been spotted in various rooms, and the sounds of voices have been heard in various places. Since there doesn't seem to be any particular room associated with the haunting there, the only pinpointed hotspot is the saloon, so grab a room and plan your vigil around a meal and drink.

Address: 1411 Airport Way
Website: www.captainbartlettinn.com
Activity: O, T, E

Fairbanks Northern Lights Hotel

Ever since a young girl passed away on the third floor of this hotel, employees and guests alike have witnessed seeing her apparition and hearing her voice. Even when the hotel closed down the third floor because of complaints—and to try and understand how to deal with this unique sort of problem—the front desk reported receiving odd phone calls from unoccupied rooms on the floor. If you plan to visit the Northern Lights Hotel, you will want to stay on the third floor (naturally) if it is open—if not, go for the second floor. There have been guests who have, on occasion, reported seeing her there, too.

Address: 427 First Avenue
Website: www.explorefairbanks.com
Activity: A, E

Gakona Historic Gakona Lodge and Trading Post

The Gakona Lodge was built in 1929 and served as a rest stop for people traveling the Fairbanks-Valdez-Eagle trails. The place really took off when the Army Corps of Engineers improved the area's roads and built a "shower house" for the place in 1942. Today the lodge is all modern and caters to travelers who just want to get away for a while. On the paranormal front, the place is known for a male entity that seems to spend a lot of time in the upstairs area of the lodge, but prefers Room 5. In this room, he is known to play pranks on folks staying in this room, like opening/closing doors, messing with the bed, turning on the radio, etc. Employees of the lodge believe the spirit to be one John Paulsen, a former regular that passed away many years ago. Others have speculated that the spirit could be that of Jim Doyle—a man who loved the area and homesteaded it in the early 1900s. Doyle even built a roadhouse (the remains of which still stand) in the area the lodge now occupies.

Address: Mile 2 of Tok Cutoff Road
Website: www.gakonalodge.com
Activity: T

Girdwood Alyeska Resort

The hotel of this upscale resort is said to be haunted by a man named Chris who, according to locals, committed suicide in the hotel a few years ago. Chris is said to haunt two rooms in the hotel: Room 721 and Room 515. In both rooms, he is known to manipulate many of the objects, such as turning the television on/off, opening/closing doors (including the dresser), and playing with the faucets in the bathroom. Recently, a visitor to the resort reported seeing a man in Room 515 standing at the entrance of the bathroom. When the visitor attempted to speak to the person standing in his room, he simply disappeared.

Address: 1000 Arlberg Avenue
Website: www.alyeskaresort.com
Activity: A, T

Hatcher Pass Motherlode Lodge

Originally known as the Little Susitna Road-house, the Motherlode Lodge was built in 1942 by Victor Cottini. Today, the lodge experiences several different types of paranormal activity—from several different entities. The first seems to be a female apparition in a red dress who is often seen on the second floor. Many witnesses have seen this apparition. The second is a young girl who seems to inhabit Room 12. Her presence is made known by her lounging on the

bed or simply playing with the bed covers during the night. The third (and final) entity seems to be an older man who hangs around on the ground floor. He is known for moving objects in the bar area and is often heard there as well. Visitors to the lodge have also seen this man standing behind them when looking in the hallway mirror.

Address: In Hatcher Pass on the bank of the
　　Little Susitna River
Website: www.motherlodelodge.com
Activity: A, E, T

Juneau The Alaskan Hotel & Bar

The Alaskan is the oldest, still-operating hotel in Juneau, Alaska (it was established in 1913), and was built to service the booming mining industry. Of course, like most hotels of the day, this also meant the place had a thriving bar and prostitution business. It is said that the ghost that haunts the Alaskan today is a remnant of that past. Dubbed "Alice" by the employees of the hotel, the spirit is said to have been one of the more desired of the ladies of the night, who was killed one evening while on duty. Visitors who stay in the hotel stand a great chance of running into her, too! Her presence is especially known in three hotel rooms: 218, 219, and 308. She is usually accompanied by intense cold spots and she has been spotted—in the form of a misty object—in the rooms, as well as on the stairs. One visitor also reported experiencing a residual effect in one of the room's bathrooms; for a moment, the modern fixtures seemed to be those of a past long gone.

Address: 167 South Franklin
Website: www.thealaskanhotel.com
Activity: C, M, R, A

Kennecott Kennecott Mines

Since 1938, the town of Kennecott (also spelled "Kennicott"), Alaska, has stood uninhabited—at least by mortals anyway. After the area's mines were pretty much tapped, the entire camp packed up and left on the train. After the area was named a historic place, the National Park Service took over (loosely) taking care of the place. Located just down the way from the town of McCarthy, visitors to the ghost town should be careful, as many buildings are in horrible disrepair. If you visit, here is what you can expect—an eerie experience that many believe is caused by the residual spirits of the camp's mining past. As with most mines, many accidents occurred in Kennecott— quite a lot of them ending with death. Could the spirits of those accidents still haunt the area? Could be. Or it could be the residual effect of past activities trapped in the area being replayed for the public? Either way, expect to hear strange voices and sounds and to see what many say are the black shadow shapes of spirits trapped in the environment. Paranormal groups who have visited Kennecott have not been disappointed, as EVPs and strange photos are common. Proceed with caution…

Address: End of Edgerton Highway/McCarthy Road
Website: www.alaskaontheweb.com
Activity: S, R, E

Kotzebue Northwest Arctic Heritage Center

Formerly known as the NANA Museum of the Arctic, the area where the new Heritage Center is being built is known for a ghost story that is sketchy at best. Locals say that a young boy drowned under the museum in a pool of water that was created when snow began to melt. This story has not been verified—though several area investigators have attempted to do so. However, most agree that the building is haunted— though most probably by spirits of long gone Alaskan Natives. The entity is said to be playful and will move items left behind (such as a toy or ball) and will often mimic sounds that will draw you into a certain room—only to discover nobody is there. The new center should be open, but check in advance before traveling there.

Address: 100 Shore Avenue
Website: www.nps.gov/cakr/parknews/nwahc
Activity: T, E

Seward The Van Gilder Hotel

Dating back to 1916, the Van Gilder Hotel has seen its fair share of interesting visitors over the years. Past overnight occupants include famous local politicians, bankers, and entrepreneurs who stayed while scouting out possible future ventures. Today, the place is known for two paranormal visitors—both are apparitions that inhabit two distinct areas of the hotel. A female spirit that seems to reside in Room 202B is often seen at the foot of the bed and often heard talking at night. The second spirit is that of a man who likes to hang out in Room 308. He, too, has been recorded speaking in this room, though witnesses have not reported seeing his apparition.

Address: 308 Adams Street
Website: www.vangilderhotel.com
Activity: A, E

Sitka Rookie's Bar and Grill

Stories surrounding the ghost of this sports bar have been circulating through Sitka for quite some time. Locals believe that the building that Rookie's now inhabits is haunted by a woman who was struck by a drunk driver just outside the place. The area where the accident is said to occur, along with the sports bar, is said to often be filled with the sounds of a female screaming in pain. Activity has also carried over to inside of the bar as well. Patrons have caught the sounds of moaning and seen dark shapes moving quickly through the bar when nobody is in that area.

Address: 1615 Sawmill Creek Road
Activity: E, S

Skagway Golden North Hotel

Oftentimes, an entire city can be known for haunted activity. Paranormal investigators usually call this type of area a "portal." When a portal is present, it can cause many places to experience a lot of activity. Such is the case with Skagway, Alaska. Of the haunts within this city, the Golden North Hotel may be the most famous, though. The hotel is primarily known for two haunted rooms: Room 14 and Room 23. It is said that a woman (who the hotel calls "Mary") died of pneumonia in Room 23 while waiting for her betrothed to return from work. Today, that room still possesses her spirit. She is often seen standing in the room—and sometimes causes visitors to experience a choking sensation in their sleep. Room 14 is the site of glowing balls of light—or orbs—that dance around the room that many say is just another form of Mary.

Address: Corner of 3rd Avenue and Broadway Street
Website: www.skagwayoutlet.com/golden
Activity: A, T, O

Skagway Red Onion Saloon

With a past that includes being the area's most well-known brothel, the Red Onion Saloon is another of Skagway's most infamous haunts. Built in 1897, this house of ill repute was notorious with travelers in the area as a place to get a drink and a woman for the evening. Though the entire saloon was moved in 1914, the spirit of at least one of the previous occupants came along with it. The upstairs area of the saloon is said to be haunted by a female apparition that makes her presence known with the scent of a strong perfume. Footsteps are heard in this area as well—sometimes extending down onto the ground floor of the building. The Red Onion Saloon has a restaurant and a museum and is well worth a visit.

Address: 205 Broadway Street
Website: www.redonion1898.com
Activity: N, E

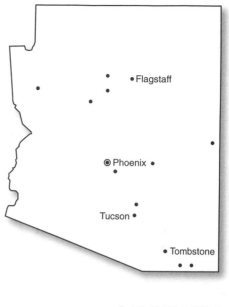

ARIZONA

Alpine Hannagan Meadow Lodge

Named after founder Robert Hannagan, the Meadow Lodge has been involved with ranching and homesteading in this area since 1926. With the establishment of a service station, restaurant, and cabins, the Hannagans serviced folks traveling along the newly formed Clifton-Springerville Highway. Several entities are said to haunt this historic lodge: a child who is heard laughing in the upstairs area, a Native American in full headdress that is seen walking outside, and a woman who is known as the "Lady of the Lodge." The latter is the most famous. She is often seen looking from upstairs windows in the lodge, as well as walking the second floor.

Address: U.S. Hwy 191, 22 Miles South of Alpine
Website: www.hannaganmeadow.com
Activity: A, E

Bisbee Bisbee Inn/Hotel La More

With a history dating back to the mid-1800s and the infamous OK Trail, the Bisbee Inn has played host to many visitors over the years—both living and dead! Probably the most common activity reported in the hotel is the sight of a young girl standing in the doorway of Room 23 (changed from the "unlucky" Room 13). The employees of the inn have dubbed this young lady "Abigail" and she has been witnessed many times—especially when the hotel has few guests. Another female is said to haunt the first floor as well. She is called "Michelle" and is said to have been a prostitute dating back to the early 1900s. The final spirit residing in the hotel—also a female—is said to be older and is seen in various rooms watching over the guests. All three spirits are reported to be of a good nature and all three make regular appearances to customers—even if it is just to lie down on their bed and mess up the covers a bit!

Address: 45 OK Street
Website: www.bisbeeinn.com
Activity: A, T

Bisbee Copper Queen Hotel

The Copper Queen has been standing watch over the town of Bisbee since 1902 and has served as a sort of "paranormal beacon" to investigators all over the world. The haunts of this hotel are well known and have been documented many times. As hotel employees will quickly tell you, the place is haunted by three entities—each of them distinct and active. The first, and probably the most famous, is a female entity believed to be Julia Lowell, a prostitute who frequented the hotel back in the day. She is known to haunt the second and third floors in rooms on the West side of the building; she does so by teasing visitors in their sleep by whispering in their ear, playing with their covers/feet, and appearing at the foot of the bed (sometimes dancing). The second ghost is a gentleman who is seen in a cape and top hat that prefers to appear as a shadow shape around the Teddy Roosevelt Room—his presence is evident by the smell of an invisible pipe. The final spirit is that of a young boy who is often heard laughing in the hallways. He is said to have drowned in the nearby San Pedro River. Rooms to rent: 210, 303, 304, 308, 312, and 412.

Address: 11 Howell Avenue
Website: www.copperqueen.com
Activity: A, S, T, E

Bisbee Oliver House Bed and Breakfast

Open year-round and located within a great area of Bisbee, the Oliver House is a comfortable and peaceful place to stay while visiting Arizona. So comfortable, that many of the local miners who used the house for boarding over the years have decided to stay on … According to the owner of the B&B, 27 people have died in the home—including one who was murdered. That man was Nathan Anderson, and he was shot to death in a room at the top of the stairs. Nathan is said to still roam the halls of the B&B and likes to open/close doors as well as bang the shutters in the Plum and Purple Sage rooms. A second ghost that haunts the house likes to visit the "Grandma" room. This is the spirit of an elderly woman who prefers to use the rocker in the room and is often seen staring out the window. The owner of the house will tell you that there are five ghosts in the house, and that one is violent (though not to guests). Could the violent spirit be Nathan? Go find out.

Address: 126 All Souls Avenue
Website: www.bisbeeoliverhouse.com
Activity: E, T, A, O, C

Chandler San Marcos Golf Resort

Serving as a Mecca of high luxury in the Southwest, the San Marcos has been providing first-class service since 1913. With visitors like President Herbert Hoover and Clark Gable, it's no wonder that Dr. Alexander Chandler—the founder of the town and hotel—would choose to stay in the hotel beyond the grave. Of course, it also helps that the ghost of a former mistress is also said to haunt the hotel (reportedly, she committed suicide on the property). Chandler, who also died in the hotel, is said to be heard at times moaning through the hallways and the areas of the first floor where people gather. The female ghost is often seen as a whispy figure in the upstairs hallways and on the staircase.

Address: 1 San Marcos Place
Website: www.sanmarcosresort.com
Activity: A, E

Douglas The Gadsden Hotel

The second incarnation of the Gadsden Hotel (built in 1929 after a fire destroyed the first version) is full of interesting stories: Pancho Villa riding into the hotel, Shelley Winters answering her hotel door nude, and Lee Marvin getting into tussles in the bar. But maybe the most interesting tale is that of a headless ghost that is said to haunt the establishment. The apparition is most often seen in the hotel's basement, but around the holidays (Christmas/New Year's) he seems to venture into the other parts of the hotel, making his presence known by moving items and wandering the halls. He is always seen as a misty shape—though some reports have described him as wearing black—and either headless or faceless.

Address: 1046 G Avenue
Website: www.hotelgadsden.com
Activity: A, T

Flagstaff Historic Hotel Monte Vista

The Monte Vista, a local hotel dating back to 1926, has many interesting tales surrounding it—some of which involve a haunting. There was a bank robber who died having his last drink in the hotel bar, two prostitutes who were thrown to their deaths from a balcony in Room 306, the spirit of a bellboy that haunts Room 210, the ghost of a strange man who hung meat from a chandelier who passed away in Room 220, and the cries of a ghostly infant that are heard from a long-empty basement. But the ghost that has made this hotel famous is that of its most active area: Room 305. Numerous reports of an older woman have been reported in this room—usually sitting in the old rocking chair that is stationed there.

Address: 100 North San Francisco Street
Website: www.hotelmontevista.com
Activity: E, A, S, R, T

Flagstaff Hotel Weatherford

Now a nationally recognized historic location, the Hotel Weatherford opened its doors for business in 1900 and hasn't stopped since. Not even for ghosts. Guests at the hotel have witnessed a female apparition that seems to enjoy hanging out in the ballroom. She is generally seen moving across the room at a high rate of speed, though she does sometimes play with the lights that hang over the pool tables. She is also known for whispering to guests in the bar area. The second story involving spirits at the Weatherford is a little more disturbing—at times, a man and woman are seen (dressed for a wedding) sitting in one of the upstairs rooms (though the room primarily known for this has since been turned into a storage area). Though it is thought to be a couple that committed suicide in the hotel in the 1930s, it is probably a residual haunt left behind by visitors long gone.

Address: 23 North Leroux Street
Website: www.weatherfordhotel.com
Activity: A, T, E, R

Flagstaff Museum Club

Known locally as one of the area's best music and dance clubs, the Museum Club is known nationally as an extremely haunted location. The bar is said to still be inhabited by a pair of previous owners that came to an untimely demise. The first to go was Thelma Scott, who fell down the stairs and broke her neck (the couple lived above the bar). Next to go was her husband, Don, who fell into despair after his wife's death and decided to take his own life in front of the fireplace. Customers who visit the club today have witnessed apparitions in the bar and on the staircase, and say that objects in the place tend to move on their own. The fireplace is also said to fire up on occasion all by itself.

Address: 3404 East Route 66
Website: www.museumclub.com
Activity: A, T

Globe Noftsger Hill Inn

If you're looking for a stay in a hotel that has a "schoolhouse" feel to it, then the Noftsger Hill Inn is for you. With rooms decked out with chalkboards and antiques, you will feel like you're visiting the school that used to exist in the building. Also occupying the premises is one of the area's most notorious residual haunts. Visitors over the years have reported hearing the sounds of children playing and phantom footsteps running up and down the halls. On occasion, these children become glowing balls of light (or orbs) that are seen shooting through walls into rooms and blasting up and down the hallways.

Address: 425 North Street
Website: www.noftsgerhillinn.com
Activity: O, R, E

Jerome Connor Hotel

The original incarnation of this hotel was built in 1898. After two fires and several remodeling jobs, the hotel is now a tribute to days past. Within the establishment, several rooms are known for a haunted past as well: Rooms 1, 2, and 4. Room 1 is known for a female entity that likes male visitors. Men who have stayed in this room report hearing whispering, female laughs, and a massive cold spot that creeps over the bed during the night to snuggle with them. Room 2 experiences a more PK (psychokinetic) style haunt with chairs that move and a ghost that likes to move/hide objects that the guests have in the room. Room 4 is haunted by an old man and his dog; both are seen and heard in this room, sometimes together.

Address: 164 Main Street
Website: www.connorhotel.com
Activity: A, T, E, C

Jerome Ghost City Inn Bed and Breakfast

Built in the Victorian Era as a boarding house, GCI is now a unique B&B with rooms that take you back to the late 1800s and rooms that are themed—such as the Northern Exposure Room. There are also two rooms that are known for being haunted. The Verde View Room is said to be haunted by a man believed to be a miner who stayed at the inn when it was a boarding house. He has been seen in the Verde View Room as well as the hallway just outside the room's door.

There is also a female spirit that is said to haunt the Cleopatra Hill Room. She has been seen on several occasions and has been heard during the night.

Address: 541 Main Street
Website: www.ghostcityinn.com
Activity: A, E

Jerome Jerome Grand Hotel

Starting out as the United Verde Hospital, the Jerome Grand Hotel has seen its fair share of sickness and death. Before becoming a hotel, the hospital serviced the area—which included many of the local mining camps—until 1950, when local mining was phased out. Paranormal activity has occurred in the hotel since it began restoration in 1994—though it is said that the ghosts were waiting in the building since operating as a hospital. A female nurse is the spirit seen most often; she seems to be a residual haunt that makes the rounds room to room to check in on patients. Another female entity is a woman in white, who is thought to be a young lady who died giving birth. She is often seen looking for her baby within the hotel and is more of an intelligent spirit, as she is often heard asking for help, her baby, etc. Other activity experienced throughout the hotel includes: coughs, whispers, voices, and the smells associated with living in a hospital.

Address: 200 Hill Street
Website: www.jeromegrandhotel.com
Activity: A, R, E, O, C

Kingman Hotel Brunswick/ Brunswick Bistro

Who haunts the Hotel Brunswick in Kingman, Arizona? It could be the Chinese railroad workers who were forced to use tunnels beneath the hotel to reach their homes after a hard day's work. Most likely, it is the spirits of the two original owners of the hotel: Mulligan and Thompson. Employees have witnessed what looks like two male apparitions climbing the basement stairs into the hotel. Other activity seems to revolve around the dining room/bar where stacks of old coins have been found stacked neatly on the bar, the sounds of old music has been heard, and dark shadows seem to scoot along the wall. Guests staying in the hotel's rooms have felt things tugging at them in their sleep—one guest even witnessed the apparition of a small boy in her room. Though it's unclear if the hotel is still open, there's still the Brunswick Bistro and Mulligan's Irish Pub in the building.

Address: 315 East Andy Divine Avenue
Website: www.kingmantourism.org
Activity: T, E, R, A, S

Oracle Acadia Ranch Museum

Built in 1882, the Acadia Ranch became a makeshift frontier hospital for tuberculosis patients shortly after opening. Like most locations associated with this horrible ailment, the Acadia saw a lot of death and misery—and it is reflected in the haunting at that location today. The two most prominent entities witnessed at the site are a nurse and an angry patient. The nurse acts much like a residual haunt and is seen "making her rounds." The male spirit—thought to be one of the many patients who died there—makes his presence known by throwing things and knocking things down. Portraits and pictures that are hung on the walls are often found lying on the floor after a night with nobody in the building. Today, the Acadia Ranch is a museum and a tribute to the past. They have limited hours, so you may want to check them out in advance via their website before visiting.

Address: 825 Mount Lemmon Road
Website: www.oraclehistoricalsociety.org
Activity: T, A, R

Phoenix Hotel San Carlos

The San Carlos was built in 1927 on the site of the area's first schoolhouse—a fact that is made even more interesting when you consider the school house was built on a site that local Native Americans say was involved with worshipping their "God of Learning." Three boys—attendees of that school—are now said to haunt the downstairs area of the hotel and the Copper Door restaurant. It is said they fell into a well and drowned while retrieving a baseball. That well still exists today in the hotel's basement. Another child, possibly from the same time period, is said to roam the hotel's rooms. She and the boys are often heard laughing and running throughout the establishment. But the most famous ghost to haunt the San Carlos is young Leone Jensen, a distraught woman who leaped to her death from the top of the hotel on May 7, 1928. The act was chronicled by the local paper and it is supposed that she did it because of a lost love. Today, she is seen as a whispy, white figure that visits guests in their rooms and walks the rooftop.

Address: 202 North Central Avenue
Website: www.hotelsancarlos.com
Activity: A, E

Phoenix Pioneer Living History Museum

Boasting over 90 acres of authentic 1800's cabins, buildings, etc., the museum/village is a living tribute to life in the old pioneer days. Even as I write this, the museum is expanding the small village and continuing to add to the grand collection of artifacts and memorabilia from the period. The haunting surrounding this location seems to be a residual effect of so many people and stories that revolve around the cabins brought to the village. With the typical activity associated with this type of haunt (glimpses of people moving about, who ignore the onlookers and the sounds of times past) the village does not hold a sense of foreboding at all, but provides a great place for people to experience this type of haunting.

Address: 3901 West Pioneer Road
Website: www.pioneeraz.org
Activity: R, E

Prescott Elks Opera House

Dating back to 1905, this opera house has been entertaining folks in Prescott for many years. Maybe it's the disposition of actors, but like many other theater/opera houses, the Elks Opera House is now said to be haunted by the spirit of an ex-actor who apparently does not know when to "exit stage left." Voices are heard in the theater when nobody else is present, as well as the sounds of a heavy pair of boots walking around. Employees have also complained about props that are moved about when needed and an uneasy feeling that seems to fill the air when individuals are left alone in the building.

Address: 117 East Gurley Street
Website: www.elksoperahouse.com
Activity: E, T

Prescott The Hassayampa Inn

Stay in this luxurious hotel and get two haunted spots in one—the Elks Opera House is just a few doors down! Named after the Hassayampa River just north of Prescott, the inn has been experiencing paranormal activity almost since the day it opened in 1927. This is due to the suicide of a young woman the hotel has named "Faith." Not long after the hotel opened, a newlywed couple checked in. The man left to pick up some cigarettes and never returned. After several days of waiting, Faith hung herself in the tower of the hotel. Since that day, Faith has haunted the hotel—mostly in Room 426, but she has also been seen in the hallways and other locations. Another spirit that is called "the Night Watchman" is also often seen in the lounge, though this spirit is thought to be more residual in nature. Faith, however, is known for waking up guests during the night by manipulating objects in the room and bathroom of Room 426 and for whispering in the ears of those staying in her room.

Address: 122 East Gurley Street
Website: www.hassayampainn.com
Activity: A, E, T, R

Tombstone Big Nose Kate's Saloon

Once called the Grand Hotel, Big Nose Kate's Saloon in Tombstone was built in 1881 and was a regular visit for old-time gunfighters. Some say the souls of several of these cowboys still reside there! They have been seen all over the building—in the bar, the basement, the front doorway, and windows, etc. Though it smacks of urban legend, the most common story you'll hear concerning the ghosts there revolves around a spirit they call the "Swamper." He was apparently a resident of the hotel who mined silver in the basement. He is said to still be there looking for his fortune today. Visit Big Nose Kate's and maybe you'll be fortunate enough to see a ghost.

Address: 417 East Allen Street
Website: www.bignosekates.info
Activity: A, S, T

Tombstone Bird Cage Theatre

With a short history—the theatre was only open from 1881 to 1889—the Bird Cage is one of the most haunted locations in all of Arizona. Whether it's because of the rough people that visited the "Cage" during its heyday or it's the proximity of so many legendary people and stories in the area, one thing is sure—a visit to this location will not be boring! Most investigators believe the haunt at the Bird Cage is a residual affair and that none of the apparitions will actually interact with you. Regardless, visitors have seen people in period dress, heard the sounds of gunshots and laughing, and even smelled the aromas of whiskey and tobacco in the air. The Bird Cage Theatre is a tourist attraction in Tombstone and can be visited quite easily—but you may want to check on how many folks are there in the period you plan to visit. The place is known for drawing a heavy crowd.

Address: 517 East Allen Street
Website: www.tombstonechamber.com
Activity: R, E, N

Tombstone The Larian Motel

Though this motel was built rather recently in 1957, the place is in proximity to many well known haunted areas of Tombstone, including the O.K. Corral and Bird Cage Theatre. Could it be that the paranormal activity from other sites has bled over into the Larian? Could be. It could also be that the property is simply built on an area with a lot of history and that the spirits who reside there are a remnant from that past. Either way, rooms 3 and 4 of this hotel are considered hotspots within the place. Room 3, the Doc Holliday Room, is known for people having things moved or taken during the night—as well as mysterious items appearing. Guests have reported feeling uneasy in this room—as if somebody is watching them. Room 4, the Wyatt Earp Room, is said to be haunted by a man from "modern times" that many believe could be a tourist who died while visiting Tombstone.

Address: 410 East Fremont Street
Website: www.tombstonemotels.com
Activity: T, A

Tucson Hotel Congress

With vintage furniture and style, as well as appliances (check out the old-time radios and the complete lack of television), you'll feel like you've stepped back in time when staying at the Congress—an upscale version of back in time! It was the upscale appearance of the hotel that led to villain John Dillinger staying as a guest—and being arrested in Tucson. The ghost that is said to haunt the Congress is thought to be a female that died from suicide there. Investigators that have checked out the hotel say that Room 242 was the site of the sad event—and that the room is, indeed, haunted with the poor soul. The spirit is said to whisper in the ears of those staying there, as well as appear to them in the form of a strange mist.

Address: 311 East Congress Street
Website: www.hotelcongress.com
Activity: E, M, A

Williams El Tovar Hotel

Perched on the rim of the Grand Canyon, the El Tovar Hotel is known for its magnificent view, as well as its past visitors (Theodore Roosevelt, Albert Einstein, and Zane Grey to name a few). Paranormal investigators who have visited the hotel say that the place is haunted and that the activity there is quite frequent. The spirits that inhabit the place are associated with the hotel's status as a "Harvey House" (meaning, it was established and owned by the infamous Fred Harvey Company). The first ghost known to haunt the place was a "Harvey Girl" and was actually buried on the premises. Her spirit is seen walking between the hotel and her grave (which is in the middle of a parking lot). The second entity in the hotel is that of Harvey himself who is often seen on the third floor of the hotel and in the kitchen where employees have witnessed him many times. For your best chance at seeing a ghost, visit the El Tovar during Christmas when Harvey is said to often participate in the festivities.

Address: Located on Center Road
Website: www.grandcanyonlodges.com
Activity: A

Williams Red Garter B & B Inn

The Red Garter—one of America's only "bed and bakeries"—has been haunted by the female ghost called "Eve" for many years. She appears in all four guest rooms and has even shown up in photographs. The spirit has been known to shake beds during the night and to be heard pacing up and down the stairs between the first and second floors. These stairs are called the "Cowboy's Endurance Test," and oddly enough, there has also been a male voice heard from that area as well. A second ghost? Possibly. Visitors to the Red Garter—especially those interested in the paranormal—rarely leave disappointed.

Address: 137 Railroad Avenue
Website: www.redgarter.com
Activity: T, A, E

ARKANSAS

Bauxite Bauxite Historical Association Museum

Built as a tribute to local mining history of this town, this museum is said to be haunted with the past memories of those miners. It is also haunted by a ghost! Whether it's a miner or someone associated with the old Masonic Lodge on the premises, visitors to the museum have reported voices, footsteps, and feeling something touching them as they wander the various exhibits. With no specifics available concerning the locations of the hauntings there, this place is ripe for a full-fledged investigation.

Address: 6706 Benton Road
Website: www.arkansas.com
Activity: E, T

Bentonville Peel Mansion Museum and Garden

Built in 1875, the Peel Mansion was a massive farmstead in the late 1800s and was known throughout the area for its expansive apple orchards. The owner of the estate, Colonel Samuel West Peel (an officer in the Confederate army during the Civil War), was the first person born in Arkansas to serve in the United States Congress. He loved the state and he loved his estate—so much, in fact, that he is said to now haunt the place. Visitors to the Peel Mansion have seen strange lights bounce around rooms and dark shadow masses that seem to shoot through an area when shadows should not be present. While there's nothing specific that points to Col. Peel as the culprit, he's as good a guess as any!

Address: 400 South Walton Boulevard
Website: www.peelmansion.org
Activity: O, S

Bentonville The Station Café

This restaurant, located just down the way from the Wal-Mart Visitors Center, has Angus burgers that are legendary throughout the area. You can order one and have a seat in the little café to keep an eye out for the resident spirit there. Though the apparition has, indeed, been seen in the dining area, it is mostly known for frequenting the area downstairs near the restrooms. Employees and patrons alike have seen the ghost, as well as heard whispers coming from areas of the restaurant where nobody is sitting. Paranormal groups that have researched the haunting say that employees have experienced poltergeist activity as well—items in the kitchen have been seen moving on their own, sometimes with force.

Address: 111 North Main Street
Website: www.stationcafeinc.com
Activity: T, A, E

Clarendon Monroe County Courthouse

Believe it or not, the current courthouse sitting at 123 Madison Street in Clarendon, Arkansas, is the fourth to do so! The first was torn down by federal troops so they could build defenses at Devalls Bluff, the second burned down, and the third lasted for a while, but was torn down to make room for the present incarnation of the building. The current courthouse was finished in 1911. Could it be the history of constant destruction and construction that keeps spirits busy in this place? Or maybe it's the public hangings that took place on the property during the 1800s. Could be. Most believe, however, that the spirit is that of John Orr, who was killed by his wife and co-conspirators. The story goes that John's wife, Mabel, and four black servants plotted to kill Mr. Orr and, after the deed was done, were lynched at the courthouse. Or at least the servants were. Mabel apparently was given the suicide route out. Regardless of the reason for the haunting, visitors to the courthouse have reported hearing odd cries coming from the basement of the building and seeing glowing balls of light on the property.

Address: 123 Madison Street
Website: www.clarendon-ar.com
Activity: E, O

Eureka Springs The 1886 Crescent Hotel and Spa

The Crescent has been known as one of America's most haunted spots for years, but before that it was known for a fraudulent doctor by the name of Norman Baker. Baker is known for profiting by scamming cancer patients out of their life savings for his "cure." Baker went to prison (for mail fraud), and the Crescent was left with the spirits of many people who died there looking for hope. Though there may be several entities in the Crescent from this era (including Baker himself), the most well-known ghost on the premises is probably that of a construction worker, who is said to have fallen and died in what is now Room 218. This ghost has been nicknamed "Michael," and he has been seen, felt, and heard in this room. In addition to 218, Rooms 202 and 424 are also known as hot spots in the hotel. Room 419 has been the site of a ghostly nurse, and the downstairs lobby of the hotel has featured the appearance of an apparition as well.

Address: 75 Prospect Avenue
Website: www.crescent-hotel.com
Activity: A, E, T, S, C, R

Eureka Springs 1905 Basin Park Hotel

Locals claim that the entire city of Eureka Springs is haunted. They attribute this to the springs for which they are famous, and a reputation for the spiritual/otherworld that started with the Native Americans who lived in the area prior to settlement. The Basin Park Hotel, in keeping with this tradition, has several haunted rooms: 307, 308, 407, and 408. All four rooms have experienced activity. Several spirits are said to walk the halls of the Basin Park: a little girl is known to visit folks in their sleep, a male spirit likes to visit the reception area by the bar, and a cowboy has been seen walking through walls into rooms and down the hallways (though his actions are considered residual since he doesn't ever seem to notice anyone around him). With a haunted tour of the premises, this is a great place to kick off a haunted visit to Eureka Springs.

Address: 12 Spring Street
Website: www.basinpark.com
Activity: A, R, E, T

Fayetteville Inn at Carnall Hall

Located on the University of Arkansas campus, the Inn at Carnall Hall was originally built as a woman's dormitory for the university in 1906. Today, it is an impressive hotel and restaurant with a unique look (Colonial Revival). Though who haunts the hotel isn't exactly known, many employees and visitors have witnessed a full-body apparition in several rooms. At times, only a partial apparition is present (meaning, the feet or the head doesn't exactly show up ...), but there's enough to know it is a ghost! There have also been reports of the spirit there sitting on the bed and moving objects in rooms.

Address: 465 North Arkansas Avenue
Website: www.innatcarnallhall.com
Activity: A, T

Forrest City St. Francis County Museum

Before beginning its current existence as a museum dedicated to fossils and artifacts pertaining to the area, the St. Francis County Museum was simply a house. The Rush-Gates house to be exact. It was built in 1906 by Dr. J. O. Rush. Perhaps it is the ghost of Dr. Rush that now haunts this museum. There is a complete rendition of his office on the premises after all. Or maybe the haunt has something to do with nearby Crowley's Ridge—a place with Native American and Civil War significance. Either way, visitors to the museum have experienced dark shadows, orbs, cold spots, and strange mutterings from within the walls.

Address: 603 Front Street
Website: www.sfcmuseum.org
Activity: S, O, C, E

Fort Smith Fort Smith National Historic Site

Known for a reputedly ruthless, but wise lawman—Judge Isaac C. Parker—the area in this park that is occupied by the old courthouse and hanging gallows of Fort Smith is said to be extremely haunted. Between 1873 and 1896, the courthouse oversaw 86 executions of men convicted of either murder or rape (both made a mandatory death sentence after the Civil War). And Judge Parker sentenced 79 of these 86. During his tenure as a judge, "Ole Isaac" handed out 160 death sentences total. Because of the huge amount of horrible death on the grounds, it is said that the park is now haunted ... and not only by those convicted of their crimes. It is also said that the ghost of Judge Parker himself walks the halls of his old courthouse.

Address: Third and Garland Streets
Website: www.nps.gov/fosm
Activity: E, S, A

It's said that he was beheaded in the line of duty while working late one night. Others say a Depression-era foreman for the railroad named William McClain is the spirit. Whichever you believe, visit the town of Gurdon and get precise directions to the stretch of train tracks, as it can be difficult to find for out-of-towners.

Address: Junction of Highway 53 and 67
Activity: O

Garfield Pea Ridge National Military Park

For two days in this area—March 7 and 8, 1862—the Confederate and Union armies fought over who would control the state of Missouri. With the defeat of Major General Earl Van Dorn, the Union army would win that battle. Today, this battle site is one of the best-preserved Civil War memorials in the country. Considering that hundreds of soldiers from both armies died at this battle, it is no big surprise that this park is thought to be haunted. Many who have taken the tour of the military park have noted seeing the flashes of men in uniform darting through the trees, as well as hearing the sounds of cannon fire and guns in the night. Most of the activity seems to take place around the area where the Elkhorn Tavern once stood. This was the site of some of the fiercest fighting during the campaign and is one of the stops on the tour.

Address: 15930 East Highway 62
Website: www.nps.gov/peri
Activity: R, A, E

Gurdon Gurdon Spook Light

Located north of the city of Gurdon, the infamous Gurdon Spook Light can be seen almost nightly along the train tracks just off highways 53 and 67. There are numerous stories concerning the light—just ask the locals—but the existence of the light itself cannot be debated. It has been recorded by video cameras and had its photo taken numerous times—even by television shows like *Unsolved Mysteries*. Most believe the light is a spectral lantern that is held in the hands of a long-dead railroad worker.

Hardy Old Hardy Hotel Antique and Collectibles Mall

This hotel-turned-mall was built in 1898 and was known for many years as one of the best hotels in the area. This good reputation lasted right up until the 1940s, when a man was murdered on the second floor. The hotel's owners have heard the footsteps of the murdered man on this same floor and have had numerous personal items moved by unseen hands. At times, they have reported seeing a misty apparition on the stairs and near the murder scene as well. Other activity includes lights turning on/off and doors opening when nobody is present. If you visit the Old Hardy Hotel, be sure to ask to see the "Murder Room" on the second floor—it's well worth the visit!

Address: 204 East Main Street
Website: www.oldhardytown.net
Activity: A, E, T

Helena Magnolia Hill Bed and Breakfast

Though paranormal investigators (as well as the owner of the B&B) have no idea who the spirit is that haunts Magnolia Hill, everyone is certain that she is there! Numerous sightings of a woman in a long dress have been reported over the years from almost every area of the house—though the most common place associated with the ghost is the stairs and upstairs hallway. Guests have also heard the sounds of footsteps, seen doors open/close, and found items in various rooms moved/thrown on the floor. The spirit of a male soldier is also thought to reside in the basement. Before the house was built, this area of Helena served as a Civil War fortification during a skirmish there. Magnolia Hill dates back to 1900 and has since been a home, a church, and a USO club during World War II. Could the haunting be associated with one of these events? Visit and find out.

Address: 608 Perry Street
Website: www.magnoliahillbnb.com
Activity: A, T, E

Hot Springs The Poet's Loft

The Poet's Loft is a coffeehouse and performer's venue that would be perfectly at home in cities like Berkeley, California, and Austin, Texas—but is, instead, located in the heart of Arkansas. Rubbing elbows with folks in this place means meeting local, budding poets, musicians, magicians, and even actors. Of course, it may also mean meeting the spirit that is said to haunt this location. With a story that involves a patron being physically held down in her seat by invisible hands, the Poet's Loft is a legendary hot spot in central Arkansas. Those who have visited the place frequently say that the ghost there is known for being seen in the kitchen and for touching customers sitting in the dining area.

Address: 514-B Central Avenue
Website: www.thepoetsloft.com
Activity: A, T

Jonesboro Foundation of Arts Forum Theatre

Over the years, the Forum has hosted numerous plays and traveling theatre groups. The place is also known for movies, hosted events, and a ghost that goes by the name of "Charlie." Charlie is known for turning lights on and off—sometimes on cue—and for generally being heard in the performance area. More often than not, if he is heard, he is laughing. Actors working in the Forum have often heard a male voice talking when nobody else was present, as well as experienced the overwhelming sensation that somebody else was present on the stage.

Address: 115 East Monroe Avenue
Website: www.foajonesboro.org
Activity: E, T

Little Rock Old State House Museum

Other than being known for President Bill Clinton's election night celebrations, this museum is known throughout Arkansas as the site of multiple ghosts. The Old State House is the oldest surviving state capitol building west of the Mississippi and is said to still house several dead politicians who once called this building their work space. Men in period dress have been seen on the second floor and voices have been heard (as well as footsteps) in almost every area of the museum.

Address: 300 West Markham
Website: www.oldstatehouse.org
Activity: A, E

Little Rock Quapaw Quarter

The area of Little Rock, Arkansas, known as the Quapaw Quarter is the oldest part of the city. This part of town has homes dating back as far as the early 1800s and houses many historic structures related to the birth and history of Little Rock: MacArthur Park, the Cathedral of St. Andrew's, and Curran Hall, to name a few. To paranormal investigators in Arkansas, the Quapaw Quarter is home to one of the state's biggest residual haunts—almost as if the entire area periodically travels back in time. Horse and carriages have been seen, as well as numerous people walking about in period dress, throughout the streets. People have heard the horses and strange conversations there as well. The old Little Rock Arsenal (in the middle of MacArthur Park) has also had sightings of a misty apparition in the building that many attribute to the Civil War and the many deaths that occurred there during that time.

Address: Downtown along Capitol Street
Website: www.quapaw.com
Activity: R, A, E

Little Rock Vino's Pizza Pub and Brewery

Vino's in Little Rock is known for three things: killer pizza, great in-house brewed beer, and a spirit that haunts the restaurant! Rumors concerning the haunting began when employees began noticing that chairs that were previously put on top of the tables at closing were suddenly back on the floor in the morning when they returned. Guests to the brewpub then started reporting strange sounds and voices in the restrooms and dining area. Then came the cold spots … Vino's is apparently haunted—most paranormal groups in Arkansas list it as a local haunted location. It is well worth a visit—even if it's to catch the sounds of a long-lost patron over a slice of pepperoni and a cold beer.

Address: 923 West 7th Street
Website: www.vinosbrewpub.com
Activity: E, C, T

Paragould Collins Theater

Actors and employees of the Collins Theater in Paragould, Arkansas, believe that the building is haunted by the original owner/creators of the theater (which was built in the early 1900s). The ghosts of this husband-and-wife team are said to be seen sitting in the balcony watching as the actors rehearse—and have even made the occasional appearance during an actual production. When the pair of spirits is seen, it is only for a moment—it seems that, as soon as they are noticed, the husband and wife will disappear right before the witnesses' eyes.

Address: 2nd Street and West Emerson
Website: www.collinstheaterparagould.com
Activity: A

Van Buren King Opera House

This Victorian theater was completely overhauled for a grand re-opening in 1979 and still has productions appearing on its stage today. During the first production ever held in the revitalized theater, there was a special guest—a ghost! The local legend goes like this: An actor in the early 1900s was beaten to death at a local train station while attempting to steal away a rich doctor's daughter. Since he was "most happy" at the theater, his spirit is said to have returned there. During various productions (as well as rehearsals) a man is often seen in a black jacket and top hat that matches the description of the actor that was killed. Usually this spirit is seen backstage, though he has been glimpsed in the auditorium area as well.

Address: 427 Main Street
Website: www.vanburen.org
Activity: A

CALIFORNIA

Alameda The Aircraft Carrier USS Hornet Museum

The eighth ship to carry the name USS Hornet now sits in a berth at the decommissioned Alameda Naval Base. While functioning during WWII, the Hornet was responsible for the destruction of approximately 1,410 Japanese aircraft. The ship itself suffered the loss of over 300 American lives—partially due to the fact that the Hornet had the Navy's highest suicide rate for the time. Whether it's the history of battles, or the loss of American lives in general, the Hornet is a haunted location today. Activity includes the apparitions of sailors moving about the ship, voices heard when nobody is there to speak, and items moving of their own accord (including doors). Be on your toes when you visit the Hornet—spirits there also like to touch visitors!

Address: 707 West Hornet Avenue
Website: www.uss-hornet.org
Activity: A, E, T

Antioch Black Diamond Mines Regional Preserve

Working as a miner has always been dangerous. If it's not "black lung" or some other horrible disease knocking you off, it was probably the horrendous working conditions. Over the years, the Black Diamond Mines in Antioch saw their fair share of these kinds of deaths. Today, that impact is evident to all who visit the preserve. The spirits left behind by these events still can be heard—especially at night. Though the activity is mostly residual (sounds of workers, digging, etc.), there is said to be at least one active spirit: Sarah Norton. Locals will tell you she was crushed to death in a horrible buggy accident. Today she is seen as a glowing white figure roaming around the mines and the nearby Rose Hill cemetery.

Address: 5175 Somersville Road
Website: www.ebparks.org
Activity: R, E, A

Arcata Humboldt Brews

With great food, beer, and music, this brewpub in Arcata, California, is a great place to hunt for ghosts. Patrons of this establishment have grown quite accustomed to the spirit hanging out over the years. Many of them have heard a strange, male voice speaking from empty areas of the main dining room and have seen glasses and barware move on their own. Employees closing the place have reported hearing footsteps in the empty areas of the building as well. Ask the folks at Humboldt Brews who haunts the place, and they'll tell you it is the ghost of a long-dead owner/businessman who decided to stay along beyond the grave.

Address: 856 10th Street
Website: www.humboldtbrews.com
Activity: E, T

Avalon Banning House Lodge

Built in 1910 by the Banning brothers, this lodge stationed on Catalina Island is known for a nearby celebrity ghost. Actress Natalie Wood drowned in the bay and is said to be occasionally seen walking on the beach—or heard yelling for help from the water. In the actual lodge, however, the ghost of the "White Lady" is said to walk. She is often seen in the common areas, on the stairs, and even walking outside between the lodge and the Isthmus Yacht Club. Visitors to the lodge have reported seeing other ghosts as well: the Banning brothers, Catherine Banning, and an old fisherman who is known to be accompanied by the smells of tobacco and the sea.

Address: 1 Banning House Road
Website: www.visitcatalinaisland.com
Activity: A, E

Bakersfield The Gaslight Melodrama Theatre and Music Hall

What is it about theatres and ghosts? More often than not, locals will claim that a theatre is haunted—even if there is no supporting evidence to back up the claim. The Gaslight Melodrama Theatre is also thought to be haunted by the folks in Bakersfield. The tale goes like this: Before the theatre moved into its present building, the location housed a toy store. The owner of this store—for some reason—became despondent and committed suicide. His ghost then moved into the store. Then, of course, the store left and the building became a theatre. During the 1980s, the place became known for almost constant activity—including the moving of props and stage settings, noises, etc. The sounds are still heard today, but not as often. The spirit in this theatre may need some prompting.

Address: 12748 Jomani Drive
Website: www.themelodrama.com
Activity: T, E

Banta Banta Inn

Featured on the 1990s television show *Sightings*, the Banta Inn is notorious for a ghost said to be the owner of the establishment who died in 1967 behind the bar (of natural causes—most say a heart attack). Since his death, owners and employees alike have seen pictures fly off the walls, bar objects move on their own, and dark, shadow-like spirits moving around in the back areas of the building. Today, the Banta Inn is not actually an "inn" in the sense you can stay there; the place is, instead, a restaurant. Grab a table—preferably close to the bar—after dark and keep an eye out for the dark shape that is said to haunt the place.

Address: 7th and G Street
Website: www.bantainn.net
Activity: S, T

Benicia The Union Hotel

Ever since a young, distraught woman hung herself in the Union Hotel, this place has experienced paranormal activity. The spirit of the young woman has been spotted in hallways, as well as most of the rooms in this hotel. In addition to the appearance of her "full bodied apparition," guests have also heard the sounds of her crying and mumbling and have witnessed lights turning themselves on and off. The hotel has even gotten reports of a pale, see-through female staring outside from one of the upstairs windows. In addition to the woman, a young boy is said to haunt the Union Hotel. His connection to the hotel is unknown, but he is most often seen in the bar/dining room area.

Address: 401 First Street
Website: www.unionhotelbenicia.com
Activity: A, E

Berkeley The Claremont Hotel Club and Spa

The present hotel that stands at 41 Tunnel Road is, literally, on the ruins of a castle that burned to the ground in 1901. The hotel was built in 1915 and has gone through several incarnations before settling on the present-day version of the Claremont. Paranormal activity in this location includes the phantom smells of smoke, as well as the spirit of a young girl. The girl is often seen and heard on the fourth floor of the hotel (employees say that the room 422 has the most reported happenings), and it is speculated that she died either in the castle, or in a fire that later occurred during its tenure as a hotel.

Address: 41 Tunnel Road
Website: www.claremontresort.com
Activity: A, E

Brookdale Brookdale Inn & Spa

With beginnings firmly rooted in the area's lumber industry (the inn was originally the headquarters of the Grover Lumber Mill), the Brookdale came into existence in 1900 as a campground and hotel to service local travelers. During the 1920s and 1930s, the place was quite popular with the rich and famous—and was even visited by President Herbert Hoover. Later on, though, the Brookdale's reputation became a little more sinister as the hotel became a haven for gangsters and the Mob. But strangely enough, the haunting of this location is associated with none of that history! There are two apparitions that are seen in the hotel—and both are young girls. The first is said to be Sarah Logan, a girl who drowned in a creek that runs through the dining room of the hotel. The second girl is yet another drowning victim who passed away because of an accident in a small hotel pool. The girls are most often seen in the lobby, lounge, and Brookroom areas of the hotel. Sarah is even said to walk up and ask guests for help, to only then disappear right before their eyes. Other hot spots include the Mermaid Room, the Fireside Room, and the Pool Room.

Address: 11570 Highway 9
Website: www.brookdaleinnandspa.com
Activity: A, E, T

Carmel La Playa Hotel

This hotel started out as a dream home for chocolate heiress Angela Ghirardelli—but was only so briefly, as she moved out a mere year later. In the 1920s, a second building was constructed with guest rooms and the place became a hotel. Since that time, the hotel has been haunted by a female spirit that many believe to be Ghirardelli herself—or maybe a cousin. It seems that locals have been passing around a story since those days that one of the Ghirardelli girls, cousin to young Angela, drowned while swimming in nearby Carmel Bay. Nobody knows for sure if this story is true. However, visitors to the hotel do say that a female voice is often heard in the hallways and hotel rooms, and that the appearance of a girl at the foot of the bed seems to indicate that there is, indeed, a ghost in the La Playa Hotel.

Address: Camino Real and 8th Avenue
Website: www.laplayahotel.com
Activity: A, E

Cerro Gordo Cerro Gordo Mines/ Belshaw House

The Belshaw house, a small two-bedroom cabin in the Cerro Gordo Mines area, was built in 1868 by Mortimer Belshaw. Belshaw made his fortune by mining gold and was well known for many years in the area as a "bullion king." Today, visitors to the mine can stay in the little Belshaw house and visit with Mortimer in person. Once the sun goes down, the small cabin is known for his spirit that is said to haunt the cabin. Guests have witnessed shadow shapes,

orbs, and weird flashes of electricity that seem to emanate from the middle of the living room.

Address: Highway 136 from Keeler, CA
Website: www.cerrogordo.us
Activity: S, O

Clovis Wolfe Manor Hotel

The upcoming Wolfe Manor Hotel (it's still in progress, so check their website before visiting) was once known as the Clovis Avenue Sanitarium and was considered one of the best/most haunted locations in California. Then the television show *Ghost Hunters* visited the place. And they got evidence—good evidence. Once the hotel is finished and you visit there, expect to hear loud voices and footsteps when nobody is present, see dark masses, and possibly see the apparition of a young woman named "Mary." Other spirits seen on the premises include a child and a tall man who are often seen standing in various doorways. Visitors to the place have also felt something or someone touching them when nobody else is present.

Address: Clovis Avenue and Santa Ana Avenue
Website: www.wolfemanorhotel.com
Activity: A, S, E, T

Coloma Sierra Nevada House

Built during the gold rush of California, the Sierra Nevada House was a notorious hotel, saloon, and brothel that serviced the thousands of miners streaming into the area to find their fortune. Since its inception, the hotel has burned down twice and has seen more than its fair share of rough times—not to mention rough people. The haunting of this location seems to mostly affect the second floor of the hotel. Room 4 is said to be the most haunted—though employees will tell you that things happen quite often in the bar and the kitchen as well. Objects move, voices are heard, and a misty figure has been seen in the aforementioned Room 4.

Address: Lotus Road and Highway 49
Website: www.sierranevadahouse.com
Activity: E, T, M

Death Valley Furnace Creek Inn and Ranch Resort

Located dead smack in the middle of Death Valley, the Furnace Creek Inn is a friendly oasis in the middle of a desert. Even the ghost that is said to haunt Furnace Creek is said to be of the friendly sort. Employees of the resort will tell you that the ghost is a former chef who worked there from 1959 to 1973. His name was James Marquez, and after he passed away (while in retirement) he decided to return to the place that made him the most happy. He is most often seen and heard in the dining room/kitchen areas of the inn—the places where he would have spent most of his time. He bangs plates, pots, and pans, and also moves random kitchen items around.

Address: Highway 190
Website: www.furnacecreekresort.com
Activity: E, T

Dorrington The Dorrington Hotel

The Dorrington was built in 1852 by John and Rebecca Gardner as a hotel/depot on the Big Trees Carson Valley Road. It was long after Rebecca passed away that hotel visitors began to report strange things happening. The first hot spot in the hotel seems to be the dining room, where witnesses have seen lights switch on and off, doors open and close, and motion detectors go off for no reason. Other ghostly happenings seem to include the sounds of young children playing on the second floor. They are often heard there, as well as stomping up and down the stairs. A popular story about Rebecca has the spirit knocking down Christmas trees during the night and her apparition appearing beside a set of Christmas lights.

Address: 3431 Highway 4
Website: www.dorringtonhotel.com
Activity: A, T, E

Eureka Abigail's Elegant Victorian Mansion

With unique gingerbread accents on the exterior of this house, Abigail's is a hard place to miss. Dating back to 1888, the mansion is a nationally recognized historic location and today it houses four unique rooms to stay in—all decked out in period furniture. Abigail's is also a great place to experience a mild residual haunting. Many people staying in this bed and breakfast have reported hearing the sounds of jazz music playing in the evening. The owners are quick to point out that they do not play music of this sort—much less over a loud speaker during the night! Not much else is reported activity-wise, but if you are a beginning ghost enthusiast, this might be a great way to get your feet wet.

Address: 1406 C Street
Website: www.eureka-california.com
Activity: R, E

Fort Bragg Glass Beach Inn

With a view that stares out over the Mendocino coastline, the Glass Beach Inn makes for a nice getaway. The house itself (built in the 1920s) has six rooms, and there's even a cottage out back for a more private evening. The spirits that are said to reside at the inn are reportedly there due to bad luck associated with a certain chair on the premises. The story goes that those who sit in this chair for any extended period (not sure exactly how long this is) end up dying shortly thereafter. Or maybe it's just coincidence that the two spirits that are said to haunt this place just happened to enjoy sitting in the same place. Either way, keep your ears perked for the sounds of walking/footsteps, voices, and furniture moving during the evening (this is in the main house). You might want to have the owner point out the chair in question, though … and avoid it.

Address: 726 North Main
Website: www.glassbeachinn.com
Activity: E

Fresno Meux Home Museum

A Victorian home that belonged to the Meux family for 81 years, the place is now a historic location and museum. Thomas Richard Meux, a Tennessean, was a captain in the army, a doctor, and an entrepreneur. Many generations of the Meux family have lived and died in this house and it is most likely that these are the souls that still walk the halls of the stately manor. Employees and visitors alike have heard phantom sighs, footsteps, and whispers throughout the house—as well as seen the misty shape of a man staring from the windows. The Meux Home Museum has had no serious paranormal investigation, so details concerning the haunting are few. Check it out for yourself and let us know how it went!

Address: 1007 R Street
Website: www.meux.mus.ca.us
Activity: E, M

Fullerton Stadium Tavern

The haunt in the Stadium Tavern has less to do with the business itself than it does with the entire complex it's located in. The Villa del Sol is said to be haunted by a spirit that visits all the businesses there. The tavern, though, is the most known location for this entity. You can tell when the spirit is in the bar by the sudden appearance of an intense cold spot. The employees of the tavern—as well as the other stores and businesses in the building—call the ghost "Chuck" and say that he is harmless. You might want to grab a drink while waiting for Chuck to show up though; encounters with this ghost are few and far between.

Address: 405 North Harbor Boulevard
Website: www.redondobrewery.com
Activity: C

Georgetown The Historic American River Inn

The American River Inn is known throughout the area for its Queen Anne architecture and collection of Old English antiques. The place was built in 1853 and was the product of—you guessed it—gold fever in California. The typical disasters associated with this vocation occurred here and in the area: mining accidents, fires, you name it. The ghost that currently visits its guests at the American River Inn is said to be one of the many miners who passed away over the years. He is known for appearing in guests' rooms, stomping down the hallways, and generally doing everything possible to make his presence known. Since the spirit is not associated with any specific room or area, you may want to ask the innkeepers where the miner is hanging out at the moment.

Address: Orleans and Main Street
Website: www.americanriverinn.com
Activity: E, A

Groveland The Groveland Hotel

Yet another product of mining and the gold rush, the Groveland was built in 1849 to service the workers as a saloon. Back then, a lot of the miners actually lived in the hotel rather than buying or building a local home. Such is the case with "Lyle." Lyle was a miner who lived in the Groveland Hotel until his death in 1927 in Room 15. After his death, Lyle stayed on in the hotel and likes to play pranks on those who stay in his room—or the rooms close by. Paranormal activity includes lights turning on/off, doors opening/closing, and items being swept from the dresser onto the floor (especially if they belong to a female). The owner of the hotel has tracked and logged paranormal activity in this hotel for many years, so make sure to touch base to get the current info on the haunting there.

Address: 18767 Main Street
Website: www.groveland.com
Activity: T

Guadalupe Far Western Tavern

With roots that go back to being a hotel, the Far West is now a restaurant with a unique menu item—a ghost! During the hotel days, it's said that a man burned to death within the building while sleeping in an upstairs room. Once the hotel was repaired—and even later when the place was turned into the present-day eatery—people started hearing strange things from the upstairs area. Things like bangs, someone walking, and moans or cries. These activities continue on today—though most of the employees of the Far Western will tell you that things don't happen that frequently. However, the occasional guest at the restaurant will still hear the odd noise coming from upstairs or feel an intense cold spot wash over them during their meal.

Address: 899 Guadalupe Street
Website: www.farwesterntavern.com
Activity: E, C

Half Moon Bay The Historic Zaballa House Bed and Breakfast

Known as one of the oldest houses in Half Moon Bay, the Zaballa House has been haunted by a spirit in Room 6 for many years—and to make matters worse, he or she is a noisy ghost! Guests who have stayed in this room report hearing the sounds of a person stomping around, keys rattling, phantom alarms sounding, and windows banging. Though it doesn't occur every single night, the room has had enough regular activity to warrant a thorough investigation.

Address: 324 Main Street
Website: www.zaballahouse.net
Activity: E, T

Ione Ione Hotel

This hotel was built to accommodate the sudden influx of miners during the 1849 gold rush. Since then, the place has burned down twice (once in 1910 and once in 1988) and been rebuilt twice. The ghost that is said to haunt this hotel is named "George" and most in the hotel believe he likes to hang out in Room 13. He is known for opening and closing the doors and windows, and he has been heard breathing and whispering in the room. Another hot spot in the hotel is the basement (check with the front desk before going down there, though) where people say they have heard a male voice calling for help.

Address: 25 West Main Street
Website: www.ionehotel.com
Activity: E, T

Jamestown 1859 Historic National Hotel

When Heinrich and Hannah Neilson created one of the area's best hotel and restaurants back in 1859, little did they know that modern-day visitors would probably best know them because of a haunting! The ghost of the National Hotel is openly talked about (it's even on their website) and stories regarding the spirit are constantly springing up. The hotel owners have named the ghost "Flo" and say she likes to haunt the front rooms on the second floor. Her apparition has been seen in almost every room up there, as well as passing through walls, going down the stairs, and hanging out in the dining room. There are diaries kept in the guest rooms that allow visitors to log their own experiences with Flo, so there's some good nighttime reading for you there as well.

Address: 18183 Main Street
Website: www.national-hotel.com
Activity: A

the kitchen would be rearranged on a daily basis. The place has now been transformed into a more upscale restaurant atmosphere, and the activity there has lessened quite a bit. Maybe the spirit just didn't like the original décor there...

Address: 500 Hartnell Street
Website: www.stokesrestaurant.com
Activity: T, E

Long Beach Queen Mary

Entire books have been written about the paranormal activity at the Queen Mary. It seems that almost as soon as this 1936 luxury liner docked permanently at Long Beach, stories started spreading about the ghosts there. The quick rundown of the hot spots there include: the main swimming pool where two girls are said to walk (they reportedly drowned there), the passageway outside the pool where the spirit of a young boy also walks, the Queen's Salon is said to be haunted by a female, the First Class Suite area is haunted by an older gentleman, and the forward storage room is said to be haunted by the sounds of children playing. Then there are the kitchen, the ship's morgue, and Shaft Alley... But perhaps the best, and most intriguing story, involves cabin B340 on the third level. Activity there happens so frequently and dramatically, that the cabin is at times closed off from the public. Call ahead and see if you can get the room!

Address: 1126 Queen's Highway
Website: www.queenmary.com
Activity: A, E, C, O, M, T

Monterey Stoke's Restaurant and Bar

Housed within the walls of an awesome Victorian house (circa 1838), Stoke's is another one of those "legendary" haunted places—at least in California. There was a time when employees and managers of this eatery would complain about the almost-constant poltergeist-like activity. Plates would be broken, guests would be harassed (the entity would grab them and pull at their clothing), and generally everything in

Moss Beach Moss Beach Distillery

Tales of the "Blue Lady" that haunts this unusually designed building have been circulating throughout the area for many years. Then, the stories were seemingly debunked almost overnight thanks to the team of television's *Ghost Hunters* finding speakers, lights, etc. throughout the bar. Since then, local paranormal investigators have come forth to state that, despite the tourist gimmicks set up in the bar, the place is, indeed, haunted. The Blue Lady is said to have been actually murdered on the beach, but her spirit has been seen throughout the restaurant/bar. Other activity includes items levitating on their own, doors opening/closing, and items disappearing to only reappear in strange locations.

Address: 140 Beach Way
Website: www.mossbeachdistillery.com
Activity: A, T

Murphys Murphys Historic Hotel

Built on the site of the Sperry-Perry Hotel (1856), the Murphys came into existence in 1945, when the original hotel was improved upon. The haunting of this historic place seems to be an almost-violent one; witnesses have reported seeing glasses explode, feeling a malevolent pressure holding them down in their sleep, and hearing an ominous voice calling for an unknown person. (The voice doesn't seem clear enough to make out the name.) Folks have also heard the sounds of a female crying and seen weird lights shoot through the walls into rooms. Though the ghostly activity does seem to be aggressive, nothing overtly bad has happened to patrons of this place. Paranormal investigators consider this place as one of the more active in California, so it's probably worth your time to visit.

Address: 457 Main Street
Website: www.murphyshotel.com
Activity: A, O, S, E, T

Newbury Park The Stagecoach Inn Museum

The Stagecoach was originally a hotel called the Grand Union and was built in 1876. When a freeway threatened to cause the demolition of the place in 1960, the hotel was named a historic landmark and the entire building was relocated to its present-day location. Whether it has always been this way, or whether it is a result of moving the property, the current inhabitants of the building claim the place is haunted. The spirit of a female, accompanied by the smell of a strong perfume, is said to have been seen in various areas of the museum. Though the original Grand Union did have a ghost (a male spirit who is said to have been murdered)—it is ap-parently only visited by the female apparition these days.

Address: 51 South Ventu Park Road
Website: www.stagecoachmuseum.org
Activity: A, N

Placerville Cary House Historic Hotel

There are lots of interesting stories about this old brick building built back in 1857. It all starts with the place being named the "Jewel of Placerville" for being one of the best hotels in all of the gold rush–era cities. Then there are the stories concerning the ghosts ... The first is about a spirit that is said to haunt Room 212—a male entity that was once a carriage driver and now likes to make noises and generally make himself known in this particular room. Another ghost story that takes place in this hotel concerns a front desk clerk that was called "Stan," who was reportedly stabbed to death for flirting with a guest who was checking in. Today, he is seen in the lobby area of the hotel and has been known to touch male guests and pinch female guests on the behind!

Address: 300 Main Street
Website: www.caryhouse.com
Activity: A, E, T

San Diego El Fandango Restaurant

Not much is known about the girl that is said to haunt this fine Mexican restaurant. Patrons have seen her on and off over the years—usually as a dark, black mass that hovers in the back corners of the dining room. On occasion, however, employees have reported that a full-bodied apparition—and, indeed, it is a woman—has also appeared sitting in one of the corner tables. It's not always the same table, it's not always the same corner, but it's always a corner table! This location is probably your best chance at seeing a ghost while eating a taco ...

Address: 2734 Calhoun Street
Website: www.elfandangorestaurant.com
Activity: A, S

San Diego Whaley House Museum

Brought into the world spotlight by the infamous ghost hunter Hans Holzer, the Whaley house has had the reputation of being an extremely haunted site for quite a long time. Holzer claimed the place to be, "Possibly the most haunted house in America." There are several spirits that roam this house, including a hanged man by the name of Jim, the former owner Thomas Whaley, and his wife and children. Pale figures, footsteps, and voices have been experienced in almost every room and every employee there has their own story about the haunting of this house-turned-museum. At times, the place even seems to shift into a residual mode with the home literally filling with the sounds of old-time music, children laughing and crying, etc. The activity is said to happen so frequently here, that even a short visit may bring a great experience.

Address: 2476 San Diego Avenue
Website: www.whaleyhouse.org
Activity: A, E, R

San Dimas Pinnacle Peak Steakhouse

There aren't many details concerning the haunting of this establishment—though employees there will nod enthusiastically if you ask about the ghost there. It is generally said that the resident spirit is a little girl—most likely a Native American—who has been seen at various times standing in the dining area. She is also known for grabbing at the servers' trays, knocking over glasses, and generally moving things around—probably in order to be noticed. Kids are often like that...

Address: 269 West Foothill Boulevard
Website: www.pinnaclepeaksteakhouse.com
Activity: A, T

San Francisco Alcatraz Island

Visiting this historic site does little to impress upon the average person the sheer amount of despair and death that happened within the walls of this legendary prison. The entire area where the prisoners were held is known to be haunted by former inmates—some of them quite famous. Al Capone is probably the most well known. The television show *Sightings* once did an investigation here—and though a lot of the information did come from a psychic, there was other paranormal activity as well, including cold spots, shadow figures, and a cell door that slammed shut all by itself.

Address: Accessible by ferry from the
　　Embarcadero
Website: www.nps.gov/alcatraz
Activity: R, S, A, E, T

San Francisco The Presidio

Stories regarding the Presidio being haunted have circulated through the military for years. Since the old Spanish fort shut down official operations and shifted to being a tourist site, these sightings and reports have continued from visitors and employees. While there is a whole book's worth of information regarding the ghosts of this massive complex, the most commonly known haunt is that of the Officer's Club. Tales of a female apparition that appears in front of the ballroom fireplace are spoken of by the employees, as well as the spirit of a male officer that is heard in various rooms. There is a strong residual effect to the complex as well—smells are often encountered coming from the non-functioning kitchen and the room where the bodies of officers were often laid in state. Sounds associated with a funeral or party are also heard in this area—as well as invisible pots and pans banging in the kitchen. The main building of the Presidio is now a rental hall for events—how about renting it for a ghost hunt?

Address: Whole area north of Lake Street
Website: www.nps.gov/prsf
Activity: A, E, N

Santa Monica The Georgian Hotel

Built during the height of Art Deco style, the 1933 Georgian Hotel is a wonder to see. The architecture and style of this place is worth the visit alone. Add in the fact that it is haunted by the "spirits" of the prohibition days, and you've got a trip indeed! The bar of this hotel is known for experiencing both residual and intelligent elements of a haunting. Sounds of people talking, laughing, and walking about have been heard in the bar on almost a daily basis for years. There is said, though, to be at least one intelligent spirit here. Employees say it is a male spirit and he will often answer with a "good morning" when greeted. At other times, he can also be heard sighing in the restaurant as if responding to comments or conversation in the area.

Address: 1415 Ocean Avenue
Website: www.georgianhotel.com
Activity: R, E

Shoshone Amargosa Opera House and Hotel

This hotel/theater was once the headquarters for the Pacific Coast Borax Company and the center of a small village that housed the miners that worked for them. Today, the small area called Shoshone (sometimes called Death Valley Junction) is home to the hotel—and not much else! Except a ghost of course. Several of them, in fact. The spirits are said to be those of old-time borax miners who make their presence known by opening and closing doors, walking the halls, and shooting through the doors of guests' rooms as a ball of light.

Address: CA127 and State Line Road
Website: www.amargosa-opera-house.com
Activity: E, O

Truckee Donner Memorial State Park

The horrible story of the Donner party and their trip across the mountains into California is a well-known tale—as well as the cannibalism that occurred among them once they became stranded in the highlands with no food left to eat. Among those who died—and were subsequently eaten—was Tamsen Donner, the matriarch of the clan. It is said that Tamsen now haunts the area of Donner Park where she met her demise. It also just so happens that this area is now a campground for tent camping! Campers have reported seeing a glowing female pass through the trees, appear suddenly in the woods, and even walk inside tents! She is known for grabbing at people as they are sleeping in their sleeping bags and generally trying to get noticed. It has been theorized that reenacting the scene of her...final circumstances...will trigger activity. (i.e., start a fire, cook some meat, and get to eating).

Address: Interstate 80
Website: www.parks.ca.gov
Activity: A, T

Volcano St. George Hotel

Two other hotels stood on the site that the St. George now occupies: the Eureka and the Empire. Both were destroyed by fires, making way for the present hotel to be built in 1862. Nobody is sure if the two ghosts who are permanent residents of this hotel are a product of either of those fires are not, but one thing is sure—the ghosts are definitely there! The first apparition—seen quite often in the hallways—is a young girl dressed in white. The second spirit is that of an elderly man walking with a cane in his hand. Both spirits are known for visiting folks in their hotel rooms and for responding to questions with knocks on the wall. Witnesses of the haunting have also reported having their beds messed up, items moved around, and hearing the sounds of talking and singing at various hours of the night.

Address: 16104 Main Street
Website: www.stgeorgehotel.com
Activity: A, E, T

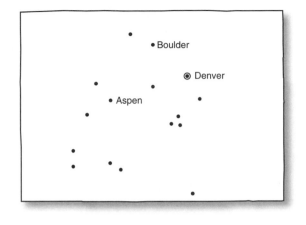

COLORADO

Arvada Yak and Yeti Restaurant

This home was built in 1864 and was known throughout the area for great food when it was called the Cheshire Cat Brewpub. It was also known for the ghost of Cora Van Voorhis. When the place was converted into the Yak and Yeti, employees began to report strange happenings from the restaurant, including pots and pans banging, chairs moving by themselves, and strange voices coming from the kitchen. Many years ago, several generations of the Van Voorhis family lived in this place; Cora died during this time period after she fell down a flight of stairs there. Shortly after Cora's death, family members reported being visited by Cora as well as an "Uncle Ned," who had also died there years before. It seems that Cora and Ned are still there today visiting with the patrons of the Yak and Yeti.

Address: 7803 Ralston Road
Website: www.theyakandyeti.com
Activity: E, T

Aspen Hotel Jerome

This historic hotel—built in 1889—has been one of the premier lodgings in Aspen since the 1950s when the place was frequented by up-and-coming writers, artists, and actors (including John Wayne, Lana Turner, and Gary Cooper). The haunting of this hotel, though, is much less glamorous. Room 310 is rumored to be haunted by the spirit of a little boy who drowned in the hotel's original swimming pool (located one floor beneath this room). Guests have reported seeing a "shivering, wet" apparition in this room. There is also the spirit of an old miner that is seen walking the halls of the hotel and heard crying. It's said that he died in the place after losing his fortune. Finally, there is also the ghost of a former maid that is said to be seen in various rooms, still pulling her weight around the place.

Address: 330 East Main Street
Website: http://hoteljerome.rockresorts.com
Activity: A, E, T

Boulder Boulder Theater/George's Food and Drink

When the Boulder Theater opened up their mini-bar, The Lounge, for its patrons to grab a pre-show bite and drink, it attracted a lot of guests—including one dead one. Not long after opening its doors, employees of The Lounge started noticing strange things happening: doors swinging by themselves, lights turning themselves on and off, and a strange black shape that was seen shooting down the stairs into the restaurant. The ghost is reportedly George Paper, a man who is said to have run the theater in the 1940s. Paper is said to have accidentally hanged himself while repairing some lights. Paper has always haunted the theater, but since opening the little restaurant, he has become more active. In honor of George's sudden spurt of energy, The Lounge has since been renamed "George's Food and Drink." Go share a meal with him there today!

Address: 2032 14th Street
Website: www.bouldertheater.com
Activity: S, T

Breckenridge Historic Brown Hotel

Dating back to the 1860s, this private residence was converted into a school, and then a hotel. Now the place is simply a bar—a bar with its own resident ghost. The old hotel is said to be haunted by a spirit called "Mrs. Whitney." It's said that this female entity is still roaming the area where she was shot and killed by her lover while staying in the hotel. Visitors have felt intense cold spots suddenly appear at times, as

well as seen doors move, faucets turn on and off, and heard a mumbling female voice from the area of the restrooms. With a rich history, and a malevolent spirit, the Historic Brown Hotel makes for an interesting meal.

Address: 208 North Ridge Street
Website: www.historicbrown.com
Activity: C, E, T

Castle Rock Old Stone Church Restaurant

This restaurant was actually a church for many years—all the way from 1888 to 1966. After that, the place sat until 1975 when it was converted into the present-day restaurant. The most common ghost story concerning the old church involves the Choir Loft area. A woman is often seen there wearing a dress. She has also been seen near the stairs, which would have been behind the altar during the old days. Other activity in the restaurant includes sugar caddies flying through the air, chairs moving by themselves, and weird electric fields that seem to appear at intervals inside the dining area. There have also been reports of cold spots and the feeling of something brushing against the backs of patrons.

Address: 210 3rd Street
Website: www.oscrestaurant.com
Activity: C, A, T

Creede The Creede Hotel and Restaurant

Another product of the silver-mining boom of the late 1800s, the town of Creede sprang into being almost overnight. The Creede Hotel (then known as Zang's) was considered one of the classy joints of the day and serviced clientele with a few more dollars to their name. Apparently, the place was so nice that some of the boarders decided to stay there … forever. Guests who stay in this hotel have reported hearing strange voices in their rooms and seeing glimpses of a pale, misty figure in the hallways. Add in the sounds of footsteps and bangs when nobody is around, and you've got a full-fledged haunting!

Address: 120 North Main Street
Website: www.creedehotel.com
Activity: E, A, M

Cripple Creek The Hotel St. Nicholas

This hotel began as a hospital created by the Catholic Order of the Sisters of Mercy in 1898. The sisters left the hospital in 1924 and the place continued to function as a private hospital until 1972. The actual hotel came into being with a new facelift and restoration in 1995. Since that time, employees of the hotel say that two ghosts have been haunting the place: "Stinky" and "Petey." Stinky is said to be a miner who worked in the Cripple Creek area and is often seen walking down the back stairway and sitting in the office at times. Petey, reportedly an orphan who was cared for by the sisters, is known for moving and hiding items in the bar area. Over the years, other areas of the hotel have had experiences as well, such as glimpses of misty apparitions, things moving, and strange sounds where nobody is staying.

Address: 303 North 3rd Street
Website: www.hotelstnicholas.com
Activity: A, E, T, M

Cripple Creek Imperial Casino Hotel

Originating as the Collins Hotel back in 1896, the Imperial was built as a place for people to live after a fire devastated most of the town. The haunting of this hotel and casino seems to involve a man named George Long, one of the men who looked over the place in the early 1900's. Apparently George fell down the stairs that lead to the basement and died as a result. Nonetheless, there were those who thought George had been killed—by his mentally ill daughter, Alice. George had, apparently, married a first cousin, and this is blamed for the woes associated with Alice. When Alice would get out of control, she would be locked in a room adjacent to the present-day hotel lobby (where the Red Rooster bar is now located). Today, folks hear the sounds of a female speaking and scratching coming from the door area of the Red Rooster, as well as things attributed to George—such as turning lights on/off, casino machines going off, and the feeling that somebody is touching you (which especially happens to women).

Address: 123 North 3rd Street
Website: www.imperialcasinohotel.com
Activity: T, E

Denver Black American West Museum

When Dr. Justina L. Ford moved to Denver in 1902, she became one of the area's first female doctors (she was also black, making her one of the first black doctors as well). Over the years of her practice, she delivered over 7,000 newborns in her home—the place where the Black American West Museum now resides. When Ford passed away in the house, it wasn't long before people started noticing strange things were happening. Doors seemed to close and open on their own accord, footsteps were often heard in empty rooms, and the whispy form of an apparition was occasionally glimpsed—an apparition that looked a lot like the veritable Dr. Ford. Visit the museum for a great look at early living in the American West—from an African-American perspective. Just keep an eye out for Dr. Ford!

Address: 3091 California Street
Website: www.blackamericanwestmuseum.com
Activity: A, E, T

Denver The Buckhorn Exchange

In addition to being one of the oldest trading centers in Colorado, the Buckhorn Exchange also possesses the state's oldest liquor license. With so many years of drinking, trading, and fighting, it's no wonder that the restaurant is now haunted. Nobody knows who the ghost happens to be—but most employees agree that the spirit is there. Activity includes tables and chairs moving by themselves, strange voices heard (also noticed by guests there), and dark shadow shapes that shoot along walls in the dining room.

Address: 1000 Osage Street
Website: www.buckhorn.com
Activity: T, E, S

Denver Lumber Baron Inn & Gardens

Named after area lumber entrepreneur John Mouat, the Lumber Baron was built in 1890 and now functions as a bed and breakfast. Before being purchased by the current owner, the house had a reputation as one of the area's most haunted houses. During the 1970s, the site was the scene of a double homicide; two teenage girls were killed in their apartment (now called the Valentine Room in the B&B)—one shot in the head and one strangled and shoved under the bed. Residents and visitors to the house have witnessed a female apparition in this room, as well as on the stairs. But it doesn't end there— according to local paranormal investigators, the place is also haunted by a male entity that is often heard speaking in empty rooms, a black female who once was a maid during the early years of the house, and an older male ghost that appears with the smell of tobacco.

Address: 2555 West 37th Avenue
Website: www.lumberbaron.com
Activity: A, E, T, N

Estes Park Elkhorn Lodge and Guest Ranch

This sprawling ranch has a main lodge, a coach house, cottages, camping, and stables! The interesting thing is there are ghost stories for almost all of them. The stable is said to be haunted by an apparition that enjoys grabbing people and knocking on the walls. The main lodge, which dates back to 1874, is also said to be haunted by the dark shadow of an apparition that's often seen in the common areas on the ground floor. Guests have also reported hearing talking in the

hallways when nobody was present, as well as their faucets inexplicably turning on during the night. Again, activity has been reported throughout the premises at the Elkhorn, so you may want to talk to the employees about current hot spots.

Address: 600 West Elkhorn Avenue
Website: www.elkhornlodge.org
Activity: A, T, E

Estes Park Stanley Hotel

What's left to say about this legendary haunted place? It was the biggest star of the movie *The Shining*; it's been featured on numerous television programs and documentaries about haunted places; and it's one of the highest probability sites for catching evidence of a haunting. Just make sure to hit the hot spots: Room 217 (Stephen King's inspiration), Room 401 (where a glass exploded on the television show *Ghost Hunters*), and Rooms 408 and 418 (which are the most haunted, according to the staff). The concert hall on the premises is also said to have a lot of activity; investigators have captured voices of a young girl who is said to have died in the building. With voices heard in almost every room of the fourth floor, as well as objects/dark shadow-shapes moving in almost every area of the hotel, the Stanley Hotel is one of the country's premier haunts.

Address: 333 Wonderview Avenue
Website: www.stanleyhotel.com
Activity: A, E, T, S, O

Evergreen Historic Brook Forest Inn & Spa

The Brook Forest Inn opened in 1919 and was considered an extremely luxurious place for the times—mostly because of running water and electricity. Today, with the addition of a stellar spa, the inn has the same reputation. It also has the reputation for being haunted—especially in the now infamous Ambassador Suite. It's said that a stable hand strangled his wife to death in this room, and then went to the stables and hung himself. The apparition of a woman has been seen in this room on a regular basis—usually walking on the balcony. At times, she is even visible from the street! In addition to this tale, there is also said to be the ghost of a small boy that roams the third floor. He's thought to be a victim of influenza who passed away in the hotel. The final spirit reported at Brook Forest seems to be that of an ex-employee. He has been spotted on the third floor as well, and witnesses say he appears as a "pale man" who stands in the hallway.

Address: 8136 South Brook Forest Road
Website: www.thebrookforestinn.com
Activity: A, T, E

Glenwood Springs Hotel Colorado

Opening in 1893 with a genuine European spa, the Hotel Colorado catered to the very rich and famous of the day, and had at least two American presidents stay there (William Howard Taft and Theodore Roosevelt). The Colorado is said to be haunted by a veritable "family" of ghosts. There is a man (thought to be Walter Devereux, the original owner of the hotel) that is often accompanied by the scent of tobacco in the lobby. There is a female apparition that's seen in the dining room area (also appearing with a scent—that of a perfume) and in various guest rooms. And there's a female child that is often seen in the hallways of the hotel. Other activity includes an elevator that seems to run by itself at times. The hot spot in the place are Rooms 551, 651, and 652.

Address: 526 Pine Street
Website: www.hotelcolorado.com
Activity: A, E, N, T

Manitou Springs Briarhurst Manor Estate

The Briarhurst is a historic home dating back to 1888. It was built by Dr. William A. Bell for his personal use, but today it functions as a restaurant and an event facility for weddings and get-togethers. Almost every room of the Briarhurst has had reports of the paranormal over the years. The places that seem to come up the most, though, are the library, the Pink Room, and the stairs. Activity in these areas is quite frequent, and seems to include getting your clothes/hair pulled, apparitions that appear before surprised guests, and the sounds of whispering voices. There have also been reports of "old time" music playing in various parts of the house, as well as mysterious cold spots that seem to follow guests around.

Address: 404 Manitou Avenue
Website: www.briarhurst.com
Activity: R, E, A, C, T

Manitou Springs The Historic Miramont Castle

Dating back to 1895, the Miramont has been a landmark in the Manitou Springs area for over a century. With a past that includes being a home, a sanitarium, and an apartment building, it's no wonder that at least one spirit has managed to linger in this wonderful place. The apparition of a woman in a black dress has been seen on more than one occasion—and has even been photographed by a visitor. She's known for peering back at you from mirrors, though she has also been heard singing and talking on the third floor. Visitors have also reported the presence of a male spirit as well—at least one witness has seen a man in a top hat and coat who walked into a wall and disappeared right before his eyes!

Address: 9 Capitol Hill Avenue
Website: www.miramontcastle.org
Activity: A, E, T

the hallways. Visitors have also reported going to their rooms in the evening and finding that their covers have been turned down for them. Friendly ghost, indeed!

Address: 312 Onarga Street
Website: www.paonia-inn.com
Activity: A, E, T

Ouray Beaumont Hotel & Spa

The Beaumont is a historic hotel (built in 1886) with a distinguished past that dates back to the gold rush. With past visitors like Sarah Bernhard, Theodore Roosevelt, and Herbert Hoover, the Beaumont has catered to folks with great taste for more than a hundred years. The ghost story concerning the Beaumont smacks of an urban legend—but even employees of the hotel will tell you that it is true. At least the haunting part anyway … It's said that a woman was killed by a jealous chef who worked in the hotel back in the early 1900s and that he was never convicted of the crime. Now, both the girl and the chef haunt the third floor of the hotel. She has been seen on various room balconies and walking the hallways; he has been seen in various rooms and even photographed peering from a mirror.

Address: 505 Main Street
Website: www.beaumonthotel.com
Activity: A

Paonia Bross Hotel Bed and Breakfast

The Bross Hotel was first opened in 1906 by a local lawman by the name of W. T. Bross. He lived in the establishment with his family while he ran an extremely successful business. When the hotel was refurbished in the 1990s, it seems that at least one guest became a bit agitated: the ghost of Mrs. Bross—the lawman's mother! Employees of the hotel think of Mrs. Bross as a friendly ghost, and suppose that the construction and revitalization of the hotel caused the spirit to become restless and to make herself known. She has been heard and seen in various rooms of the hotel, as well as seen walking

Redstone The Historic Redstone Castle

Ever since John Cleveland Osgood completed this massive castle in 1902, strange stories have circulated about it. After Osgood died in 1927, visitors to the castle would report feeling the presence of somebody in the room with them and smelling cigar smoke. During his tenure at the castle, Osgood managed to work his way through three wives—a fact that made for interesting talk back in the day. It seems that at least one decided to hang around with him in the castle to this day! Several witnesses have stated that the smell of perfume will suddenly appear in various rooms.

Address: 58 Redstone Boulevard
Website: www.redstonecastle.us
Activity: A, N

Silverton The Grand Imperial Hotel

The "G. I.," as it's known to locals of Silverton, has been the social center for the mining community since the late 1800s. Today, the G. I.'s jovial social atmosphere continues—even if the mining has all but dried up. Over the years, employees of the Imperial have stated that this hotel is haunted. Details concerning the spook there are not that detailed, but the reports have been consistent over the years. The ghost has been dubbed "Dr. Luigi" by the folks at the establishment and he is known for making a lot of noise in various rooms on the second floor. One report puts Luigi appearing to customers in the lobby as well, though this doesn't seem to be the norm for this spirit. Check in with the hotel to get more updated information concerning hot spots and sightings in this location.

Address: 1219 Greene Street
Website: www.grandimperialhotel.com
Activity: A, E

South Fork Historic Spruce Lodge

The Spruce Lodge offers traditional rooms for rent, modern rooms/cabins, and has an RV park for those who want to bring their own mobile lodgings. Of course, you'll have to stay in the lodge itself if you want to experience the haunting there. With a past that includes functioning as a hotel, a boarding house, and a restaurant, the Spruce has been serving the public for over 80 years. The current owners knew, though, what they were getting into when they purchased the place: footsteps heard during the night, lights turning themselves on/off, and doors that seem to open and close of their own accord. An apparition of a woman has been reported in the lodge, as well as a girl who's been seen peering from an upstairs window. Hot spots in the place include Rooms 1, 6, and 7 (though it seems that activity has occurred almost everywhere). Other activity at this location includes the sound of footsteps, dark shadow people (seen in various locations), and the sensation of being touched while you sleep.

Address: 29431 West Highway 160
Website: www.sprucelodges.com
Activity: A, E, T

Trinidad Tarabino Inn

Completed in 1907, the house that's now called the Tarabino Inn was built by two of six Tarabino brothers who moved to the United States from Piedmont, Italy. It served as a home for the two brothers and their families for many years before being sold and changing hands many times over the years. The inn is now said to be haunted by the spirit of a female who has appeared to the owners several times. She is usually seen standing at the foot of the stairs while dressed in a long gown. They have also heard the sounds of footsteps and smelled cigar smoke at odd times in the house. However, some of the activity seems to point at a residual haunting. Guests who have stayed in the inn have reported hearing the sounds of a party— or of a huge family—laughing and talking on the ground floor. Even the owners have heard some of these sounds, as well as smelled the scents of "Christmas" in the house.

Address: 310 East 2nd Street
Website: www.tarabinoinn.com
Activity: R, A, E

Victor Victor Hotel

Built in 1899 as a bank, the Victor Hotel has been in operation since 1992. The building itself lay dormant for many years before the current owners renovated and got the Victor going. In addition to holding the funds and monies of area businessmen, the bank is said to also have held the bodies of the dead during the winter months (they would wait until the spring thaw, when the ground was soft, to bury them). This is said to be the cause of the haunting of this hotel. Activity in the hotel includes an elevator (in itself a treasure as it's the old "bird cage" style) that seems to run by itself, a ghost by the name of "Eddie" who haunts Room 301 (said to have died when he fell down the elevator shaft), and an extremely haunted fourth floor where the aforementioned bodies were kept. It's there that employees hear voices, see the apparitions of doctors and patients, and are woken in the middle of the night by people walking around, though nobody is there.

Address: 4th Street and Victor Avenue
Website: www.victorhotelcolorado.com
Activity: A, E

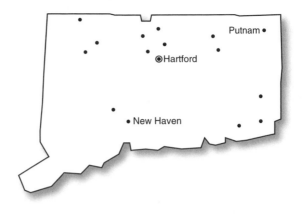

CONNECTICUT

Coventry Nathan Hale Homestead Museum

Nathan Hale was a Revolutionary War hero who was executed by the British after being captured as a spy—but the house that stands at the Homestead Museum was actually more known for Hale's parents, Deacon and Abigail Hale (his stepmother), rather than Nathan. The haunt at the homestead became known locally when a former owner said that he saw the apparition of Deacon Hale staring at him through the front window. Later, he would add that a family servant—a girl named Lydia Carpenter—also haunts the house. Visitors to the museum have heard the sounds of chains clanging, footsteps, and voices.

Address: 2299 South Street
Website: www.coventryct.org
Activity: A, E

East Granby Old New-Gate Prison

Originally a mine, the Old New-Gate Prison came into being when a place was needed to house prisoners during the Revolutionary War. The place continued to function as such through the Civil War. Over the course of this place's history, many deaths have occurred within this location. Tour guides will point out a place where a man was crushed to death while mining there (a place that is also said to be haunted) as well as locations where prisoners were killed trying to make their escape. Paranormal activity at the prison includes voices, orbs, and residual sounds associated with mining there. Take the tour they offer—this is the best way to note the spots where tragedy struck those who inhabited the place.

Address: Located along Newgate Road
Website: www.eastgranby.com
Activity: S, O, R, E

East Hartford Makens Bemont House

Known locally as the Huguenot House, this historic building is located in the heart of Martin's Park in East Hartford. Along with the Goodwin Schoolhouse and the Burnham Blacksmith Shop, the home is part of a complex/living museum that's managed by the Historical Society of East Hartford. The structure was originally built by Edmund Bemont in 1761 and it served his family for many generations until the last living relative, Adolph Rosenthal, donated the property to the historical society in 1968. Paranormal activity began in the house when it was moved from Tolland Street into the park. Employees and visitors alike began seeing a male and female apparition there (dubbed "Benny" and the "Blue Lady"). Many believe the female spirit to be one Abigail Bemont, wife of Edmund, but this isn't certain. Activity includes the sounds of knocks/bangs and objects moving during the night—in addition to sightings of the actual phantoms!

Address: 307 Burnside Avenue
Website: www.hseh.org
Activity: A, E, T

East Windsor Jonathan Pasco's

This restaurant is named after the famous Revolutionary War hero that built this building as his home in 1784. Today, Pasco's is known for its delicious food, great beer list, and the spirit of Pasco himself, who is said to still walk the halls of his famous home. The owners of the restaurant—as well as other employees—have said that they have noticed doors opening and closing of their own accord, felt intense cold spots mysteriously appear, and have heard the sounds of talking and walking in the upstairs area of the restaurant when nobody was supposed to be up there.

Address: 31 South Main Street
Website: www.jonathanpascos.net
Activity: O, C, E, T

Griswold Homespun Farm B&B

With a history that dates back to Simon Brewster and the early 1700s, this historic location functioned as a dairy and area orchard for over 200 years while it was in the Brewster family. Today, it is a bed and breakfast with a whole new family that runs the place—though you can argue that Simon Brewster has never left … It's said that the spirit of Brewster still walks the home and likes to make himself known to visitors by walking loudly through the hallways, whispering in people's ears, and generally watching the proceedings that take place in his old house. The second floor is said to be more active than the first—though activity does happen there on occasion.

Address: 306 Preston Road
Website: www.homespunfarm.com
Activity: E

Hartford Old State House

Before this historical building was even built, the site of the Old State House was already a notorious one. This was the place where witches were hung—the first of which occurred in 1647. After the State House was erected, reports of ghostly activity began filtering from the place. These rumors and reports persisted through the years, even as the house became a museum. During the 1970s, famed psychic researcher Lorraine Warren and her husband, Ed Warren (a demonologist), visited this site and declared it to be haunted by not only a witch, but the ghost of one of the former museum employees, Joseph Steward. Visitors today have reported seeing apparitions, as well as hearing the footsteps and residual sounds of a phantom meeting taking place.

Address: 800 Main Street
Website: www.ctoldstatehouse.org
Activity: A, E, R

Litchfield The Litchfield Inn

The Litchfield Inn is one of those places that people point at and whisper about when they pass—and the small town of Litchfield, Connecticut, has been doing just that for many years! It is said locally that the place is haunted by the spirit of a Native American woman. She has been seen in the front yard outside the premises, as well as peering from ground-floor windows. A former employee of the inn told a Connecticut paranormal investigator that the apparition of the girl has been seen many times in the inn—especially on the ground floor in the common areas. It's said that she likes music, and that playing it will draw the woman out into the open to make an appearance.

Address: 432 Bantam Road
Website: www.litchfieldinnct.com
Activity: A

Mystic The Captain Daniel Packer Inne Restaurant and Pub

This extremely old, but well-kept site was built in 1756 by Captain Daniel Packer, a seafarer who knew that travelers needed a place to rest while journeying between Boston and New York. Since the establishment is right along the Mystic River, he would also be responsible for ferrying them across the water to continue their journey. Today, this pub and restaurant is said to be haunted. Though the exact entity isn't known (many think it is Packer), the telltale signs are all there: strange sounds, voices, orbs, and doors that seem to always open and close by themselves.

Address: 32 Water Street
Website: www.danielpacker.com
Activity: E, O, T

New Haven Fort Nathan Hale

Fort Nathan Hale was constructed in 1807 from the remains of Black Rock Fort—a massive barracks that was burned by the British in 1779 during the Battle of New Haven. During the Civil War, a second fort was built beside the first, but neither saw any action—at least not any action of the war type. The whole area surrounding Fort Nathan Hale is considered a massive haunted hot spot. Numerous sightings of green balls of light, ghost soldiers, voices, etc., have been reported here for over a hundred years. Many think the ghosts are a remnant of the battle that took place there—though locals have also said that the balls of light go back to the days of area settlers and that the spirits could be those of Native Americans buried in the area.

Address: 50 Woodward Avenue
Website: www.fort-nathan-hale.org
Activity: O, A, E

New London Lighthouse Inn Resort

Designed by William Emerson (the creator of Central Park in New York), the Lighthouse Inn was originally home to Charles S. Guthrie, a massive figure in the steel industry. The home was built in 1902 and was originally called Meadow Court. It was converted into an inn in 1927 and it has remained so since. Under the inn is a set of passageways that is said to be haunted—there are footsteps heard here, as well as cold spots and orbs present—and it doesn't stop there. There are several ghosts within the place: a bride who is said to have died while falling down the stairs (she is seen there, as well as in the hallways and guest rooms) and several child spirits (who are usually heard in the hallways). Customers have also made sporadic reports of being watched and touched while staying in the Lighthouse Inn.

Address: 6 Guthrie Place
Website: www.lighthouseinn-ct.com
Activity: E, T, O

New London New London Ledge Lighthouse

Considered one of the most unique lighthouses in all of America, the Ledge began operation at the mouth of the Thames River in 1909. If you believe the haunted history of this lighthouse, it wasn't long after that that a man named "Ernie" would have taken his life by cutting his throat and falling into the waters below. Of course, this info is courtesy of paranormal researchers Roger and Nancy Pile, not known fact. What is known, however, is that the haunting of the lighthouse is well documented; whether it's the infamous video of Japanese thrill seekers getting frightened on YouTube or the television series *Scariest Places on Earth*, Ledge Lighthouse is a media darling and a place that frightens those who visit. Project Oceanology offers tours to the lighthouse, so jump on board and visit Ernie while you're in the area!

Address: One mile offshore from the town of New London
Website: www.oceanology.org
Activity: E, T, S, A

New London The O'Neill Monte Cristo Cottage

The Monte Cristo Cottage—owned and operated by the Eugene O'Neill Theatre Center—was the boyhood home of playwright Eugene O'Neill. The place is a historic site and has drawn tourists from all over the world (and not just fans of the theatre). The house is said to be haunted—some say by Eugene himself, others say his mother, Ella Quinlan O'Neill. Eugene spent his summers in this house after his youth, and even wrote some of his best work here (*Ah, Wilderness!* and *Long Day's Journey Into Night*), so he may haunt the place where he spent so many happy days. As for his mother ... well, that's a different story. She was an addict (morphine) and spent many horrible days in the house—once even attempting suicide. Whether it's Eugene or Ella, visitors have heard voices and footsteps, as well as seen misty figures walking through the rooms.

Address: 325 Pequot Avenue
Website: www.theoneill.org
Activity: M, E

Norfolk The Blackberry River Inn

Known for a female ghost called the White Lady, the Blackberry River Inn is a great local place to stay if you want a high probability for seeing an apparition. With a residual haunting atmosphere, the spirit of this unknown woman is said to walk almost nightly down the main hallways of the second floor of this inn. She has also been spotted walking a small path between the main house and a small cottage that resides close by. Nothing is heard or felt concerning the White Lady—only seen. Keep your vigil of either of these two locations in the wee hours after the other guests have gone to sleep for your best chance of an encounter.

Address: 538 Greenwoods Road
Website: www.blackberryriverinn.com
Activity: A, R

Preston Captain Grant's, 1754

Constructed by Captain William Gonzales Grant in 1754 for his wife, this house has been used as a garrison for soldiers (during the Civil War), a safe haven for runaway slaves and (today) as a historic inn. Employees of the inn—as well as numerous guests who have stayed there—have said that they believe the place to be haunted...and by none other than the wife of old Captain Grant: Mercy Adelaide Grant. She is said to be a "prophetic" ghost that appears when a person is in need within the house. In addition to Mercy, there has also been activity in the inn that points to a child ghost—including laughing, voices, and the pattering of little feet. The child is also thought to be one of the Grant family members and is often encountered in various rooms and hallways of the inn.

Address: 109-111 Route 2A
Website: www.captaingrants.com
Activity: A, E

Putnam The Bradley Playhouse

This old theater was opened to the public in 1901 and has been rumored to be haunted almost since the day of its first performance. The principal spirit of the place is said to be a woman named Victoria who is known for haunting the balcony of the theater. She is usually there when the area is empty—though she has also been known to completely leave that area and visit with those on stage. Other activity has occurred in the basement and backstage areas as well. As a visitor to the playhouse, you may want to try and get a sight of the ghost from the balcony; at least, if she doesn't show there, you have a good view of the stage!

Address: 30 Front Street
Website: www.thebradleyplayhouse.info
Activity: A

Seymour Carousel Gardens

The Carousel Gardens mansion was built in 1894 by William Henry Harrison Wooster as a home for him and his wife. Today, the place is a restaurant and banquet hall and has been known throughout the area as a haunted place since the famous Warren duo (Lorraine and Ed) visited the house and declared it to be so. Some of the activity reported in the home include a ghost cat who has been seen on the second floor, the sounds of bangs and things breaking, and a female apparition by the name of "Ruth" who is known to hang out in the bar area. Ruth has been seen moving bar glasses, making cutlery fly across the room and tugging on people's clothing as they dine.

Address: 153 North Street
Website: www.carouselgardens.com
Activity: A, T, E

Simsbury Sage American Grill

Known to locals for years as the Chart House Restaurant, area paranormal groups have held that this location has been haunted for many years. Visitors to the place have witnessed chairs moving by themselves, as well as heard the sounds of voices and footsteps. According to at least one investigator, the place was inhabited by a dark entity during the years the place was the Chart House—an entity with malicious intent who fed off dark feelings and acts perpetrated here many years ago. What acts are these, you ask? Who knows? The place has since changed into the Sage American, but is still considered to be haunted by most. You would probably need to visit to find out for yourself.

Address: 100 South Water Street
Website: www.sageamerican.com
Activity: E, T

Tolland Daniel Benton Homestead

The Daniel Benton house was built in 1720 and was the home of the Benton family for over 200 years. This means that many members of this family lived and died within these walls (dying in your own home was the norm of the period). During the Revolutionary War, the homestead was the site of a mini-prison, courtesy of the house's basement. One of the prisoners held there—a soldier from that war—is now said to haunt the house. But he is not alone ... A female apparition (believed to be Elisha Benton, a girl who died of smallpox within the home) is also seen at times walking the grounds of the property—as well as peering from the place's ground floor windows.

Address: Located on Metcalf Road
Website: www.tollandhistorical.org
Activity: A, E, S

Torrington The Yankee Pedlar Inn

Originally called Conley's Inn (after the original owner, Frank Conley), the Yankee Pedlar was first opened in 1891. It's said that Conley's bedroom in the inn is the central location for the haunting that occurs here. Visitors who have stayed in this room have reported hearing voices, seeing doors open/close by themselves, and feeling the presence of somebody standing over them as they sleep. But paranormal activity is not limited to just this room. Almost every area of the inn has had something happen—so make sure to check out all the common areas of this place as well (especially the lobby and hallways).

Address: 93 Main Street
Website: www.pedlarinn.com
Activity: A, E, T, O, C

West Hartford Noah Webster House

Sightings of a female apparition at this location have been reported on many "haunted websites" over the years. It's reported that she is seen peering from the downstairs windows. Workers within the Noah Webster museum have said, though, that they have never witnessed this. They have experienced a door opening to the basement and strange voices/bangs that seem to come from the attic area. Nobody is sure who the apparition—if there is one—seems to be, but there does seem to be some paranormal activity in this old house. The Noah Webster place is now a museum and can be visited by the public. Tour the house and decide if it is haunted for yourself.

Address: 227 South Main Street
Website: www.noahwebsterhouse.org
Activity: A, T, E

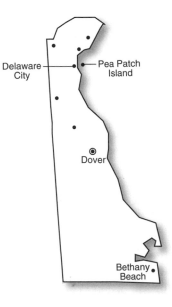

Delaware
City

Pea Patch
Island

Dover

Bethany
Beach

DELAWARE

Bethany Beach Addy Sea Bed and Breakfast

John M. Addy built this luxurious home for his family in 1902, and they lived in this house for several generations before the current owners took possession and turned the place into a bed and breakfast. According to visitors, the Addy Sea is haunted—in three spots actually. Room 1 of the B&B is said to have a spirit that likes to shake the bed and bathtub when you are in them. Room 6 is said to be plagued with the sounds of voices and an old-time organ playing. Room 11 is said to be visited by the apparition of a former worker, Paul Dulaney. Other hot spots include the hallways and the attic/roof (where footsteps are often heard).

Address: 99 Ocean View Parkway
Website: www.addysea.com
Activity: A, E, T, R

Dover Leone's Lookerman Exchange

This bar and restaurant has a relatively new history. Prior to its recent renovation, the employees there reported seeing strange shadow shapes that would completely black out windows and walls, and shoot at a high rate of speed across the room. Inexplicably, strange fires started spontaneously in random locations throughout the restaurant as well. The basement area of the exchange also seems to be a hot spot—though you may have to settle for visiting the main dining/bar area. Other activity in the place includes glowing balls of light, voices, and the occasional chair moving.

Address: 1 West Loockerman Street
Website: www.loockerman.com
Activity: S, O, T, E

Dover Woodburn Mansion

The home of the present-day governor of Delaware is known as Woodburn and was built in 1798 by Charles Hillyard III. The first time a ghost was reported within Woodburn was in 1815, when the Bates family (the residents at the time) was entertaining a local preacher. The devout Methodist reported seeing a man on the stairs in a powdered wig and short breeches. The man, thought to be Hillyard himself, is still seen to this very day … along with a young girl in a dress and bonnet. Tours of the historic place are made available to the public—visit their website for dates and times.

Address: 151 King's Highway
Website: http://woodburn.delaware.gov/
Activity: A, T, E

Middletown Locust Grove Farm

This old farmstead is as known for its fabulous gardens as it is for its regular events. With tours, several festivals, and a yearly corn maze, visitors to Locust Grove are always in for an adventure—especially if they happen to catch a glimpse of the resident spirit. Over the years, reports have circulated in this area concerning the ghost of a young boy who is often seen within the house. It's thought that he was probably a family member who died of natural causes in the home. Additional paranormal activity on the farm includes the sounds of voices, footsteps, and objects being knocked about.

Address: 1084 Bethel Church Road
Website: www.visitdelaware.com
Activity: A, E

New Castle Amstel House Museum

This is the first of two houses in New Castle built by Dr. John Finney—and both of them are now haunted, as well as connected by a tunnel that runs between them. So it is possible that the ghost of the two houses is one and the same. Many believe the spirit within the Amstel house is that of John or his son David. It's said that the third floor is the area with the most activity—including doors opening/closing, lights turning on/off, and the sounds of heavy footsteps. Visit the museum's website for their hours of operation and to plan your trip there.

Address: 2 East Fourth Street
Website: www.newcastlehistory.org
Activity: T, E

New Castle David Finney Inn

As mentioned above, the David Finney Inn is connected to the Amstel House by an underground tunnel. Unlike the Amstel House (which is a museum), the David Finney is a bed and breakfast, so you can actually stay here after taking a tour of the museum. Much like the other home, the third floor is also said to be the most haunted. It experiences much of the same ghostly activity as the Amstel House—a fact that has led many investigators/visitors to believe that maybe both houses are actually haunted by the same entity. Sleep here and visit Amstel and you've hit both places in one easy shot!

Address: 216 Delaware Street
Website: www.newcastlecity.net
Activity: T, E

Newark Cooch's Bridge

This was the location of the only battle fought in Delaware during the Revolutionary War—and the first battle where the Stars and Stripes were proudly flown. The battle was fought on September 3, 1777, and was, unfortunately, lost by the colonial troops as ammo ran low. The area was subsequently taken by the British. Today, the bridge is located along Highway 95 outside the city of Newark. The place is said to be haunted by the spirits of the fallen troops of this battle. Locals over the years have witnessed glowing orbs/apparitions and heard the residual sounds of a battle taking place.

Address: Highway 95
Website: www.cityofnewarkde.us
Activity: O, A, R

Newark The Deer Park Tavern

There are a lot of interesting tales about this circa-1851 tavern. It is said to stand on the grounds of another place called the St. Patrick's Inn, which burned down many years ago. Famous guests to the former location included George Washington and the creators of the Mason-Dixon Line. It's also said that Edgar Allan Poe visited the famous inn and (supposedly) wrote the poem "The Raven" there. More recently, the Deer Park is known for their Mug Club and a ghost that is said to haunt the stairway. Numerous people have heard strange noises from the stairs, including footsteps, coughing, and voices.

Address: 108 West Main Street
Website: www.deerparktavern.com
Activity: E

Newark Salem Church Road

Ahh...there's nothing like a good legend involving witches and ghosts. The story is even better when the ghosts *are* witches! During the infamous witch hunts and trials of early America, local folklore holds that an entire family was found guilty for practicing the dark arts and was summarily hanged along an old dirt path in the area. This path eventually evolved into a road: Salem Church Road. Today, travelers along this road often spot dark shadow shapes, ghost lights, and even the occasional apparition walking. Though tales of roads like this have been cataloged in almost every state, paranormal research groups in this area have reported that this

activity does, indeed, happen here and that your chances of seeing the same events are high.

Address: Self Explanatory
Website: www.cityofnewarkde.us
Activity: A, O, S

Pea Patch Island Fort Delaware

Dating back to 1859, Fort Delaware was famous during the Civil War as a place where Confederate soldiers did not want to end up—prison. Most believe the haunting here has to do with the prison as well. Because of the huge number of lives that were lost during the war, the entire fort grounds is said to be haunted. Thankfully, you can now take a quick ferry over to the island and tour the place. Some hot spots you may want to concentrate on are the dungeon area (where many prisoners died), the parade grounds (where apparitions of soldiers are seen), and most areas of the actual fortress.

Address: Reach the Island via Ferry from Delaware City
Website: www.destateparks.com
Activity: A, S, O, C, E, T

Smyrna Smyrna Museum

Built sometime around the year 1800, the house that is now called the Smyrna Museum was best known for being a barracks during the War of 1812. During the Civil War, the place was used as a center for drafting soldiers into the Union army. The paranormal activity that occurs in this museum has been reported by several visitors, as well as museum staff members.

While there's nothing concrete in the reports—mostly just the weird sounds of things moving and voices—quite a few people have reported feeling an overwhelming sense of something watching them while they are in the building.

Address: 11 South Main Street
Website: www.delawarebeautiful.com
Activity: E

Wilmington Bellevue Hall

Originally a home to the famous DuPont family of Delaware, Bellevue Hall is a place that has gone through many changes. When William du Pont Jr. bought the place, it was a Gothic Revival castle—but this wouldn't last. He quickly set about transforming the place into an exact replica of Montpelier, the home of President James Madison. Today, the structure is the centerpiece of the wonderful Bellevue Park. According to locals (and employees), the house is now so haunted that the second and third floors cannot be rented out (its primary source of income is from conferences held on the first floor). The off-limits areas have been plagued with the sounds of footsteps, laughing, crying, voices, whispers—pretty much every noise in the haunted handbook!

Address: 720 Carr Road
Website: www.destateparks.com
Activity: E, T

Wilmington Dead Presidents Pub & Restaurant

The old buildings that make up the pub and restaurant at this establishment were once two individual places—homes, actually. They were built in 1806, and over the years since the families moved out of these buildings, many businesses and ventures have lived and died there. Today, though, there is a thriving business—a place that's said to be haunted. Some say the ghost is that of a regular patron who slipped, fell, and died there in the 1960s—others say it's haunted because the basement area of one of the houses was once a chapel where the dead were laid out for viewing. Either way, visitors have witnessed things moving around the kitchen and dining areas, including dishes that have been thrown at employees. Voices and laughs have been heard in the same areas as well.

Address: 618 North Union Street
Website: www.deadpresidentspub.com
Activity: E, T

Wilmington Rockwood Museum

The Rockwood mansion/museum was built somewhere between 1851 and 1854—researchers are unsure of the actual date—by Joseph Shipley in a Gothic Revival style. The place served as his family home for many years, until it finally passed down into the hands of the Bringhurst family (descendents of Shipley). The house has been known throughout the twentieth century and beyond as a place that's haunted by strange, glowing balls of light. Witnesses have seen them inside the empty house at night (usually seen from the street by passersby) and even shooting through rooms while tours were taking place! Today, Rockwood offers overnight ghost tours and sleepovers, as well as the usual museum tours during the day.

Address: 610 Shipley Road
Website: www.rockwood.org
Activity: O

Woonsocket Mount Saint Charles Academy

Founded by the Brothers of the Sacred Heart in 1924, the Mount Saint Charles Academy is one of those places that's been rumored to be haunted for quite some time. This is mostly due to stories on the Internet. Unfortunately, the exact details concerning the haunt vary, but they usually involve shadow shapes on the property, apparitions of people seen around the main building, and various orbs/glowing balls of light. But investigators in Delaware back the story up and say that much of the activity there has been witnessed and documented. The Academy is a junior/senior high school in the area, so be respectful when touring the grounds—or just stop by the office there and let them know you're visiting.

Address: 800 Logee Street
Website: www.mountsaintcharles.org
Activity: S, O, A

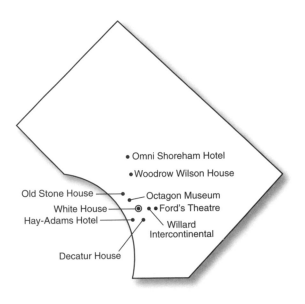

- Omni Shoreham Hotel
- Woodrow Wilson House

Old Stone House —• Octagon Museum
White House —◉ • •Ford's Theatre
Hay-Adams Hotel —•
Willard
Intercontinental

Decatur House

DISTRICT OF COLUMBIA

Decatur House on Lafayette Square

Built by famous naval hero Nathan Decatur, this house dates back to 1818. It would be in this home where Decatur would die of wounds that resulted from a famous duel with a fellow naval officer. Activity in the house includes the apparition of Decatur—and also his wife Susan—being spotted in various places, as well as the sounds of footsteps, bangs, etc. The home has been investigated by local paranormal investigators and they, as well as the folks who work on the premises, believe the place is, indeed, haunted. Today, the place is a museum that hosts numerous interesting exhibits. They also allow people to rent the place for events. Maybe a ghost hunt?

Address: 1610 H Street Northwest
Website: www.decaturhouse.org
Activity: A, E

Ford's Theater

The spirit of Abraham Lincoln is quite a busy one! Besides being seen in the Parker House (where he died), the White House, and the Capitol building, it's also said that Lincoln haunts Ford's Theater, where he was shot by John Wilkes Booth. Famed Civil War photographer Matthew Brady is said to have taken a photo of the spirit while documenting the theater for the murder trial of Booth (the photo is included here). Of course, the ghost could also be attributed to one of the estimated 22 workers who were killed in the building when it collapsed about 30 years later. Today, the place has been fully renovated and is completely safe—unless you are afraid of seeing a possible spirit roaming the grounds! Some believe the ghost is Lincoln; some think it's Booth. Actors over the years have felt his presence on the stage and many have claimed to see the apparition in the box where Lincoln was shot.

Address: 511 10th Street Northwest
Website: www.fords.org
Activity: A

The Hay-Adams Hotel

Long before this place was a hotel, it was the home of historian Henry Adams and his wife Marian. While they lived there, Marian collapsed and died in front of the downstairs fireplace one evening and was later found by her husband. Today, the Hay-Adams Hotel is still haunted by the very presence of Marian. Persistent cold spots are found on the first floor (including the area near the fireplace) and her apparition has been said to visit people staying in the hotel. She is said to be full of despair and a frightening sight to those who have witnessed the ghost.

Address: 16th and H Street Northwest
Website: http://www.hayadams.com/
Activity: A, C

Octagon House

The Octagon Museum is said to be (probably) the single most haunted location in all of Washington, D. C. Whether or not this is true can be debated; however, it is true that there are probably more stories of ghosts and spirits in this location than in any other. Dating back to 1799, the Octagon House is said to have had at least two women leap to their deaths from the stair landings, as well as a man who was shot to death in one of the upstairs bedrooms. Other ghostly stories include Dolley Madison returning from the grave to visit the house (the Madisons stayed here for a spell) and haunted tunnels beneath the home that were once used to shuttle slaves during the Civil War. Activity includes the sounds of a residual haunt (carriages, parties, etc.), a female who screams and a male voice that's often heard on the stairs and in the upstairs area.

Address: 18th Street and New York Avenue
Northwest
Website: http://www.nps.gov/history/nr/travel/
wash/dc22.htm
Activity: A, R, E

Old Stone House

Possibly the oldest haunted building in Washington, D. C. (it was built in 1795), the Old Stone House is said to be inhabited by a very angry spirit that employees call "George." The entity is said to walk the third floor (especially in the bedroom) and is known to push people, yell in an angry voice, and to pace violently back and forth across the hard floor there. When the house was a bordello, it was whispered that George did even crueler acts in the bedroom, including rape and murder! A local psychic who went into the Old Stone House declared the place to be haunted by at least ten different spirits (something that has been, in part, corroborated by witnesses who have seen a female apparition on the staircase). Today, the house is run by the park service and can be toured.

Address: 3051 M Street Northwest
Website: http://www.nps.gov/olst/planyourvisit/
    directions.htm
Activity: A, E, T

Omni Shoreham Hotel

This luxurious hotel is said to have a haunted executive suite—a suite with five rooms, no less! Needless to say, this may be one of the most comfortable locations to investigate the paranormal in Washington, D. C. The ghosts who inhabit the area are said to be a girl named Juliette Brown, who was a housekeeper, and a girl named Helen, who was an adopted daughter of the hotel owner. Activity in the suite includes the sounds of a female talking, as well as an apparition that is said to be seen walking through the room or standing at the foot of the bed when people are sleeping there. Guests have reported having their luggage and personal items moved, and even finding the place to be cleaned up while they were absent!

Address: 2500 Calvert Street Northwest
Website: www.omnihotels.com
Activity: A, E

The White House

Stories of ghosts in the White House have circulated D. C. almost since the place came into existence in the late 1700s. The first presidential inhabitants—President John Adams and his wife Abigail—are numbered among the first ghosts to haunt the place. Abigail is said to roam the East Room. Other presidential spirits include Abraham Lincoln (in the Lincoln Bedroom), William Henry Harrison (in the attic), and Andrew Jackson (in the Rose Bedroom). Fortunately, most of the haunted locations in the White House are included on the tour there, so head on over and check it out (just make sure you can get on the tour list by contacting your local U.S. representative).

Address: 1600 Pennsylvania Avenue Northwest
Website: www.whitehouse.gov
Activity: A, E, C, O, S, T

Willard InterContinental Washington

With a rich history that includes the visitation by presidents (including Abraham Lincoln), royalty, and celebrities, it's no wonder that the Willard is considered a great local site in Washington. Of course, it could also be because the place is also considered a great local haunted place. It's said that the hotel's front lobby is visited on a regular basis by the spirit of former president Ulysses S. Grant. During his presidency, Grant would make almost daily visits to the hotel to chat with people in the lobby, discuss politics, and have a drink and smoke (resulting in the term "lobbyists"). Today, the presence of Grant's ghost is announced by the smell of a fine cigar appearing out of nowhere, as well as the feeling of a strange presence.

Address: 1401 Pennsylvania Avenue Northwest
Website: www.washington.intercontinental.com
Activity: N

Woodrow Wilson House

This house, built in the Georgian Revival style, was completed in 1915 and was later purchased by Wilson in 1921. After his presidency, Wilson and his family would live here until his death in 1924. During the 1960s, this house was investigated as a haunted location by famed paranormal researcher Hans Holzer. During this investigation, Holzer came to the conclusion that the place was haunted by Woodrow Wilson and that, through a psychic, the ghost was communicating with those who lived there. Visitors, as well as employees, have experienced cold spots, strange sounds, and glimpses of an apparition in the place over the years. Today, the house is open for tours to the public. Go to their website for dates and times.

Address: 2340 S Street Northwest
Website: http://www.woodrowwilsonhouse.org/
Activity: A, E, C

Tallahasse ◉ •

Jacksonville

Daytona
Beach

Sarasota

Miami

Key West

FLORIDA

Apalachicola Gibson Inn

This historic house (listed on the National Register) is said to be haunted by the spirit of a sea captain who was brought into the house to recover from sickness. The man is said to have died in the home from complications arising from his pneumonia—and he never left! Employees, as well as guests of the inn, have reported a male apparition that is often seen walking the halls and even visiting patrons in the middle of the night. He makes his presence known in rooms by pulling the covers off the bed, and he is often heard walking in the upstairs area. Guests have even reported hearing the piano (which is located downstairs) playing during odd hours of

the night and—after inspection—found to have nobody playing it.

Address: 51 Avenue C
Website: www.gibsoninn.com
Activity: A, E, T

Bartow The Stanford Inn

This Victorian bed and breakfast was built as a home by local attorney W. L. Wilson in 1906. Since then, it has survived as an inn and now a B&B. The house recently appeared in the movie *My Girl* and has been featured in several prominent magazines as a tourist attraction. The house is also said to be haunted! The ghost is thought to be one of the former innkeeper/owners. The apparition of the man is said to be seen—and often heard—on the stairs of the

B&B. This spirit is usually considered the culprit when doors open/close by themselves, lights turn on/off, and items are suddenly found in odd locations throughout the place.

Address: 555 East Stanford Street
Website: www.thestanfordinn.com
Activity: A, E, T

Brooksville Hernando Heritage Museum

Before becoming a museum, this place was known as the May-Stringer house. It dates back to the mid-1800s and holds a lot of local history. It also holds a lot of personal history for the May and Stringer families who lived there—including the deaths of many loved ones on the premises. These deaths are considered the source of the paranormal activity at this location. One of the ghosts said to haunt the place is that of a young girl who is often heard crying for her mother. She is also held responsible for numerous toys and exhibitions being moved or shifted over the course of the evening. There is possibly a second entity in the house—another female according to the accounts of investigators who have worked in the house. She has also been heard and recorded there. The museum offers regular ghost tours and events, so visiting the spirits at this location is quite easy.

Address: 601 Museum Court
Website: www.hernandohistoricalmuseum.com
Activity: E, T

Cassadaga Cassadaga Hotel

In addition to being a haunted hotel, the Cassadaga is also famous for being the centerpiece of an entire paranormal community! Known as a spiritualist center, the area is home to numerous psychics, mediums, fortune-tellers, etc.—many of whom actually will visit you in the hotel to give you a personal reading. As for the haunting, the place is said to be inhabited by a male spirit who is accompanied by the scent of a cigar. There are also two little girls who are often heard laughing and playing in various places throughout the hotel. The hotel owners and employees are openly fond of their ghosts, so let them know you are hunting their spirits when you check in, and you'll get the most current information regarding the hot spots there.

Address: 355 Cassadaga Road
Website: www.cassadagahotel.net
Activity: A, E, T, O

Cedar Key Island Hotel & Restaurant

The building that now houses the Island Hotel is said to have been constructed between 1859 and 1860. After a hurricane, a fire, and the collapse of local business, the hotel fell on hard times in the early 1900s. Today, the building is a much happier place—even considering the fact that the place is haunted. Hotel employees will tell you that the building is haunted by 13 ghosts, including a boy, a soldier, a prostitute, past guests, and more. Hot spots in the hotel include the second floor (where the soldier is seen), Rooms 27 and 28 (where the apparition of a female prostitute is seen and often felt), and Room 29 (a location said to be haunted by Bessie Gibbs, a resident of the hotel for over 26 years). The hotel has been featured on several television shows, as well as in print, so you may want to learn more about the varied and numerous spirits of this place prior to visiting.

Address: 373 2nd Street
Website: www.islandhotel-cedarkey.com
Activity: A, O, S, E, T

Clearwater Belleview Biltmore Resort

Built in 1897, the Belleview has played host to many historic and celebrity guests over the years. It seems that ever since this upscale hotel opened its doors, it has been considered one of the best places to stay in the area. So good, in fact, that at least one guest has decided to stay on after death. The hotel is said to be haunted by a female apparition that is often seen walking around the upper floors in a wedding dress. Glimpses of a male apparition in uniform have also occurred sporadically in this hotel—as well as strange phenomena that most believe to be paranormal: lights turning themselves on/off, elevators running with nobody in them, and the sounds of banging and footsteps that seem to originate from the top floor.

Address: 25 Belleview Boulevard
Website: www.belleviewbiltmore.com
Activity: A, E, T

Clewiston Clewiston Inn

The Clewiston opened doors for business in 1938 and has been considered a haunted hotel for over 20 years. It's said the place is occupied by three ghosts. The kitchen area of the hotel is said to be the haunt of a former chef who likes to bang/move pots and pans. The first floor of the hotel is said to be haunted by a female apparition who has been seen numerous times by employees and guests. Finally, the second floor has a permanent resident in the form of a female spirit who stayed after dying from a heart attack in a room. Activity occurs in the hallways, the stairs, and many of the guest rooms. The hotel even claims to have a photograph of one of the female spirits hanging in the lobby!

Address: 108 Royal Palm Avenue
Website: www.clewistoninn.com
Activity: A, E, T

Daytona Beach Daytona Playhouse

The Daytona Playhouse is reportedly the site of a ghostly love story. The place is said to be haunted by the spirits of a man and woman who are thought to have been lovers during the early days of this place's history. Though it sounds like an urban legend, or one of the plays that would premier in the playhouse, investigators in Florida say the history and story holds water. The man apparently went to Spain to participate in the wars there and died while doing so. Of course, this was unknown to his lover, who waited for him in Daytona. After the man did not return, she eventually committed suicide by leaping into the Halifax River where she drowned. The playhouse is now haunted by both spirits, who have reunited within this building, and celebrate their reunion by stomping around, moving props, and making the occasional appearance backstage.

Address: 100 Jessamine Boulevard
Website: www.daytonaplayhouse.org
Activity: A, E, T

Deland Putnam Hotel

The original version of this historic hotel burned down in 1917, but was rebuilt to accommodate a sudden boom in population in Deland during the early 1920s (the second version actually opened in 1923). Aside from the fire, the story of the hotel is pretty much on point with most older hotels in America—unless you include the story of a murder-suicide that's said to have taken place there. Details concerning the act are sketchy, but hotel employees love to tell the story anyway. Apparently, a visiting couple got into an argument, which ended with the husband murdering the wife, then him committing suicide. Since then, apparitions of a male and female have been seen on the upper floors of the hotel, as well as a shadowy shape (most believe to be another form of the male entity) that is often seen shooting through various rooms.

Address: 225 West New York Avenue
Website: www.deland.org
Activity: A, S

Fernandina Beach Fort Clinch State Park

Construction on this historic—but never battle-tested—fort began in 1847, but was never finished. What was constructed, though, was used as a post during the Civil War and the Spanish-American War. Paranormal investigators have said that this area is haunted by the soldiers who had a nice station at the fort before moving on to other harsher battles; since their time at Fort Clinch was a good one, their spirits returned for more duty. Activity includes orbs, voices/whispers, and strange mists that are seen to move against the wind.

Address: 2601 Atlantic Avenue
Website: www.floridastateparks.org/fortclinch/
Activity: O, M, E

Ft. Lauderdale Stranahan House

Located on the historic River Walk of Ft. Lauderdale, the Stranahan House was built in 1901 as a trading post before becoming the permanent residence of Frank and Ivy Stranahan. Permanent because it's said that both former residents still haunt the house today. Frank is often seen walking in and out of the bathroom, as well as in the hallways. Also, strange moans that many say are male in origin seem to emanate from the walls throughout the house. The spirit of Ivy seems to enjoy the gift shop area of the house. Her presence is associated with the sudden smell of perfume and the feeling of someone pressing close to you. The Stranahan house is a great piece of Florida history and a great place to experience a haunting.

Address: 335 Southeast 6th Avenue
Website: www.stranahanhouse.org
Activity: A, E, N, T

Gainesville Sweetwater Branch Inn

Though called an "inn," the Sweetwater is actually two historic homes that now function as bed and breakfasts. Once known as the McKenzie house and the Cushman-Colson house, the Sweetwater is a living tribute to Victorian life and one of the most well-preserved historic locations in the state. On the paranormal side, you will want to stay in the blue house (McKenzie house). This is the area that's said to be haunted—specifically the rooms in the home's attic. Many natural deaths occurred in this home when it was still part of the McKenzie family, so nobody is sure who the ghost is. Regardless of the identity, visitors have reported feeling watched in the rooms, as well as feeling a heavy pressure on them as they slept. A face has been seen by one of the employees several times in one of the windows, and dresser drawers in the rooms have also been known to open and close on their own.

Address: 625 East University Avenue
Website: www.sweetwaterinn.com
Activity: A, E, T

Key West Fort East Martello Museum & Gardens

This museum is full of wonderful exhibits, but none have captured the public's eye and imagination like the infamous "Robert the Doll." The doll is said to have belonged to Robert Otto (called Gene by all who knew him), a boy brought up in a harsh/stern family in Key West. He possessed the doll his entire life and treated it like a person, allowing it to "eat" at the table, have his own furniture, and sleep with Gene. When Gene died, the doll was placed in the attic—but not for long. The doll would inexplicably move about the house and be found in random rooms. Laughter and voices would occur around the doll as well. One servant even claimed to have found the doll standing at the end of her bed with a knife! The doll is on display at the Martello now. Does the ghost of Gene still follow his beloved doll? Most say yes. Find out for yourself.

Address: 3501 South Roosevelt Boulevard
Website: www.kwahs.com/martello.htm
Activity: E, T

Lake Worth Lake Worth Playhouse

Once known as the Oakley Theatre, this place opened for business in 1924 and is considered one of the area's best examples of Art Deco architecture. Over the years, the playhouse has seen a lot of tragedy, including lean years (with the business changing hands many times), hurricanes, and the general ravages of time. Today, the playhouse is a thriving theater and is considered by paranormal investigators who live in this area to be haunted. Most activity involves two areas: the prop room of the theater (where strange footsteps and bangs are often heard) and the dressing room (where a misty apparition is often seen by actors and employees of the playhouse).

Address: 713 Lake Avenue
Website: www.lakeworthplayhouse.org
Activity: A, E

Maitland Enzian Theater

Already considered a unique institution in the Maitland area (they serve food and drink with their movies), the Enzian also distinguishes itself from other movie theaters in the area by being haunted! Many times over the years, patrons have found themselves watching something other than the movie on the screen. On moonless nights, a floating face/head will appear in a corner of the theater, move around a bit, then shoot through the wall toward the adjoining restaurant (called the Nicole St. Pierre Lounge as of this writing). This spectacle has been seen multiple times by credible witnesses and is even spoken about by employees. Consider it the second half of a double feature when you visit.

Address: 1300 South Orlando Avenue
Website: www.enzian.org
Activity: A

Marco Island Olde Marco Island Inn & Suites

Built on the grounds of a now extinct Native American tribe (the Calusa), the Olde Marco dates back to 1883 when Captain Bill Collier opened up the place to service the public. The inn changed hands several times over the years, but is still operating to this day. The paranormal activity here isn't attributed to any particular person, but it has been experienced quite a bit over the years. The activity includes hearing voices/footsteps, feeling permeating cold spots, and finding objects that have been moved throughout the place. The best part about this location is the fact that activity has been reported in almost every room of the actual inn—so your chances of experiencing something out of the ordinary are high.

Address: 100 Palm Street
Website: www.oldemarcoinn.com
Activity: E, T

Miami Miami River Inn

This inn was constructed between the years of 1906 and 1910, but was almost completely renovated during the 1980s. Perhaps it was this renovation and redesign that caused one of the state's strangest residual hauntings to begin. On almost a nightly basis at this inn (around 11 p.m.), there is a complete audio reenactment of someone angrily entering a room and destroying the furniture! It's said that you can hear footsteps, see the door handle shake, and then hear the sounds of various items being smashed to pieces. But it doesn't just stop with the audio experience. Visitors have also reported feeling their room vibrate (like furniture is being moved) and a strange scooting sound that sounds almost as if something (or someone) is being dragged across the room.

Address: 118 Southwest South River Drive
Website: www.miamiriverinn.com
Activity: R, E, T

Micanopy Herlong Mansion Bed and Breakfast

Built somewhere in the neighborhood of 1845, this simple pine farmhouse was the home of Zeddy and Natalie Herlong who eventually turned the place into the Greek Revival masterpiece that exists today. When the original Herlong family passed away, the house is said to have become the subject of a major family squabble; all six offspring of the Herlongs fought over who would own the property. One of the siblings, Inez Herlong Miller, is said to have died in the house while visiting her old room (actually she went into a diabetic coma and never recovered). It's the ghost of Inez that's said to now walk the halls of the Herlong mansion. Other activity includes the sounds of a female voice, footsteps, and the occasional moving object.

Address: 402 Northeast Cholokka Boulevard
Website: www.herlong.com
Activity: E, T

Monticello 1872 John Denham House

This historic Italianate mansion began as a home for a local Scottish cotton trader. Today it is a historic bed and breakfast that has been featured in numerous publications for its splendor, luxurious accommodations, and (of course) a ghost. It's said that the haunted center of this establishment is the Blue Room and that the area is known to be haunted by a female entity the employees call "Aunt Sarah." Activity in this area includes cold spots, shadow shapes, orbs, and the sounds of a female talking or laughing. The idea of this house being haunted is no sur-

prise to those who live in the area, though. It is said locally that the entire city of Monticello is a portal to the other side and that hauntings in this town are quite the norm.

Address: 555 West Palmer Mill Road
Website: www.johndenhamhouse.com
Activity: C, S, O, E

Ocala Seven Sisters Inn

Already a unique place to stay in Florida due to the sheer number of themed rooms (like the China, Egypt, and India rooms), the Seven Sisters Inn is actually two places in one. There is a pink house that's said to be haunted by a friendly presence and a purple house that reportedly has a more ominous entity within. Hot spots include the Paris Room (where an elderly man is often seen sitting in a chair—and even throwing it once), the Grand English Room (reputedly haunted by a female apparition), and the African Safari room (considered to be inhabited by a male spirit as well). Be sure to also check out the stairs in the pink house where a worker claims to have been dragged by a spirit!

Address: 820 Southeast Fort King Street
Website: www.sevensistersinn.com
Activity: A, S, T, E

St. Augustine St. Augustine Lighthouse & Museum

The original watchtower that stood where the current St. Augustine Lighthouse now resides was built in the late 1500s. It eventually fell to disrepair and the current incarnation of the lighthouse was erected in its place in 1874. With this much history, it's only natural that a certain amount of tragedy would happen. A man named William Harn died of tuberculosis on the site, and three young girls (two were daughters of superintendent Hezekiah Pittee and one was a servant girl) were drowned in an accident involving a rail car (used to truck supplies into the lighthouse). Paranormal activity on this site includes voices, bangs, and dark shadow shapes that are all experienced within the actual lighthouse. The museum on the grounds is the site of a male apparition in uniform, who is seen roaming the place.

Address: 81 Lighthouse Avenue
Website: www.staugustinelighthouse.com
Activity: A, S, E, T

St. Augustine St. Francis Inn

This historic site holds a lot of local history. It was built in 1791 by Gaspar Garcia, an officer in the Cuban army during the Second Spanish Colonial period. In 1845, the place became an inn and made it through Union occupation during the Civil War to survive as a hotel until today (though ownership has changed hands a few times). It is said that this inn is haunted by the spirit of a former servant named Lily. She is easy enough to find in the house—they named the room she likes to stay in Lily's Room. Her appearance is usually marked by the sounds of items being moved and low-volume whispers/moans. It's also thought that a male entity—a soldier who is said to have once fallen in love with Lily, then committed suicide—also haunts

the place. There have been witnesses who have reported seeing a male apparition in period dress walking the halls there.

Address: 279 St. George Street
Website: www.stfrancisinn.com
Activity: A, E, T

St. Petersburg Renaissance Vinoy Resort & Golf Club

Decked out in Art Deco glory, the Vinoy has been a top-notch getaway in the area since the 1920s. Activity in this hotel includes the sounds of heavy footsteps in the Grand Ballroom (an area that is now carpeted) and the appearance of a female apparition that's always seen dressed completely in white. She is most often spotted on the fifth floor of the hotel—along with a male spirit dressed in 1920s clothing that likes to hang out in Room 521. There have been numerous reports of both apparitions, as well as the sounds of whispers, talking, and things moving in rooms throughout that floor of the hotel.

Address: 501 5th Avenue Northeast
Website: www.marriott.com
Activity: A, E, T

Tampa Cuban Club

Built in 1917, the Cuban Club has been the social center for Cuban-Americans in the Tampa area for many years. The bottom floor of this building—the cantina/bar area—is said to be haunted by a little boy who's known for playing with items left there. There is also an elderly gentleman in old-time clothes who has been seen standing by the railing overlooking this area. The theater of the club is reportedly haunted by two apparitions as well: the spirit of an actor who's said to have hanged himself on the stage, and the ghost of a former board member of the club who was shot in the face after an argument. Both apparitions are seen on the stage area. The stairs between the ground floor and the second floor also has an apparition—a woman that wears high heels. She is heard here as well as in the ballroom, where the sounds of her heels hitting wooden floors are clearly distinguished.

Address: 2010 Avenida Republica de Cuba
Website: www.cubanclub.org
Activity: A, E, T

Venice Pelican Alley Restaurant

Servicing as a local fishing-camp bar for over 50 years, the Pelican Alley is known for more than just serving up awesome seafood. Employees of this restaurant claim that the place is haunted by a previous owner. They (along with many of the patrons) have witnessed items moving of their own accord in the kitchen and dining room, seen doors open/close by themselves, and experienced the presence of someone or something standing beside them. One particular customer report involved a female who visited the restaurant and made a trip to the restroom. As she was returning to her table, she heard the sounds of heavy footsteps following her. She never turned around, but sat down at her seat expecting someone to pass by. Of course, there was nobody there.

Address: 1009 West Albee Road
Website: www.pelicanalley.com
Activity: E, T

GEORGIA

Americus Windsor Hotel

The Windsor was built in 1892 to attract tourists from the north who wanted to escape the harsh winters. With 100 unique rooms, the Windsor underwent a multimillion dollar renovation and reopened to an eager public that included former President Jimmy Carter. The Windsor is said to be haunted by a former employee by the name of Floyd Lowery. Though he died of natural causes, he loved the hotel so much he has decided to stay and roam the third floor. He also has company there. In the early 1900s, it was said that a housekeeper in the Windsor was pushed down an elevator shaft along with her young daughter. Both died and now roam the hotel as well. Hot spots in the place include the third-floor hallways, third-floor rooms, the Grand Dining Room, and the staircase.

Address: 125 West Lamar Street
Website: www.windsor-americus.com
Activity: A, E

Atlanta Anthony's Fine Dining

Also known as the Pope-Walton house, construction of Anthony's began in 1797 and continued all the way through the Civil War in the 1860s. Today the place is a fine dining restaurant (it says so right in the name) that specializes in seafood ... and is thought to be haunted. Employees who have had time alone in the house—especially at night—have seen the apparition of a woman they believe to be Annie Barnett, a former resident in the late 1800s. She is often seen and heard around the staircase area. Other activity includes, incredibly, the sight of a ghost cat and the sounds of children laughing and playing on the second floor. One of the spirits (probably not the cat) is also known to turn lights on and off when employees are leaving.

Address: 3109 Piedmont Road
Website: www.anthonysfinedining.com
Activity: A, E, T

Atlanta Georgia Aquarium

According to employees of the Georgia Aquarium, this location typically does not house ghosts or paranormal activity—at least that was true until they received an exhibit that included remnants from the wreckage of the Titanic. It's said that the Iceberg Room of the exhibit is haunted by the spirit of an old man—possibly a fatality from the sinking of the ship. There are also the ghosts of a young man dressed in ship's uniform that likes to hang around the exhibit of dishes, from the ship, and a Native American

spirit that seems to be walking the area called the Cold Water Quest. The Georgia Aquarium, ghosts aside, is a great place to visit—the Titanic exhibit is clearly even better. Take a trip to the aquarium before the exhibit and the spirits move on (if it ever does).

Address: 225 Baker Street
Website: www.georgiaaquarium.com
Activity: A, E

Atlanta The New American Shakespeare Tavern

The Shakespeare Tavern is a unique place in Georgia. Besides being a dinner theater where one can watch loud, boisterous plays and music while enjoying authentic English pub fare, the theater is said to be haunted by three spirits—two male and one female. There is the male spirit that seems to enjoy walking through the male dressing room and the props department, a female spirit (that seems to be a former actor) that's often sighted in the female dressing room, and a black shadow person that has been spotted by employees and patrons on/above the stage area. The sounds of items moving and unusual banging also accompany the presence of these lost souls.

Address: 499 Peachtree Street Northeast
Website: www.shakespearetavern.com
Activity: A, E, T

Augusta Ezekiel Harris House/ Augusta Museum of History

This house is owned and operated by the Augusta Museum of History and is, in itself, a piece of history and a museum collection. Built in 1797, this old estate has had paranormal stories swirling about it for almost 200 years! The stories usually concern one of three ghosts thought to reside here. The first is that of a soldier said to be dressed in a Revolutionary War uniform who was, supposedly, hung in the house. Besides being seen on the stairs (and sometimes on the front porch), it's rumored that people have seen his disembodied head rolling down the steps! The second spirit seen is a black woman who's thought to be a former slave. She is often seen walking through rooms on the first floor. And finally, there is a young white woman, who is often glimpsed staring from a second-floor window—and seen on the porch as well.

Address: 1822 Broad Street
Website: www.augustamuseum.org
Activity: A, E

Augusta The Partridge Inn

This historic inn was built in 1836 as a private residence, but was converted into a hotel in 1892 by a vacationing Morris Partridge. At the height of its elegance, the place was the site of a gala for President Warren G. Harding—at the lowest point of its existence, the place fell into disrepair after struggling as an apartment complex in the 1960s and 1970s. Today, the hotel thrives again and is known for, among other things, a ghost by the name of "Emily." Emily is said to be a bride-to-be from the late 1800s who was staying in the hotel when she received news of her betrothed's death. She is often spotted in the hotel walking the halls while wearing her bridal gown. The sounds of a female crying and footsteps have also been reported in the hotel.

Address: 2110 Walton Way
Website: www.partridgeinn.com
Activity: A, E

Braselton Braselton Town Hall

The building that houses the town hall in Braselton, Georgia, was once the residence of the founding family of the town. William Harrison Braselton and his wife, Pallie Darby Braselton, built the house around 1909, and the town of Braselton was born (though not incorporated until 1916). City employees who work in the building say that a ghost that they have dubbed "Little John" haunts the place. Though it cannot be verified through public record, it's rumored that John was a mentally challenged boy who

resided in the home's attic. When the place is closing for the day, it's reported that John then emerges from the attic and is heard walking the floors and stairs. The sounds of things moving and banging are also heard. In addition to this, many believe the place is also the source of a residual haunting that features a female apparition and guests who are heard having a dinner party of sorts on the first floor.

Address: 4982 Highway 53
Website: www.braselton.net
Activity: E, T, R

Covington Gaither Plantation

This antebellum home gained notoriety for being haunted when it was featured on the television show *Ghost Hunters*. It's said that the place is haunted by a former owner of the house and his daughter. Residual sightings of soldiers dressed in Confederate army uniforms have also been spotted on the property. Today, you can rent the entire place for an event, so visiting it is not a challenge. While there, check out Cecilia's Bedroom, which is said to be haunted by the room's namesake. Employees have reported seeing an apparition, as well as seeing things move and hearing voices and footsteps throughout the house. If the area is open, the attic is also thought to be haunted as well—by spirits left behind from the Civil War. There is also a chapel outside the main house that is reportedly visited by the wife of a former pastor who was killed by the "holy man."

Address: 270 Davis Ford Road
Website: www.gaitherplantation.com
Activity: A, E, T, S

Dawsonville Amicalola Falls State Park Lodge

Amicalola means "tumbling waters" in Cherokee—an appropriate name for this place located in the heart of the Chattahoochie National Forest. This area of the forest was known to the Cherokee people for being a place of the dead—

a place where people went for spiritual reasons and to celebrate those who've passed away. The lodge at this park is built right smack in the middle of this area! Experiences in the lodge include items that move on their own, doors that open and close by themselves, and severe drops in temperature that paranormal researchers refer to as "cold spots." Employees in the place will tell you that the ghosts like the kitchen, but activity is said to have occurred in almost every area of the lodge.

Address: 418 Amicalola Falls State Park Road
Website: www.amicalolafalls.com
Activity: E, T, C, O

Fayetteville Holliday-Dorsey-Fife House Museum

This museum was built in 1855 and was the home of several prominent families in the area (all listed in the name). The place is thought to be haunted by a relative of one of these families: Doc Holliday. Witnesses claim that a man dressed as a gunslinger has been seen in one of the upper windows. Holliday did, indeed, live in the area with his relatives, but left in the 1870s because of his declining health. There is reputedly a second ghost within the HDF house as well. This one is thought to either be John Manse Dorsey or Solomon Dorsey—both former residents. Solomon actually died in the house in 1901. Activity seems to revolve around the second floor and the attic (where a skeleton once hung during the 1800s). In addition to ap-

paritions, people have heard the sounds of footsteps and voices.

Address: 140 Lanier Avenue West
Website: www.hdfhouse.com
Activity: A, E

Fort Oglethorpe Chickamauga National Military Park

The haunting of Chickamauga is one of the most famous in the country—especially in the realm of haunted Civil War sites. Over the years since the famous battle that took place in 1863, people visiting the park have experienced an apparition (though some claim it to be a creature) that has been dubbed "Old Green Eyes." Some believe it is a headless soldier that roams the park, moaning in pain. Others say the entity dates back to the Native Americans who lived in the area. In addition to this bizarre entity, the wooded areas of the park are said to be in the throes of a residual haunt that dates back to just after the battle. Once the Battle of Chickamauga was over, there were more than 35,000 casualties. Women working in the medical tents, searched the area with lanterns for the wounded. Today, spirit lights that many believe to be these lanterns are often seen floating through the trees.

Address: Lafayette Road at Ft. Ogelthorpe
Website: www.nps.gov/chch/
Activity: A, E, R, O, S, T

Grantville Bonnie Castle Bed, Breakfast & Events

This Victorian Romanesque home dates back to 1896 and has served as host to at least two former United States presidents: Jimmy Carter and Franklin D. Roosevelt. But neither is the most famous visitor to this bed and breakfast. That distinction belongs to "Mary," a female spirit that's said to haunt the second floor of this place. Her apparition has been spotted, as well as heard, in the hallways (the sounds of her footsteps and voice have been reported in various rooms as well). One local report also says that the apparition of a former owner also haunts the house. He has reportedly been seen in the front parlor area, as well as in the front yard.

Address: 2 Post Street
Website: www.bonniecastle.org
Activity: A, E

Kennesaw Kennesaw Mountain National Battlefield Park

This is the second of two haunted Civil War battle sites in Georgia—though this one is lesser known than that of Chickamauga. The battle here was a small one (relatively speaking), though it still resulted in over 5,300 dead soldiers. The haunting of this battlefield is said to be a residual one that takes place during the dusk and dark hours. The park closes at sunset, so you'll have to settle for the dusk. The sounds of cannons firing, soldiers yelling, and the armies crashing through the trees are said to take place on a regular basis. Others have said strange mists and orbs float through the area along with the apparitions of the soldiers still fighting after all these years.

Address: 900 Kennesaw Mountain Drive
Website: www.nps.gov/kemo/
Activity: A, E, R, O, M

Lavonia Southern Oaks Inn

Little is known about the haunting of this Greek Revival home. The inn—which is really not an inn since there are no rooms for rent—serves as a local event location. And most of these are weddings. Local paranormal researchers say that the house is haunted by a husband and wife—

previous owners of the inn—and that the spirits have been there since the furnishings/décor were updated to look more modern. It's reported that the spirits like to move the furniture around and to relocate items throughout the house—especially in the kitchen. Visit this location to learn more about the specific haunting there. Since the inn is available for events, consider this as a possible pay-to-play area.

Address: 30 Baker Street
Website: www.southern-oaks-inn
    -weddings.com
Activity: A, T

Macon Hay House

Originally called the Johnston-Felton-Hay house, this building is currently a museum with furniture and decorations that date back to the home's origins (when it was built between 1855 and 1859). Museum employees and visitors alike claim the place is currently inhabited by the spirit of an elderly woman that has been seen and heard by people touring the house. There is a hidden room (included on the tour of the house and museum) that's said to be the hiding spot of the spirit. In this room, there's a small window that's visible from the outside, and passersby have stated seeing the old woman staring through this window on quite a few occasions.

Address: 934 Georgia Avenue
Website: www.georgiatrust.org
Activity: A, E

Marietta Marietta Museum of History/ Kennesaw House

This museum is housed within the historic Kennesaw House—an old cotton warehouse that dates back to 1845. Over the years this building has been used as a hotel, a Confederate hospital, a morgue, and a place for retail shopping. With such a mixed background, it's no wonder that the place is considered haunted. Most of the stories concerning this location, though, involve its role as a hospital/morgue during the Civil

War. Over the years, visitors to the building's basement have reported experiencing a residual haunting, where the sights and sounds of an active hospital have taken place around them. A war-era surgeon has also been spotted in the actual elevator! Folks touring the museum have also reported seeing the apparition of a woman (believed to be a member of the Fletcher family who lived in the place in the 1800s) in the museum area.

Address: 1 Depot Street
Website: www.mariettahistory.org
Activity: R, E, A

Milledgeville Old Governor's Mansion

Dating back to 1839, this fine example of High Greek Revival architecture was the home of Georgia's governors for more than 30 years. During General William Sherman's famous "March to the Sea" in the Civil War, this place was used for a while as Sherman's headquarters. After the war, the capital of Georgia was moved to Atlanta, and the house became simply a house. It's said that the ghost stories involving this estate have been circulating throughout the area since the early 1900s. Activity in the mansion includes a female apparition that's seen on the first floor and numerous smells that are said to be associated with a spirit named "Molly." According to folks there, Molly was a past cook who decided to stay on beyond the grave.

Address: 231 West Hancock Street
Website: www.gcsu.edu/mansion/
Activity: A, N

Rutledge Hard Labor Creek State Park

Within this state park is an area called Camp Rutledge. This area is said to be haunted by the spirits who have wandered in from a small graveyard located within the park's boundaries. Said to be disturbed by park visitors—much less the camp—these spirits are thought to be active throughout the area, though they are typically only noticed where the cottages are for rent.

The most common entity seen is that of a man who is rumored to have been a farmer in the area during the early 1800s. There is also a small boy who is known for moving items within the cottages. Both ghosts have been spotted many times, and a local ghost hunting group has even collected data at this site that confirms the activity and haunting.

Address: 5 Hard Labor Creek Road
Website: http://gastateparks.org/info/hardlabor/
Activity: A, E, T

Savannah 17 Hundred 90 Inn and Restaurant

Housed within two buildings that date back to … well … 1790, this inn is perhaps the most haunted location in Savannah. If it isn't the most haunted, then it's at least the most well-known haunted spot there. The site is said to be haunted by the spirit of a woman called Anna Powers. Local history states that Powers committed suicide by leaping from a third-floor balcony into the courtyard. Her apparition has been witnessed numerous times in almost every area of the inn and restaurant—but the area she likes the most is Room 204. Sounds of a young woman talking, laughing, crying, etc., are heard in this room, as well as feeling the overwhelming sense that someone is present with you. Visitors sleeping in this room have also reported feeling touched, having the covers pulled, and experiencing intense cold spots there.

Address: 307 East President Street
Website: www.17hundred90.com
Activity: A, E, T, C

Savannah The Ballastone Inn

Though lesser known than some of its haunted peers in Savannah, the Ballastone Inn is no less haunted than others—and certainly is no less historical. Dating back to the late 1800s, this property has been a family home, a boarding house, a hotel, and the administrative offices of the Girl Scouts of America. The spirit that haunts this fine establishment dates back to the Civil War and is said to be Sarah Anderson, the wife of a local general who was instrumental in the defense of the city of Savannah during the war. Sarah is often witnessed standing by the front door, roaming the second-floor hallways, and lurking in the elevator.

Address: 14 East Oglethorpe Avenue
Website: www.ballastone.com
Activity: A

Savannah Forsyth Park Inn

This former home dates back to 1893 and over-looks one of the city's most beautiful areas, Forsyth Park. Visit the park while you are at this inn to set the tone for your stay in Savannah. With tons of Spanish Moss drooping from the trees, you'll be ready to experience the entity that's said to reside in this old home—that of "Lottie." It's reported that this female spirit once lived in the place and went insane after poisoning her own mother to death there. Lottie now walks the hallways as well as visits people staying in the inn's luxurious rooms—though the two hottest spots are the stairs and the fountain in the courtyard (she's been witnessed in both areas more than once). The sounds of her walking, as well as her voice/laughing, have also been heard many times in the inn—especially on the second floor.

Address: 102 West Hall Street
Website: www.forsythparkinn.com
Activity: A, E

Savannah Kehoe House

This historic home was constructed in 1892 by William Kehoe and is a fine example of Queen Anne architecture. The house remained in the Kehoe family for many years until it was sold and turned into a funeral home. Today, the place is a bed and breakfast—and whether it's because of the house's past (dealing with the dead) or maybe just the general history there, the Kehoe House is said to be haunted. The majority of the paranormal reports involve young female spirits that many believe to be the twin daughters of the Kehoe family. These girls reportedly died while playing in one of the chimneys inside the house. Rooms 201 and 203 are considered the most haunted. There have been quite a few sightings of the apparitions in these rooms, as well as the sounds of children—though these types of stories have been told about almost every area of this house.

Address: 123 Habersham Street
Website: www.kehoehouse.com
Activity: A, E, T

Savannah The Pirate's House Restaurant

A notorious haunted location that has been featured on many television shows/programs over the years, the Pirate's House is a paranormal favorite in Savannah. The Herb Room of this restaurant is rumored to be one of the most active hot spots in the state, with almost constant activity that involves intense cold spots and the sensation of being touched. In the past, the house was used by pirates to ferry merchandise to customers—and over the course of doing business—many of them died while "trading" within the place. Employees have seen the apparitions of sailors, heard the sounds of heavy boots walking, seen utensils/items move by themselves, and experienced almost every other kind of paranormal activity in the restaurant. Get the Herb Room if you can, but if you can't, don't worry—every room in this place is said to be haunted!

Address: 20 East Broad Street
Website: www.thepirateshouse.com
Activity: A, E, T, S

Stone Mountain The Village Inn Bed and Breakfast

Built in the early 1820s as a roadside inn, this location is one of the oldest structures in the area. It has survived many harsh years, including an attack by General Sherman during the Civil War (he took no pity on the owners there because they allowed the place to be used as a Confederate hospital). Whether it's because of the folks who died here while serving the Confederacy or it's the circumstances surrounding one of the numerous people who simply stayed at the place, the inn is said to be haunted. A misty apparition has been seen many times in the hallways of the upper floor, as well as in the bedrooms. Others have reported seeing objects move, doors open/close by themselves, and hearing the sounds of singing that seem to emanate from the walls.

Address: 992 Ridge Avenue
Website: www.villageinnbb.com
Activity: A, E, T

Valdosta Vito's Rock 'n' Roll Pizzeria & Lounge

This place was known as a haunted hot spot when it was called Warren's Blue Bayou. Now that the place is a pizzeria … well … the story remains the same. Employees have reported finding chairs removed from tables (where they are stacked neatly for the night), seeing objects move in the kitchen, and catching the glimpses of a dark, shadowy entity shooting through the main dining room. Many believe the haunting dates back to the days when the place was originally a home. The story goes that the owner of the house committed suicide in the home by hanging—though this bit of history cannot be verified. At any rate, the ghostly happenings in this location have occurred through the habitation of two businesses and at least one family!

Address: 500 North Ashley Street
Website: www.myspace.com/vitospizzeria
Activity: A, S, E, T

Waimea Falls Park
Ko Olina
Honolulu
Lana'i City
Kailua-Kona
Honaunau

HAWAII

Honaunau Pu'uhonua o Honaunau Park

For ancient Hawaiians, the area that occupies this park was a place of refuge. Whether you were in fear of execution, fleeing crimes, or simply seeking a place with peace and quiet, this was it. It was said you could work off the crimes that you had committed at these temples, thereby commuting your sentence. Local conjecture is that the activity in this park stems from those who died but are still trying to find this sanctuary. Others believe the spirits that haunt this area come from the bones of former tribal chiefs who are buried in the temple. Either way, spiritual activity has been reported from this area for hundreds of years.

Address: Located on Highway 160
Website: www.nps.gov/puho/
Activity: A, E, T

Honolulu Hilton Hawaiian Village Beach Resort & Spa

This upscale hotel makes for a nice getaway. With a spa, a swimming pool, and a beachfront location, who could argue? For a ghost hunter,

this place makes for an even nicer vacation when you consider the spirit of the "woman in red" who is said to wander the halls of this hotel. Dating back to the 1940s, there are numerous tales of hotel employees and patrons witnessing this apparition. Locals will tell you that the woman was the victim of a horrible, jealous man who murdered her in one of the hotel's rooms many years ago. Some hint she is part of a local legend involving a spirit who warns of impending volcano eruptions—but then, she's been seen many more times than there's been eruptions!

Address: 2005 Kalia Road
Website: www.hilton.com
Activity: A

Honolulu Honolulu National Airport

This is possibly the only haunted airport known in the United States. At least, the only one that I know of! The garden area of this airport is said to be haunted by an apparition that folks have witnessed wandering the area, waiting to get on planes. The spirit, known to push carts and touch people, is often seen as a whispy apparition that seems to shoot along the wall. There have been other reports of the paranormal in this airport as well—from airport personnel no less! At least two pilots have reported seeing a strange, disembodied head/face that's covered in blood either on or near Gate 31. This experience has also been witnessed by one of the ground crew.

Address: 300 Rodgers Boulevard
Website: www.honoluluairport.com
Activity: A, M

Honolulu Iolani Palace

Building on this spacious palace began in 1879. It was intended to be a place that would establish the Hawaiian royal family as the legitimate governing body for the area. The king and queen held many lavish parties at this palace and opened the path for the United States to recognize Hawaii. Unfortunately, this place was also the site of the overthrow of the Hawaiian throne and the imprisonment of the queen. Many died during these turbulent times, and it's said that the female spirit that wanders the grounds outside this palace is a product of that violence. She is often seen as a glowing, white figure roaming the courtyards. Employees who now guide the tours through the grounds have reported also seeing a black shadow mass, which seems to dart among the areas around the palace.

Address: 364 South King Street
Website: www.iolanipalace.org
Activity: A, S

Honolulu Waikiki Parc Hotel

This upscale getaway is loaded with amenities: a top-notch spa, a killer restaurant, and a ghost that works for the hotel. It's said that this hotel is haunted by a former employee. A machine that allows employees to punch in/out on the premises still records this employee every day as "punching in." In addition to this, at least two hotel employees have reportedly seen a strange apparition that appears to look like said worker near the time clock.

Address: 2233 Helumoa Road
Website: www.waikikiparc.com
Activity: A, T

Kailua-Kona Hulihe'e Palace

This palace was the vacation area for Hawaiian royalty that inhabited the islands for many years. Today, it is a museum that is operated by the Daughters of Hawaii and features many examples of local furniture, art, and décor. Much like the Iolani Palace, this place is haunted by an outside apparition—only in this case, the ghost is said to be that of a little boy. He has been spotted in various locations outside the palace—tour guides will be happy to point out the most recent sightings—and is known to vanish when you approach him. Nobody is sure who the boy is, but many believe he was probably a local native that served the royal family.

Address: 75-5718 Ali'i Drive
Website: www.daughtersofhawaii.com
Activity: A

Kailua Kona-Kona Village Resort

Dating back to ancient times—1965 actually—this resort is a unique and exciting getaway with individual bungalows, an upscale restaurant, and a location right next to the ocean. The hotel has three zones where guests can stay: Sand, Lava, and Lagoon. For those wanting to experience the paranormal, you will want to stay in the Lagoon zone. It's reported that this area experiences the sights and sounds of a residual haunting that dates back to the times of tribes and ritual dances. Guests have heard chanting, voices, and drums late at night and have seen everything from orbs to black masses to glowing apparitions. Most eerie of all are the reports from some guests who have heard a high-pitched scream.

Address: Queen Ka'ahumanu Highway
Website: www.konavillage.com
Activity: R, O, S, A, E

Ko Olina Ihilani Resort & Spa

This high-class resort located on the beach boasts 387 guest rooms and 36 suites of comfort. Amenities include a golf course, a spa, and a locally renowned restaurant. It's said that the seventeenth floor of this hotel is haunted. The story goes that a woman who was vacationing in this hotel passed away in her room of natural causes. She now roams the halls and visits those who stay on the seventeenth floor, completely unaware that she has passed away. Witnesses of the apparition say that she appears to be trying to speak to them, but quickly dissipates after being seen. Nobody has attempted to capture her words via Electronic Voice Phenomena, but it would be interesting to hear what she wants to say.

Address: 92-1001 Olani Street
Website: www.ihilani.com
Activity: A

Lana'i City The Lodge at Koele

Looking more like a country manor than a hotel, this Four Seasons resort is tucked in the middle of two world-ranked golf courses. It's also said that the place is built over an area known as a sacred burial ground (but then, this seems to be the case of most places in Hawaii). Regardless, tales of fleeting apparitions and dark shapes have been reported here almost since its inception. The hotel is said to even have pictures of the apparitions that were taken during a photo shoot. The ghosts do not seem to be attached to one spot of the hotel as much as they seem to be everywhere! Could this be the effect of being over these sacred grounds? Who knows? Visit the lodge, play some golf, and maybe you'll spot an entity for yourself.

Address: 1 Keomoku Highway
Website: www.fourseasons.com/koele/
Activity: A, S

O'ahu Waimea Falls Park

Stories concerning the paranormal have circulated about this hot spot for hundreds of years. The native Hawaiians who inhabited this area were known for human sacrifice—and this park is located right in the middle of the ceremonial and burial areas. Local legend tells of a tribal chief who regularly made sacrifices here in the late 1700s and made the mistake of killing a visiting British soldier. Since then, there have been several deaths that have resembled this act. Many believe it is the vengeful spirit of the chief still making sacrifices—many believe it is simply coincidence. Either way, glowing apparitions, voices, and the sounds of tribal chanting have been reported from the "lookout" area of this park.

Address: 59-864 Kamehameha Highway
Website: www.hawaiiweb.com
Activity: A, E

IDAHO

Arco Craters of the Moon National Monument & Preserve

This area was formed over 2,000 years ago when a volcano in the area erupted. The Shoshone Indians decided that this marked an area of particular significance and created a village at this site. It's said that at one time or another, a second Native American tribe intruded upon the Shoshone, forcing the Shoshone medicine man to bring the wrath of the volcano down upon the intruders. Since then, the Shoshone have thought of the place as one of power and evil. Because of the deaths of so many due to the eruption, the place is also thought to be haunted by the spirits of the Native Americans who perished here so many years ago. Activity is marked by the appearance of glowing balls of light and misty apparitions that are seen roaming the grounds.

Address: Southwest of Arco on Highway 20/26/93
Website: www.nps.gov/crmo/
Activity: O, M

Athol Farragut State Park

Located on the shores of Lake Pend (Idaho's largest lake), Farragut State Park was once the Farragut Naval Training Center. The actual center is now a museum and is one of several activities available to park visitors—along with 4,000 acres of boating, hiking, and camping. There is also a building standing in the park that was once a prison during World War II— this is the location considered to be haunted. While in service, it's reported that several deaths occurred in the building—including a suicide. Employees who have worked in the park, and particularly in this building, say that an apparition in the form of a "bald man in uniform" walks the prison. He has been witnessed many times, along with objects that move on their own and voices that seem to emanate from the long-empty cells.

Address: 13550 East Highway 54
Website: www.visitidaho.org
Activity: A, E, T

Boise Egyptian Theatre

The Egyptian opened its doors in 1927 with the play *Don Juan* and has been steadily presenting shows and events for the last 75 years. It's believed that the Egyptian is haunted by an apparition that likes to walk the stage and the projection booth of the theatre. Employees call the ghost "Joe" and have seen the apparition as a "real life" style apparition and as a black, man-shaped shadow. People have also been touched by an unseen presence, as well as heard the sounds of a male voice coming from the projection booth area. It's also believed that a female apparition walks the place—a woman dressed in 1920's attire. The haunting of this theatre is well known in the area—a local television station did a story about the ghost. Catch an event at this historic theatre and maybe you'll catch a glimpse of the spirit as well.

Address: 700 West Main Street
Website: www.egyptiantheatre.net
Activity: A, E, T, S

Boise Night Moves Gentleman's Club

One of the few "adult-oriented" haunts listed in this book, Night Moves is a strip bar located in the heart of Boise, Idaho, nightlife. Besides witnessing the usual fare at such a bar, many visiting this establishment have also seen an apparition in the dark corners of the club. Employees have reported seeing the apparition as well, and say that the ghost who resides there loves to shake the chandeliers/lights and to occasionally throw objects about the place. Though it would, on the surface, seem to be kind of a scary ghost, those who work there say the spirit is friendly and is probably just enjoying the sights.

Address: 4348 West State Street
Website: www.nightmovestopless.com
Activity: A, T

Boise Old Idaho State Penitentiary

This correctional facility dates back to 1870 when the new state of Idaho needed a territorial prison to house the convicts of the day. Over the years, the place grew, and more and more prisoners made their way to this stronghold. After several riots on the premises, the prison was finally closed down in 1973 and turned into a historic location. Today, tours make their way through the facility and experience many paranormal things quite often. Activity includes voices, footsteps, and the feeling of someone brushing past you as you walk the halls. This location has been investigated by many paranormal groups—on and off television—and none have left disappointed. These groups have all reported the same information: the Idaho State Penitentiary is haunted by the spirits of many past inmates, and they are active!

Address: 2205 Old Penitentiary Road
Website: www.idahohistory.net/oldpen
Activity: A, C, E, T

Boise Owyhee Plaza Hotel

This hotel has been servicing downtown Boise since 1910. The recently renovated hotel now contains two locally renowned restaurants. Of course, the place also contains at least one spirit— a ghost that likes to visit with folks in the meeting rooms! Over the years, several hotel employees have reported seeing an apparition in the meeting rooms, as well as other areas, including the basement, the upstairs hallways, and the kitchen. The only guest room associated with the spirit is said to be Room 136, where it was reported that a guest saw the apparition of a woman standing over her as she woke up in bed. This incident was reported to the front desk and the woman was moved—the guest that is, not the ghost. She's still there…

Address: 1109 Main Street
Website: www.owyheeplaza.com
Activity: A, E

Coeur d'Alene Bates Motel

This hotel is said to be haunted by a noisy spirit (literally a poltergeist—the German word for a ghost of that type). The spirit in this motel moves items around within and between rooms, opens/closes doors, and turns lights on/off in various rooms. In the wee hours, the ghost also likes to walk the halls—apparently with heavy boots on—as the sounds of footsteps are often heard in the night. The Bates Motel was once the officer's quarters for the Farragut Naval Base, and the spirit seems to have an affinity for Rooms 1 and 3. Check in with the front desk to find out where the most recent/current activity is taking place.

Address: 2018 East Sherman Avenue
Website: www.visitidaho.org/placestostay/
   hotels-motels/bates-motel
Activity: E, T

Gooding Get Inn Bed and Breakfast

This hotel was originally part of Gooding College and was later transformed into a hospital for those sick with tuberculosis. Untold numbers died within these halls before the hospital was eventually shut down. Today, the place has been converted into a bed and breakfast, but the spirits of the sick and dead seem to still linger within these halls. Apparitions that have been spotted include an older man in a white lab coat, a woman dressed in period clothes, and a little girl (who is usually seen either with or around the young woman). Other activity includes the sounds of footsteps, whispers, and bangs in areas where nobody is staying or working.

Address: 301 University Street
Website: www.getinnidaho.com
Activity: A, E

Idaho City Donna's Place

This Idaho City landmark is known for more than just collectibles (though the place has and sells an extensive line of NASCAR and Anheuser-Busch memorabilia)—it's also the location of one of the area's most infamous ghosts. The building is thought to be haunted by a female apparition that loves to make herself known to employees and customers alike. Sometimes she is seen, but most often she makes herself known by responding to questions by knocking on the wall or ceiling. She is also known to touch folks while they are shopping. Most believe the ghost dates back to the times when the area was a residential strip of homes that serviced the mining industry.

If you're a fan of NASCAR, Budweiser, or ghosts, Donna's Place is the place for you!

Address: 200 Main Street
Website: www.donnas-place.com
Activity: A, E, T

Lewiston Lewiston Civic Theatre

This building was built by the Lewiston Methodist Church in 1907 and serviced the Methodist community for many years. The current theatre moved into the establishment in 1972 and has been presenting shows and events to the community ever since. The theatre is said to be haunted by two ghosts: a little girl and a man who was once the theatre director. The little girl is often seen sitting on the stairs and heard crying backstage. Nobody is sure who this spirit is or where she came from (though it's assumed it has something to do with the church that was there rather than the theatre). The man, as mentioned above, is thought to be a former director of the theatre who simply couldn't bear to be away. He is often seen sitting and watching the shows, as well as walking through the seats after the place is closed.

Address: 805 6th Avenue
Website: www.lctheatre.org
Activity: A, E

Murtaugh Sidewinders Bar and Grill

This eating and drinking establishment is said to be haunted by a poltergeist-like entity. The ghost has reportedly been seen in the place several times by employees—usually in the form of a shadowy figure walking across the main area—but the bulk of the activity revolves around things being moved. Lights have turned themselves on and off, the jukebox is said to do the same, and bar utensils and items have been moved by unseen hands. In addition to this activity, patrons have also said that they have heard the sounds of a piano playing in the distance—almost as if the music is coming from very far away.

Address: 109 West Archer Street
Activity: A, S, E, T

Nampa Pete's Tavern

Known as one of the area's better drinking holes, Pete's is also known for a strange room that is in the back of the bar called "The Cave." During prohibition, it's said that employees of the tavern would serve alcohol in this room, and it was one of the few local speakeasies. The Cave is also reported to be haunted. It's said that the room contains at least two entities—one male and one female. Voices in this room have been recorded several times, and people who have spent quality time in the area have also reported hearing whispers, feeling something touching them, and experiencing intense cold spots that seem to spring up out of nothing. Though nobody has seen an actual apparition, the activity in this establishment has occurred frequently enough to declare the place haunted.

Address: 11 12th Avenue South
Website: www.petestavern.net
Activity: E, T, C

Pierce Cedar Inn

This hotel was constructed in 1927 to service area railroad crews working on the line there. Once the railroad was finished, the inn continued to do business until the present day. Many visitors have reported strange sounds in the old hotel at night. Guests have asked to switch rooms or simply complained after experiencing a night of constant banging, footsteps, and voices in the halls. Could it be rowdy railroad workers still hanging out? Possibly. One thing is for sure: the activity happens rather frequently and rather loudly—and not in just one part of the hotel. This is a place where you may want to check in with the front desk about the current ghostly happenings to get the skinny on the current hot spots.

Address: 412 South Main Street
Website: www.minersshanty.net
Activity: E

Preston Deseret Industries Thrift Shop

This secondhand goods store run by the Church of the Latter Day Saints is said to be haunted by a spirit that is also seen in many of the shops up and down State Street. This store is reputedly the ghost's favorite stop and is known to play pranks on the people there, like turning lights on and off, closing doors, and playing with clocks and phones. Many different types of electronic phenomena seem to happen with this spirit—meaning, that this ghost likes to play with the electricity! Besides messing with the lights, the ghost seems to get a kick out of activating the fire alarm and generally making a nuisance of himself to the patrons.

Address: 36 South State Street
Website: www.prestonidaho.org
Activity: T

Soda Springs Enders Hotel & Café

Built in 1917, this historic hotel now features a café, a bar/lounge area, and a gift shop. The second floor of the hotel is a museum, so when you spend the night here, you will be on the third floor. The haunting of this hotel became a hot local story when a ghost was reportedly caught in a photograph taken in the hotel's basement. Employees will tell you, though, that it doesn't stop there. Footsteps, voices, and even an apparition have all been heard/seen in the basement and on the second and third floors of the hotel. People disagree on whether the spirit is a male or female entity (ghost hunters have claimed a little of both)—and the picture is of no help in that regard. Visit the Ender's Hotel and maybe you can figure it out!

Address: 76 South Main Street
Website: www.visitidaho.org
Activity: A, E

Chicago

⊙ Springfield

ILLINOIS

Alton McPike Mansion

Built in 1869 for Henry McPike, this place has been a home, a boarding house, and a small business college. In the 1950s, though, the place was abandoned and vandals ransacked the home. Today, the house is in the process of being renovated and can be visited for tours and overnight stays. The paranormal activity revolves around the spirit of a man who is thought to be Paul Laichinger—a former resident of the house in the early 1900s. While some have reported several spirits in this house (including the apparition of a former female servant), this entity has been witnessed the most. Visitors to the McPike mansion will want to spend most of the time in the cellar, as this seems to be the center of activity. Expect to possibly witness apparitions and

orbs, as well as hear the sounds of footsteps and voices.

Address: 2018 Alby Street
Website: www.mcpikemansion.com
Activity: A, E, T, O, C

Alton Mineral Springs Hotel

Founded in 1914, this hotel was promoted as a place of healing. The mineral waters native to this area were supposed to heal people and make them healthy. These days, the Mineral Springs is a mini-mall, which can make following the various ghost tales a bit confusing—especially since most of the stories involve areas of the hotel that now are part of various shops and attractions. Orient yourself by taking the ghost tour that the mall offers. This will help if for no other reason than to get the hot spots there. The place is reportedly haunted by at least two spirits—both male—that tend to visit the old lobby and bar areas of the hotel. There's also an old swimming pool that's no longer in use in the building's basement. Many claim that this area is the most haunted of the hotel.

Address: 302 East Broadway
Website: www.mineralspringshauntedtours.com
Activity: A, S, C, E, T

Cave In Rock Cave-In-Rock State Park

This state park features a giant cave that overlooks the Ohio River. During the early 1800s, this cave was home to a tavern, brothel, and gambling house—and was the site of many a murder. When the place was raided (due to its notorious standing) by police, over 60 bodies were recovered from inside the cave. Today, the site is known in the area for a residual-style haunting. Passersby on the Ohio have reported hearing the sounds of the gambling hall conducting business—as well as screams and moans from those who were killed in the horrible place. The park offers camping, so staying there and visiting the cave is only too easy.

Address: Just Outside Town on the Ohio River
Website: www.stateparks.com/caveinrock
Activity: E, R

Chicago Congress Plaza Hotel

The Plaza dates back to a time when the streets were lined with gaslights and passersby walked on cobblestones. Built in 1893 as an annex to the Louis Sullivan's Auditorium Building, the hotel was added on to in 1902 with a South Tower (an area that now houses the Gold Room). Today, this hotel is said to be haunted by (probably) some of the infamous past visitors—including several prominent Chicago mobsters. The ballroom area is considered most haunted, but most parts of the hotel have had some type of activity—including voices, footsteps, and shadowy shapes seen moving along the walls. Employees working in the hotel's kitchen have also reported that various appliances are known to turn themselves on/off, and utensils have been witnessed moving by themselves.

Address: 520 South Michigan Avenue
Website: www.congressplazahotel.com
Activity: S, E, T

Chicago Ole St. Andrew's Inn

This Scottish-American bar has been serving up pub-grub and ghost stories for many years now. It's infamous with the college crowd and neighborhood locals who talk about the spirit of Frank Giff as if he's still a regular. Giff is a former owner who just doesn't know when to quit working! He likes to move bar glasses, play with women's hair, and gently squeeze patrons' legs—especially if they are drinking vodka (said to be Giff's drink of choice). Frank is said to have passed away in the bar after a night of drinking, so maybe the attention spent on the vodka drinkers is a type of warning. When you visit this location, be sure to talk to the bartenders about the spirit—they know all the stories and will keep you informed concerning the current tales and hot spots in the bar.

Address: 5938 North Broadway Street
Website: www.chicago.com
Activity: T

Chicago Red Lion Pub

Built in 1882 in the aftermath of the great fires of Chicago, the building that now houses the Red Lion has been a place of many names. The first bar that resided there was called Dirty Dan's and was a western-themed affair. The Red Lion was built by John Cordwell in 1984 to serve as a traditional pub and a tribute to his father who passed away in England. It's said that John's father now haunts the bar. He is often seen and felt in the area of a stained glass window (an area that commemorates his death). But he is not alone! Other spirits are thought to include a cowboy from the western-bar days, a woman who appears with the scent of lavender, and a man who is seen walking the stairs. Visiting this pub is a must for the paranormal tourist, as it is, without a doubt, one of the most well-known haunted locations in the city.

Address: 2446 North Lincoln Avenue
Website: www.redlionchicago.com
Activity: A, E, T, S, C

Clarendon Hills Country House

This place dates back to 1922, when the first floor was a tavern and store and the second was the home of the Kobel family. Today, it's a restaurant and nobody lives on the second floor—unless, of course, you include the ghost! Customers and employees alike have been reporting strange occurrences for many years. Tales include doors slamming, voices talking away in empty rooms, and a female apparition that has been seen in the dining area (as well as the storeroom on the premises). There are several theories concerning the identity of the girl—including that she was a former employee, or a girl from the prohibition days who visited the place as a "lady of the evening," or a customer who was killed in an auto accident just after visiting the place.

Address: 241 55th Street
Website: www.burgerone.com
Activity: A, E, S

Decatur Avon Theatre

This theatre opened in 1916 as a place for the upper crust to go and watch movies. Opening up just a couple weeks after the Lincoln The-atre (also in Decatur), the Avon did not want to compete with the live performances. Instead, the Avon found its own niche with film. But like the Lincoln, the Avon is reported to be haunted. The spirit that resides here is thought to be Gus Constan, a former owner of the theatre before the place was bought out. It's said that Gus was, literally, thrown out of the theatre, but got his revenge by returning in the afterlife. Employees say that Gus moves props, and likes to watch invisible shows after the theatre is closed to the public—the sounds of applause and laughs have been heard in the empty seats at night. Gus has also been known to touch employees/visitors to the theatre, as well as appear to surprised people in the office area.

Address: 426 North Water Street
Website: www.theavon.com
Activity: A, E, T

Decatur Lincoln Square Theatre

Seating over 1,300 people, this theatre was considered a modern marvel when it was constructed in 1916. Over the years, of course, this all changed as the theatre slowly decayed and soon fell out of use. But with a renovation in the early 1990s, the Lincoln is now back in action—ghost and all! The theatre is said to be haunted by an old stagehand who worked in the place in the early 1900s. His presence is usually noted by the sounds of footsteps and whispers—as well as the appearance of a shadowy apparition that likes to hang out in the balcony area. The spirit has also been seen on the metal spiral staircase in the rear of the building. Witnesses have experienced all of this activity, as well as cold spots and the strange sight of seats moving by themselves—as if an invisible spectator is sitting there.

Address: 141 North Main Street
Website: www.lincolnsquaretheatre.com
Activity: S, C, E, T

Elizabethtown Grand Rose Hotel Bed and Breakfast

This house was originally the home of James and Elizabeth Mcfarlan and was built in 1812 overlooking the Ohio River. It was later made into a hotel for folks traveling along the same river. After years of service, the Mcfarlan family sold the place to Sarah Rose, an employee who loved the area and changed the name to the Rose Hotel. Today, the place is a popular local B&B and a place where small-town weddings are often held. All of this business is well received by the spirit of Sarah, who's said to still be within the Rose Hotel. People have claimed to have seen a female apparition walking the second floor, as well as climbing the stairs. Other activity includes the sounds of a female voice and items that seem to be moved during the night.

Address: Corner of Route 45 and Route 146
Website: www.rosehotelbb.com
Activity: A, E, T

Grafton Ruebel Hotel

This hotel was built in 1884 by Michael Ruebel and was more known in the area for its saloon than it was for the rooms. During World War II, this hotel was used by Coast Guard sailors who patrolled the Mississippi River. But not long after the war, the place closed down when business in the town of Grafton pretty much dried up. The current incarnation of the hotel opened in 1997 and has pretty much been considered a haunted location since then. It wasn't long after

opening that the hotel employees began getting reports that a little girl was haunting the second floor. Guests have reported seeing her on the stairs, in the hallway, and in several rooms that are close to the stairs. She is always seen wearing a long dress, but she is never heard.

Address: 217 East Main Street
Website: www.ruebelhotel.com
Activity: A

Grand Tower Devil's Backbone Park

This RV campground is located on the outskirts of Grand Tower, Illinois, and is right on the bank of the Mississippi River. If you walk north along the river, you will eventually run into two local, notorious landmarks: the Devil's Bake Oven and the Devil's Backbone. The backbone is simply the ridge that overlooks the river, which robbers used as a place to catch boats traveling the river off guard. The oven is a giant rock and the remains of a house that once stood here. The house was the lodging for the boss of a local iron factory and his daughter. It's rumored that the daughter committed suicide in the house (after her lover left town) and now haunts the area. Witnesses over the years have reported hearing the sounds of a female crying and screaming (especially during thunderstorms), as well as seeing a female apparition walking the path between the ruins of the house and where the factory once stood.

Address: 236 Park Road
Activity: A, E

Highland House of Plenty

Timothy Gruaz built this house for his family in the mid-1800s. He made his living by running a general store, and then a newspaper that was popular during the time. When he left the house, it passed on through several other families before evolving into several restaurants. The current eating establishment is called the House of Plenty, and it is the premier dining establishment in Highland, Illinois. Nobody is sure who haunts this restaurant, but many locals suspect that it is probably a family member who passed away at some point over the years. Regardless of who the spirit is, diners have reported the usual sounds associated with a haunting: footsteps, shuffling, bangs, and voices. Locals will also tell you that sometimes you can see a "ghost light" from one of the basement windows.

Address: 802 Ninth Street
Website: www.houseofplenty.net
Activity: O, E

Joliet Patrick C. Haley Mansion

This house is actually a castle—a castle built by a former mayor of Joliet, Patrick C. Haley. The entire place is built of limestone (a characteristic that paranormal investigators will tell you often marks a haunted location), though the inside is filled with fine woods, stained glass, and six fireplaces. The house became locally infamous for its haunting when it was investigated back in the 1970s. Investigators then said (and still repeat today) that the place has at least three entities in it: an old woman (said to be a former resident), a young boy (who also lived there), and a young woman who is thought to be the boy's nanny. Activity in the house has occurred often and includes the sounds of voices, screams, and the loud bangs of slamming doors/windows.

Address: 17 South Center Street
Website: www.patrickhaleymansion.com
Activity: A, E, T

La Salle 9th Street Pub

It's been rumored locally that this bar has been haunted for many years. The tale goes like this: Half of the bar was once a home that was simply next door to the tavern. A woman who lived in this house hated the bar and constantly complained about the place. After she passed away (inside the house), the house was purchased by the tavern and added on to the existing structure by knocking down a few walls. Instead of simply "turning over" in her grave, the woman

decided instead to haunt the pub. People have reportedly heard the woman speaking in the area by the pool tables, as well as felt cold spots, and seen pool cues/balls move by themselves. Could the old lady be haunting the 9th Street Pub? Go see for yourself.

Address: 253 9th Street
Website: www.9thstpub.com
Activity: E, T

La Salle Hegeler Carus Mansion

This Victorian home is over a hundred years old and was the residence of a wealthy local man named Edward Hegeler, who made his fortune in the metal industry. In addition to building this 57-room mansion, Hegeler also founded and built a local publishing house that was quite popular in the day. People who live in the neighborhood have been telling paranormal tales about this house for a very long time. Stories include seeing faces in the windows, hearing voices screaming from within the walls, and witnessing glowing orbs of light dashing between rooms. Today, the Hegeler Carus Foundation resides in the house and offers tours, as well as unique goods in the small shop within. Residents of La Salle will be quick to point out directions to the mansion, as well as give you some of the local tales concerning the place.

Address: 1307 Seventh Street
Website: www.hegelercarus.org
Activity: A, O, E

La Salle Kaskaskia Hotel

This Colonial Revival hotel first opened its doors in 1915 with 107 rooms and special amenities that marked the Kaskaskia as the area's most luxurious place to stay. The sixth floor of this hotel was originally made as a club room for the Illinois Valley Manufacturer's Club, but today it serves as a ballroom—a haunted ballroom. It's reported that the ghost of a young girl who fell to her death from this area (to the ground outside) now resides there. She is often heard dancing in the ballroom—music and all. Other activity in this hotel includes voices/whispers, items that move with nobody present, and the eerie sounds of footsteps in the lobby.

Address: 217 Marquette Street
Website: www.kaskaskiahotel.com
Activity: E, R, T

Okawville Original Springs Mineral Spa & Hotel

The current Original Springs that stands today is the second incarnation of the place. The original burned in 1892 (only to be rebuilt in 1893). The hotel was famous in the late 1800s for the reputed healing powers of the water found there. Based on this reputation, the hotel featured a famous spa, and the magical water was distributed throughout the area. Today, the place is more famous for the haunting said to occur there. With two apparitions (a female who has been seen on the second floor and a male known to visit guests in their rooms), dark shadow shapes, and strange sounds that fill the night, the Original Springs makes for a great haunted getaway. Hot spots (in addition to the second-floor hallways) include the suite where a former owner died (now called Room 28) and the area surrounding the swimming pool.

Address: 506 North Hanover Street
Website: http://members.tripod.com/
    okawvillehotel/
Activity: A, S, E

Palestine Fife Opera House

The David Fife Opera House first opened its doors in 1901 and featured all types of live performances for the town of Palestine. According to old newspaper articles, when the Fife was in operation, the entire town's electricity would dim! In addition to the opera house, other businesses have resided in this building, including a tavern, a hardware store (ran by Fife), and a mortuary! As seems to be the case with most theaters, the Fife was first considered haunted in the 1950s. Activity includes the sounds of music and voices, glimpses of a shadowy apparition (usually seen on the stairs), and footsteps. The Fife still hosts events and features a store—so you can visit the place for yourself.

Address: 123 South Main Street
Website: www.fifeoperahouse.org
Activity: A, S, O, E

Prairie du Rocher Fort de Chartres State Historic Site

This site dates back to the 1700s, when the French controlled the Mississippi River, as well as this entire area of the United States. The actual fort (which has been partially reconstructed by the Illinois Historic Preservation Agency) was built in 1750 and was abandoned by French troops in 1771 ... but something from their stay has remained behind. People say that the strange sight of men on horses and wagons walking in a slow parade has been seen at this location many times. Most believe it is a funeral procession, but nobody can be sure of this. Some say it only happens on the Fourth of July (some even say it only happens when the Fourth of July falls on a Friday), and some believe it happens whenever the moon is full. Either way, it seems to be a residual haunting and an intriguing one to catch, if possible.

Address: 1260 State Highway 155
Website: www.ftdechartres.com
Activity: A, E, R

Springfield Dana-Thomas House

Designed by famous architect Frank Lloyd Wright, the Dana-Thomas house was built literally over the top of another house and was completed in 1904. The house is said to be haunted because of extensive "Spiritualism" rituals that were performed in the place during the early 1900s. Spritualism was very popular at the time, and Susan Dana was a firm believer. She had also had several people very close to her pass away as she lived in this home. With séances, table tipping sessions, and psychic experiments being conducted in the place, could she have summoned back one of these dead relatives? Who knows? In later years, though, visitors and residents of the area reported experiencing voices, footsteps, shadow-shapes, and a glowing ball of light within the house.

Address: 301 East Lawrence Avenue
Website: www.dana-thomas.org
Activity: O, S, E

Springfield Inn at 835

Finished in 1909, this house-turned-inn was built for a florist named Bell Miller. The place was the talk of the town and even spawned a new upscale neighborhood that the locals called 'Aristocracy Hill.' The spirit that is said to haunt this place has few details—the folks that work there don't know who it is or where he/she came from. They do know that the elevator in the inn has worked by itself, that they have heard voices in empty rooms and that books have been seen moving by themselves. Reports of guests experiencing the phenomena have trickled in over the years as well. Regardless of who the apparition is, activity at this location seems to be of a harmless nature, so this could make a great introductory paranormal experience for budding ghost hunters.

Address: 835 South Second Street
Website: www.innat835.com
Activity: E, T

St. Charles Historic Hotel Baker

The haunting of this historic hotel (it was built in 1926 by the renowned Colonel Edward Baker) is based around a love story—a love story gone very wrong! The tale goes that a woman who worked as a maid was carrying on a love affair with a male worker in the hotel. One night, after a drunken bout of gambling, the man broke up with the woman and stormed out of town. The woman tried to continue on without him, but finally gave in to depression, waded into the neighboring Fox River and drowned. Whether this story is true or not cannot be determined; however, employees of the hotel (as well as guests over the years) have reported hearing the ghostly sounds of a woman crying within the hotel. Her apparition is said to visit folks within their rooms and to tug on their sheets as they sleep.

Address: 100 West Main Street
Website: www.hotelbaker.com
Activity: A, E, T

Utica Starved Rock Lodge

If you book a room at this lodge, you will want to pick one that is actually within the lodge itself, rather than one of the outside cabins. It's the lodge that's reported to be haunted. Employees have been relating strange tales of paranormal activity for many years. Many believe the spirits that reside in the lodge are Native Americans left behind by a great battle—an affair that forced one tribe to starve to death. Others say that the spirits are those of a couple that was murdered in the neighboring park during the 1960s. The paranormal occurrences usually include cold spots, orbs, and doors opening/closing by themselves. One guest who stayed in the lodge also reported a strange black apparition that was seen shooting into the dining area.

Address: Routes 178 and 71
Website: www.starvedrocklodge.com
Activity: A, S, O, C

Woodstock Woodstock Opera House

This historic location was built in 1889 as an all-purpose town hall and community center—the library, the city court, and the fire department were all housed within these walls back then. In addition to these functions, the structure also had an auditorium that would host plays and events. Over the years, the city offices moved out of the building, but the opera house continued on. Like many other theaters, the Woodstock is said to be haunted by a former actor that the employees dub "Elvira." Elvira is reported to hang out in seat DD113 and to love messing with the visiting performers' props and costumes in the backstage area. Elvira seems to get the blame for most things that go awry in this theatre, but that aside, most people who work in the place have reported experiencing paranormal activity.

Address: 121 West Van Buren Street
Website: www.woodstockoperahouse.com
Activity: E, T

INDIANA

Evansville Willard Library

Named after Willard Carpenter, a local notable, this library was his dream. He tried to live long enough to see it finished, but this did not happen. The library was finished in 1885, two years after his death. Strangely enough, it is not Willard who's said to haunt this location. The ghost that walks these halls is known as the "Lady in Gray" and is thought to be one of the Carpenter daughters named Louise. Over the years, many paranormal investigators have attempted to document activity at this place—and most have been successful. Employees, visitors, and investigators have experienced cold spots, black shadows, voices, and the occasional misty figure of … you guessed it … a woman in gray! If you visit the library's website, you may catch a glimpse of the spirit as well—the site features live webcam feeds from various cameras stationed throughout the library.

Address: 21 First Avenue
Website: www.willard.lib.in.us
Activity: A, E, C, S

Fortville Ivy House Bed and Breakfast

This home was built in 1921 by Jess E. Ferrell so he could live on the highest point in the city of Fortville. In addition to top-notch upscale furnishings and lodging, this B&B boasts one of the state's best door collections. Yes, that's right, door collections. Each one is unique and has its own story. Taking a tour of the home is a great way to learn about each of them—and if you ask nicely, you'll get the stories concerning the resident ghost. The owners of the home believe they inherited the spirit after they purchased an antique piano. Since the purchase, they (along with guests who have stayed there) have heard the sounds of the spirit banging and walking around on the second floor. Reportedly, you can actually hear the phantom footsteps of the spirit walking down the hall and stopping just outside a bedroom door.

Address: 304 North Merrill Street
Website: www.ivyhousebb.com
Activity: E

French Lick French Lick Springs Hotel

The mysterious healing waters of the nearby springs have been attracting people to the French Lick Springs Hotel since 1845. This massive hotel features 443 guest rooms and tons of amenities to please most everyone. The haunting of this hotel has been talked about in this area for many years and involves several stories. First off, there is the spirit of Thomas Taggart (a former owner), who is said to haunt the service elevator. Then there is a room that was supposedly the site of a double suicide and is now haunted by the couple. Finally, there is the completely haunted sixth floor that's rumored to be visited by a woman during the night—a woman who is often heard laughing or talking in the hallways.

Address: 8670 West State Road 56
Website: www.frenchlick.com
Activity: A, E, T, N

Gary Indiana Dunes State Park

With more than 2,100 acres of fun, this park is a huge draw for folks who want to swim and sunbathe on the shores of Lake Michigan. For those who are attracted to tales of the paranormal, the place is also a huge draw—mainly because of the ghost of "Diana" or "Diana of the Dunes." This spirit is reported to be that of a local woman named Alice Gray, who lived along the lake with her boyfriend. It's said that her boyfriend killed her, though he was not convicted of the crime. Local investigators will tell you that Alice Gray was a real person who died from wounds that hinted at murder, and that Alice does, indeed, still walk these shores.

Address: 1600 North 25 East
Website: www.duneland.com
Activity: A, E

Indianapolis Hannah House

Built in 1858 by Alexander Hannah, this house has had a haunted reputation for so long that almost no one remembers it as a "normal" house. The basement was used as a stop on the Underground Railroad where hundreds of escaped/freed slaves took refuge on their journey north. It's thought that not all the slaves who passed through this place managed to leave, though. A fire reportedly killed a group of them at one point, and they were all buried right there at the site of the accident. A lot of the activity in the basement (cold spots, voices, choking sensations, and apparitions) are all said to be a product of this incident. In addition to this, there is an upstairs bedroom that's haunted by an old woman who has been seen there many times. And if that's not enough, the stairs are haunted by old Alexander himself.

Address: 3801 Madison Avenue
Website: www.thehannahmansion.org
Activity: A, E, C, T, R

Indianapolis James Allison Mansion

Known as one of the best examples of an Arts and Crafts Country Estate, this mansion dates back to the early 1900s and a man named James Allison. Allison was known for his work in the auto industry and was instrumental in pioneering the sport of auto racing. Today the mansion is part of the Marian College campus and can be visited there. The paranormal activity stems back to a time when the house was used for dorms. During that period, many who stayed there reported hearing strange cries from the basement, voices in the attic, and objects that seem to move or even disappear from the various rooms.

Address: 3200 Cold Springs Road
Website: www.nps.gov/nr/travel/indianapolis/
Activity: E, T

Indianapolis Slippery Noodle Inn

Known as Indiana's oldest bar (it dates back to 1850), the Slippery Noodle is also famous for great live music, trivia nights, and the ghost of a former slave that walks the basement! Before becoming the establishment it is today, the Noodle served as an Underground Railroad stop during the Civil War and later became a brothel. Ghosts from both of these eras now remain in the place. The spirit of a black male has been seen and heard in the basement, and the apparition of a young woman has been spotted several times on the first-floor balcony.

Address: 372 South Meridian Street
Website: www.slipperynoodle.com
Activity: A, E, C, T

Jeffersonville Old Bridge Inn Bed and Breakfast

Just across the way from Louisville, Kentucky, this quaint house was built in 1836. Over the years, the place has belonged to several prominent Jeffersonville families and eventually became a place of business. It's rumored that the spirit of a former owner—most likely Charles Hancock (a descendent of the Declaration of Independence notable John Hancock)—still resides in the house. The spirit of this man has visited folks sleeping in the upstairs rooms and has been heard on occasion speaking from the rooms that have nobody in them. This spirit is known to be a "nice entity," so if you are looking for a haunted, non-threatening getaway, the Old Bridge Inn may just be the ticket for you.

Address: 131 West Chestnut Street
Website: www.oldbridgeinn.com
Activity: A, E

Lawrenceburg Whisky's Restaurant

Formerly a home, then a factory, this restaurant is a local haunted favorite. The spirit of a woman (probably a past inhabitant) has been witnessed in the Malt Room of this restaurant. Employees and patrons alike have experienced paranormal activity in this room that includes the appearance of her apparition and the sensation of her tugging on folks' clothes. It's been reported that she can be detected by the scent of a powerful, old-fashioned perfume that seems to permeate the room. The spirit of this woman is said to be nice and only wants to be noticed, so grab some food and a drink, and maybe she'll make an appearance for you!

Address: 334 Front Street
Website: www.whiskysrestaurant.com
Activity: A, E, N, T

Lewisville Guyer Opera House

This historic theater was built over the remains of one of the town's biggest disasters—a massive gas explosion that destroyed much of downtown Lewisville, including the home and offices of Dr. O. K. Guyer (the man the opera house is named after). Over the course of many years of entertaining the Lewisville community, tragedy has struck this place several times. At least one death is said to have occurred during a show (that of a little boy), and turbulent financial times have also contributed to the despair, and subsequent deaths, of several former operators of the opera house. Today, the spirit of the little boy who died in his seat still walks the theater. People say his apparition can be seen in the aisles after the place is closed and several actors have reported hearing a child's voice at times in the backstage area.

Address: 110 West Main Street
Website: www.guyeroperahouse.net
Activity: A, E

Madison Ohio Theatre

The original theatre that occupied this space was called the Little Grand, and it burned down to the ground in 1836. Two years later, the Ohio Theatre opened its doors. When the original theatre burned—as far as anyone knows—there was nobody inside. Despite this, the place has been rumored to be haunted ever since the new theatre was built. According to locals, the spirit of this place likes to hang out in the balcony area of the theatre and has been heard screaming. Besides the burning theory, many have also attributed the haunting to either a dead stagehand or actor (both of whom are rumored to have committed suicide). Visitors to the Ohio have also experienced cold spots, strange orbs, and voices throughout the theatre as well.

Address: 105 East Main Street
Website: www.ohiotheatremadison.com
Activity: A, E, O, T

Mitchell Whispers Estate

This unique lodging dates back to 1899 and is full of interesting stories. Besides the ghost tales that follow, a room in this house has a bed from the movie *Interview with the Vampire*. Folks often ask to stay in this room (asking for the "vampire room"). There have been several recorded deaths in this house—including one of the original owners, Jessie Ruth Gibbons and her 10-month-old daughter—so it's not hard to believe the place is haunted. Activity is your usual assortment of odd sounds—footsteps, voices, bangs, etc.—and they are heard in almost every area. One of the neat things about this location, though, is the ability to document your own sighting—they have a photo/video page on their website, as well as testimonials from eyewitnesses. You can also revisit the place via the live webcams that have been placed within the house.

Address: 714 West Warren Street
Website: www.whispersestate.net
Activity: A, E, T

Morristown Kopper Kettle Inn

The building that currently houses the Kopper Kettle started out as part of the Junction Railroad, and then became a tavern in 1858. After that, the place changed hands many times over the years, but always stayed a family-run business. With so many families living and working beneath this roof, it's no wonder that the place is considered to be haunted. Though nobody is sure who haunts the place, most of the people who have spent any amount of time in the place believe the inn is, indeed, haunted by somebody. With the sounds of voices, footsteps, and mysterious bangs, activity is sporadic, but present. Check in with the folks there to get the current activity report.

Address: 135 West Main Street
Website: www.kopperkettle.com
Activity: E

Munster Munster History Museum

Before becoming the Munster History Museum, this house dates back to 1910 and was home to the Kaske family. Before that, the place was an inn, but it burned down in 1909. Investigators have been unable to determine whether or not anyone passed away on the property during that fire, but during the Kaske family's occupation of the home, there were definitely deaths—all of natural causes. Whether it's a spirit left behind by the fire, or one of the souls of the Kaske family, the museum is considered haunted by employees and visitors alike. Most believe the spirit is that of Wilhelmina Kaske, who passed away in the front bedroom of the house. A female figure has been seen in that area, as well as peering from upstairs windows.

Address: Ridge Road at Columbia Avenue
Website: www.munsterhistory.org
Activity: A, C, E, T

Nashville Story Inn

With roots that go back to 1851 (when the place was a general store), the Story Inn is one of the original structures in the town of Nashville (then called Storyville). The ghost stories concerning the Story Inn could fill a book—and, in fact, have filled many books. This inn has a tradition of keeping journals in the bedrooms and many of them are lined with eyewitness accounts of the resident spirit called the "Blue Lady." One bedroom within the house has had so many occurrences that the owner changed the name of the room from the Garden Room to the "Blue Lady Room." They even have a photograph of their resident spirit—one that appears to show the Blue Lady peering from an upstairs window.

Address: 6404 South State Road 135
Website: www.storyinn.com
Activity: A, E, C, T

New Albany Culbertson Mansion

Now a haunted house in the sense that it has staged scary attractions within, the Culbertson mansion has roots that go back to the late 1800s. The real haunting of this house goes back to these days—specifically 1888—when the carriage house was a place that stabled the Culbertson family's horses and provided rooms for the family's servants to live in. It's said that a bolt of lightning struck the carriage house one stormy night, starting a fire that destroyed everything and everyone within. Later, when the place became a rental property, keeping tenants became a problem. With strange cries, smells and bangs, people who lived in the house usually didn't last long. At least this was true of all of the residents with the exception of one—a doctor who's reported to have slaughtered his entire family in the place!

Address: 914 East Main Street
Website: www.hauntedculbertson.org
Activity: A, E, T, C

South Bend Tippecanoe Place

Dating back to 1889, this location was built by Clem Studebaker to be his family home—and the place remained so for some time. The mansion was also the social epicenter for the South Bend area for years until the Studebaker family moved away. Since then, the place has been a Red Cross center, a school, and a museum. Today, it is a fine-dining establishment. Paranormal activity has been reported by visitors for a while now—with most of it coming from the waiters and bartenders. According to these tales, people have witnessed bar glasses floating in the air, seen items moving by themselves, and heard mysterious sounds that seem to come from the downstairs dining area.

Address: 620 West Washington Street
Website: www.tippe.com

Address: E, T

Valparaiso Inn at Aberdeen

This historic home dates back to over 150 years ago, when the town of Valparaiso was in its infancy. Additions and makeovers to the house have occurred sporadically throughout the years—with the most recent taking place in 1995. Folks around town in Valparaiso have been whispering stories about the ghosts at this inn for many years. These stories usually involve people who were shuttled through the house when it was (possibly) part of the Underground Railroad. Sometimes the tales involve the deaths of former residents, or the sightings of the spirit of a young girl, who is often seen sitting on the front steps/porch of the house. It's rumored that the spirit of the girl likes to roam the house as well—guests have seen the fireplace in the Aberdeen Suite of the house turn on by itself during the night.

Address: 3158 South State Road 2
Website: www.innataberdeen.com
Activity: A, E, T

Vevay Schenck Mansion Bed & Breakfast

This mansion-turned–bed and breakfast was constructed in 1874 by Benjamin Franklin Schenck. The place is a "Second Empire" masterpiece that features four porches, seven balconies, and eight chimneys. Residents of Vevay say the house is haunted by a woman called the "Lady in White," who is dressed in a Victorian-era dress and walks the halls of the mansion on the second floor. Guests at the B&B who have witnessed the apparition during the day and night say that she ignores those around her and simply walks past them—a sure sign of a residual haunt. But this is contradicted by the people who have also said to have heard voices, footsteps, and the sounds of things moving within their rooms during the night.

Address: 206 West Turnpike Street
Website: www.schenckmansion.com
Activity: A, E, T, R

Warsaw Barbee Hotel

Known as one of the haunts (pun intended) of famous mobster Al Capone, this hotel dates back to the early 1900s, when it was considered a high-style resort. Capone reportedly would rent the entire place to avoid running into any trouble and always stayed in Room 301 of the hotel. This room is now rumored to be haunted by the spirit of Capone, who is said to be seeking the solace and solitude he often found here when he was still alive. The entity makes its presence known to guests and employees by the smell of cigar smoke—a habit Capone was known for. Other ghostly activity on the premises includes the apparition of an old man that's seen on the stairs and a dark, shadowy apparition that's often spotted sitting in the booths within the bar.

Address: 3620 North Barbee Road
Website: www.barbeehotel.com
Activity: A, S, N, E

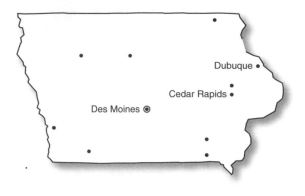

IOWA

Bentonsport Mason House Inn & Caboose Cottage

This Mormon-built home was constructed in 1846 as a hotel to serve travelers in the area moving along the river. During the era of the Civil War, the hotel served a second purpose as a regular stop along the Underground Railroad for escaped slaves. The owners of this location believe that the Mason House is inhabited by five separate entities. With a past that includes the deaths of three previous owners, a doctor amd several patients, as well as a murder, this comes as no surprise. Hot spots in the place include Room 5 where the spirit of a young boy is said to pull on people's clothing during the night (he is also known for being spotted on the second-floor landing), Room 7 (where a Mr. Knapp was murdered), Room 8 (the site of a floating face/head), and the bedrooms on the third floor where the spirit of an older woman has been seen many times.

Address: 21982 Hawk Drive
Website: www.masonhouseinn.com
Activity: A, E, T

Cedar Rapids Brucemore Mansion

This Queen Anne–style mansion dates back to 1886 and the Sinclair family. The house changed family hands two times—to the Douglas and Hall families—before the inhabitants completely died out in 1981, leaving the place as a trust organization. Today, the home offers tours of the grounds and the house, and is said to be haunted by a spirit that dates back to the early 1900s. A professor from the University of Chicago even visited the house back then to offer insight into the haunting, but to no avail. Visitors and employees working at the house have reported activity that seems to occur most often in the library. The activity includes voices, laughter, glowing balls of light, and books/items that move by themselves.

Address: 2160 Linden Drive Southeast
Website: www.brucemore.org
Activity: E, O, T

Cedar Rapids Coe College

The legend concerning the ghost of Helen has been passed down through the students and faculty of this school throughout the twentieth century. She is thought to have been a student of Coe College who died of influenza during a horrible outbreak in the early 1900s. After the girl passed away, Helen's parents donated an expensive grandfather clock to the school—and Helen attached herself to it because it was from her home. Originally in Voorhees Hall on campus, the clock now resides in Stuart Hall and is still said to be haunted. At night, the spirit of Helen is said to emerge from the clock and to walk the halls of the building.

Address: First Avenue at College Drive
Website: www.coe.edu
Activity: A, E

Cherokee American Theatre

This theatre dates back to the 1920s, and ghost stories concerning the place are just about as old. Over the years, patrons and employees alike have reported hearing the voice of a woman in the empty seats and seeing glimpses of an apparition in the backstage area. Local paranormal investigators say that the place is haunted by a woman who is thought to possibly be Hazel Goldie, the wife of a former owner and ticket booth worker in the old days. Tales of Mr. Goldie haunting the place are told as well—though it seems that most experiences within the theatre seem to involve a female presence.

Address: 108 East Main Street
Website: www.fridleytheatres.com
Activity: A, E

Council Bluffs Historic Dodge House

Built in 1869, this house was the home of General Grenville M. Dodge, one of Iowa's most historic characters. Several generations of the Dodge family lived in this place and it's thought that the ghost who resides in the home-turned-museum is a remnant of that past. Paranormal groups in the Council Bluffs area have reported that the Dodge House is haunted by the spirit of a little girl who is thought to mainly hang out near the old servant's quarters. Several "ghost photos" have been taken of the small girl—mostly from the exterior of the house because the employees do not allow inside photography. If you want to capture a photo of the girl, concentrate on the front door. There are several photos that seem to indicate the female apparition likes to look through the door's small windows.

Address: 605 3rd Street
Website: www.dodgehouse.org
Activity: A

eral days later. Who are the spirits in this place? Who knows? Visit and maybe you'll find out!

Address: 200 Pearl Street
Website: www.up.com
Activity: A, S, E, T

Council Bluffs Pottawattamie County Jail

This prison was built in 1885 and served as the area's jail until 1969. Today, the Historical Society of Pottawattamie County keeps up the place and offers tours. Over the course of this jail's history, this "revolving cage" prison was the home of thousands of criminals—with at least two who died on the premises. Strangely enough, it's thought that an ex-employee haunts the place—a jailer by the name of J. M. Carter. Paranormal activity in the prison includes voices, footsteps, bangs, and the occasional sighting of a shadowy figure. Many visitors over the years have reported feeling the overwhelming sensation of an entity watching them from within the cells, so tread softly at this site.

Address: 226 Pearl Street
Website: www.thehistoricalsociety.org
Activity: S, E

Council Bluffs Union Pacific Railroad Museum

Even before the Union Pacific moved its museum into this building, it was thought of as haunted. The previous occupants—a library—reported many strange occurrences over the years, including books that flew off the shelves, voices in the stacks area, and the sounds of heavy footsteps on wooden floors (even in areas that had been carpeted). Today, the haunting is said to continue. Dark shadowy shapes are seen darting through the hallways, voices are heard, and items turn up missing only to reappear sev-

Dakota City Humboldt County Historical Museum

Stories surrounding this site have carried on in the Dakota City area for many years—stories that are quite varied and interesting! The first involves the place being haunted by the spirit of a professional wrestler named Frank Gotch, who died locally and is rumored to walk within the place. Another story involves a fisherman who drowned in the Des Moines River and has been spotted peering from the windows there. But when these stories are boiled away, the only real activity that has been reported in the place involves ghost lights that are said to be seen from the streets when passing by the place.

Address: County Road P56
Website: www.humboldtiowahistory.org
Activity: O

Decorah Luther College

Founded in 1861, this university was originally a center and church for the local Norwegian community. Today it is a learning center for approximately 2,500 students. On the campus is a building called Larsen Hall, which is reportedly haunted by the spirit of a young woman named "Gertrude." Though this story smacks of an urban legend (Gertrude is, in fact, blamed for everything that happens within Larsen Hall, including missing items, fire alarms going off, etc.), many residents of this dorm say the stories of Gertrude are true. Witnesses say that they have seen the apparition of the woman, as well as experienced strange residual effects in the building, such as seeing items within rooms that are not really there—items that date back to the 1800s.

Address: 700 College Drive
Website: www.luther.edu
Activity: A, T, R

Dubuque The Grand Opera House

Tales involving ghosts at this site began when the theater's custodians started reporting strange occurrences to the local police department. According to the reports, the sounds of voices were heard in the seating area (of course nobody was there) and props used during live performances were being moved from one place to another. This theater dates back to 1890, but the paranormal activity seems to have started sometime during the 1920s. In addition to the voices and other activity, the most dramatic incident at this site involves the recent sighting of a pair of female apparitions sitting in the audience area.

Address: 135 8th Street
Website: www.thegrandoperahouse.com
Activity: E, T, A

Dubuque Historic Mathias Ham House

This Victorian/Gothic mansion dates back to 1856 when it was built by local miner and entrepreneur Mathias Ham. The Ham family lived and died in this home, with the final member of the immediate family, Sarah Ham, being the last to live there. While Sarah was there, it's docu-

mented that she was attacked during the night by a pirate who approached the house from the neighboring Mississippi River. She shot the man, who then dragged himself to the river and died. Today, visitors and employees report hearing ghostly voices, footsteps, and noises within the house. Passersby also report the sighting of a ghost light within the windows, as well as along the pathway that leads from the house to the river.

Address: 2241 Lincoln Avenue
Website: www.mississippirivermuseum.com
Activity: A, O, E

Fairfield Top of the Rock Grill

Known locally as the haunted Red Rock Tavern, the Top of the Rock Grill has been investigated several times by local paranormal teams. All have decided that this location is, indeed, haunted. Employees have reported experiencing ghostly happenings within the old building for many years—happenings that include items moving by themselves in the kitchen, voices/whispers in the bathrooms, and the sounds of people moving/walking in the upstairs area when the place is supposed to be empty. Nobody knows who exactly haunts the place, but over the years the building has had several major fires and was the location of a set of apartments on the upper floor. Could the spirit be the remnant of one of these times/events?

Address: 113 West Broadway Avenue
Website: www.topoftherockgrille.org
Activity: E, T

Marion Carlos O'Kelly's Mexican Café

It's rare that a chain-type restaurant or establishment is reported as a haunted location—probably because most of them are built fairly recently and not much in the way of tragedy occurs. But this Mexican restaurant differs. It's reported that this place is haunted by a noisy spirit that likes to play with the dining room chairs/tables, move things in the kitchen, and generally make a nuisance of itself throughout the restaurant. Though none of the activity is thought to be of a malicious nature, it's definitely thought to be of an annoying one. Over the years, many employees and customers have witnessed the events that, strangely enough, seem to happen more during the daylight hours rather than the night. Sounds like a good place for lunch...

Address: 3320 Armar Drive
Website: www.carlosokellys.com
Activity: T, E

Marion Granger House Museum

Considered one of the best examples of middle-class Victorian architecture in the area, the Granger house is a living testament to ninteenth century Iowa. The house was built in the 1840s and was the home to the same family for over a hundred years. Many generations of this family lived and died within the house, and at least one of the latter is said to still walk the halls of the place. Ghostly reports concerning the museum include faces peering from windows, shadow masses in the halls, and the sounds of walking/moving coming from the upper floor when its known to be empty. The museum offers tours to the public—catch one to check out life in the olden days and maybe you'll catch a glimpse of the ghost as well.

Address: 970 Tenth Street
Website: www.marion-historical-society.org
Activity: A, E

Villisca Villisca Axe Murder House

On June 10, 1912, this house was the site of one of Iowa's most gruesome murder scenes. During the night, the family of J. B. and Sarah Moore was slaughtered by the hands of a madman wielding an axe. Two adults and six children (two were young girls visiting the family) were all killed and were found dead by a neighbor in their horrible state. Paranormal activity in this house is said to have started in the 1930s, when a female resident reported seeing a male apparition standing beside her bed with an axe. That family soon left the house, only to be replaced by another who experienced the sounds of children crying during the night. The current owners—and numerous visiting investigators—have also reported strange events in the place that include apparitions, voices, footsteps, bangs, and the sounds of children.

Address: 323 East 4th Street
Website: www.villiscaiowa.com
Activity: A, E, C, T

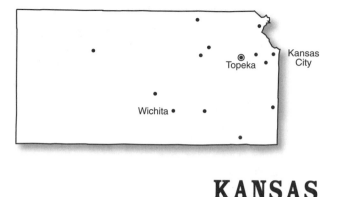

Topeka ⊙   Kansas
Topeka   City

Wichita •

KANSAS

Atchison Tuck U Inn at Glick Mansion

Erected in 1873 for former Kansas governor George Glick, this house underwent a massive renovation in 1912 that transformed the place from a Victorian-style mansion into a Tudor Revival manor. This is the current style of the Tuck U Inn, a historic bed and breakfast located in Atchison—a town known throughout Kansas for being full of dark history and mysteries. The ghost that resides at this mansion, though, is anything but dark. Employees of this B&B say the spirit is benevolent and only wishes to be noticed. Activity is pretty mild as well, including the sounds of footsteps, doors that open/close by themselves, and the usual bangs and knocks associated with a haunted home.

Address: 503 North Second Street
Website: www.glickmansion.com
Activity: E, T

Beaumont Beaumont Hotel

Situated in the beautiful Flint Hills of Kansas, the Beaumont Hotel was constructed in 1879 as a stagecoach station. The place was known as the Summit Hotel back then and was a regu-

lar stop for rich cattle barons, railroad magnates, and businessmen. During those years, the place also did a little bit of darker business—a brothel. Reportedly, there was a proprietor of this hotel who found out his wife was becoming overly fond of a rancher named "Zeke." So the innkeeper shot and killed the rancher on the second floor of the hotel. Today, Zeke is thought to haunt the Beaumont. He likes to move chairs in front of the doors to rooms, turn on radios during the night, and walk the hallways on a regular basis (made evident by the sound of spurs). Guests have reported seeing the apparition of a cowboy on the second floor as well.

Address: 11651 Southeast Main Street
Website: www.hotelbeaumontks.com
Activity: A, E, T

Coffeyville Brown Mansion

W. P. Brown solicited the firm of Wilder and Wright of Kansas City, Missouri, to build this mansion around the turn of the century. With three stories, sixteen rooms, and Tiffany glass/chandeliers, construction was finished in 1906. W. P. and his wife Nancy lived in the home with their son Donald until the boy died in 1911 at the age of 11 from complications arising from diabetes. After he died, the Brown family closed up Donald's room, and it remained that way until Nancy passed away 26 years later—a mere two months after W. P. passed away. So, who haunts the Brown mansion? It could be W. P. (people say they smell the scent of a pipe at times), Nancy (the sounds of a female crying have been reported), the daughter Violet (an apparition has been seen of a female dancing in the ballroom), the son Donald (heard humming in his bedroom), or maybe it's the former butler, Charlie. You know what they say—the butler did it. After all, his apparition is often seen sitting in a chair in the former servants' room.

Address: 2019 Walnut Street
Website: www.coffeyville.edu/thornburg/
    brownmansion/
Activity: A, E

Fort Riley Custer House

Known as a frontier outpost and for the exploits of the infamous "Buffalo Soldiers," Fort Riley was built in 1853 to guard the ever-expanding Western frontier. Today, the place is an active military base and home to the 1st Infantry Division (The Big Red One), so you will need to get a visitor's pass to get on the base (an easy task at the gate, though only open to U.S. citizens). The Custer House Museum on the base is generally regarded by those who serve there as being haunted. It's said that exhibits have been known to be moved during the night—and at least once, moved directly in front of visitors! Other activity includes strange sounds and glimpses of a pale apparition that many believe to be Custer himself (though the actual house he lived in is elsewhere on the base).

Address: On the U.S. Army Base
Website: www.kansastravel.org
Activity: A, T, E

Fort Scott Fort Scott National Historic Site

Named for General Winfield Scott, this former fort started out as a small camp in 1842. The place grew to a full-fledged fort when nearby Fort Wayne was abandoned by the U.S. Army as a post. This status, though, was short-lived. In 1855, the last remnants of the post were sold off as the entire garrison of this fort was moved to Fort Riley (though the place would briefly be used again during the Civil War). Today, the area is a historic site and open for tours. The haunting of this former fort seems to mostly be of a residual nature—the apparitions of long-dead Civil War soldiers are often seen walking the grounds. The former officer's quarters located here are also said to be haunted. Since serving the army, the place also functioned as the "Free State Hotel" and an orphanage. The sound of children playing has been heard, as well as glimpses of a pale apparition peering from the former hotel's windows.

Address: U.S. Highway 64 at 59
Website: www.nps.gov/fosc/
Activity: A, E, R

Hanover Hollenberg Pony Express Station

This was a location along the famed Pony Express route that served as a way station for pioneers traveling along the California and Oregon trails. Located on the Hollenberg ranch—a place that was operated by local rancher Henry Hollenberg—this station is known for more than just the brave souls who delivered the mail. This location is also the site of an infamous residual haunting. It's said that the riders of the Pony Express still ride through the area and are sometimes seen—though, they are most often reported as "heard." Phantom riders, the sounds of horses galloping, and the cries of men yelling at their mounts are experienced at this eerie site.

Address: 2889 23rd Road
Website: www.kansastravel.org
Activity: R, A, E

Hays Fort Hays State Historic Site

This outpost was originally constructed to protect railroad workers and travelers of the Smoky Hill Trail in 1865. The fort was located right in the middle of lands that were occupied by the Cheyenne and Arapaho Indian tribes, and it kept peace in the area until 1889. It was originally called Fort Fletcher (named after Governor Thomas C. Fletcher of Missouri) and was the home to people like Wild Bill Hickok and Buffalo Bill Cody. The ghost that haunts this area is known to locals as Elizabeth Polly. There is a memorial for her located on the old grounds of this fort. She is said to have died while helping the soldiers of Fort Hays recover from a cholera epidemic. Her spirit is often seen walking the area of the fort called Sentinel Hill and is known to locals as the "Blue Light Lady."

Address: 1472 Highway 183
Website: www.kshs.org/places/forthays/
Activity: A

Hutchinson Hutchinson Public Library

This public library is a modern facility and the literary center of events for the entire Hutchinson area. They offer many reading programs and stock a mean shelf of books. Of course, this isn't the only draw to this library. The place is also rumored to be haunted. The ghost is said to be Ida Day, who was a librarian here for many years. After her death, people started reporting the sounds of footsteps, a female voice, and odd bangs coming from the basement. Over the years, the sightings of Ida have expanded to include seeing her full-bodied apparition and the strange sight of books moving by themselves.

Address: 901 North Main Street
Website: www.hutchpl.org
Activity: A, E, T

Kansas City Strawberry Hill Museum and Cultural Center

This Victorian home was built in 1887 by John G. Braecklein for John and Margaret Scroggs. The Scroggs family lived in this residence for 32 years until 1919, when it became an orphanage for children whose parents died at the hands of an influenza epidemic. The orphanage ran continuously until 1988, when it was closed down. It was then that the structure was converted to its current form, a museum dedicated to preserving the Slavic heritage of Kansas City. The museum is reportedly haunted by the infamous "Lady in Red"—a spirit who is thought to be one of the many homeless taken in by the orphanage. She's known to appear to visitors and ask, "Where's the house of the priest?" Her apparition has been witnessed all over the house along with that of another entity thought to be a male member of the Scroggs family.

Address: 720 North 4th Street
Website: www.strawberryhillmuseum.org
Activity: A, E, C, O

Lawrence Eldridge Hotel

Originally the site of the Free State Hotel (a place that pre-dates the Civil War), the second incarnation of this hotel was built in 1856 after the original was burned to the ground by pro-slavery raiders. In 1863, the second version of the hotel was also burned down—this time by Quantrill's Raiders when they attacked the city of Lawrence and killed over 150 people. The third hotel was called the Hotel Eldridge and it stood the test of time (though it did close briefly due to financial woes). The paranormal activity in this hotel is quite interesting; it's said that Room 506 is a "portal" into the spirit world. People have witnessed multiple apparitions, ghost lights, black shadow masses, etc., in this room. The activity occurs throughout the fifth floor of the hotel and includes doors that open/close by themselves and the sounds of footsteps.

Address: 701 Massachusetts Street
Website: www.eldridgehotel.com
Activity: A, O, S, E, T

Manhattan East Stadium Purple Masque Theatre

Finding this theatre can be half the challenge to investigating/visiting this case! The place is part of the East Stadium of Kansas State University (if you visit their website below, you can find directions to the theatre, as well as its performances). Employees, as well as acting troupes, of the Purple Masque will tell you all about the exploits of the resident ghost they have dubbed "Nick." He is thought to be a football player who died (from overexerting himself at practice) in the building when it was still a functioning stadium. Activity in the theatre includes items moving by themselves, voices, and the occasional glimpse of ole Nick himself.

Address: 17th Street and Anderson Avenue
Website: www.k-state.edu
Activity: A, E, T

Shawnee Heaven on Earth Salon-Spa-Gifts

With haunted restaurants, hotels, museums, and state parks, it's no wonder that a spa would be haunted in Kansas as well! The Heaven On Earth is an upscale spa without the upscale prices—and even does charity work for the area in the form of a "locks of love" program that provides hair for chemo patients. Employees of this spa have reported experiencing an entity on the premises who likes to move/knock things around. Other activity includes cold spots and strange sounds that seem to emanate from the bathroom area. The activity does seem to be sporadic, so this may be a low-probability site to check out…but if you need a haircut and spa treatment, why not visit a haunted one?

Address: 11004 Johnson Drive
Website: www.heavenonearth-salon-spa
   -gifts.com
Activity: E, T, C

Topeka Kansas State Capitol Building

This Capitol building was a massive and extended undertaking. Construction began in 1866, but it would take over 37 years for the place to be fully finished. Over the course of construction, nine people died on the premises, and it's said that the ghostly manifestations that occur here are related to this fact. It's also told locally that a woman, distraught over her legal affairs, killed herself by leaping from the stairs that lead up into the dome of the Capitol (a place that is now included on the tour if you feel like trekking up almost 300 stairs!). Activity in the building includes voices, the sounds of cries/footsteps, and the apparition of a woman seen at the bottom of the staircase.

Address: 10th and Jackson Streets
Website: www.kansastravel.org
Activity: A, E

Wichita Broadview Hotel

Built in 1922, this hotel is a living tribute to the Roaring 20s and even offers a "Flapper Tour" of the establishment. But the biggest attraction for many at this hotel won't be offered on that tour: Clarence the ghost! It's said that Clarence checked into the hotel many years ago with his wife. While staying there, he caught his wife messing around with another man, so Clarence gunned his wife down then committed suicide by leaping from an upper-story balcony. Clar-ence has since been seen and heard often in this hotel and has even been known to call the front desk from rooms known to be empty. In addition to this activity, visitors have also experienced voices in their rooms, doors opening by themselves and finding their bathroom items misplaced or moved within their room.

Address: 400 West Douglas Street
Website: www.broadview-hotel.com
Activity: A, E, T, C

Wichita Kansas Aviation Museum

The Art Deco masterpiece that is this museum was dedicated in 1935. It existed as the Wichita Municipal Airport until it was shut down in 1984. During its years of operation, the place was a key terminal during World War II and later became an Air Force base for training purposes. The building was transformed with a massive renovation into a museum in 1991. As for the haunting at this location, nobody is sure who the entity is or could even be. Regardless of this, the activity continues there: glimpses of a strange apparition that appears to be a male, voices, footsteps, and the sounds of someone trying to open doors there.

Address: 3350 South George Washington
   Boulevard
Website: www.kansasaviationmuseum.org
Activity: A, E, T

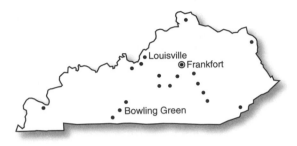

KENTUCKY

Ashland Paramount Arts Center

Originally called the Paramount Theatre, this center first opened its doors in 1931. It was built for movies, but the place has been used for virtually every type of entertainment over the years. The story surrounding the haunting of this theatre goes back to the 1940s. It's said that a man working for a construction team stayed alone at the theatre while his co-workers went to go get lunch. When the workers returned to the scene, the man who was left behind was dead. Since then people have been seeing the apparition of the construction worker in the theatre, as well as experiencing strange voices and cold spots.

Address: 1300 Winchester Avenue
Website: www.paramountartscenter.com
Activity: A, C, E

Bardstown Jailer's Inn Bed & Breakfast

This B&B makes for an extremely unique experience—besides the fact that the place is haunted, the Jailer's Inn was actually a functioning jail. The Nelson County Jail in fact. The mini-prison operated from 1797 until 1987. Today, you can stay in one of the old cells of the jail—an area that is considered to be one of the most haunted there. The other five rooms in this establishment are more modern and "normal." The activity here seems both "intelligent"and residual. Guests who have stayed in the cell room have reported hearing voices, seeing shadowy shapes, and experiencing an extreme amount of bad feelings. People staying in other areas have also experienced the sounds of prisoners talking, footsteps, and odd knocks and bangs during the night.

Address: 111 West Stephen Foster Avenue
Website: www.jailersinn.com
Activity: S, C, E, R

residual type that simply reflects past services within the church, but with the appearance of an actual spirit and objects being moved within the place, it's fair to say the entity there seems intelligent as well.

Address: 604 Poplar Street
Website: www.bbonline.com/ky/christophers/
Activity: A, E

Bardstown The Old Talbott Tavern

This bed and breakfast has roots that go back to 1779 when the place was a stagecoach stop and tavern for weary travelers. Over the years, many famous folks have stayed at this place, including Abraham Lincoln, Andrew Jackson, and Jesse James. It is actually Jesse who claims the distinction of seeing the first ghost here! He said that while staying in the tavern, a strange man appeared in his room as if he had stepped from a mural or came through the door. Jesse opened fire on the intruder, but the man simply vanished. The bullet holes are still present in the wall where this occurred. More current ghost stories concerning Talbott involve a woman who hung herself from the second-floor chandelier and the spirits of children heard playing on the second floor.

Address: 107 West Stephen Foster Avenue
Website: www.talbotts.com
Activity: A, E, T

Bellevue Christopher's Bed & Breakfast

This bed and breakfast was once a church, and gets its name from the patron saint of travelers. It dates back to the 1800s, and it was a functioning church all the way up until 1996. Then the place was purchased by a private owner and transformed into this luxury getaway. Not long after renovating and opening the place, people starting experiencing strange things here: apparitions walking the stairs, a phantom piano playing during the night, and the sounds of voices and footsteps coming from empty rooms. Most think the haunting is probably a

Berea Historic Boone Tavern Hotel & Restaurant

This hotel and restaurant are named after famed woodsman Daniel Boone. It was built in 1909 as lodging for visitors to Berea College—which was preferable to staying at the college president's house (as they did before). This hotel is actually owned by the university and continues to run today as strong as ever. Strangely enough, the ghost stories associated with the hotel involve the spirit of a young "slave boy" who is said to have died while traveling the Underground Railroad. Nobody seems to know how a boy who died many years before this place was even built managed to get here, but people will tell you it's true. Activity includes the apparition of the boy, as well as the sounds of crying and voices.

Address: 100 Main Street North
Website: www.boonetavernhotel.com
Activity: A, E

Brandenburg Doe Run Inn

This mill-turned–bed and breakfast was constructed between 1780 and 1790 along the Doe Run Creek—a place discovered and named by Squire Boone, brother of famed Daniel. In 1901, the place was transformed from the mill into the Sulfur Wells Hotel, and subsequently becamethe Doe Run Hotel in 1947. The current incarnation came into being in 1958. As for the ghost here, nobody is sure who the spirit is supposed to be—it could be almost anyone that lived and died in the place since 1901. But the spirit is known for untying people's shoes, hanging out in the dining room, and lingering on the stairs between the first and second floors.

Address: 500 Doe Run Hotel Road
Website: www.doeruninn.com
Activity: E, S, T

Cumberland Benham School House Inn

This former schoolhouse dates back to 1926, when it served the community as a combination high school and elementary school for children who lived in the area's coal camps. Today it is a 30-room guest house that, along with the nearby Kentucky Coal Mine Museum, pays tribute to the area's mining history. The haunting of this location seems to be of the residual nature, and reflects sounds and events that were all too common: the sounds of children laughing and running through the halls. This was, of course, an everyday occurrence until the school shut down in 1992. Many people have experienced this event here, and the reporting of this activity has become common.

Address: 100 Central Avenue
Website: www.benhamschoolhouseinn.org
Activity: R, E

Frankfort Liberty Hall Historic Site

This tourist destination is actually the site of two houses: Liberty Hall (1796), built by famous Kentuckian John Brown, and the Orlando Brown House (1835). The Liberty Hall house is the one considered to be haunted. It's reported that at least three spirits inhabit this house—including a soldier who walks the grounds and an opera singer who disappeared while attending a gala—but the most famous spirit in this location is the "Gray Lady." This female apparition is thought to be a woman named Margaret Varick, a relative of the Brown family, who died while visiting the place. People have witnessed the gray apparition of Margaret many times in the house, as well as heard her talking in empty rooms. Other activity at Liberty Hall includes strange lights, cold spots, and doors that open/close by themselves.

Address: 202 Wilkinson Street
Website: www.libertyhall.org
Activity: A, E, T

Franklin The Octagon Hall Museum

Dating back to 1859, this unusual structure was the home of Andrew Jackson Caldwell and his family. It remained their property throughout the Civil War, all the way until 1918 when it was sold. Activity here is blamed on the house being used as a hospital during the Civil War—a place where many soldiers died performing their duty. There is also a story that involves a young girl named Mary Elizabeth, who is said to have burned to death in the kitchen when her dress accidentally caught fire from the stove. Experiences at the Octagon Hall Museum include the sounds of a young girl laughing/crying/talking, voices of soldiers, apparitions, and a spirit who likes to lounge on upstairs beds.

Address: 6040 Bowling Green Road
Website: www.octagonhall.com
Activity: A, E, T

Harrodsburg Harrodsburg Spring Park

This public park is located on a property that once housed a local hotel called the Graham Springs Hotel. Local lore tells us that during that hotel's tenure, a young woman checked in with a fake name and died of mysterious causes during a social event. The hotel buried the unknown woman in their back lot (now part of the park). Today, the spirit of this woman is said to haunt the park. If you search for it, you can actually find the headstone of the girl; you'll know it by the strange words written on it: "Hallowed and hushed be the place of the dead. Step softly. Bow head." The ghost is known to linger in the area around this grave and has been spotted many times over the years.

Address: Highway 68 South
Website: www.harrodsburgky.com
Activity: A

Lexington Gratz Park Inn

This upscale hotel is named after famous Kentuckian Benjamin Gratz and is located in the area of the Gratz Park Historic District. Tales regarding the haunting of this hotel have been told for years in the town of Lexington—as well as all over Kentucky. According to locals, the building that now houses the hotel was originally owned by the city—and back then the basement was the morgue. Needless to say, that area—as well as most other areas of the hotel—is now considered to be haunted. Witnesses have reported seeing an apparition of a young girl (known as "Anna") playing in upstairs hallways, as well as the spirits of men (of which the most famous is "John") that have been seen within actual guest rooms. People have also complained about noise coming from the "fourth floor" of this hotel—a strange event since the hotel only has three floors ...

Address: 120 West Second Street
Website: www.gratzparkinn.com
Activity: A, E

Lexington Henry Clay Estate

Construction on Henry Clay's beautiful estate began in 1809 and was an ongoing project for many years. Clay, along with his wife, lived in the estate until his death in 1852. The property then was passed down to James Clay, who completely tore the home down and rebuilt it. Since then, the house has belonged to a university, been a home again, and is now a museum that's overseen by the Henry Clay Memorial Foundation. It's said that the spirit of old Henry is still in the house to this day. His apparition has been seen by several employees and guests over the years, and is known for hanging out in the downstairs parlor area. Other activity in the house includes the usual unknown bangs and knocks, as well as footsteps.

Address: 120 Sycamore Road
Website: www.henryclay.org
Activity: A, E

Lexington Loudoun House

This Gothic-style estate is now home to the Lexington Art League, a place where exhibits, events, and workshops are held to support the local art community in the area. Long before they moved into this historic residence, the Loudoun was considered to be a "haunted house" by the community. According to locals, the house is subject to both a residual and intelligent haunting. On the intelligent side, a woman is said to be seen walking throughout the place. She is wearing a Victorian-era dress, and she is usually accompanied by the scent of perfume. On the residual side, people have also reportedly witnessed what sounds like a formal event—the sounds of music and voices engaged in merriment in the downstairs areas of the house.

Address: 209 Castlewood Drive
Website: www.lexingtonartleague.org
Activity: A, R, E, N

Louisville The Brown Hotel

This hotel was built in 1923 at a cost of over $4 million dollars by famous Louisville resident J. Graham Brown. Brown practically lived in this place as he ran the hotel until his death in 1969. The hotel was shut down in 1971 and was turned into the local Board of Education building. Apparently, this didn't sit too well with Brown. Soon after the board moved in, they started seeing and hearing strange things in the hall, including the apparition of Brown himself. In the 1980s, the Brown Hotel reopened with all new upscale furnishings and was completely remodeled—and the ghost stayed. Guests have reported still seeing his apparition walking the halls, as well as hanging out in the front lobby.

Address: 335 West Broadway Avenue
Website: www.brownhotel.com
Activity: A, E

Louisville The Louisville Palace

This place started out in 1928 as Loew's The-atre, located along Louisville's famous "movie row." The theatre ran continuously until 1978, when it was shut down (the property changed hands to become a nightclub). It would be the early 1990s before the theatre would get yet an-other makeover to become the place it is today. During construction, it's reported that workers began to see an apparition of a "man in glasses" in different locations throughout the theatre. Soon, they began to hear voices as well. Once the theatre opened, activity continued in the form of an apparition and strange malfunctions in the projector room. Most believe this spirit is that of Ferdinand Frisch, a man who worked at Loew's Theatre and died of a heart attack in the basement.

Address: 625 South 4th Street
Website: www.louisvillepalace.com
Activity: A, E, T

Louisville The Seelbach Hilton

This hotel is like a ticket straight into the 1920s. Art Deco décor and furnishings create an atmo-sphere that makes this place a living time capsule. Over the years, the Seelbach has been known for many famous visitors, including Al Capone (a frequent drinker in the Oakroom lounge) and F. Scott Fitzgerald (who wrote about the hotel in his book *The Great Gatsby*). The ghost in this ho-tel is famous as well. She is known as the "Lady in Blue" and is said to be the spirit of a woman who committed suicide in the hotel by leaping down an elevator shaft. Her apparition has often been seen in the hotel—usually accompanied by a strange, sweet perfume.

Address: 500 Fourth Street
Website: www.seelbachhilton.com
Activity: A, N

Louisville Waverly Hills Sanitorium

What more can be said of this haunted loca-tion? It's appeared in television shows, movies, numerous books, and even more websites. The haunting of this former tuberculosis sanito-rium is said to be one of the most intense and active in the United States. Activity includes apparitions, shadow people, voices, residual sounds of the past hospital, and objects that move by themselves (one of the common tech-niques used for investigating this place includes placing a small ball on the floor for the spirit to roll). Waverly offers tours, overnight stays, and even sells merchandise to promote the haunt-ing here. Word on the street, though, is that the owners are talking of turning the place into a hotel, so getting free-run of the place may be a thing of the past very soon. Better visit now, or plan on staying there once it reopens as a hotel.

Address: 4400 Paralee Lane
Website: www.therealwaverlyhills.com
Activity: A, S, E, T, C, O

Mammoth Cave Mammoth Cave National Park

This cave has been visited by explorers, tourists, and locals since 1816. In 1841, a doctor by the name of John Croghan decided to set up a tuberculosis ward within the cave, hoping that the damp, cool air would be helpful to his patients. This, of course, did not work, and when the patients all passed away, the doctor moved on. The dead were buried at the entrance of the cave—alongside many others who were already interred at this location. For many centuries prior to this, local Native American tribes had been burying their dead within the cave because they thought of the place as holy ground. If this isn't enough to cause the cave to be haunted, consider the fate of explorer Floyd Collins. Collins died when he became pinned down by a falling boulder while exploring the cave. Visitors to the cave have reported hearing voices, seeing apparitions, and experiencing strange phenomena at this location for many years.

Address: 1 Mammoth Cave Parkway
Website: www.nps.gov/maca/
Activity: A, E, T, C, S

Paducah C. C. Cohen Restaurant & Bar

This restaurant is as proud of their ghost story as they are their menu. Don't believe me? Just look on their website and see which gets top billing! The spirit that inhabits this circa 1865 building is said to be a woman by the name of Stella. She is thought to be Stella Cohen Peine, a resident of the building who died here in 1980 when it was still a private residence. The bar has decorated the upstairs balcony area to resemble Stella's living room, complete with a picture of her hanging on the wall. Maybe this

is why she haunts the place—it looks like home! At any rate, activity here ranges from voices, to footsteps, to items being moved around in the dining room and kitchen on an almost nightly basis.

Address: 103 Market House Square
Website: www.cccohen.com
Activity: A, E, T

Perryville Perryville Battlefield State Historic Site

On October 8, 1862, this area erupted into a battle that would become the largest in the state of Kentucky during the Civil War. At least 7,600 people were killed or wounded during this fight—and it would become the South's last attempt to keep Kentucky as a Confederate state. Union troops, the victors, took time to bury their own dead after the battle, but the Confederate soldiers were left to rot in the sun. Maybe this is the reason the area is said to be haunted. Visitors to the park have reported hearing the sounds of battle, seeing apparitions of soldiers and men on horseback, and witnessing strange glowing balls of light that are often seen dancing across the battlefield.

Address: 1825 Battlefield Road
Website: http://parks.ky.gov/findparks/
   histparks/pb/
Activity: A, E, R, O

Renfro Valley Aunt Polly's Crafts & Collectibles

This place is the oldest original house in Renfro Valley and is a fine example of a classic Kentucky log cabin–style home. Aunt Polly's is known for their handmade crafts, antiques/collectibles, and homemade jellies and jams. The place is also known for Aunt Polly—a woman buried in the cemetery directly across the street from this store. According to local lore, Aunt Polly became upset when she was buried in the cemetery rather than on her own property at the store, so now she has returned to haunt the place. Visitors to the store have reported experiencing an overwhelming sense of "creepiness," cold spots, items moving by themselves, and the sounds of a person in the upstairs area when it's known to be empty.

Address: Hummel Road off U.S. Highway 25 North
Website: www.rockcastlecountyky.com
Activity: E, C, T

Richmond White Hall State Historic Site

Underneath the walls of this historic site is yet another historic site—a mansion by the name of Clermont that was built in 1798 by Revolutionary War General Green Clay. In the 1860s, Clay's son, Cassius, decided to build over the top of Clermont and re-dubbed the property White Hall. Today, the place is a living museum that you can tour to catch a glimpse of Kentucky's historic past. Of course, the house is said to be haunted by Cassius, himself. With a background that included murders, duels, and war, it's no wonder his spirit is damned to stay behind. Many sightings of Clay, as well as several other spirits (thought to be a man Clay killed in the library, his wife, and his daughter) have been witnessed numerous times in the house, along with the sounds of voices and footsteps. It's thought that the third floor of the house is the most haunted.

Address: 500 White Hall Shrine Road
Website: www.whitehallclermontfoundation .org
Activity: A, E

Springfield Historic Maple Hill Manor

This antebellum home, built in the famous Greek Revival style, was constructed by Thomas Irvine McElroy. Here he ran a plantation of over 600 acres and raised a family along with his wife Sarah Jane Maxwell. During the Civil War, the home was briefly used as a hospital and a temporary camp, and later the place became a foster home that raised over 300 children. With so many memories in one house, it's no wonder that the place is haunted. Some of the activity seems to be associated with the war (spectral soldiers are sometimes spotted on the property) and some with the foster home (the sounds of children), but the most frequently spotted apparition in this house is said to be Sarah. She is often seen walking the halls, and even making the occasional appearance in a guest room.

Address: 2941 Perryville Road
Website: www.maplehillmanor.com
Activity: A, E

West Point Ditto House Inn

This Federal-style home served as General William Tecumseh Sherman's headquarters briefly during the Civil War and was then used as a hospital to treat officers wounded and dying from battle. During the years since then, the place has been a bank, a boarding house, and a private residence. Today it is a bed and breakfast. The haunting of this house has been featured on several television programs going back to the 1990s and is fairly well known throughout the area. It's said that spirits from the Civil War hospital who died in the house are now seen walking the halls and the grounds. Though most stories seem residual in nature, some witnesses say a spirit has touched them or spoken to them.

Address: 204 Elm Street
Website: www.innsite.com/inns/A004689
Activity: A, R, E, T

Wilder Bobby Mackey's Music World

Originating as a slaughterhouse in the 1850s, Bobby Mackey's Music World has a unique and unsettling history. Once the slaughterhouse closed for business in the late 1800s, a local occult group began using the property to make sacrifices, utilizing the well there much like the slaughter house did—to drain blood. In 1896, though, it was discovered that two men in the cult used the place for a whole different purpose: to murder and dispose of a woman named Pearl Bryan. Bryan's head was never found—even when the two murderers (Scott Jackson and Alonzo Walling) were offered a lesser sentence than death if they revealed where they put it. The two men were executed and the old slaughterhouse became home to several Mob-run nightclubs before the property was finally purchased by country-western musician Bobby Mackey. Paranormal activity is common and intense, and includes screams, voices, objects moving, and spirits who grab/push people. In addition to the spirit of Bryan, many believe the evil entities of Jackson and Walling are also present. But the most famous ghost here is "Johanna," the benevolent spirit of a former stripper who committed suicide on the property. Pick up Mackey's song of the same title to learn more about her story.

Address: 44 Licking Pike
Website: www.bobbymackey.com
Activity: A, E, T, C, S

LOUISIANA

Baton Rouge Old Louisiana State Capitol

This historic building is one of the best examples of Gothic Revival architecture in the United States—looking more like a castle than an administrative building. The building was constructed in 1847 at a location overlooking the Mississippi River where the famous "red pole" was said to be. The site now hosts the Museum of Political History and is open to the public for visiting most days. As for the paranormal activity—this dates back dozens of years to when the Capitol building was used by various veterans' organizations after the 1930s/World War II. Employees would report hearing footsteps and voices, see doors close by themselves, and catch glimpses of a shadowy apparition (that was known to shoot up the ornate circular staircase). Sightings have continued until the present day and the current museum has even allowed the place to be investigated.

Address: 100 North Boulevard at River Road
Website: www.sos.louisiana.gov
Activity: S, E, T

Baton Rouge Spanish Moon

This modern bar and nightclub features more than just daily drink specials and live music. It's also the location of an apparition that nobody can seem to explain. The spirit appears to be that of a young man—though witnesses to the event can only say for certain that the entity is male. He is often seen throughout the main floor of the nightclub close to closing or after-hours when folks are cleaning up. In addition to this apparition, the place experiences bar glasses and items that seem to levitate or move by themselves, as well as the usual bangs and knocks associated with a haunting. You may want to check this location's website for their live music schedule and plan a visit when there is no band playing to experience this haunting for yourself.

Address: 1109 Highland Road
Website: www.thespanishmoon.com
Activity: A, E, T

Cheneyville Loyd Hall Plantation

This massive plantation goes back to 1820 when William Loyd (a relative of the famous Lloyd's of London family) built the original house on the property. William was an extremely disliked person—his own family made him drop an 'L' from the Lloyd last name. Local Native Americans would often shoot arrows at the front door of the house to show their dislike of the man as well (still evident in the door, though it is now the door to the dining room). During the Civil War, Loyd worked as a double agent and eventually met his demise in his own front yard, where he was hanged. There are other recorded deaths in the place as well, including a suicide by Inez Loyd. As a result of this history, this location is charged with almost every type of paranormal activity: apparitions, moving objects, strange smells, and the sounds of music/voices that are heard throughout the house.

Address: 292 Loyd Bridge Road
Website: www.loydhall.com
Activity: A, E, T, N

Destrehan Destrehan Plantation

There are several good reasons to visit this historic plantation home, including the mansion itself (built in 1787), a plantation store, and an authentic document called the "Jefferson Document" that names a Destrehan family member to the Orleans Territorial Council and was signed by Thomas Jefferson himself. Of course, you could also visit to experience the haunting of this plantation. The mansion is reportedly haunted by Stephen Henderson, a resident of the home during the days of Jean Lafitte (who often visited the place). His apparition, along with another male entity, is often sighted at different locations on the property—though the ballroom seems to be the most common hot spot for activity. In addition to the apparitions, visitors have experienced voices, footsteps, and the periodic slamming of the front door.

Address: 13034 River Road
Website: www.destrehanplantation.org
Activity: A, E, T

Destrehan Ormond Plantation Manor

This former sugar plantation dates back to 1789 and is a rare example of the French West Indies–style home that was so popular along the Mississippi River during that era. Soldiers used the place as a makeshift base during the infamous Battle of New Orleans and occupied the place again during the Civil War when Union troops took over the area. During the late 1800s, the manor was purchased by Senator Basile LaPlace who grew rice on the plantation, but he didn't stay long. The Ku Klux Klan soon identified LaPlace as an enemy, then shot and hanged him alongside the road in front of the plantation. It's said his spirit now roams the grounds. But the haunting doesn't end there…Witnesses have experienced a female apparition as well (seen as a young girl) who's thought to be one of the many who lived and died within the place over the centuries.

Address: 13786 River Road
Website: www.plantation.com
Activity: A, E

Garyville San Francisco Plantation

Built in 1856 by Edmond Bozonier Marmillon, this location is one of the most unique structures in all of Louisiana. With hand-painted ceilings, faux marbling, and antique furnishings designed by John Henry Belter, the residents of this house never spared a detail in creating a wonderful place to live. And that's just what the family did for many generations—they lived and died in this house. This is why the mansion is considered to be haunted to this day. It's rumored that the house is inhabited by as many as three ghosts: the spirit of a small boy, who is heard crying during the night; the ghost of a young girl, who is seen near the stairway (thought to be a young daughter who died after falling down the stairs); and the apparition of an older man, who is seen on the top floor and around the area of the roof.

Address: 2646 Highway 44
Website: www.sanfranciscoplantation.org
Activity: A, E

Houma Southdown Plantation House/ Terrebonne Museum

This circa 1859 home is the centerpiece of an area that's known for growing and selling sugar. William J. Minor was one of the original owners of the house (and eventually the only owner), and it would be his family that would occupy the premises all the way up until 1932. The house would retain its association with sugar after the Minors left, as the place was purchased by a sugar corporation. Today, the property is a museum dedicated to the history of the house, as well as the area industry. The haunting of the museum is thought to be the spirit of someone from the Minor family, since many of them lived and died in the house over the years. A ghostly figure is often spotted walking the halls of the house, and even passersby over the years have whispered tales of an eerie face seen peering from the windows of this mansion.

Address: 1208 Museum Drive
Website: www.southdownmuseum.org
Activity: A

Lafayette T. Frere's House Bed & Breakfast

This Acadian-styled home was built using local Louisiana red cypress wood in 1880. With a giant porch and rooms filled with antique furniture, it's easy to find yourself swept back to the days when Cajun settlers occupied most of the area. In addition to the history associated with this house, there is also at least one darker tale—the tale of a young girl and her ghost. The story goes like this: A young female resident was found one day accidentally drowned in a nearby cistern full of water. When the local priest was called to give her the last rites, he refused, saying she had committed suicide. The spirit, unhappy with this decree, now roams the house waiting for absolution. She is thought of as a "nice" spirit, and the activity in the home includes the sounds of music, objects moving by themselves, and the sounds of footsteps walking the halls at night.

Address: 1905 Verot School Road
Website: www.tfreres.com
Activity: E, T

New Iberia Joseph Jefferson Mansion/ Rip Van Winkle Gardens

Famous American actor Joseph Jefferson had this home built for him in 1870. Jefferson was a well-known actor and was noted for playing the role of Rip Van Winkle—something he did a remarkable 4,500 times! After his death, the house was sold to John Lyle Bayless of Kentucky, who lived there and created the Rip Van Winkle Gardens—25 acres of beautiful foliage that surrounds the mansion. The home is governed today by a foundation and is open to the public for tours. Stories concerning the haunting of this historic place usually involve one of two spirits. The first is that of a small girl, who has been seen on the main floor and in the servant areas. The second is the spirit of a man, who is often witnessed upstairs in the hallways and peering from a window. The girl, though, is usually the ghost that is seen—and heard. The most recent activity reported is the sound of the girl crying in the downstairs hallway.

Address: 5505 Rip Van Winkle Road
Website: www.ripvanwinklegardens.com
Activity: A, E, T

New Iberia Shadows on the Teche

This antebellum masterpiece dates back to between 1831 and 1834. The incredibly fascinating and detailed history of this house includes stories of politicians, businessmen, the Civil War, and family life in Louisiana. Today, all of this history, as well as the house itself, can be visited and toured (check the website for hours of operation). The ghost stories associated with this property are the natural product of many generations of people living and dying within a single home. The only spirit of name that is thought to be here is that of Mary Moore, the matron of the home who died while her property was occupied by Union troops during the Civil War. Activity includes lots of voices/footsteps heard on the second floor and in the attic. There have been glimpses of a misty figure, but it's not certain if it was just a mist, or if it was an apparition.

Address: 317 East Main Street
Website: www.shadowsontheteche.org
Activity: A, M, E

New Orleans 1891 Castle Inn

This Gilded Age mansion is one of the more unique places to stay in the Garden District of New Orleans. It's minutes away from all the fun in the French Quarter, but is quieter and cleaner. The employees of this inn will tell you right off the bat (if you ask) that this location is most certainly haunted—probably by two ghosts! The haunted reputation started with a guest witnessing a male apparition standing in Room 11. Soon after, strange occurrences started happening on a regular basis. More people starting seeing the apparition of the man on the front porch and in other rooms—then people started reporting seeing the spirit of a young girl. Other noted activity includes faucets turning themselves on, footsteps, objects moving, and lights turning on/off. The male ghost is thought to be a former paid servant of the inn, while the girl is believed to be a person who drowned on the property back in the days when the place was a sprawling plantation.

Address: 1539 Fourth Street
Website: www.castleinnofneworleans.com
Activity: A, E, T

New Orleans Beauregard-Keyes House

This place was originally built for Joseph LeCarpentier in 1826 and is called a "raised center hall" house—a popular style back in the day in New Orleans. It's now called the Beauregard-Keyes house for its two most famous residents: Civil War Confederate General Pierre Gustave Toutant Beauregard and author Frances Parkinson Keyes. The house is said to be the site of a strange residual haunt—when the Civil War was a thing of the past, and Beauregard died of natural causes, it's said his spirit returned to this place—and brought with him the sounds of the actual war. People passing by during the evening have heard the sounds of battle cries, gunshots, and cannon fire coming from the house.

Address: 1113 Chartres Street
Website: www.neworleansmuseums.com
Activity: R, E

New Orleans Dauphine Orleans Hotel

Records of this site date back to 1775, with the hotel's most notable area, the Audubon Cottage (where John James Audubon painted his *Birds of America* pictures from 1821–22) still serving as a meeting room. Pretty much the rest of the hotel owes its existence to Samuel Hermann, who created the bulk of the hotel in 1834 to exact specifications. The building also served as a bordello while this area of New Orleans was known as Storyville. The ghost that is said to haunt this hotel is reputed to be a Civil War soldier—a Confederate soldier, actually. He is often seen throughout the hotel, as well as in the courtyard. In addition to appearing to unsuspecting hotel guests, he's known for walking and talking in the hallways of the second floor.

Address: 415 Dauphine Street
Website: www.dauphineorleans.com
Activity: A, E

New Orleans Hotel Maison de Ville

This classic French Quarter establishment offers three places to stay (but check to make sure they are all available): the main building, a carriage house, and seven cottages that suit almost every taste. It's also located right in the heart of all the action in New Orleans! The paranormal experiences that have taken place here are few and far between—so you might want to ask about current activity if you visit. There are several ghost stories that are told about this hotel, but the one you'll encounter the most features the apparition of a soldier who is often seen walking near the cottages. He is known for visiting Cottage 4 and getting attention by touching guests, turning the radio on/off, and making general noises within the place to get the current guests' attention.

Address: 727 Rue Toulouse
Website: www.hotelmaisondeville.com
Activity: A, E, T

New Orleans Hotel Monteleone

In 1886, local cobbler Antonio Monteleone purchased the Commercial Hotel in the French Quarter and thus began the Hotel Monteleone. Four generations of the family have now owned and run the hotel since then. There have been five major renovations as well—the fourth being the biggest. (In 1954 the original building was razed and a new one was built.) The paranormal activity in this hotel has been ongoing since then and has been witnessed by numerous employees and guests. It's been said that there are many spirits in the place—and eyewitness accounts would support this. The most common activity in the hotel includes a door in the restaurant that opens by itself on almost a daily basis (this is a locked door, mind you), a female apparition that is spotted on the second floor (thought to be a former maid), and the spirits of small children, who are heard more than seen running and playing in the halls. The hotel staff also believes that the ghost of a former employee, William Wildemere, is also present there. Check in and check it out for yourself!

Address: 214 Rue Royale
Website: www.hotelmonteleone.com
Activity: A, E, T

New Orleans Le Pavillon Hotel

This 1907 hotel is another Gilded Age masterpiece of New Orleans and has been a staple of visitors to the Crescent City for decades. Originally called Hotel Denechaud, the place survived both World Wars and the Depression with its reputation still intact as one of the area's premier places to stay. In 1970, the hotel changed ownership and underwent a major renovation—upgrading the furnishings to an even more luxurious level. This renovation is also thought of as the catalyst for the hotel's sudden burst of paranormal activity—though the stories concerning the spirits there date back to the early 1900s. It's said that the spirit of a young girl named "Ada" roams the halls, as well as three other spirits (two male, one female) that date back to the 1920s. Guests and hotel employees have experienced voices, glimpses of apparitions, and heard reports from guests who have heard strange noises during the night.

Address: 833 Poydras Street
Website: www.lepavillon.com
Activity: A, E

New Orleans Madame John's Legacy

Some say that this site is the oldest in New Orleans—or at least it shares that title along with the Ursuline Convent. There was a fire in 1788 that took out most of the area, and this location was built that same year. The Legacy is a great example of the classic Creole home of the time and was mentioned in a story by George Washington Gable called "Tite Poulette" in 1879 (this story is also the source of its current name). The house gained more fame in the area when it was featured briefly in the movie *Interview with the Vampire*—in a scene that shows several coffins being loaded from a home. As for the spirit that resides here, this haunting has been known for many years to folks in the Quarter. Nobody is sure who the ghost is supposed to be, but most agree the place is haunted, as enough witnesses have reported hearing voices/footsteps and seeing a pale apparition peering from windows.

Address: 632 Dumaine Street
Website: http://lsm.crt.state.la.us/madam.htm
Activity: A, E

New Orleans Muriel's Jackson Square

Studying the history of buildings in the French Quarter is a great task indeed. With two major fires happening during the area's history, most buildings/houses are in their second or third incarnation. This location suffered at the hands of the 1788 fire, but was rebuilt by Pierre Jourdan into his home. Since that time, various parts of the building have been a saloon, a grocery store, a bar, and a restaurant. Today, Muriel's resides in this historic building—a place known for a great Sunday jazz brunch, a tasty bistro-styled menu, and the spirit of ol' Pierre, who is still hanging out at the property. The area of the restaurant known for this activity is called the Séance Lounges, and employees, as well as guests, have had many experiences there. Activity in the restaurant includes items moving by themselves, strange voices/footsteps, and the shadowy shape of Pierre himself!

Address: 801 Chartres Street
Website: www.muriels.com
Activity: S, E, T

Shreveport Shreveport Municipal Auditorium

This Art Deco auditorium (one of the best examples of the period in Louisiana) first opened for business in 1929. Over the years, many famous musicians have performed here—including "the King" himself, Elvis Presley. Part of the site's questionable history, though, includes the possible use of the auditorium's basement as the city morgue. It's thought that during the "Louisiana Hayride" days, the morgue was located here mainly because there was really nowhere else to put it. Whether this story is true or not, one thing is certain, this place is haunted! Locals will tell you so, paranormal investigators will tell you so, and if you tour the site, you will probably agree. Things that have been experienced here over the years includes apparitions seen on the main floor, strange moans and cries coming from the basement, and shadowy shapes seen in almost every corner of the auditorium.

Address: 705 Elvis Presley Avenue
Website: www.ci.shreveport.la.us
Activity: A, S, E

St. Francisville The Myrtles Plantation

This is another one of those legendary haunted places that most ghost hunters feel like deserves a special pilgrimage at some point. The basic story is this: Judge Woodruff and his family lived in the house during the early 1800s. A slave girl named Chloe was caught eavesdropping on a family conversation and punished by having her ear cut off. In an attempt to get back on the family's good side, Chloe decided to bake a cake laced with oleander (it was one of the Woodruff girls' birthday), then miraculously cure the child. Unfortunately, she overdid it on the poison and killed the wife and both daughters. The other slaves on the plantation, fearing harsh retribution, beat Judge Woodruff to the punch and hung Chloe in the front yard. She is now said to roam the plantation and has been seen and heard numerous times over the years. If you plan to visit Myrtles, consider renting the "Slave's Quarters" area as this is considered an extremely active spot.

Address: 7747 U.S. Highway 61
Website: www.myrtlesplantation.com
Activity: A, E, S, T, C

St. Martinville Bienvenue House

Dating back to 1830, the Bienvenue makes a great headquarters for checking out local attractions like Bayou Teche, the Evangeline Oak, and the historic St. Martin of Tours Catholic Church. In days past, this location was called the Bonin House and the Evangeline Hotel. It was during the latter period that a gruesome murder took place on the property that took the lives of innkeeper Isabel Robertson and her invalid daughter, Belle. It's thought that at least one of them haunts this property (probably Belle). The bed-ridden Robertson would often ring a bell to signal to Isabel that she needed something—a sound that is still heard today in the girl's bedroom. Other activity includes objects moving and lights that turn on/off by themselves. Stay in the "Evangeline Room" for your best chance at experiencing the paranormal here.

Address: 421 North Main Street
Website: www.bienvenuehouse.com
Activity: E, T

Sunset Chretien Point Plantation

Located outside the city of Lafayette, this Deep South plantation is mostly known for the staircase in the home that was duplicated for a scene in *Gone With the Wind* (when Scarlet O'Hara is seen shooting a Union soldier). Built in 1831, this house has been a local favorite haunted location for over a century. Many tales have been told about the house—and the tradition continues today. The story that you will usually hear—and is a true tale—concerns the former mistress of the house, Felicity Chretien. Once in the early 1800s, her home was attacked by thieves. One managed to get inside, but was immediately shot dead by Felicity. She then armed her servants and they staved off the remainder of the attackers. For years, the blood stains of the dead man were clearly evident on the stairs. It's said that the spirits of Felicity and the dead "blackguard" are still present in the house. Passersby have reported seeing apparitions in the house, as well as hearing voices and moans.

Address: 665 Chretien Point Road
Website: www.chretienpoint.com
Activity: A, E

Vacherie Oak Alley Plantation

The oldest residents of this infamous plantation would be, without a doubt, the rows of live oak trees that line the property. At best estimate, the trees were probably planted in the early 1700s by a settler. Construction of the massive estate began in the late 1830s and continued for many years as the Telesphore/Roman family settled into Oak Alley. The Romans continued to live in the mansion throughout the Civil War and up until the plantation was sold in 1866 at an auction. Since then, the place has changed hands many times. Today it is a bed and breakfast, living museum, gift shop, etc. The haunting of this grand estate started with the sighting of an apparition in the area called the "Lavender Room." Employees closing for the day saw the shadowy shape of a woman peering from a window as they were leaving—a woman who closely resembled a previous owner, Mrs. Stewart. Sightings of the woman in the Lavender Room have happened several times, as well as glimpses of a male apparition known to be seen in the kitchen area. Other activity includes the sensation of being touched, objects moving by themselves, and voices heard in empty rooms.

Address: 3645 Highway 18
Website: www.oakalleyplantation.com
Activity: A, E, T, S

West Pointe a La Hache Woodland Plantation & Spirits Hall

Captain William Johnson built this house to headquarter a massive sugar plantation in the 1830s. From this vantage, he built his empire along with the help of famed pirate Jean Lafitte.

Today, the place is virtually unchanged—except that many of the slave quarters were knocked down by Hurricane Betsy in the 1960s. In their stead, the owners moved the historic St. Patrick's Catholic Church (built in 1883) from Homeplace, Louisiana. It now sits on the site of the slave quarters and is called Spirits Hall. But these aren't the only spirits on the property…This bed and breakfast is said to be haunted by a friendly, but mischievous, spirit that loves to play with things and move them around. Many guests have reported having their objects moved in their room during the night. Talk with the owners about the activity there—you'll love to hear their tales along with a nice mint julep…

Address: 21997 Highway 23
Website: www.woodlandplantation.com
Activity: E, T

Winnfield Southern Colonial Bed & Breakfast

In addition to offering upscale B&B lodgings with southern hospitality (no extra charge), this lodging is known for hosting weddings and events in the Winnfield area. The architecture is unique in that a wraparound second-story porch was added amidst the standard columns of a Greek Revival–styled home. As for the ghost at this location, not a lot is known. Locals will tell you the place is haunted—as will the owners/employees, if you ask. The spirit is reported to move objects within guests' rooms as they sleep, and visitors have reported hearing odd bangs, knocks, and whispers.

Address: 801 East Main Street
Website: www.southerncolonialbedand
    breakfast.com
Activity: E, T

MAINE

Bar Harbor Coach Stop Inn

This bed and breakfast is Bar Harbor's oldest inn and dates back to 1804. It originated as a carriage/coach stop (hence the name) and now functions as a five-room mini-inn. The ghost that roams its halls is known to locals as "Abbe." She has been seen in the reflection of mirrors within the house and tends to show up when any music is being played. In addition to this, guests have reported hearing strange sounds during the night and seeing flickering/glowing lights in various areas of the home. Where would the spirit of young Abbe most likely hang out in the B&B? How about in the room that's named after her? Stay in this room for your best chance of having a paranormal experience.

Address: 715 Acadia Highway
Website: www.coachstopinn.com
Activity: A, E, O

Biddeford City Theater

After a fire destroyed the original opera house in Biddeford on December 30, 1894, the city decided to build a newer—and more ornate—version. It managed to open in January of 1896. After several successful years of entertaining the locals, this theater suffered a tragedy when singer Eva Gray collapsed and died on stage on October 30, 1904. It wasn't long after Eva was gone that actors and theater employees began reporting strange activity—voices, footsteps, and the appearance of her apparition. If this isn't enough, locals also say that a second spirit (thought to be a former theater manager called "Mr. Murphy" resides in the place as well. He's known for manipulating items in the backstage area, as well as playing with the house lights.

Address: 205 Main Street
Website: www.citytheater.org
Activity: A, E, T

Boothbay Harbor The Opera House at Boothbay Harbor

With a history dating back to the 1890s, this opera house operated for a while as a lodge for the famed Knights of Pythias. The knights held their meetings in this building, as well as ordained new members to the organization. After building a new lodge, the knights moved on and the place was transformed into an opera house/theater. During the 1940s, folks visiting the theater began reporting strange happenings in the upper floor: voices, footsteps, and the sounds of someone playing the piano were often heard. Though employees aren't sure of who the spirit is, it's widely believed the ghost is that of a man dubbed "Earl Cliff," who was said to be a piano player for the opera house. Paranormal activity continues in the building, so catch an event at this location to also catch a glimpse of a ghost!

Address: 86 Townsend Avenue
Website: www.boothbayoperahouse.com
Activity: E

Dedham The Lucerne Inn

Sometime in the early 1800s, this inn was built alongside a lake on land granted to John Phillips for his service during the Revolutionary War. It was subsequently known for many years as the "Lake House." In 1814, the home was converted into a halfway house—but not in the correctional institution sense! It was called a halfway house because the place was the only stop on the trail between the cities of Bangor and Ellsworth. The home offered food, drink,

and lodging for travelers along this trail, and eventually the house evolved into the inn that it is today. To experience the paranormal here, you will want to rent Room 8. Visitors who stay there experience voices, shadowy figures, and items moving in the room. It's thought that this is the product of some poor traveler who passed away at the inn sometime in the past.

Address: 2517 Main Road
Website: www.lucerneinn.com
Activity: E, S, T

Fryeburg Admiral Peary House

Originally called the House of Three Gables, this house (built in 1865) became the residence of Robert E. Peary in 1877. Peary would go on to be the first explorer to journey to the North Pole. Over the years, several local prominent families would follow Peary and live in this house before the place finally became a bed and breakfast in 1988. Since the B&B's opening, people have been seeing the spirit of a little girl throughout the house. She's described as a Caucasian female around seven or eight years old. Employees have reported having no knowledge of who the girl could be—and yet the witnesses continue to come forward. Check in with the staff after you arrive to get information regarding the most current sightings of the apparition.

Address: 27 Elm Street
Website: www.admiralpearyhouse.com
Activity: A

Greenville The Greenville Inn

It would take ten years for local lumber baron William Shaw to finish this house (1885–1895). It would remain a family estate until the place was eventually converted into an inn. The haunting of this inn involves the strange tale of a man dubbed locally as "Boots Berry." Boots was born in Room 302 of the Greenville Inn, and he gained notoriety while working there when he saved a family from a runaway horse carriage. Unfortunately, Boots's luck would not last, and he eventually ended up in prison, where it's said he learned to tap dance. After his release, Boots returned to the inn and, according to the story, managed to save a girl who was trapped on the icy roof. Boots lowered the girl to safety, then promptly fell to his own death. Since that day, people have reported hearing the sounds of tap dancing coming from the area of Room 302.

Address: 40 Norris Street
Website: www.greenvilleinn.com
Activity: E

Kennebunk The Kennebunk Inn

With origins dating back to 1799, when the place was the home of one Phineas Cole, this inn has been serving the public since 1928. It was originally called The Tavern, but changed its name to the current moniker in the 1930s. According to employees at this inn, the spirit of Silas Perkins (a former innkeeper at the place) walks the halls and has been witnessed many times by those who work there, as well as guests. Perkins is known for moving items (usually barware, though he has also manipulated silverware and other things) and for visiting patrons within their rooms. It's in the latter that folks experience cold spots and a man's voice speaking from the darkness.

Address: 45 Main Street
Website: www.thekennebunkinn.com
Activity: E, T, A

Kennebunkport Captain Fairfield Inn

This Federal-style mansion was built in 1813 by James Fairfield and his wife Lois Walker. The home remained in the family for over a hundred years (long after the death of Captain Fairfield in 1820) before moving into the hospitality business. The inn has nine rooms today—each with its own style and unique name. Unfortunately, it isn't any of these upscale accommodations that are known for the ghost. Instead, it's reported that a shadowy apparition is often witnessed in the basement. The spirit is thought to be Captain Fairfield, and he makes himself known by appearing before startled employees and guests who venture into his area. Though his visage has been described as "dark" and even "scary," it's generally thought that the entity is quite benevolent and is simply avoiding the guests and folks tramping through his home.

Address: 8 Pleasant Street
Website: www.captainfairfield.com
Activity: A

Kennebunkport The Tides Inn By-the-Sea

This location was actually built originally as an inn (not a family home) in 1899 by Emma Foss. She hired a famous architect of the time, John Calvin Stevens, to design and oversee construction. She dubbed the building the "New Belvidere." Emma ran the establishment for some time before she passed away in her treasured inn—and now she is said to haunt the place as well. Visitors to the place have reported seeing the apparition of Emma in various locations within the inn, as well as hearing a female voice coming from hallways and empty rooms. The current owners like to say that Emma will let them know when she disapproves of any "improvements" made there. Stay at the Tides and you may get a visit from Emma as well.

Address: 252 Kings Highway
Website: www.tidesinnbythesea.com
Activity: A, E

Ogunquit Ogunquit Playhouse

Evolving from a small summer playhouse, this now-legendary theater has been serving the public since 1933. Of course, the actual building that now houses the playhouse didn't come about until 1937. This was when Walter Hartwig purchased the Weare Farm plot and had the theater built on the premises. Since its inception, there have been no notable tragedies within the playhouse—at least nothing that would cause the place to be haunted. The spirits that are reported to roam this area date much farther back than any theatre group. The apparitions of Revolutionary War soldiers have been witnessed both inside and outside the Ogunquit and seem to be trapped in the thrall of a residual haunting.

Address: 10 Main Street
Website: www.ogunquitplayhouse.org
Activity: R, A

Poland Spring Poland Spring Resort

This sprawling complex has many places to stay in/choose from: there's the Presidential Inn (built in 1912), the Maine Inn, the Motorcourt Inn, and several cottages. The original inn to grace this property (The Wentworth Ricker Inn, built in 1797) no longer stands, but the grounds have never stopped hosting guests since that original premises was built by local legend Jabez Ricker. Tales of ghosts roaming the resort also date back quite a few years. Guests and employees alike have been whispering about apparitions, voices, and strange knock/bangs in various locations on the compound for years. Most of the paranormal activity, though, seems to occur in the Presidential Inn portion. This building is where most of the more dramatic stories take place—primarily seeing an apparition.

Address: 543 Maine Street
Website: www.polandspringinns.com
Activity: A, E

Portland Portland Museum of Art

This museum is the oldest art establishment in the state of Maine and it houses more than 17,000 objects of art. These pieces are divided and shared by three separate historic buildings. This museum also shares a ghost with another nearby location, the Maine College of Art. It's rumored locally that the late Captain Asa Clapp roams both institutions and has been witnessed in both places as well. Before becoming what they are today, these two places were known as the Clapp house and the McLellan-Sweat house. Both were owned by Asa, and it's thought that he haunts these two locations because he could no longer haunt his own former residence. (When Asa's wife passed away, her will decreed that the mansion be torn down and a marker be erected in its place.) It seems only natural that poor old Asa would migrate to other family properties.

Address: 7 Congress Square
Website: www.portlandmuseum.org
Activity: A, S, E

Rockland The Berry Manor Inn

This inn is an award-winning establishment with twelve guest rooms—eight are in the actual house and four are in the carriage house. To experience the paranormal in this bed and breakfast, you will want to stay in the main house. Dating back to 1898, this Victorian manor was home to Charles H. Berry, the nephew of famed Civil War general Hiram Berry. The spirits are said to harken back to this time—three women in Victorian dresses are often seen standing by the windows in the downstairs area of the home—and are even spotted by locals passing by the place! Because the spirits are only witnessed in this same state, it's thought that they are the remnants of a residual haunt—three women forever trapped in time, sipping tea in the parlor ...

Address: 81 Talbot Avenue
Website: www.berrymanorinn.com
Activity: A, R

Rockland Captain Lindsey House Inn

This home-turned-inn was built by yet another sea captain (yes, Captain Lindsey) in 1835. The current owners were themselves sea captains as well—so maybe this would explain how they came to know that one of their spirits in the home is the now-expired mariner. Or maybe they know this because of a now-infamous trip made to the inn by a group of "spiritologists" who claimed that the place is now haunted by more than 30 entities! Along with Lindsey, the group reported that a former owner (T. B. Severance), a young boy (called "Jeffrey"), and a little girl (dubbed "Emmy") also walks the halls of this inn. But perhaps the most interesting ghost of all is that of "Ensign." This male spirit is said to be aggressive (but not menacing) and is thought to be the source of most of the activity. Stay in a first-floor room to experience events here that include items moving, footsteps and doors opening/closing by themselves.

Address: 5 Lindsey Street
Website: www.lindseyhouse.com
Activity: T, E

Rockland Limerock Inn

Marked by its grand turret, this Victorian home is graced with a wraparound porch, beautiful gardens, and a great location—just minutes away from most of the area's attractions. All of this makes for a great B&B experience. But before becoming a place for local accommodations, the house was simply a home—home to an area physician named Dr. Lawry. For years, Dr. Lawry did house calls—only they were in his house! Patients would travel from far and wide for his services, and the front parlor of this inn was his waiting room. Today, the residual effect of all these years of service can still be experienced here—the sounds and sights of patients waiting in the parlor. Spirits staring from upstairs windows have also been witnessed by passersby on the sidewalk. The staircase in this inn is said to be a particularly good hot spot to see and hear the entities.

Address: 96 Limerock Street
Website: www.limerockinn.com
Activity: R, A, E

Searsport 1794 Watchtide by the Sea

Built on land deeded to General Henry Knox (the nation's first secretary of war), this inn dates back to the year in its name. Over the years, it ping-ponged between being a private residence and operating as an inn/teahouse. Today, it has ponged into the latter and has undergone a massive renovation that's transformed it into a top-notch getaway. So, who is the spirit said to reside in this inn? Nobody knows. It's thought the ghost is that of a child, but it could also be the mischievous spirit of an adult. The ghost is known for playing "jokes" on guests staying at the inn by messing with them in their sleep and moving their items. The spirit is also a wanderer, so check in with the innkeeper for the most current locations of the sightings.

Address: 190 West Main Street
Website: www.watchtide.com
Activity: E, T

Searsport Carriage House Inn

Featured on the program *If These Walls Could Talk*, this inn dates back to 1874 and Captain John McGilvery. With a past that includes operating as an army barracks, serving as a base for American painter Waldo Peirce, and being haunted, this inn is sure to please all comers. Tales of the spirits here have been circulating the area for quite some time—and started when locals reported seeing apparitions peering from the place's upper story windows. Paranormal investigators who have visited the house say that there are two ghosts within the place—and the ghosts make themselves known to the public by whispering to them, knocking on the walls, and playing ghostly music during the night.

Address: 120 East Main Street
Website: www.carriagehouseinmaine.com
Activity: A, E

Tenants Harbor The East Wind Inn

The story of this cozy inn sounds like something from a mystery movie. Visitors to the East Wind have reported feeling an ominous presence on the third floor (especially in Rooms 12 and 14)—an entity that's said to actually hold people down in their beds while they sleep. According to local records, this floor was used for Masonic rituals during the 1800s (the building dates back to 1860) and all the way up until the 1920s, when the place was converted into the Wan-e-set Inn. A psychic who visited the East Wind reported feeling the presence of an angry woman on the third floor who was murdered during the 1800s. When local investigators looked into these reports, it was uncovered that a woman had, indeed, been stabbed and strangled in the immediate area during this period. Could she now haunt the East Wind Inn? If not she, then it seems at least somebody is there. Expect the following activity: moans/voices, cold spots, and the occasional glimpse of a misty apparition.

Address: 21 Mechanic Street
Website: www.eastwindinn.com
Activity: A, E, C, T

Wiscasset The Musical Wonder House

Build in 1852 as a "double house," these two homes served the Clark, Wood, and Scott families for decades before becoming the museum it is today (dedicated to the art and industry of the music box). Over the years, several females (specifically in the Scott family) have died here, but, interestingly, the spirit that haunts the museum is said to be that of a male! It's rumored locally that the entity of a man is often seen sitting on a couch in the parlor area. This same man has also been witnessed on the stairs, in the kitchen, and roaming the upstairs area. Folks aren't sure who the ghost is, but it's a safe bet he's probably the remnant of one of the aforementioned families who lived there. Other activity in the museum includes voices and footsteps.

Address: 16 High Street
Website: www.musicalwonderhouse.com
Activity: A, E

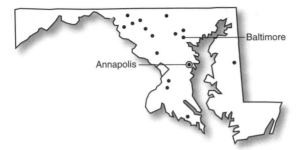

MARYLAND

Annapolis Middleton Tavern

This location claims to be one of America's oldest, continuously run taverns. The building dates back to 1740 and is decorated with objects from the previous three centuries. Employees say that the place is inhabited by a friendly spirit they call "Roland." Roland has been seen staring out the dining room windows toward the harbor and is dressed in a patriot-style outfit. Experiencing Roland can be as easy as having a meal at this tavern (which is in itself a good thing, since they have a great menu and food). In addition to appearing in full form, patrons have also reported seeing Roland as a dark, shadowy shape shooting across the dining room. Other activity at Middleton includes footsteps, dishes moving by themselves, and the phantom scent of cigar smoke (smoking is not allowed in the premises).

Address: 2 Market Space
Website: www.middletontavern.com
Activity: A, S, T, N, E

Annapolis Rams Head Tavern

The earliest documentation concerning a business at this address goes back to 1794 and a tavern called the Sign of the Green Tree. During this period, the tavern gained a reputation of being haunted—reputedly by the spirit of a young girl named Amy. Today, employees (as well as the numerous patrons who have had an experience) will tell you that Amy is still around. They'll even point out her old bed post for you. Annapolis residents will also tell you that Amy is not alone in the tavern; others have witnessed the apparition of a Civil War soldier walking the grounds. The Rams Head has several locations (including a road house), so make sure you visit the one in Annapolis to catch a glimpse of Amy or the soldier.

Address: 33 West Street
Website: www.ramsheadtavern.com
Activity: A, E

Annapolis Reynolds Tavern

This is the second of two haunted taverns in Annapolis and is also one of the finest Georgian structures in the area. The building has always been a tavern (at least as far back as anyone can remember), even when it doubled as the Reynolds' home. One of the tavern's most famous visitors in the old days was George Washington. It's said that George even had a crush on the woman of the house—an act that got him chased out of the place and all the way down the street by Mr. Reynolds! The ghost of this tavern is also an interesting tale. The spirit is reported to be Mary Reynolds, a young woman who began her time in the tavern as a housekeeper. Young William Reynolds fell in love with the girl, so they got married and eventually became the residents of the property. Mary's apparition has been witnessed in the tavern on several occasions, as well as the phantom sounds of her voice.

Address: 7 Church Circle
Website: www.reynoldstavern.org
Activity: A, E

Baltimore The Admiral Fell Inn

This classic, European-styled hotel is located in a great area of Baltimore, and besides being in the proximity of the usual amenities (shopping, dining, etc.), there are lots of nearby haunts (literally). There are also several area ghost tours that you can take to familiarize yourself with these areas, including one hosted by this hotel. In the Admiral Fell itself, the ghost stories usually involve the spirit of a nurse that's seen all around the hotel. She is said to be a remnant of the Anchorage Mission House—a hospital for soldiers that existed as the original occupant of the building. People have reported seeing and hearing this nurse for many years, along with

a male entity who is thought to have died in Room 413. Housekeepers who take care of this room are extra wary, as many of them have also heard voices and felt cold spots there.

Address: 888 South Broadway
Website: www.admiralfell.com
Activity: A, E, C, R

Baltimore Fort McHenry National Monument

With a rich history that extends back through the Civil War and the War of 1812, Fort McHenry has been the site of naval bombardments, the inspiration for our national anthem, and an area of rioting during the War Between the States. The haunting of this fort is thought to be of a residual nature, as visitors have reported hearing cannons firing, men shouting, and answering gunfire. On occasion, the spirits of two local soldiers are also said to be seen: Lt. Levi Clagett and Pvt. John Drew. Local investigators suggest visiting the park close to sundown, as this seems to be when most activity occurs. You will have to take a "water taxi" to reach the fort from the inner harbor, so plan ahead for visiting this haunted location!

Address: Fort Avenue off Lawrence Street
Website: www.nps.gov/fomc/
Activity: R, E, A

Baltimore The Horse You Came In On Saloon

According to local legend, the poet/writer Edgar Allan Poe entered this bar on October 3, 1849, had a few drinks, stumbled outside, and was found dying a few hours later. The part concerning Poe's death is, of course, fact. What is legend is whether or not he visited this saloon. Historians have disputed Poe's visit on this night, but others have staunchly claimed the story to be the truth. The story is also supported by the ghost of old Edgar himself. Employees and visitors to this saloon have reportedly witnessed Poe's apparition in the upstairs area of the bar, as well as experienced other paranormal activity as well: voices, cold spots, and heavy phantom footsteps.

Address: 1626 Thames Street
Website: www.myspace.com/thehorselive
Activity: A, E, C

Baltimore Radisson Plaza Lord Baltimore

Intended to be an Art Deco masterpiece, this hotel was built in 1928 and named after George Calvert, the Lord of Baltimore (the founder of Maryland). Located in downtown Baltimore, this hotel has serviced numerous politicians, celebrities, and visiting luminaries over the years. Today, you can visit and be accommodated in a great location in relation to several downtown haunted areas. But of course, you need look no further than this hotel's ballroom to find a ghost! Employees have reported seeing male and female apparitions in this area of the hotel (most likely a residual haunt from years past). In addition to this, guests have witnessed the spirit of a young girl playing and crying on the nineteenth floor of the hotel (she is usually seen with a ball in the hallway there). Nobody is sure who the girl could be, but it's thought that she's a past guest.

Address: 20 West Baltimore Street
Website: www.radisson.com/lordbaltimore
Activity: A

Baltimore USS Constellation

This version of the Constellation (there have been three ships with this name) has been residing in retirement in Baltimore harbor since it was last decommissioned on Feb 4, 1955. During the ship's years of service, the crew of the Constellation saw all types of missions: war (Civil War), humanitarian aid, and training. Perhaps it's because of these activities that the old warship is now considered haunted. Activity on the vessel includes the appearance of several apparitions, ghost lights, and the sounds of footsteps/voices in the lower decks. Among the spirits said to roam the ship are three past servicemen (Neil Harvey, Thomas Truxton, and Carl Hansen), a small boy, and a man who is said to have hanged himself on the top deck (who could also be a sailor, but folks aren't sure). Take a tour of the ship to get your shot at experiencing the paranormal on this craft.

Address: 301 East Pratt Street
Website: www.constellation.org
Activity: A, E

Baltimore The Waterfront Hotel

As hard as it may seem to believe, the Waterfront began its career as a private residence (a really huge one) in 1771. When the Civil War broke out, the city of Baltimore needed a place to house and feed troops, so the property was converted into a tavern for this purpose. Today, the location is a top-notch restaurant. According to locals, the Waterfront is also haunted. People have heard voices and footsteps coming from the upper floors, as well as having seen bar stools moved. It's rumored that there was a death in the building in the late 1970s, but this hasn't been confirmed; however, paranormal investigators have visited this hotel and determined that activity is present on the premises. Catch a meal at this restaurant, and ask about the most current sightings to increase your odds of experiencing something.

Address: 1710 Thames Street
Website: www.waterfronthotel.us
Activity: E, T

Boonsboro Old South Mountain Inn

With close proximity to another haunted Maryland site, Antietam National Battlefield, this place makes a great base for exploring the area. Other attractions in the vicinity include Harper's Ferry and several state parks. This inn dates back to 1732 and is said to have been a favorite stop for people like Daniel Webster and Henry Clay over the years. During the Civil War, the place was briefly used as the headquarters for General D. H. Hill prior to the battles of Stone Mountain and Antietam. The paranormal activity at this inn is thought to be a result of the war. Phantom soldiers have been seen in and outside of the inn, as well as other apparitions thought to be residents of the inn back in those days. Other activity includes doors that seem to shake (like someone's trying to open them), voices, and footsteps in empty rooms.

Address: 6132 Old National Pike
Website: www.oldsouthmountaininn.com
Activity: R, A, E, T

Clinton Surratt House Museum

This plantation home dates back to 1852 and has served over the years as a tavern, a post office, and a headquarters for the local Confederate underground. The home is named for its most famous resident—Mary Surratt—a woman who was executed in connection with the assassination of President Abraham Lincoln. The house can be toured by the public and has many attractions to offer visitors—including the apparition of Surratt herself! Tales of her walking the halls of this house date back to the 1940s, when the place was a tavern. She would often be seen along with the apparition of John Wilkes Booth (he stopped at the house while attempting to escape authorities after assassinating the president). Patrons still tell stories today of hearing voices and footsteps in the museum (mostly on the upper floor) and seeing Mary doing her rounds.

Address: 9118 Brandywine Road
Website: www.surratt.org
Activity: A, E

Ellicott City The Diamondback Tavern

Formerly known as the Tiber River Tavern, this locally owned bar and grill was created by a group of guys who wanted a laid-back place to watch sports and enjoy reasonably priced food and drinks. But not long after moving in, they realized they got more at this tavern than they had bargained for! Guests would tell of hearing voices, and employees would report objects being moved in the bar area. A local paranormal team was called in, a few pieces of evidence were gathered, and now the place celebrates their haunted status by hosting Halloween events. The activity is sporadic and oftentimes subtle in this joint, so you may want to question your bartender about any recent sightings before choosing your spot for a vigil.

Address: 3733 Old Columbia Pike
Website: www.diamondbacktavern.com
Activity: E, T

Ellicott City The Judge's Bench

This pub gets its unique name from the history of the property. During the 1800s, judges would take their break from the nearby courthouse and visit the site for a bite to eat. Back then it was a grocery store. Today it is a bar and grill.

So who haunts the pub? Locals will tell you it is a young girl named "Mary." The legend says that Mary hanged herself on the third floor (though nobody seems to know who Mary was). And how does she make herself known today? By flushing toilets. She does other things as well—she's been heard talking in the area of her supposed death, as well as walking around (more like stomping). Is it still haunted? According to local paranormal investigators, it is.

Address: 8385 Main Street
Website: www.judgesbenchpub.com
Activity: E, T

Elkton Elk Forge Bed and Breakfast Inn and Retreat

This top-notch spa has been compared to some of the greats in Europe. The massages and food here are said to be the best in the state, if not the entire northeastern United States! Back in the 1700s, this inn was actually part of a large mill. When the Revolutionary War brought English troops through the area, they demanded flour from the miller. He obliged them, but gave them a little something extra—ground up glass mixed into the flour. When the troops saw what he had done, they returned and hanged the miller for his "treason." It is the miller who is thought to haunt this B&B. His apparition has been witnessed, along with the sounds of his voice and his footsteps. Talk to the owners there about their paranormal activity—they will point out the miller's favorite hangouts.

Address: 807 Elk Mills Road
Website: www.elkforge.com
Activity: A, E

Frederick Schifferstadt Architectural Museum

This Colonial German building was built in 1758 by Joseph Bruner as a frontier home and a refuge for travelers. The house is now a living shrine of architecture and a testament to living during the French and Indian War. Stories concerning the place being haunted began when visitors and employees starting hearing a strange voice speaking in German. When they would investigate, nobody would be found. Soon, other activity started to be noticed as well, including the sounds of footsteps, doors opening/closing, and small items being mysteriously moved during the night. It's thought that there are actually two spirits in the museum now: Joseph and Elias Bruner. Two separate voices have been heard speaking in the foreign language, and it would make sense that these two would stay along in the place that they treasured so much.

Address: 1110 Rosemont Avenue
Website: www.frederickcountylandmarks
     foundation.org
Activity: E, T

Glen Echo Clara Barton National Historic Site

Clara Barton devoted her life to helping the needy and eventually formed the American Red Cross. When she wasn't chasing her life's pursuits, she spent her time at her home in Glen Echo. She lived at this house for the last 15 years of her life and passed away in her own bedroom there at the age of 90. But this didn't stop Clara from staying. To this day, people who visit this historic site report seeing the apparition of old

Clara walking the halls, as well as hearing her voice. Most of the local stories involving this house usually involve seeing Clara peering from a window, or through the front door.

Address: 5801 Oxford Road
Website: www.nps.gov/clba/
Activity: A, E

Hagertown The Hager House

This circa 1740 home is built of uncut field-stones that have been fitted together to form the walls—a building technique that made the place practically impregnable to area Native Americans. It was presented to one Elizabeth Kershner as a wedding present from her new husband Jonathan Hager. The Hagers operated a frontier trading post out of their home until they eventually sold it to a man named Jacob Rohrer. The place remained in the Rohrer family until 1944, when it became a historical landmark. It's thought that the ghostly happenings at this house are a product of the Rohrer family. A woman dressed in 1800's clothing is often seen on the second-floor staircase and hallway. Other activity includes strange screams from the basement, dark 'shadow people' who walk the halls, and the phantom smell of a pipe.

Address: 110 Key Street
Website: www.hagerhouse.org
Activity: A, E, N

Keedysville National Museum of Civil War Medicine

It seems only natural that the National Museum of Civil War Medicine would be located in the historic Pry house. During the Civil War, the home was used to treat the wounded that rolled in from the Battle of Antietam. In the 1970s, the Pry house caught fire and local firefighters responded. By the time they reached the blaze, though, the entire second floor had collapsed. So imagine their surprise when they could see a woman screaming for help through one of the second-floor windows! The home was rebuilt and eventually became the museum it is today. And it is still haunted by the poor woman upstairs. Her apparition is often seen, as well other activity there: doors opening/closing by themselves, voices, and footsteps.

Address: 18906 Shepherdstown Pike
Website: www.civilwarmed.org
Activity: A, E, T

New Windsor Yellow Turtle Inn

This "bed and brunch" was at one time called the New Windsor Castle Hotel and has been serving as local accommodations for over a hundred years. Learning about the ghosts at this location can be quite a feat. According to the owner of this inn (mostly via her website) she is constantly learning about new spirits on the property. Some of the more intriguing ones are Sarah (who lived on the property and was thought to be a servant girl to a Dr. Baker), Leon (thought to be the spirit of a gardener who earned his name by rearranging the letters on a "Noel" sign), and Sally (a little girl in her early teens that was witnessed by a guest). Apparitions are abundant here—and the owner has a pretty liberal policy concerning ghost hunting during your stay. Just check in when you get there and learn the house rules, as well as get the most current sighting reports!

Address: 111 South Springdale Avenue
Website: www.yellowturtleinn.net
Activity: A, T

Rockville Beall Dawson House

This antebellum home was quite the popular location during the Civil War. First, the Confederate army under General J. E. B. Stuart decided to make the house and yard their encampment for an extended period of time, while waiting for the Union army to make their move. Once they did, and the Rebels moved on, Union army General George McClellan took the place over. Whether it's a product of the war, or simply a natural result of so many family members living and dying within the place, the Beall Dawson House is considered to be haunted. They host Halloween tours on the premises every year, so this might be the best time to get the staff talking about their resident spirits. Most of the activity sounds like a residual haunt, but people do (on occasion) report the odd apparition as well.

Address: 103 West Montgomery Avenue
Website: www.rockvillemd.gov
Activity: R, A

Scotland Point Lookout State Park

With beginnings that include being a popular summer resort, you would never believe this spot to be full of dark and deadly history. It all started when the resort was taken over by the government to be used as a hospital for wounded Union soldiers during the Civil War. Soon, the place added a Confederate prison and hosted (at its peak) over 20,000 prisoners of war. Three forts were built to guard the area (Fort Lincoln still stands today), and a lighthouse was eventually erected. Today, this lighthouse is the paranormal

center for ghostly activity at this park. Famed parapsychology Hans Holzer claimed that the Point Lookout Lighthouse was one of the most haunted in America. Phantom soldiers are also seen in various areas of the park and seem to still be suffering the tragedies of those who ended up here during the Civil War.

Address: 11175 Point Lookout Road
Website: www.dnr.state.md.us
Activity: A, R, E, S

Sharpsburg Antietam National Battlefield

On September 17, 1862, over 23,000 soldiers were either killed, wounded, or found missing after a full day of fighting at this Civil War battlefield. And it wasn't long after the battle that people started noticing strange things happening there. More and more visitors were hearing and seeing the sights of a large and active haunting. There are many specific spots within the park that experience activity, but the most significant location is that of "Bloody Lane." In addition to the activity mentioned above, other interesting tales from this spot include the sounds of Christmas music, dark shadow shapes shooting through the trees, and a unique battle cry: *Faugh a ballaugh!* This was the motto of the Irish Brigade that fought during this battle. Perhaps they are still fighting to this day…

Address: 5831 Dunker Church Road
Website: www.nps.gov/ANTI
Activity: A, R, S, E

Towson Hampton National Historic Site

When this massive estate was completed in 1790, it was the largest home in the United States. Studying the history of this house is like taking a sociology course—over the years its occupants have included slaves, their owners, servants, blue collar workers, etc. This variation of occupants can also be said of the spirits here. Depending on who you talk to, up to nine ghosts are said to haunt this property. The most frequently encountered include Priscilla Ridgely (the wife of the original owner—her apparition is often seen wandering the halls there), Cygnet Swann (an occupant of the house who died of mysterious causes in the 1800s—she's usually seen in the northwest bedroom where she died), and Tom the Butler (who worked in the home his whole life—he's been heard and seen on the ground floor). Other hot spots on the property include the stables, the parlor, and the great hall room of the house.

Address: 535 Hampton Lane
Website: www.nps.gov/hamp/
Activity: A, E, T

Urbana The Historic Landon House

This house was originally a silk mill in the 1750s in the state of Virginia. It was relocated to Maryland in 1840 to service the community as an all-women's school. The academy would later switch to a military school. During the Civil War, General J. E. B. Stuart hosted a ball at the academy, and all was well until the Battle of Antietam occurred. In the aftermath of that battle, the school was hastily made into a field hospital that serviced the wounded and dying from both sides. The haunting of the Landon House seems to be the remnants of this period—battle sounds, cries of the wounded, and music from the era have all been heard.

Address: 3401 Urbana Pike
Website: www.landonhouse.com
Activity: R, E

Waldorf Dr. Samuel A. Mudd House Museum

This place was the home of Dr. Mudd and his wife Sarah Frances Dyer. The two of them raised nine children in the house and had quite the estate at one time. When the Civil War broke out, Mudd clearly sided with the Confederacy—this was evident if for no other reason than he was a slave owner. When the war was over and President Lincoln was assassinated, imagine Samuel's surprise when his old friend, John Wilkes Booth, came to visit for a while. Mudd (supposedly) had no idea of Wilkes's crime or had any participation in it. This didn't stop charges from being levied against him, though. It would take a presidential pardon to clear his name, and to this day it is hotly debated whether or not Mudd was a co-conspirator in the assassination of Lincoln. What is less debated, though, is whether the Mudd house is haunted. Employees and visitors alike have been witnessing strange events here: shadowy apparitions, voices echoing in empty rooms, and books/photos that seem to move on their own.

Address: 3725 Dr. Samuel Mudd Road
Website: www.somd.lib.md.us/MUSEUMS/
  Mudd
Activity: A, S, E, T

Springfield

Boston

MASSACHUSETTS

Ashland Stone's Public House

This pub was built in 1834 by a local farmer and soldier named John Stone. It was originally a hotel that serviced folks traveling along the railroad and was called the Railroad House. Stone died in 1858, but the inn continued operating well into the twentieth century. In 1976, Leonard "Cappy" Fournier bought the place and business once again graced the inn after a long period of disrepair, and the place also began to earn its reputation as a haunted location. Fournier would tell tales of objects moving, frightened psychics who fled the premises, and an upstairs area that creeped out anyone brave enough to enter. Today, it's said that there are many spirits within this pub, including Stone himself. Visit and see what you experience—if it's available and open to the public, be sure to check out the upstairs area.

Address: 179 Main Street
Website: www.stonespublichouse.com
Activity: A, E, T

Barnstable Beechwood Inn

This small inn has been recommended to tourists of this area by over 50 travel books and has been named an Editor's Choice by *Yankee Magazine*. But long before servicing the public, the place was simply a home—a Victorian home that dates back to the 1800s. It wasn't long after the owners purchased the place that they began to experience paranormal events in the house. On several occasions, the apparition of a woman dressed in white was witnessed, as well as heard. These sightings have also occurred with visitors who have stayed at the Beechwood over the years—with the spirit even playing small pranks on certain guests. Apparently, the ghost likes to toy with things in the guest rooms and moves items around during the night. The spirit of the woman has been seen in many areas of the house, so check in with the owners when you get to the inn to stay in a room with current activity.

Address: 2839 Main Street
Website: www.beechwoodinn.com
Activity: A, E, T

Boston Cutler Majestic Theatre

When the Majestic opened its doors in 1903, it was considered one of the grandest theatres in all of New England. The designer was John Galen Howard, an MIT-trained architect renowned for his studies at the L'Ecole des Beaux Arts. For decades, the place featured opera and theatre productions before transforming itself into a movie venue, and, after being renovated, is still open for service. The ghosts of this theatre have been talked about for many years—though you don't always hear the same story. It seems that there are varying opinions on who exactly haunts the theatre. Some say it's a small girl, others say the ghost is that of a past actor, and many believe the spirit to be that of a mayor who died on the premises. Regardless of who the spirit is, hot spots in the theatre seem to be the third set of balconies and the backstage area.

Address: 219 Tremont Street
Website: www.maj.org
Activity: A, E, T

Boston Omni Parker House

This hotel has been part of the Boston skyline since 1855. Prestigious visitors traveling along the Freedom Trail often stayed at the Parker House for the modern amenities of the time—a tradition the hotel continues today. Many believe that the original owner, Howard Parker, still roams the place. His apparition has been seen many times in the hallways and in guest rooms—especially on the ninth and tenth floors (levels that were built after Parker's death—he's probably checking out the new area). But perhaps the most well-known story involving the haunting of this hotel is that of Room 303. It's reported that a man committed suicide in this room during the 1940s, and that activity there includes phantom smells, cold spots, and voices. Call ahead to see if you can get this room, but note this: at times, this room has been converted into storage due to constant reports from guests staying there.

Address: 60 School Street
Website: www.omnihotels.com
Activity: A, E, C, N

Brewster The Captain Freeman Inn

Not much is known about this Victorian home or its spectral resident. Since this bed and breakfast opened up and local tourists started patronizing the place, rumors started circulating about the haunted happenings at this inn. It's said the ghost there is called "Roberta" and that she dates back to the early 1900s. She has been witnessed roaming the inn's hallways, as well as the guest rooms. She has even been seen by passersby who have seen her peering from the windows. This is a location that you will simply have to visit to unravel the particulars of the haunt there—but, hey, isn't that part of the fun?

Address: 15 Breakwater Road
Website: www.captainfreemaninn.com
Activity: A

Charlemont The Charlemont Inn

Travelers along the Mohawk Trail have been patronizing this historic establishment since it was first built in 1787. Set deep in the mysterious Berkshires, the Charlemont boasts 16 rooms (two are suites), an on-site restaurant, and a tavern. Visitors to the inn have reported experiencing strange things there for decades—this activity even extends to the employees/owners. Most folks believe there are multiple entities at the inn (some are Elizabeth, Fidelia, Sam, Louis, Elisa, and Norman), with several of the spirits attributed to past owners. Hot spots in the Charlemont include Rooms 18, 19, 21, 22, and 23, though there have been reports of voices, cold spots, and items moving in almost every room. The chance of seeing something paranormal for yourself is high at this location—

just get the grand tour when you visit and pay attention to the most recent stories.

Address: Route 2, Mohawk Trail
Website: www.charlemontinn.com
Activity: A, E, T, C, N

Concord Concord's Colonial Inn

Though the original structure dates back to 1716, the inn has only been in operation since 1889 (only 120+ years...). In addition to providing accommodations in the area, the place has also functioned in several other capacities over the years, including a military storehouse, a family store, and a private home. Residents have included Henry David Thoreau (who stayed here while attending Harvard) and Captain John Minot (thought to possibly be the ghost who now haunts the inn). Reports of the paranormal here are a fairly recent event and only date back to the 1960s. A couple was staying in Room 24 when they witnessed an apparition who approached their bed during the night. This room continues to be the most haunted area (though activity has since spread around a bit). You can read about the ghost stories of this location on their website—just be sure to try and snag Room 24 when you visit!

Address: 48 Monument Square
Website: www.concordscolonialinn.com
Activity: A, E

Eastham Penny House Inn & Day Spa

This Cape Cod bed and breakfast is as relaxing as it is historic. In addition to getting the usual amenities of a top-notch getaway, the place also has an on-site day spa that offers massages, full body treatments, and manicure/pedicures. If you stay in any of the 12 rooms of this inn, there is a great chance you may encounter the resident spirit—especially if you stay in the "old side" of the house. The ghost is said to be a female who was (probably) a past owner. Folks have dubbed the spirit the "Goodnight Ghost" due to numerous encounters with her by peo-ple curling up for sleep. Locals, and even the press, say that the ghost is "mischievous" and is known for playing pranks on visitors by moving their items, touching them in their sleep, and whispering to them.

Address: 4885 State Highway
Website: www.pennyhouseinn.com
Activity: A, E, T

Essex Windward Grille

This old farmhouse-turned-restaurant can actually be termed as "ancient"—at least in relation to the history of the United States. It dates back to 1680 and existed most of these long years as a family home. Its reputation in the area as a great restaurant began with its predecessor, the Hearthside (though Windward is now considered a fine establishment as well). Tales of ghosts wandering this eatery are nothing new to locals in Essex—especially since it was featured on the television show *Ghost Hunters*. Reported activity in the restaurant includes dishes moving by themselves, voices (including the sounds of a child/baby crying), and shadowy apparitions that seem to enjoy the bar area.

Address: 109 Eastern Avenue
Website: www.windwardgrille.com/
Activity: A, T, E, S, C

ceased former resident Dr. Tripp). If you visit, the two biggest hot spots in this B&B seem to be the Dimmick and Tripp Rooms. In these locations, people have heard voices/footsteps, seen objects move/turn on and off, and seen the apparition of a woman. Occurrences are said to happen regularly here, so your odds of experiencing something are good.

Address: 40 Main Street
Website: www.villagegreeninncapecod.com
Activity: A, E, T

Fall River Lizzie Borden Bed and Breakfast

Setting aside for a moment the grisly murders that took place in this house-turned-B&B and the highly publicized trial that followed, this location is yet another of those "haunted pilgrimages" that most paranormal investigators will want to make at some time. Sightings of a female apparition have been ongoing for some time, as well as other commonly reported activity: footsteps, voices, cold spots, etc. Guests who stay at this historic crime scene can actually sleep in the bedrooms where members of the Borden family were brutally hacked to death. The place has been featured in numerous television shows, books, etc., so researching this case and narrowing down your hot spots is no real challenge.

Address: 230 Second Street
Website: www.lizzie-borden.com
Activity: A, E, T, C

Falmouth Village Green Inn

Dating back to 1804 and Braddock Dimmick, this inn has spent most of its years as a family home—first to the aforementioned Dimmick family, then followed by the Tripp family, and today's owners, the Crosby family. The current owners also number among those who have witnessed strange events in this inn—including the apparition of an old man seen entering the parlor (thought to possibly be the now-de-

Groton The Groton Stagecoach Inn Grill and Tavern

Originally built in 1678, this place was simply known then as the Groton Inn. With over 300 years of continuous service, the Groton is one of New England's longest-running accommodations. It's also one of the area's longest-running ghost stories. Guests have reported strange happenings for decades. With several apparitions seen on the site, as well as rumors of spectral Native Americans, activity here is ongoing and frequent. Room 10 is said to be the most haunted, as the spirits of a woman they refer to as the "Gray Lady" and a Civil War soldier have both been seen in this room (as well as other areas of the inn). Other activity includes objects being moved (dishes, room items, etc.), the cries of the aforementioned Native Americans, and strange footsteps/voices.

Address: 128 Main Street
Website: www.grotonstagecoachinn.com
Activity: A, T, E

Lenox The Mount Estate & Gardens

This massive estate was built in 1902 and construction was overseen by Edith Wharton herself. She based the design, as well as the decoration, of the place on her book *The Decoration of Houses*. She used the estate as a writer's retreat until the fall of her marriage. At that point, she moved to France and the home was sold in 1911 to become a school for girls. Wharton herself was afraid of ghosts and would allow no books on the subject in her home, so it's quite ironic that her home is considered haunted today (and possibly by her). The house has been featured on quite a few haunted television programs, and the place even hosts ghost tours on site. So what can you expect at this location? Typical sightings include the sounds of voices/footsteps, shadowy apparitions and doors slamming shut for no apparent reason. The Mount is open most days—though they have seasonal hours in the winter—but ghost tours are usually only available on Fridays. Check out their website for more information.

Address: 2 Plunkett Street
Website: www.edithwharton.org
Activity: A, S, E, T

Nantucket The Wauwinet

Though it sounds more like urban legend than ghost story, the Wauwinet Inn is said to be haunted by the spirit of a woman—an apparition that likes to stay just out of sight (though she is accompanied by the scent of a heavy floral perfume). Locals report that the spirit at this resort is known for appearing out of the cor-

ner of your eye—when you turn to look at the ghost, she is suddenly gone! Strange tales of Native American burial sites also circulate the area, but this has never been proven. On the more believable side of the events at this inn, eyewitness accounts also include voices, the sound of running water, and lights turning themselves on and off.

Address: 120 Wauwinet Road
Website: www.wauwinet.com
Activity: A, E, T

North Adams Houghton Mansion

This mansion (also known as the North Adams Masonic Temple) became famous overnight when visitors from the television program *Ghost Adventures* had a strange paranormal evening on the premises. Named after Alfred Charles Houghton, this house was built in the 1890s and saw a lot of Houghton family tragedy—including the suicide of a servant. He shot himself after he inadvertently caused the deaths of two family members in a car accident not far from the premises. The aforementioned television program featured some of the activity that reportedly occurs quite often in the house: voices that sound like a young girl, shadowy apparitions, and heavy footsteps. The place is only open to the public by arrangement, so you will need to visit their website to set up an event or to visit the mansion.

Address: 214 Church Street
Website: http://houghton-mansion.tripod.com/
Activity: A, S, E

Orleans The Orleans Inn

Though this place was originally called Aaron's Folly, it has thrived for over a hundred years. During the early 1900s, the inn was actually a boarding house (and rumored to be a brothel), but converted to a full-time hotel just after World War II. It wasn't long after guests started spending more time at the inn that paranormal activity began being reported. Current guests and visitors, as well as the on-site employees, have had recurring encounters with a female spirit that they have dubbed "Hannah." It's thought that Hannah is a remnant of the brothel days—that she was a young woman who was murdered while working there. She is known for appearing (on occasion) to folks during the night, opening/closing doors, and playing with the lights.

Address: 3 Old County Road
Website: www.orleansinn.com
Activity: A, T

Pittsfield The Thaddeus Clapp House

This bed and breakfast has roots that go back to the very founding of the town of Pittsfield. The Clapp family was instrumental in not only settling the area, but bringing in some of the biggest industries to the city, including the railroad, several mills, and the first area electric company. It's unclear, however, who exactly haunts this house. According to local tales, a playwright by the name of Peter Bergman visited this home and had a famous encounter with a spirit. Bergman spoke of his strange visitation many times and was quite open about the haunting. But finding stories about the ghost since Bergman is quite a task. Check in with the B&B concerning more recent paranormal activity before visiting—though this Berkshires stop would prove entertaining and pleasurable even without the addition of a ghost!

Address: 74 Wendell Avenue
Website: www.clapphouse.com
Activity: A, E

Quincy Regina Russell's Tea Room

With services that include psychic, tarot, and palm readings, this tea room already has quite a lot of paranormal appeal. But throw in a ghost/haunting, and it becomes a must-see! Workers at Regina's have been witnessing a female apparition (wearing a long dress) standing by the fireplace ever since the place opened in 1970. She is also said to be able to call you by name (if she knows it) and has been heard whispering from dark corners of the place. Regina's now performs fortune readings over the telephone (see their website for more info), but if you want a chance to see the ghost, you will have to visit in person!

Address: 40 Franklin Street
Website: www.rrtearoom.com
Activity: A, E

Salem Hawthorne Hotel

This hotel has been the premier accommodation in Salem since 1925 and now includes a small, four-room bed and breakfast called the Suzannah Flint House. But you will have to stay in the actual hotel if you want to have a paranormal encounter. The Hawthorne (named after famed writer Nathaniel Hawthorne) was built on the site of the old Salem Marine Society and it's thought that the activity there is a throwback to the days of sailors who would visit the area. Activity in the hotel includes doors opening/closing by themselves, objects being moved (especially in the 'lower deck' library and in rooms on the sixth floor), and the feeling of an entity touching guests as they sleep.

Address: Essex Street at Hawthorne Boulevard
Website: www.hawthornehotel.com
Activity: A, T

Sandisfield New Boston Inn

With a rich past that includes training soldiers for the Revolutionary War, this inn dates back to 1737. For tourists who enjoy a nice, historic atmosphere and a paranormal experience, this is one place that can supply both! Though activity has been reported throughout the premises, it's said that Room 4 is the most active. Guests in this room have reported hearing objects being moved and voices that come from out of nowhere. Other hot spots in the inn include the game room (where a woman named Harriet was killed by a lover in 1805), the bar area, and the actual hallways of the inn. The spirits in this location are well known to the employees, so be sure to ask them about the most current sightings to get fresh information.

Address: 101 North Main Street
Website: www.newbostoninn.com
Activity: E, T, A

Sudbury Longfellow's Wayside Inn

When David Howe built an extension to his house in 1716 to service travelers along the Boston Post Road, he had no idea just how long the inn/tavern would stay in operation. The famous poet Henry Wadsworth Longfellow visited the inn in 1862 and loved the place so much that he wrote a book about it (*Tales of a Wayside Inn*). Today the place has ten guest rooms and still offers food, drink, and lodging for the weary tourist—as well as one of the area's most interesting ghost tales. The place is said to be haunted by one Jerusha Howe, a member of the original Howe family that ran the place. Jerusha died an old maid after spending her life waiting for a lover who never returned to her. Today, she likes to personally meet and greet male visitors to the inn by touching them, whispering to them in the night and making her presence known with the scent of citrus. Hot spots in the inn include Rooms 7 and 9.

Address: 72 Wayside Inn Road
Website: www.wayside.org
Activity: A, E, T, C, N

Washington Bucksteep Manor

The haunting of this bed and breakfast became famous overnight when the *Ghost Hunters* team visited for an investigation. Tales of a ghostly monk walking the property have circulated this area—and specifically this home—for quite a while. Employees have reported seeing the apparition of the monk, as well as hearing voices, feeling someone touching them, and finding objects in the house moved during the night. Though the television series found nothing unusual, sightings of the monk continue to this day. Stay at this scenic B&B and maybe you can spot the ghost walking the grounds.

Address: 885 Washington Mountain Road
Website: www.bucksteepmanor.com
Activity: A, E, T

West Springfield Piccadilly Pub Restaurant

This 1829 home was built by a man named Charles Ashley and was known as the "Ashley House" for decades after his death. Since then, the place has changed owners and purpose numerous times over the years. Today it is a pub/restaurant with modern fare. Apparently, at least one past owner likes the newest incarnation—a ghost called "Mr. Vincent" has been witnessed numerous times by employees and guests alike. The basement is reputedly the most haunted area (ask if you can go down there), but the main area of the restaurant has also seen the shadowy apparition, as well as heard the odd sounds of footsteps and voices.

Address: 1506 Riverdale Street
Website: www.piccadillypub.com
Activity: A, S, M, E

Yarmouth Port The Colonial House Inn

The history of this home-turned-inn is almost as old as our country—and has many elements associated with early America. Located along the historic Old King's Highway, Josiah Ryder built this house in the 1730s. After two additions and numerous owners (some of them historic in their own right), the place is now an upscale Cape Cod getaway. Ghostly hot spots in this inn include the area of the widow's watch (where a person reportedly commit suicide by hanging) and Room 208 of the "Nantucket" addition, as well as Rooms 102 and 107 of the main house (said to be plagued with the screams and cries of young children). While there, be sure to visit

the bar area as well. Patrons have experienced the sight of apparitions here—apparitions that are also known for touching visitors!

Address: 277 Main Street
Website: www.colonialhousecapecod.com
Activity: A, E, T, S

Yarmouth Port Old Yarmouth Inn

Known as the oldest inn in Cape Cod (the place was built in 1696), the Yarmouth has had quite a few owners over the years—as well as residents/on-site businesses. The paranormal experiences at this inn are thought to be a product of a past resident who operated a dental office on the first floor of the house. Once the family would go to bed at night, he would creep up a set of servant's stairs in the rear of the inn to visit his mistress. Some believe it is his spirit that roams the halls to this day. Other theories involving possible entities in the inn include a slave (who would have shuttled through along the Underground Railroad), a young woman (who reportedly burned to death in an upstairs room), and random guests who may have passed away in the building over the years. Activity in the inn includes bangs/knocks in empty rooms, intense cold spots, and apparitions.

Address: 223 Route 6A
Website: www.oldyarmouthinn.com
Activity: A, M, C, T, E

MICHIGAN

Allegan Old Jail Museum

When this jail was built in 1906, it not only housed the local criminals, it served as the home for the sheriff and his family. Today it stands as a museum with over 10,000 artifacts that's run by the Allegan County Historical Society. Tales of spirits roaming the cells of this jail are well known in the area, but, perhaps what is less known is the ghost that's been seen in the "home area" of the jail. She has been witnessed on several occasions and appears to be someone from the early twentieth century. Paranormal investigators visiting this site have had great luck in the cells, as well as the house (especially in the solitary confinement area). This museum isn't open every day, so you will want to check

their hours on their website before making the trek over.

Address: 113 Walnut Street
Website: www.allegancountyhistoricalmuseum
  .org
Activity: A, E, O

Augusta Brook Lodge Hotel & Conference Resort

This historical lodging is owned and operated by Michigan State University. The place originally served as a family home to Dr. W. E. Upjohn (founder of the Upjohn pharmaceutical company) and was purchased along with 40 acres of land in 1895. Dr. Will (as friends called him) would later die on the property—in a cabin that you can now rent. The cabin is called the "Doctor's Cottage" and is thought to be haunted by its namesake. While no apparition has been seen, many who have stayed in this area have demanded to be moved to another room after spending an uneasy evening hearing footsteps and phantom music, as well as experiencing the constant feeling of being watched by someone unseen.

Address: 6535 North 42nd Street
Website: www.hfs.msu.edu/brooklodge/
Activity: E

Bay Port Sweet Dreams Inn Victorian Bed & Breakfast

The Bay Port area of Michigan is one of the oldest settlements in the state, dating back to the 1800s. Local paranormal experts tend to attribute most of the stories and tales of ghosts to this fact. Such is the case with Sweet Dreams. The owner of this B&B is quite open about the haunting and believes the spirit to be that of Ora Wallace, the daughter of an early-era local businessman, William Wallace. Ora is said to spend most of her time these days visiting people who stay in rooms on the third floor. She's known to touch people in their sleep, open/close doors, and whisper from the dark corners of the rooms. If this isn't enough, there is also the possibility of a second entity who is believed to be the first wife of Wallace.

Address: 9695 Cedar Street
Website: www.myspace.com/sweetdreamsinn
Activity: E, T

Belding Alvah N. Belding Memorial Library

After the original public library burned down in a massive fire in 1893, the city of Belding was left with a wandering library that moved into a drug store, and then city hall. It would take until 1917 for a new library to be constructed. It was finished in 1918 and later named after the most instrumental person involved with its creation, Alvah Belding. So who haunts the place? Nobody knows. Being a library, there hasn't exactly been a lot of exposure to death

(books don't count). Most believe the haunting involves the land the library is situated upon, or perhaps a past building/home that resided in the location prior to the library's existence. Again, nobody knows. One thing is certain, though, visitors to the library's children's section have been seeing more than books. The apparition of a young girl is rumored to roam this area and the sounds of her laughing have been heard by many.

Address: 302 East Main Street
Website: www.belding.michlibrary.org
Activity: A, E

Brimley Point Iroquois Lighthouse

In 1622 the Ojibwa Indians fought a massive battle against invading Iroquois at the head of the St. Mary's River. Today, the Point Iroquois Lighthouse stands at this location, guarding against the accidental grounding of boats sailing Lake Superior. Light first burst forth from this landmark in 1857, and it kept steady watch over the waters until it was extinguished in 1962 (for a new water-based lighthouse). The lighthouse can be toured today (it's part of the Hiawatha National Forest), and even features a gift shop. If you're lucky, you might even catch a glimpse of a shadowy apparition here. The entire area, including the interior of the lighthouse and adjoining house, is haunted by those who perished during the battle between the tribes. There is also said to be the ghost of a small girl (who was eaten by a bear in the area) that's been seen walking the grounds.

Address: 6 Mile Road
Website: www.exploringthenorth.com/
    ptiroquois/iroquois
Activity: A, C, E, S

Calumet The Calumet Theatre

This theatre first opened on March 20, 1900, with a production of *The Highwaymen*. It has since provided live entertainment and movies on pretty much a constant basis. If you visit the

Calumet for a play, you will not be disappointed; however, if the theatre is not your favorite form of entertainment, you can also take one of the tours. With less noise, this may be your best shot at seeing one of the resident ghosts. When an actress forgot a key line during a play in 1958, she claimed the spirit of one Madame Helena Modjeska appeared to her and helped. Others have since claimed to see the female apparition, along with a second entity who is thought to be a young girl named Elandra Rowe. Activity seems to happen on the stage, as well as in the backstage area, and includes voices, apparitions, and the usual bangs/knocks.

Address: 340 Sixth Street
Website: www.calumettheatre.com
Activity: A, E, T

Central Lake Murphy's Lamplight Inn

Rumors circulated this area for decades that the earlier version of this inn was actually a brothel that catered to the wealthy. Though this has never been proven, it is not unlikely, considering the sheer number of owners of this property. While this area recovered from the Depression, the inn fell into disrepair and struggled to remain open—and it didn't help that guests began to report seeing ghosts. The current incarnation of the inn, Murphy's Lamplight, is a restaurant and bar and is known for its down-home service. Visitors to the Lamplight still report seeing the spirits, though. Eyewitnesses to the paranormal activity say that it is an entire family (a man, a woman, and a young girl) that haunts the place and that they like to hang out in the bar. They have been seen dancing, as well as staring through the windows.

Address: 2535 North Main Street
Website: www.murphyslamplight.com
Activity: A

Charlevoix Stafford's Weathervane Restaurant

This top-notch dining experience began as a grist mill in the late 1800s. People would bring their grain down along the Pine River to the mill for processing and then continue down the river with the flour. It was converted into an eatery during the 1950s and now features a bar made from planks that came from a wrecked ship. When the owners of the mill turned the place into a restaurant, they had no idea that a ghost from the mill's past would turn up—and, literally, it was a ghost of the mill's past! As was common in the 1800s, a lack of safety standards made milling a dangerous job, and this mill claimed the life of at least one miller. Today, he walks the Weathervane and makes his presence known by moving dishes/barware, along with the sounds of footsteps and cold spots that seem to appear periodically in the dining room.

Address: 106 Pine River Lane
Website: www.staffords.com/weathervane
Activity: T, E, C

Chelsea The Purple Rose Theatre

Actor Jeff Daniels is the founder/executive director of this community theatre that is known for productions that appeal to people of all backgrounds and incomes. Tales of the paranormal have circulated this theatre (as they seem to do with most theatres) among the actors and personnel for years. These claims usually include the acts of doors slamming shut, strange knocks/bangs, and the occasional glimpse of a misty apparition sitting in the audience area. No serious investigation has ever been made in this theatre (though one group with psychics is said to have visited), but tales of the spectral visitors persist. Catch one of the many productions presented at this theatre and keep an eye out for at least one transparent patron...

Address: 137 Park Street
Website: www.purplerosetheatre.org
Activity: A, E, T

Detroit Cadieux Café

This family-run business is one of the area's (if not the country's) best Belgian bars/eateries. Their top-notch mussels and beer, as well as convivial environment have even been featured on Anthony Bourdain's television show *No Reservations*. The current owner of the Cadieux also believes that the place is haunted. The apparition is thought to be Yvonne Devos, the owner's mother and previous matron of the café. She has been seen wearing a dress and hanging out in the bar area, as well as sitting at a table. Fortunately, Yvonne is not alone in the Cadieux—her husband, Robert, is also said to haunt the basement. If this isn't enough to pique your interest, throw in the third apparition of a man (seen entering through the front door) and objects that seem to move on their own, and it all adds up to one great way to have beer and mussels.

Address: 4300 Cadieux Road
Website: www.cadieuxcafe.com
Activity: A, T

Detroit Detroit Symphony Orchestra

Founded in 1914, the DSO gained legitimacy in 1917 when Russian pianist Ossip Gabrilowitsch took over as music director. Ossip was the son-in-law of famous writer Mark Twain, and intimate friends with composers like Gustav Mahler and Sergei Rachmaninoff. His leadership compelled the community to build an orchestra hall (which subsequently opened in 1919). Yes, indeed, Ossip certainly loved the DSO—so much so that he is said to still reside there. Visitors, as well as employees, have seen Gabrilowitsch in the offices, as well as walking the backstage area. Strange voices, cold spots, and the sounds of footsteps have also been experienced.

Address: 3711 Woodward Avenue
Website: www.detroitsymphony.org
Activity: A, C, E

Detroit Doubletree Guest Suites Fort Shelby

This newly restored hotel used to be known to locals in Detroit as the Fort Shelby Hotel (the name when it opened in 1916). Prior to the restoration, the decrepit hotel sat for quite some time unoccupied—except for the Anchor Bar, a business that rented a portion of the building. Local legend states that a homeless man named Al worked for the bar and would sneak into the abandoned hotel at night to sleep. Unfortunately for Al, sleeping there would prove his horrible demise—the plumbing in the bar busted, sending human waste from the restrooms into the old hotel. This had been going on unnoticed for years until a rare inspection uncovered several feet of sludge-like waste in the building. And right in the middle of it all was the bones of old Al; still stuck in the muck where he died. Now that Doubletree has completely redone the building to the tune of $90 million, old Al seems sort of out of place walking the halls of this upscale hotel—yet he does. His apparition has been seen in the lobby, as well as the hallways of the establishment.

Address: 525 West Lafayette Boulevard
Website: http://doubletree1.hilton.com
Activity: A

Detroit The Whitney

This impressive mansion was constructed between the years of 1890–94 for Detroit luminary David Whitney. It was designed in the rare Romanesque Revival–style and is the finest example of this architecture in the city. The place has 52 rooms, 20 fireplaces, and a secret vault. If that isn't impressive enough, consider that Whitney had electricity installed in his home by Thomas Edison himself! Today, the estate hosts events—both public and private—and is open for private dining, so if you decide to visit be sure to check their calendar. As for the ghost in this location, witnesses say it is a male and that he likes to move objects in the house. Could it be Whitney? Sure, why not? The spirit could also be a remnant of the Wayne County Medical Society that resided in the place after the Whitney family left. Either way, expect to feel cold spots and to hear strange sounds while you visit the house.

Address: 4421 Woodward Avenue
Website: www.thewhitney.com
Activity: A, C, T

Dowagiac The Beckwith Theatre Company

This nonprofit theatre company was formed in 1990, though the actual theatre has roots that date back to the late 1800s. Many musical luminaries have visited the Beckwith over the years, including John Philip Sousa who directed his own music here. It's said locally that this theatre is haunted by the spirit of a young girl who is suspected to have disembarked from an "orphan train" that passed through the area during the Depression. Activity at the theatre does seem to be prankish in nature (which would somewhat confirm the spirit to be a child). People working there will find their belongings, as well as props moved and sometimes hidden. Visitors to the Beckwith have seen the little girl on occasion, as well as heard her whispers and laughter.

Address: 100 New York Avenue
Website: www.beckwiththeatre.org
Activity: A, E, T

Fenton Fenton Hotel Tavern & Grill

This hotel was built to serve folks traveling along the railroad (circa 1856) and was originally known as the Vermont House. Later the name was changed to the Fenton House by owner Abner Roberts, and so it has remained until today. With an attached tavern, the Fenton makes for a great one-stop getaway—especially for the paranormal tourist! Regulars and employees of the hotel and tavern all have their stories concerning the ghosts—and they will tell them to you with very little prodding. First there's the male apparition known for sitting at the bar, then there are the random voices and sounds that are heard throughout the premises, and then there's the shadowy entity known for walking the third-floor halls. Needless to say, this is the place to visit if you want an encounter (and it is open to the public)!

Address: 302 North Leroy Street
Website: www.fentonhotel.com
Activity: A, S, E

Frankenmuth Frankenmuth Historical Association Museum

Once known as the Kern Commercial House Hotel, this museum features exhibitions and artifacts from the area's old Franken colonies. Nobody is sure who the resident ghost is, though with a past that includes a hotel and saloon (as well as a newspaper), it's entirely possible the spirit dates back to one of these periods. Employees of the museum (as well as folks who live in the area) have been talking about the apparition in this old building for years—and sightings of the entity have taken place fairly often. Most reports revolve around the front, or first, section of the museum, though other stories/accounts have placed activity throughout the building.

Address: 613 South Main Street
Website: www.frankenmuthmuseum.org
Activity: A

Grand Haven The Grill Room

The website for this upscale restaurant describes itself as a "luxurious chop house and grill." And from the reviews, the description sounds accurate enough. But long before the place served up food, it was a hotel that dated back to 1873. Throughout the early 1900s, the Gildner Hotel serviced the area as one of the few accommodations open to the public. But the hotel didn't last, and a string of restaurants came through before the Kirby House/Grill Room managed to stick around and take off. Employees at the Kirby, though, have reported strange happenings for a long time—tales of a phantom in a cowboy hat in the upstairs areas and the apparition of a little girl that has been seen so often that the restaurant now calls her "Emily."

Address: 2 Washington Avenue
Website: www.thegilmorecollection.com/grillroom
Activity: A

Grand Rapids The Grand Inn and Conference Center

This fairly modern hotel was once known as the Presidents Inn, but that place eventually made way for the newly renovated Grand Inn. Like most hotels that stick around for a while, the Presidents had its fair share of tragedy—though locals will tell you it was actually more than its fair share! Stories of strange events happening in the Grand are now common in Grand Rapids and usually include apparitions walking the halls, trouble with the phones and lights in the rooms, and strange whispers/voices around the pool. While this hotel doesn't necessarily advertise its haunted status, the stories are more than well known there, so feel free to talk to employees about current activity.

Address: 3221 Plainfield Northeast
Website: www.grandinngr.com
Activity: A, E, T

Grayling Rayburn Lodge Bed and Breakfast

This log cabin–styled lodge dates back to the mid-1900s and has a rather unique ghost story/urban legend. According to the tale, at one point the lodge had stood abandoned, or at least it was empty and not operating. A group of teenagers visited the place, snuck in, and decided to host an impromptu séance. When they were finished, one of them noticed a strange man coming toward them from the adjoining Au Sable River. He was dressed like a lumberjack and was pointing toward the group when he suddenly vanished. Scared, the group fled the place, but one boy began to violently throw up. Eventually, they all made it to their vehicles and out of the area. To this day, locals will tell you that the ghost of the man in flannel still walks the grounds around this lodge. If you visit and don't immediately run into him, consider checking out the amenities of this beautiful lodge instead.

Address: 1491 Richardson Road
Website: www.rayburnlodgebnb.com
Activity: A

Gulliver Seul Choix Point Lighthouse

This 1892 lighthouse became instantly known for its paranormal activity when it appeared on an episode of the television show *World's Scariest Places*. The site is said to be haunted by Captain Joseph Townsend who passed away and was embalmed on the property in 1910 (he was a caretaker there). It's thought that his spirit stuck around because of the long time that passed before he could be buried (heavy snows forced the Townsend family to keep the corpse in the basement until the first thaw). Of course, this didn't happen in the actual lighthouse, but in the caretaker's house. Visitors to the lighthouse have smelled strange cigar smoke (usually in the bedroom where Townsend died), heard voices throughout the place (but especially in the basement), and found items rearranged in the off-hours.

Address: 672N West Gulliver Lake Road
Website: www.greatlakelighthouse.com
Activity: A, N, E, T

Holland The Felt Estate

Located on the outskirts of the town of Holland, the Felt mansion dates back to 1928 when it was completed just in time for the Great Depression. To make matters worse, the Felt family (Dorr and Agnes) both suffered a strange fate; it was only six weeks after they moved into their dream home that Agnes passed away in the house. Dorr would grieve, but not for long. A year and a half later, he died in the mansion as well. The house would struggle through WWII, and then become a seminary. After that, it was used as part of a prison. Strange uses, indeed, for a house of the Roaring 20s. In the early 2000s, ghost tours were held on the now decrepit property to raise money for its restoration—they were held here, because visitors who had been sneaking into the abandoned property had been telling tales of shadow people, full-blown apparitions, and horrible moans coming from the place. Some claim the ghost of Agnes Felt is in the house. Others believe the spirits are from the prison. Either way, the occasional report of paranormal activity still comes from the mansion. Catch a tour and check it out for yourself.

Address: 6597 138th Avenue
Website: www.feltmansion.org
Activity: A, S, E

Holly The Historic Holly Hotel

Though this inn-turned-restaurant suffered a devastating fire in 1978 (the second to hit the property), most of the site has managed to stay true to its historic roots (so much so that it is listed on the United States Register of Historic Places). Before becoming the Holly Hotel, the business was called the Hirst Hotel—named after the owner. Mr. Hirst is thought to be one of several folks now haunting the place. The owners of this restaurant are pretty open about their ghosts—there's even some great info concerning the haunting directly on their website—so don't be afraid to ask them about their spirits. Besides hearing about Mr. Hirst, they'll tell you about their female entity as well: Nora Kane. Both spirits like to make their presence known by scent (tobacco and perfume, respectively), but the most commonly reported activity is the sound of strange, phantom laughter.

Address: 110 Battle Alley
Website: www.hollyhotel.com
Activity: A, N, E

Marshall The National House Inn

This bed and breakfast is the oldest operating hotel in the state. It was built in 1835 by Colonel Andrew Mann but really didn't hit its stride until the railroad came through the area in 1844. From that time on, this "railroad hotel" served thousands of guests over the years until slowing business forced a closure in 1878. Since then, the building has been used for many different functions, including a factory, an apartment building, and a doctor's office. Today you can stay in one of fifteen rooms and experience the rich history and tradition of this inn. You can also experience a great haunting! When renovations began on this B&B and antiques started being brought in, people started noticing the apparition of a woman in early 1900's clothing. Locals believe her to be a resident of the place when it was an apartment building. Other activity at the site includes cold spots, voices, and the constant feeling of someone watching you.

Address: 102 Parkview
Website: www.nationalhouseinn.com
Activity: A, E, C

Marquette The Landmark Inn

Originally dubbed the Northland Hotel, service began at this establishment in 1930. It continuously accommodated visitors until the 1980s when it closed due to its poor state and lack of business. The place was completely renovated and reopened with all new amenities. If you check out the Landmark's website, you can learn all about the upscale lodgings, the on-site restaurant, and read some of the ghost stories concerning the inn. The spirit of a librarian is said to haunt the Lilac Room, a prostitute is often spotted in the hallways, and the apparition of a young woman has been known to move barware and other items in the North Star Lounge. Though stories of the ghosts in this inn

seem to include most areas of the hotel, you may want to snag the Lilac Room.

Address: 230 North Front Street
Website: www.thelandmarkinn.com
Activity: A, E, T

Petoskey Stafford's Perry Hotel

In 1899, 20 luxury resorts were built on Little Traverse Bay overlooking Lake Michigan. Today, one of them still stands—the Perry Hotel (named after the owner, Dr. Norman J. Perry). With 79 guest rooms and three restaurants to choose from, the Perry is the high mark of indulgence for visitors. Locals, as well as hotel employees, will tell you that their ghost is a woman who committed suicide on the premises in 1902. Her apparition is often seen walking in the garden area of the hotel. There have been tales of the spirit being seen inside the hotel, but these are rare. The ghost at this hotel prefers to stay outside, so think about eating alfresco while you're there…

Address: 100 Lewis Street
Website: www.staffords.com/perry-hotel-4/
Activity: A

Presque Isle Old Presque Isle Lighthouse

Featured in numerous books and television programs, this is a legendary Michigan haunt. Being the first of two lighthouses to bear this name, it was erected in 1840 and functioned until it was replaced (by the New Presque Isle Lighthouse) in 1870. Since then, private owners have made the lighthouse and adjoining cottage a summer home. In 1992, the current owner of the light-house, George Parris, passed away on the premises, leaving his wife, Lorraine, behind to watch after the property. It wasn't long before Lorraine started seeing strange things, including a light in the now-inoperable lighthouse and the apparition of George himself. Many residents in the area (as well as boats and planes going by) have witnessed the spectral light coming from this lighthouse. Take a tour and maybe you'll see it as well.

Address: 4500 East Grand Lake Road
Website: www.keepershouse.org
Activity: A, O

Saginaw J. B. Meinberg and Woody O'Brien's

This restaurant and pub is quite modern—even if the building it's located in is a little bit older. The building was used as a tavern way back in the early 1900s and is still a favorite hangout for locals today. Ask the patrons about the ghost located there and you will get an earful. Apparently everybody has seen and knows about the phantom barmaid that's still waiting on the customers. Most believe she dates back to the earlier tavern days, but nobody has a name to attach to the (sometimes seen) face. Other activity includes barware moving and footsteps when the pub is empty enough for people to actually hear them.

Address: 116 South Hamilton Street
Website: www.myspace.com/meinbergs
Activity: A, E, T

St. Clair Murphy Inn

When the current owners completely renovated this 1836 boarding house, they had no idea that they would be unleashing a haunting in the house! Originally called the Farmers House (and later on, the Scheaffer Inn), this Irish-decorated pub and inn has seven rooms for rent and a great on-site bar/restaurant/live music lounge. Paranormal investigators who have visited/

stayed at the inn have reported encountering a female apparition who walks the place. She's most often seen in the Lancaster Room (and the neighboring Devonshire Room), but occasional sightings of the spirit have occurred in almost every guest room. The owners of the inn have had reports of the activity from guests, but most everyone believes the entity to be quite friendly.

Address: 505 Clinton Avenue
Website: www.murphyinn.com
Activity: A, E

Traverse City Bowers Harbor Inn

This summer retreat for J. W. Stickney and his wife Genevive was originally constructed in the 1880s. It would later become the Bowers Harbor Inn and a favorite place to visit on the Old Mission Peninsula. With a fantastic location along the West Grand Traverse Bay, the inn makes a great place to stay while exploring the great outdoors. Of course, you can also explore the actual inn and attempt to catch a glimpse of their resident ghost: Genevive Stickney. The story goes that Mr. Stickney had an affair with a nurse who lived with them (she took care of Genevive) and when he died, he left all his money to her (though Genevive got the house). Eventually, Genevive fell into despair and hanged herself from an elevator shaft in the house. Guests have since seen her apparition in mirrors there, as well as appearing in photographs taken inside the inn. Other activity includes items moving, paintings that fall off walls for no reason, and lights that turn on/off with nobody around.

Address: 13512 Peninsula Drive
Website: www.bowersharborinn.net
Activity: A, T

Ypsilanti Michigan Firehouse Museum

The building that holds this museum dates back to 1898 and served as an area firehouse for many years. It's only too ironic that the place would suffer two fires itself—once in 1901 and once in 1922. When the second occurred, the fire chief was Alonzo Miller. Alonzo passed away and his grandson took over the station—and the paranormal activity began! Today, a museum resides in the location and the strange happenings are said to still occur. These include doors opening/closing by themselves, strange knocks/bangs in all areas of the building, and mysterious whispers/voices that seem to emanate from the very walls. The activity is said to be quite frequent (one door in particular is said to open on almost a daily basis), so be sure swing by this historic and entertaining museum.

Address: 110 West Cross Street
Website: www.michiganfirehousemuseum.org
Activity: E, T

MINNESOTA

Annandale Thayer's Historic Bed & Breakfast

If you read the information listed on Thayer's website you will learn that the place is motorcycle friendly, the employees will care for your special dietary needs, and that the place is haunted by a friendly spirit—one who is treated just like any other guest. For the "haunted tourist," Thayer's is a godsend. With paranormal package deals that include ghost hunting classes, tours, and stays in haunted rooms, this B&B makes for a trip that can't be missed. So who haunts Thayer's? According to the website, as well as paranormal investigators who have visited, there are two spirits walking the place: Gus and Caroline Thayer, caretakers of the small inn during the late 1800s when it was known as the Annandale House. They are said to visit most rooms

and are known for moving items around in the rooms, as well as appearing in person.

Address: 60 West Elm Street
Website: www.thayers.net
Activity: A, T

Anoka Billy's Bar & Grill

Located within walking distance of the Mississippi River, this classy pub may have the area's best ribs and chicken. If you visit, be sure to check out their weekly specials, and to ask about their interesting past. The building that Billy's now occupies was once the second incarnation of the Jackson Hotel (built in 1885 after the first hotel burned in a great fire). Not long after the Jackson opened, a man named Peter Gross was killed out front (he actually was shot out front, and died inside the hotel). In addition, the Jackson was said to be running a makeshift brothel on the premises. The hotel continued to operate into the 1950s, and then became an apartment building. Visitors to Billy's, much like the folks who lived in the apartments, now say a female apparition walks the restaurant (thought to possibly be Mrs. Jackson, a former owner of the hotel). Other activity includes items moving and strange voices heard on the third floor.

Address: 214 Jackson Street
Website: www.billysbargrill.com
Activity: A, E, T

Duluth Charlie's Club

This bar and billiards center is much like any other scattered all across the United States: bands play, people socialize, and cold drinks are served with a smile. But unlike most nightclubs, this place is rumored to be haunted. According to local history, this club was a tavern and brothel in the early 1900s, and it did good business until it burned down. Because of the shady business, it's thought that any ladies of the night who died were not reported to the authorities. Today, one of these ladies is still hanging out at Charlie's. Employees call the spirit "Sadie," though this may or may not have been her name while alive. Sightings of Sadie have occurred quite often, along with the apparition of a man who is thought to be a deceased regular of the place.

Address: 5527 Grand Avenue
Website: www.angelfire.com/band2/charlies/
Activity: A

Duluth Glensheen, The Historic Congdon Estate

This historic mansion was built 1905–08 and would serve as home to Chester and Clara Congdon for the rest of their lives. Indeed, the Congdon family would occupy this home all the way until 1977! Glensheen now hosts tours to the public and offers an upscale place for private events. It's unfortunate that the ghost story concerning this estate involves the horrible demise of the last Congdon to live in the home, Elisabeth. She was murdered in the house along with her nurse Velma Pietila. To make matters worse, all signs pointed to her daughter, Marjorie, and her husband, Robert Caldwell, as the culprits. The two were arrested and prosecuted for the crime (Marjorie would later be acquitted and Robert would commit suicide). Locals who have visited the mansion say that strange things happen there: shadowy apparitions have been seen on the premises (especially in the area of the murder), whispering voices have been heard, and objects have been witnessed moving by themselves.

Address: 3300 London Road
Website: www.d.umn.edu/glen/
Activity: A, E, T, S

Hastings LeDuc Historic Estate

This Gothic Revival masterpiece was erected in 1865 by General William LeDuc and his wife Mary. After serving in the Civil War, General LeDuc wanted to start a family, and this began by moving the family to Hastings. He would go on to work in politics and become a local entrepreneur who had luck in the railroad business. When Mary passed away in 1904, William and his daughter Alice turned to spiritualism to cope with her passing. He died in 1917, and the home changed hands several times before passing to the Minnesota Historical Society. Today, the property is in the process of being turned over to the city of Hastings. As for the haunting, it's said that at least two ghosts have been seen on the property. The first is a male apparition that most believe to be either General LeDuc or a man named Carroll Simmons (an owner of the house in later years), who has been spotted throughout the place. There's also a female apparition (assumed to be Alice LeDuc), who is usually blamed for cold spots, doors opening/closing, and objects moving on their own.

Address: 1629 Vermillion Street
Website: www.dakotahistory.org/LeDuc/home
Activity: A, C, E

Hibbing Greyhound Bus Museum

This museum not only has examples of antique buses, but has displays and attractions that can take you back to the sounds of 1914 traffic! When you're finished with your tour, you can even visit the on-site gift shop to take home gifts for the family. What you cannot take home, though, is the spirit who reportedly walks the museum. Employees have been reporting strange shadow masses and voices in parts of the museum (usually in the Sunrise and Montana areas) for a long time. Paranormal investigators were called in, and evidence was gathered that seems to support the haunting of this location. When you visit, mention your interest in the paranormal to the guide and you may get a few extra stops on the tour.

Address: 1201 Greyhound Boulevard
Website: www.greyhoundbusmuseum.org
Activity: S, E

Luverne Palace Theatre

What is it about theatres that seem to attract spirits from beyond? Like most older venues with a long history of hosting plays and performances, the Palace is rumored to be haunted. The place was built in 1915 by Herman Jochims and, along with his wife Maude, he managed the place during the era of silent films. Herman would handle the projector and Maude would play the piano/organ. Today, both of them haunt the theatre. Herman is usually seen standing in the balconies and is thought to be the spirit who moves things in the backstage area. Maude likes to hang out in the area of the old pipe organ—and according to some witnesses, is still playing it (even though it has been broken for many years).

Address: 104 East Main Street
Website: www.palacetheatre.us
Activity: A, E, T

Minneapolis First Avenue and the 7th Street Entry

With a reputation that places First Avenue in the center of the Minneapolis music scene, it's no wonder that most people who live in the area have heard of the club. Musicians and bands travel from all over the world to play this venue. But long before the club opened its doors in the 1970s, the place was an Art Deco masterpiece bus station. The press hailed the Greyhound station as a modern wonder when it finished construction in 1937. The apparition that has been seen in the First Avenue is thought to date back to this station. Most of the activity takes place in the restroom area, and it's reported that the spirit of a girl is the culprit. Local legend puts the girl as a suicide victim that took her own life in one of the bathroom stalls. She is generally blamed when things go awry on the stage, or (especially) when a spectral girl is witnessed walking the area…

Address: 701 First Avenue North
Website: www.first-avenue.com
Activity: A, T

Minneapolis Municipal Building Commission

The foundation of this building was first laid in a Masonic ceremony in 1891, and after construction was finished, the place served as a center for the city of Minneapolis. Over the years, many different offices and departments have resided here—including the city jail, which was located on the fourth and fifth floors. Imagine the prison officers' surprise when inmates began reporting an apparition of a man in boxer shorts walking the fifth floor! It didn't take long for the ghost story to get around, and soon reports of the spirit were springing forth from inmates and guards alike. It's thought that the spirit is that of John Moshik, a man who was hanged on the premises for killing a person during a robbery. In addition to the adult-detention area (as the prison level is now named), Moshik has been seen in the hallways and tower areas.

Address: 350 South 5th Street
Website: www.municipalbuildingcommission
.org
Activity: A

Sauk Centre Palmer House Hotel, Restaurant and Pub

This upscale hotel was built to replace the Sauk Centre House hotel that burned down in 1900. It was the first place in the area to feature electricity and became famous when author Sinclair Lewis mentioned it in one of his works. When Mr. Lewis penned these words, he had no idea he would be writing about the place he would walk in the afterlife! It's said that Sinclair now haunts the Palmer House, along with the spirits of a child, a man (dubbed "Raymond") and former prostitute (named "Lucy" by the folks there). Employees have been witnessing strange happenings at this hotel for decades, and chances are high for you to experience the paranormal as well. Hot spots in the place are Room 11, Room 18, Room 22 (haunted by Raymond), Room 17 (Lucy's hangout), the hallways (where the child plays), and the basement. Activity includes voices, cold spots, objects moving, and of course the apparitions themselves.

Address: 500 Sinclair Lewis Avenue
Website: www.thepalmerhousehotel.com
Activity: A, E, T, C, S

Silver Bay Split Rock Lighthouse

After a slew of ships were destroyed by a fierce gale coming off Lake Superior, locals demanded that a lighthouse be built on their shore. Building began and the place was completed and running by 1909. It functioned for 59 years before being handed over to the state as a historic site. Rumors that the place is haunted seem to date back to the 1980s. The tale goes like this: A man was once leaving the lighthouse as the place closed for the day. When he got into his car, he realized he had lost his wallet inside. He returned to find the lighthouse already locked up, but noticed an old man was staring at him from an upstairs window. He attempted to get the man to let him in, but he was ignored and he eventually left. When he returned the following day for his wallet, he asked who the old man was who wouldn't let him in. The staff did not know—and said there was nobody in the building. Is the old man still there? Maybe you should go check...

Address: 3755 Split Rock Lighthouse Road
Website: www.dnr.state.mn.us/state_parks/
split_rock_lighthouse/
Activity: A

St. Paul Forepaugh's Restaurant

This upscale, and constantly praised, French restaurant is housed in a Victorian mansion that was built by a man named Joseph Forepaugh. Forepaugh lived in the home along with his wife Mary, their two children, and several servants. Unfortunately, Joseph's fortunes would not last, and when finances took a dire turn, he decided to commit suicide by shooting himself in the head. Strangely, it's said that a servant named

Molly became so despondent about the death, that she followed suit by hanging herself in the house. Of course, rumors circulated that Joseph may have had an affair with Molly, but the truth of this is unknown. Regardless, local legend places both of them in the house to this day. Joseph's apparition has been witnessed many times on the ground floor (especially in the dining room), and Molly has often been seen and heard in and around the third floor.

Address: 276 South Exchange Street
Website: www.forepaughs.com
Activity: A, E

St. Paul Minnesota Public Radio's Fitzgerald Theater

Mostly known today for the radio show *A Prairie Home Companion* (as well as the film, which was shot there), the history of this theater dates back to 1910. It was patterned after the famous Maxine Elliot Theater in New York and was originally called the Sam S. Shubert Theater. The name was changed when Garrison Keillor spearheaded the movement to rename the place for St. Paul native F. Scott Fitzgerald. Today, the place is reportedly haunted by two spirits: an old stagehand named "Ben" by the staff and a woman who is thought to be an actress (employees call her "Veronica"). The female has only been heard (the sounds of her singing often resonate from the stage area), but Ben has been witnessed many times as a dark, shadowy shape that roams the place.

Address: 10 East Exchange Street
Website: http://fitzgeraldtheater.publicradio.org
Activity: A, S, E

St. Paul Ramsey County Courthouse

This Art Deco skyscraper has been servicing the St. Paul area since 1932 and still functions to this day. The place offers tours of the building—and even has information on their website for self-guided tours. If you decide to go this route, make sure to spend some quality time walking the old halls and checking out the lobby. These are the two areas known for ghostly activity. Shadow masses have been seen in these areas, and the sounds of voices and footsteps have been heard as well. The haunting of the courthouse is thought to be the product of hangings that took place on the property, but nobody attributes the activity to one specific person. Workers who were involved with renovating the place in the early 1990s reported strange things happening the entire time they were there, including finding their tools and equipment constantly being moved, voices, and strange shadows.

Address: 15 West Kellogg Boulevard
Website: www.co.ramsey.mn.us/cm/manager/
CourthouseTours
Activity: A, S, E, T

St. Paul Wabasha Street Caves

This location makes for an interesting night out; they host "swing nights" with swing jazz music and have a top-notch café right inside. But in the old days, the place was a notorious speakeasy, as gangsters made the Wabasha Caves their regular haunt. If you don't feel like dancing when you visit, you can opt to take one of the tours—these include a "gangster" tour and a spooky tour that's offered in the fall. (Of course, you can take the normal tour as well and still visit all the hot spots here.) Employees and patrons will tell you that the place is haunted by the aforementioned gangsters (at least the ones who died in the line of duty) and that they make themselves known by the sounds of spectral music and appearing as glowing orbs of light shooting across the caves.

Address: 215 Wabasha Street South
Website: www.wabashastreetcaves.com
Activity: E, O

Stillwater Warden's House Museum

The warden of the Minnesota Territorial Prison lived in this house from 1853 to 1914, when the prison itself was relocated to the city of Bayport. During this time, 13 different wardens occupied the home. Today, the place stands as a remnant of the area's past and a tribute to life in the early 1900s. It's said that a former inmate of the nearby prison and a woman (thought to be Gertrude Wolfer, daughter of former warden Henry Wolfer) now haunt the museum. Activity was first documented when neighbors witnessed a woman in a dress standing within the premises after closing (staring from an upstairs window). Since then, she and the prisoner have both been seen several times. Other activity includes cold spots and strange sounds that seem to come from empty rooms.

Address: 602 North Main Street
Website: http://wchsmn.org/museums/
   wardens_house/
Activity: A, C, E

Stillwater Water Street Inn

When the lumber industry boomed in the late 1800s, the city of Stillwater responded by building the Lumber Exchange Building. It was connected to the train depot and featured many shops on the premises for the local lumber barons and townsfolk to use. When the lumber industry dried up for the most part, the building continued to provide offices and small businesses for the area. In 1994, work began on the building to transform the place into the inn, restaurant, and pub it is today. If you want a paranormal

encounter at this location, it's recommended that you hang out in the pub. Back in the old days, this area was a rowdy saloon that had its fair share of violent incidents. It's said that a Confederate soldier was killed while drinking at the saloon and that his spirit can still be seen today—as well as heard and smelled (strange scents of body odor have been experienced).

Address: 101 Water Street South
Website: www.waterstreetinn.us
Activity: A, E, N

Taylors Falls The Old Jail Bed & Breakfast

This place was opened in 1869 as a saloon. The owners had a brewery just up the way, so they used a cave that connected the two properties to store their beer. As the saloon grew in popularity, so did incidents at the place, so a jail was soon erected next door to handle the troublemakers. If you visit the place today, you will find that the saloon and jail are now both part of a bed and breakfast—and you can stay in either building. Paranormal activity happens, of course, in the actual jail cottage. The spirits of past inmates are said to still be in the building and they like to get noisy! They bang on the original jail door that still remains there, they stomp during the night, and they like to talk a lot in the wee hours.

Address: 349 Government Street
Website: www.oldjail.com
Activity: E

Two Harbors Black Woods Grill & Bar

This local chain has five locations, so if you visit their website make sure you are getting directions to the restaurant in Two Harbors! This location is the original eatery of the chain and the one thought to be haunted. It wasn't long after the restaurant moved into the old building that employees started noticing strange things happening: heavy footsteps that almost seemed to follow you, the sensation of someone touching/

breathing on you, and the strange sight of a ghostly woman in white who would approach you and vanish before your eyes! There are a lot of local stories concerning why this place is haunted, all the way from the grounds being cursed to blaming it on former tenants (some believe the place was once an orphanage), but the truth is yet to be found. If you're looking for great food, though, and a chance to see a ghost, this may be a good bet!

Address: 612 7th Avenue
Website: www.blackwoods.com
Activity: A, E, T

Tupelo •

• Vicksburg
◉ Jackson

MISSISSIPPI

Columbus Highland House Bed & Breakfast

This classic Greek Revival masterpiece (built in the early 1900s) features many of the amenities of an upscale hotel, including an exercise room, a pool, and a theater. This is the second house to stand on this site—and the second place built by W. S. Lindamood. He was forced to construct a new home after his first home was burned to the ground by a housekeeper who was angry when he spurned her advances. Perhaps it is this housekeeper that now haunts the B&B. Visitors have heard voices and witnessed doors opening/closing by themselves. Local paranormal investigators visited the home and, though their findings were inconclusive, managed to

get compelling evidence that suggests a female spirit is walking the grounds.

Address: 810 Highland Circle
Website: www.discoverourtown.com/MS/
  Columbus/
Activity: E, T

Columbus Temple Heights

This mansion is considered one of the best period restorations in the state of Mississippi. The house dates back to 1837 and has features of both a Greek Revival and Federal-style home. It was built as a family home for General Richard T. Brownrigg, but he would barely visit the estate before selling it. Eventually, it fell into the hands of Reverend J. H. Kennebrew, whose family would live in the mansion until 1965.

Today, the place can be toured and even rented for special events; just know if you do so, that you may have an extra guest there. Owners over the years at Temple Heights have reported hearing mumbling voices and the sounds of breaking dishes in the home. Most believe the spirit is that of Elizabeth Kennebrew, the last member of the family to live in the house. Descriptions of the late Lizzie match the eyewitness accounts of a female apparition that has been seen walking the grounds.

Address: 515 Ninth Street North
Website: www.columbus-ms.info
Activity: A, E, R

Ellisville Deason Home

Dating back to 1845, this house was the property of Amos and Eleanor Deason. During the Civil War, the Deasons were visited by Major Amos McLemore, who was hunting a band of men that was accused of deserting the Confederate army. During the evening, a group of these men (known as the Leaf River Rowdies) broke into the home, and their leader (one Newt Knight) shot McLemore dead. Today, it's thought that McLemore now haunts the Deason home—or does he? After several paranormal investigations at this location, it's clear that a least one female walks the house (her voice has been recorded via EVP) and some believe that Newt Knight may even haunt the place as well. So who is the female spirit? Most signs point to a young Virginia Hollomon, who died in the home and even had her funeral there. The house is currently being renovated, but with a little luck will open for regular tours by the Daughters of the American Revolution (the owners of the house). If you visit, expect to hear voices, see objects move, and (hopefully) see the apparition of poor Jennie.

Address: Deason Street at Anderson Street
Activity: A, E, T, S

Jackson Old State Capitol Building

This massive structure was erected in 1839 and once simultaneously held all three branches of the Mississippi state government. Today, you can tour the premises or simply visit the on-site museum to explore this haunted location. Over the years of its operation, the place experienced at least one death (most think there were probably more)—a legislator who died of a heart attack while at work. Employees and visitors who experience paranormal activity in the building often blame the politician, though evidence gathered by local investigators suggests at least two spirits walk the old Capitol. Eyewitness accounts of the haunting include seeing lights that turn on/off, the sounds of footsteps, bangs/thumps from empty offices, and doors that open/close by themselves.

Address: 100 North State Street
Website: http://mdah.state.ms.us/museum/oldcap/
Activity: E, T

Meridian Grand Opera House/MSU Riley Center

Two half-brothers, Israel Marks and Levi Rothenberg, built this theater in 1889 along with the neighboring building that once functioned as a department store (and is now a conference center). The opera house was originally going to be a hotel, but the plans were scrapped halfway through construction and a theatre was built instead. The place has been renovated many times over the years and now is part of the Mississippi State University campus. Visitors to this Romanesque/Empire–style theater have been reporting sightings of a spectral lady for decades. Most believe the spirit is that of an ex-actor who must have had a strong attachment to the premises. This ghost is usually seen on the actual stage and is even occasionally heard singing in the wee hours.

Address: 2206 Fifth Street
Website: www.msurileycenter.com
Activity: A, E

Meridian Merrehope Mansion

This massive estate is one of the few remaining Antebellum homes still standing in the city of Meridian. During the Civil War, the area fell under the onslaught of General William Tecumseh Sherman who declared that "Meridian no longer exists." To look at the house today, you'd never believe it started as a three-room cottage for Juriah Jackson. When Mr. John Gary purchased the property in 1868, most of the present rooms were added on. It is the daughter of Mr. Gary (Eugenia) that's rumored to walk the house today. Employees have witnessed her apparition (they recognize her from a portrait that still hangs in the home today) on numerous occasions and say that she is joined in the afterlife by a second spirit that likes to hang out in the Periwinkle Room. Both spirits are known for moving objects and making loud bangs/knocks throughout the place.

Address: 905 Martin Luther King Drive
Website: www.merrehope.com
Activity: A, E, T

Natchez Dunleith Historic Inn

Before this house was built, a home by the name of Routhland stood on this property. In 1855, lightning struck this house and burned it to the ground. The inheritors of the estate, Charles and Mary Dahlgren, decided to build another home. They lived there for three years until Mary died. Charles sold the home to Alfred Vidal Davis, who renamed the place Dunleith. The house has been a bed and breakfast since 1976 and now includes an on-site restaurant and tavern. The ghost story concerning this location goes back to Routhland and a young woman who's called "Miss Percy." According to legend, Percy died on the property while pining away for a lost love and she now walks the halls of Dunleith. She's been seen and heard in most areas of the main house, so you may want to ask about current sightings when you visit so you can stay in the best hot spot.

Address: 84 Homochitto Street
Website: www.dunleith.com
Activity: A, E

Natchez King's Tavern

Richard King built this establishment in the late 1700s and it functioned as an area inn, tavern, and post office. Dark legends concerning its history began when three skeletons were found within the walls of the place during renovations in the 1930s. It wasn't long before tales of murder and the place being haunted started circulating. It's said that one of the infamous Harpe brothers killed a baby in the tavern (for crying) and that King himself may have murdered a mistress that was threatening to break news of his affair to his wife (thought to be one of the three skeletons, along with those of two men who were either accomplices who were done in, or murdered slaves). Paranormal experiences on the premises include the sounds of a baby crying, a female apparition (usually seen on the second floor), and intense cold spots that seem to follow patrons.

Address: 619 Jefferson Street
Website: www.natchezms.com
Activity: A, E, C

Natchez Linden Bed and Breakfast

The main house section of this B&B dates all the way back to 1790, with the newer wing being added on in 1818. Linden gained area notoriety when the film *Gone With the Wind* copied their front door for the home "Tara" in the movie. The place features six guest rooms—and almost as many ghost stories! It's thought that the house is in the throes of a strong and unique residual haunt; a phantom horse-drawn carriage has been seen out front, as well as the strange sight of a female apparition on the roof! Of course you'll be staying in the actual home, so you may want to direct your attention to the second floor where the ghost of a man is often seen (he appears to be a product of the 1920s/30s as he is always seen with a top hat and cane).

Address: 1 Linden Place
Website: www.lindenbandb.com
Activity: R, A, E

Ocean Springs Aunt Jenny's Catfish Restaurant

Besides the fact you can eat some of the state's best catfish and fried chicken at this restaurant—you'll be eating it in a home that dates back to 1852. And if that isn't enough history, consider the fact that the surrounding oak trees on the property are over 500 years old! Unfortunately, there isn't as much history known about the ghost that's reported to haunt this restaurant. With any house as old as this one, there were certainly births, deaths, and funerals held on the property, so it's probably safe to assume the spirit is a natural result of one or more of these affairs. Activity in the place usually happens on the second floor and includes voices, odd footsteps/bangs, and items that seem to be moved during the night.

Address: 217 Washington Avenue
Website: www.coastseafood.com/jennys
Activity: E, T

Pascagoula Longfellow House National Historic Site

Though this house was built in 1850 for a New Orleans businessman named Daniel Smith Grahams, the mansion is mostly known for the later Pollock/Moore family who called the house Bellevue. The property stayed in their family all the way into the 1940s, when it was sold and converted into a hotel called the Longfellow House. Rumors circulating about the house being haunted have made the rounds in Pascagoula for decades—going back to folks who actually stayed in the hotel. Guests would complain about heavy footsteps in the halls at night, as well as low-pitched voices that seem to come from dark corners. Urban legend says the ghost is that of a slave who was beaten to death on the property, but this has never been proven. But if you believe eyewitness accounts, there is a male spirit walking the halls of this historic home.

Address: 3401 Beach Boulevard
Website: www.stateparks.com/longfellow_house
Activity: S, E

Pass Christian The Blue Rose Restaurant and Antiques

This 1848 cottage-style home was built by Hugh Fitzpatrick, and the place remained in his family through several generations before changing hands many times over the years. While the Pass Christian area struggled with the woes of yellow fever, it's said that the family residing in this house suffered the loss of a daughter named Letty. She was around 13 years old and suffered from mental illness, so she seldom strayed far from the house. Perhaps it's because of this that her spirit is now said to roam the home today. Current owners of the Blue Rose, as well as past owners, have witnessed the girl's apparition many times, along with witnessing objects moving by themselves (doors, objects, etc.). Today you can visit this location; it has a restaurant, an antique shop, and you can even rent out the upper floor for private events.

Address: 120 West Scenic Drive
Website: http://bluerose.passchristian.net/
Activity: A, T

Tupelo Tupelo Community Theater

With roots that go back to the days of vaudeville, the Lyric Theatre (home of the TCT) was constructed in 1912 by R. F. Goodlett. During the 1930s, the theater underwent renovations to transform the place into a movie venue (and also upgraded to a new Art Deco look). It wasn't long after this makeover, though, that the city of Tupelo was struck by a terrible tornado in 1936. Most of the buildings were leveled, but the Lyric survived. As the town coped with the aftermath of the tragedy, the Lyric was used as a hospital, and then as a mortuary. It's because of the latter that folks deem the theater to be haunted. Employees and visitors alike have reported hearing voices/footsteps, seeing shadowy apparitions, and finding theatre props moved during the night.

Address: 200 North Broadway
Website: www.tctwebstage.com
Activity: A, S, E, T

Vicksburg 1902 Stained Glass Manor

Junius and Fannie Johnson built this house with the help of famed architect George W. Maher (one of the many teachers of Frank Lloyd Wright) and they would both live in the house until their respective deaths. Junius died after suffering wounds during a tornado in 1919, but Fannie lived to a ripe old age, passing away in 1931. Today, this bed and breakfast features six rooms for rent and even a carriage house—but

you will want to stay in the main house to experience the paranormal here. It's said that Fannie still walks the halls of her beloved home and that her apparition is often seen around her old bedroom. There have also been visitors that say a young boy haunts the top floor/attic of the house. Dark rumors state that Fannie may have been privy to the "mercy killing" of a crippled/mentally impaired boy in that area, and that it is his spirit that is often heard in the attic.

Address: 2430 Drummond Street
Website: www.vickbnb.com
Activity: A, E, T

Vicksburg Anchuca Historic Mansion and Inn

The name *Anchuca* comes from the Choctaw language and means "happy home." It's thought to be the oldest columned home in Vicksburg (it was built in 1830, but the columns were added in 1847), and it was built for a local politician named J. W. Mauldin. While Vicksburg endured a siege by the Union army during the Civil War, the house was used to shelter those whose homes were destroyed. Anchuca is reportedly haunted by a former owner of the house called "Archie." Staying at this mansion-turned–bed and breakfast is a must when visiting Vicksburg. But if you can't, don't despair—there is a café on the site that you can visit as well. Since most sightings of Archie take place in the parlor and the dining room, you still might be able to catch a glimpse of the apparition.

Address: 1010 First East Street
Website: www.anchucamansion.com
Activity: A

Vicksburg Annabelle Bed & Breakfast Inn

When you visit this B&B, you get two historical buildings in one. In addition to the actual house itself (a Victorian-Italianate built in 1868), you also get the 1881 guest house that sits with a fantastic view of the Mississippi Delta. Annabelle's is part of the Historic Garden District of Vicksburg and is linked to yet another haunted house, Cedar Grove. John Klein, the original owner of Cedar Grove, built this home for his son Madison. And much like the former, Annabelle's is considered haunted. So who haunts this home? Is it a member of the Klein family, or yet another owner who lived and died in the place over the years? No one is sure. But witnesses of the paranormal activity on these premises have experienced voices, cold spots, and items being moved. Check in with the current owners—they will catch you up on the activity happening at this B&B!

Address: 501 Speed Street
Website: www.annabellebnb.com
Activity: E, C, T

Vicksburg The Duff Green Mansion

This home was built as a wedding gift for one Mary Green by her newlywed husband Duff in 1856. Prior to the Civil War, the mansion had a reputation for entertaining the elite in the city of Vicksburg, but when the city fell under siege, Green wisely offered the place as a hospital for both sides of the battle lines. Union soldiers were treated on the top floor, while the Confederate troops were cared for on the ground floor. The basement was used as a surgery center, and it's said that hundreds of men suffered amputations in this area. Since those days, the home has been an orphanage, a retirement home, and now a bed and breakfast. If you stay at the mansion, you may want to consider renting the Dixie Room. Visitors who have slept here have witnessed the apparition of a Confederate soldier—an apparition that's missing one leg! Other activity in the house includes voices, cold spots, and the feeling of being watched.

Address: 1114 First East Street
Website: www.duffgreenmansion.com
Activity: A, C, E

Vicksburg Vicksburg National Military Park

When General John C. Pemberton surrendered to General Ulysses S. Grant on July 4, 1863, it pretty much signaled the beginning of the end for the Confederacy. The siege of Vicksburg had cost both sides almost 3,000 men's lives, as well as over 11,000 wounded. This extended battle—as well as the impending surrender of the South—would leave Vicksburg in a state that would take a hundred years to recover from. The park that commemorates this battle has over 1,300 monuments and a complete Union gunboat on display. These alone would make visiting the park a must, but when you add in the paranormal events that have taken place in the park, you have a trip that can't be missed! All of the battle areas (especially around the fortifications) have had reports of phantom battle sounds, the cries of men, and strange misty apparitions that can be seen even in the daytime. Most of the activity seems to be residual in nature—and the events get more active when the site hosts Civil War reenactments.

Address: 3201 Clay Street
Website: www.nps.gov/vick
Activity: R, M, E

West Point Waverley Mansion

The area in and around Columbus, Mississippi, is behind the cities of Vicksburg and Natchez only when it comes to hauntings in the state of Mississippi. Waverley is on the outskirts of town (and technically in the city of West Point) and is considered one of the best of the local haunts. The house was built by Colonel George Hampton Young in 1852 and the Young family lived in the home until the last member of the family, Captain William Young, passed away in 1913. After years of decay, the house was completely restored by the Snow family and is now open to the public for tours. It wasn't long after the place opened, though, that folks started asking about a strange young girl that they had seen inside. This is the spirit that roams Waverley. It's thought that she is a member of the Young family who passed away in the mansion. Her apparition, as well as her voice, has been witnessed many times in the mansion.

Address: 1852 Waverley Mansion Road
Website: www.wpnet.org/waverley_mansion
   .htm
Activity: A, E

MISSOURI

Boonville Old Cooper County Jail

When this small jail closed down in 1978, it was the longest continuously running prison in the state of Missouri. It dates back to 1848 and is built entirely of limestone (something that may be of interest to paranormal investigators). Famous outlaw Frank James was briefly held at the jail until locals (sympathetic to the James brothers) dismissed the case. The state later deemed staying in the old, iron cells as "cruel and unusual punishment" (read some of the testaments to such written on the cell walls) and forced the place to close. Since then, it has existed as a living museum and a place for resident spirits to hide! Since hangings took place right on the property, it isn't hard to believe that the place is haunted. The resident spirit is said to be that of a young male prisoner who

likes to make himself known by banging the cell doors and appearing as a dark shadow mass.

Address: 614 East Morgan
Website: www.mo-river.net/history/cooper/
    old_jail/jail
Activity: S, E

Branson The Shepherd of the Hills Outdoor Theatre

Located on the outskirts of Branson, this theatre was founded by a Kansas minister named Harold Bell Wright. Harold moved to the area when he was diagnosed with tuberculosis and he founded the spot now known as Inspiration Point in 1896. This area of the Ozarks was a hotly disputed chunk of land during the Civil War, and it saw a lot of troops from both sides march through—and even skirmish—at times. Imagine the surprise of theatre patrons when they saw an unusual Confederate soldier march through the middle of a production of the play Baldknobbers. Their surprise would grow even larger when the soldier would vanish before the entire crowd. Since then, this apparition has been seen on many occasions and can be sought in the lands surrounding the outdoor theatre.

Address: 5586 West Highway 76
Website: www.oldmatt.com
Activity: A

Bridgeton Payne-Gentry House Museum

This museum is a historic home (it dates back to 1870) and once functioned as a local doctor's office. The original homeowners, Elbridge and Mary Elizabeth Payne, lived in the home for several years until Elbridge died. Mary then had to raise the Payne children in the home by herself. One of the Payne children, Will, would add the office to the house in order to treat patients on the property. The second child, Mary Lee, would marry a man named William Gentry and continue to live in the home for many years. During this time, tragedy struck the family when Mary Lee died while giving child birth. It is Mary Lee that's said to still walk the house today (though there are also outrageous legends concerning numerous ghosts in this home). Employees of the museum, and even visitors (including paranormal investigators who have checked out the site), have reported seeing shadowy apparitions, hearing voices, and seeing the spirit of Mary Lee Gentry in various corners of the house.

Address: 4211 Fee Fee Road
Website: www.museumsusa.org/museums/
    info/1164434
Activity: A, S, E

Caledonia Caledonia Wine Cottage

This stage stop inn was erected in 1824 by Jacob Fischer. The place featured a three-story main house and a slave house out back. Tunnels connected the two places, as well as provided a route for the slaves to enter the fields for work. During the Civil War, the wounded from the battle at Pilot's Knob were brought to the cottage for treatment. The Union soldiers took command of the inn and kept "contagious" prisoners locked in the attic. The Confederate troops were treated along with the troops from the North, but when they got better they were moved into the basement, which became a makeshift dungeon of sorts. If you stay at this mini-B&B (they have two rooms you can rent on the third floor) or if you just visit for wine and food (they get rave reviews for their fine cuisine), pay attention to your surroundings. Almost every area has had paranormal activity, to include shadowy apparitions, voices (usually of an old woman), and objects that seem to move by themselves (such as the door that leads to the slave house).

Address: 128 South State Highway 21
Website: www.caledoniawinecottage.com
Activity: S, E, T

Carthage Grand Avenue Bed and Breakfast

This Victorian mansion was built by S. H. Houser in the early 1900s—though he wouldn't stay in the home for long. After declaring bankruptcy, the house was sold to Albert and Belle Carmean and they would reside in the place along with their son, Carl. In 1933, Albert passed away in the house, and they held his funeral right there on the site. If you visit Grand Avenue today, you will want to check out their murder mystery dinners (locals say they are a blast) and rent one of the four unique rooms on the property. The chances of encountering a spirit is equal in each of the rooms—mostly because the ghost of old Albert is usually encountered in the common areas. You will know he's around when you smell the phantom scent of cigar smoke (a habit that he was known for).

Address: 1615 Grand Avenue
Website: www.grand-avenue.com
Activity: E, N

Carthage Kendrick Place

This area of Carthage was once known as Kendrick Town, and it was named for the same person that the house is principally known, William Kendrick. Kendrick purchased the still-new home in the 1850s from the original owners, the Rankin family. The home currently belongs to a preservation organization called Victorian Carthage, Inc., and they offer tours of the property as well as make the place available for private events. During the Civil War, the town of Carthage was torched—and most of the pre-war buildings and houses were burned to the ground. The Kendrick house was briefly used as a makeshift headquarters as troops secured the area. This is why folks witness a Confederate soldier walking the grounds. But he is not alone—there is also a female spirit in the place that most believe to be a member of one of the many families who lived and died in the home over the years. Activity at this location includes voices, misty apparitions, and the usual bangs/knocks of a haunted house.

Address: 131 Garrison Street
Website: www.kendrickplace.com
Activity: A, M, E

Columbia Jack's Gourmet Restaurant

The location of this well-known eatery has had an infamous reputation over the years. During the 1920s, it was known as a rowdy drinking hall that featured as many fights as it did beers. As with most establishments of this sort, it didn't take long for the local university students to find out about it, so it quickly turned into a favorite hangout after a Missouri Tigers home game. These days, though, Jack's is known for legendary steaks and gourmet fare—and the spirit of a young girl. She is said to be Sarah Haden, a young woman who died in the premises long before the bar business moved in (some place her as far back as the late 1800s). Others say the ghost is the product of the rough-and-tumble atmosphere that existed when "Jack's Coronado Inn" was reputedly a gangster hangout. Either

way, stop in for a great meal and the chance to see the lovely Sarah.

Address: 1903 Business Loop 70 East
Website: www.jacksgourmetrestaurant.com
Activity: A

Columbia The Tiger

This hotel opened in 1928 with high hopes of serving the public and providing reliable accommodations for area travelers. Unfortunately for them, the Great Depression rocked the country and poor business forced the property to convert into a flop house that provided cheap lodgings for folks who were down and out. It's said that, at its worst, the basement was parceled into small areas that only had room for a single bed and sink. During these harsh times, quite a few people passed away in the place from malnutrition and poor health—and at least one of these people has stayed on beyond the grave! Employees and guests of the Tiger have been reporting strange footsteps, voices, and cold spots in the hotel for decades. Check in with management there for current sighting reports before choosing your room.

Address: 23 South 8th Street
Website: www.thetigerhotel.com
Activity: E, C

Excelsior Springs The Elms Resort & Spa

The Elms is Missouri's own "healing waters" story. Much like other hotels that marketed their natural spring water for its curative properties, this resort began as a wooden inn parked alongside the springs. Unfortunately, the close proximity of water did nothing to keep the place from burning to the ground in 1898. So they built again and finished the new hotel in 1909—and fire revisited them and burned this version as well. The third incarnation of the hotel opened in 1912 and has managed to stay flame-free for almost a century. And though neither fire claimed any fatalities, the Elms is reputedly haunted by two ghosts. The first is said to be a male gambler from the 1940s who's often seen and heard around the lap pool. The second is a spectral maid said to be witnessed in a 1920's uniform wandering the halls and rooms on the third floor.

Address: 401 Regent Street
Website: www.elmsresort.com
Activity: A, E

Hannibal Garth Woodside Mansion

This historic bed and breakfast (circa 1871) has played host to at least one significant Missourian over the years: Samuel Clemens (a.k.a. Mark Twain). John and Helen Garth grew up with Clemens, and when they returned to live in Hannibal after a long hiatus, they corresponded with him regularly. Clemens would also send them copies of his new books, as well as stay with them while in Hannibal. But did he love them and the place enough to visit in the afterlife? Some locals believe so. Visitors to the house have reported smelling the spectral scent of a pipe in the room named for Clemens, as well as witnessing strange orbs of light. Just remember that this B&B has a main house, a secondary house, and cottages—you will want to stay in the main house.

Address: 11069 New London Road
Website: www.garthmansion.com
Activity: N, O

Hannibal LulaBelle's Restaurant & Bed & Breakfast

Back in the 1800s, the appearance of a new town brothel was reason for great celebration, so when Hannibal finally got their "place of ill repute" in the early 1900s, they were slightly behind the curve. It wasn't long, though, before this particular bordello earned a strong reputation for its women and fun—especially for the madam/owner, Sarah Smith. The place thrived on gambling, drinking, and prostitution all the way into the 1950s, when it was finally be-

sieged by local clergy and forced to close. Staying at LulaBelle's is like getting four places in one—there's the restaurant and three separate B&Bs scattered among three buildings. You will want to stay in the actual LulaBelle's, though. The rooms with the most activity include the Jaded Jewel, Angel of Delight, and the Farmer's Daughter. Activity in these areas include disembodied voices, heavy footsteps, items moving on their own, and the feeling of being touched by somebody within the rooms!

Address: 111 Bird Street
Website: www.lulabelles.com
Activity: E, T, S

Hermann Wine Valley Inn

Stationed in two historic structures (the Begemann and Kimmel buildings) this must-visit site in Hermann features a gift shop that sells area wines (an industry that has gained Hermann no small amount of notoriety in the last few decades). There are rooms located in both buildings, but if you want to splash in some paranormal fun during your visit to Missouri's wine country, you will want lodgings in the Begemann (which has more rooms to choose from anyway). So who haunts the place? Paranormal investigators who have stayed in the inn say there is a male spirit—possibly a past owner—who walks the halls. He makes himself known by charging the air with electricity, appearing as a shadowy apparition, and whispering from dark corners of the rooms.

Address: 403 Market Street
Website: www.wine-valley-inn.com
Activity: S, E

Independence 1859 Jail, Marshal's Home & Museum

This limestone jail was constructed during a massive buildup of animosity between those who supported the southern states and pro-abolitionists who were pouring into Missouri on their way to Kansas. Violence and guerilla warfare had already broken out between the two states, and this prison held those who opposed the pro-Union marshals who tried to keep the peace. When Jackson County became "depopulated" by state order (due to rising tensions along the Missouri/Kansas border), the area became known for its bloody clashes. At least three officers were killed on the property, including a marshal who was gunned down by Quantrill's Raiders. Touring the jail will allow you to experience its history—as well as (hopefully) experience the residual haunt left behind by all this tragedy. Employees and guests have heard strange voices in the cells, as well as seen misty apparitions and dark shadow people.

Address: 217 North Main Street
Website: www.jchs.org/jail/museum
Activity: A, M, S, E

Independence Vaile Mansion

This "wedding cake" styled Victorian home was the residence of Colonel Harvey Vaile, an Independence native that made his fortune through mail sales. The place was finished in 1881, and business thrived for Vaile until allegations of mail fraud were made. Mrs. Sylvia Vaile, despondent about impending criminal actions against her husband, decided to take her own life by overdosing on morphine. Later, Harvey was cleared of all wrongdoing, but not before it cost him his wife. When Vaile died, the home became an inn, then an asylum, and then insolvent and unused. The mansion is in the process of restoration today and can be toured (check the hours and dates for tours on their website). While you check out the architecture of the place, keep an eye out for poor Sylvia. Over the years, locals have reported seeing her spectral image peering from windows, as well as walking the halls (especially in the upstairs area).

Address: 1500 North Liberty Street
Website: www.vailemansion.org
Activity: A

Ironton The Parlor Bed & Breakfast

This Victorian home was built by Ironton native Charles J. Tual in 1908, and the place remained in his possession for many years until he passed away. At that point, the home had several owners (and even functioned briefly as a funeral home). One of the current residents, Jeannette Schrum, had a grandmother who worked on the property as a maid during the 1930s. Schrum's familiarity with the home resulted in her purchasing the place and transforming it into a themed B&B in 2000. It's themed because the business openly promotes the fact that it is haunted. Visitors, as well as the owners, have witnessed a female apparition on the property—a woman believed to be Jeannette's grandmother. She has been seen in the downstairs parlor/kitchen, as well as in the upstairs Waterfall Room. Other activity includes the sounds of a woman's voice and objects that are manipulated.

Address: 203 South Knob Street
Website: www.theparlorbandb.com
Activity: A, E, T

Jefferson City Governor Thomas Fletcher House

The haunting of this historic Missouri site (built circa 1851) has been documented by several prominent governors and has been related to the press by such people as Jean Carnahan (one-time first lady of the state) on the show *If These Walls Could Talk.* The spirit of a little girl is thought to haunt the upper floors of the mansion, and she has been seen and heard there for almost a hundred years. She's said to be the daughter of Governor Crittenden who withstood threats from the infamous James gang to fight state crime. The governor was so concerned for his family that Carrie (the daughter) was constantly guarded. Her apparition has been witnessed so many times on the site that a statue was erected of her in front of the place (check out the fountain there).

Address: 401 Elm Street
Website: www.jeffcomo.org
Activity: A, E

Joplin Prosperity School Bed and Breakfast

The origin of this B&B dates back to 1907 when the city of Prosperity needed a school to service the area—and it did so all the way up until 1962. The building then sat empty for many years until the current owners opened up accommodations as a B&B in 2002. It seems that visitors started witnessing paranormal events in the building almost from day one. This spurred the owners to keep a journal of different eyewitness accounts in the place—as well as to host some of the biggest names in the paranormal field (including Jason and Grant of TAPS, John Zaffis, and Chris Moon). Expect to encounter dark, shadow apparitions scooting about the place, as well as the apparition of a young girl (check out the photo here in this book), and the voices of children.

Address: 4788 County Road 200
Website: www.prosperitybandb.com
Activity: A, S, E

Kansas City Alexander Major's Historic House & Museum

Alexander Major was instrumental in creating the early economy of Kansas City. He operated a freight service that delivered goods to outposts west of the city, as well as organized the now-famous Pony Express. His home in K.C. dates back to 1856 and is now located in a city park. It underwent a major renovation in 1984—an event that's said to have kicked up the paranormal activity there—and is now open for public tours. On-site employees pretty much wave away any ideas about the place being haunted, but locals insist they know better. During the mid-1900s, a woman by the name of Louisa Johnston lived on the property, and it's reported that she died there while trying to restore the house to its earlier glory. It is her spirit that neighbors of the park have reported seeing within the home.

Address: 8201 State Line Road
Website: www.visitkc.com
Activity: A

Kansas City Hotel Savoy

This historic hotel was constructed by the Arbuckle brothers (famed for their coffee at the time) in 1888 and is decorated with Art Deco and Art Nouveau touches that still speak of the days when the Savoy was the benchmark of local elegance. For locals, though, the place is more known for the award-winning Savoy Grill located on the property—and for the ghost stories that seem to circulate about this hotel. These tales started when the hotel had some down years after World War II. The place was used as cheap apartments, and people staying there would report the apparition of a woman walking the halls. Since the hotel started operating as such again (and underwent major renovations) the sightings have increased. An employee who was staying in Room 505 reported a spirit that kept moving things in his room, as well as the sounds of a female voice. It's thought the ghost is Betsy Ward, a woman who died in this room many years ago. Other hot spots include the seventh floor and the basement.

Address: 9th Street and Central Avenue
Website: www.savoyhotel.net
Activity: A, E, T

Kearney Jesse James Farm

What more can be said concerning the infamous James gang—and, specifically, Jesse James himself? His antics through the years have been labeled everything from atrocious all the way up to heroic. This farm was where Jesse and Frank grew up, along with a stepbrother named Archie, who was killed there when a Pinkerton detective threw a small bomb inside (thinking Jesse was there). The haunting of this area seems to differ between what happens inside (viewed by the staff there) and what happens outside (that local witnesses report). Inside, the activity seems to be of a mild nature and includes cold spots and high EMF readings (blamed for making folks there feel like they are being watched). But outside, people report the usual sights and sounds associated with a strong residual haunt: phantom guns shot, horses, and voices are heard emanating from the empty yard.

Address: 21216 James Farm Road
Website: www.jessejames.org
Activity: E, R

Lee's Summit Longview Mansion

When this massive estate was first built, it was the largest construction project in the history of the United States. It was finished in 1914 and locals declared the place to be "the world's most beautiful farm." Owner and millionaire Robert A. Long included 51 buildings on this property, along with a full racetrack for horses, a school, and a church. At its peak, over 200 people were living and working on this farm! Now that the place is open for private and public events (as well as tours), sightings of a female apparition have become one of the main attractions. It's believed that the woman is Lula Combs, a relative who died in the home after a lengthy coma. In addition to the actual appearance of her specter, witnesses have reported hearing her voice, finding the bed in her old bedroom rumpled, and smelling her perfume on occasion.

Address: 3361 Southwest Longview Road
Website: www.longviewmansion.com
Activity: A, E, T, N

Lexington The Oliver Anderson House

When prosperous slave owners began relocating into Missouri, it was not uncommon for massive mansions to start springing up. Such is the case with this house built by Oliver Anderson in 1853. Little did the Anderson family know, the area around the home (and, indeed, all of Lexington itself) would become the location of a battle during the impending Civil War. Union soldiers would occupy the city, evict the Anderson family (who would eventually end up in Kentucky), and use the house as a makeshift hospital for their own wounded soldiers. Like many sites associated with the Civil War, the home is now considered haunted. Spectral soldiers are said to be seen on the front steps (the location where three southern prisoners were killed), and the sounds of the wounded are heard from within the house.

Address: 1101 Delaware Street
Website: http://www.mostateparks.com/
     lexington/andhouse
Activity: A, E, R

New Franklin Rivercene Bed & Breakfast

This massive estate was built by riverboat captain Joseph Kinney in 1869. He owned a ferry service that would transport people and cargo between Montana and New Orleans, and when he built this Second Empire masterpiece, it was so opulent that the Missouri governor's mansion was modeled after it. Today, the place is an area favorite for overnight accommodations and a killer breakfast. If you decide to visit, keep an eye out for a member of the Kinney family who's still around: Noble Kinney. According to several sources, Noble died at the young age of 26 after tumbling down the grand staircase in the home. Over the years, family members—as well as B&B guests—have bumped into Noble on occasion.

Address: 127 County Road 463
Website: www.rivercene.com
Activity: A, T

New Haven Boondocker Inn

Though this place may have once been an inn—or even a restaurant—it is now a rental facility for events. It's also a prime place for budding paranormal investigators to train (especially if you have a group that can chip in toward the rental). The haunting at this location became well known in the area when a local paranormal group published findings that claimed there were four spirits in the building: a man wearing boots, a young girl, a boy (who was heard screaming), and a woman (who was said to have been witnessed walking the place in a flowered shirt). Who are these people haunting the place? No information regarding this was released—or, for that matter, even researched. So if you want a "no questions asked" kind of investigation, you may want to consider renting the Boondocker.

Address: 9487 Highway 100
Website: www.boondockerinn.com
Activity: A, E, C, S

Potosi Sweet Memories Sandwich & Ice Cream Shop

In addition to the ice cream, it's said that the spirit of this home-turned-eatery is also quite sweet. The ghost is allegedly the wife of a previous owner named Harriet Van Allen. She lived there with her husband, Garrett Van Allen, in the 1870s and passed away in the home. Visitors to the historic house (it was built in the mid-1800s) have reported numerous instances of objects on the tables, as well as in the kitchen, moving by themselves. When the activity gets going, previous owners have even reported seeing the apparition of Harriet appear in the dining room, as well as hearing her voice in the same area.

Address: 105 West Breton Street
Website: www.sweetmemoriesshop.com
Activity: A, E, T

Sedalia Hotel Bothwell

There are many reasons to visit this jazz-era hotel (circa 1927), including the Ivory Grille and Lounge, the Ragtime Store where you can buy hits of the time, and rooms that take folks back to the days of flappers and swing music. For the paranormal traveler, the Bothwell offers one more attraction—an entire floor of haunted rooms! It's said that the third floor of this hotel is one massive hot spot. Numerous guests have reported hearing voices, seeing apparitions, and finding items missing in their rooms during the night. Though none of the experiences have been of a "scary" nature, the constant activity has created quite a stir among the hotel staff, who now approach the third floor with a certain amount of caution. You may want to check in with them prior to selecting your accommodations—they probably know more about the events happening there and should be able to direct you to the most active rooms.

Address: 103 East 4th Street
Website: www.hotelbothwell.com
Activity: A, E, T, S

Springfield Gillioz Theatre

When this theatre opened in 1926, the crowd waiting outside was five times its capacity! The place became an instant sensation and folks traveling along the newly created Route 66 would often kick off their journey with a "talking picture" show. The theatre became so well known that Clark Gable personally sent them a postcard in 1934 for screening his film *It Happened One Night.* By the 1970s, though, the place was in a whole different state—the furnishings had fallen into disrepair and crowds were venturing elsewhere for their entertainment. Today, with new owners and a new renovation, the theatre and has once again opened to much local fanfare. But, in addition to the plays now showing there, the place is also attracting folks who want to catch a glimpse of a ghost. Sightings of a spectral boy began in the 1960s and is said to still occur today. Your best chance of an encounter is supposed to be the restroom area, so drink lots of liquid prior to your visit!

Address: 325 Park Central East
Website: www.gillioz.org
Activity: A

Springfield Pythian Castle

This grand building began as an orphanage that was founded and operated by the Knights of Pythias in 1913. During World War II, the U.S. government acquired the property for use as a veteran's hospital and a place for entertaining troops, until it was eventually sold as surplus in 1993. The castle gained notoriety when it appeared in a movie called *Children of the Grave* and evidence was uncovered that seemed to suggest the grounds are haunted by the hostile spirit of a male from the orphanage. These days, the castle is used for events—and has even hosted ghost tours—so you may have to rent the place to get access to it. If you have the opportunity to explore this castle, though, pay attention to the area where the orphanage offices once were. Also check out the access tunnels in the basement, which is where witnesses saw a large, black apparition approach them.

Address: 1451 East Pythian Street
Website: www.pythiancastle.com
Activity: A, S, E, T

Springfield University Plaza Hotel

Sometimes a place is haunted simply because of where it's located. Such is the case with the Plaza. Before the Civil War, it's said that the area the hotel now occupies was once a plantation house. When the area came under conflict, the man of the house was killed and the property was razed by Union soldiers. It would be many years later before the hotel would be built, but apparently the ghost of the "Colonel" stuck around and waited. Though the hotel doesn't advertise their resident spirit, local stories and sightings have been happening enough to keep the haunted reputation alive and well. Stocked with great on-site amenities (like two pools, a sundeck, and a sauna), this place makes for a great investigation. Just keep an eye out for the Colonel in his favorite spots: the ballroom and the rear hallways of the hotel.

Address: 333 South John Q. Hammons Parkway
Website: www.upspringfield.com
Activity: A

Springfield Walnut Street Inn

This inn is actually three locations in one: the main house where you can stay in one of six rooms, a carriage house (with four rooms), and a cottage with two additional rooms. If you want to experience the haunting of this inn, you will want to stay in the main house, though. It's reported that the Rosen Room of the house is haunted by the spirit of an elderly lady. She has been seen several times in this room, as well as in the hallways there. Before becoming an inn in 1987, the place, which dates back to the 1890s, was known as the McCann-Jewell house. Over the years, several prominent area families lived in the home, including the Dennis, the Jewell, and the Rosen families. It's thought that the spirit is probably a remnant left behind by one of these residents.

Address: 900 East Walnut
Website: www.walnutstreetinn.com
Activity: A, E

St. Charles Little Hills Winery Restaurant

Located in the heart of the historic Main Street area of St. Charles, this restaurant is a rather modern affair in a very old town! Perhaps the haunting of this location has more to do with the history of the town itself (early settlers of the area date back to 1769), rather than the restaurant. Either way, dozens of witnesses have confessed to seeing the strange sight of a male and female apparition dressed in period clothing walking about the place. When things go missing (or are simply moved without explanation), the spirits are usually blamed. Grab a meal at this restaurant (and if you are able, have a glass of their wine that's made not too far away) and check in with the servers for more current info regarding the spirits.

Address: 501 South Main Street
Website: www.littlehillswinery.com
Activity: A, T

St. Charles Mother-in-Law House Restaurant

This home has a unique and curious history. In 1866, Francis Kremer decided he would build his house in a unique style: He would put his family on one side of the property, and then he would build a separate, second half of the house for his mother-in-law. Both sides were made to be exactly the same so nobody would be upset, and both sides were lived in by the Kremer family for several generations. The restaurant that occupies the place today is well known for its great location (in the historic section of St. Charles) and its great mix of steaks and seafood. Of course, it's also known for the resident ghost. The spirit is said to walk the northern part of the house—the section that the mother-in-law lived in—so it's thought that she is probably the person haunting the restaurant. The activity here usually includes glasses and utensils moving, as well as the sounds of footsteps.

Address: 500 South Main Street
Website: www.motherinlawhouse.com
Activity: E, T

St. Genevieve La Maison de Guibourd-Valle

This early Missouri home dates back to 1806 and features a unique form of early architecture known as *poteaux sur-sol,* or "post on sill," style. It served as a home for early settler Jacques Guibourd, and then for the Valle family, all the way up until 1971 when Anne Valle passed away. At that point, the home became a living museum that still displays many of the Valle family antiques. Ghost stories concerning this home started when a resident, Jules Valle, saw a unique sight there in 1939: He reported seeing three men materialize in front him within the house—but only from the waist up! He said they were dressed in old "Spaniard" clothing and that they paid him no attention whatsoever. During the years since this initial sighting, many others have stepped forth to state seeing the exact same residual activity.

Address: 4th Street and Merchant Streets
Website: www.stegenevievemissouri.com/
  guibourdvallehouse
Activity: R, A

St. Genevieve Main Street Inn B&B

This bed and breakfast has been serving up great food and wonderful accommodations for the local populace since 1882. Of course, it did this under the original name of the Meyer Hotel before undergoing a major renovation and a name change a century later. The spirit that now walks the grounds here is said to be a man who died in the hotel during the late 1890s. He's known for generally making a lot of noise on the top floor and making a nuisance of himself during the wee hours. Locals will tell you that the inn's resident ghost is completely harmless and simply wants to be noticed. Go there and maybe you'll notice him as well...

Address: 221 North Main Street
Website: www.mainstreetinnbb.com
Activity: E

St. Joseph Glore Psychiatric Museum

In the mid-1800s, the state of Missouri opened a series of insane asylums to service those with mental health conditions in various corners of the state. The Glore Museum occupies the halls of "State Lunatic Asylum No. 2." The founder of the museum, George Glore, spent more than 40 years working with the mentally ill in Missouri and wanted the museum to stand as a testament to the history of mental health care. Though the place does feature many innovations of psychiatry over the years, there are also some of the horrors of past "treatments" on display. In addition to these exhibitions, it's said you can experience some of the paranormal here. Since many asylum patients spent their entire lives within the walls (and probably were even interred in the morgue there), it seems only natural that they would stay in the place they know so well. Activity on the grounds includes apparitions (sometimes seen as shadow shapes), voices, and intense cold spots.

Address: 3406 Frederick Avenue
Website: www.stjosephmuseum.org
Activity: A, S, E, C

St. Louis Bissell Mansion Restaurant & Murder Mystery Dinner Theatre

Captain Lewis Bissell (commissioned by President Thomas Jefferson) moved to St. Louis after serving in the War of 1812 and helping found the city of Omaha, Nebraska. His land overlooking the Mississippi River was known to passersby on riverboats as Bissell's Point, and the actual mansion was added in the 1820s. In addition to being one of the area's most historic homes, the place is known locally for its murder-mystery dinner productions—and, of course, for the haunting of the house. Though it's not certain, most believe the male spirit who resides there is none other than the Captain himself. He has been witnessed inside and outside the home—though the inside appearances are not as common as those of the female apparition seen there! She has been witnessed on the stairs many times (wearing a long dress) and is thought to be a past resident as well.

Address: 4426 Randall Place
Website: www.bissellmansiontheatre.com
Activity: A, E, T

St. Louis Jefferson Barracks

This sprawling complex offers days of historical and paranormal fun. It was the country's first "Infantry School of Practice" and dates back to 1826, when it was built to supplement the area arsenal. It was a key location during the

Black Hawk War, as well as the later Civil War. The national cemetery in the complex is a mute testament to just how many lives have died in area battles. For the haunted traveler, there are several hot spots for you to explore. Start with the museum on the grounds, which once was used as a powder magazine/storage facility and was also where soldiers during the WWII era witnessed a ghost with a bullet hole in his head roaming the area. The second place to visit is the veteran's hospital—the area in and around this building has been the stomping grounds for a Civil War–era soldier who has even spoken to people lucky enough to have spotted him.

Address: 251 County Road 63125
Website: www.stlouisco.com/parks/j-b
Activity: A, E

St. Louis The Lehmann House Bed & Breakfast

Making the journey to Lafayette Square in St. Louis is like taking a trip back in time—a trip that's filled with the antique elegance of the old city and the history of area founders. This B&B began as a home for Edward S. Rowse in the 1860s, but is more known for later residents Frederick and Nora Lehmann. Frederick was a prominent lawyer in his day, and he maintained this Romanesque Revival home for many years until his death. After a massive renovation in the 1990s, the Lehmann House is now open for business as a B&B. Discussions concerning its ghosts are quite common, so feel free to broach the subject with the current owner. She will point out the hot spots, including the dining room where Mr. Rowse passed away many years ago. Activity here includes dark shadows, voices, and the sounds of things moving/banging.

Address: 10 Benton Place
Website: www.lehmannhouse.com
Activity: S, E, T

St. Louis The Lemp Mansion Restaurant & Inn

The haunting of this mansion has been national news since *Life* magazine published an article about the ghosts there in 1980. During the years the Lemp family (rich beyond measure due to a lucrative beer brewing business) resided in the house, there were three suicides. Later, the home was operated as a boarding house for the poor, and tales of ghostly apparitions began to circulate. Today, the property has been completely renovated by the Pointer family and it has a top-notch restaurant and bar right in the mansion. Guests (as well as employees) continue to experience the paranormal in this house, including apparitions, voices, and objects that seem to move on their own. There have been many notable photographs of spirits in this house as well (take a look at the photo I took during a brief visit to the house). Consider staying in the top floor of the house if you visit—dark rumors state a boy died in this area (dubbed "Zeke" by paranormal researchers) and that this area is extremely active.

Address: 3322 DeMenil Place
Website: www.lempmansion.com
Activity: A, E, T, C, S

West Plains The Avenue Theatre

This Art Deco landmark was opened in the 1950s to screen movies to the local population. To supplement the income of the theatre, they also started featuring musical acts (much to the enjoyment of the people of West Plains). But all of this wasn't enough; by the 1980s, the business was struggling to the point that they closed the theatre altogether. A local organization (Arts on the Avenue) then decided the place might be great for plays, so the doors opened once again in 1990 to a production of *The Mousetrap*. With over a hundred plays now under their belt, it only seems natural that actors working in the building would start reporting that the building is haunted (most theatres are you know ...). Activity in this theatre includes the sounds of a baby crying (heard in the upper seating areas), missing props (thought to be taken or hidden by the spirit there), and strange flickers of light when the place is dark.

Address: 307 Washington Avenue
Website: www.theavenuetheatre.com
Activity: O, E, T

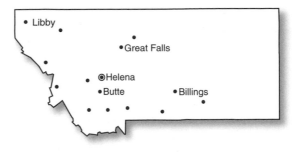

MONTANA

Alberton Ghost Rails Inn

This site was constructed in 1909 as a housing area for workers along the Milwaukee Railroad—and when the same company pulled up stakes and left the area, the entire city of Alberton basically shut down. Today, this nine-room guesthouse takes folks back to the time of railroad travel and carriage rides—and the haunting of this inn harkens back to a previous owner, Bertha Brash. Bertha passed away in the building while doing her daily cleaning routine. Since then, people who stay in Room 5 of this inn have experienced an apparition who likes to touch them while they sleep (or lounge on the bed). There have even been reports of the ghost sitting on the bed with them—sometimes pinning their

legs momentarily. Other sightings of Bertha have taken place in Room 8 and in the downstairs kitchen.

Address: 702 Railroad Avenue
Website: www.ghostrailsinn.com
Activity: E, T

Billings Moss Mansion

This mansion-turned-museum was built entirely of red sandstone in 1903 and was the home of Preston Boyd Moss and family. It was designed by famed New York architect Henry Janeway (creator of such places as the original Waldorf Astoria), and it now displays many fine antiques from the early twentieth century. During the years the Moss family lived in the estate (all the way until 1984), there were several family deaths on the premises, including Preston himself. Ghostly sightings became news in the area when the final Moss resident of the house, Melville, was on his death bed. A nurse that was taking care of him reported walking into Melville's bedroom and seeing the apparition of young girl standing by the bed. Since then, sightings of the girl have happened on and off over the years—

as well as glimpses of a male apparition on the stairs (thought to be Preston).

Address: 914 Division Street
Website: www.mossmansion.com
Activity: A, E

Billings Parmly Billings Library

This library is the first to have served this area—as well as the entirety of Yellowstone County, Montana. It was donated to the city in 1901 by the Billings family in honor of Parmly Billings. Parmly was the son of the city's founder, Frederick Billings. Today, the place is quite modern and offers a phenomenal collection of books for the local populace. But not everyone travels to this library for books. There are a couple resident spirits in the building. Witnesses say the apparition of a man in work clothes and boots has been seen walking the second floor and that a female ghost is often glimpsed in the basement. Both spirits seem to do their own thing and ignore those who see them, so it sounds like a typical residual haunt. But who are they? This might take some research. Good thing you're at a library! Interestingly, this is the newest building to house the library; the original building is also considered haunted as well (read the next entry).

Address: 510 North Broadway
Website: http://ci.billings.mt.us/
Activity: A, R

Billings Western Heritage Center

This location was the original site of the Parmly Billings Library (it's written right on the front of the building) that was built in 1901. It's a museum these days that features the rich heritage of the area, as well as numerous traveling exhibits. The WHC is a Smithsonian Institute affiliate, so the standard is set extremely high for this facility. So when a place like this states it is haunted, people tend to listen! Tales of the haunting there include finding a child's footprints in the attic area, as well as seeing the apparition of an elderly gentleman in the basement. The WHC holds "haunted events" around Halloween and has even been investigated by paranormal groups in the past. Check their online calendar for their on-site events, as well as the museum's hours.

Address: 2822 Montana Avenue
Website: www.ywhc.org
Activity: A, T, E

Butte Silver Bow County Courthouse

This ornate public building was built in the Beaux Arts style and rivaled the cost of the state Capitol when it was constructed in 1912. The haunting that occurs here is thought to be a product of the previous building (a courthouse), as well as a prisoner who was hanged on the property by the name of Miles Fuller. When Fuller was hung on a "portable gallows" that the prison would bring out for events like this, he was immediately taken to be buried. Local legend states that a strange burst of thunder occurred as they were putting the coffin into the ground. Was this a grim foretelling of events to come? Must have been—it's Fuller's apparition that's often seen walking the grounds in and around the courthouse. Other activity experienced on the property includes cold spots, dark shadow shapes seen in the hallways, and doors that seem to open and close by themselves.

Address: 155 West Granite Street
Website: www.butteamerica.com
Activity: A, T, C

Butte The World Museum of Mining

With a century of mining under its belt, it's no wonder the city of Butte would feature a museum dedicated to the trade. The place is located on the Orphan Girl Mine yard and it features numerous exhibits like "Hell Roarin' Gulch." The claim this mine is located on dates back to 1875, and like most mines, it suffered many tragedies and losses over the years, including cave-ins and work-related accidents. Perhaps it's because of these events that the place is now inhabited by the spirits of the dead. Most paranormal experiences take place in and around the actual mine shaft and usually include voices and pale apparitions of men in turn-of-the-century attire. Of course, it's also possible that spirits have returned to the area because of the great lengths the museum has gone to while re-creating an authentic-looking mining town.

Address: 155 Museum Way
Website: www.miningmuseum.org
Activity: A, E

Crow Agency Little Bighorn Battlefield

On June 25, 1876, Lt. Col. George A. Custer and approximately 263 soldiers found themselves fighting to the death against thousands of Sioux and Cheyenne Indians. Army scouts warned Custer that their army had been spotted, but he refused to change his tactics and led the entire unit to total destruction. If you visit Crow Agency, you can see the markers where soldiers lost their lives, as well as visit the memorial there. The entire area is, according to local paranormal experts, part of a massive residual haunting that includes the sounds of battles and cries of the wounded. Apparitions of Native Americans (and soldiers) have been seen as well. The nearby 1894 stone house (used by cemetery caretakers in the early 1900s), in addition to the visitor's center, has also reported

activity over the years that includes apparitions and voices.

Address: Interstate 90 at Junction 212
Website: www.nps.gov/libi/
Activity: A, R, E

Deer Lodge Old Montana Prison Museum

This territorial prison began operations in 1871 and it provided a place for imprisoning criminals all the way until 1978. After closing, the Powell County Museum & Arts Foundation took over the complex (with a 99-year lease no less), and they now host tours of the site for the general public. In addition to touring the yard and the old cells, you can see exhibits of makeshift prison weapons, prisoner art work, and objects that tell the story of the prison guards who worked at this location. Like most old prisons, there were questionable "rehabilitation" techniques used there—such as "the hole," where prisoners would be isolated in a dank, dark area. The hole is thought to be one of the catalysts of the haunted activity there (along with general depression and misery). Hot spots on the property include the aforementioned hole, the area where prisoners were hanged, and the cells themselves.

Address: 1106 Main Street
Website: www.pcmaf.org
Activity: A, S, E, C, T

Dillon Bannack State Park/Meade Hotel

Bannack was founded almost overnight in 1862 when a frontiersman named John White discovered gold in the area. By 1864, Bannack was named the territorial capital of Montana. Mining continued in this area into the 1950s before the gold started running out. At that point, the town literally shut down and the state of Montana turned the entire area into a state park. The Meade Hotel is a remnant left behind that was built in 1875 to serve as a courthouse there. In 1890, it was converted into a hotel to handle the influx of profiteers. Today it stands alone as a landmark in the park. Talk to the park rangers about seeing the inside of the place—it was folks like them (workers at the park) who first started telling of the ghostly activity here. Sights of shadowy apparitions, as well as the strange sounds of disembodied voices and music, have been witnessed here for over 40 years.

Address: Bannack Bench Road off Highway 278
Website: www.bannack.org
Activity: A, S, E

Ft. Benton Grand Union Hotel

This circa 1882 hotel gained a new lease on life when it was carefully restored by the joint efforts of the National Trust for Historic Preservation, the U.S. Parks Department, and the Montana State Historic Preservation Office. The Grand is actually seven years older than the state of Montana and opened to great fanfare in the city of Fort Benton. The hotel would provide upscale accommodations for travelers journeying up the Missouri River by steamboat and stay in operation until the 1980s. After closing briefly, the business reopened with its new makeover in 1999, and it wasn't long before guests to the new rendition of the hotel began reporting strange glimpses of "see-through" men, hearing the sounds of guttural voices, and experiencing a strange vibe in certain areas. Local investigators visited the Grand and declared the hotel to be, indeed, haunted. Keep an eye out in the lobby, as well as the hallways for your own ghostly vision.

Address: 1 Grand Union Square
Website: www.grandunionhotel.com
Activity: A, E

Great Falls Beacon Icehouse

This place is like most bars/nightclubs in the country: they offer drink specials, provide a place for locals to cut loose, and feature live music on the weekends. But unlike other venues, the Beacon is also known by locals to be haunted. Rumors about ghosts began when employees started telling of doors shutting by themselves, lights turning themselves on, and a basement that universally gives everyone the creeps. The place was investigated by a local paranormal team, but the results were inconclusive. Meanwhile, the reports continue. If you decide to catch a drink or a show at the Beacon, you may want to hang around close to the bathroom. This seems to be the area with the most activity.

Address: 1349 13th Street Southwest
Website: www.beaconicehouse.com
Activity: T

Hamilton Daly Mansion

This house is the result of three massive renovation jobs that were conducted in 1889, 1897, and 1910—all ordered by the same owner, Marcus Daly. Unfortunately, he died before the third incarnation was finished, which turned the Victorian-style home into a Georgian Revival mansion. And as hard as it is to believe, this glorious estate was abandoned after the last member of the Daly family (Margaret Daly) passed away in 1941. A trust would take over the property in 1986, and the place now hosts weddings, events, and tours. Haunted tales concerning the house began when employees reported that a painting (called "Musicale") was found mysteriously moved during the night. They would put the painting back where they had hung it, only to repeatedly find it moved again in the morning. It wasn't long before other events started happening as well—including the phantom scent of roses and sightings of a pale female apparition in the house. Most believe the spirit is that of Margaret (called "Mrs. Daly" by the workers there) and that the best place to encounter her is around her old bedroom and the painting she seems to enjoy so much.

Address: 251 Eastside Highway
Website: www.dalymansion.org
Activity: A, T, N

Helena Carroll College

This Catholic institution was established in 1910 as the Mount St. Charles College, and it currently has a yearly enrollment of approximately 1,400 students. The school was renamed in honor of Bishop Carroll, who ran the place during World War I and was instrumental in the success of the college. Today, there are two separate hauntings on this campus: St. Charles Hall and St. Albert's Hall. The former is known for the apparition and phantom bloodstains of a student who died on the fourth floor (reputedly by committing suicide). St. Albert's is supposed to be the place that an apparition of a nun is often seen on the top floor. She is thought to be a member of the convent that once resided on the campus and to have died of natural illness.

Address: 1601 North Benton Avenue
Website: www.carroll.edu
Activity: A

Helena Grandstreet Theatre

This former Unitarian church was built in 1901 and it has one of the state's most unique ghost stories. When a local woman by the name of Clara Bicknell Hodgin passed away in 1905, her family donated an expensive Tiffany window to the church she loved so much, and it was promptly installed on the property. Later, in 1933, the city would end up using the church as a temporary library as they repaired the town's library (it was damaged during an earthquake). The window was removed and stored when the temporary library left the building and the church sat unused for some time. When Broadstreet Productions took over in 1976 and created the Grandstreet Theatre, the Tiffany window was reinstalled—and strange things suddenly began

to happen. People on the property began to hear voices, see lights turn on/off, and doors seemed to close without any help. Apparently, Clara has returned to watch over her window ...

Address: 325 North Park Street
Website: www.grandstreettheatre.com
Activity: E, T

Helena The Myrna Loy Center

This media center started serving the area in 1976 as the Helena Film Society. It was located on the second floor of an office building, and it thrived. When they received a major grant in 1985, they moved to the historic Lewis and Clark County Jail building and changed the name to the current moniker. Long before the MLC moved into the jail, locals had been telling stories of the ghosts that walked the halls there. And it wasn't long before visitors to the MLC started seeing things for themselves—especially in the basement area. Activity includes voices, shadow masses that move along the walls, footsteps, and the sounds of cell doors clanging shut. In addition to watching live performances, the Myrna Loy Center is available for rentals—so you may want to consider getting the place all to yourself.

Address: 15 North Ewing Street
Website: www.myrnaloycenter.com
Activity: A, S, E, T, C

Kalispell The Conrad Mansion Museum

Charles and Alicia Conrad moved to Kalispell with their two children (Charles and Catherine) in order to build a family home. But before the home was even finished, they had a third child named Alicia Ann, who would be three by the time the house was finished in 1895. Unfortunately, Charles Sr. would only live in his new estate seven years before he passed away from complications arising from tuberculosis. But the house remained in the family until 1974, when Alicia Ann would leave the house to the city of Kalispell. Today, the place is a museum and features many of the original furnishings of the Conrad family—including an actual family member! Employees of the museum have witnessed the apparition of Alicia Ann in the home several times. She was once seen walking down the second-floor hallway and down the stairs and has been witnessed in her old bedroom. Other activity includes a rocking chair that moves on its own, voices, and the sounds of "female footsteps."

Address: 330 Woodland Avenue
Website: www.conradmansion.com
Activity: A, E, T

Libby Sportsman's RV Park

As you read this book, you will undoubtedly read many passages concerning the haunting of restaurants, hotels, and museums. But how about RV parks? This is a haunted location tailor-made for those who love to travel in rooms on wheels! Before this park was created, the ruins of an old hotel were there—the Riverside Inn. The Riverside was known for seedy characters, and is said to have experienced an unordinary number of murders, over the years. Eventually the place burned down (some believe on purpose by angry workers who traveled to the area to work on the Libby Dam). Now, visitors say a shadowy apparition of a man wearing a long cloak is often seen walking the area of the RV park where the hotel once stood. Is he a murdered gambler/visitor from years past? Fire up the family truckster and go have a look.

Address: 11741 North Highway 37
Website: www.libbymt.com
Activity: S

Pray Chico Hot Springs Resort & Day Spa

This location could possibly be the most popular haunted getaway in the entire state of Montana. It definitely is the most well known. Tales of the famous "White Lady" that roams the halls of this resort have been whispered over camp fires for decades. Stories started when two security guards working in the main lodge witnessed a glowing white female apparition in the third-floor lounge. Since then, numerous employees and guests have seen the ghostly woman on the third floor—especially in and around the infamous Room 349. It's said that the spirit likes to move a rocking chair in this room. Most believe the ghost to be Mrs. Percie Knowles, the wife of Bill Knowles, who built the place in 1900.

Address: 1 Old Chico Road
Website: www.chicohotsprings.com
Activity: A, E, T

Red Lodge The Pollard Hotel

This hotel dates back to 1893, and it was the first brick building in the town of Red Lodge. In 1902, Thomas F. Pollard took possession of the property and changed the name from the Spofford Hotel to its current name. After Pollard passed away, the hotel changed names many times before going back to its earlier moniker in 1991 with an all new makeover. The haunting of this hotel is a popular story with folks in Montana—and a well known one as well. Paranormal investigators travel a great distance to stay on the Pollard's third floor to experience the female apparition that has been witnessed there numerous times. If you don't want to stake out the hallway there, your best chance to see the ghost is in Room 310 (where she likes to play with the lights and visit people during the night) and Room 312 (where she has been known to touch people sleeping and even hold them down on the bed). Additional activity includes spectral flashes of light and disembodied voices that support the belief that the spirit is that of a woman.

Address: 2 North Broadway
Website: www.thepollard.com
Activity: A, E, T, O

Virginia City Fairweather Inn

Staying in Virginia City is like traveling in a time machine back to the 1800s—and this inn is your ticket to ride! Originating as a private home for a tailor named Martin Lyon, the home turned into a boarding house when Martin was robbed and killed on the way home. His wife, Anna, operated the business until she died in 1896. The inn then became the Anaconda Hotel and Saloon. While this place was in operation, the owners came to a horrible demise. Frank McKeen died in 1918 and his wife Amanda (now depressed) committed suicide in the building right after. The Fairweather is now haunted by the spirit of Amanda McKeen. If you stay in one of the luxurious rooms there (they've redecorated the place with fantastic Victorian-era furnishings), you will want to keep an eye out for a female apparition. She tends to hang around the common areas of the first floor.

Address: 307 West Wallace
Website: www.aldergulchaccommodations.com
Activity: A

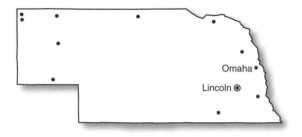

NEBRASKA

Alliance Alliance Theatre

What would make a spirit want to haunt a theatre? Entertainment? Don't ask the employees of the Alliance, because they don't know either. In fact, not much is known at all concerning the haunting of this movie venue—except that it is, indeed, haunted. This theatre began in 1903 as the Charter Hotel, but was converted into a "talking pictures" house in 1938. It's decorated in an Art Moderne style and has undergone several major renovations over the years. So does the haunting have something to do with these new makeovers? Maybe it's because of its past as a hotel? Who knows? Employees will simply tell you that weird things happen here, including shadowy figures that are seen in the building and the sounds of footsteps echoing from the theatre when it's empty.

Address: 410 Box Butte Avenue
Website: www.gejutheatres.com
Activity: S, E

Brownville Captain Meriwether Lewis
Museum of Missouri River History

The only thing better than visiting an antique ship, is visiting one that has an entire museum located within it! This vessel launched in 1931 to assist the U.S. Army's Corps of Engineers with channeling the Missouri River and keeping it open to navigation. The museum on board is a living exhibit of life during the Western Expansion period of the country (for both settlers and Native Americans) and can be toured most days. While you're there you may want to pay attention to the piano located on the ship. It's said this piano is often played by an invisible musician! Tales of phantom piano music playing on this boat are pretty well known in Brownville—and the employees may be able to tell you even more concerning their resident ghost!

Address: Located on Missouri River in Downtown Brownville
Website: www.meriwetherlewisfoundation.org
Activity: E, T

Chadron Olde Main Street Inn

When the O'Hanlon family moved to Nebraska they knew they would be building a massive home. It was constructed in 1890, and they spared no expense despite living in an area still considered remote by city standards. During the infamous incident at Wounded Knee, the house was used briefly by General Nelson Miles as a perfunctory headquarters. Today, the place is a bed and breakfast that features one of the area's best bar/lounges, the Longbranch Saloon. As for the ghost, he is known to the residents of the inn as "Jack," and he is often blamed for things that go awry in the place. If a glass or piece of kitchenware is found missing or suddenly moved, Jack did it. Strange sounds? Jack did it. Poor Jack. On a real note, the spirit is said to be friendly and likes to hang out on the stairs (phantom footsteps have been heard there many times). Check in with the owner/innkeeper to get current sightings of their spirit and more information regarding their haunting.

Address: 115 Main Street
Website: www.oldemainstreetinn.com
Activity: E, T

Crofton The Historic Argo Hotel

Possibly the most well-known haunted location in the state of Nebraska, the Argo has had so many stories spun about it that it's hard to keep up with it all! It is known that the hotel was constructed in 1911 and was originally called the Argo (though it would change hotel names a couple times). It is also a fact that, at one point, the building functioned as the New Meridian Sanitorium—a place that treated diseases like cancer and operated more as a hospice for the dying, rather than a hospital. It would be in 1994, when the current owners would once again renovate the building and restore it to the Argo Hotel. It was also during these renovations that ghostly activity started surfacing. Glimpses of apparitions in hospital gowns, the sounds of cries, and instances of objects moving started happening on a regular basis. Then there's the basement…It's said to be haunted by a female spirit dubbed "Alice." She's thought to have died while giving childbirth in the place and is now seen roaming the hotel looking for her baby.

Address: 211 West Kansas Street
Website: www.theargohotel.com
Activity: A, E, T, C

Fairbury TrailBlazers Restaurant

This restaurant is well known locally for their great service and eclectic menu. But get folks in Fairbury talking about ghost stories and the strange happenings of TrailBlazers will almost certainly come up. Nobody is able to put a name to the specter that's said to haunt the building (which is much older than the restaurant and once functioned as a Montgomery Ward's department store), but eyewitness accounts of dishes and silverware moving by themselves and strange sensations of cold spots/someone brushing past you seem to be common. While no apparition has been seen (at least that's been documented), it does seem like this location is rather active. Order yourself a great meal and ask your server about the tales concerning the restaurant—you may just have a good reason to leave a good tip!

Address: 500 4th Street
Website: www.fairbury.com/pages/dining/
    trailblazers
Activity: T, C

Harrison War Bonnet Creek Battlefield Site

When word of Custer's defeat at the Battle of Little Big Horn made its way to Nebraska, the Cheyenne Indians decided they would make their move as well. They left their reservation at Red Cloud Agency and began the trek north. But the U.S. Army would respond with troops led by General Wesley Merritt. The result was a battle that took place at this site on July 17, 1876. The Cheyenne were badly defeated (though this news was less publicized than the exploits of Buffalo Bill Cody during the battle). Today, there is a monument to mark the battle—one that has tales of a residual haunting circulating about it. It's said that if you visit the place during the evening, you can hear the phantom sounds of horses, men shouting battle cries, and screams of pain. Check in with the park online for their hours and events.

Address: Pants Butte Road off Highway 20
Website: www.nps.gov
Activity: A, E, R

Lincoln Johnny Carson School of Theatre and Film

This theatre is part of the University of Nebraska–Lincoln campus. It can be found in the Temple Building, which is located on Q Street. The building was built in 1906 as a student activity center, but was recently changed to the current name listed above (mostly due to a large donation to the university from Johnny Carson's estate). Since the location became a theatre for live performances, there have been sightings of a male apparition (it's rumored that he is the ghost of a stagehand who died in an accident in the 1940s)—especially during any production of the play *Macbeth*. There is also supposed to be a second entity that's sometimes described as the ghost of a former teacher, or of a little girl, depending on the situation. Unless you're seeing *Macbeth* there (an actual apparition is supposed to appear during this show), activity may include items being thrown and the sounds of footsteps.

Address: 215 Temple Building
Website: www.unl.edu/TheatreArts/
Activity: A, E, T

Lincoln Nebraska State Capitol Building

Since Franklin Pierce passed the Kansas-Nebraska Act in 1854 (which essentially created Nebraska), there have been five state capitol buildings. The first two were in Omaha, but then it was decided to move the state capital to the city of Lincoln. The current version of the Capitol was finished in 1932, and it was the third to be built on this site. Over the years since its completion, there have been several accidents on the premises that have resulted in the death of someone—and it's thought that these are the "someones" now haunting the place! The stairs that lead up the tower are said to be the location of the most activity—including shadow masses that shoot up the stairs, voices, and the sounds of footsteps. But most disturbing of all are the tales of screams that are heard in various locations throughout the building.

Address: 1445 K Street
Website: www.capitol.org
Activity: S, E

Nebraska City Super China Buffet

How many places can you visit where you can see paranormal activity and eat some great Chinese food as well? Well, at least one in the state of Nebraska! Before this 100-plus item buffet moved into the building, several other businesses ran their operations at this address, including a hardware store and a second restaurant. When things of a shadowy nature started happening at Super China, people started talking about dark rumors surrounding these previous businesses. It's said that the spirit walking the buffet is either the former owner of the hardware store (he died of natural causes in the place while working) or the son of the owners of the former restaurant (who, according to local legend, committed suicide). Either way, activity at this eatery includes items that are moved by invisible hands and "muttering" voices that seem to emanate from the air.

Address: 14330 Jefferson Davis Highway
Website: www.superchinabuffet.com
Activity: E, T

Omaha Brother Sebastian's Steakhouse & Winery

Built by restaurateur Loren Koch in 1977, this themed restaurant is well known throughout Omaha for its extraordinary steaks. In 1996, the place suffered a devastating fire that resulted in the entire restaurant having to be rebuilt—so that's exactly what they did. For the paranormal tourist (especially one who loves beef), Brother Sebastian's is a breath of fresh air. Good food and good spirits (pun intended) are to be had at this establishment. The food is so good in fact, that the ghost on this property is that of a former customer named Bill Wolcott. It's reported that old Bill loved the restaurant and ate there almost every day—right up until he died of cancer. When the restaurant reopened after the fire, customers started asking who the man was that was standing against the stone wall. The wait staff would, of course, go look and find nobody there. In addition to sightings of Wolcott's ghost, people have also seen doors open on their own and found candles lit by themselves during the night.

Address: 1350 South 119th Street
Website: www.brothersebastians.com
Activity: A, T

Omaha Hummel Park

When over 200 acres of land was donated to the city of Omaha, the city decided to create a park and name it after one of their long-standing park superintendents, J. B. Hummel. The park features playgrounds, picnic areas, and an overlook above the Missouri River that's called "the Devil's Slide." Local legends concerning ghosts that roam the park date back to when the area was a fur-trading post created by Jean Pierre Cabanne in 1823. It's said that Cabanne drove local Native Americans from the area despite it being a place where they buried their dead. Add in a generous helping of folklore that includes cults performing sacrifices on the property, and you've got one helluva haunted location! Reported activity here includes glowing balls of light that shoot across the grounds, the sounds of screams/cries, and bizarre mists that (on occasion) seem to resemble the walking dead.

Address: 11808 John J. Pershing Drive
Website: www.ci.omaha.ne.us/parks/
Activity: O, M, E

Omaha O'Connor's Irish Pub

This Irish pub was founded in 1998, and it is the headquarters of the local St. Patrick's Day parade. In addition to getting typical pub grub and drinks there, they even have a party room that can be rented for special/private events. Local paranormal investigators have visited this pub—at the request of employees there—because of strange reports concerning shadow masses shooting by the entry to the kitchen area, as well as roaming around the second-floor bar. There has also been at least one instance where an employee closing for the night has heard the sounds of someone walking on the second floor—even though there was no one inside. Information regarding the haunting of the pub is still forthcoming (check in with the staff to see what happened), but the activity does seem to still be happening. It might well be worth your time to have some fish and chips at O'Connor's.

Address: 1217 Howard Street
Website: www.oconnorsomaha.com
Activity: S, E

Scribner Old Hotel Café and Saloon

When the Hardner Hotel was built in 1901, it was considered a modern facility with all the amenities of a big city hotel. During the depression, though, business became so slow at the Hardner that they eventually closed up shop. Though the building is still known locally as the "old hotel," the property only features a restaurant on the site these days. There are also numerous urban legends/ghost stories surrounding the site. These started when the place sat empty for many years. Tales of hotel patrons committing suicide, as well as being murdered, have circulated the area and even made their way into several publications. According to those who have visited the café, the grounds are haunted and most of the activity happens on the now-empty second and third floors. But on occasion, experiences do bleed into the restaurant—activity includes shadow shapes, voices and unexplained cold spots.

Address: 503 Main Street
Website: www.scribnernebraska.com
Activity: E, S, C

Sidney Fort Sidney Museum and Commander's Home

The city of Sidney was mapped out in 1867 as a frontier outpost for workers constructing the Union Pacific railroad. Because of constant at-tacks from area Indian tribes, an army outpost was eventually added on called Sidney Barracks. In time, the small garrison expanded into a full fort that functioned until 1894. The home that houses the Fort Sidney Museum was used as the residence for the post commander at Fort Sidney, and it's said that at one point during its tenure, the wife of one of the commanders fell down a set of servants' stairs and died. Specifics concerning this event are unavailable (and may just be urban legend to support the activity there), but scattered reports of a female apparition have circulated this area for some time. She has been seen within the house, and it's rumored that a local magazine even took a photo of the ghost.

Address: 6th and Jackson Streets
Website: www.cityofsidney.org
Activity: A

Valentine Centennial Hall and Museum

This museum began as a schoolhouse that was built in 1897 (the oldest surviving school in the state of Nebraska). The school was the only source for a primary and secondary education in the area for many years until other local towns began creating their own schools. In 1978, the place was converted into a museum that hosts displays of area history. For people who are interested in the paranormal, this museum offers the chance to see a great residual haunting. Visitors and workers alike on this property have heard the sounds of children playing and have seen their misty apparitions. Local legend says there is also an active spirit on the site (reputedly a girl who was poisoned by a bad clarinet reed and died on the property), but this hasn't been verified. The staff of the museum is used to getting questions about their haunting, so don't be afraid to get more current information when you visit.

Address: Third Street and Macomb Street
Website: www.visitvalentine.com
Activity: R, A, E

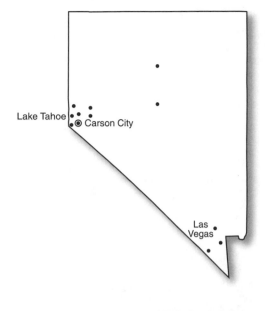

Lake Tahoe
Carson City

Las
Vegas

NEVADA

Austin International Café & Bar

The city of Austin was founded in 1862 after a horse (owned by W. H. Talbott) kicked up a chunk of rock riddled with gold. The sudden onslaught of miners and prospectors to the area resulted in a population of over ten thousand within a year! It was decided that a hotel was needed, so the International Hotel (built in 1860 in Virginia City) was moved to its present-day location in Austin. Needless to say, with so much gold flowing through the hands of Austinites, the area was sure to draw outlaws, gamblers, and other seedy characters—and the International saw a great many of them. Perhaps it's for this reason that the spirit of a former owner named "Tommy" is said to still look over things at this café and bar. The hotel itself is closed, but you can get a great steak (or other home-cooked

meal) here, as well as a drink, and keep an eye out for the male apparition. He is usually seen by the bar, or heard stomping around in the empty second-floor area.

Address: 59 Main Street
Website: www.internationalcafeandsaloon.com
Activity: A, E

Battle Mountain Nevada Hotel

This small town sprung into existence when the neighboring city of Argenta abandoned their mines to move closer to the Central Pacific Railroad in 1870. It wouldn't be long before local amenities began to spring up to support not only folks traveling by rail, but also the numerous surrounding mining towns. The Nevada Hotel was one of these institutions. With rooms for rent and an on-site saloon, the Nevada was the social center of Battle Mountain in the 1880s and 1890s. Today, you can't rent a room at the hotel (they don't have any), but you can visit the casino and bar, where maybe you'll see some of the paranormal occurrences that have been reported over the years. Most of the stories involve strange cold spots that seem to follow patrons, as well as the phantom sounds of voices and footsteps that come from the upper floor of the old hotel.

Address: 36 East Front Street
Website: www.battlemountaintourism.com
Activity: E, C

Boulder City Boulder Dam Hotel

In addition to being only minutes from hopping downtown Las Vegas, this historic hotel is pretty much a one-stop stay in Boulder City. It has a highly rated restaurant, on location shopping, and even a museum that celebrates the history of the city, as well as the neighboring Hoover Dam. The hotel was built to house workers on the dam—though it's probably more known for its famous guests over the years (people like Bette Davis, James Cagney, and Henry Fonda). Unfortunately for the hotel, once the dam was finished, business began to wane. This caused the unfortunate demise of the hotel's major shareholder, Raymond Spillsbury, who committed suicide on the property. Today, the spirit of Raymond is said to walk the halls of this hotel. Sightings of his apparition, as well as smelling the scent of phantom cigarette smoke, occur on a regular basis. The basement is said to be a

particularly active area—though you may want to get current sightings info from the staff there. They are quite used to discussing their resident spirit.

Address: 1305 Arizona Street
Website: www.boulderdamhotel.com
Activity: A, E, N

Carson City Brewery Art Center

This limestone building dates back to 1860 and is built from the same quarry that supplied the stone for the Nevada State Capitol Building. The Carson Brewery Company brewed its famous Tahoe Beer at this facility from 1862 until 1948. In 1975, the BAC was formed to supply locals with a place to enjoy live events and entertainment—a tradition that lives on today. The haunting is, reputedly, the product of a former building superintendent—a mason by the name of James P. Maar. Maar worked in the place for some time and even attended meetings with his local lodge there. His apparition has often been seen in the ballroom and theater areas of the center, and his disembodied voice has been heard around the main entrance.

Address: 449 West King Street
Website: www.breweryarts.org
Activity: A, E

Carson City Carson City Mint

Designed in 1866 by the Supervising Architect of the Treasury, Alfred Bult Mullet, the mint was created to assist with the sudden wealth in the area due to mining. It functioned until 1899, when it was reduced to an assay office, and then eventually became the Nevada State Museum. According to locals, two spirits haunt this historic mint: Osborne Parker and Abraham Curry. Parker was a worker who was crushed to death in the basement when some minting equipment fell on him in 1872. Strange noises and footsteps that are often heard in the basement are usually attributed to him. Curry was a former superintendent of the building who passed away in

1873. His apparition has been seen and heard in various offices within the building.

Address: 600 North Carson Street
Website: www.nps.gov/nr/travel/nevada/usm
Activity: A, E

Carson City Nevada State Governor's Mansion

When Acting Governor Denver Dickerson moved into this mansion in 1909, Nevada had already been a state for 45 years. And it wasn't long after moving in that his daughter, June Dickerson, was born in the house (the only child to have this distinction). This happened before the building was even opened to the public in 1910. Though this massive estate is said to be haunted by as many as three spirits, the reality is that only two have been seen—and they have always been seen walking down the second-floor hallway. Most likely, this site is experiencing a residual haunting that involves the first ladies of the house, Una and June Dickerson. But whether it is them or not, what is seen is the strange sight of a glowing woman in a long dress, followed closely by the spirit of a little girl.

Address: 600 North Mountain Street
Website: www.nps.gov/nr/travel/nevada/
  gov.htm
Activity: R, A

Crystal Bay Cal Neva Resort, Spa & Casino

San Francisco entrepreneur Robert P. Sherman wanted a place he could take his real estate clients to that would be away from the city bustle for a weekend of wining and dining, so he built the Cal Neva in 1926, modeling it after the cabin in the Broadway play *Lightnin'*. When it burned down in 1937, the resort was quickly rebuilt by Norman Biltz and Adler Larson—this is the area that now makes up the Indian Room, the Circle Bar, and the casino. During the 1960s, Frank Sinatra even (briefly) owned and frequented the place. Since the Cal Neva is already considered the oldest casino in the United States, it probably comes as no surprise that there were a lot of gangsters/mobsters that made the lodge their second home. It was also used for a lot of illicit rendezvous (such as the reputed visit by Robert Kennedy to Marilyn Monroe). If you visit the upscale resort today, you can join in with the rich tradition of gambling and enjoy the amenities of a quality spa. You can also stay in the cabin that is said to be haunted by Marilyn herself! Though she is known to haunt up to six different locations, there have been eyewitnesses that have claimed to have seen the apparition of Monroe sobbing in the corner of the cabin.

Address: 2 Stateline Road
Website: www.calnevaresort.com
Activity: A

Dayton Gold Canyon Steakhouse

This eatery gets rave reviews for their food, as well as for its great location (the center of Dayton's historic district). But a hundred years ago, the building that now hosts the restaurant was a local boarding house. It's said by local historians that the town of Dayton (thought to be one of the two possible "oldest towns in Nevada") was the site of many a gunfight—and at least one happened right outside what is now the Gold Canyon Steakhouse. One man was shot dead, and one was hung the following day for murder. Today, employees of the restaurant report seeing and hearing a male entity that's dressed in the attire of a gunslinger. His apparition has been witnessed within the dining room, and the sounds of his footsteps and voice have been heard in the kitchen as well. The story of the ghost is well known among those who work here, so check in with them to get more current tales regarding the haunting.

Address: 160 Main Street
Website: www.goldcanyonsteakhouse.com
Activity: A, E

Incline Village Thunderbird Lodge Historical Site

Construction on this lodge began in 1936 by George Whittell and it would remain his personal residence until his death in 1969. It has since been added onto several times and is now open for tours (via bus and boat) and events. After you visit the gift shop on the premises, let your tour guide know that you are interested in the "haunted history" as well. You will be shown the small building with the indoor pool (where a worker is said to have fallen and died), as well as locations within the main lodge where the apparition of Whittell is said to be "felt" and seen. Paranormal investigators who have visited Thunderbird have captured interesting audio clips that do seem to support the idea of paranormal activity at this location—but, as is usual with haunted places, you will have to sort the fact from fiction since much of the information has been supplied by so-called psychics.

Address: 969 Tahoe Boulevard
Website: www.thunderbirdlodge.org
Activity: A, E, T, C

Las Vegas Planet Hollywood Resort & Casino

Paranormal events at this not-so-paranormal chain started when the property was still called the Aladdin Hotel. Much like the Aladdin, Planet Hollywood is an upper-crust getaway for the trendsetter, as well as those who simply want to stay in a hotel with a top-notch casino—and the place is, of course, still thought to be haunted.

Though there aren't many pieces of information regarding the spirits, the sheer number of experiences leads one to believe that the resort is, indeed, haunted. For years, guests have claimed to hear voices and the sounds of footsteps stomping through the hallways (sometimes right up to their door). Reports of shadowy apparitions and items found moved during the night have occurred on occasion as well.

Address: 3667 Las Vegas Boulevard South
Website: www.planethollywoodresort.com
Activity: S, E, T

Primm Whiskey Pete's Hotel & Casino

This Western-themed hall of gambling is named for a legendary figure from the area (yep, you guessed it, Whiskey Pete). Pete McIntyre was an area miner who died of "miner's lung" in 1933 and was buried with his casket standing on end. When the casket was dug up and moved to accommodate a new building on this property, it's said that ghostly activity started occurring. Employees of the casino have seen Pete playing with the silverware and barware, and he is often blamed for turning lights on/off and messing up the covers in rooms of the hotel. Guests have claimed to have seen a "grizzled old miner" walking right through the middle of the casino floor, and the spirit has even made the occasional appearance in a guest room.

Address: 31900 Las Vegas Boulevard South
Website: www.primmvalleyresorts.com/
   hotel_whiskey
Activity: A, E, T

Reno Lake Mansion

The history of this home is as interesting as the ghost story that takes place there. When Myron C. Lake (one of the founders of the city of Reno) saw the house in the late 1870s, he fell in love with it and immediately purchased it. It remained in his family until 1971, when the place was scheduled for demolition. A preservation organization took possession of the home, though, and had the house moved three miles away. It seems unbelievable, but this would happen again. In the late 1990s, the city would decide to expand their convention center, which would result in the house moving again to the downtown area. According to employees of this living museum, if the house is haunted, it is a subtle haunt—yet, paranormal investigators in the area insist that the place does have a resident spirit. Seeing or hearing anything at this location, though, may mean spending some real time there, so you may want to rent the mansion.

Address: 250 Court Street
Website: www.lakemansion.com
Activity: A, E

Reno Washoe County Courthouse

This public facility dates back to 1911 and is a Classic Revival masterpiece by architect Frederic Delongchamps. It was built around, literally, the first version of the courthouse (a brick two-story affair built by Septimus F. Hoole), and it would be added on to again in the 1940s and the 1960s. Because of severe reforms to the divorce law in the state of Nevada in 1931, it's said that over 30,000 divorces were granted in the next 10 years! Could a place be haunted because of the sheer number of broken households that have passed through this building? Could be. The haunting could also have something to do with the turbulent history of the general area as well. Either way, courthouse employees have experienced dark shadow shapes in the hallways, whispering disembodied voices, and doors that open/close by themselves.

Address: 75 Court Street
Website: www.washoecourts.com
Activity: S, E, T

Virginia City The Gold Hill Hotel

Originally named the Riesen House, the Gold Hill is said to be the oldest hotel in the state of Nevada. It dates back to the early 1860s and was an integral part of the community during the great silver and gold rush. Much like pioneers of the mining industry who visited Virginia City, you can stay at this hotel (as well as eat and drink at the on-site saloon). Just remember to keep an eye out for the resident spirits there. In 1986, the new owners of this hotel did a massive renovation—one that included adding on a new kitchen, dining room, and eight more guest rooms. Apparently the ghosts on the property did not appreciate this change, because this was when activity started happening. Though the entire place is known for the haunting (the sounds of children laughing have been heard in almost every area), the hot spots are Rooms 4 and 5. Room 4 is occupied by a female spirit the staff calls "Rosie" because of the scent of roses that accompanies her. She's known for moving items and hiding the belongings of people who stay there. Room 5 is the grounds of a male entity dubbed "William," who is known for speaking aloud in the room, appearing with the smell of tobacco, and moving items within his domain.

Address: 1540 Main Street (Highway 342)
Website: www.goldhillhotel.net
Activity: E, T, N

Virginia City Mackay Mansion Museum

This circa 1860 Victorian mansion was home to John Mackay, a local pioneer of the mining industry, but was built originally as the "Gould and Curry Office" for a man named George Hearst. Today, it is a museum that offers exhibits of period furnishings and mining artifacts. The place is also a local favorite for weddings and events. On the paranormal side of things, the ghosts of this mansion became big news when actor Johnny Depp witnessed a female apparition on the second floor (he stayed at the house while shooting the movie *Dead Man*). Since then, visitors have seen this female apparition—as well as two other spirits in the house. There's a female servant who is often witnessed on the stairs (as well as the second floor), and a male entity (thought to be a former resident of the place, dubbed "the Colonel") that's often witnessed in the kitchen and dining room.

Address: 129 South D Street
Website: www.mackaymansion.com
Activity: A, E, S, T

Virginia City Piper's Opera House

This historic theater is listed by the League of Historic Theaters and live performances have been occurring there since the 1860s. Of course, this is the third version of the opera house; the first two incarnations of the venue burned to the ground in 1875 and 1883. The current opera house was finished in 1885 and has pretty much functioned non-stop since then. You will want to catch a production at this theatre while you visit Virginia City. It's said that during live performances, a female apparition will often appear in a long dress standing at the top of the balcony there. When there's no performance, the only paranormal activity reported is the strange scent of lavender that seems to emanate from thin air. So take time out from hitting all the local saloons to get some culture injected into your trip.

Address: 12 North B Street (Drawer J)
Website: www.pipersoperahouse.com
Activity: A, N

Virginia City Silver Queen Hotel

In 1876 when this hotel was first opened to the public, the local Comstock Lode was making people wealthy on a daily basis. Miners and other visitors flocking to Virginia City would often stay at the Silver Queen (or at least visit to catch a glimpse of the famous "Silver Dollar Lady" painting that features a dress with over 3,000 silver dollars) while mapping out their claims in the area. At some point during this period, a couple stayed in the hotel and had one hulluva fight! It's reported that a strange residual haunt now occurs at this hotel that includes the phantom sounds of a man and woman hurling insults at one another in the wee hours of the night. This activity has been heard many times and has been documented by several paranormal investigation groups. Other ghostly happenings include voices in the halls, misty apparitions, and cold spots that inhabit the rooms along with the guests.

Address: 28 North C Street
Website: www.visitvirginiacitynv.com/
    lodging_silverqueen
Activity: R, A, E, C

Virginia City St. Mary's Art Center

Housed within a historic hospital (the St. Mary Louise Hospital, circa 1875), this center was built by the Sisters of Charity and one Father Patrick Manogue. After the site experienced a fire on the fourth floor in 1940, it closed up shop and remained unoccupied until 1964. It was then that the place became the art center it is today. SMAC offers classes on art instruction (as well as photography) to the local populace, and hosts events on the property. It was during one of these events that a witness saw what appeared to be a ghostly nun walking the second floor of the building. Since then, many people have come forward to speak out about their own experiences with the "White Nun" of St. Mary's. She is usually seen on the second floor where she is thought to simply be "making the rounds," but (on occasion) she has also been spotted on the stairs between the first and second floors. Other activity on the property includes the residual sounds of a hospital in operation—including the cries of the injured/dying.

Address: 55 North R Street
Website: www.stmarysartcenter.org
Activity: A, R, E

Virginia City Sugarloaf Mountain Motel and Market

Many paranormal investigators that make the trek to infamous Virginia City use the Sugarloaf as their "headquarters" while exploring the area. This could be because of its history (it dates back to 1878, when the building opened as a boardinghouse), or maybe the great location (it's in the heart of the downtown area on C Street), or even the on-site market that allows the purchase of food/drinks before heading out to investigate a new spot in town. But the most likely reason for staying at this motel is the fact that it, too, is considered a haunted location. The activity is thought to be a byproduct of the days when part of the motel was used as a local jail. If you want to stay in one of the haunted rooms at Sugarloaf, simply make reservations in one of the "historic rooms" listed on their website. It's in these locations that people experience shadowy apparitions, hear voices, and find personal belongings moved during the night.

Address: 430 South C Street
Website: www.sugarloafmountain-motel.com
Activity: S, E, T

Washoe Bower's Mansion

Fueled with the instant fortune they got from the Comstock mining boom, Lemuel and Eilley Bower built this home in 1863. The place was designed by architect J. Neeley Johnson (a former governor of California) and is a combination of Georgian and Italianate styles. The house remained in the Bower family until Lemuel died in 1868—then it was lost to foreclosure. In 1946 the mansion-turned-resort was handed over to the state of Nevada, and it now resides in a park along with a swimming pool. The place can be toured today (check their website for days/hours) and it is the location of a sad haunting. After Lemuel passed away in the home, it's said that Eilley turned to Spiritualists for help in contacting her dead husband. Many séances were held on the property before Eilley joined her husband in the afterlife—or did she? Some believe her spirit is still in the house. A female apparition, as well as voices and footsteps, has been witnessed in the upstairs area of the mansion.

Address: Franktown Road off U.S. Highway 395
Website: www.nps.gov/history/nr/travel/
    nevada/bow
Activity: A, E

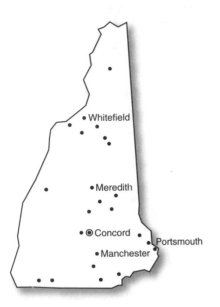

NEW HAMPSHIRE

Alton Alton Town Hall

This area of New Hampshire was first settled in the mid-1770s, but it would be the late 1800s before the city of Alton would make its first giant leap into the financial world. A local company (Rockwell Clough Company) would manufacture the world's first corkscrew, and the product would be a hit! The current town hall in Alton was constructed in 1894 (at a whopping cost of $15,000) and has pretty much functioned since then. Over the years, strange reports have come from this building—mostly from folks who have to work there on a daily basis. It seems that at least one spirit occupies this civic location, and that spirit is noisy! Eyewitnesses to the paranormal activity at the town hall have heard strange, disembodied voices in the hallways (as well as the sounds of heavy footsteps), found furniture moved during the night, and seen doors open and close with the help of invisible hands.

Address: 1 Monument Square
Website: www.alton.nh.gov
Activity: E, T

Bretton Woods Mount Washington Resort

When Joseph Stickney built this luxurious resort in 1902, it was one of the most modern and upscale hotels in the country. As such, it served as a place for him and his wife, Carolyn, to host the rich and famous from all over the world. But when Joseph passed away just a year later, Carolyn was left behind to care for the resort. She eventually remarried a man named Prince Luncinge from France and moved there to live with him. But when he, too, passed away, she returned to the hotel and lived there the rest of her life. But it would take more than mere death to keep Carolyn out of Mt. Washington. To this day, her apparition is seen on the premises in the tower suites (especially in Room 314 that contains her old bed). Lights are known to turn on/off, voices are heard, and the sounds of spectral music emanate through the hallways.

Address: Route 302
Website: www.mountwashingtonresort.com
Activity: A, E, T

Dixville Notch The Balsams Grand Resort Hotel

This massive and beautiful hotel first opened as the Dix House, a small summer inn that serviced visitors just after the Civil War. The owner, George Parsons, named the business after a local Revolutionary War hero, Colonel Timothy Dix. In 1895, an inventor named Henry S. Hale bought the property and renamed it the Balsams. Today, the hotel provides first-class accommodations, as well as an award-winning restaurant for the weary New Hampshire traveler. The Balsams is also considered one of the most active haunted locations in the state. Employees have documented ghostly activity at this location since the 1950s! There is reputedly a female apparition that walks the third floor of the hotel (and has been seen in many of the rooms there), as well as a male apparition that has been seen on the first floor and in Room 120 (considered the hottest of the hot spots). Though the identity of the female is unknown, it's thought that the spirit of the man is a circa-1930s bandleader that drowned in nearby Lake Gloriette. Other activity in this location includes voices, shadowy apparitions, and the residual sounds of past visitors.

Address: 1000 Cold Spring Road
Website: www.thebalsams.com
Activity: A, R, E, S

Durham Three Chimneys Inn

Known locally as one of the oldest homes in the state of New Hampshire, this inn dates back to 1649. After being extensively renovated in the 1990s, the house was opened to the public as a luxurious bed and breakfast. Tales of the house being haunted have been passed down for over a hundred years. It's thought that the spirit of a girl named Hannah is within the home. Hannah was reputedly a member of the Valentine Hill family (the original owners of the place). Employees have witnessed her apparition standing by the bar, as well as felt her touching them while they slept. She is also known for disturbing electronic equipment in the inn and playing with the furniture in the front parlor area. But she may not be alone. According to reports from guests, there are also glimpses of a male apparition on the property.

Address: 17 Newmarket Road
Website: www.threechimneysinn.com
Activity: A, S, E, T

Enfield Shaker Inn at the Great Stone Dwelling

Followers of this unique religion created their community in Enfield around 1793. Known as the United Society of Believers in Christ's Second Appearing (commonly called "the Shakers"), their beliefs included the avoidance of sex and the use of community, or "family," dwellings. This location was the largest of this type of housing and was finished in 1841. When the Shaker community pretty much died out in 1923, the community closed shop (maybe they should have rethought that whole "no sex" thing) and left. The great stone dwelling eventually became the property of the Enfield Shaker Museum, and the inn/restaurant opened in 1998. Since its opening, employees and visitors alike have felt the presence of the long-gone Shakers in the building—in the form of ghosts! Witnesses have reported shadowy apparitions, doors opening on their own, and the sounds of footsteps. The most common hot spot at the inn is Room 15, where a rocking chair is said to move with nobody in it.

Address: 447 Route 4A
Website: www.innsite.com/inns/B007761
Activity: S, E, T

Fitzwilliam Amos J. Blake House Museum

This house served as a home and office for Amos Blake, a local attorney, from 1865 until 1925 when he passed away. Of course, it was a house long before Amos ever ventured inside! The place was built in 1837 (next door to the Fitzwilliam Inn) and served as a headquarters for quite a few businesses before Amos moved in. Today it is a living museum, and the Fitzwilliam Historical Society regularly hosts events at the house. On the paranormal side, employees and visitors have reported seeing the apparition of a small boy (that once walked through the middle of a room in front of several people) and the misty spirit of a cat. Additional activity in the museum includes disembodied voices and the sounds of items moving.

Address: 66 Route 119
Website: www.fitzhistoricalsociety.org
Activity: A, E, T

Franconia Sugar Hill Inn

Living in the White Mountains region of New Hampshire—especially during Colonial times—has always been a difficult affair. Nobody knew this better than the Oakes family, who moved to the area and built this house in 1789. They would endure the harsh winters and remain in the home for many years. In 1924, a large addition was added on to the house and it opened as the Caramat Inn. Later, cottages would be added and the name would change to its current moniker in 1972. Today, the place has new ownership and the inn is known for its fantastic spa and dining. But during the 1980s, the locals heard tales of Sugar Hill being haunted—a reputation that has stuck with the inn. The spirits at this location seem to be rather benign and pretty much leave the guests alone, though regular glimpses of them are reported. There is a ghostly elderly couple that's been witnessed walking through the house, and the shadowy apparition of a man that has been seen in the kitchen and dining room (thought to possibly be a past owner who passed away on the premises).

Address: 116 Scenic Route 117
Website: www.sugarhillinn.com
Activity: A, S

Gilford Kimball Castle

This massive and historic estate was the brainchild of Benjamin Ames Kimball. He purchased the property (300 acres of it) in 1895 and built the castle between the years of 1897 and 1899. Constructed using materials from Europe (even the stone masons were brought in from Italy), the place served as a headquarters for Kimball as he managed the Concord and Montreal Railroad. Kimball died on the property in 1919, but the family kept the estate until the 1960s, when it was given to the state. But it would be long into the 1980s before any renovation and restoration efforts took place. Today it is a tourist attraction that you can visit—much like the paranormal group TAPS did. Activity includes a female apparition that walks the caretaker's house, the sounds of phantom horses in the stables, and a second female entity that's often witnessed in the actual castle. This spirit is thought to be Charlotte Kimball, the last remaining member of the Kimball family, who donated the property to the state—with the stipulation that nothing "commercial" would be done with it. If this isn't enough to get you to swing by the castle, it's also reported that Benjamin Kimball himself may walk the halls there...

Address: 59 Lockes Hill Road
Website: www.kimballcastle.com
Activity: A, E, T, S

Hart's Location The Notchland Inn

This 1862 inn (with thirteen guest rooms, as well as two cottages) sits squarely in the middle of the Mount Washington Valley along Nancy Brook. The brook, as well as Nancy Pond and Nancy Mountain, are all named after a woman who is the subject of a strange, local tale. It's said that a girl named Nancy Barton froze to death while chasing after her fiancé in the area where the Notchland Inn now resides. According to the story, he had stolen Nancy's dowry money and was now fleeing to the city. The Notchland now has her gravestone in their parlor! Visitors have occasionally related paranormal tales to the owners of the inn that include spirits writing on the mirrors and moving objects within the rooms. But is the ghost really Nancy? At least one patron stated that the name "Abigail" had been scrawled on his bathroom mirror while he stayed on the premises.

Address: 2 Morey Road
Website: www.notchland.com
Activity: E, T

Hopkinton Blaser's Fireside Tavern

This neighborhood restaurant serves as a local gathering place for those who are interested in a good pint or a romantic meal overlooking nearby Kimball Lake. Of course, you can also visit the tavern to share a nice ghostly tale that concerns the place. The original owners of the place, Joseph and Lucinda Mills, moved to the area and built the main building here to be their home in 1858. After their deaths, the place was passed down to their son Frank and his wife—and they, too, resided there until she died in 1924. Frank tried to live on without his beloved, but in the end decided to commit suicide in 1926—right there in the upstairs area of the present-day tavern. Sightings of the spirit of old Frank have become commonplace in the restaurant these days—as well as the sounds of male laughter, bar items moving on their own, and candles that light themselves.

Address: 157 Main Street
Website: www.firesidetavern.com
Activity: A, S, E, T

Jackson Eagle Mountain House

The original version of this farmhouse inn opened in 1879. The place later expanded into two additional buildings to accommodate visitors that came for the winter sports. In 1915, a fire destroyed the main inn and forced the owners to rebuild a new place the following year. New owners of the EMH completely restored the property in 1986, and it wouldn't take long for the place to become a nationally recognized historic property. It's said that this inn is haunted by two spirits, a boy and a woman known to the employees as the "Lady in Red." While the boy is only heard there (usually laughing in the hallways or around the offices), the woman has been seen and heard in almost every area of the third floor. Activity there includes her disembodied voice, cold spots, and the sight of her apparition roaming the halls.

Address: 179 Carter Notch Road
Website: www.eaglemt.com
Activity: A, E, T, C

Jackson The Inn at Jackson

Kate Corrine Baldwin (a member of the Baldwin family known for their line of pianos) came to this area in 1902 to live in her new summer home. She built the place after visiting the area several times (and staying in nearby Wentworth Hall) and finding it to her liking. She stayed there off and on until 1922. At that point, new owners took over the house and turned it into Gray's Manor, a local inn. After a string of new names and new owners, the place eventually came to be known as the Inn at Jackson after the current owners took possession in 2005. Locals came to know the inn as a haunted location when a previous innkeeper stated experiencing strange things there during a night with no power. It's said glowing orbs of light shot up the stairs, footsteps were heard on the second floor, and a water faucet kept unexplainably turning itself on in Room Two. Since then, sporadic reports of similar activity have been reported—presumably by the spirit of a man called "Jason," who is thought to have been a worker who committed suicide on the property.

Address: Main Street and Thorn Hill Road
Website: www.innatjackson.com
Activity: O, E, T

Littleton The Beal House Inn

This unique and historic home dates back to 1833 (when it was a farmhouse for Nathaniel Flanders and family), and it features four guest suites, three guest rooms, and a three-star rated restaurant on the property. It's called the Beal House after Justus and Marjorie Beal, who started operating an inn out of the house in 1939. Since then, the property has changed owners several times, but the place is thriving today and offers a great getaway for folks traveling in the White Mountains. Over the years, at least one of the owners had a unique experience in the inn. It seems she was sleeping in the room that was once Mrs. Beal's bedroom when she woke during the night to see a female apparition walk through the door of the room out into the hallway. When she got up and looked, the ghost was gone. It's thought that the spirit is that of Marjorie and that she's still looking over things at the old inn.

Address: 2 West Main Street
Website: www.thebealhouseinn.com
Activity: A, E

Manchester Palace Theatre

This theatre began as the dream of a local immigrant named Victor Charas. In 1914, Victor organized the construction of the Palace (designed to resemble another theatre that shares the same name in New York City), and it first opened to the public on April 9, 1915. Today, the rich tradition of bringing live performances to the local populace is alive and well. In 2007, a regional paranormal group visited this theatre and came to the conclusion that the place is haunted by a female apparition (who is usually spotted on the stage). But the ghost story would become nationally known when it hit the television series *Ghost Hunters*. Hot spots in the theatre include the reception room (where a male moaning is often heard), the balcony area of the theatre (where it's rumored a man committed suicide), and the backstage area (where props are known to move on their own). Catching a production (hopefully, along with a reception) at this location is a must for the paranormal traveler.

Address: 80 Hanover Street
Website: www.palacetheatre.org
Activity: A, E, S, T

Meredith The Nutmeg Inn

This historic house has been lovingly restored to be one of the area's best accommodations and features eight rooms, each with a private bath. If you take a walk around the place, you'll notice that this circa 1763 home still has the original flooring, wall paneling, and fireplaces—something you don't see too often in a place this old. Rumors concerning the Nutmeg being haunted began when one of the residents reported feeling a strange entity. According to the tale, she was in Room 4 practicing her music lessons when a dark shadowy apparition appeared. A strong sense of dread overcame her, so she fled the area. Since then, local paranormal enthusiasts have made Room 4 a regular pilgrimage. You may want to visit as well—with experiences that still include the dark apparition, voices, and intense cold spots, the Nutmeg Inn has all the symptoms of a haunted house.

Address: 80 Pease Road
Website: www.bbhost.com/nutmeginn/
Activity: S, E, C

Merrimack The Common Man

Reports of a ghost at this location began when a restaurant called Hannah Jack Tavern occupied the building. The premises dates all the way back to 1794, when Matthew Thornton (one of the signers of the Declaration of Independence) built the place to be his home. After the aforementioned tavern closed, the Common Man moved in. (Warning: there are several restaurants of this name, so make sure you visit the one in Merrimack!) This is the location you can visit for some good New England food and to hopefully catch a glimpse of one of the two spirits that allegedly walk the grounds. The apparition of a man has been seen on the ground floor of the restaurant, and the ghost of a Native American is thought to reside in the basement. The restaurant does host functions, so this may be a great place for a paranormal party.

Address: 304 Daniel Webster Highway
Website: www.thecman.com
Activity: A, E

Merrimack Tortilla Flat

How many times have you thought to yourself, "I sure wish I could eat some great tacos while I was ghost hunting." If this has ever crossed your mind, then fret no more. You can do so at Tortilla Flat. Not much is known about this location or its history (other than the fact that it has been a Mexican restaurant for the last 30 years), but it has appeared in several regional books that feature haunted places and area paranormal investigators have made the place a regular stop over the years. Activity in the eatery includes a shadowy apparition that has been seen regularly, the sounds of footsteps/voices, and kitchenware that's known to be moved by invisible hands—sometimes right in front of an astonished patron's face! I bet they were eating tacos...

Address: 595 Daniel Webster Highway
Website: http://tortillaflat.userworld.com/
  fax_menu_merrimack
Activity: A, S, E, T

Nashua Country Tavern Restaurant & Pub

This restored farmhouse originated in 1741 and is the site of one twisted ghost story. Though it smacks of urban legend, employees of the tavern (as well as numerous locals) will tell you that the tale is true. It seems that the house was originally occupied by a sea captain and his wife (named Elizabeth Ford). While at sea, Elizabeth had an affair with another man and became pregnant. When the captain returned home and found his wife with a new child, he promptly killed both of them and buried them on the property. Since then, the ghost of Elizabeth has been seen in the pub numerous times. She likes to hang out in the women's restroom (where she tugs on girls' hair) and to stare out windows that overlook the parking lot. When she's in the mood, she even plays with the dishes and silverware laid out in the dining room.

Address: 452 Amherst Street
Website: www.countrytavern.org
Activity: A, T

New Castle Portsmouth Harbor Lighthouse

The bulk of this lighthouse dates back to 1878, when it was built inside the shell of an older lighthouse (that dated back to 1804). It served the area through the Civil War while neighboring batteries and Fort Constitution kept the peace in the area. The haunting of this lighthouse became well known when the television program *Ghost Hunters* visited the property. On the show, it became apparent that the lighthouse, as well as the neighboring caretaker's house, is haunted. Tales of a female apparition walking the grounds, as well as that of a long-gone lighthouse keeper have been reported in the area for many years. Additional activity on site includes the sounds of voices and footsteps in the lighthouse, as well as shadow shapes and voices in the house. Take a tour of the lighthouse and maybe you'll see one of the ghosts as well!

Address: Route 1B Portsmouth Harbor
Website: www.portsmouthharborlighthouse.org
Activity: A, E, S, T

Portsmouth Star Island

Is there a haunted location in New Hampshire that the television show *Ghost Hunters* hasn't been to? Luckily, yes. But this isn't one of them. When John Smith came to this area in 1614, the place was already known locally to the fisherman—and the Isle of Shoals would eventually become one of the busiest ports in North America. Today it's just as busy, but now it's because of the world-renowned resort. Hot spots on Star Island include Cottage E of the resort (where the spirit of a little boy is said to visit people who stay there), the Charles Vaughn Cottage (now a museum that's said to be plagued with phantom footsteps and voices), and the Doctor's Cottage (where the apparition of a man who committed suicide is often seen). Of course, the main hotel (called the Oceanic Hotel) is considered haunted as well. Guests who stay on the fourth floor have heard all kinds of strange sounds while staying there—including voices, doors opening, and items being dragged across the floor.

Address: Island off Coast of Portsmouth
Website: www.starisland.org
Activity: A, S, E, T, C

Rindge Rindge Historical Society

Originally known as the Hoyt-Allen House (circa 1800), this museum features artifacts and exhibits that illustrate the rich history of the town of Rindge. The place is operated by the Rindge Historical Society who works with area schools through an outreach program and offers tours of the home (check their site for dates and hours). Though employees have known about the strange occurrences that seem to happen in the museum on a regular basis for some time, locals learned about their resident spirit when paranormal groups were brought in to investigate the activity. According to their findings, the place is haunted by a shadowy male apparition that has been seen staring from an upper-story window, and is sometimes accompanied by the scent of tobacco. Witnesses have also experienced seeing objects moving by themselves, hearing disembodied voices, and feeling the sensation of constantly being watched in the place.

Address: 24 School Street
Website: www.town.rindge.nh.us/History
Activity: A, S, E, T, N

Tilton The 1875 Inn at Tilton

Built in the year of its name, the place was originally constructed as a country inn to service area travelers. Over the years, the building has endured many trials and tribulations, including housing the police station (located in the basement), suffering a fire (that broke out in the neighboring building, but damaged part of the inn), and expansion (into an adjoining area that once was a barber shop). The building was completely renovated by the current owners in 2001, and it now contains 12 guest rooms and an on-site bar called the Olive Branch Tavern. It wasn't long after the new owners moved into the place, though, that reports of paranormal activity started filtering in. It began with the sighting of a young female apparition in the Samuel Sanborn Room. Soon, more guests were stepping forward with similar tales of the young spirit—sometimes occurring in the Mary Baker Eddy Room as well. It's thought the ghost is that of a girl named Laura, who died in the aforementioned fire.

Address: 255 Main Street
Website: www.1875inn.com
Activity: A, T

Whitefield Spalding Inn

If there was ever a hotel that was stamped with approval for being haunted, it would be the Spalding. The place was recently purchased by paranormal investigators Jason Hawes and Grant Wilson (co-founders of the group TAPS and the stars of the television series *Ghost Hunters*) and was even featured in an episode of the program.

While renovating the property, it seems that members of the two families experienced disembodied voices and caught glimpses of shadow shapes. During the televised investigation, several pieces of paranormal evidence were gathered, including a couple EVPs, eyewitness accounts of a door opening, and a "hot spot" (similar to a cold spot, only... well... hot). Is this conclusive evidence of a haunting? Maybe not. But it should be enough to intrigue you into a visit to investigate the place for yourself. In addition to getting a great stay (with an on-site eatery called "2 Kings Restaurant & Pub"), the place also hosts regular events with other members of TAPS.

Address: 199 Mountain View Road
Website: www.thespaldinginn.com
Activity: A, S, E, T

Windham The Windham Restaurant

Though this Colonial-style house was built in 1812, the actual farm that it's on goes all the way back to 1729. With great food in a rustic atmosphere, the Windham makes for one of the area's best romantic getaways. The haunted happenings of this eatery started when the place was a French restaurant. Waitresses (especially if they had blond hair) would complain of something tugging at their hair and messing with their jewelry. When the Windham opened in the home, it wasn't long before the staff and patrons started seeing the apparitions of a young boy, a young girl, and a man. Both child spirits have been witnessed on the second floor, and the man (dubbed "Jacob" by employees) has been seen at least once on the first floor. It's thought that the entities are a byproduct of the Dinsmore family (the original occupants of the house). Additional activity includes the sounds of children laughing (usually on the second floor), the disembodied voice of a man (heard in the basement), and numerous objects that have been witnessed moving by themselves.

Address: 59 Range Road
Website: www.windhamrestaurant.com
Activity: A, S, E, T

Wolfeboro Tuc' Me Inn Bed & Breakfast

When it comes to haunted B&B's, it's always nice to have a unique paranormal attraction to look forward to. At the TMI, this would be the piano that's said to be played by a spectral musician! But don't visit just for the ghost—this circa 1850 Federal-styled Colonial inn was built by Reverend Asa Piper, a local entrepreneur who co-owned a nearby lumber mill. He spared little to no expense in creating his house, and the inn today is quite the historical structure. There are seven rooms for rent—each with its own flair and style. For the haunted traveler, any of the rooms will do. In addition to the ghostly piano music that's heard in the house, the sounds of voices and footsteps have also been detected in the second-floor hallways (and it sounds like a small child).

Address: 118 North Main Street
Website: www.tucmeinn.com
Activity: E

NEW JERSEY

Bay Head The Grenville Hotel & Restaurant

Wycoff Applegate built this hotel in 1886 on land purchased a few years earlier by Anna Nunemaker (the owner and operator of a sugar plantation in the West Indies). In 1922, the hotel was sold to Nellie Georgette, who renamed the property "The Georgette," and so it stayed all the way until 1945 when the Grenville Corporation purchased the place. Today the hotel has a new owner and a recent renovation (1987), and it stands as a Victorian masterpiece with a four-star rated restaurant. Ghost stories concerning the Grenville began all the way back in the 1950s and were started by employees who claimed to hear the sounds of children playing in empty hallways, as well as once seeing a child spirit walk through the front lobby. The activity continues today and includes misty apparitions that are seen in the hallways and the sounds of furniture moving during the night.

Address: 345 Main Avenue
Website: www.thegrenville.com
Activity: A, E, T

Boonton Darress Theatre

This circa-1919 theatre has its roots in vaudeville and silent movies, but this changed during the 1940s with the advent of "talking pictures." At that point, the venue became a full-time movie house. When business to the theatre slowed down in the 1960s, the theatre briefly became a pornography-based venue, but this didn't last and the place closed in the late 1970s. After a makeover and a new owner, the Darress is back and offering live performances, as well as film screenings to an eager Boonton populace. Like most theatre ghost tales, the Darress is thought to be haunted by a former actor who performed there in the old days. Activity includes the sounds of singing/music (usually coming from the stage) and chairs that seem to move on their own, which was witnessed several times in the backstage area of the theatre.

Address: 615 Main Street
Website: www.darresstheater.com
Activity: E, T

Cape May Historic Hotel Macomber

This seashore hotel is a Shingle-style mansion (circa 1915) that features an on-site solarium, the Union Park Dining Room, and a ghost called "Lilly." Local rumors say that the spirit is that of a young woman who died in the house from choking on a chicken bone. Though this cannot be verified, it is true that patrons have witnessed a female apparition walking through the middle of the second floor (Union Park) dining room. What's more, according to employees, Lilly isn't alone in the hotel. The Macomber's hottest spot for ghostly activity (and the place you will want to stay) is the notorious Room 10. This room was a regular stay for an elderly woman in the 1920s who now visits the area from beyond the grave. It's said that staying in this room could mean experiencing dresser drawers that open by themselves, door knobs rattling, and (if you're lucky) the appearance of the actual woman.

Address: 727 Beach Avenue
Website: www.hotelmacomber.com
Activity: A, E, T

Cape May The John F. Craig House

This Victorian inn was constructed in 1866, but when the home needed some extra rooms, a separate house (that was built sometime before 1850) was attached. The bed and breakfast is strategically located for exploring the area—though with fun events like "afternoon tea" and daily waffle challenges happening at breakfast, you may spend more time at the inn than you think. Cape May is known in New Jersey for its paranormal leanings, hosting ghost tours around town and openly celebrating their local psychic and author, Craig McManus (he often hosts séances and events at the John F. Craig House). The spirits that occupy this location are as well known as any other in town. Room 4 (a.k.a. the Susan Byrd Room) is said to be occupied by a female spirit who has been heard and seen in this area (thought to be a former resident of the home, Emma Craig) and Room 2 (a.k.a. the Lucy Johnson Room) is where ghostly hands have been known to manipulate objects.

Address: 609 Columbia Avenue
Website: www.johnfcraig.com
Activity: A, E, T, C

Cape May The Southern Mansion

This elaborate and massive estate house was built in 1863 for George Allen and his family, and it remained their homestead until the last member of clan, Ester Mercur, passed away on the premises. The home would then become a boarding house, then an apartment complex, then … finally … a top-tier bed and breakfast that opened in 1996. In addition to accommodations, this B&B offers tours and rentals for events, so the whole gamut of paranormal opportunities awaits you at this fabulous location! On the paranormal side of things, it's said that the last member of the Allen family (the aforementioned Ester) is still hanging around the mansion. She is known to appear with the scent of lilacs and to mostly be seen in the kitchen area and the upstairs hallway.

Address: 720 Washington Street
Website: www.southernmansion.com
Activity: A, E, N

Clinton The Red Mill Museum

Sitting along the Raritan River, this mill is still serving the local population by hosting festivals and events, as well as tours of the mill/museum. Inside, you will find artifacts and displays that take you back to the time when the mill was first built in 1810. If you're in the area close to Halloween, they even host a haunted house on the site—a fact that's ironic because the mill itself is considered to be haunted! Employees of the museum have experienced a strange residual effect in the main area there (the alarm bell will ring and the sounds of footsteps are heard on the second floor), as well as experienced an entity that has touched people in the museum. But perhaps the most commonly reported activity is that of a spectral girl that's often seen and heard in the mill's sewing room.

Address: 56 Main Street
Website: www.theredmill.org
Activity: A, E, T, R

Collingswood Collings Knight House

This living museum is operated by the Friends of Collings-Knight House, which offers tours of the home, as well as the occasional event. The house was originally located in the middle of a 62-acre farm, and construction took place between 1824 and 1827. In 1948, the last member of the family sold the estate to Charles H. Chase, who later donated the property to the city as a historic site. Tales concerning the haunting are nearly as old as the house itself. Locals will tell you that the property "has always been haunted" and current activity is no sur-

prise to them. Workers who spend enough time on the site (as well as paranormal groups who have had the privilege of investigating there) report that voices, footsteps, and shadow shapes are common on the premises. This house is in constant need of funds to maintain the property—contact them about donations and possibly renting the venue for your own ghost hunt.

Address: Collings Avenue at Browning Road
Website: www.collingsknighthouse.org
Activity: S, E

Columbus Olde Columbus Inne

Strange tales and commonly reported sightings of ghosts have made this inn one of the most popular haunted sites in New Jersey. In fact, nearly every area paranormal group has made the place a training ground for new investigators. The place presents a challenge because of the sheer amount of urban legend and lack of historical information available to the investigator. On the legend side, tales of multiple apparitions (including a Native American that's been seen sitting on a barstool in the on-site tavern and a pair of female ghosts that are seen in various areas) have been reputedly witnessed, and there are even stories that say the infamous "Jersey Devil" was born on this property. The basement is reported to even contain an old jail cell, which just further adds to the mystique. On the history side, there's simply not much of it—other than the building likely dates back to the mid-1800s. This location is a perfect place to have a good meal and to unravel an even better mystery.

Address: 24491 West Main Street
Website: www.oldecolumbusinne.com
Activity: A, E, T, S, C

Haddon Township The Ritz Theatre Company

This circa 1927 theatre was the venue of choice for vaudeville players back in the day. The art form ran strong at this location right up until moving pictures became the current fad and took over. Over the years, the theatre has managed to stay in almost constant operations (even when this meant showing the occasional porno flick during the 1970s) and continues today with live performances/productions. Like a lot of theatres constructed during this period (what is it about the 1920s?), the Ritz is rumored to be haunted. Actors and employees alike have reported seeing strange, glowing balls of light shoot across the stage and bounce around in the backstage area. Add in props that move on their own and the occasional voice, and you have a pretty good ghost story.

Address: 915 White Horse Pike
Website: www.ritztheatreco.org
Activity: O, E, T

Hoboken The Brass Rail Restaurant & Bar

This restaurant hearkens back to the days of jazz, swingers, and early 1900's nostalgia. The food manages to stay upscale without being pretentious, and the drinks are known for being second to none. Interestingly, the residual haunting that's said to occur here is reminiscent of an activity that's all too commonly associated with the Brass Rail: weddings. This eatery is one of the area's best caterers for this kind of affair—and it's said that in the wee hours (after the restaurant is closed) a phantom wedding procession walks through the middle of the premises. There's a ghostly bride, a groom, and even the ladies/gentlemen in wait trailing behind them. Though no other activity has been reported, those who have worked at the Brass Rail state the place has a "vibe" about it that suggests visitors are never quite alone.

Address: 135 Washington Street
Website: www.thebrassrailnj.com
Activity: A, R

Jersey City The Virginia Tavern

Sometimes the most enjoyable part of investigating a ghost story is simply unraveling the mystery of a place. The Virginia Tavern is just such a story. Not only is there little-to-no information about the property online, but even the patrons are unaware of any history the building may have. This, of course, means that you must visit this site. Worst-case scenario, you'll have a couple tropical drinks (reportedly the specialty of the bar) and have a fun night out. Best-case scenario, you'll get to see the dark apparition that has been reported in the tavern. For years, locals have whispered stories concerning patrons being touched by ghosts, bar glasses flying across the room, and odd cold spots that seem to suddenly appear at random. Most of the accounts take place right there in the main area, so getting to the hot spots is no problem. Getting the history … well, that may be a problem.

Address: 130 Mallory Avenue
Website: www.virginiatavern.com
Activity: S, T, C, N

Mays Landing The Abbott House

This Victorian home was built in the 1860s by local attorney Joseph E. P. Abbott and his wife Adeline. The place remained in the Abbott family for many generations before changing hands and becoming the bed and breakfast it is today. If you visit, you will find a wonderful place to stay that features a pool, a nice veranda, and a nearby view that overlooks the Great Egg Harbor River. Local legend places the B&B in the middle of a sinister ghost story. According to the tale, Joseph was quite the disciplinarian and would often lock his child, David, in a closet for punishment. As a result of this trauma, visitors today can see and hear David still hanging out on the second floor. He's said to appear to children and to be preceded by the sounds of a ball bouncing.

Address: 6056 Main Street
Website: www.innsite.com/inns/A104986
Activity: A, E, T

Morristown Jimmy's Haunt

What's better than visiting a place with the word "haunt" right in its name? The spiritual activity here is almost as famous as the restaurant and nightclub (it's even featured on their website right along with their menu). The building dates back to 1749 and was originally called the John Sayre House. On May 11, 1833, Judge Samuel Sayre, his wife Sara, and their maid Phoebe were beaten to death by a lunatic named Antoine Le Blanc (a recent immigrant from France). Le Blanc was executed for the deed, then "dissected" by a local mortician for study. A picture of the "death mask" of Le Blanc actually hangs in Jimmy's today! Over the years, the place has been several businesses (including the Winchester Turnpike Inn and the Wedgewood Inn) and reports of constant paranormal activity came from all of them. The tradition continues today—patrons who hang out at Jimmy's report that the spirit of Phoebe is still around. She's known for moving the chandelier, opening/closing doors, and whispering to guests.

Address: 217 South Street
Website: www.jimmyshaunt.com
Activity: A, R, E, T, C

Mount Holly Burlington County Prison Museum

This national historic landmark first opened its doors in 1811 and pretty much stayed in constant use until 1965. This was mostly because the place was built with a lot of modern amenities that allowed for actual rehabilitation of the prisoners. The haunting of this prison began while prisoners were still on the premises. In 1833, a man named Joel Clough was hanged for stabbing a woman to death. Immediately following the execution, guards (as well as other prisoners) started hearing a strange moaning that would come from the area of Clough's cell—the area of the prison that's known as "the Dungeon." This area was used for the solitary confinement of prisoners who had been sentenced to death and were awaiting their punishment. Today, you can visit the museum, as well as attend hosted events there. While you tour the exhibitions, keep your eyes and ears open—sightings of shadowy apparitions and the strange sounds of disembodied voices are commonly reported in the prison.

Address: 128 High Street
Website: www.prisonmuseum.net
Activity: A, S, E

Neshanic Station Neshanic Inn

Formerly known as Murphy's Crocodile Inn, the Neshanic Inn is an area hot spot for the young folks who enjoy live music and a night on the town. While still operating as Murphy's, the place gained a local reputation for its ghost. Employees would regale the patrons with tales of a spooky basement and lights turning themselves on. Today, it's thought that the activity continues (though they don't really promote their haunting like many similar locations in New Jersey). Check in with your bartender or waiter at the inn and get more current reports of the paranormal activity—and keep an ear cocked toward the basement door. In addition to playing with the lighting, the ghost is also known for occasionally speaking aloud.

Address: 102 Woodfern Road
Website: www.myspace.com/crocinn
Activity: E, T

Ocean City The Flanders Hotel

It's rare that a hotel is actually proud of their ghost, so when the Flanders actually commissioned a picture to be painted of their resident spirit, it was major local news. Sometimes referred to as "the Lady in White," employees simply call the ghost there "Emily." She is so popular with the hotel that they even named their café after her! The Flanders has been looming over the boardwalk of Ocean City since 1923, and it makes for a great location for touring the beach. Your best chance of catching a glimpse of Emily (or at least hearing her) is to hang out in the "Hall of Mirrors." In this area, it's said that ghostly laughter and singing is often heard. Other activity in the hotel includes prank-like incidents such as items being moved, doors being unlocked/locked, and light bulbs being unscrewed in rooms. If it's open to the public, you may want to visit the basement as well ... Emily was recently seen there in all her glory.

Address: 719 East 11th Street
Website: www.theflandershotel.com
Activity: A, E, T

Ocean City Ocean City Mansion

If you prefer staying at a bed and breakfast over a massive chain-style hotel, and you enjoy getting the whole "spa treatment," Ocean City Mansion is the place for you. This B&B features differently themed rooms (and even has full cottages/bungalows outside the house you can rent)—but not all of them are known for ghostly activity. To experience the paranormal at this location, you will want to stay in the Honeymoon Suite or one of the other rooms located in the main house area. When the current owners first took over in 1997, they started hearing strange footsteps coming from the second floor of the home, so a local paranormal group was called in to investigate. Data was collected and evidence was gathered that supports the idea that OCM is haunted. Expect to hear strange sounds (including voices) and items moving in this location.

Address: 416 Central Avenue
Website: www.ocmansion.com
Activity: E, T

Ocean Grove Ashley House

Formerly known as the Angel Nook Inn, this bed and breakfast dates back to 1875 and represents a lot of local history. Today, they feature five guest rooms in this Victorian masterpiece and offer food with a New Orleans flair. Locals heard about the haunted happenings of this B&B when a guest reported feeling someone touch them while they were sleeping. Soon, more visitors reported the same feeling—including one woman who, while waiting for her husband to return from jogging, felt a ghostly finger run up her back. Others have related stories involving a spirit actually lying on the bed with them. Check in with the innkeeper to get more info concerning your stay at Ashley House; you will want the room with the most activity to experience the friendly spirit at this location!

Address: 14 Surf Avenue
Website: www.ashleyhousenj.net
Activity: E, T

Perth Amboy The Proprietary House

This place was the home of the last Royal Governor of New Jersey and was built in 1764. It is the last house of this nature to remain standing—though this was no easy task. After numerous years of abandon and neglect (not to mention area vandals), the state took over in 1967, and the property now hosts events, as well as tours (yes, even ghost tours). Hot spots in the old mansion include the drawing room, where the shadowy apparition of a man is often seen (and thought to possibly be the spirit of William Franklin, the illegitimate son of Benjamin Franklin and the last royal governor of the state), and the second floor that's said to be haunted by the spirit of a young boy who was killed on the premises. Pay attention as you tour this home—shadow shapes and the sounds of footsteps are commonplace at this site.

Address: 149 Kearny Avenue
Website: www.proprietaryhouse.org
Activity: A, S, E, T

Pittsgrove Ye Olde Centerton Inn

Dating back to 1706, this former stagecoach stop served as a welcome lodging and hot meal for many a weary traveler journeying between Greenwich and Philadelphia. It survived the Revolutionary War and managed to continuously serve the public through multiple owners and even more years. These days, the inn is known for its food and spirits (even the non-haunted spirits—*Wine Spectator* gave the business an award of excellence in 2008), as well as its ghosts. With six private dining areas in the inn, you will never want for a place to eat! The downstairs is said to be haunted by the spirit of a past server in the old tavern. His disembodied voice is often heard, and he is often blamed for silverware and glassware being moved. The upstairs dining areas are the stomping grounds of a young female ghost thought to be a past family member who lived on the site. The sounds of her laughing and playing have been heard in this area, and it's reported that she likes to appear with an intense cold spot.

Address: 1136 Almond Road
Website: www.centertoninn.com
Activity: E, T, C

Point Pleasant Magee's West Side Tavern

This tavern has been the subject of numerous legends and stories in Point Pleasant for over a hundred years. Though they still serve drinks and offer live entertainment (much like they would have during their early years), it's fair to say that quite a few folks journey to Magee's to experience the paranormal. Tales that surround the place include two ghosts known as "Captain John" and his daughter that are part of a residual haunting—one that points to abuse on the part of the father—as well as the building being used as a morgue after a notorious sea accident that occurred in 1846. Activity in the tavern includes spectral voices, items moving on their own, and shadowy apparitions that are thought to be those who lay in state on the premises. Be sure to check out the cool painting of Captain John hanging there as well!

Address: 2114 Route 88
Website: www.myspace.com/mageeswestside
  tavern
Activity: R, A, E, T, S

Somerset Van Wickle House

This Dutch-style house was constructed in 1722 for Symen and Geradina Evert, and it was built in one of the area's best locations along the Raritan River. Over the centuries, this home has endured wars (including British occupation during the Revolutionary War) and numerous generations of husbands, wives, and children. Now operated by the Meadows Foundation, you can tour the home, as well as host an event or wedding there (wow, imagine getting married in a haunted house!). This location plays host to one of New Jersey's strangest hauntings— while a couple was living in the home during the 1970s, the man of the house witnessed five simultaneous apparitions standing at his bed! Even current visitors have reported seeing the apparition of an elderly woman, as well as constantly finding things moved and hearing doors slam.

Address: 1289 Easton Avenue
Website: www.themeadowsfoundation.org/
  van-wickle
Activity: A, E, T

Surf City Surf City Hotel

The original portion of this building was constructed in the late 1800s, and was known as a popular drinking spot for those who worked at sea. During the 1940s the business expanded—not only physically, but in their clientele as well. It suddenly became a popular vacation spot. Today, you can stay here, as well as enjoy the food and entertainment on the premises. For the paranormal tourist, the hotel is even better. According to local history, a ship known as the Powhattan sank just off shore from the hotel in 1854 after encountering a storm, which resulted in over 300 people drowning. Bodies washed up on the beach for a month following the accident, and many of them were taken to this hotel. Darker rumors circulated as well that the hotel owner at the time, Edward Jennings, was caught robbing the dead who washed ashore and was soon killed on the premises. So who haunts the hotel? Mr. Jennings? Or maybe the dead from the shipwreck? Nobody knows. But activity is experienced at this location—and it includes misty apparitions, such as the site of a ghostly mother and child and the sounds of disembodied voices.

Address: 8th Street and Long Beach Island
  Boulevard
Website: www.surfcityhotel.com
Activity: A, M, E, S

Vernon The Vernon Inn

Originally known as the Vandegriff Hotel, this site was erected in 1833 by a local tavern owner named John Vandegriff. It served as lodgings, as well as a famed local meeting house, and was later renamed the Vernon House by new owner Thomas DeKay. In 1936, the property suffered a massive fire that destroyed the top half of the building, but this was replaced. It was the first of several renovations that have occurred over the years (with the most recent being in 2003). The haunting of the inn is well known to the staff of this restaurant, so you will want to mention that you are interested in their tales to get the most current information regarding their spirits. They will most definitely tell you of the shadowy apparitions seen on a regular basis there, as well as the full-bodied apparition of a man in a long coat that walked through the middle of the dining room.

Address: 340 State Road 94
Website: www.thevernoninn.com
Activity: A, S, E, T

Wharton Knotty Pine Pub

There's not much history concerning this location—unless you include the Knotty Pine's long-standing reputation has for its food and drink. It was purchased by new owners in 1997 and is one of the area's most popular hangouts with the younger crowd. In addition to the beer, the place serves up pub grub and regular servings of local sports. Though this is probably enough to attract you for a night out, you may want to consider the paranormal activity there as well. Employees, as well as patrons, have joked about the strange things that are seen and heard on this property—things like items moving by themselves, shadowy shapes darting through the place, and even the occasional female voice.

Address: 242 East Union Turnpike
Website: www.knottypinepub.com
Activity: S, E, T

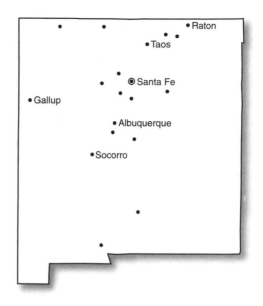

NEW MEXICO

Albuquerque Andaluz Hotel

This newly remodeled hotel was one of the more popular haunted spots to visit in New Mexico when it was called the La Posada de Albuquerque Hotel. It dates back to 1939, and it was the first hotel built by New Mexico native Conrad Hilton (of Hilton hotel fame). In addition to fine accommodations at the Andaluz, the restaurant there (Lucia) is one of the best in the area. While it was still the Posada, though, reports of the paranormal were a common event. The hotel's fourth floor is reputedly haunted by the spirit of a female dressed in a 1940's-style outfit, complete with a hat, as well as an elderly woman in a pink dress. The seventh floor and the second-floor ballroom are other areas the ghosts like to visit as well. Activity was fairly common in the Posada, so there's

no reason to assume it has stopped just because the hotel got a face-lift. You should visit, though, to find out for yourself.

Address: 125 Second Street Northwest
Website: www.hotelandaluz.com
Activity: A, E, T

Albuquerque Bernalillo County Courthouse

When Bernalillo County built a new courthouse in 2001, the old version of the building became obsolete. But, being of historical value (the former building dates back to 1926), the city has decided to clean up the building for use (most likely as a museum in the near future, or city offices). During this massive cleanup, workers on the site began experiencing a few strange things. They noticed that objects in the basement seemed to be moving on their own—including a book that was actually thrown in the direction of the workers at one point. The word paranormal didn't get used until one of the community service members witnessed the apparition of a little girl in the area. According to the report, she was wearing a school uniform and she vanished right before the surprised worker's eyes.

Address: 1 Civil Plaza
Website: www.bernco.gov
Activity: A, T

Albuquerque Bottger Mansion of Old Town

When Charles Bottger worked at the Sunnyside Tavern in the 1890s, he probably had no idea that he'd end up marrying the tavern-owner's wife! But that's exactly what happened—after his boss died, of course. Bottger married the widow, Michaela, and in the process acquired all the land in the area. The old house on the property was demolished in 1908, and the current mansion was constructed. These days, the house is a bed and breakfast. Tales concerning the haunting of the B&B began when a former owner reported sensing the presence of several spirits on the premises. It wasn't long before guests starting having experiences as well—especially in the Stephanie Lynn Room. Sightings of a misty apparition, cold spots, and the apparition of a woman (thought to be a long-gone member of the Bottger family) have been witnessed. Employees also believe a male spirit inhabits the manor. They call him "Charles" and hold him responsible for items moving, cold spots in the lobby, and a disembodied male voice that's often heard.

Address: 110 San Felipe Street Northwest
Website: www.bottger.com
Activity: A, E, C, T

Albuquerque Church Street Café

Located in the historic Casa de Ruiz, this café is a veritable time machine—as well as a wonderful restaurant. The place was built during the early years of Albuquerque (sometime after 1706) and is thought to be the oldest home in the city, if not the state. Amazingly, the house remained in the Ruiz family all the way until 1991, when the last resident of the family, Rufina G. Ruiz died at the age of 91. And even though the place is now a café, it's said that the old adobe home is still inhabited by a member of the Ruiz family: Sara Ruiz, mother of Rufina. Sara has been heard yelling in the restaurant (this started during renovations) and has even been witnessed walking through the dining room (a waiter reported seeing her in a long, black dress). Customers have reported hearing her as well, and employees note that Sara will often get their attention by tossing small stones when she wants to be noticed.

Address: 2111 Church Street Northwest
Website: www.churchstreetcafe.com
Activity: A, E, T

Albuquerque High Noon Saloon

This restaurant—known for outstanding margaritas and Mexican food—is located in one of the oldest original structures of old-town Albuquerque (circa 1785). Several area families lived in the old adobe home over the years, and it's thought that one of the couples who resided there is still visiting restaurant patrons today. With a pair of apparitions, paranormal activity is relatively high at this location. A male spirit has been witnessed in the lounge area of the eatery (seen wearing a long cloak) as well as smelled (the usual scent of smoke). And a female apparition roams the main dining room (she has been seen and heard there several times). Additional activity in the restaurant includes barware moving by itself and shadow shapes seen on occasion in the dining room.

Address: 425 San Felipe Street Northwest
Website: www.999dine.com/nm/highnoon/
Activity: A, S, E, T, N

Albuquerque La Placita Dining Rooms

This eatery has been serving up quality Mexican food since 1931, though the actual adobe building the restaurant occupies goes back to before the 1880s. In its early history, the property served as a frontier outpost and trading center, as well as a home for the Armijo family. At least two spirits are reported—a male and a young female—and activity is common enough that a visit to the restaurant is warranted. The male entity is known for calling out to employees by name and is usually blamed for sudden cold spots that appear in the dining room. The female spirit is that of a child. She has been seen and heard in the restrooms, where she is known to play with the lights and water, as well as surprise the occasional guest by appearing in the mirror behind them!

Address: 206 San Felipe Street Northwest
Website: www.laplacitadiningroom.com
Activity: A, E, C, T

Aztec Miss Gail's Inn

This state-registered historic site was built in 1878 and then converted into a local hotel in 1907 by a local man named George Stone. Today, the feel of the place is more B&B than hotel. The locals in Aztec are more than familiar with the haunted status of Miss Gail's Inn—stories concerning the ghosts in the old building have been passed down for almost a hundred years. According to local legend, there's a tree outside the inn that was used to hang folks in the old days. Because of this, at least one deceased criminal now stalks the inn. He's said to hang out in Room 7 and is known for speaking with an angry voice and making loud sounds that startle those who stay there. In addition to this spirit, there is also a female apparition that has been witnessed on the stairs. She's said to come down the stairs directly at you, ignore you, and disappear before your eyes!

Address: 300 South Main
Website: www.missgailsinn.com
Activity: A, E, T

Chama Foster's Hotel, Restaurant and Saloon

This structure, the oldest commercial building in the city of Chama, was built in 1881 to accommodate folks traveling along the Denver and Rio Grande Western Railroad. If you are interested in experiencing a rail trip much like travelers in the 1800s, you may consider booking a trip on the Cumbres and Toltec Scenic Railroad. After the trip, you can stop in at Foster's for a nice meal and the chance to see something paranormal. Though most activity happens in the upper area of the hotel, it's said the occasional bit of activity occurs in the restaurant as well. The place is thought to be haunted by the female apparition of a judge who was poisoned to death in the hotel, as well as a cowboy who's been seen walking the hotel's halls. If this isn't enough, there's even been the report of a child ghost seen crying in the hotel. If you decide to spend the night, you will want either Room 21 or Room 25—these rooms are hot spots that get a lot of attention.

Address: 393 South Terrace Avenue
Website: www.fosters1881.com
Activity: A, E, T

Cimarron St. James Hotel

This Old West hotel and saloon was a regular stop for criminals like Jesse James and Clay Allison. It was constructed in 1872 by Henri Lambert, and during its lawless years, over 25 people died violently in the place. In 1985, new owners took control of the historic hotel, remodeled it, and soon opened doors for business once again. At least, almost the whole hotel opened to the public... Room 18 is said to be so haunted that it is not available to the general public. Gunslinger Thomas James Wright was killed in this room and is said to be a malicious spirit in the afterlife. For a nicer paranormal experience, consider staying in Room 17, where a female apparition (thought to be Mary Lambert, the wife of the original owner) appears with the scent of roses. Other eyewitness accounts on the property includes glowing balls of light that shoot through the hotel, a male apparition seen standing by the bar, and whispered voices that are heard throughout the building.

Address: 217 South Collison Avenue
Website: www.exstjames.com
Activity: A, S, O, E, T, C, N

Cloudcroft The Lodge Resort and Spa

This mountain retreat dates back to 1899 and the Alamogordo and Sacramento Mountain Railway. It was originally known as Cloudcroft Lodge until 1909, when the place burned down to the ground. The second incarnation was finished in 1911 and has provided upscale accommodations and dining for thousands of visitors. With paranormal tourists, The Lodge is a holy pilgrimage—all due to the spirit of a woman named "Rebecca." Paintings (and even stained glass representations) of Rebecca hang throughout the resort, and their restaurant is even named for her! What's less known, though, is that she may not be alone. Many who stay at The Lodge report that a second entity is there as well (some believe this spirit is another female, but some say it is the lumberjack from Rebecca's story). As for Rebecca, local legend says she was murdered by her jealous lumberjack boyfriend sometime in the 1930s. Since then, she likes to frequent Room 101 (a.k.a. the Governor's Suite), where she plays with the phone, and Room 104, where guests reported hearing her voice and seeing her standing beside the bed. Rebecca has also been seen in the lounge and is known to move barware/silverware.

Address: 1 Corona Place
Website: www.thelodgeresort.com
Activity: A, E, T, C

Eagle Nest Laguna Vista Lodge

This lodge features a saloon-style restaurant that actually used to be the lobby of yet another hotel, the El Monte Hotel (built sometime in the 1890s). In addition to rooms in the "Guney" as locals call the place, you can also sleep in one of the cabins on the property. But if you want a chance at seeing a ghost, you should book your room in the main lodge. The female spirit that haunts the Laguna Vista is part of a local legend that says she was a bride who was deserted in the hotel by her new husband. She was afraid of leaving and missing his possible return, so she ended up working at the hotel until she passed away there. Now she looks for her husband forevermore in the lodge. She's usually seen wearing a dress and wandering the area by the hidden staircase. She's also been known to occasionally play a piano that's in the building.

Address: 51 East Therma Street
Website: www.lagunavistalodge.com
Activity: A, E, T

Gallup El Rancho Hotel

This hotel was constructed in 1937 as a home for movie stars visiting the area and working on local films. The original owner of the place was R. E. Griffith (brother of director D. W. Griffith, famous for the film *Birth of a Nation*). He created a place where folks like John Wayne and Errol Flynn would feel at home, and could also cut loose in the off hours from filming. Perhaps it's one of these past stars who now walk the halls of the El Rancho in the afterlife. Employees and guests have both witnessed strange, shadowy apparitions in the halls of the hotel, as well as heard the sounds of voices and footsteps on the upper floor. Tales of the ghostly activity are well known to those at the hotel, so you may want to ask around a bit about the activity before settling on a room.

Address: 1000 East Route 66
Website: www.historicelranchohotel.com
Activity: S, E, T

Jemez Springs Jemez State Monument

Located just a short distance from Albuquerque, this state site contains the ruins of a city built by the ancestors of the Jemez Pueblo people, as well as a church that dates back to 1610 and the earliest Spanish settlers of the area. For years, visiting this area has been a local "legend trip" for teenagers who want a good scare—or just want to dare someone to do something scary. For paranormal investigators, though, this site is one of the region's best residual hauntings. Visitors have experienced the sights and sounds of the priests and settlers who inhabited the area so many years ago. When it isn't shadowy apparitions, it's misty figures and glowing balls of light that roam the area. Be sure to check the park's website for their hours. Since most of the activity is witnessed at night, you probably will want to visit in the winter months.

Address: State Highway 4
Website: www.nmmonuments.org
Activity: A, R, E, S, O

Lamy Legal Tender Saloon & Restaurant

This unique location is part of the Lamy Railroad & History Museum. It's part of a complex that includes a restaurant, rooms for rent (for events and such), and even an old-style, train car café called the Lamy Station Café. The Legal Tender was built in 1881 as the Browne and Manzanares General Store, but was later turned into the Pink Garter in the 1950s. If ever there was a one-stop location where a person could learn about local history and encounter the paranormal, this is it! There are said to be three ghosts on the premises of the Legal Tender. There is a female spirit who's often witnessed climbing the stairs into the parlor area. Then there's the young girl who's been seen sitting on the stairs. Finally, there is the dark apparition of a male gunslinger who's thought to have been gunned down there.

Address: 151 Old Lamy Trail
Website: www.lamymuseum.org
Activity: A, E

Las Vegas Historic Plaza Hotel

Though lesser known than Las Vegas, Nevada, the history of New Mexico's city of the same name is just as interesting. This was the last Spanish colony to be established in North America, and it was a regular stop for frontiersmen journeying along the Santa Fe Trail. In 1882, Romero and Jean Pendaries built the Plaza Hotel to handle the sudden influx of railroad passengers needing a place to stay. Since then, the hotel has had its ups and downs—as well as several owners. Today, though, the business thrives once again and offers a historic saloon and hotel for the discriminating traveler. So good, in fact, that a former owner of the property (Byron T. Mills) has decided to stick around forever. It's reported that his apparition has been seen many times in Room 310 of the hotel. If you can't get this room, don't be disappointed, because on occasion he has also been smelled (via cigar smoke) and heard in the saloon.

Address: 230 Plaza Street
Website: www.plazahotel-nm.com
Activity: A, E, N

Los Alamos Bandelier National Monument

This park is currently being renovated—but you can still visit to see the remnants of the Pueblo people who lived in this area so many years ago. There are several trails (of varying difficulty) that will guide you through the park's sites and back to the ancient stomping grounds of the Anasazi people (who in themselves have quite a few legends told about them). Most of the spooky tales regarding this area come from hik-ers and campers who have visited and seen quite a few unexplainable things. These include ghost lights, strange mists that almost seem to follow the living, and the sounds of moans/cries. Since Native Americans lived in this area for hundreds of years, it stands to reason that hundreds died (and were probably buried) in the park. For your best chance at witnessing something for yourself, you may want to obtain a backcountry camping permit so you can journey into the areas that contain cliff-side dwellings.

Address: 15 Entrance Road
Website: www.nps.gov/band
Activity: R, M, E, O

Los Lunas The Luna Mansion

This estate was home to Solomon and Adelaida Luna, descendants of the Luna and Otero families who came to New Mexico in the 1530s. The house was built by the Santa Fe Railway in exchange for passage through the family's lands and was constructed in a combination of Victorian and Colonial styles (circa 1881). If you visit the mansion, you will be doing so for one of the area's best steaks, and to have a drink in the Spirit Lounge located in the upstairs of the house. The current (and new) owners gave the lounge this name because of the ghost stories concerning the home. It's said that the spirit of Josephita Otero still resides in the mansion and that she's often seen on the stairs that lead from the front door to the upstairs area, as well as in the actual lounge itself. When you visit there, though, choose your seat carefully—several witnesses have seen Josephita sitting in the lounge area and you don't want to sit on her …

Address: 110 West Main Street
Website: www.lunamansion.com
Activity: A

Madrid The Mine Shaft Tavern

The first (and original) incarnation of this tavern burned to the ground in 1899, which eventually made way for today's version that opened for business in 1947. Unfortunately for the bar, though, the local mining industry would completely dry up in 1954 and transform the small town of Madrid into a ghost town. When you visit the place today, you will find the tavern, as well as a great local museum and theater. According to employees of the restaurant, the spirit of a woman named "Madeleine" now shares the space with them. Strange events in the tavern include barware that moves on its own, voices, and the occasional glimpse of a strange woman (usually in the reflection of a window or mirror) that's said to be the apparition of Madeleine herself.

Address: 2846 Highway 14
Website: www.themineshafttavern.com
Activity: A, E, T

Mesilla Double Eagle Restaurant

Whether you visit this restaurant for the "World's Largest Green Chile Cheeseburger" (an offering on the Pepper's Café menu) or for their highly praised Sunday brunch, you will want to stay for the wonderful atmosphere (circa 1840s adobe mansion) and the interesting ghost story. The legend goes like this: In the 1850s, Carlotta Maes was the señora of the house. She returned home one day to find her son, Armando, in the arms of their maid, Inez. In a rage, she attacked them with a pair of scissors, stabbing each of them one time. They both died in the home and are now said to haunt the place to this day—specifically in the area of Carlotta's Salon, which was the bedroom in which they passed away. Patrons of the eatery have seen both apparitions, as well as heard the sounds of disembodied voices and seen various pieces of cutlery/barware move.

Address: 2355 Calle de Guadalupe
Website: www.double-eagle-mesilla.com
Activity: A, E, T

Mountainair Shaffer Hotel

Clem Shaffer was an artist who moved to Mountainair to advance his art. After his first wife died, he married a local by the name of Lena Imboden and built the place that's now the Shaffer Hotel in 1908. In addition to providing lodgings to the paranormal traveler, the hotel also has a restaurant and curio shop. As for the ghosts, they are said to be the original Shaffer family—known to hotel employees as "Pop" and "Ma." They have been seen in various hallways of the hotel—sometimes in full apparition form, sometimes as a shadowy shape darting through the building. Other activity on the premises includes items moving on their own, disembodied voices, and the overwhelming sensation of someone watching/standing behind you.

Address: 103 West Main Street
Website: www.shafferhotel.com
Activity: A, S, E, T

Raton Shuler Theater

This landmark is owned and operated by the city of Raton and features live performances, as well as theater productions, on a regular basis. It was built by Dr. James Jackson Shuler (a local surgeon, former mayor, and theater enthusiast) in the early 1900s. The first performance at the theater was the play, *The Red Rose,* which opened on April 27, 1915. Dr. Shuler is said to have loved the theater so much that he now visits the place from beyond the grave. Activity in the theater includes footsteps and voices heard in the stage area, props that magically move in the backstage area, and sudden cold spots that portend the presence of Mr. Shuler.

Address: 131 North 2nd Street
Website: www.shulertheater.com
Activity: E, T, C

Santa Fe La Fonda on the Plaza

This hotel is a paranormal pilgrimage for investigators who live in New Mexico (or any neighboring state) and has been a well-known haunted location for decades. When this hotel was built in 1922, it was erected on the site of a previous inn that dated back to the 1600s! In 1925, it became an infamous "Harvey House" that provided upscale service to stars and locals alike—a tradition that the hotel continues today. The previous inn at this location was for a time used as a local courthouse—and even held executions right on the property. A remnant from this past, Judge John P. Slough, is now said to haunt La Fonda. He was killed on the property and now walks the halls of the hotel. A second apparition is seen in the dining room as well; it's thought that this spirit is that of a man who lost his fortune and leapt to his death down a well ... a well that used to stand in the center of the present-day dining room. His spirit is seen approaching this spot, then disappearing!

Address: 100 East San Francisco Street
Website: www.lafondasantafe.com
Activity: A, E

Santa Fe La Posada de Santa Fe Resort & Spa

This upscale resort has every amenity for the discriminating traveler, including a spa, the restaurant Fuego (an award-winning eatery), and nearby winter sports. Prior to providing such luxuries, though, the place was simply a mansion and farm to Abraham Staab and his wife Julia (circa 1882). It would later become an artists' colony and then a hotel. But according to local legend (and more than a few witnesses),

Julia never left! She passed away in what is now Room 256, which is said to be one of the hottest spots for paranormal activity in the hotel. Her apparition, as well as her voice, has been experienced in this room. Julia has also been seen on the stairs and standing by the fireplace (of course you can also see her via the painting that hangs downstairs, too). There is a lesser-known male spirit on the premises as well, but you may want to get information regarding this entity straight from the hotel staff when you visit, as he is seldom seen.

Address: 330 East Palace Avenue
Website: www.laposada.rockresorts.com
Activity: A, E

Socorro Fort Craig National Historic Site

Established in 1854, this frontier fort played a vital role in the Indian campaigns, as well as the Civil War. The infamous Buffalo Soldiers were stationed at this fort, as well as military luminaries like Kit Carson and Captain Jack Crawford. Much of this history can be seen at the park today via reenactments and by visiting the ruins of the old fort. Like many other military parks, Fort Craig is considered to be haunted—though most of the activity suggests a residual haunting. The sounds of guns and cries of pain have been heard (thought to be remnants of a Civil War battle that occurred here on February 21, 1862). There is also an apparition of a Confederate soldier that has been seen by on-site caretakers/employees.

Address: 901 South Highway 85
Website: www.blm.gov/nm/st/en/prog/
   recreation/socorro/fort_craig
Activity: A, R, E

Taos Kit Carson Home & Museum

Thought to date back to 1825, this house was the home to famed Army General Christopher Houston Carson and family. It was purchased as a wedding present for his wife in 1843, and it remained their home for 25 years. Today it is a living museum that features artifacts and exhibits of the area, as well as Carson himself. Kit died in 1868, but according to many of the locals, he never left his home in Taos. People who tour the home have reported seeing an apparition in uniform, as well as hearing an "old time" voice speaking around them. Other activity includes cold spots, spikes in the electromagnetic fields, and the feeling of something (or someone) brushing by you as you walk through the halls of the old house.

Address: 113 Kit Carson Road
Website: www.kitcarsonhome.com/kc/
Activity: A, E, T, C

NEW YORK

Albany Professor Java's Coffee Sanctuary

This café was established in 1995 to help folks get away from their hectic day-to-day troubles by offering good food, coffee, and a place for meetings/gatherings. But this location wasn't always such a jovial atmosphere—this café is housed within a home that dates back to the 1940s. It served as family lodgings for several generations, but became known as a local drug hangout in the 1980s. Then the current owner purchased the property and built this sanctuary. There have been several apparitions witnessed in the place—including a man wearing a suit, a young woman, and a small boy (though he's usually heard laughing). The spirits are most likely a remnant of a family that lived in the house—but maybe you should do some research while you're there. Professor Java's does have WiFi.

Address: 217 Wolf Road
Website: www.professorjavas.com
Activity: A, E

Alexandria Bay Boldt Castle

Construction on this massive estate began in 1900 when the proprietor of the Waldorf Astoria Hotel, George C. Boldt, decided he wanted a home that would be reminiscent of a Rhineland castle. He summered there for four years while scores of stone masons and other craftsmen worked on the property. Then tragedy struck. In 1904, George's wife, Louise, passed away. He demanded all the work to stop on the mansion, and he abandoned it. It was acquired in 1977 by the Thousand Islands Bridge Authority and is now open for tours and events. Since it has been opened to the public, there have been quite a few sightings of a female apparition peering from one of the upper windows in the castle. Others have said to have seen her walking in the halls as well. Most believe it is the spirit of Louise Boldt, who tried to rejoin her husband in the castle only to find him gone.

Address: Collins Landing (Island)
Website: www.boldtcastle.com
Activity: A

Appleton The Winery at Marjim Manor

Housed within a mansion house that dates back to 1854 (originally called Appleton Hall), this winery offers regular tastings and hosts events. Prior to making award-winning wines, though, the estate was a retreat for the Sisters of St. Joseph convent—though this has no bearing on the ghost stories associated with this location. Sightings of a male apparition have occurred (thought to possibly be Lewis Merritt, a member of the original family of the home that was shot and killed there), as well as the sounds of footsteps and voices. Of course, you don't have to visit just for the ghosts. Pick up a bottle or two of your favorite vino and check out this wonderful, historic manor.

Address: 7171 East Lake Road
Website: www.marjimmanor.com
Activity: A, E

Aurora Aurora Inn

This stop along the Erie Canal was originally known to travelers as the Aurora House. It was built by Colonel E. B. Morgan in 1833 to service those passing through the area by water or by stagecoach. When a fire burned down the main portion of nearby Wells College in 1888, students used the inn as temporary lodgings. Today, the place features ten guest rooms and lakeside dining for tourists. As for the ghost... well, locals have named the spirit the "White Lady." She has been seen and heard in various parts of the inn—though you may want to check in with the innkeeper prior to selecting your room. Since the haunting is well known here, they may be able to make room suggestions based on your paranormal tastes.

Address: 391 Main Street
Website: www.aurora-inn.com
Activity: A, E

Bethany Rolling Hills Asylum

If not the most well known haunt in New York, Rolling Hills has to at least be the most visited. It first opened in 1827 to assist those in the county who couldn't care for themselves. Since then, it has been a nursing home and an antique mall, but is now a research center for the paranormal. It's said that over 1,000 died at the asylum over the years—mostly due to illness, poverty, and the poor treatment that was given to the poor residents in the beginning. If you choose to visit, or even investigate, this site, be prepared for a massive place with a lot of ghosts! With four floors, over 100 rooms (including a morgue and underground tunnels), and a carriage house out back that dates back to 1790, get ready for a long night. Hot spots include the Recreation Room (where voices are often heard), the "Stinky Room" (where foul odors are said to follow you), and the Solarium (where the apparition of a little girl is said to hang out).

Address: 11001 Bethany Center Road
Website: www.rollinghillsasylum.com
Activity: A, E, T, N, C, O

Buffalo Buffalo Central Terminal

This unique Art Deco station was first opened by the New York Central Railroad in 1929. It operated pretty much until 1956 when travel along the railway became less popular. It would struggle, changing owners and purpose several times, before being taken over by the Central Terminal Restoration Corporation in 1997. They are currently renovating the facility—though they do host events (like ghost hunts with TAPS from the television series *Ghost Hunters*). As you can imagine, those who work on the premises are now quite familiar with the haunting of the station. Activity includes sightings of multiple apparitions, the sounds of voices, and shadow shapes that have been witnessed in almost every area of the terminal.

Address: 435 Paderewski Drive
Website: www.buffalocentralterminal.org
Activity: A, R, E, S

Buffalo The Iron Island Museum

This museum is housed within a historic church/funeral home that dates back to 1885. Though they do have exhibits that include area artifacts and donated items, the most popular draw is the ghosts. So much so, that the place offers self-guided ghost tours, guided ghost tours, and even overnight investigations (for a reasonable price). And if you visit their website, you can check out some of the evidence that's been gathered by local paranormal groups, as well as the infamous TAPS. Activity is a regular event at Iron Island and usually includes shadowy apparitions, objects being manipulated, and the sounds of spectral voices. As you have probably figured out, getting to tour this location—and even investigate it—is a relatively easy affair, so you will want to make this museum a stop when you swing through Buffalo.

Address: 998 Lovejoy Street
Website: www.ironislandmuseum.com
Activity: A, S, E, T

Buffalo Buffalo and Erie County Naval & Military Park

This massive museum has three whole naval vessels and exhibits that are dedicated to the military history of the area. For many years, locals have talked about the haunting of one of the ships located at this park. Specifically, the USS The Sullivans. This Fletcher-class destroyer was named in honor of five brothers who died when the USS Juneau sunk during the Battle of the Solomon Islands—and these are the souls that are said to now walk the ship that bears their name. Sightings of multiple misty apparitions, as well as the sounds of footsteps and chains dragging, are often encountered on the ship. George Sullivan is said to be the most active of the five spirits—when the Juneau was struck by a torpedo, he was the only brother to not die instantly. It's said he drowned while frantically searching for his four brothers on the lower decks.

Address: 1 Naval Park Cove
Website: www.buffalonavalpark.org
Activity: A, M, E, T

Canandaigua Sutherland House

Here is a reputedly haunted location that deserves some more investigation. This bed and breakfast is a Victorian masterpiece that dates back to 1885. It features five rooms, three porches, and an outside patio—and is within walking distance of several top-notch restaurants. Before being transformed into this B&B, though, the home was known in the neighborhood as "the haunted house"—mainly because of its "spooky" appearance. Passersby would tell of seeing shadowy apparitions darting to and fro in the property, and of even hearing ghostly sounds. So does the house still have ghosts? You might want to visit and find out for yourself...

Address: 3179 State Route 21 South
Website: www.sutherlandhouse.com
Activity: S, E

Candor The Edge of Thyme Bed and Breakfast

This historic property that once functioned as a summer home for Dr. Amos Canfield and his wife, Rosa, is now a magnificent B&B that features four rooms and one suite. It also commands a great location along the Finger Lakes and makes for a great vacation. The paranormal stories surrounding this B&B are quite interesting. Reportedly, there are two spirits in the home. The first is a woman who has been seen wearing a long dress—often sitting in a rocking chair. She is also known for playing with perfume bottles and opening windows. The second entity is thought to be a Civil War soldier. The sounds of his heavy boots stomping across a wooden floor are often heard (despite the place being carpeted) in the downstairs/common areas where he likes to hang out.

Address: 6 Main Street
Website: www.edgeofthyme.com
Activity: A, E, T

Captree Island Fire Island Lighthouse

For thousands of European immigrants traveling to New York City, the Fire Island Lighthouse was the first thing they saw. The original was built in 1826, but it wouldn't last long due to being too short to be effective. When it was torn down, the bricks were used to help build the new lighthouse that was finished in 1858. The lighthouse functioned all the way until 1973, when it was finally decommissioned. Today it is a tourist attraction with an on-site gift shop. As for the ghost, it's said the spirit is that of a former caretaker of the original lighthouse. After his daughter passed away right there on the premises, and his wife left him to return to her family, he grew depressed and eventually hanged himself in the lighthouse. Paranormal activity here includes doors/windows opening by themselves, the sounds of footsteps and laughter, and a glowing spectral light that seems to indicate the caretaker is still trying to light the way.

Address: 4640 Captree Island
Website: www.fireislandlighthouse.com
Activity: E, T, O

Cooperstown The Otesaga Resort Hotel

This Federal-style hotel occupies 700 feet of lakefront property and has a commanding view of Lake Otsego. The resort dates back to 1909 and is one of the more upscale accommodations in this area of New York. The lake itself is also worth the visit—author James Fennimore Cooper often included Lake Otsego in his novels under the name "Glimmerglass." The haunting of the Otesaga is well known with the locals in Cooperstown—especially with those who have worked on the property. Though the Glimmerglass Room is said to be the hottest spot there (people often see apparitions and hear voices there), ghostly activity happens all over the hotel. The activity usually includes seeing spirits in period attire, hearing disembodied voices, and finding beds/rooms messed up that had nobody in them.

Address: 60 Lake Street
Website: www.otesaga.com
Activity: A, R, E, T

East Aurora The Roycroft Inn

This inn was first opened in 1905 to handle the sudden influx of visitors that came to check out the Roycroft Arts and Crafts Community. The hotel, as well as the movement, was founded by Elbert Hubbard, who was a writer and philosopher. When you visit the inn, you will find 28 exquisite guest suites, a wonderful restaurant, and even a gift shop that offers goods made in the Arts and Crafts style. According to several sources, this inn is also said to have ghosts. Shadowy apparitions are seen throughout the premises. Some say it's haunted because of a fire on the property (though I could not confirm this event happened), some say the ghost is that of Elbert himself (he died in 1915, leaving the inn to be run by his son, Bert), and some have no idea why the place is haunted—though they say it is, indeed, that. With accommodations and dining this nice, visiting to explore the ghost story for yourself will be a welcome trip.

Address: 40 South Grove Street
Website: www.roycroftinn.com
Activity: S, E

East Hampton The Mill House Inn

Originally constructed in 1790 by the Parsons family, this house was purchased by Patrick Lynch in 1860. He would remodel the place in 1898, adding a second story and a porch, and the home would remain in the Lynch family until 1973. At this point, it was converted into a bed and breakfast. The B&B features wonderful rooms that have the feel of antique surroundings, but are decked out with modern amenities. For the paranormal traveler, the Mill House is a great stay, indeed. They openly discuss their haunting (it's even mentioned on their website) and believe the spirit to be Patrick Lynch. Activity is mild at this location—though persistent—and of quite a benevolent nature. Plan a great weekend getaway in a scenic part of the state and explore the old Mill House Inn.

Address: 31 North Main Street
Website: www.millhouseinn.com
Activity: A, E, T

Garrison The Bird & Bottle Inn

This location was originally called Warren's Tavern and it was first opened in 1761. It thrived as a stagecoach stop on the Old Albany Post Road and made for comfy accommodations and dining for those traveling between Albany and New York City. During the Revolutionary War, the Continental army used the tavern as a local headquarters, and the business thrived until 1832 when it was closed down. The current inn opened in 1940 and features two guest rooms, a suite, and a cottage for visitors. Of course, most visit for their wonderful restaurant, which recently won a Wine Spectator Award of Excellence. When you stay at this inn, you will want to ask for the Emily Warren Room. Emily was a member of the original family that owned the property. It's said that she now haunts the Bird & Bottle and particularly likes to hang out in her old room.

Address: 1123 Old Albany Post Road
Website: www.thebirdandbottleinn.com
Activity: A, E, T

Geneva Belhurst Castle

You will probably be hard-pressed to find more luxurious accommodations than those at this magnificent estate. In addition to staying in the actual castle, you can also get a room in the Vinifera Inn or White Springs Manor—but if you want to experience anything of the paranormal sort, you will want a room in the castle. There are a few different stories about the ghosts of Belhurst: there are the sounds of a baby crying and a woman singing in the Billiard Room, the apparition of a man that hangs out in the men's room, and then there's the story of the "White Lady." She's said to be an opera singer who came to the states after she had fled from

Spain. She has been seen standing on the balcony of the Billiard Room (despite its name, it is a guest room you can rent) and even walking outside the property. Guess which room you should rent when you visit…

Address: 4069 Route 14 South
Website: www.belhurst.com
Activity: A, E

Johnstown The Olde Knox Mansion

This 42-room Victorian bed and breakfast features ornate furnishings, an antique fireplace that came from a castle in Italy, and an on-site conservatory. It's also located at the base of the beautiful Adirondack Mountains. Local filmmakers shot part of the documentary *14 Degrees* (it's about hauntings) at this location, and it has been investigated by at least one local paranormal group. Visitors to the mansion have seen apparitions walking on the property (it's thought that Rose Knox haunts the home and that one of the spirits is a long-deceased gardener who worked there), heard voices speaking from empty rooms, and pretty much experienced most every type of paranormal activity imaginable. Many say this is one of the most active haunted spots in the state—which is good news, considering how nice the mansion is.

Address: 102 West 2nd Avenue
Website: www.fultoncountyny.com/
  knoxmansion/
Activity: A, E, T, O, C

Lake George Fort William Henry Museum

This location was the subject of James Fenimore Cooper's novel *The Last of the Mohicans*—though the history related in that book is not quite accurate. This fort was constructed during the French and Indian War in 1755 and operated until 1757. Though it didn't last long, the fort was the center of a lot of action—and even more history. In paranormal circles, Fort William Henry is considered one of the state's best residual hauntings. Sightings

of Revolutionary-era soldiers and the sounds of battle are said to happen so often that the museum even offers ghost tours of the property. Within the museum itself, the favorite stop is the area that once functioned as a small prison. Visitors have said to have heard the sounds of moans and cries coming from the section where prisoners were held.

Address: 48 Canada Street
Website: www.fwhmuseum.com
Activity: R, A, E

Lancaster Lancaster Opera House

During the 1800s, it was fashionable for town halls to contain a theater. The Lancaster was built with just this in mind. It first opened in 1897, and it featured musicals, traveling productions, and recitals for many years until World War II. At that point, the space was needed to pack parachutes and then to conduct air raid drills once the war was over. Today you can still catch a show at this wonderful venue, as well as rent it out for your own event. Much like other theaters of this era, the Lancaster has a haunted reputation. Actors have reported seeing apparitions wearing clothes from the 1920s and hearing the sounds of footsteps following them as they leave for the night.

Address: 21 Central Avenue
Website: www.lancopera.org
Activity: A, E

Little Falls Beardslee Castle

Augustus Beardslee built this massive manor in 1860. He modeled the castle after those in Ireland and constructed the place close to the railway to expedite his travel on business (he was a major investor of the New York Central Railroad). The estate would go on to endure two fires, multiple owners, and several renovations to make the restaurant that resides there today. When you have a meal at this historic site, you will be treated to gourmet fare and one of the area's most extensive wine lists. There are several ghost stories concerning the castle. The first involves the spirits of Native Americans said to roam the area after they were blown up in the 1700s (while attempting to raid a munitions dump located on the property). Then there's the story of ghost lights and a phantom child that's been seen outside the property (the scapegoat for several accidents that have occurred there), as well as the spirits of Abigail and "Pop" Christensen. Abigail is said to be a bride who died in the castle, while Pop was the first owner of the restaurant. Pop committed suicide there when he learned he was terminally ill.

Address: 123 Old State Road
Website: www.beardsleecastle.com
Activity: A, E, O, T

Liverpool Ancestors Inn at the Bassett House

This bed and breakfast has four rooms available for overnight guests and is just minutes away from downtown Syracuse. The home was once the property of George and Hannah Bassett—and when you discuss the ghostly happenings at this house, they are usually the ones that get the credit. It's said the spirits like to greet guests to the B&B by turning on the lights there and by showing up in photographs as a blur. The current owners of the property have reported hearing door knobs rattling during the night and finding the lights on after they have turned them off. Locals also say there is a spirit in the B&B known as "Tim." It has been reported that this entity likes to visit with folks who aren't feeling very well and that he's been seen several times on the second floor there.

Address: 215 Sycamore Street
Website: www.ancestorsinn.com
Activity: A, T

Napanoch Shanley Hotel

Built by Thomas Rich in 1845, this location was known in the old days as Hungerford's Hotel. In 1895, the entire property burned to the ground, but a replacement hotel was built right back up the same year. It would go on to have several new names and owners, but the place was pretty much then the way it is now: cozy, comfortable, and in a great location. The Shanley is also extremely open about their haunting. So much so, in fact, that half their website is devoted to the spirits that reside there! Paranormal activity happens in almost every area of the hotel, but here are a few suggestions for those who wish to stay there. Rose's Room is known for a spirit that likes to lie on the bed. Marguerite's Room is known for a male apparition who likes to appear to startled guests and ask for "Marguerite." Then there's the Sun Room, which is one of the most active with disembodied voices, objects being manipulated, and the a ghost that likes to touch people.

Address: 56 Main Street
Website: www.shanleyhotel.com
Activity: A, E, T, C, O, N

New Paltz Mohonk Mountain House

It's said that the entire village of New Paltz is haunted—though locals don't seem to be able to say why. The area was settled in the 1670s by Huguenots that fled Mannheim, Germany, during the Esopus Wars, though it wouldn't officially become a city until 1828. The Mohonk, on the other hand, was founded in the 1870s after Alfred Smiley fell in love with the area while visiting. Much like it did in those days, the massive resort offers accommodations, dining, a spa, and lots of things to do outdoors. They also offer a Halloween "haunts" weekend that has become one of the area's more popular events. But who haunts the hotel? Here's where things get fuzzy. Much like the city of New Paltz, people have varying opinions, but no specifics. It's generally agreed that apparitions are seen, voices are heard, and spooky things happen—but there are no names to attach to the spectral faces. This is a wonderful location that warrants your own investigation...

Address: 1000 Mountain Rest Road
Website: www.mohonk.com
Activity: A, E

New York City The Algonquin Hotel

This hotel contains a lot of history. Whether it's the literary luminaries of the city hanging out at the Round Table, or it's the social elite discussing future business ventures (it's said *The New Yorker* magazine was brainstormed in just this manner), The Algonquin is all about movers and shakers. It first opened in 1902 and was an island of opulence in the already trendy neighborhood of Manhattan—a tradition that continues today. Even the ghosts are an upscale affair at this hotel! During the 1920s, a literary group called "The Vicious Circle" used to meet at the hotel to discuss their projects and to dissect pieces of literature and theater. Though they would disband during the Great Depression, it's said that at least one of them has stuck around to haunt the place. It's said that strange noises are heard on the thirteenth floor—and that a photo of Dorothy Parker is often found removed from the wall. Could Dorothy Parker haunt this hotel? Why not? It's worth a look.

Address: 59 West 44th Street
Website: www.algonquinhotel.com
Activity: E, T

New York City Bridge Café

This eatery began as a simple grocery store and "wine and porter bottler" back in 1794. It was operated by Newell Narme for several years before changing hands and eventually becoming a string of saloons/boarding houses. Of course,

in most venues of this sort back then, you also had gambling, prostitution, and excessive violence. It's because of the latter that patrons (and employees) now see shadowy apparitions, hear phantom footsteps, and smell the strong scent of lavender perfume in the café. Then again, you may not smell the perfume at all, since you will be partaking of the wonderful food that's served at the restaurant.

Address: 279 Water Street
Website: www.bridgecafenyc.com
Activity: S, E, N

New York City Hotel Chelsea

Primarily known for the plethora of artists and musicians who have resided there, the Chelsea is a historic hotel that dates back to 1883. Famous visitors to the place include Bob Dylan, Allen Ginsberg, and Eugene O'Neill—though, perhaps, the stories involving Dylan Thomas and Sid Vicious may be the most well known. Thomas fell into a coma that eventually led to his death after drinking 18 whiskeys in a row—and is now said to haunt the hotel. Vicious' girlfriend, Nancy Spungen, was stabbed to death in Room 100 of the hotel (most believe Sid did it), so now this area is said to be haunted as well. Other ghosts in the hotel include Thomas Wolfe (who is said to haunt the eighth floor) and several others without celebrity status. If you're not staying in Room 100, check in with the hotel staff for your room selections, as this hotel is full of ghostly locations.

Address: 222 West 23rd Street
Website: www.hotelchelsea.com
Activity: A, E, T

New York City Hotel Thirty Thirty

Known more in paranormal circles for its previous moniker—the Martha Washington Hotel—this posh set of accommodations is quite unique for the area. With its historic exterior (the hotel first opened in 1903) and its modern Scandinavian-styled interior, the property is as beautiful as it is comfortable. When the hotel first opened at the turn of the century, it was the only area lodgings made exclusively for women. During the 1940s, many of the Hollywood starlets of the day would use the hotel as a base while visiting New York (actress Veronica Lake even worked there after her career took a nosedive). It is also female apparitions that are witnessed in the property. Guests and employees alike have seen and heard them over the years and attribute the haunting to women who took up residence in the building over the years.

Address: 30 East 30th Street
Website: www.thirtythirty-nyc.com
Activity: A, E

New York City Merchant's House Museum

This museum has been called the best example of a Federal-style house in the Manhattan area (and there are hundreds of these homes in this area). It was built in 1832 for a wealthy merchant by the name of Seabury Tredwell. He and his wife, Eliza, raised eight children in the home—and the place remained in the family until 1933 when the last member died there (Gertrude Tredwell). The haunting of the museum has been featured on television programs, articles, etc., and is now quite well known. The spirit of Gertrude is said to hang out around her death bed and the second floor in general. She has been seen and heard there—along with the sounds of the downstairs piano playing spectral music during the night.

Address: 29 East 4th Street
Website: www.merchantshouse.com
Activity: A, E, T

Oyster Bay Raynham Hall Museum

In addition to the exhibits featured within this living museum, you can also take a stroll through one of the area's best gardens. When the house was first purchased in 1738 by Samuel Townsend, it was a simple four-room house. But after a massive renovation in 1851 by Solomon Townsend II, the house became the Gothic Revival masterpiece it is today. When you tour this site, ask the museum guides about their ghosts—the mansion has several interesting ghost stories. The first tale involves several key characters from the Revolutionary War. After two officers were overheard discussing the traitor Benedict Arnold, the information led to the hanging of a British officer, John Andre. This man is said to still visit the house in the afterlife. Then there's the spirit of Sally Townsend, one of the daughters of the house who fell in love with a British officer, and the ghost of a former servant thought to be Michael Conlon.

Address: 20 West Main Street
Website: www.raynhamhallmuseum.org
Activity: A, E, T, S, N

Raquette Lake The Brightside on Raquette

This unique lodge is only accessible by boat, but you can grab a ride out when you get to Raquette Lake Village. This property was once the home to Joe and Mary Bryere, who migrated to the lake in 1880. The resort was first opened in 1891 and was an instant hit for those who wished to get away into the country, but still have all the amenities of a luxury stay. This tradition still continues at the Brightside today. As for the ghosts—they are a well-discussed subject at the lodge (just check out the write-up on their website). According to the tale, a couple checked into the resort in the 1970s during a winter storm. The husband decided to dare a trip into the village by crossing the ice on the lake while his wife sat by the window and waited for him to return. He never did. Since then, guests have reported seeing the female apparition (especially when somebody plays the old piano in the Great Room). But if you really want a fun paranormal trip, ask for the lodge's "Ghost Room."

Address: On Raquette Lake
Website: www.brightsideonraquette.com
Activity: A, E, T, O

Rochester The Auditorium Theatre

Operated and maintained by the Rochester Broadway Theatre League, this venue dates back to 1928 and is known throughout the area for its massive productions. Large-scale musicals, such as *The Phantom of the Opera* and *Miss Shanghai*, are featured quite often—and have been since the Roaring 20s. With Art Deco furnishings, one of the best-preserved antique Wurlitzer organs, and a constant barrage of quality theatre, this location should make for a wonderful visit. Paranormal activity at the theatre includes shadowy apparitions that dart across the stage and the spirit of an old man that's been seen and heard in various parts of the building. The old man is thought to be a local named "Tommy," who used to visit the Auditorium quite often to socialize with folks.

Address: 885 Main Street East
Website: www.rbtl.org
Activity: A, E, S

Saratoga Springs The Adelphi Hotel

Whether you find anything haunted at this gorgeous hotel or not, you will not regret your visit to this location! Built as an Italian villa for William McCaffery in 1877, the current owners of this unique hotel purchased the property in 1977 and slowly renovated the place room by room. All their love and care for this historic site shows in the hand-stenciled walls and ceilings, the plush furnishings, and the individually decorated and renovated guest rooms (39 total). Tales concerning the Adelphi being haunted have circulated around the town since the building sat slated for demolition. Passersby would claim to see a woman dressed in a blue Victorian-era dress walking through the property and staring from windows. Since the hotel opened in 1980, there have been a couple incidents, but nothing overtly paranormal. Plan yourself a wonderful trip and spend the night in this unique getaway—who knows, maybe you'll see the "Woman in Blue" for yourself.

Address: 346 Broadway Avenue
Website: www.adelphihotel.com
Activity: A

Smithtown Katie's of Smithtown

This double-decker bar features a lot of drink specials, live DJ music, and karaoke nights—pretty much typical fare for an American drinking establishment. What is not typical, though, is the haunting of the bar! Built on the grounds of a former hospital, the building that houses Katie's dates back to the early 1900s—as do several of the spirits there. A male apparition (thought to be a past patron named Charlie Klein) has been seen several times on the premises, as has a female entity dressed in 1920's attire. Additional activity includes the sounds of footsteps/voices and items moving of their own volition. Katie's was featured in an episode of the television program *Paranormal State*, so their haunting is now widely known. If you feel the need for a night on the town, you may consider visiting this haunted hot spot.

Address: 145 West Main Street
Website: www.katiesofsmithtown.com
Activity: A, E, T

Staten Island Garibaldi Meucci Museum

This Gothic Revival home (circa 1840) was once the residence of inventor Antonio Meucci and his wife Ester. Italian revolutionary Giuseppe Garibaldi stayed with Meucci in his home prior to earning fame for helping unify Italy. This museum commemorates both men (Meucci is said to have been the "true inventor of the telephone") and is open to the public most days. When the museum staff started experiencing paranormal goings-on, they consulted with local investigators. Activity in the museum includes the sounds of coughing/moaning, glimpses of shadowy apparitions, and various voices heard throughout the old home. Most believe one of the spirits on the property is Ester; she died in the house and was even buried in the front yard. Most also believe she is not alone …

Address: 420 Tompkins Avenue
Website: www.garibaldimeuccimuseum.org
Activity: S, E, C, T

Staten Island Wedding Cottage at the Old Bermuda Inn

This Victorian estate dates back to 1832 and was once the parsonage for the local St. Luke's Church (during the 1840s). Today it is a bed and breakfast that also hosts (you guessed it) weddings. They feature four suites and two mini-rooms, as well as one of the best breakfasts in the area. The home was once the residence for Martha Mesereau and her husband—but when the Civil War broke out, he was called to duty and soon perished in combat. Martha became a recluse and eventually died alone in the home. Locals say that she can now be seen peering from her bedroom window (now a din-

ing room) and her apparition has been seen within the house several times (usually on the staircase). The sounds of her crying have also been heard, and it's said she likes to turn on lights in the house—a habit that dates back to when she would light a candle to wait for the return of her husband.

Address: 2512 Arthur Kill Road
Website: www.weddingcottage.com
Activity: A, E, T

Upper Jay Wellscroft Lodge

This majestic Mission-style estate was constructed in 1903 as a summer home for Jean and Wallis Craig Smith. Now a bed-and-breakfast style lodge, the property is known for personal touches like a gaming room, reading nooks, and a cozy bar. It's also in a great location—snuggled in the middle of Adirondack Park and minutes away from Lake Placid. The lodge seems like the last place to be haunted, though the story of the "Lady in Red" is quite known in the area. Her apparition has been seen quite a few times on the staircase, as well as gazing out the front windows of the mansion. Guests have also, reportedly, heard the sounds of phantom music playing in the house on occasion.

Address: 158 Route 9N
Website: www.bedbreakfasthome.com/
  wellscroftlodge/
Activity: A, R, E

Victor Valentown Museum

Operated by the Victor Historical Society, this museum has certainly embraced its haunting since appearing on the television program *Ghost Hunters.* They offer year-round ghost hunts at an extremely low price, so this makes for a perfect spot for the beginning paranormal investigator. The museum was originally known as Valentown Hall and was constructed in 1879 by Levi and Alanson Valentine. It's filled with displays of early period merchants and antiques, which for an interesting visit even without the ghosts. But if you are there for them, you may want to check out the stairway that leads to the second floor, where the sounds of footsteps and the sighting of a shadow mass has been seen. There has also been activity on the third floor, where a ballroom used to exist (though you may need permission to enter this area). This area was the site of a murder when a young man shot another for courting his girl.

Address: 7370 Valentown Square
Website: www.valentown.org
Activity: S, E, T

Walton Octagon Farm Bed & Breakfast

Built in a rare octagon shape, this former dairy farm features five rooms in the main house and a small cottage for rent. They also have a great on-site farmers' market and one of the best breakfasts you'll ever eat (called the "Generous Farmer's" breakfast). According to several sources, the property also has one of the most unique and tragic residual haunts in the state. It's said that a young bride was riding a horse when she was thrown by the animal. She struck her head on a stone and instantly died. This spectral sight is now repeated in the wee hours, much to onlookers' surprise. This story does, indeed, smack of urban legend, but witnesses insist the tale is true.

Address: 34055 State Highway 10
Website: www.octagonfarmbandb.com
Activity: R, A

Warwick Silvio's Italian Villa

This restaurant dates back to the late 1700s and a Revolutionary War veteran named Levi Ellis. The property was added onto in 1811, and again in the mid-1800s by the owner of the time, Gilbert Drew, who renamed the place Maple Glen Farm. The haunting of this spectacular Italian eatery involves a dark tale that took place in 1972. The resident at the time, Roy Vail, was working in the barn when his sister was brutally murdered in the home. After suffering rumors of his involvement in the deed, Roy decided to commit suicide in the area of the restaurant that is now known as the Peach Room. When you visit this haunted location, be sure to try out their killer appetizers (like their carpaccio and fried calamari), and keep your senses peeled for paranormal activity. Shadowy apparitions have been seen and the sounds of voices and phantom footsteps are often heard.

Address: 274 Route 94 South
Website: www.silviositalianvilla.net
Activity: S, E, T

Youngstown Old Fort Niagara

This Colonial-era fort has guarded the mouth of the Niagara River for over 300 years. At various times, the post has been alternately controlled by the French, the British, and (of course) the Americans. The last time it faced conflict was during the War of 1812, but the U.S. Army would take until 1963 to fully withdraw from the site (the Coast Guard is still there today). For years, visitors to the old fort have noted strange happenings. Things like the apparitions of soldiers, the sounds of guns/cannons firing, and the strange sight of a headless man! The headless apparition has been seen in the old French Castle in the fort—and the tale dates all the way back to the French occupation of the post. According to the legend, two officers engaged in a duel after having a dispute. The winner of the sword fight wasn't satisfied with just beating his opponent—after his foe had fallen, he decapitated the man and threw the head into the Niagara River.

Address: 2 Scott Avenue
Website: www.oldfortniagara.org
Activity: A, R, E

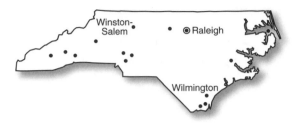

NORTH CAROLINA

Albemarle Albemarle Opera House

When F. E. Starnes, D. F. Parker, and J. C. Parker built this building in 1907, they had no idea that one of their descendants would own the place today! The site was built as an opera house to entertain the local public, and it did so between the years of 1908 and 1913. After that, it was turned briefly into a movie theater and then (morbidly enough) it became an annex to the neighboring undertaker's shop. Today, the building is mostly empty, though Starnes Jewelry is still there as it has been for many decades. Paranormal activity in the opera house is thought to be because of a flu epidemic that swept through the city in 1917. This outbreak was the reason that the place was used to store the bodies that would not fit in the undertaker's shop next door (called Huneycutt's). Every business that has operated out of this building has since experienced misty apparitions floating through walls, strange voices that speak from thin air, and snippets of phantom ragtime music.

Address: 127 West Main Street
Website: www.albemarleoperahouse.com
Activity: A, R, E, M

Asheville Asheville Seasons Bed and Breakfast

Located in the heart of Asheville's historic district of Montford, this B&B makes for an intimate stay in a busy city. The place features five guest rooms and is only minutes away from many notable sights. Since the home was built in the early 1900s, it has either housed a family or been family owned and operated—and this is true of the ghost there as well. The spirit at this location is known as "Grace" and is thought to be the great-grandmother of a former resident. She is known for being quite friendly to the guests who stay at the house. It's said that if you stay in Grace's old room, she just may crawl into bed with you and give you a hug—an event that has happened a few times over the years. Just hope that her phantom dog doesn't join her. There has been at least one sighting of her apparition walking with her canine companion.

Address: 43 Watauga Street
Website: www.asheville seasons.com
Activity: A, E, T

Asheville Barley's Taproom & Pizzeria

This small restaurant chain has businesses in North Carolina, South Carolina, and Tennessee, but it's this site in Asheville that's reputedly haunted. The eatery is located in a former appliance store that was constructed in the 1920s, and it was the first restaurant created with the name "Barley's." The ghost on this property is said to be Will Harris, a killer who went on a shooting spree in Asheville in 1906. Harris became enraged when a local girl refused to divulge the whereabouts of his former girlfriend, Mollie Maxwell. When the police arrived on the scene, a shootout ensued that took five lives. Harris escaped, but was caught two days later and shot over a hundred times by the angry posse. As was the norm for the day, Harris' body was placed on display downtown in the area where Barley's now resides. As for the restaurant today, ghostly activity includes the sounds of voices and footsteps, as well as a shadowy apparition thought to be Harris himself!

Address: 42 Biltmore Street
Website: www.barleystaproom.com
Activity: S, E, T

Asheville The Grove Park Inn Resort & Spa

The resort on this property was built from granite boulders that came from nearby Sunset Mountain. It opened in 1913 to much fanfare and was the vision of St. Louis native E. W. Grove who made a fortune selling his "Grove's Tasteless Chill Tonic." Staying in this upscale hotel may set you back a pretty penny—but it may be worth it if you manage to secure the infamous Room 545. During the 1920s, a woman fell to her death from a nearby balcony and is now thought to haunt this room. Employees dub the female apparition "the Lady in Pink," or sometimes, "the Pink Lady." She has been witnessed in this room, as well as the adjoining hallway, numerous times, and guests have made a lot of strange reports concerning their stay in Room 545. Most of the stories include doors locking by themselves or the sounds of voices/footsteps—but on occasion, they include the spirit actually appearing in the room as a hazy, pinkish apparition.

Address: 290 Macon Avenue
Website: www.groveparkinn.com
Activity: A, M, E, T

Asheville The Smith-McDowell House Museum

It's hard to believe that this house-turned-museum was built almost 20 years before the American Civil War. The care taken in restoring the home by the Western North Carolina Historical Association is amazing, as is the furniture and artifacts on display within the antebellum home. The Smith and McDowell families lived in this house until the outbreak of the aforementioned war, but because of the economic turmoil that enveloped the area after the conflict, the house changed hands to Alexander Garrett in 1881. And on it went until the place was transformed into a school dormitory in 1951. So who haunts this museum? Opinions vary on the specifics, but it's generally accepted that there are at least two spirits on the premises. There is a female apparition that has been seen and heard in the kitchen (along with the sounds of old music), and then there is a darker entity that tends to scare folks in the area around the old cistern.

Address: 283 Victoria Road
Website: www.wnchistory.org
Activity: A, S, E, R

Balsam Balsam Mountain Inn

This inn really is located in the North Carolina mountains and is the product of three years of work (1905–08). In addition to their great rooms and suites, this hotel is known for their massive on-site library and their regular "songwriters night" events. You may have even heard of their ghost, "Henry." He has been featured in several books, as well as on the Travel Channel. He's said to hang out in Room 205 of the inn, where he has been seen, heard, and felt. At other times, Henry has been witnessed in the hallway outside this room (there's been at least one eyewitness account in Room 207, too, but some claim this is a possible second spirit on the premises). Seeing and hearing ghosts are a relatively common report—but how about getting a back rub from a ghost? According to one guest at the inn, this is exactly what happened.

Address: 68 Seven Springs Drive
Website: www.balsammountaininn.com
Activity: A, E, T

Chapel Hill The Carolina Inn

John Sprunt Hill funded the building of this inn in 1924 so that alumni and visitors of the University of North Carolina would have a place to stay. In 1935, he donated the place to the school with the stipulation that all profits from the inn would be used to fund the university library's North Carolina Collection—a tradition that continues to this day. The resident spirit of this inn is said to be a man named William Jacocks. He was a research physician who actually lived in the inn for 17 years before he passed away. The second floor was the location of his "quarters"—an area that is now several guest rooms due to a renovation in 1990. People who stay in one of these rooms often report finding their things rearranged and even getting locked out.

Address: 211 Pittsboro Street
Website: www.carolinainn.com
Activity: E, T

Chapel Hill The Horace Williams House

This home is owned by the University of North Carolina, but is maintained by the Preservation Society of Chapel Hill. The house offers tours, hosts regular events, and features displays of historic items within. The major portion of the place was built in 1840, but significant improvements were made on the house over the years by the various individuals who lived there. Though most of these residents are pretty historic in and of themselves, the home is most known for its last resident, Horace Williams. He was a professor at the university, and when he died, he left the house to them. But according to members of his family, Horace is still there. Tales of people seeing items moving on their own and regular sightings of Williams' ghost seem to confirm the haunting as well. While you tour the home, make sure you swing by Horace's old rocking chair. He is known for often sitting in the rocker, and it has been seen moving with nobody in it many times.

Address: 610 East Rosemary Street
Website: www.chapelhillpreservation.com
Activity: A, T

Hickory 1859 Café

This restaurant of "casual elegance" features live music in addition to its wonderful food and drink. While you're there, take a look at your surroundings as well—this café is housed in one of the area's oldest homes (guess when it was built...). The original owner was a man named Henry Link, who used the premises for his home and a general store. Could the female apparition who's seen on this property be a family member? Perhaps. Over the years, though, there have been several families who have lived in this location. Either way, employees of the café have seen a blond-haired spirit in the dining room, as well as in the reflection of mirrors. According to locals, the owners even have a photo of the spectral woman.

Address: 443 2nd Avenue Southwest
Website: www.hickoryonline.com/1859cafe/
Activity: A

Huntersville Historic Latta Plantation

This classic southern plantation home was at one time nestled in the middle of 100 acres of cotton and crops. When it was built in 1800, two slaves worked these fields, and at the height of its history, 34 slaves would live on the property and tend to over 700 acres! Prior to the Civil War, James Latta would pass away and the home would change hands to one David Harry—who would then sell the place to William A. Sample, who had the misfortune of living on the plantation during the war. Visiting the plantation today is like stepping back in time. Of course, this is what Mecklenburg County (the owners of the living museum and farm) wants. Tales of the plantation being haunted go way back. Previous owners would tell of strange sounds of children playing that would seem to be heard from a great distance, as well as small shadowy apparitions that were often seen darting about the house. They reckoned the place was haunted by the Latta family. What do you reckon?

Address: 5225 Sample Road
Website: www.lattaplantation.org
Activity: A, S, E, R

Kure Beach Fort Fisher

The fall of Fort Fisher to the Union army during the Civil War (January 15, 1865) was one of the many signals that the Confederacy was coming to an end. Fort Fisher was General Lee's last remaining line of supply and support in the war, so its defeat was devastating to the Army of Northern Virginia. If you head over to the visitor's center on the site today, you can learn a lot more about the history of this post and even tour the grounds. You may also learn about Confederate General Chase Whiting, who was left with the duty of surrendering the fort when it was overcome—and was seriously wounded in the act. He was taken to a northern prison where he died. Many believe General Whiting returned to Fort Fisher once he passed away—his apparition has been seen walking the area of the final battle and the old fort.

Address: 1610 Ft. Fisher Boulevard South
Website: www.nchistoricsites.org/fisher/fisher
Activity: A

Lake Lure The Lodge on Lake Lure

This lodge-style bed and breakfast began in 1938 as a retreat for the North Carolina State Patrol. They maintained and visited the place all the way until 1968 when it was sold to a private owner. Now open to the public, you can stay overnight at the lodge in one of their spacious rooms, or simply visit for a meal. As for the ghost there…well, you will want to check out Room 4 to meet this male spirit. He's said to be the former George Penn, a state patrolman who was killed in the line of duty—and the person for whom this lodge was dedicated to when it opened! Folks who stay in Room 4 have reported seeing a man walking through the middle of the room, through the wall, and into the hallway. Others have seen him in the same area, but appearing as a shadowy mass that seems to stand in one corner. Which version will show up when you visit?

Address: 361 Charlotte Drive
Website: www.lodgeonlakelure.com
Activity: A, S

Manteo Fort Raleigh National Historic Site

The mystery surrounding this site has endured through centuries of searching and doesn't look to be solved any time soon. Between 1554 and 1590, Sir Walter Raleigh sponsored the colonization of this area by English settlers, and ships were dispatched to do so. Due to complications involving a war with Spain and the great distances involved with traveling, at one point, there was a three-year gap with communications. By the time John White, an emissary for Raleigh, got back to the settlement, it was completely deserted. One hundred sixteen men, women, and children had vanished. Over the years, there have been several hypotheses about what happened (and a couple good fictional accounts as well), but the whole affair is still a mystery. Today, the entire area is said to be the stomping grounds of Virginia Dare, the first English child born in the New World and one of the youngest to go missing. Since nobody knows what Virginia looked like, it is most likely assumed that the female apparition who is seen here is Dare. Keep an eye out if you visit the area—Virginia is also known for appearing as a spectral deer.

Address: 1401 National Park Drive
Website: www.nps.gov/fora/
Activity: A

Midland Reed Gold Mine

In 1799, a 12-year-old boy named Conrad Reed found a 17-pound chunk of gold while fishing. After it served as a household doorstop for some time, his father sold the gold for a pauper's price. Later, he learned the error of his asking price and soon exploited the mine for a good deal of money. Today, you can tour the site of the gold mine and even take a trip into the tunnels. While you're down there, you will want to keep an ear cocked for the sounds of a woman complaining. Don't bother looking for her, though, because you won't see her. She's long dead. In the years after this area's gold rush, a family by the name of Mills moved in. William Mills and his wife, Eleanor, lived a simple life, but it's said that she was a constant nagger. One day she fell and hit her head, killing her instantly. William mourned her death, but his sorrow turned to fear when he heard her once again complaining in the house. So he took her body and threw it down the mine shaft. Tourists have reported hearing the phantom voice of Eleanor while touring the dark mine shafts. She complains to this day.

Address: 9621 Reed Mine Road
Website: www.nchistoricsites.org/Reed/reed
Activity: E

New Bern Attmore Oliver House

This living museum is owned and operated by the New Bern Historical Society and features eighteenth- and nineteenth-century furniture, Civil War artifacts, and a strange doll collection. The house itself is the biggest attraction, though. It was built in 1790 and it served as home for the Chapman and Attmore families for several generations. During the Civil War,

Hannah Attmore lived in the house along with three brothers—all of whom joined the Confederate army. Two of the brothers died, and Hannah stayed in the house along with her husband William Oliver. The historical society bought the house in 1954 and has had the place since. As for the haunting, the story goes like this: During the turn of the century, a smallpox epidemic broke out in the area, so two members of the family (thinking they were probably sick) decided to sequester themselves in the locked attic. Meanwhile, the servants who watered and fed the folks got the worst of the disease and died. The starved corpses were later found in the attic and, to this day, the upper story of the house (as well as the attic itself) is said to be the site of strange happenings that include voices, pounding on the walls, and items moving on their own.

Address: 511 Broad Street
Website: www.newbernhistorical.org
Activity: E, T

Raleigh Mordecai House

At one time, this house was the centerpiece of a 5,000-acre farm. The oldest portions of the home date back to 1785, when Joel Lane built the house for his son, Henry. Not long after the house was built, Lane sold some of his land to the state of North Carolina for the purpose of building a capitol city. This is the modern-day city of Raleigh. Henry's property would remain in the family and was passed down to his daughter Margaret, who married a man named Moses Mordecai. After Margaret passed away, Moses stayed in the family by then marrying her sister, Ann! In 1826, an addition was made onto the house that turned the look of the place into a Greek Revival–styled masterpiece—and that's how the manor looks today if you visit it for a tour. As for the ghost, it is assumed that the occasionally seen female spirit is a long-gone member of the Lane or Mordecai families. She is often seen walking the upstairs areas and is said to be wearing a long, black dress. She

is also known for playing with the downstairs piano and messing with people's hair in the upstairs restroom. While there, be sure to check out the Andrew Johnson birth house nearby—it, too, is thought to be haunted!

Address: 1 Mimosa Street
Website: www.nps.gov/nr/travel/raleigh/mor
Activity: A

Southport The Brunswick Inn

Located on the mouth of the Cape Fear River, this bed and breakfast makes for a great headquarters when exploring the Victorian homes of Southport. The place was built in 1792, so the Brunswick is a great deal older than even most of the "antique" homes that are marketed in the town's waterfront district. The inn has three guest rooms—each with a private bath and fireplace—and one on-site ghost named "Tony." It's thought that Tony is the spirit of a harpist who used to perform at the house (then called the Brunswick Hotel) until he drowned in an accident in 1882. Tony's known for playing with guests' items in their rooms and for generally hanging out in the library. Over the years, the owners of the inn have built up quite a catalog of interesting tales concerning Tony, so talk to them about current activity there before choosing your room!

Address: 301 East Bay Street
Website: www.brunswickinn.com
Activity: A, E, T

Wilmington Battleship North Carolina

This battleship participated in every major naval offensive of World War II and managed to escape the conflict to be decommissioned in 1947. There were casualties on board during the war, though. Ten sailors lost their lives and 67 were wounded during their duty onboard, which is why the ship is now considered to be one of the most haunted areas in North Carolina. Numerous visitors over the years (as well as the on-site caretaker) have experienced hearing voices, seeing a male apparition (said to have blonde/white hair), and feel unexplainable things brushing past them in the hallways of the ship. Additionally, reports have also been made of shadowy apparitions that seem to shoot down the stairs at a high rate of speed on the lower decks. So keep your eyes open when you tour the ship—you just may see a ghost!

Address: 1 Battleship Road
Website: www.battleshipnc.com
Activity: A, S, C, E, T

Wilmington Bellamy Mansion

This magnificently columned mansion is also known as the Museum of History and Design Arts. The house had barely finished construction when the Civil War broke out—an event that forced Dr. John D. Bellamy and his family out of the property. The place was used as the headquarters for Union troops that occupied Wilmington, and after the war, it took a presidential pardon from President Andrew Johnson to get the house returned to the family. Workers at this museum have heard so many tales concerning their resident spirits, that nothing seems to faze them any more. Not even the wheelchair that seems to keep letting itself out of storage and ending up in different places of the house. It is assumed that this act is the work of the late Ellen Bellamy, who died in the house in 1946 (it was her wheelchair). Other activity in the home includes the sounds of voices and the full-bodied apparition of a Union soldier, who has been seen walking the main floor there.

Address: 503 Market Street
Website: www.bellamymansion.org
Activity: A, E, T

Winston-Salem The Historic Brookstown Inn

This inn, as well as the on-site restaurant, The Cotton Mill, is within walking distance of old Salem (a Moravian town that dates back to 1766). During the old days, this inn functioned as an area textile mill—and as you make your way through the place, you will get a bit of the feel of those times thanks to the early American décor and the exposed beams/bricks. If you take a break from hunting for the ghost at this inn, be sure to check out the graffiti wall on the fourth floor. It's literally covered with inscriptions and such from the women who worked in the mill over the years. It's generally thought that one of these past female workers now haunts the place as well. Employees and guests at the inn have experience hearing a strange disembodied female voice that's said to either call you by name, or to say the word "mercy" over and over again.

Address: 200 Brookstown Avenue
Website: www.brookstowninn.com
Activity: E

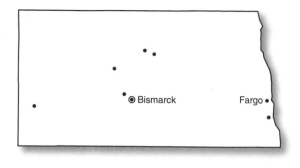

Bismarck   Fargo

NORTH DAKOTA

Abercrombie Fort Abercrombie

This post was created in 1858 to stave off the possible Native American encroachment of the states/territories of Minnesota, North Dakota, and South Dakota. It suffered a siege by the Sioux in 1862 and stood staunchly through the Indian Wars and the American Civil War. Today, the Friends of Fort Abercrombie care for the post and have recently opened a new interpretive center on the site. In addition to all this history, you may want to visit the fort to experience one of the state's best residual hauntings. Perhaps it's a remnant of the aforementioned siege, but visitors to the site have reported hearing the phantom sounds of battle, as well as seeing the apparitions of soldiers and Native Americans. They pretty much do their own thing and ignore the observer, so it also makes for a pretty tame haunted location as well.

Address: Off Broadway Street
Website: www.ftabercrombie.org
Activity: A, E, R

Anamoose Sage Hill Bed & Breakfast

Built in 1928, this location was originally a schoolhouse that was built by Colonel Samuel White (resulting in the name "The White School"). Until it closed in 1968, this rural school treated 100 or so students to hot showers, good food, and wind-powered electricity—luxuries that most of these children did not have at home. The property was purchased in 1996, renovated, and then opened as an area bed and breakfast. According to local tales, it wasn't long after inhabiting the building that the new owners of the B&B began experiencing paranormal happenings. Lights would magically turn on and off, and a strange moaning voice would be heard in the cellar. Locals say it is haunted by a former schoolmaster and a student who were burned to death there—but this bit of history is unconfirmed. Either way, with disembodied voices, phantom scents, and things moving on their own, it appears that Sage Hill is quite haunted, indeed.

Address: 2091 33rd Street Northeast
Website: www.sagehillnd.com
Activity: E, T, N

Bismarck Apple Creek Country Club

Though you may have to be a member of the country club to play golf at this facility, the on-site Boston's Bar & Grill is open to the public. It's said that the country club is haunted by a former chef of the restaurant and that his apparition has been seen several times on the premises. Unfortunately (or maybe fortunately?) he is not alone. Reports of a second entity have also made their rounds through the course. Locals say a janitor was found dead when the staff returned one morning to open for the day (apparently he died of natural causes while working) and now he is still cleaning the club in the afterlife. Well, maybe not cleaning—more like making banging sounds, and occasionally taking a walk around the premises.

Address: 8921 East Highway 10
Website: www.applecreekcountryclub.com
Activity: A, E, T

Bismarck Liberty Memorial Building

This building holds the State Library and is called "Liberty Memorial" because it was built as a tribute to locals who died in World War I. Construction lasted from 1920 until 1924, and the place was fashioned in a Federal style with limestone exterior—a fact that may intrigue paranormal investigators (limestone is said to conduct spiritual energy). Ghost activity began while the local Historical Society occupied a portion of the premises. Sightings of a male apparition, as well as hearing his disembodied voice, became so common that members of the society referred to the ghost as "the Stacks Monster." Eventually, the society found new lodgings and moved out of Liberty Memorial—but they still tell tales of the spirit that would call them by name and blanket them with the feeling that they should immediately flee the building.

Address: 604 East Boulevard Avenue
Website: www.library.nd.gov/history
Activity: A, E, T, S

Fargo The Children's Museum at Yunker Farm

This lively museum is housed within the historic home of a local man named Newton Whitman. He built the home in 1876, and it was the first brick home to be located in the Dakota Territory. The house was eventually sold to the Yunker family—and it later became the home of the museum. Employees have reported experiencing a friendly ghost on the premises that's thought to be a member of the Yunker family. They have dubbed the spirit "Vanessa," and she is generally thought to hang out in the upper floor of the house. Paranormal activity in the museum includes doors that open and close by themselves, an elevator that has a mind of its own, and the feeling of a friendly presence that's often experienced when the building is empty.

Address: 1201 28th Avenue North
Website: www.childrensmuseum-yunker.org
Activity: E, T

Garrison Stoney End Restaurant & Cabin Fever Lounge

Located along the Lewis and Clark Trail, this home-style restaurant and lounge is the source of a lot of local talk. Besides providing a place for residents to get in a good meal, to grab a drink, and to play some billiards, the Stoney End has also provided hours of interesting talk—the kind of talk that's usually done over campfires or while you're watching a scary movie. Urban legends concerning this location run amok with stories that tell of a male entity who was rumored to have been murdered on the site of the restaurant. Sometimes it's in the actual eatery where he died, and sometimes it's simply told that he died somewhere outside the restaurant. Either way, patrons have claimed to see the apparition, as well as hear him speaking from thin air.

Address: 3956 Highway 37 East
Website: www.stoneyendsupperclub.com
Activity: A, E

Harvey Harvey Public Library

Sometimes the legend concerning a haunting is so tragic that it overshadows the mystery surrounding the paranormal activity. Such is the case with this library. For the locals who work in the building—and even live in the city of Harvey—there is no doubt that the property is haunted. Prior to becoming the library, the place was simply a local home. On October 2, 1931, a woman named Sophie Eberlein-Bentz was murdered by her husband in this house. When the library moved into the site (on the anniversary of her death, no less, in 1990) they immediately noticed strange things were happening. Lights would mysteriously blink on and off, items would disappear only to reappear later on, and strange shadow shapes would be witnessed moving among the books. If you feel the need to grab a good read while you're visiting North Dakota, be sure to swing by this library to say hello to Sophie.

Address: 119 East 10th Street
Website: www.harveynd.com
Activity: E, T, S

Mandan Fort Abraham Lincoln

In addition to the fort itself, the Fort Abraham Lincoln Foundation keeps up the On-a-Slant Indian Village and the Custer House—the source of paranormal activity on this ex-military installation. The fort was established in 1872 to protect the city of Bismarck, which was located on the other side of the Missouri River. Lt. Col. George Armstrong Custer commanded the Seventh Cavalry at this fort and it would

be from here that he would make his last ride to perish at Little Big Horn. The foundation recently rebuilt the Custer house that was on the post, and it's said that Custer has returned to the place! Maybe he didn't want to roam the actual area of his death, so he returned to be indoors again. Activity in the museum home includes cold spots, voices, doors opening/closing by themselves, and the common feeling of being watched.

Address: 4480 Fort Lincoln Road
Website: www.fortlincoln.com
Activity: C, E, T

Medora Chateau de Mores

This unique home holds a lot of local history. The original owners, Antoine Amadee, the Marquis de Mores, and his wife (Medora von Hoffman), built this place and moved in after establishing an area meat-packing plant that did very well. Later, the town would be named after Medora and the marquis would pass away while living abroad. If you visit this house-turned-museum today, you will hear more of this history as well as get to see some of the actual furnishings of the De Mores family. The spirit that walks the property is thought to be one of the De Mores (though there's some debate as to whether it is Antoine or Medora). Activity there includes spectral lights that glow in the place during the evening hours and strange cold spots that seem to follow you at times. You might also want to swing by the De Mores State Park on Main Street—there you can see a statue of old Antoine himself.

Address: 3448 Chateau Road
Website: www.medora.com/what-to-do/
    ?Chateau-de-Mores
Activity: O, C

Medora Rough Riders Hotel

This newly renovated hotel was built in 1884 by George Fitzgerald and was originally named the Metropolitan. It was constructed to handle the sudden surge in population after the Marquis de Mores started his meat-packing plant (see the previous listing) and a local stagecoach line. In 1903, the name of the hotel was changed to its current moniker in honor of Theodore Roosevelt (the first president to visit the city of Medora). The hotel is currently undergoing an expansion that will add a whopping 68 rooms, as well as an expanded dining room. Tales of the hotel being haunted began about 30 years ago when the hotel was under different ownership. Guests who slept on the top floor would report being bothered by the sounds of a young boy playing in the hallways. Of course, there would be no "young boy" in the building. To this day, locals say the boy can be heard and sometimes seen in this same area. If you visit after the expansion is finished, be sure to stay in the original area to experience this spirit.

Address: 301 3rd Avenue
Website: www.medora.com/rough-riders/
Activity: A, E, T

Toledo •

Sandusky •
Cleveland •

• Akron

◉ Columbus

• Cincinnati

OHIO

Akron Akron Civic Theatre

Marcus Loew knew when he built this theatre in 1929, that he was actually constructing a center for social life in Akron. It was designed by architect John Eberson to resemble a Moorish castle, and it was the area's only "atmospheric theatre" (its ceiling is made to appear as the night sky with stars and clouds). The venue underwent a massive renovation in 2001 to the tune of $19 million and is now once again the center of the artistic community. For quite some time, tales concerning ghosts at the civic theatre have been whispered by locals. Most sound like urban legends—but then witnesses say they do see paranormal happenings there. There's the story of a former janitor who's said to still be cleaning and a ghostly male actor that's been seen hanging out backstage and in one balcony. A darker tale

also tells of a woman who committed suicide in the canal at the rear of the theatre and is occasionally seen wandering there.

Address: 182 South Main Street
Website: www.akroncivic.com
Activity: A, S, E, T

Chillicothe Crosskeys Tavern

The lighthearted pub atmosphere of this restaurant and bar is the draw for the locals—though you may be more attracted to the history and haunting of this location. The building dates back to the 1800s, though it has only been a tavern since the turn of the century. The ghost has been dubbed "Harold" by the staff, and he's thought to be the victim of a murder that happened in either the nearby alley, or in the tunnels

255

that are said to run beneath the structure (stories vary). Of course, the facts support neither story, since there's no record of a murdered Harold there. What is known, though, is that glasses have been seen moving by themselves, lights turn on by unseen hands, and the sounds of footsteps/whispers have been heard in the basement.

Address: 19 East Main Street
Website: www.crosskeystavern.com
Activity: E, T

Chillicothe Majestic Theatre

Long before this theatre occupied the area it does now, a Masonic hall was located there. The hall was built in 1853, and it played host to traveling productions, musical acts, and community events for many years. In 1904, the Masonic Opera House was purchased by A. R. Wolf and remodeled. It would change hands several more times—each time being slightly improved—until it was appropriated by a nonprofit in 1990. These days, the theatre hosts classes and events to the public, much like it did in the 1800s. As for the haunting, it's said to be the product of a bad moment in time. When the Spanish flu hit nearby Camp Sherman in 1918, the theatre was used as a temporary morgue. Locals dub the alley adjacent to the property "Blood Alley" and say this area, along with the entirety of the theatre itself, is the site of paranormal activity—things like misty apparitions and disembodied voices and screams.

Address: 45 East Second Street
Website: www.majesticchillicothe.org
Activity: A, M, E, T

Cincinnati Hilton Cincinnati Netherland Plaza

When this hotel first opened in 1931, it received rave reviews. It's unique architecture (French Art Deco) and lush decorations made for an enjoyable upscale retreat. Today, the hotel is owned by the Hilton chain, but still maintains the high level of comfort and style that made the Neth-

erland so popular back in the day. Of course, the hotel is also known for the "Lady in Green," their resident spirit. According to local legend, the spirit is the wife of a construction worker who died while building the place. When the property underwent renovations in 1983, several workers told of seeing the green apparition walking the area known as the Hall of Mirrors.

Address: 35 West Fifth Street
Website: www.hilton.com
Activity: A

Circleville Round Town Players Community Theater

Located within the historic Memorial Hall (circa 1890), this theater has been pleasing local crowds since the 1960s. They offer regular productions of plays and musicals in a cozy setting—despite the reputation that the area they occupy is haunted. Rumors of ghosts date back to a library that was located in the building—librarians and patrons would report seeing the apparition of a Union soldier and say that books would move by themselves. Now that a theater operates there, tales persist. Activity is said to include apparitions (a little girl and a woman dressed in white now accompany the soldier), objects moving (doors, props, etc.), and the sounds of voices and footsteps are heard throughout the building.

Address: 165 ½ East Main Street
Website: www.roundtownplayers.com
Activity: A, S, M, E, T

Cleveland Agora Theater

Maybe Ohio should be known as the "Land of the Haunted Theaters"... Much like the others listed here, the Agora has had haunted legends swirling around about it for many years. Known as one of the preeminent music venues in the state, the Agora dates back to the 1960s, though the theater itself is much older (it was originally called the Metropolitan Theatre and was built in 1910). If you decide to catch a musical show here, keep an eye out for the apparition that's said to visit with folks onstage. Witnesses say the spirit is dressed in a yellow raincoat and that he is often seen on the catwalks.

Address: 5000 Euclid Avenue
Website: www.clevelandagora.com
Activity: A

Cleveland Franklin Castle Club

Though this is a private club, the place does offer rentals for private events and host the occasional event, so check the calendar on their website before planning a visit. Housed within the historic Franklin Castle (circa 1865), members of this club get private meals and the added perk of getting to stay on the property overnight—if the place doesn't seem too spooky to you. For years, the locals have looked upon this Gothic structure with a mixture of awe and dread. Tales about the place include the murder of a young girl (said to be Karen Tiedemann), secret passages and cabinets (one, reportedly, was filled with human remains), and the victims of an axe murderer. Visitors have reported seeing the apparition of Karen, hearing the spectral cries of infants and encountering misty apparitions in the club. This location was certified as haunted by the infamous Hans Holzer when he investigated the haunting there in 1976.

Address: 4308 Franklin Boulevard
Website: www.franklincastleclub.com
Activity: A, E, M, O, T, C

Cleveland Johnny Mango World Café & Bar

Known for Tex-Mex food, a juice bar, and meatless entrées, Johnny Mango's is a local favorite. Of course, you can also just swing by for a beer and a chance to glimpse one of their on-site spirits. According to several sources, Johnny Mango's is plagued by up to three ghosts—all entities who passed away in or around the building prior to the restaurant moving in. The most well-known ghost is "Margaret," a female apparition that's often seen there. It's said she died in the 1800s from a trolley car accident. Most of the activity in the bar just seems to be of the "hey, look at me" variety, so drop by and give it a shot.

Address: 3120 Bridge Avenue
Website: www.jmango.com
Activity: A, E, T

Cleveland Squire's Castle/North Chagrin Reservation

Located in the North Chagrin Reservation (a park located in Cleveland), Squire's Castle dates back to the 1890s. It was built by Feargus B. Squire as a gatekeeper's house for his manor house—a structure that was never actually built. Squire was the owner of the Standard Oil Company, and he planned to use some of his vast wealth to put up a permanent estate on the 522 acres he purchased in Cleveland. Instead, he ended up selling the gatehouse and land in 1922. Local legend says that the spirit of Rebecca Squire now haunts the castle, despite the fact that she died in Wickliffe, Ohio, in 1929 (long after the property was sold). So who haunts the place? It could be that Rebecca came here after she died (ghosts have been known to do that), or it could be that the spirit is altogether somebody different. Either way, locals have reported seeing a pale apparition in the castle and hearing ghostly moans.

Address: Located in Park on Chagrin River Road
Website: www.clemetparks.com
Activity: A, E

Columbus Harrison House Bed & Breakfast

The majority of this home was built in 1890, though the owner (Amos Solomon) would add on to the structure several times. Solomon lived in the house until 1907, at which point he moved away and began leasing the property. Several tenants and owners later, the B&B is now in capable hands and offers wonderful accommodations that are within walking distance of many local attractions. It wasn't long after the new owner took over, though, that she started noticing strange things around the house. Things like imprints on the newly made beds (like someone invisible just sat there) and objects turning up in strange places. Visitors then started relating strange tales of seeing apparitions in the guest rooms: the spirit of a young boy and man once appeared before a young guest, and the ghost of a woman was seen by a psychic.

Address: 313 West 5th Street
Website: www.harrisonhouse-columbus.com
Activity: A, E, T

Columbus The Ohio Statehouse

Though the cornerstone of this massive building was laid in 1839, it would be 1861 before construction was finished. It was designed in the Greek Revival style that was so popular back then, and the first legislature met there in 1857. Visiting the statehouse is a lot of fun—they have a café and museum gift shop, and even feature tours that are open to the public. And if you visit during the Halloween season, you might even get to take one of their haunted tours. So, who haunts the building? According to the locals, it's a former senate page named Tom Bateman. The residual sight of old Tom headed down the stairs to the east exit is said to happen every day around 5 p.m. Of course, Tom gets the blame for other things that happen around the statehouse as well—things like

the lights flickering, doors slamming, and objects being moved during the night.

Address: 1 Capitol Square
Website: www.statehouse.state.oh.us
Activity: R, A, T

Columbus Thurber House

This Victorian home is now a museum that reflects the way of life that James Thurber would have experienced while living there (1913–17). You can tour the first two floors of the home and see most of the common areas, the five bedrooms the family lived in, and the bathroom that Thurber hid in when he heard a ghost running through the house! He wrote about this experience in a story he titled "The Night the Ghost Got In." According to Thurber, he would hear the sounds of footsteps running up the stairs, see books flying across the room, and witness shadowy apparitions walking in front of windows. All of this is activity that's said to still occur today in the old house. Most believe the spirits of the home stem from a fire that took out the Ohio Lunatic Asylum and many of the area homes that once stood at this location (seven died in the fire).

Address: 77 Jefferson Avenue
Website: www.thurberhouse.org
Activity: E, T, S

Fairport The Fairport Harbor Marine Museum and Lighthouse

The lighthouse at this museum has been watching over Fairport Harbor and Lake Erie since 1825. It functioned until 1868, and then was replaced by a newer version that was operated until 1925. Over those many years, there were a number of lighthouse keepers who resided on the property—though none are as interesting as Captain Joseph Babcock and his wife. During his service, Mrs. Babcock grew ill and was bedridden, so she was given a number of cats to keep her company. Once she was well, and the family moved on from the lighthouse, all the cats were accounted for, but one. A gray cat was missing. Years later, a curator of this museum, Paula Brent, starting seeing a strange sight: the ghost of a gray cat running through the museum, and even lying on her while she was sleeping (she lived on the property). Later, a mummified gray cat (now on display in the museum) was found in a crawlspace under the building, which solidified the idea that a cat is, indeed, haunting this location.

Address: 129 Second Street
Website: www.ncweb.com/org/fhlh/
Activity: A, T

Gallipolis Our House Museum

This living museum dates back to 1819 and a man named Henry Cushing. It functioned as a tavern and local restaurant—though their on-site ballroom was what made the place so popular with the locals. General Lafayette visited the tavern in 1825 (an event the museum celebrates every year) and the Cushings ran the business until 1865. In 1944, the owners of the property donated the old tavern to the state, and it is currently operated by the Ohio Historical Society. Members of the society, along with visitors to the museum, number among those who first noticed the paranormal activity at Our House. According to their reports, the sounds of a woman singing and phantom footsteps are heard in the building.

Address: 432 1st Avenue
Website: www.ohsweb.ohiohistory.org/places/
  se10/
Activity: E

Granville The Buxton Inn

If it's not amazing enough that this inn has been continuously operating since 1812, how about the fact that it's still operating in its original building! Orrin Granger built the property (then known as a tavern) to service travelers journeying by stagecoach between the cities of Columbus and Newark—though it would also function as a local post office and a ballroom for gala events. Today it functions, more or less, like a bed and breakfast, so you can rent a room on this property while you hunt for the ghosts. Sightings of spirits date back to the 1920s when a resident of the tavern, Fred Sweet, reported seeing a ghost standing in the kitchen eating a piece of pie! It's thought the spirit is old Orrin looking over the property, though he isn't alone... Witnesses have also seen a "Lady in Blue" in the inn who is presumed to be Ethel Bounell, a former innkeeper there.

Address: 313 East Broadway Street
Website: www.buxtoninn.com
Activity: A, E, T

Greenville Bear's Mill

Gabriel Baer built this mill in 1849—and, unbelievably, this water-powered structure still operates today (the only mill of this type to still do so in Ohio). Prior to the building of this property, President James Monroe had granted the area's water rights to Major George Adams in 1824. When Baer purchased the land and these rights from him, construction on the mill had already begun. More recently, the mill was purchased by Charlie Andrews in 1947. Charlie was an advocate of healthy living and even won a court case against the city of Greenville for polluting the area's water. He began the tradition of creating organically produced flours and meals—a tradition that continues today in the on-site store. Stop by, take a tour, and buy some quality health food products—and be sure to keep an eye out for their resident spirit. The ghost is said to be an elderly man (possibly Baer or Adams), and his apparition has been seen many times.

Address: 6450 Arcanum-Bear's Mill Road
Website: www.bearsmill.com
Activity: A, E

Kenton Hardin County Historical Museum

Located within the Sullivan-Johnson House (circa 1896), this museum contains a set of extremely unique exhibits. The halls are filled with such items as toys that were made at the nearby Kenton Hardware Company, the Frederick Machetanz Collection of Alaskan Art and Literature, and a display dedicated to Civil War hero Lt. Jacob Parrot (the first person to ever receive the U.S. Medal of Honor). Of all the strange sights, though, the strangest is probably the spirit of Louella Sullivan! She was the first occupant of the house and a local artist—and she's said to still roam the halls of her old Victorian home. Visitors and employees have seen her apparition walking in the basement, heard the sounds of her phantom footsteps, and even smelled her perfume on occasion.

Address: 223 North Main Street
Website: www.hardinmuseums.org
Activity: A, E, N

Kingville Kingville Public Library

The oldest portion of this library, the meeting room, dates back to 1894. It was called the Kingville Free Reading Room and was operated by the Linnean Literary Society of Kingville. In 1918, the building was physically moved to its present-day location, which contained a school back then. In 1927, the school burned down and the haunted happenings began. Though there are, reportedly, several spirits in the library, the most commonly encountered ghost is a man wearing a tall black hat. He's usually seen in the old reading room section of the library, where he's said to look at the surprised witness and then walk into a wall of books. Other activity includes dark shadow shapes and the sounds of whispering voices.

Address: 6006 Academy Street
Website: www.kingsville.lib.oh.us
Activity: A, S, E

Lafayette The Red Brick Tavern

This historic stagecoach stop was erected in 1837 to service travelers journeying between the cities of Springfield and Columbus. It was built by William and Mary Minter, who operated a tavern and lodgings. In 1854, the third floor of the tavern was used as a school for local children, and several families leased a portion of the Red Brick for their home. The tavern has been visited by a number of influential people over the years (including six U.S. presidents)—though the most important visitors these days are their patrons. If you visit, you'll be treated to a top-notch meal in a wonderfully historic site. As for the ghost, it's said the spirit is a female member of the Minter family who is thought to have committed suicide on the property. Her apparition, along with the sounds of her whispering and footsteps, has been witnessed many times.

Address: 1700 Cumberland Road
Website: www.historicredbricktavern.com
Activity: A, E

Lebanon The Golden Lamb

When Jonas Seaman applied for a license to operate a "house of entertainment" in 1803, he had no idea he would be creating the oldest continuously operating business in the state of Ohio! The current version of the Golden Lamb was constructed in 1815 (though the third story was added on in 1844 and the fourth story was built in 1878). Visit the property today and you'll find a restaurant, a bar (the Black Horse Tavern), and some of the most historic lodgings in the state. If you're lucky, you'll also see the ghost of "Sarah!" She's named after the room she likes to hang around in (Sarah's Room), though she's generally thought to be Eliza Clay, the daughter of Henry Clay who passed away on the premises in 1825. There is also a male spirit in the inn, who most believe to be Charles Sherman, a former Supreme Court Justice who died while visiting the Golden Lamb in 1829.

Address: 27 South Broadway
Website: www.goldenlamb.com
Activity: A, E, N

Logan A Georgian Manner Bed and Breakfast

Is it possible to experience "Southern hospitality" in an Ohio bed and breakfast? According to the folks at Georgian Manner, yes indeed! With five beautifully decorated rooms, a wonderful view of Lake Logan, and one of the best breakfasts you'll eat north of the Mason-Dixon Line, they make a good case. For the paranormal tourist, the deal is even sweeter when you consider the possibility of bumping into the ghost of John Engle. He was the original builder and owner of this house and he was murdered in 1898 when he drank poisoned coffee. Though his wife was acquitted of the crime, most believe she was the culprit (she had been trying to divorce the man for some time). John's restless spirit is said to now visit with people staying in his old home. Interestingly, at least one source also reports that locals have seen spectral children playing on the front porch as well.

Address: 29055 Evans Road
Website: www.georgianmanner.com
Activity: A, E

Loveland The Historic Loveland Castle

Also known as Chateau Laroche, this castle is the headquarters for the Knights of the Golden Trail, a group based out of Ohio that follows the rules of chivalry and the Ten Commandments. Both institutions were founded by Harry Andrews who decided to build the place after touring numerous castles just after World War I. Harry was declared dead during the war, and by the time he corrected the mistake, his wife had married another. The castle is now available for rent for events. Ghost stories concerning the castle began when members of the knights started noticing strange things on the grounds there. Things like shadowy apparitions, doors slamming shut for no reason, objects being moved with nobody around, and even disembodied voices. Though it's thought there are several spirits in the castle, one in particular is known for protecting the place. It's said that when someone speaks ill of the castle, the ghost will give them a friendly shock to remind them to be respectful.

Address: 12025 Shore Road
Website: www.lovelandcastle.com
Activity: A, S, E, T

Lucas Malabar Farm

Created by Pulitzer Prize–winning author Louis Bromfield, Malabar Farm dates back to 1939. He created the property to illustrate the merits of land conservation and responsible farming. During his tenure, he wrote several books about the area—and one that featured two very prominent local murders. The first was the murder of a man by a local eccentric woman named Phoebe Wise—a woman who is now said to walk Reformatory Road in the afterlife. The second story concerns Ceely Rose, a woman who murdered her entire family on the property where Malabar Farm now sits. When you tour this park, make sure to visit the old barn there. This is the site of most of the ghostly activity. A shadowy apparition and the sounds of a disembodied voice are often heard in this area.

Address: 4050 Bromfield Road
Website: www.malabarfarm.org
Activity: S, E

Mansfield Ohio State Reformatory

Ranking right up there with Waverly Hills Sanitorium and Myrtles Plantation, this location makes the short list of must-see haunted places in the United States—and is probably the most well known paranormal spot in Ohio. Featured in numerous television programs, movies, and books, the prison was built in 1886 and has been the site of many historical moments. For example, Civil War soldiers trained at a post (Camp Mordecai Bartley) that was located there (while the place was a territorial prison) and famous author O. Henry was once incarcerated in the prison. If you take a haunted tour of the reformatory, you will get to hit most of the hot spots (like "the Hole," the warden's office, and the numerous cells), so keep an eye out for apparitions and shadow shapes that are said to be seen throughout the complex. If you have the time, you may want to take a stroll down Reformatory Road, too. It's said the ghost of Phoebe Wise (see above entry) is often seen walking there.

Address: 100 Reformatory Road
Website: www.mrps.org
Activity: A, E, S, T, O, C

Marion The Harding Home

This location was the site of Warren G. Harding's "front porch" campaign that catapulted him into the White House. This historic house (circa 1891) is now a living museum that's decorated with the original furniture and furnishings that Warren and his wife, Florence, kept there during their tenure. Adjacent to the home is the original "press house" that managed Hardin's campaign, which is now a museum dedicated to the former president. Both properties can be toured and feature a lot of attractions, including the spectral sight of old Warren himself! Though he passed away in San Francisco while in office, his spirit has been witnessed in his house. It's said he is often seen walking the parlor (and heard as well, as the sounds of footsteps are a common occurrence) and that his presence often causes the clocks on the premises to go awry.

Address: 380 Mt. Vernon Avenue
Website: www.ohsweb.ohiohistory.org/places/
c03/
Activity: A, E, T

Maumee Fallen Timbers Battlefield

When General "Mad" Anthony Wayne and his Legion of the United States troops defeated a confederacy of Native Americans led by Chief Little Turtle in 1794, the way was opened for Ohio's statehood. You can visit this battlefield today and experience this history—as well as one of the state's biggest residual hauntings. It's said that if the conditions are just right (such as a stormy night) visitors can see and hear the clash between the soldiers and Indians. Thirty-three Americans were killed in the fray, though the total death count would be much more, and the anniversary of all this bloodshed (August 20) is, reportedly, the most active night.

Address: Along the Maumee River
Website: www.fallentimbersbattlefield.com
Activity: R, A, E

Maumee Wolcott House Museum Complex

Though the Wolcott House is the centerpiece for this massive tourist attraction, the grounds contain seven historical buildings (including a schoolhouse and a train depot). Tours are offered on a regular basis (check the website for hours) and make for an interesting and fun-filled afternoon even without the presence of a ghost. But while we're on the subject of ghosts, the Wolcott House (circa 1836) is said to have 'em. Employees and visitors alike have told of entities touching them while walking through the structure and hearing the sounds of footsteps and whispers. The house was the home of James Wolcott, his wife Mary, and their family, so most believe the spirit is a remnant of that household.

Address: 1035 River Road
Website: www.wolcotthouse.org
Activity: E, T

McConnelsville The Twin City Opera House

Originally built as the town hall and theater, this opera house was a highly contentious project back in the day. It took an absent mayor and a Democratic majority to get the property built—a task that took over two and a half years. The grand opening was in 1892, and much like that day, the opera house is pleasing crowds today. When you take a closer look at this theater, the place has several secrets. First, there are the tunnels that run under the building that were used to shuttle actors to and from a neighboring hotel (and rumored to be part of the Underground Railroad), Next, there's the secret stairs that were uncovered in the 1980s. And then there's the ghost. The apparition of a former usher named Everett has been seen in the theatre a number of times. There's also the spirit of a woman who's been heard singing and playing the piano.

Address: 15 West Main Street
Website: www.operahouseinc.com
Activity: A, E

Medina Spitzer House Bed and Breakfast

This is a location that's hard to miss. How many bright-pink Victorian houses do you think there are in Medina? It dates back to 1890 and was the home of General Ceilan Milo Spitzer—though these days, it's home to folks like you who are looking for a wonderful weekend away from home. The B&B features four guest rooms, a quaint garden (often used by locals for weddings), and, according to locals, two ghosts. The dining room is said to be the site of a disembodied male voice, and a female apparition has been seen in Anna's Room—though the Ceilan Room is said to be a close second with paranormal activity.

Address: 504 West Liberty Street
Website: www.spitzerhouse.com
Activity: A, E

Mentor James A. Garfield National Historic Site

This house was constructed in 1832 by James Dickey, but was acquired by James Garfield in 1876. He lived there while serving as a U.S. Representative, and even ran his "front porch" campaign for president from there. Local reporters dubbed the property "Lawnfield," and after Garfield was assassinated, his wife built the first ever presidential library right there in the home. When you tour this historic house you'll get to experience all this history. So, does James Garfield haunt his old house? Nope, his wife does. Visitors report hearing her in the upstairs area of the home, and it's said that during renovations, she would keep her house neat by arranging all the tools for the workers while they were away.

Address: 8095 Mentor Avenue
Website: www.nps.gov/jaga/
Activity: E, T

New Vienna Snow Hill Country Club

If you've ever wanted to visit a haunted location and then go outside and play a round of golf, then this location is just for you! The club is semi-private, which means you can join them for extended access, but even without membership you can eat at the restaurant—the site of paranormal activity at the club—or even stay for one of their "Ghost and Dinner" events (which even allows you to stay overnight). As for the ghost—well, most believe the spirit is a member of the family that built the original log cabin that became the club (circa early 1800s), or is a remnant of the days when the existing structure functioned as an area tavern. Activity includes spectral voices, shadow shapes, and items moving of their own volition.

Address: 11093 SR 73
Website: www.snowhillcountryclub.com
Activity: S, E, T

Newbury Punderson Manor

Located within Punderson State Park, this massive estate is an English Tudor–styled manor house that dates back to the early 1800s and a man named Lemuel Punderson. He built this house alongside the lake and lived there many years until he passed away mysteriously (some say he drowned himself in a golden bathtub). Today it is a Xanterra property that features overnight accommodations and the locally renowned Cherry Dining Room restaurant. The haunting of Punderson Manor is the stuff of campfire legend. The tales include a spectral girl who's said to rise from Punderson Lake (a teenage girl drowned there in 1977), park rangers who once encountered an intensely cold spirit on the stairs inside the manor (and the female entity laughed at them), and the grisly visage of a dead lumberjack who hanged himself from the rafters in the dining room. When you visit, you will want to rent Suite 231 (also known as the Windsor Suite or the Blue Room) where the sounds of moans are heard, the doors are said to burst open, and an apparition actually sits on the bed with you.

Address: 11755 Kinsman Road
Website: www.pundersonmanorresort.com
Activity: A, E, T, C

Painesville Rider's Inn

With this location you get a bed and breakfast and phenomenal restaurant all in one stop! This makes the place a prime haunted getaway. Built as a stagecoach stop in 1812, the history of this inn includes functioning as an Underground Railroad location during the Civil War and even operating as a speakeasy during the 1920s. On the B&B side of things, the place offers eleven rooms—each with its own homey touch. On the restaurant front, the fare is traditional (with some recipes that were found in a nineteenth-century cookbook found in the attic) and can be eaten either in the pub or in Mistress Suzanne's Dining Room—a spot named for their resident spirit. Suzanne was the wife of Joseph Rider and she died amid suspicious circumstances a mere six weeks into the marriage. Sightings of her apparition, as well as experiencing her simple welcoming presence, occur quite often in the inn.

Address: 792 Mentor Avenue
Website: www.ridersinn.com
Activity: A

Ripley The Rankin House

Overlooking the Ohio River, this historic landmark served as the end of a perilous trek for thousands of black Americans journeying along the Underground Railroad. It was the home of Reverend John Rankin and dates back to 1828.

Rankin was a fierce abolitionist who wrote letters on the subject of freedom and even formed the Ripley Anti-Slavery Society. If you're interested in visiting this site, you will need to set up an appointment via their website. It will be well worth your time. In addition to all this history, you also get to experience some unique paranormal activity. The inside of the property is, reportedly, haunted by the spirit of a dog, and folks who brave the climb up the hundred steps out front often hear the disembodied voices of those who came before.

Address: 6152 Rankin Road
Website: www.ripleyohio.net/htm/rankin
Activity: A, E

Sandusky Hotel Breakers

Perched on the tip of Cedar Point, this hotel has a commanding view of Lake Erie. It has stood over a hundred years and features quick access to all the nearby fun (such as the amusement and water parks). It also features several ghost stories. If you talk to the employees, you'll most likely hear the tale of Room 169 and the spirit of Mary. Local legend says a girl of this name hanged herself in this room after having a fight with her betrothed (though there's no history to back this up). Other hot spots include the east wing of the hotel (where apparitions have been seen) and the nearby Frontier Trail (the site of a phantom woman who walks the area searching for her long lost lover).

Address: 1 Cedar Point Road
Website: www.cedarpoint.com
Activity: A, E, T

Somerset Clay Haus Restaurant

If you like to have a good meal—say, steak and seafood—with your paranormal activity, then the Clay Haus may be the spot for you. It's located within the historic former home of Phillip Grelle who purchased the property in 1812. Some elements of the original house can still be seen there today (such as the downstairs tavern that once was the family's main living area). Another feature of the original house is the witnessing of entities in the restaurant. The stairs seem to be the center of the activity. The sounds of people stomping up and down them are heard—and the apparitions of three men have been seen there as well. One of these spirits, a man dressed in dark clothes, has since been seen several times near the "Blue Room" in the eatery.

Address: 123 West Main Street
Website: www.clayhaus.com
Activity: A, E

Trinway Prospect Place Estate

Locations don't get much more ghost-hunter friendly than this historic manor. With regular tours (of the ghostly type) and the freedom for paranormal groups to rent the entire house for their own ghost hunts, Prospect Place makes for the perfect investigation spot. The house dates back to 1856 and was a stop along the Underground Railroad prior to and during the Civil War. The owner at the time, George Willison Adams, was a staunch abolitionist and a member of the Lords of the Valley, a group of men with wealth who helped fight slavery. Hot spots in the estate include the basement (where the spirits of those who traveled the railroad are said to still reside), the ballroom (where a dark entity haunts what's thought to be the product of slave voodoo practice), and the ground floor where the ghost of Constance roams (a girl who died after sustaining a fall).

Address: 12150 Main Street
Website: www.prospectplace-dresden.com
Activity: A, S, E, T, C

Worthington The Worthington Inn

The oldest part of this property dates back to 1831. It was the home for Rensselear W. Cowles and his wife. After he passed away, new owners expanded upon the house and created an inn in 1852 called the Bishop House, then it was called the Union Hotel, then the Central House. Fi-nally, the current owners gave the place its current moniker and restored the inn back to all its Victorian glory. With the property changing hands so many times, it's no wonder that the ghost would be that of a previous owner. The spirit of George Van Loon is said to hang out in the old section of the inn and is heard doing his old daily ritual of closing up for the night. Since the inn no longer offers overnight accommodations, you will have to settle for a great meal at this location.

Address: 649 High Street
Website: www.worthingtoninn.com
Activity: E, T, N

Zoar The Cobbler Shop B&B and Antiques

The city of Zoar was a communal living space for German immigrants who decided to flee Europe because of the heavy taxation being levied against them. The State Church there (Lutheran) had been steadily increasing taxes to pay for the Napoleonic Wars. The village was formed in 1817, and this property was created to be their cobbler shop. It also served as a home for up to three families. With five guest rooms in the bed and breakfast, three families can still be accommodated there today. As for shoes, well there are examples (antiques) that are on display, but they aren't making any new pairs, though some antiques are for sale in their shop. The ghost on this property is said to appear quite menacing—even if he is of a mild nature. Witnesses say the male spirit is dressed in a long, black cloak and is often seen and heard in the hallways there.

Address: 121 East Second Street
Website: www.cobblershop.com
Activity: A, E

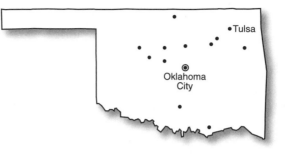

OKLAHOMA

Claremore Belvidere Mansion

Located just off downtown Claremont, this spacious Victorian masterpiece was built in 1907 for John and Mary Bayless. Unfortunately, John would never see construction on his new home finished. He passed away a mere six months before the home was done. These days you can visit the mansion's Victorian Gift Shop to take a look around—or even take part in one of their special events. If you do visit, be sure to ask the employees about their resident spirits. They will tell you the place is haunted by John and Bland Bayless (his daughter). A guest visiting the mansion noted a strangely dressed man on the front porch when she went in. When she asked who the man was, and gave a description of him, the staff was amazed that it matched the description of John. As for Bland, she committed suicide in the early 1900s and is now seen and heard throughout the mansion.

Address: 121 North Chickasaw Avenue
Website: www.rogerscountyhistory.org
Activity: A, E, T

Cushing Cushing Country Club

This community club is much like any other in the United States: it has a restaurant, a golf course, and a swimming pool. But unlike other country clubs, the one in Cushing is said to be haunted. Employees have reported seeing a shadowy apparition that appears in the dining room and likes to move items on the various tables there. They called in a local paranormal group, which investigated the site (and did manage to get a couple good audio clips), but got largely inconclusive findings. Is the place haunted? Maybe. There does seem to be paranormal activity there. If you decide to catch a meal at the CCC, try dining in the Pink Room, which is reportedly the most active area.

Address: 4615 East 9th Street
Website: www.cushingcountryclub.com
Activity: S, E, T

Durant Fort Washita

When the U.S. government set up this fort in 1842, it was the southwestern-most military post in the country. It was also smack-dab in the middle of Choctaw Indian territory. Interestingly, unlike other army posts stationed in Native American territory, this particular fort was created to protect the tribe. But when the Civil War broke out, the troops abandoned the area—only to admit Confederate soldiers from Texas. After the war, the entire site was handed over to the Choctaw. There are several interesting haunted tales concerning the fort—not the least of which is the story of "Aunt Jane." Prior to the Civil War, Jane was a local settler who was robbed and killed by frontiersmen. Since this act, her headless apparition has been seen many times over the years. Then there's the spirit of a Civil War–era soldier, who's said to menace those who visit the old barracks at the fort, as well as reports of a malicious entity who grabs and harasses people who enter the Bonahan Cabin.

Address: 3348 State Road 199
Website: www.okhistory.org/outreach/military/ fortwashita
Activity: A, S, E, T, C

El Reno Fort Reno

Before you take a tour of this wonderful and historic site, swing by the visitor's center. They will supply you with all the info you need to find your way around the grounds. Fort Reno was established as a military outpost in 1874 during the Indian Wars to maintain a presence among the Cheyenne and Arapaho tribes. In 1876, the outpost moved across the North Canadian River to the other side and added a saw mill and corrals. The fort functioned all the way through World War II and even housed German prisoners of war for a time. Today it is run by a local nonprofit organization that is constantly renovating the post. There are two areas that are said to experience paranormal activity: a Victorian house where visitors have witnessed shadow shapes and the apparitions of small children, and the grounds themselves, where the residual sounds of soldiers, as well as apparitions, are seen and heard.

Address: 7107 West Cheyenne Street
Website: www.fortreno.org
Activity: A, S, E, R

Fort Gibson Fort Gibson

This early western fort was created in 1824 as a jumping off point for frontiersmen and explorers journeying west. It was abandoned in 1857 after there was no longer a need for a military post in this area. But during the Civil War, it was reoccupied to keep the peace among the local tribes. Of course, the haunting of this fort has nothing to do with any war. It concerns the legend of Vivia Thomas, the daughter of a wealthy Bostonian who journeyed to Fort Gibson for revenge. When she was abandoned by her lover (an officer in the army stationed there), she traveled to the fort, disguised herself as a man, and enlisted in the army. She shot the officer dead as he traveled to visit a local Indian woman, but she was immediately sorry for her deed. She would go to the grave of the soldier and weep each night—until she froze to death on top of his grave. To this day, people in the area claim to see a female apparition walking the grounds of the old fort.

Address: 907 North Garrison Street
Website: www.okhistory.org/outreach/military/ fortgibson
Activity: A

Guthrie Blue Belle Saloon

This location was one of the first drinking establishments in the state of Oklahoma. It opened in 1889 and featured a downstairs tavern and upstairs bordello—sort of a one-stop-shopping spot for Old West gunfighters (just check out the bullet holes in the ceiling there). Over the years, several prominent men of the time visited the Blue Belle, such as Teddy Roosevelt and Tom Mix (an actor who actually bartended there for a spell). In the paranormal realm, there have been several visitors as well. A former madam of the bordello, called "Miss Lizzie" by the staff, is said to be seen along with two young girls. Named Claudia and Estelle, they are thought to have worked there and to have come to a bad end. There is also the spirit of a man who's been seen in the main bar area. He's dressed in turn-of-the-century attire and is quite the grouchy spirit. He has been known to use profanity to get patrons' attention.

Address: 224 West Harrison Avenue
Website: www.bluebellesaloon.info
Activity: A, E, T, S

Guthrie The Old Santa Fe Depot of Guthrie

When the railroad first made its way into Guthrie in 1887, the city already had a nice depot waiting. The first train rolled into town with over 1,000 passengers wanting to homestead in the area, and many more trains just like this followed. This sudden influx of people to the city created a need for many new amenities, including a bigger and better depot. The Santa Fe Depot was constructed in 1889 to meet this need (though today's version was actually an add-on built in 1903). Today, it services the community as a museum, restaurant, and event center. You will especially want to visit the eatery there; it was one of the infamous "Harvey House" establishments and it holds a lot of history in itself (and this is before you've even gone into the museum!). As for the ghostly activity here, it seems mostly residual in nature. Glimpses of spectral people in dated clothing and the sounds of "conversations" and "chattering" are heard in various areas of the property.

Address: 409 West Oklahoma Avenue
Website: www.theoldsantafedepotofguthrie.com
Activity: R, A, E

Guthrie Stone Lion Inn

This location is actually called the Haunted Stone Lion Inn right on their website! There's nothing better than when a place acknowledges its haunting and openly discusses their ghost(s). This mansion was built in 1907 for F. E. Houghton and family and is a massive house, indeed. With three floors of typical Victorian rooms (including a ballroom on the third floor), the Stone Lion makes for a great bed and breakfast stay. In addition to featuring six unique guest rooms, the B&B also hosts murder mystery evenings and offers fine dining. There are two spirits that reside in this property. The first is that of a young girl thought to be Augusta Houghton, who died in the home when she was eight years old (she was sick with whooping cough, but it's generally accepted that she probably died from an overdose of medicine that contained codeine). She is known for playing on the third floor, where she is often seen and heard. The second entity is that of an older man that's been seen on the first floor and in the basement. He is thought to be a remnant of the days when the mansion was used either as a boarding house or a funeral home. His apparition is usually accompanied by the strong scent of a cigar.

Address: 1016 West Warner Avenue
Website: www.stonelioninn.com
Activity: A, E, T, N

Oklahoma City The County Line

How many times have you gone to a paranormal investigation and thought to yourself, "I wish I had some barbeque right now..." Well, when you visit the County Line in OKC, you will get a little of both! When it comes to food, this restaurant needs no introduction, as their smoked meats rank as one of the best in the area. The paranormal side of the house, though, is a little less well known. During the 1930s, this building was the home of a speakeasy called the Kentucky Club. It was a tavern, bordello, and gambling hall that appealed to the upper crust of the region and was a regular stop for famed criminal Pretty Boy Floyd. Since the restaurant moved into the property, employees have been seeing "shadow people" walking the dining room and hearing disembodied voices throughout the main area. It's thought that one of the spirits there is a man called "Russell," who is said to have been murdered in the dining room after flirting with another man's girlfriend (this was when the place was a bar). Additional activity includes glassware moving by itself and voices coming from the attic (where the bordello was once located).

Address: 1226 Northeast 63rd Street
Website: www.countyline.com
Activity: S, E, T

Oklahoma City Langston's Western Wear

This "cowboy heaven" was established in 1913 and is generally accepted to be the oldest western wear store in Oklahoma (though, wouldn't all stores in the 1800s have had "western wear"?). There are quite a few outlets for this clothing chain, but the original location in OKC is within the historic "Stockyards City." During the 1930s, this building was actually a dancehall that was witness to a horrible crime. A girl named Patty, who worked in the hall, was shot and killed there (in the area of the store that's now "Women's Boots"). Her sister, Rose, was so distraught that she committed suicide in one of the hotel rooms located in the upstairs area of this store. Patrons of Langston's have since reported seeing the two girls in various areas of the shop—but especially on the second floor. Disembodied voices and objects moving top the list of paranormal activ-

ity—with at least one customer saying she was shoved by an entity.

Address: 2224 Exchange Avenue
Website: www.langstons.com
Activity: A, E, T

Oklahoma City The Overholser Mansion

This house was built in a "chateau" style in 1903 and was the residence of Henry Overholser and family. Henry was instrumental in the early growth of OKC by constructing over thirty-five buildings, two opera houses, and the U.S. courthouse in the city. Henry passed away in 1915, but his wife, Anna, continued to live in the home with their daughter, Ione, and her husband, David Perry. Anna passed away in 1940, but the mansion remained in the family until 1972, when the current owners purchased the place from Perry. You can now tour the house, as well as rent it for special events and occasions (such as a ghost hunt). The home itself has had ghost tours during the Halloween season, as well as paranormal investigations. Activity in this haunted house includes disembodied voices, the sounds of footsteps, and the pale apparition of a woman (thought to be a member of the Overholser family) who's been seen in the area of the downstairs music room.

Address: 405 Northwest 15th Street
Website: www.overholsermansion.org
Activity: A, S, E, O

Oklahoma City The Skirvin Hilton Hotel

When the Skirvin Hotel opened its doors in 1911, it was the grandest hotel in the American Southwest—and that's exactly what owner W. B. Skirvin intended! In 1930, the hotel added a new wing that increased the room capacity and raised the height of the hotel by 14 stories. Unfortunately, this is also the same period when the hotel suffered a great tragedy—a young maid who worked in the building leaped from one of the upper floors with her infant, killing both of them instantly. Dark rumors swirled that Mr. Skirvin had an affair with the maid and that the baby was their "love child," but this has never been confirmed (and is highly unlikely considering Skirvin's advanced age at that point). Since that act, the spirit of this maid has been seen in the hotel numerous times. The employees call her "Effie" and say she likes male visitors at the hotel. Patrons have heard her disembodied voice (sometimes saying seductive things), witnessed her apparition (with at least two accounts stating she was naked) and seen a maid's cart moving on its own. Even more disturbing, though, are the phantom sounds of a baby crying that have been heard in several rooms.

Address: 1 Park Avenue
Website: www1.hilton.com
Activity: A, E, T

Ponca City 101 Ranch and Wild West Rodeo

This annual affair just celebrated its 50th anniversary and is still going as strong as ever. Its roots go back to the old 101 Wild West Show and, of course, the 101 Ranch. The ranch was founded in 1893 by George Miller and was run by him and his wife, Molly. Many of the early Western films were shot at this ranch because of the on-site structures, such as the old school, a hotel, and general store. In addition to the rodeo, a portion of the old ranch is now a historic monument and park. This is what you want to concentrate on—in this area are the foundations of an old house (called the "White House") and the remains of what used to be the ranch. The park and surrounding climes are considered to be haunted. According to locals, passersby have seen shadowy apparitions and heard the sounds of strange voices/music that seem to emanate from the air around them.

Address: 1609 Donald Avenue
Website: www.poncacity.com/101_ranch
Activity: S, E

Sapulpa Sapulpa Historical Society Museum

This unique museum is three-stories tall and a sort of mini-village in and of itself. Instead of simply showing exhibits of the area's past, this historical society decided to re-create businesses that would have existed in the early 1900s. There's a blacksmith shop, a sheriff's office, and even a boarding school all housed in the museum. There's also an exhibit that's not listed in the brochure—a ghost! Employees and visitors alike have heard disembodied voices and seen glimpses of misty shapes in the museum—so a local paranormal group was called in. Several great EVPs were captured and personal experiences were had. Though there's no name or face to attribute to the spirit(s), it's generally thought that it dates back to when the building (called the Wills building, circa 1910) was an area hotel.

Address: 100 East Lee Avenue
Website: www.sapulpahistoricalsociety.com
Activity: M, E, T

Shawnee The Ritz Theatre

Originally a dry-goods store (circa 1897), the building was transformed into a theatre when the place was expanded later that same year. It was known as the Cozy, and it featured vaudeville acts that traveled through the area. The name was changed to its current moniker in 1926 when the place started showing "talking pictures." Today, the calendar for the theatre looks much the same—only the productions are of a more serious nature. Also of a serious nature is the spirit that's said to roam the grounds. Employees say the ghost is that of Leo Montgomery, a projectionist there between 1913 and 1965 until he passed away on the premises while working (heart attack). Glimpses of a male apparition in 1930's styled clothing have been seen in the theatre, and the sounds of disembodied voices are heard as well. But is the spirit of Leo all alone? Some say no. Many locals also swear that a female apparition roams the theatre (dubbed "Amelia") that dates back to the brief period that the building was used for boarding.

Address: 10 West Main Street
Website: www.theritzshawnee.com
Activity: A, E, T

Tulsa Brady Theater

Though this theater was first called Convention Hall (and operated as such), it still pretty much functioned as it does today. That means this place has been featuring live entertainment on a regular basis since 1914. Thanks to an Art Deco makeover in 1930, the theater is also as historic as it is entertaining. The same can be said of the ghost there. The spirit is reportedly a famous singer by the name of Enrico Caruso, who became sick while visiting Tulsa to perform. He died almost a year later, but returned to the place where he contracted his malady. His apparition has been spotted on the property, along with other shadow masses that paranormal investigators believe point to additional souls walking the building. In 1921, this theater stood in the center of one of the city's most heated clashes, the Tulsa race riots. Quite a few folks were killed, and many of their bodies were held in the theater, which was used as a temporary morgue at the time.

Address: 105 West Brady Street
Website: www.bradytheater.com
Activity: A, S, E, T

Tulsa Cain's Ballroom

If you were making the rounds in the 1930s, this place would be known to you as the "Home of Bob Wills." And Bob Willis would be known to you as the "King of Western Swing." Of course, this information is still heavily disseminated in Cain's Ballroom these days. This ex-garage (built by local entrepreneur Tate Brady in 1924) was transformed into a dance hall in 1930 by Madison "Daddy" Cain, and it featured all the prominent performers of western swing. This tradition is carried on today in that the venue features cutting-edge music on a regular basis. As for the paranormal activity, it is a subtle affair. Most of it involves "spooky feelings." But on occasion, employees and fans have experienced strange things like lights turning themselves on/off and feeling sudden blasts of cold air.

Address: 423 North Main Street
Website: www.cainsballroom.com
Activity: C, T, E

Watonga Roman Nose Park and Lodge

This park is named for Chief Roman Nose, a Cheyenne warrior who famously converted to the "white man's ways," then moved back to this area of Oklahoma to become disillusioned by the adoption of a European lifestyle. He encouraged his fellow Native Americans to rebel against these ways and to return to their own traditions. This is something you can do as well when you visit the park—outdoor activities are abundant in this area and include fishing, horseback riding, and boating. When you visit, though, stay in the resort. Employees have dubbed an entity that walks there "Henry" and believe he was a Cheyenne chief. Henry is known for moving things in the lodge, as well as appearing before the occasional surprised guest there. The spirit is well known by those who work in the resort, so feel free to get current ghost info when you check in.

Address: Highway 8A
Website: www.watonga.com/romannose/
Activity: A, E, T

Wynnewood Eskridge Hotel Museum

This is one of those rare concepts that just seems to work—a hotel that is now a living museum. The Eskridge Hotel was built in 1907, the same year that Oklahoma received statehood. Pinckney Reid Eskridge was the owner of the business and he ran it successfully for many years until a severe decline in patronage brought on the hard times. In 1973, the Wynnewood Historical Society purchased the property and transformed it into the area's most popular tourist attraction. Of course, it wasn't long after the society took over that strange things began to occur around them. Usually it was strange shadows that seemed to dart through doorways and down the halls, but then they started noticing mannequins (used for displays) would be moved and in different positions than when they closed the night before. Disembodied voices and heavy footsteps followed, and so they called in a local paranormal group. Hot spots in the museum include Room 28 and the "Doctor's Room."

Address: 114 East Robert S. Kerr Boulevard
Website: www.wynnewoodokla.com/tourism
Activity: A, S, E, T

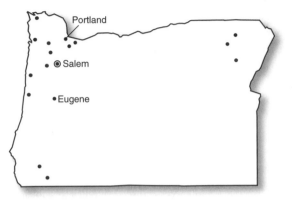

OREGON

Astoria Liberty Theater

The city of Astoria is one of the oldest settlements in the country west of the Mississippi River—and it was a rough town with many infamous gunfighters and criminals roaming the region. When residents decided to add a little culture to their lives, they constructed the Liberty. This theater is one of the better examples of old "palace style" vaudeville venues that once were so popular. It is currently a nonprofit and is in the process of renovating, though it is open for events (plays and music) and can be rented for your own use. The Liberty has pretty much always been considered a haunted location. Their ghost is said to be a male spirit that employees call "Handsome Paul." His apparition has been seen many times there and is said to be wearing a tuxedo and hat. Other activity in the theater includes items floating through the air and the occasional sound of a door slamming shut.

Address: 1203 Commercial Street
Website: www.liberty-theater.org
Activity: A, E, T

Baker City Geiser Grand Hotel

Dating back to 1889, this luxurious hotel has seen its fair share of hard times. After starting out as the finest accommodations between Portland and Salt Lake City, the building functioned as a brothel and a hospital before returning to its former glory in 1997. Stories concerning the numerous ghosts that are said to roam this location began when construction workers witnessed several apparitions on the property. Spirits in the hotel include a female from the

1930s, the ghost of an old saloon dancer, the apparition of a former cook that hangs out in the kitchen, and the spirit of a man who was murdered in the hotel (his shooting is said to have resulted in the first ever murder conviction in the county). With so many ghosts roaming the halls, almost every area of the hotel is considered a "hot spot," though employees may recommend Room 203, where ghostly sounds are heard on a regular basis.

Address: 1996 Main Street
Website: www.geisergrand.com
Activity: A, E, S, T, R

Elgin Elgin Opera House

This structure was originally a performance center and the local city hall. It was built in 1912 with the hopes of driving illegal businesses out of the area, including a well-known brothel. It is now a historic site and is listed on the national register. Live performances, as well as movies, still continue in the venue so visiting the opera house poses no challenge. Strangely, though, to experience the paranormal happenings at this location, you may not need to go inside at all. According to local investigators, this site is one of the state's better residual hauntings. It's said that, on occasion, the strange appearance of two gunslingers fighting it out will appear on the front steps of the theater. The apparitions are said to both fire their guns, then fall to the ground as if shot.

Address: 104 North 8th Street
Website: www.elginoperahouse.com
Activity: R, A, E

Eugene Bijou Art Cinema

This theater was designed by the first dean of the University of Oregon's School of Architecture, W. R. B. Willcox, in 1925. It is a rare (for the area) Spanish Mission–styled structure that currently screens art films and rare pieces of cinema that aren't found in most theaters. But in the past, the place functioned as a church (it was originally the United Church for Christ) and a funeral home (the McGaffey-Andreason Mortuary). Patrons of the cinema house have reported leaving the theater often feeling "drained" of energy. Others experience the sensation of a presence around them. Glimpses of shadowy apparitions have also occurred in the building. The Bijou has two separate theaters—and both have had their fair share of activity. A local paranormal group investigated this location and confirmed that the place is, indeed, haunted.

Address: 492 East 13th Street
Website: www.bijou-cinemas.com
Activity: A, S

Forest Grove The Grand Lodge

Built as a retirement home for Master Masons and followers of the Eastern Star, this grand resort features two bars, a pub, and an on-site restaurant (Ironwork Grill). It was completed in 1922 (at least the first portion of it), but a smaller cottage was added in 1927 to house orphans of area masons. In 1999, the masons left the lodge to move on to newer facilities and McMenamins took over management—and reopened the place a year later with accommodations, dining, and one of the area's most unique spas. They also play host to several spirits on the property. Paranormal activity is, in fact, so prevalent here that the hotel keeps a diary of ghostly reports at the front desk! When you check in, be sure to mention you are an amateur ghost hunter and you will be assigned an "active" room (the most well known are Rooms 216, 224, and 228). Be sure to keep an eye out for the lodge's most infamous ghost as well. She is known as the "Lavender Lady" and is said to appear with the scent of said flower.

Address: 3505 Pacific Avenue
Website: www.thegrandlodge.com
Activity: A, R, E, N, T

Independence Lenora's Ghost Tavern

You know you're in for a great paranormal outing when the location has the word "ghost" right in its name! This tavern dates back to the early 1900s and was originally operated by a woman named "Lerona" (I guess the owners thought "Lenora" would sound better). She reputedly ran a brothel on the premises, in addition to the usual vices of drinking and gambling. According to locals, Lerona became distraught when her lover was killed in World War I, so she climbed to the roof of the building and dived through a skylight. She was found lying dead in front of the present-day bar (it's said that there are bloodstains there to this day). Since then, patrons have reported seeing the apparition of a woman in a long dress in the bar area, as well as upstairs. Even passersby have said to have seen a pale woman peering from a second-story window.

Address: 114 South Main Street
Website: www.myspace.com/lenorasghost
Activity: A

Jacksonville McCully House Inn & Cottages

This historic property features three guest rooms in the original McCully house: the McCully Room (named for the original owners of the house), the Girls Room (named for their daughters, Mary Bell and Isadora), and the Dolls Suite (located in the attic). According to those who have stayed in the inn, any of these rooms stand a chance of being visited during the night by the home's ghost. Guests have reported seeing a pale, female apparition walking the halls—only to disappear through a door. Take time from hunting for the spirit to visit the on-site restaurant, the

Garden Bistro. They are well known for their fine cuisine and wine selection.

Address: 240 East California Street
Website: www.mccullyhouseinn.com
Activity: A

La Grande Hot Lake Springs Hotel

In addition to a hotel and restaurant, this location features a museum, an RV park, and a gift shop. The whole thing was created by a local artist, David Manuel, who has a studio and bronze foundry on the site. But long before this complex was ever renovated, the hotel existed as a sanitarium and a spa. Folks who stay in the hotel have heard the screams and cries of the past residents there, as well as seen the apparition of an old man (who's rumored to be a former caretaker that committed suicide on the property). Ironically, though, most are not frightened by the activity—probably because most of it is of a residual nature. Visit their website for more information regarding the hotel, as well as the other sights located at Hot Lake Springs.

Address: 66172 Highway 203
Website: www.hotlakesprings.com
Activity: A, R, E

McMinnville Hotel Oregon

This location is one of five haunted spots owned by McMenimins in Oregon that's featured in this book! The locally renowned company is known for purchasing historic structures, upgrading them (while retaining their old charm), and reopening them to the public—and Hotel Oregon is no different. It was first built in 1905 as the Hotel Elberton, and it now features fine overnight accommodations, three bars/pubs on the premises, and the annual McMinnville UFO Festival! As for the ghost ... he is affectionately called "John" by employees there. He has been seen and heard on the first two floors of the hotel and is said to hang out in the cellar bar there. Most eyewitness accounts of the encounters with this spirit involve hearing the sounds of heavy footsteps following them, then when the witness stops to look, the sounds immediately cease.

Address: 310 Northeast Evans Street
Website: www.mcmenamins.com
Activity: A, E, T

Newport The Oar House Bed and Breakfast

This former home was completely renovated in 1993 with modern amenities and whirlpool tubs. It features five rooms with private baths and is within walking distance of many area attractions. It was originally constructed circa 1900 using materials washed up on the beach from shipwrecks and served as a boarding house for sailors. Later on, the property evolved into a brothel—but it wouldn't be one of the ladies of the night that would haunt the place—It would be the maid. Employees call her "Mary" and say that she lived in the building while working for the brothel. She stayed so she could keep an eye out for a beau that was supposed to meet her there. When several years had gone by without him showing up, the girl committed suicide. Now her apparition is seen in the sitting room and walking the second floor of the B&B.

Address: 520 Southwest 2nd Street
Website: www.innsite.com/inns/A000918
Activity: A, E

Oregon City McLoughlin House

This living museum is part of the Fort Vancouver National Historic Site. It was the home of John McLoughlin, a local doctor who served as the "factor" for the fort between 1825 and 1845. It was moved from its original location (where it was built in 1845) to the park in 1909. Prior to the move, though, the place functioned briefly as a hotel, then a brothel, and then a boarding-house. Today, you can visit the museum, as well as the graves of McLoughlin and his wife, Marguerite, that are located just outside the house

(they were moved along with the home). If you're lucky, you may even see ol' John himself! His giant apparition is often seen stalking the halls of his old house (he's sometimes also seen as a giant shadow shape). Locals also claim that Marguerite is there as well (and possibly others), as people have reported seeing a ghostly female staring out a second-floor window.

Address: 713 Center Street
Website: www.mcloughlinhouse.org
Activity: A, S, E, T

Portland The Bagdad Theater and Pub

This theater was constructed by Universal Pictures and first opened in 1927. It was designed with an Arabian flair—a look that was popular after the release of Douglas Fairbanks' film *Thief of Baghdad*. If you enjoy having a beer or a bit of food with your movie, then you need look no further than the Bagdad. And you're especially in luck if you like a ghost with your movie as well. The haunting of this theater is a subtle affair—most often the reports are a simple "feeling" of someone or something watching them. But on occasion, the odd patron will tell of a dark, shadowy apparition that's been seen around the restrooms and intense cold spots that seem to fall down upon the unwary moviegoer.

Address: 3702 Southeast Hawthorne Boulevard
Website: www.mcmenamins.com
Activity: S, C, E

Portland Pittock Mansion

Built circa 1914, this house originally belonged to Oregon pioneers Henry and Georgiana Pittock. They lived in the home until their deaths in 1918 (Georgiana) and 1919 (guess who), though the Pittock family would retain the estate well into the 1950s. After the place was damaged in a 1962 storm, the city purchased the property. Now it is a museum that illustrates life in turn-of-the-century Portland. Ghostly tales concerning the mansion have circulated for some time—pretty much since the house was opened to the public. The apparition of an old woman has been seen in the basement and the sounds of footsteps have been heard on the ground floor of the house as well. Another piece of interesting activity seems to involve a Pittock family photo that is often found to be moved around the house during the night—employees will hang the portrait, only to return the next morning and find it somewhere else.

Address: 3229 Northwest Pittock Drive
Website: www.pittockmansion.org
Activity: A, E, T

Portland   White Eagle Hotel and Saloon

This unique bar/café actually hosts an upstairs hotel, so you can stay at this location while you look for ghosts in the saloon! It originally opened in 1905 to serve the area's Polish community as a tavern—and it has had strange tales involving ghosts and "Shanghai tunnels" (underground holding areas for kidnapped women sold into prostitution) told about it almost as long. Activity includes menus moving through the air, disembodied voices, and the odd encounter with one of the White Eagle's two resident spirits: Rose and Sam. According to local legend, Rose was a prostitute who was murdered on the second floor, and Sam was a Polish worker, who was killed there as well. Since they are usually seen on the second floor (where the rooms are located), staying at the hotel is a must. But don't forget the saloon! Sam is said to also hang out around the bathrooms and barware has been seen moving on its own.

Address: 836 North Russell Street
Website: www.mcmenamins.com
Activity: A, E, T, S

Salem   Historic Bush House Museum

This 1878 Italianate-style mansion is the permanent residence of some of the area's best vintage furnishings—as well as unique varieties of roses (located in Bush's Pasture Park outside). The home originally belonged to Asahel Bush II, and he lived in it until his death in 1913. The place remained in the Bush family, though, until 1953 when A. N. Bush passed away. The paranormal activity here is said to be the product of a horrible family secret—though it sounds more like an urban legend than reality. Reputedly, the Bush family had a young daughter who was either mentally challenged, or became schizophrenic (stories vary), so they "kept" her in the basement away from visitors and other family members. The poor girl is said to have lived her entire life in the basement—and eventually died there. When the sounds of a female voice (and even cries) are heard on the property—or other activity is witnessed (such as cold spots and shadow shapes)—this female entity is blamed.

Address: 600 Mission Street
Website: www.salemart.org
Activity: S, E, C, T

Salem   Mission Mill Museum

This museum is a living tribute to the Thomas Kay Woolen Mill, which functioned between 1889 and 1962. In addition to this, the site features a working church (that can be rented for events and meetings), a parsonage, and two historic houses (the Jason Lee House and the Boon House). There are several supernatural stories concerning this compound, including a spectral groundskeeper that's been sighted several times walking the grounds. The mill itself is said to have a residual haunt where the sounds of the old machines are still heard along with several voices. And the Jason Lee House (the home of the founder of Salem) is haunted by a little girl who has been seen standing on the front porch. Interestingly, all of this only scratches the surface. Nearly every historic structure on the site has a story—and all of this can be explored by you when you visit the mill.

Address: 1313 Mill Street Southeast
Website: www.missionmill.org
Activity: A, E, T, S

Troutdale Edgefield Manor

Built in 1911, this grand estate served as an area "poor farm" for many years. It was a self-sufficient communal dwelling where people of little means all pitched in to survive. It shut down in the 1950s and was later converted into a nursing home. In 1990, McMenamins slowly transformed the property into a mini-village that now contains an inn, several pub/bars, and even a brewery. If you stay in the manor, you will not lack for things to do and see—especially if you're looking for ghosts! There are several well-known stories about this estate—including the apparition of a woman who likes to wake guests and the phantom sounds of children playing in the halls. But perhaps the most infamous spirit at this resort is the young girl that's said to haunt "Althea's Room." She has been known to appear during the night and start singing for the startled guests sleeping there.

Address: 2126 Southwest Halsey Street
Website: www.mcmenamins.com
Activity: A, R, E, T

Wheeler Old Wheeler Hotel

When the Rector Hotel and its adjoining annex outlived its design, it was replaced in 1920 with the Wheeler Hotel. During the 1930s, though, things took several bad turns when the Depression (coupled with one of the worst fires in this area ever) crippled the local economy. As a result, the hotel was closed and the Rinehart Clinic moved in—and stayed until the 1980s. These days, the place is a hotel again and it has a fresh, new makeover and new owners to boot! There are seven rooms for rent (and you can even combine them to create a "suite" if you like), though most activity seems to happen in Room 3 (at least one paranormal group that stayed in the hotel recorded great evidence in this area). The owners/innkeepers are quite aware of their invisible guests—they were the first to notice them there when they began remodeling—so feel free to broach the subject with them. Activity includes voices, footsteps, and shadowy apparitions.

Address: 495 Highway 101
Website: www.oldwheelerhotel.com
Activity: S, E

Wolf Creek The Wolf Creek Inn

Where do you begin when a place simply has so much history and haunted tales? This inn was constructed in 1883 and originally called the Wolf Creek Tavern. It is Oregon's longest continuously operating hotel and is currently owned and operated by the state. During the heyday of black and white film, luminaries like Clark Gable and Carol Lombard stayed at the inn (and you can stay in the rooms they enjoyed). This location has been rumored to be haunted for decades—with its most famous ghost possibly being the author Jack London, who stayed at the inn and used it for inspiration while finishing his book, *Valley of the Moon.* He has been seen and heard in the room that's named for him. Other stories include locals being attacked by a vampire while camping in the area (some say the vampire/spirit was even witnessed once in the inn) and the apparition of a former stagecoach driver that walks the main floor (an interesting tale in that the "man" was actually found to be female while she lay dying at the inn).

Address: 100 Front Street
Website: www.thewolfcreekinn.com
Activity: A, E, T

Yachats Heceta Head Lighthouse

This lighthouse, along with the neighboring keeper's house, is listed on the National Register of Historic Places. They date back to 1894 and are in pristine condition. The lighthouse itself can be toured almost daily (check their website for hours) and has an adjoining gift shop in the old generator shed. The keeper's house is now a bed and breakfast that you can stay in (though during the day, it is an interpretive center)—and after you hear the stories about this B&B, you will want to! The old house is said to be haunted by the apparition of an elderly lady that is known as "the Lady in Grey" and "Rue." She is thought to be a past caretaker's wife (possibly Mrs. Frank DeRay), and she has made several dramatic appearances over the years. Employees, the on-site caretakers, and guests have all seen this pale spirit floating toward them in various areas of the house—but the hot spots seem to be the second-floor hallway, the kitchen, and the attic. Once she was even heard screaming!

Address: 92072 Highway 101 South
Website: www.hecetalighthouse.com
Activity: A, E, T

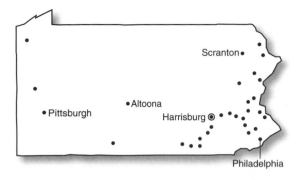

PENNSYLVANIA

Allentown King George Inn

Established in 1756 during the French and Indian War, this crossroads tavern was quite the multi-purpose location. It served as a town hall, courthouse, and church for early Colonials living living in the area—and even had a drill field for soldiers behind the building. Now a nationally recognized historic site, the King George is an upscale restaurant that presents a unique dining experience—you can eat with a ghost! Employees at the inn have heard phantom footsteps, seen full-bodied apparitions (usually a Revolutionary-period soldier, but a woman and child have been witnessed as well), and found doors opened by unseen hands.

Address: 3141 Hamilton Boulevard
Website: www.kinggeorgeinn.com
Activity: A, E, T

Altoona Railroaders Memorial Museum

This museum is dedicated to the railroad industry and its impact on the Industrial Revolution—and life in Altoona in general. It's located in the old Penn Central Railroad complex (one of the largest hubs of rail activity in the country at one point) and features displays like the private rail car of Charles M. Schwab. The haunting of the museum became well known when the location appeared on the show *Ghost Hunters.* Employees have witnessed shadowy apparitions walking throughout the museum and heard the sounds of footsteps. Their resident spirit is thought to be a man who worked on the railroad and is even featured in a photograph that's hanging in the museum.

Address: 1300 9th Avenue
Website: www.railroadcity.com
Activity: A, S, E

Bedford Jean Bonnet Tavern

Though Jean Bonnet purchased this property in 1779, it actually dates back to the 1760s. The tavern played an important part in the Whiskey Rebellion of 1794 (it served as a meeting place) and years before had operated as a French trading post. Tourists today are treated to a top-notch restaurant experience and lodgings in one of four traditionally apportioned rooms. Since this location is a well-known haunted spot in this area, you may want to book your room well in advance before visiting. Employees and patrons alike have been witnessing paranormal events in this old tavern for many years and the rooms can fill up fast. Experiences in the building include seeing apparitions (sitting at the bar and in the hallways), hearing the sounds of voices and heavy footsteps, and finding objects moved when nobody was around.

Address: 6048 Lincoln Highway
Website: www.jeanbonnettavern.com
Activity: A, R, E, T

Bethlehem Sun Inn

This piece of Moravian architecture dates back to 1758 and has played host to numerous key figures in America's history. People like George Washington, John Adams, and Samuel Adams enjoyed the hospitality of this Colonial inn back in the day. Today you can enjoy visiting this living museum—and even rent the property for your own events. This is also a location that's comfortable with its haunting—the story of the inn's ghosts has been featured in the press and a local paranormal group even conducts public ghost hunts on the property. According to these sources, the spirit of a former caretaker Hughetta Bender now resides in the building. She was the founder of the Sun Inn Preservation Association, and it's reported she poured a lot of love into the inn.

Address: 564 Main Street
Website: www.suninnbethlehem.org
Activity: A, E

Cashtown Cashtown Inn

Of all the haunted areas associated with the American Civil War, the climes around the battlefield of Gettysburg are said to be the most active. During the conflict, this inn served as the headquarters of General A. P. Hill in 1863. Functioning as one of the state's oldest hostelries, the property had been servicing travelers in the region since 1815—a tradition that's carried on today. You can rent one of their seven rooms (and dine there as well) as you explore the Gettysburg battlefield and other haunted sites in the area. The paranormal activity at Cashtown mainly stems from when the property was used as a makeshift hospital during the battle. The residual sights and sounds of doctors working on patients have been witnessed on the lower levels of the inn and the A. P. Hill room is the site of objects moving and people feeling touched during the night. But you may want to rent the General Lee Suite—this is said to be the most haunted spot.

Address: 1325 Old Route 30
Website: www.cashtowninn.com
Activity: A, R, E, T

Conneaut Hotel Conneaut

In 1893, Exposition Park added on a brand new hotel—the Exposition Hotel—to provide upscale accommodations for those vacationing at the lake. In 1903, the hotel was completely overhauled (and mostly demolished) to be rebuilt into the Hotel Conneaut. The building would endure new additions and a horrible fire that took out a good chunk of the hotel to be what it is today—a great getaway for those wanting to visit the Conneaut Lake Park. It's also a great getaway for those interested in the paranormal. A ghostly couple is said to still dance in the ballroom and the spirit of a former employee (called "John" by those who work there) hangs out by the fireplace. But they're not alone—the ghost of a little girl has been witnessed in various hallways, and a spectral bride, named "Elizabeth," likes to visit people in their rooms.

Address: 12382 Center Street
Website: www.clphotelconneaut.com
Activity: A, E, T

Douglassville Covatta's Brinton Lodge

Some places just attract ghosts. To hear the locals talk about this historic lodge, haunted tales about this property have circulated for over a hundred years! Dating back to the early 1700s, this early tavern served as a stop along the Schuylkill River. It was transformed into a family home in 1890 and then into the present day lodge in 1927—though it was a private club back then. As for the tales … Well, there's the "Lady in White," who's been seen many times. Then there's the spirit dubbed "Dapper Dan" that likes to pinch ladies and breathe into their ears (said to hang out in the second-floor meeting area). There is also the apparition of an older woman that hangs out in guests' rooms on the third floor. Some say there are also the ghosts of a little girl and Caleb Brinton himself on the property. Brinton Lodge is now a restaurant and bar, so stop in and say hello to all the spectral guests.

Address: 1808 West Schuylkill Road
Website: www.brintonlodge.com
Activity: A, E, T, C

East Berlin Bechtel Victorian Mansion B&B

This wonderful home was built by local architect Joseph Dise for William G. Leas. It was finished in 1897, and it would remain in the Leas family for 85 years until it was purchased by Charles and Miriam Bechtel and turned into a bed and breakfast. Now under new ownership, the mansion makes for quite a fun visit. With six guest rooms and several romantic package deals you can purchase, this B&B would make a great paranormal getaway for a couple. As for the haunting, the activity is attributed to one or more members of the Leas family. Quite a few of them passed away on the premises, though most believe that the active spirit is Flossie. She died of spinal meningitis in the house at the age of 22. Activity in the manor includes shadowy shapes that are seen, objects moving by themselves, and the apparition of a young woman who stands on the turret balcony.

Address: 400 West King Street
Website: www.bechtelvictorianmansion.com
Activity: A, S, T, N

Gettysburg Farnsworth House Inn

John McFarland built the original portion of this house in 1810—though it was added on to in 1834. During the Civil War, the Sweney family (owners of the property at the time) watched as Confederate sharpshooters took position in the home's windows to pop shots at Union soldiers during the three-day Battle of Gettysburg (just check out the hundreds of bullet holes that riddle the structure's south side). If you stay in one of their nine guest rooms—or even just grab a traditional dinner at the restaurant—you will not be disappointed. The attic of the inn is said to be haunted by a Confederate soldier who still feels guilt for accidentally shooting and killing a local girl named Jennie Wade. He is joined by the spirit of a girl named "Mary," who has been seen and heard wandering the second floor of the inn as well. For those staying overnight, consider choosing the Sarah Black Room—reportedly, the most haunted room in the house.

Address: 401 Baltimore Street
Website: www.farnsworthhouseinn.com
Activity: A, E, T

Gettysburg Gettysburg Hotel

Now owned by the Best Western hotel chain, this historic site was once a local tavern. It was erected in 1797 by a local man named James Scott, and it was a regular visit for Colonials of the day. During the Civil War, the property was appropriated to service as a hospital. Hundreds of men were carried from the front lines to be operated on at this location—and Abraham Lincoln would deliver his famous Gettysburg Address just a short distance away. Remnants of the war and its effect on the city are still visible at this hotel—as is a remnant of a different sort. Visitors have reported seeing a spectral nurse walking the halls of this location. Dubbed "Rachel" by those who work there, the apparition is quite famous. Stop by and see Rachel when you're in the area—and be sure to have one of the city's best meals at the Centuries on the Square restaurant there.

Address: 1 Lincoln Square
Website: www.hotelgettysburg.com
Activity: A, E

Gettysburg Gettysburg National Military Park

Considered the turning point of the American Civil War, this historic battle tallied over 51,000 casualties and secured the way for a Union victory. The bloody clash lasted for three days (July 1–3, 1863) and forced General Robert E. Lee to withdraw his troops to Virginia (and to abandon his invasion of the north). For paranormal enthusiasts, Gettysburg represents holy ground. Numerous sites around the battle have documented hauntings and even more visitors have had their own ghostly experience while traveling through this area. But in the end, the battlefield itself is probably the most haunted spot in the region. Reports of spectral soldiers walking the grounds and the sounds of warfare have been associated with almost every area of the park—but you may want to spend a little extra time at Little Big Top, the Devil's Den, and Cemetery Ridge.

Address: 1195 Baltimore Pike
Website: www.nps.gov/GETT/
Activity: R, A, E, O, M

Gettysburg The Lightner Farmhouse Bed & Breakfast

This historic (circa 1862) home built by Isaac Lightner had a front-row seat for the famous Battle of Gettysburg. And much like every other property that dates back to those three infamous days, the house was used as a hospital for Union troops. Visitors today are much luckier than those of that time—this Federal style B&B features six rooms in the main house, or you can stay in a private cottage (it was the original summer kitchen). While there, you will want to take a walk of the property. This location is said to have a residual haunting that takes visitors back to the days of the war. The sights and sounds of spirits from that era are seen in and around the farmhouse and on the grounds where the old Civil War barn used to reside.

Address: 2350 Baltimore Pike
Website: www.lightnerfarmhouse.com
Activity: R, A, E, O

Harmony Harmony Inn

Austin Pearce was a well-respected area businessman. He had his hands in banking, the region's railroad industry, and even operated a mill. He built this Italianate-style mansion in 1856, but business would turn sour for poor Mr. Pearce. He would sell the house, which would go on to become the Ziegler Hotel. These days, even though it has the word "inn" in the name, the place is a restaurant. With contemporary cuisine in historic surroundings, the eatery is well known with the locals for their quality atmosphere—though for some, their experience may include paranormal activity. Objects in the dining room are known to move by themselves, and many who dine at the inn say they can actually feel a presence beside them. Local legend says one of the ghosts is a man named Barney, who died from a fall there (though there's no history to really back this up) and a psychic has stated that there's the spirit of a handicapped girl in the building.

Address: 230 Mercer Street
Website: www.historicharmonyinn.com
Activity: A, T, C

Jim Thorpe The Inn at Jim Thorpe

Cornelius Connor built the White Swan Hotel in 1833 to cope with the sudden influx of people to the area. The coal industry was booming and the hotel would serve as food and lodgings for the workers. When the building burned down in 1849, it was rebuilt as the New American Hotel. Today the business is called the Inn at Jim Thorpe—and it is much like the New American was back in the day: upscale period furnishings decorate the rooms and the historic grounds make for a pleasant stay away from home. The haunting of this inn is quite a public matter—articles and even television reports have been made about the subject. It's said that visitors have found their belongings moved during the night, and sightings of apparitions (sometimes appearing as shadows) happen regularly. Room 211 is known for the television turning on and off by itself, and the spirit of a woman dubbed "Madeline" has been seen wearing a Victorian dress.

Address: 24 Broadway
Website: www.innjt.com
Activity: A, S, E, T

Jim Thorpe The Old Jail Museum

This massive stone structure served as the Carbon County Prison from 1871 until 1995. It has a segregated cell system with a men's floor, a women's floor, and solitary confinement cells in the basement. The old jail was the site of the Molly Maguire hangings in the 1800s. It's reported that one of those that were hanged (Alexander Campbell) actually placed a handprint on a cell wall, saying that it would remain as proof of his innocence. Despite numerous cleanings, the print is said to be visible today.

The jail offers tours (even the ghost type) of the premises today, so make a lap through the old structure and see if you experience the ghostly voices and touches that others have reported in the past.

Address: 128 West Broadway
Website: www.theoldjailmuseum.com
Activity: S, E, T

Lafayette Hill General Lafayette Inn & Brewery

This inn (originally knows as the Three Tuns), along with the neighboring St. Peter's Church, played an important role during the Revolutionary War. General Lafayette used this location to fend off an attack by British soldiers and to escape into the night. Through this skirmish—and the entirety of the war—the inn stood. It underwent a massive renovation in the 1990s and now offers lodgings (in an adjacent guest house), a restaurant, and an on-site brewery (just check out their old-style meads). There have been several apparitions spotted on the property: an elderly woman has been seen in the upstairs dining room, an old man in a dressing gown was witnessed walking toward the kitchen, and a pair of ghosts have been seen in the yard. Most disturbing of all, though, is the story of a young woman who was murdered on the property and now roams the second-floor club room of the inn.

Address: 646 Germantown Pike
Website: www.generallafayetteinn.com
Activity: A, E, T, C

Lebanon Inn 422

Though this inn dates back to 1880, the legend associated with it is much older. Prior to the home's construction, a house existed at this site that belonged to Anne Caroline Coleman. It was built for her by her parents as a graduation gift. It's said that she was in love with a man whom her parents did not care for. As a result, she was sent away to her sister's home in Philadelphia, where she committed suicide. Of course, it

turned out her parents had bad taste—the man was James Buchanan and he would go on to be President of the United States. When you stay at this historic inn, you get a wonderful on-site restaurant—and if you're lucky, you'll get to catch a glimpse of Anne herself! According to many sources, the spirit of the poor woman has been seen in the house and is known for helping out around the place.

Address: 1800 West Cumberland Street
Website: www.inn422.com
Activity: A, T

Lumberville Black Bass Hotel

Built in the 1740s, this hotel served as a sanctuary for those traveling through the wilderness of early Pennsylvania. During the Revolutionary War, the owners of the inn were staunch supporters of the Crown (called Tories), and it's said that they even turned George Washington away when he asked to stay there. There have been numerous notable visitors to the hotel, and much of the furnishings are even of a high pedigree, but the property has had some rough times in recent years (mostly due to floods). But with new owners, the Black Bass proudly offers eight beautiful suites and a restaurant that features a great view of the Delaware River. The ghosts at this hotel are interesting as well. The first is said to be a past owner named Hans, who was stabbed to death during an argument, and then there's the spirit of a woman who's been seen on the second floor (where the guest rooms are located) sitting on a bed with a gun in her lap.

Address: 3774 River Road
Website: www.blackbasshotel.com
Activity: A

Malvern General Warren Inne

With history dating back to 1745, this property has seen it all. It was originally called the Admiral Vernon Inne, but was renamed the Admiral Warren Inne for the naval commander who defended the colonies during the French and Indian War. The tavern there would become a popular Tory hangout at the onset of the American Revolution (thanks to the loyalist inclinations of owner John Penn) and would even be a site associated with the Paoli Massacre (a local blacksmith was tortured on the third floor). After the colonists won the war, the name of the hotel was changed to its present day moniker in honor of the hero of Bunker Hill. Today, the inn offers eight guest suites, an on-site restaurant, and even a tavern for those who just want to stop in for a drink. You may also run into one of the ghosts that are said to be in the building. Most paranormal events involve phantom Revolutionary War soldiers, though there's also a spirit in the tavern who's known for breathing on the necks of women.

Address: 16 Village Way
Website: www.generalwarren.com
Activity: A, T

Marietta The Railroad House Inn

This haunted inn features eight rooms (decorated with period furnishings), an on-site tavern, and a restaurant that features American cuisine. It dates back to 1823 and was built to service those traveling through the area by railroad. Men working the Susquehanna River would stay in the house—as well as gamble and drink there—and before the town's official train station was built, folks would purchase their train tickets in the inn as well. It is probably due to all the people coming through—and their trials and tribulations—that the Railroad House is now haunted.

For those who want to be in the middle of the paranormal action, you will want to rent Room 9. It's said to be the center of the activity—activity that includes disembodied voices and a dark entity that often gives visitors the "creeps." For the less brave, consider Room 5 (the site of the apparition of a little girl) or hang out in the garden where a female spirit is said to approach single men.

Address: 280 West Front Street
Website: www.therailroadhouse.com
Activity: A, S, E, T

Milford Cliff Park Inn

This massive resort has something for everyone. In addition to lush accommodations, the property also has a restaurant, spa amenities, and a golf course. Throw in a handful of haunted stories and you have a destination that can't be missed! Located next to a scenic overlook, this historic inn has a commanding view of the Delaware Valley. When you stay there, you will want to rent either Room 10 or 11, which are said to be the most haunted. These rooms are said to be visited by a female spirit called "Sally." She has been seen and heard there and is known for opening doors for guests. Other spirits on the premises include the "Lady in Brown," who's been seen on the staircase (rumored to be a woman that committed suicide at the cliffs), a male entity that hangs out in the kitchen (called "Uncle Stew"), and the male spirit of a former maintenance person that the staff calls "Walt."

Address: 155 Cliff Park Road
Website: www.cliffparkinn.com
Activity: A, E, O, T

Mount Joy Bube's Brewery

There's always something going on at this livery brewpub and restaurant. Whether it's live trivia, karaoke nights, or their on-site ghost tours, Bube's is the center of nightlife in Mount Joy. There are actually three separate establishments in the complex: the Catacombs restaurant, the

Alois Martini Bar, and the Biergarten restaurant. Alois Bube purchased this historic brewery in 1876, and in its heyday it had an on-site hotel and tavern (now the Alois bar). The property was massively renovated in 1968 and today you can enjoy beer brewed in the Bavarian style that made Bube so popular during his lifetime. If you take the ghost tour, you will get to see most of the hot spots in this location—such as the bar located in the former hotel and the catacombs themselves. Activity includes shadowy apparitions, items moving by themselves, and disembodied voices.

Address: 102 North Market Street
Website: www.bubesbrewery.com
Activity: S, E, T

New Hope Logan Inn

Sometimes when a place is haunted, it's really haunted. Such is the case with the Logan Inn. It was built in 1722 by the founder of New Hope, John Wells, to operate a ferry service. It was expanded into a full tavern in 1727 and was a popular hangout for Colonial settlers in the area. It would gain the name "Logan" a hundred years later in honor of a local Lenni-Lanape chief that took James Logan's name. The inn features upscale accommodations (16 rooms total) with antique furnishings and a highly praised on-site restaurant. For ghost enthusiasts, consider renting Room 6 on the property. It's also known as "Emily's Room" and is named for Emily Lutz, the mother of a former owner. She's thought to visit with folks in this area and often appears as a glowing apparition accompanied by the scent of lavender. Other hot spots include the bar area (where the spirit of a soldier is seen) and the lobby/common areas (where people have spotted a male apparition and a young girl who's often heard crying).

Address: 10 West Ferry Street
Website: www.loganinn.com
Activity: A, O, N, E

New Hope Wedgwood Inn

Known as the "Painted Lady" of the town, this Victorian bed and breakfast dates back to 1870. The inn is named after the British inventor Josiah Wedgwood (and even has Wedgwood blue colored walls and authentic Wedgwood china). The site is famous for the fact that General George Washington camped at this location (along with about 1,200 soldiers) prior to crossing the Delaware River in 1776. The inn features eight guest rooms with various amenities (including Jacuzzis, fireplaces, and porches), so be wise when you choose your room! There's also said to be two ghosts on the premises. First there's the spirit of a little girl called "Sarah" that's said to have passed away in the tunnels that run under the house, and then there's the ghost of Joseph Pickett, an artist who lived in the area.

Address: 111 West Bridge Street
Website: www.wedgwoodinn.com
Activity: A, E, T

New Oxford Chestnut Hall Bed and Breakfast

Enjoy a complete Victorian experience when you visit Chestnut Hall. In addition to the beautifully apportioned home, you will also be treated to a magnificent garden and early morning tea in the parlor. The house dates back to 1890 and was built for Alexander and Sarah Himes. It would remain in their family until the 1970s and would become a B&B in 2004. And when a place is operated by the author of a book on hauntings, you know you're in for a good paranormal stay! The property is said to be haunted by the ghost of a little girl named Alice. Guests who stay at Chestnut Hall have reported seeing and hearing this spirit in most areas of the house.

Address: 104 Lincoln Way West
Website: www.chestnuthallbb.com
Activity: A

Philadelphia Betsy Ross House

The oldest portion of this home dates back to 1740 (though other sections of the house would be added later). Over the years, the property was used as a combination of business and home, with wares being displayed on the first floor and the family typically living on the upper levels. It is, of course, known for its most famous resident, Betsy Ross, who lived in the house between 1773 and 1785. She's said to have sewn the first ever American flag on the premises. Employees have been experiencing strange things during their tenure, such as seeing shadowy apparitions, hearing phantom voices, and feeling the sensation of being grabbed. When you visit, check out the gift shop there as well. A security guard was killed in this area, and it's said the sounds of a male voice have been heard.

Address: 239 Arch Street
Website: www.betsyrosshouse.org
Activity: S, E, T

Philadelphia Cornerstone Bed & Breakfast

Can a guardian angel haunt a home? Some say yes—and the haunting of this B&B just may be one of those places. This Victorian masterpiece was constructed in 1865 as a family residence—and today it is a family-run business. They offer six guest rooms, a great breakfast, and an easy walk to area attractions. As for their ghost—or angel—the dim apparition of a female has appeared on occasion to the owners of the B&B, as well as guests. It's said the entity is preceded by the strong scent of a perfume and is known for gently touching people on the forehead. Angel or ghost? It's your call. Visit the Cornerstone and find out.

Address: 3300 Baring Street
Website: www.cornerstonebandb.com
Activity: A, N, T

Philadelphia Eastern State Penitentiary

When this massive prison first opened in 1829, it offered a whole new system for reforming criminals. It was termed the "Pennsylvania System," and it involved keeping inmates completely isolated from each other—sort of a long-term solitary confinement. When they (briefly) interacted with each other, the prisoners would wear masks that would prevent them from speaking to one another. It's ironic that this sort of inhumane treatment was actually created by a reform group of the day. Now a historic site, the prison offers tours and is an infamous haunt for paranormal investigators. Hot spots on the property include cell blocks 4 and 12, as well as the death row area. Witnesses have seen apparitions and shadow masses, as well as heard disembodied voices and the sounds of cells slamming shut.

Address: 22nd and Fairmount Avenue
Website: www.easternstate.org
Activity: A, S, E, T

Philadelphia Fort Mifflin

This early British outpost served as a key location during the American Revolution. It guarded the Delaware River and after the American army took the post, it became the site of the single largest bombardment of cannon fire in North America. This occurred in 1777 when the British army attacked the post for five consecutive days. Visitors to the fort today get to see the old barracks, officers' quarters, and blacksmith shop, as well as tour the grounds. For paranormal tourists, there are several key spots in the fort you will want to see. The officers' quarters is known for a female apparition who's heard screaming (thought to be Elizabeth Pratt). Casemate 5 is the site of a "faceless apparition" that's been witnessed many times. And then there's the smithy that's said to be haunted by a former blacksmith named Jacob Sauer.

Address: 1 Fort Mifflin Road
Website: www.fortmifflin.us
Activity: A, S, E, T, C

Philadelphia Independence Hall

Most people visit this location for one major reason: the Liberty Bell. But Independence Hall is only part of a much larger attraction, the Independence National Historic Park. You need a ticket to tour this site (they are free, but must be obtained through their website) so plan in advance for this trip. Originally known as the Pennsylvania State House, this historic site took 21 years to complete. It was started in 1730 and when it was finished, it would witness a staggering amount of history (including the meeting of the Second Continental Congress, the signing of the Declaration of Independence, and the adoption of our national flag). Check out all these exhibits, but make sure you also visit the clock tower. The apparition of an eighteenth-century man has been seen there. Others say the spirits of Benedict Arnold and Ben Franklin haunt the hall as well.

Address: 143 South Third Street
Website: www.independencevisitorcenter.com
Activity: A

Pittsburgh Frick Art & Historical Center

Why not inject some art into your life during your next paranormal road trip? Housed within the historic Frick Mansion (also known as Clayton), this living museum contains unique pieces of art, as well as a glimpse of life during the 1880s. The grounds also contain a café, a museum shop, and the Car and Carriage Museum. Henry and Adelaide Frick lived in this beautiful home between 1882 and 1905, and it would be Helen Clay Frick who would transform the place into an art museum. While you are checking out all the exhibits on this property, take a look around for their ghost. It's said the main house is haunted by a female apparition that was a member of the Frick family. Interestingly, sources don't seem to agree who the ghost is, though. Some say it is Adelaide looking over her old house, yet others insist the spirit is Helen.

Address: 7227 Reynolds Street
Website: www.frickart.org
Activity: A, T

Reading Emily's

Originating as a hotel in 1827 (built by one Benjamin Dickinson), this historic restaurant is a favorite with folks in Pennsylvania. With an upscale but simple menu, a fantastic wine list, and special holiday fare, visiting Emily's is an easy decision. It's even easier if you are a fan of history and hauntings. There have been many owners of this property (especially during the years it functioned as a hotel)—and most of them have had their share of paranormal experiences. The sounds of laughter have been heard around the restrooms and stairs, the dining room has been the site of objects moving, and a shadowy apparition has been seen in almost every area of the building. Nobody knows who the ghost is—the name "Emily" was arbitrarily given to the entity—but many believe she could be a girl who died in a fire on the premises years ago.

Address: 3790 Morgantown Road
Website: www.emilysrt10.com
Activity: S, E, T

Scranton Andy Gavin's Eatery and Pub

Originally known as Kaplan's Bar, this pub is housed within a building that's more than a hundred years old. As soon as the current owner purchased the place, he started hearing stories about the place being haunted. According to the tale, the previous owner had heard phantom footsteps and found things missing while reno-vating the second story of the building (an area that would become apartments). Since Andy Gavin's has opened, employees of the pub, as well as patrons, have had many experiences with the entity they now call "George." The spirit is known for moving around barware and having fun in the bathrooms (locking stalls, turning off the lights, etc.).

Address: 1392 North Washington Avenue
Website: www.myspace.com/andygavinspub
Activity: E, T

Scranton The Banshee Pub

This classic Irish pub has one of the grandest bars in all the state. It's over 50 feet long and made of wood salvaged from the very building the pub is located in. The building itself dates back to the 1800s and is said to have been used as a temporary morgue during the Spanish flu epidemic of 1918. Whether this is true or not, one thing is certain: This bar is haunted! Numerous sightings of an apparition of a little girl have occurred, as well as the spirit of a man dressed in black. Additional activity includes things moving of their own volition, disembodied voices, and a possible negative entity that's said to be in the basement.

Address: 320 Penn Avenue
Website: www.banshee-pub.com
Activity: A, T, E

St. David's The Radnor Hotel

This posh Main Line hotel features one of the best eateries in the area, the Glenmorgan Bar & Grill. It's also in a great location for exploring local attractions such as Valley Forge, Haverford Square, and the Philadelphia Museum of Art. Local paranormal investigators say the Radnor is also a great place to sleep with a ghost! Interestingly, the haunting of this hotel seems to only involve one room: Suite 309. According to the reports, this room is the stomping grounds of a female apparition that's known for appearing floating in the air over sleeping guests. It's said she then glides to the door and through it into the hallway. With no background story, or further information, this is a haunting that's begging to be explored—just make sure you get Room 309!

Address: 591 East Lancaster Avenue
Website: www.radnorhotel.com
Activity: A

Tannersville Tannersville Inn

Previously known as the Tannersville Hotel, this location dates back to 1825. It was purchased in 1834 by Manasseh Miller, who transformed the local tavern into a major stagecoach-stop hotel. Miller and the property would prosper and grow for the next 50 years—unlike others who lived at this location. Local history states that the infamous "Learne Massacre" occurred there—an event that involved a family being massacred by local Indians. Today there are no accommodations at the inn; instead, the place offers a tavern and restaurant. You can choose to eat in their famous greenhouse area, the parlor, or (weather permitting) the veranda. As for the ghosts, they are said to be in almost every corner of the property. Whether they are the souls of those who visited the hotel, or those of the Learne family, is unknown. Either way, employees and guests have reported seeing and hearing strange things at this inn.

Address: Route 611 and Warner Road
Website: www.tannersvilleinn.com
Activity: A, E, T, S

Trumbauersville Trum Tavern

Established in 1752, the original tavern on this site was founded by Elisha Parker. It would later be known as the Jacob Fries Tavern during a period in the late 1700s when an uprising against the government (called Fries Rebellion) would force John Adams to send troops to the property. Though the tavern is now more of a modern bar and grill, there is as least one aspect that's still historic—the ghosts! The spirit of Jacob Fries is said to still be walking the second floor of his old business. He is usually blamed when items go missing or objects are found moved during the night.

Address: 1 East Broad Street
Website: www.trumtavern.com
Activity: E, T

Union Deposit Union Canal House

This restaurant and inn began as a tavern in the 1700s that served travelers journeying through the region. It was originally known as Ye Olde Tavern and, along with the nearby Fort Swatara, is one of the town's original structures. The two properties are actually connected by a tunnel, and it's said that during the French and Indian War (as well as the Revolutionary War) soldiers would use the tunnel to go for a drink. You can now get a drink at this historic site as well. With on-site accommodations and a restaurant that features fantastic seafood, the Union Canal House makes for a great getaway. You will want to rent Room 104 if you decide to stay. This area is said to be haunted by a female spirit who's been seen and heard there (a medium once told the owners the ghost was named "Rebecca"). You can also keep an eye out for paranormal activity while you get that drink—the bar is said to be the site of objects moving on their own and folks experiencing the sensation of being touched by unseen hands.

Address: 107 South Hanover Street
Website: www.unioncanalhouse.com
Activity: A, E, T

Womelsdorf The Stouch Tavern

Dating back to the 1730s and an innkeeper named Jacob Seltzer, this tavern has been servicing the local community for many years. It was purchased in 1785 by Conrad Stouch who renovated the property and created a stagecoach line that ran between Harrisburg and Reading. Though the tavern has been visited by folks like George Washington, no guest is as important these days as you! Swing by and check out their wonderful menu—as well as bar selections. You can keep an eye out for ghostly activities while you dine there. The haunting at this location is quite mild: objects move, shadows are seen, and footsteps are heard.

Address: 138 West High Street
Website: www.stouchtavern.com
Activity: S, E, T

Wrightville Accomac Inn

History hangs heavy in this inn. Of course, with past visitors like Samuel Adams and the Marquis de Lafayette, this comes as no surprise. Before the construction of this inn in 1875, the property was the site of a well-known ferry service and hotel. It was also the site of a well-known local murder. Johnny Coyle was the son of the owner and operator of Coyle's Ferry—one of the many names for this location. When he was spurned by a local girl named Emily Myers, he shot and killed her. The trial was a local sensation and Johnny ended up hanging for the deed. According to several sources, his spirit now occupies the Accomac Inn—and Emily's ghost is possibly there with him. Stop in at this eatery for a wonderful upscale dining experience—and keep an eye out for the paranormal. Activity at this restaurant includes objects moving, phantom voices, and the aforementioned spirits roaming the property.

Address: 6330 River Drive
Website: www.accomacinn.com
Activity: A, E, T

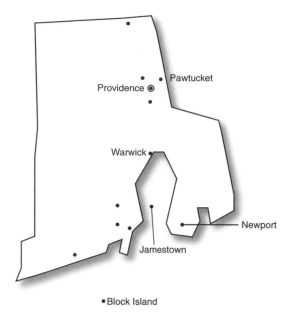

RHODE ISLAND

Block Island Harborside Inn

Located in the heart of Block Island's main town, this inn commands a spectacular view over the neighboring Old Harbor. With over a century of service, the inn currently treats customers to wonderful accommodations within reach of area sites and attractions. In addition to featuring Victorian architecture, this location also features a Victorian ghost. For years, guests who have stayed in Room 302 of the Harborside Inn have reported seeing, hearing, and feeling the spirit of a woman wearing a black dress. The "feeling the spirit" reports involve actually being touched or gently pushed by the apparition while staying in the room. There have been occasional bits of activity that have spread out into the adjoining hallway, but you will want to

rent this room to get your best chance at experiencing the paranormal.

Address: 213 Water Street
Website: www.blockislandreservations.com
Activity: A, E, T

Charlestown General Stanton Inn

This establishment dates back to 1667 and a man named Thomas Stanton. In addition to serving as his home, the place was used as a school house to teach local Native American children (in the room that is now known as the Indian Room on the property). The building was converted into a stagecoach-stop inn just after the Revolutionary War and was known for over a hundred years as one of the area's best gambling stops. Today, the site is known for most of the same amenities (minus the gambling) A good meal and room can be had here for all—if you don't mind the possibility of running into an apparition! Sightings of a man dressed in suspenders and a farm hat have occurred in the Washington and Williamsburg Rooms, as well as experiencing the feeling of someone touching you. As for activity in the rooms ... well, it's said that Room 5 is the most active, but this is because it connects to the attic where people have seen objects flying through the air!

Address: 4115 Old Post Road
Website: www.generalstantoninn.com
Activity: A, T, E

Cranston Sprague Mansion

Tales of ghostly happenings have filtered from this mansion since 1928. It's reported that a local woman named Ethel Duckworth was in the wine cellar when she felt someone touch her arm. Since the Cranston Historical Society purchased the place in 1966, many more things have occurred as well. A black shadowy apparition was witnessed on the stairs, footsteps have been heard in and near the doll room, and a female apparition wearing a Colonial dress was witnessed standing in the old governor's bedroom. Employees at the mansion have dubbed the male entity there "Charlie the Butler." Today, you can tour this museum home, or rent it for events and weddings. Maybe you'll even be greeted at the door by the butler ...

Address: 1351 Cranston Street
Website: www.cranstonhistoricalsociety.org
Activity: A, S, E, C

Jamestown Fort Wetherill State Park

The foundations of this fort go all the way back to the Revolutionary War and the earthen works that were placed on the site to ward off the British (though the place would fall with the occupation of Newport). A tower was later added to the site in 1800 and "Fort Dumpling" was

established just across the water from Fort Adams. It would be 1900 before the property was expanded into a large post and renamed Fort Wetherill in honor of Captain Alexander Wetherill. Today it is a park that's open to the public, and a great place to visit along Newport Harbor. Reports of glowing apparitions/balls of light have circulated the area for decades—as well as tales of ghosts that throw rocks, touch visitors, and walk the grounds around the old fort. Check the park's website for their hours of operation—with limited nighttime access, this may be a great location for a daytime investigation.

Address: On Fort Wetherill Road
Website: www.riparks.com/fortweth
Activity: A, O, E, T

Narragansett South County Museum

This museum is part of Canonchet Farm, a local public park, and it was founded in 1933 (though it did move a few times over the years). The farm served as a summer home for a former state governor—Colonel William Sprague—and his wife Kate. But the remnants of their massive estate are long gone since the place burned down in 1909. The visitors center and the caretaker's cottage date back to the time of the Sprague family, but the museum itself was simply built on the grounds of the old mansion. Because of the property's history, it's said that the place is haunted. Spectral figures have been seen walking throughout the museum (and even walking through the front door from the parking area), and employees have returned to work to find museum pieces moved during their absence.

Address: 100 Anne Hoxsie Lane
Website: www.southcountymuseum.org
Activity: A, T

Newport Castle Hill Inn and Resort

This massive home was established in the nineteenth century by marine biologist Alexander Agassiz. In addition to featuring the usual Victorian elements from that day, the place also has the remnants of a mini-lighthouse on the property (now a really neat Turret Suite). Though you can choose to stay in luxurious beach houses/cottages at this resort, you will have to stay in the actual mansion to see their resident spirit. Employees say the entity is a female that ceaselessly walks the halls of the old house. Glimpses of her have occurred in various areas, and her voice is occasionally heard. Additional activity in the inn involves barware/silverware that seems to move on its own in the dining room.

Address: 590 Ocean Drive
Website: www.castlehillinn.com
Activity: A, E, T

Newport Belcourt Castle

This Louis XIII–style hunting lodge was designed by Richard Morris Hunt and was constructed in 1894. Believe it or not, the property was originally a bachelor pad for local magnate Oliver Hazard Perry Belmont, the son of the Rothschild banking representative of America. Today, you can tap the sheer elegance of this place for your own event or wedding as the lodge is available for rental. Though there have been several ghost stories for some time, activity in the castle seemed to increase after the death of Donald Tinney, one of the owners of the home. Workers in the estate have witnessed his apparition in the ballroom, standing on the balcony (mind you, this is the same room that already had tales of armor moving by itself). This is in addition to the spirit that is already walking the halls there—that of a monk. If you tour the home's chapel, you will see a statue of this monk. The spirit likes to hang out by this statue and has been witnessed several times by the owners, as well as visitors to the house.

Address: 657 Bellevue Avenue
Website: www.belcourtcastle.com
Activity: A, E, O

Newport Hotel Viking

Having recently undergone a massive renovation (to the tune of $6.2 million), this circa-1926 hotel makes for a wonderful getaway when visiting Newport. With on-site amenities like the One Bellevue restaurant and Spa Terre right there on the premises, you may not even leave the hotel. This is especially true if you decide to spend some of your time investigating the haunting there. Known to paranormal groups in the area as one of the best residual haunts in the state, the Hotel Viking's ghostly activity sounds like a scene straight out of *The Shining*. It's reported that, at night, you can actually hear what sounds like a massive party going on somewhere in the lower level of the hotel. Of course, if you take a look around, you'll find there's no such thing going on. Capturing audio evidence of the phenomena may reveal more details concerning the haunt (such as what era it harkens back to), so be sure to pack your digital recorder.

Address: 1 Bellevue Avenue
Website: www.hotelviking.com
Activity: R, E

Newport Villa One Twenty

This Italianate-style mansion was designed by famed architect Richard Upjohn for Hamilton Hoppin and his family in 1856. It has gone by several names over the last few years, including the Inn at Shadow Lawn (the name that most paranormal investigators know the place by).

The haunting of this bed and breakfast concerns a tale that involves past residents at the turn of the century. It's said that a past owner of the home was a local doctor who married a wealthy woman, but was not particularly in love with her. While they lived here, he cheated on her with many local women until she became fed up with the behavior and shot him dead in the front driveway. She was found innocent of wrongdoing (mostly because there were no witnesses), but she lived alone in the house until her death (she had been universally shunned by the locals for the act). Today, if you stay in the inn, you may run into her. Her apparition has been seen, and her disembodied voice has been heard throughout most of the home.

Address: 120 Miantonomi Avenue
Website: www.villaonetwenty.com
Activity: A, E

Newport The White Horse Tavern

This location is one of those rare places that can actually be termed "ancient"—at least in American terms. It was constructed in 1652 as a residence for Francis Brinley and he lived there until 1673 when he sold the place to William Mayes (who turned the place into a local tavern). For over a hundred years, the tavern served as the colony courthouse (as well as meeting hall) in addition to serving food and drink there. The name was changed to the White Horse Tavern in 1730 and so it has remained since (except for a brief period when the place functioned as a rooming house). The spirit who lingers on this property is said to be a man who died suddenly while staying overnight on the property (they offered rooms for guests in the "old days"). He was buried quickly and poorly because of fears that he might have carried a disease. This man is now seen hanging out by the dining room fireplace. His apparition has been witnessed many times, along with the sounds of him walking the downstairs area. Witness this ghost while you enjoy a wonderful meal at this tavern (just remember that the dress here is business casual!).

Address: 26 Marlborough Street
Website: www.whitehorsetavern.us
Activity: A, E

North Kingstown Hoof Fin Feathers Carriage Inn

This restaurant is a favorite with locals in the area—not just for the wonderful food they serve, but for the sheer number of spooky tales told about it. This, of course, was magnified when the television show *Ghost Hunters* visited there and broadcasted their activity all over the country! According to the staff of the eatery, quite a few spirits roam around this old carriage house, which dates back to the 1760s. There's the apparition of an older woman, who's been seen in the newer dining room; the "women of the night," who have been witnessed in the older dining room; the ghost of the "burnt girl," who has been seen in the banquet hall; and a little boy, who walks the main floor. Additional activity in the restaurant includes voices (one employee had a spirit whisper her name) and sudden cold spots.

Address: 1065 Tower Hill Road
Website: www.hooffinfeathers.com
Activity: A, E, C, T

North Providence Ruffstone Tavern

This casual dining establishment is known for their killer version of Seafood Diana—as well as their other pub grub and menu items. The building dates back to the 1800s and managed to survive through two world wars and quite a few owners. The current version still retains much of the Irish pub feel that it had in years past, but has managed to update their look as well. This location was another haunted place investigated by TAPS on their television show. Though they didn't find much to support the idea of the place being haunted, it is still generally thought to have paranormal activity. The apparition of a man in a top hat smoking a pipe was seen in the main room and items have been known to move in the kitchen, as well as the dining room (including the door that connects the two areas).

Address: 17 Metcalf Avenue
Website: www.providenceri.com
Activity: A, T, N

Pawtucket Slater Mill

The Old Slater Mill Association was founded in 1921 to preserve the history of this mill, as well as the textile industry that was so valuable to this area. A complete restoration was made, and the property opened for tours in the 1950s. If you visit the museum today, you will find more of a complex than a single museum. With the Slater Mill (circa 1793), Wilkinson Mill (circa 1810), and the Sylvanus Brown House (circa 1758) on the grounds, there's plenty to see. The ghost stories, though, seem to involve just the two mills. In the Slater Mill, the spirits of children who died working there have been seen and heard in the building (especially in the bell tower and machine rooms). The attic area is also known for motion detectors going off by themselves

and sudden, intense cold spots appearing. The Wilkinson Mill also has its fair share of activity, including a waterwheel that moves (even when there's no water to turn it) and a machine shop that tends to scare most employees that enter.

Address: 67 Roosevelt Avenue
Website: www.slatermill.org
Activity: A, E, C, T

Wakefield Brookside Manor

This Colonial-style manor house features five guest rooms (each with its own fireplace) and over eight acres of gardens, ponds, etc., that you can explore. The home has an original "keeping room" that features a walk-in fireplace that dates all the way back to 1690! It's reported that this bed and breakfast is now haunted by Charles Fletcher, a former owner. He lived in the house between 1921 and 1965 and is the primary reason for the elegance of the home. (He extensively added on to the property while he resided there). The apparition has appeared at times in the house to owners of the property, as well as guests, and is even known for moving items (such as pillows) around in the guest rooms. He's thought to mostly hang out in the older section of the house, so plan your visit around staying in this area.

Address: 380-B Post Road
Website: www.inntravels.com/usa/ri/
    brooksidemanor
Activity: A, T

Warwick Aldrich Mansion

This 75-acre estate was once known as Indian Oaks and it took 16 years to finish it (construction began in 1896). It served as home for Senator Nelson W. Aldrich, and was the location of one of the most celebrated weddings of the day, the joining of Abby Aldrich and John D. Rockefeller Jr. This tradition is carried over today in the fact that this mansion can be rented out for your wedding as well! They even offer a top-notch catering service. The haunting of this home serves as a reminder that not everything that happened there was a good thing. According to local history, one of Nelson's daughters, who wasn't as fortunate as Abby, ended her own life by leaping from an upper-story balcony. She is the person that's said to walk the estate today. Sightings of a female apparition in the house, as well as a female disembodied voice have been heard throughout the upper floor.

Address: 836 Warwick Neck Avenue
Website: www.aldrichmansion.com
Activity: A, E

SOUTH CAROLINA

Abbeville The Abbeville Opera House

During the early 1900s, Abbeville was a stop-over for famous traveling production companies journeying between New York and Richmond. The city decided to capitalize on this by building an opera house to entice these productions to perform locally. This resulting theater was finished in 1908 and was a massive success. Today, that tradition is as strong as ever. In the early decades of the theater's operation, the practice of segregation was still going on in South Carolina, and a "Negro section" was in place in the theater—this area of the theater is thought to be the source of the opera house's haunting. Though any record of wrongdoing in the balcony is nonexistent, visitors watching performances have noticed a shadowy apparition in the area. It's said that at night, when the theater is empty, voices are heard as well.

Address: 100 Court Square
Website: www.theabbevilleoperahouse.com
Activity: S, E

Charleston The Battery Carriage House Inn

Samuel N. Stevens purchased this land in 1843 and later that year built the original house on this property. In 1859, he sold the place to John F. Blacklock, who moved in just in time to see the outbreak of the Civil War. He abandoned the newly purchased home, and it was sorely battered during the Siege of Charleston. Because of this, he sold the home—and this tradition of renovating and selling the property would continue through several families until the 1980s when the mansion finally began to function as an inn. With several great hot spots to stay in, the Battery makes for a great paranormal getaway. Sightings of a male apparition (dressed in gentlemanly attire) and a headless spectral torso are the main activity at this location. You will want to rent Room 3 (where shadow shapes and glowing orbs have been witnessed), Room 8 (where the torso has made an appearance and shutters mysteriously bang within the room), or Room 10 (the stomping grounds of the gentleman spirit who has been seen and heard on many occasions).

Address: 20 South Battery
Website: www.batterycarriagehouse.com
Activity: A, S, E, T

Charleston Boone Hall Plantation & Gardens

This 1800s plantation house (as well as the surrounding fields that feature fruits and vegetables that you can pick) has been open to the public since 1956. It's a popular place for weddings and events—though you can also visit and take one of the offered tours there as well. The home is said to be the stage for a sad, but interesting, haunting. According to the story, a young girl named Ammie Jenkins, who lived in the house, was shot in the chest with an arrow (that entered through an upstairs window). She staggered down the stairs but died on the thirteenth step. The legend states that bloodstains remained on this step for decades and were avoided by folks in the home (though nothing is said of the boy that supposedly shot the girl for spurning his love). Ammie is now said to haunt the house and, reputedly, has been seen and heard there. Other activity on the site includes the residual apparition of a Confederate soldier who has been seen walking the front yard of the plantation.

Address: 1235 Long Point Road
Website: www.boonehallplantation.com
Activity: A, R, E

Charleston Dock Street Theatre

This historic theatre (circa 1809) was first known to locals as the rough and tumble Planter's Hotel. Before closing down (mostly due to public petitions to close the place), the hotel was known for constant fights, as well as gambling and prostitution. The theatre, on the other hand, brought instant culture to the city—a tradition that continues today with the Charleston Stage production company, which (along with the city) is currently renovating the theatre to the tune of $20 million. It's said in the paranormal community that renovations will often kick up activity, so maybe this will get the two spirits there ramped up for their grand re-opening in 2010! It's said that the spirit of actor Junius Brutus Booth (father of John Wilkes Booth) haunts the theatre along with a prostitute dubbed "Nettie" by employees. Voices, items moving, and shadow shapes make up the typical sightings at this theatre.

Address: 135 Church Street
Website: www.charlestonstage.com
Activity: S, E, T

Charleston Fort Sumter National Monument

Getting to this island monument is easier than you think—now that the area is automobile accessible! So there's no excuse for missing this historic and haunted site. On April 12, 1861, the Civil War officially broke out when this fort was attacked by Confederate troops who could not abide Northern soldiers occupying their area. The Confederacy would win the battle and hold the fort throughout the war, despite several attempts by the North to retake it. The ghost that walks Fort Sumter is said to be Private Daniel Hough, one of the two Union fatalities that happened during the first conflict at the fort. It's thought that Hough is buried on the parade field of the fort—and this just happens to be the area where his spirit is seen.

Address: Island off Sullivan's Island
Website: www.nps.gov/fosu/
Activity: A

Charleston The Meeting Street Inn

Located in the historic district of old Charleston, this inn dates back to 1874, when the property served as a home to Adolf Tiefenthal and family—as well as a saloon, restaurant, and wholesale market. In 1886, the property changed hands and became the Atlantic Brewing and Ice Company, triggering a series of owners and businesses that would eventually lead to the modern-day inn (founded 1981). The current owners took over the place in 1992 and, after renovating it, offer a great place to tour and to stay in while visiting Charleston. It's generally thought by locals that the inn is haunted by two members of the Tiefenthal family. After Adolf died, his wife remarried and continued living in the building—an event he did not particularly like. Adolf is said to hang out in Room 303 of the inn and makes his presence known by banging around in there, as well as occasionally locking the door to the room (from the inside). Room 107 is reputedly the area haunted by the widow Tiefenthal—her apparition has been witnessed there, as well as the sounds of her disembodied voice.

Address: 173 Meeting Street
Website: www.meetingstreetinn.com
Activity: A, E, T

Charleston Poogan's Porch

Since this place opened in 1976, it has been universally hailed as one of Charleston's finest eating establishments. It has been featured on television programs and in magazines, and is generally thought to be the best "low country" eatery in the state. The restaurant is located in a former house that dates back to 1888, and the spirit that roams the place was a resident during this era. The ghost is thought to be a woman named Zoe St. Amand, who lived in the house many years before passing away there. Her apparition has been seen by employees, patrons, and even folks staying at the neighboring Mills House Hotel. She's typically seen wearing a long black dress and is usually considered the culprit when pots and pans are found moved in the kitchen and the odd bang/knock is heard in the restaurant/dining room.

Address: 72 Queen Street
Website: www.poogansporch.com
Activity: A, E, T

Pawleys Island Litchfield Plantation

This historic plantation dates back to the 1700s, with the earliest known owner being Peter Simons. When he died in 1794, his two sons split up the 2,000-acre estate, and the strip along the shoreline, now known as Litchfield, was sold to the Tucker family in 1796. Dr. Henry Tucker and his family lived in the home for a hundred years before the property began a series of ownership changes. Today, the bed and breakfast–style house makes for great accommodations while visiting the area (as well as a unique place to hold a meeting or event). The house is the result of many renovations and additions over the years, including one massive makeover done by Dr. Henry Norris in the 1920s. It's said that Dr. Norris enjoyed the home so much that he now inhabits the place in the afterlife. His apparition has been seen walking the halls, and his presence is sometimes accompanied by an unusual cold spot.

Address: 290 Kings River Road
Website: www.litchfieldplantation.com
Activity: A, C

Union The Inn at Merridun

This antebellum mansion dates back to 1855 and was originally known as the Keenan Plantation. Before becoming a bed and breakfast in 1992, the house was home to many families over the years. Among these was the Duncan family (Thomas and Fannie), who inherited the property in the early 1880s. It was Thomas that renamed the plantation "Merridun" after the three major families that lived there (Merriman, Rice, and Duncan). It is Thomas and Fannie are said to haunt the inn today—along with the spirit of a black servant who once worked there. All three apparitions have been witnessed on the property (Fannie has even been seen without a head!), sometimes accompanied by a scent (cigars, perfume, etc.), or disembodied voice.

Address: 100 Merridun Place
Website: www.merridun.com
Activity: A, E, N

Winnsboro Fairfield County Museum

This historic facility has functioned as a family home (for Richard Cathcart and his brood), a school, and a hotel/boardinghouse over the years. During these long decades, many a soul has lived and died within these walls. So is it possible that at least one of the departed is now forever immortalized in a mirror? Employees of the museum think so. The mirror in question hangs over a mantel and is said to be imprinted with the face of an older woman who, presumably, died on the property at some point over the years. Whether this is true or not (or the face is simply a product of "matrixing"), one thing is certain—visitors to the museum often report feeling the presence of an older woman there in the house. The occasional bit of paranormal activity, such as dark shadows and finding objects moved, does occur in the home in addition to the woman, so visiting the museum is well worth your time.

Address: 231 South Congress Street
Website: www.midnet.sc.edu/fairfieldmus/
Activity: S, E

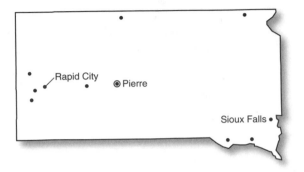

SOUTH DAKOTA

Custer The Black Hills Playhouse

This theater is part of a camp and lodge that dates back to 1933. The production group that performs in the playhouse was founded in 1946 by Dr. Warren M. Lee, though they wouldn't get an actual theater until 1955. It was built on the site of an old dining hall that burned down three years earlier. Today, the playhouse is as strong as ever (not to mention the CCC Camp Lodge). Paranormal activity at this location is said to hearken back to the days when the lodge housed post-Depression workers. It's thought that the spirit who has been heard in the backstage area of the playhouse is the daughter of one of these past workers. The entity likes to hang out in the costume area and even, on occasion, will move pieces of clothing and props there. The most commonly reported activity, though, is the phantom sounds of footsteps.

Address: 24834 South Playhouse Road
Website: www.blackhillsplayhouse.com
Activity: E, T

Custer Custer State Park

This state attraction offers a rather unique and sinister tale for the paranormal traveler. Local legend tells of a location there that's said to house a veritable army of evil spirits. This area is known as Little Devil's Tower, and it is located along one of the many trails within the park. According to the tale, local Native Americans would avoid this area because of the evil spirits—something that is almost completely ignored today when you see the sheer amount of campers and hikers who visit this area. Your best chance to experience something at Custer State Park is to camp there as well. Set up some night-vision video cameras and see what you get. According to investigators who have stayed there, the strange sight of glowing orbs of light is common, as well as strange cries and moans heard coming from Little Devil's Tower.

Address: 13329 State Highway 16A
Website: www.custerstatepark.info
Activity: O, M, E, A

Deadwood Bullock Hotel

This hotel dates back to 1895 and was built after Sheriff Seth Bullock's hardware store burned to the ground in 1894. It contained a saloon and gambling hall and even served as Bullock's own accommodations for a great while. Today's version of the hotel has the same feel (and many of the same amenities) of Seth's day, including a bar that seems to transport you back in time to the Victorian era. Perhaps it's because of this that Seth is said to still be hanging out in his hotel. He did actually die in the place (Room 211 to be exact) in 1919. He likes to appear to guests who stay in his room, as well as roam the halls with the other ghost on the property. This entity is thought to be a young girl, and her apparition has been seen in several rooms (205, 207, and 209) as well as heard in various spots throughout the hotel. According to employees, reports of paranormal activity have also come from Rooms 302, 305, 313, and 315.

Address: 633 Main Street
Website: www.historicbullock.com
Activity: A, E, T, C

Deadwood Historic Adams House

This circa 1892 home is part of a small complex that includes a museum, a gift shop, and a cultural center. The house was the home of Harris and Anna Franklin and features Queen Anne–styled architecture. It pretty much stayed in the Franklin and Adams families until it was turned (briefly) into a bed and breakfast. Eventually, it was donated to the city that turned it into the living museum it is today. Stories concerning the place possibly being haunted began when the bed and breakfast operated. The owner would receive complaints from guests of an old man walking through their room. Since there were no people of this description staying at the B&B (especially none that could go through walls), they came to the conclusion that W. E. Adams was still hanging around there. Today, the activity includes a rocking chair that moves by itself, the sounds of footsteps, the sudden scent of tobacco, and even the occasional glimpse of the apparition.

Address: 22 Van Buren Avenue
Website: www.adamsmuseumandhouse.org
Activity: A, E, T, N

Hill City 1880 Train

When the gold-mining boom hit the Black Hills of North Dakota in 1874, the area would be changed forever. Fortunes would be made, battles would ensue, and the Dakota Territory would become quite the popular place. Once the railroad came through, the movement of product (as well as passengers) became a much easier task and facilitated the economic growth of the entire area. When you buy a ticket to ride this train, you get 2½ hours of historic travel through the Black Hills country—and, possibly, you may get to meet a ghost! Just not on the actual operating train. Scattered throughout the train yard are remnants of trains past, and it's among these relics that folks are said to encounter the occasional apparition, as well as hear disembodied voices. If you don't see a spirit here, head over to the High Liner Eatery for a meal (it's housed in a train car there), as reports of a strange apparition wearing a brown suit have occurred at this restaurant.

Address: 222 Railroad Avenue
Website: www.1880train.com
Activity: A, E, S

Hill City Alpine Inn

This inn dates back to the 1880s and was originally known as the Harney Peak Hotel. It was located in the heart of Main Street, Hillyo (the original name for the town), which was known to the locals as the "One Mile of Hell" (due to the high number of saloons, gamblers, and gunfights there). Over the years, the inn has endured two major fires and years of neglect after it shut down in 1934. Today, it's back in operation and features top-notch dining and accommodations. Because of its rowdy past, it's generally thought by paranormal investigators that the Alpine Inn is haunted. Tales of phantom footsteps, voices, and strange lights have filtered from the hotel over the years and is said to still happen to this day. If you visit, get a room on the second floor—this area is generally regarded as the most active.

Address: 225 Main Street
Website: www.alpineinnhillcity.com
Activity: E, O

Hot Springs The Toal House Bed and Breakfast

For the paranormal tourist, you may have heard of this place by its former name, the Villa Theresa Guest House B&B. It was a stop for anyone traveling through South Dakota who wanted to encounter a ghost. It is now known as the Toal House, and it has many of the amenities that you'd expect at a full-service hotel. Long before the place was a B&B, though (by any name), it was called the Sioux City Club, a gentleman's club with gambling, booze, and you name it. It was created by Chicago businessman F. O. Butler, and it operated for many years before turning into a private residence. The first new owner to take over the property had lots of interesting tales about the house, including a strange residual scene that involved a male apparition knocking a female apparition down the stairs. During this particular witness' residence, a third apparition was also seen—said to be a mean-looking man who would perch on the stairs and glare at the home's inhabitants. Other activity includes items moving by themselves (to include a dog), the smell of perfume (in upper story rooms), glowing balls of light, and the disembodied head of F. O. Butler himself!

Address: 801 Almond Street
Website: www.toalhousebnb.com
Activity: A, R, E, T, O, N

Lake City Fort Sisseton State Historical Park

This frontier fort was constructed in 1864 and was originally named Fort Wadsworth. It was created to guard the Dakota Territory from attacks by Native American tribes. The park, located in the Coteau des Prairies area of the state, still features many of the fort's original parts, including the officers' quarters, the barracks, and even a guardhouse. You can host events at this park, as well as do the usual outdoor activities, so visiting this location is even easier than most in this book. As for the paranormal activity, park employees have reported strange lights that have been seen on the property for decades. Much like other places that experience such "ghost lights," it's said they seem to bob around for a while and then disappear, much to the astonishment of those who are watching.

Address: 11907 434th Avenue
Website: www.sdgfp.info
Activity: O

McLaughlin Major James McLaughlin Heritage Center

The history of Major McLaughlin is a fascinating trip through this area's history. He was appointed an Indian Agent for the Standing Rock Sioux Agency and was instrumental in the arrest of Sitting Bull in 1890 (an event that spurred a gunfight and the death of the Sioux chief). The heritage center is located in the former home of McLaughlin and is said to be the major's residence in the afterlife. Guests and employees alike have reported experiencing strange activity in the center, including seeing dark shadow shapes, hearing disembodied voices, and seeing the occasional sight of McLaughlin in person! Of course, while you're there, you will want to take in the exhibits and history that this center holds as well.

Address: Main Street at Highway 12
Website: www.museumsusa.org/museums/
info/1159883
Activity: A, S, E

Midland Midland Pioneer Museum

This unique museum offers glimpses of the area's past, as well as unique (and large) displays. Before planning your visit, though, be sure to check the hours and dates on their website—they are typically only open during the summer months. Some of the things you will see at the Midland Pioneer Musuem include early tractors and cultivators, a completely furnished schoolhouse, and the original 1907 Chicago and Northwestern train depot. As for seeing the spirit that roams these grounds, you will want to go to the area that used to be a local bank. Over the years, quite a few visitors have noticed strange sounds in this area (such as hurried/whispered voices, the stomps of heavy boots, and a gasping/heavy breathing sound) and found things "rearranged" during the previous evening.

Address: 25121 Capa Road
Website: www.midlandsd.com/PioneerMuseum
Activity: E, T

Rapid City Hotel Alex Johnson

Alex Johnson was the vice president of the Chicago and Northwestern Railroad and founder of this hotel. The place first opened in 1928 and features hints of Native American architecture that Johnson intended to honor the neighboring Sioux nation. Even the magnificent lobby of this hotel reflects this homage in the décor and design. As for the paranormal activity at the hotel…well…where do you begin? Probably on the eighth floor, which is said to be the area the "Lady in White" roams. She is presumed to be the spirit of a past suicide and she's been seen on this floor many times—along with the sounds of crying and of a piano playing. The infamous Room 812 is said to be haunted by a second female, who either committed suicide by leaping from the window there or was pushed out (most think the latter). Almost constant activity is reported in this room. Employees say the hotel is also haunted by its founder—sightings of a male apparition have occurred over the decades in various locations in the hotel.

Address: 523 Sixth Street
Website: www.alexjohnson.com
Activity: A, E, T

Rapid City The Sports Rock

This sports bar is known for its pizza, calzones, and an abundance of televisions tuned to popular sports events. But before they moved into this building, the property was infamously known as one of the area's most active haunted locations when it was called Hooky Jack's. At the turn of the century, an area police officer named

John Leary was injured in a mining accident that cost him both of his arms—resulting in him having two hooks placed in their stead and earning him the nickname "Hooky." He passed away in 1916 after being struck by a car, but he lived in this building and has since haunted the place. Though most of the activity seems to happen on the upper floors, strange things happen in the restaurant as well—including glimpses of spectral faces, voices, and the occasional orb of light seen scooting through the bar.

Address: 321 7th Street
Website: www.sportsrockpizza.com
Activity: A, E, O

Sioux Falls Orpheum Theater Center

The Orpheum first opened its doors in 1913 to feature touring vaudeville acts and live entertainment. In 1954, a local theater group (Community Playhouse) took over the business and have since hosted productions there. The venue is listed on the National Register of Historic Places and, much like the other Orpheum (located in Memphis, Tennessee), is considered to be haunted. Actors who work on the site call the ghost there "Larry" and say he only wants to be noticed. During the 1950s, Larry was once seen in the center of a glowing ball of light, and in the 1970s, a stage manager once saw him standing on the stage in all his glory. It's said that Larry likes to play with items left in the theater and that he is usually accompanied by an intense cold spot (sometimes this is all that's experienced when he appears). Catch a performance at this historic theatre and see if you can spot Larry hanging out there!

Address: 315 North Phillips Avenue
Website: orpheum.sfarena.com
Activity: A, O, C, E, T

Springfield Libby's Steakhouse

Finding information regarding this eatery is next to impossible—even when you contact the restaurant itself! They will tell you about their wonderful menu (they are known as one of the best steakhouses in the area) or even make a reservation for you, but not much is related concerning the history of the site. What is known locally is that the place was once a family-run drug store by the name of Hoch Drugs and that tales concerning a ghost on the property have been around for a very long time. It's rumored that a young female (most likely a member of the Hoch family) died on the property and that she now haunts the basement of the restaurant. It's said that when the basement door is left open, strange things happen in the eatery: silverware/barware moves on its own, a girl's voice is heard, and a sort of "eerie feeling" sweeps over the place. Stories concerning the ghost grew locally when a former employee confessed to having seen the apparition of a little girl in the basement that vanished when he approached her.

Address: 818 South 8th Street
Website: www.springfieldsd.com
Activity: A, E, T

Yankton Mount Marty College

This Catholic college is a private institution, but most of the school's grounds can be toured (check in with the front office for times/dates). The college is named for a Benedictine missionary named Martin Marty, who visited the area in 1876 to minister to Native Americans. Since its inception in 1936, the place has had several ghostly tales told about it. Whitby Hall is reportedly so active that they had to actually shut it down for a couple of years, hoping the ghostly activity would cease. Multiple apparitions have been witnessed in this building. One of the dorms, Corbey Hall, is also the location of multiple sightings—including the spirit of a female that's been seen in the elevator. And if that's not enough, the campus itself is also generally thought to be haunted by a male spirit that's been seen and heard all across the campus. He likes to appear as a shadowy apparition and is often heard tromping behind you as you walk the grounds.

Address: 1105 West 8th Street
Website: www.mtmc.edu
Activity: A, E, T

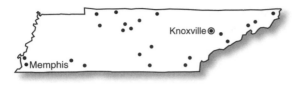

TENNESSEE

Adams The Bell Witch Cave

This is arguably one of the most well-known ghost stories in the country. Numerous books, television shows, and even movies have featured the tale. According to the legend, when John Bell purchased land for his home and family to reside on, it upset a neighbor by the name of Kate Batts (who had sold a portion of her land in the deal). She felt she was shortchanged in the sale. After she passed away, strange things started happening in the Bell home. Things that included knocks and bangs through the night, objects moving on their own, and physical attacks on John and Betsy Bell. People came from miles around to witness the activity—including Tennessee politician Andrew Jackson. After John died (reportedly from being poisoned by Kate), the activity pretty much dried up. You can visit the site of these paranormal attacks and take a tour of the Bell Cave and Cabin. Strange things are said to occur there even to this day.

Address: 430 Keysburg Road
Website: www.bellwitchcave.com
Activity: A, E, T

Athens The Keith Mansion

This bed and breakfast dates back to 1858 when it was built by architect Thomas Crutchfield for Colonel Alexander Hume Keith and his family.

It would take many years to completely finish the home (partly due to the Civil War and the Union troops that occupied the house in 1863). The mansion would remain in the Keith family for over a hundred years before undergoing a renovation and being transformed into the B&B it is today. According to several sources, the house is now haunted by a spirit that most believe to be a soldier that passed away on the premises (during its occupation, portions of the home were used as a makeshift hospital). Rent one of their wonderful rooms (there are five), enjoy a wonderful meal (the current owner is a chef), and hopefully you will experience the paranormal as well. Activity in the mansion includes disembodied voices and objects that tend to move on their own (doors, rocking chairs, etc.).

Address: 110 Keith Lane
Website: www.keithmansion.com
Activity: E, T

Bolivar Magnolia Manor Bed & Breakfast

Built by Judge Austin Miller in 1849, this B&B served as the location for a pivotal moment in history. Prior to the Civil War Battle of Shiloh, Generals Grant, Sherman, Logan, and McPherson met and lodged in this home to discuss the impending battle that would take place down the road at Pittsburg Landing. You can soak up this history—as well as the paranormal history—of this house when you stay in one of their four luxurious rooms (decorated in period furniture and furnishings). Ghostly activity has been recorded in all four rooms (and also in the cottage out back that was once used to house servants), though the three rooms on the second floor seem to get the most attention. The B&B was featured in the movie *Ghosts of War*, as well as on the television show *If Walls Could Talk*. Activity on the premises includes disembodied voices (male and female), the sightings of apparitions (thought to possibly be Annie, Lizzie, and Austin Miller), and objects that seem to be manipulated by invisible hands.

Address: 418 North Main Street
Website: www.magnoliamanorbolivartn.com
Activity: A, S, E, T

Calhoun Pinhook Plantation House B&B

This historic location has a mysterious—and somehwat unknown—history. It's generally thought that the home dates back to 1810 and the Alexander family, which moved in from neighboring Asheville, North Carolina. The house sat on 641 acres and featured a ballroom that was the social center for the area (and the site of a duel at one time)—and at one point was occupied by both sides of the Civil War. The bed and breakfast now offers patrons three period-styled rooms in a location that can't be beat for exploring the outdoors. There are several ghost stories about Pinhook (though you can probably get more from the innkeepers there) that are pretty well known. The first involves a residual scene that takes place in the "gathering room" there—it's said a spectral monk is seen holding court over a group of other spirits. But the most well-known ghost is that of the "Lady in the Grey Gown." She is usually seen climbing the stairs to the second-floor rooms, though she is also known for whiling away the hours in a certain rocking chair.

Address: 692 Pinhook Road
Website: www.pinhookplantation.com
Activity: A, R, E, T

Castalian Springs Cragfont of Middle Tennessee

The original version of this home was a log cabin built in 1786 by George and James Winchester. After George was killed by Indians, James decided to build a grander manor on the property, so the construction of such began in 1798 (it was finished in 1802). It would change hands many times over the years before the state of Tennessee took it over in 1958 and made the place a historic site. They offer tours of the property and you can even rent Cragfont for weddings. There are several ghost tales concerning this house. First, there's the spirit of James that many have claimed to witness there. Then there's the story of Malvina—she looked over the property during the Civil War while her husband and son fought for the Confederacy. Locals claim to see the spectral face of Malvina peering from the windows, looking out over her old plantation grounds.

Address: 200 Cragfont Road
Website: www.cragfont.com
Activity: A, R, E, T

Dover Riverfront Plantation Inn

Originally known as the Crow House (circa 1859), this bed and breakfast offers five guest rooms and on-site dining for the discriminating traveler. It's also in spitting distance of area sites like Fort Donelson and Land Between the Lakes. During the Civil War, troops camped on the front lawn of this property and even used part of the home as a hospital. Perhaps it is because of this that the place is now considered haunted. Several area paranormal investigators have visited this property and found interesting evidence. Activity on the premises is said to include the sounds of moans/cries (maybe from the wounded who were treated?) and doors that open/close by themselves.

Address: 190 Crow Lane
Website: www.innsite.com/inns/A002927
Activity: E, T

Franklin Carter House

This historic home was, literally, right in the middle of the Battle of Franklin during the Civil War (just check out the bullet holes that riddle the structure). As the battle took place in the surrounding fields, the house was used by Union troops as a command center while the family took shelter in the cellar. Tragically, one of the Carter family's sons, Tod Carter, was injured fighting for the Confederacy right in his own front yard. He was carried into the family home, where he died in his bedroom two days later. His spirit is now said to haunt this area. Other ghosts in the house are said to include

Tod's sister, Annie, who has been seen walking there and the ghost of a young child who died from a fall that was incurred in the house. The Carter House is a living museum and they offer a long and wonderful tour of the property. It is a must-see when traveling through this area.

Address: 1140 Columbia Avenue
Website: www.carter-house.org
Activity: A, E, T

Gatlinburg Rocky Top Village Inn

This modern lodge was run by famed songwriter Felice Bryant (co-writer of such songs as "Rocky Top" and "Bye Bye Love") until she passed away in 2003. Her husband, and co-writer, Boudleaux Bryant, preceded her in death in 1987. The inn is still in operation, though, and offers the public 89 guest rooms/suites and two comfy cottages. According to locals, this inn was the site of a double homicide. Two employees were brutally killed in the back office of the site—and most believe their spirits are still at the Rocky Top. Sightings of an apparition in the parking lot and hanging out by the fountain have occurred several times and guests have also reported hearing the sounds of screaming during the night.

Address: 311 Historic Nature Trail
Website: www.rockytopvillageinn.com
Activity: A, E

Greeneville The General Morgan Inn

Built in 1884 to service travelers along the railroad, this old hotel offers modern amenities (spa, wireless Internet, etc.) in a historic setting. Tales concerning the haunting of this inn are well known throughout the area—even with the on-site staff (so asking them about current activity may not be a bad idea). It's said that a female spirit named "Grace" likes to hang out in the restaurant there (now called Brumley's, but known to most paranormal investigators by its former name, The Green Room). She is supposed to have been a waitress when the inn was called the Grand Central Hotel, so it's fitting that Grace is known for moving around silverware and taking spoons from tables. Many believe, though, that not all of the paranormal activity can be blamed on Grace. Before this hotel was constructed, this location was the resting spot of the De Woody Tavern (a rough establishment for the times) and is also thought to be the spot General Morgan was shot and killed in 1864 during the Civil War.

Address: 111 North Main Street
Website: www.generalmorganinn.com
Activity: A, E, T

Hurricane Mills Loretta Lynn's Ranch

In addition to being an award-winning songwriter and musician, Loretta Lynn is also known for her psychic abilities! Though it's not publicized, she has always had this power (she, reportedly, predicted her own father's death and even saw his ghost when she visited her old family home). After she moved into this old plantation house with her family (an area you can tour almost daily), they started noticing strange things—like female apparitions walking through the room! Sightings of two spectral women (dressed in long gowns with their hair up) happened several times, along with a Civil War soldier who was once witnessed standing beside Loretta's bed. Other activity includes the sounds of moans and chains that come from a cellar and phantom footsteps. Keep in mind, you can also stay at this ranch when you visit—there's an RV park and a campground right on the premises.

Address: 44 Hurricane Mills Road
Website: www.lorettalynn.com/ranch/ranch
Activity: A, E, T, R

Jonesborough Hawley House Bed & Breakfast

This property has the distinction of being the oldest home in Tennessee's oldest town! It was built in 1793, but was added on to several times over the years. Today, it is a B&B that features three guest rooms and top-notch service. When the Hawley family moved into this historic site—and performed extensive renovations of the property—they noticed the sounds of female voices coming from the second floor. Though it hasn't been proven, it's thought that the house may have served as a brothel at some point and that the spirits heard there are possibly a remnant of those days. It's said that the ghosts there only like to perform when men are about—so this may support the idea that their spirits were ladies of the night.

Address: 114 East Woodrow Avenue
Website: www.bbonline.com/tn/hawley/
Activity: E, T

Jonesborough Historic Eureka Inn

Dating back to 1797, this location was originally the home of Robert and Harriett Mitchell. It was purchased from them in 1851 by William Henry Maxwell, who added onto the house and allowed the local court to sequester juries there during trials. After functioning for a bit as a boardinghouse, the place was renovated and transformed into a hotel in 1900. The inn has 14 rooms these days—most decorated in period furnishings while having most of the amenities you would expect at a modern chain hotel. According to some visitors, the inn also has a couple of resident ghosts. Paranormal investigators visited this site and reported seeing a shadowy apparition walking by and hearing the sounds of disembodied voices/footsteps. However, you may want to conduct your own investigation.

Address: 127 West Main Street
Website: www.eurekajonesborough.com
Activity: S, E, T

Knoxville Baker Peters' Jazz Club

This restaurant and music venue is located within the historic Baker-Peters mansion. The home dates back to 1840 and is the site of an interesting ghost story. Abner Baker was a soldier during the Civil War and was hanged shortly after the end of the conflict for killing a Union army veteran at the Knoxville courthouse. Abner's father, Dr. Harvey Baker, had been killed in the mansion by Union soldiers during the war, so most believe he murdered the veteran for revenge. It's said that Abner now haunts the jazz club. Employees and patrons have witnessed glasses moving on their own, and heard the voice/sounds of an invisible guest in various areas of the mansion. You'll get to see a lot of haunted locations while touring through this area of Tennessee, but you probably will not find another spot with food this good, so you may want to visit!

Address: 9000 Kingston Pike
Website: www.bakerpetersjazzclub.com
Activity: E, T

Manchester J. P. Adams Tower House Museum and B&B Inn

This bed and breakfast contains a mini-museum and even offers tours of the house on occasion (yes, ghost tours, too). It was built by J. P. Adams as his family home—and it remained as such until 1943. If you choose to stay in this comfy location, you will want to keep an eye out for the family of ghosts that is said to reside on the property. Sightings of old John occur in the front parlor and around the Civil War exhibit displayed there. Of course, you may also run into his wife, May, or their son, Marion, as well. Both of them tragically died while the house was being built and both of them are now seen/heard in the house. May cries when a storm is passing through, and Marion is known to appear as either an apparition or a ball of light in the upstairs bedrooms.

Address: 300 West Fort Street
Website: www.innsite.com/inns/B009891
Activity: A, O, E

McMinnville Falcon Rest

This circa 1896 mansion was built by Clay Faulkner, the creator of "Gorilla Jeans," for his wife Mary. They would live there together until Clay's death in the house in 1916. The place would go on to become a hospital and nursing home before becoming the B&B it is today. The Falcon Manor portion of this property offers guest rooms for the public—and then there's on-site dining (the Victorian Tea Room) and a gift shop as well. It wasn't long after opening, though, that the owners started witnessing some pretty strange acts. The sounds of footsteps and whistling were heard near the staircase (close to Clay's old bedroom) and then a guest reported seeing the apparition of a woman in a dress and bonnet standing by the front door.

Address: 2645 Faulkner Springs Road
Website: www.falconrest.com
Activity: A, E, T

Memphis The Inn at Hunt Phelan

This antebellum home dates back to 1828 and it has the history to prove it! Eli and Julia Driver purchased the home in 1850 and made significant improvements to the property before their son-in-law, William Richard Hunt, took over the place during the Civil War. The home was briefly occupied by General Leonidas Polk (during the planning of the Battle of Corinth) and General Ulysses S. Grant (who planned the siege of Vicksburg there)—but Hunt was long gone with the family furnishings, which had been trucked out by Confederates using a train car. The family would also abandon the house briefly during the outbreak of Yellow Fever in Memphis—and this is also the source of the home's haunting. It's said a caretaker stayed behind to guard the family gold while the family left the city to avoid getting the "Black Vomit." Unfortunately, he died and is now said to still be guarding the house and its treasure to this day (of course no gold was ever found—or probably even existed). Grab a gourmet meal at the inn's restaurant, or better yet, a room on the premises, and watch out for their invisible guard.

Address: 533 Beale Street
Website: www.huntphelan.com
Activity: A, E, T

Memphis National Ornamental Metal Museum

Though this location seems to make many of the "most haunted" lists around Memphis, nothing at the property indicates the spirits are malevolent in any way. Once the home for the officers of the nearby military hospital (long closed), this museum compound includes a library, a smithy, and a foundry on the site. They still create metal masterworks at this museum, as well as celebrate their craft. If you visit and want to see the paranormal, you will want to tour the library house. This old home was once the residence of the hospital's head physician—and he liked to take his work home with him. The home had a basement morgue that connected to the old hospital (via a tunnel) where the doctor could perform autopsies. While the museum was undergoing a renovation, workers who were in the house reported seeing shadowy entities and hearing disembodied voices in the old morgue. Add in the apparition of a man who has been witnessed on the second floor and you've got one great haunt!

Address: 374 Metal Museum Drive
Website: www.metalmuseum.org
Activity: A, S, E

Memphis Orpheum Theatre

Originally called the Grand Opera House, this theatre dates back to 1890. In 1907, the name was changed to its current moniker when the venue became part of the Orpheum Circuit of vaudeville shows. Unfortunately though, the Orpheum would burn to the ground during a striptease performance by Blossom Seeley. The theatre was rebuilt in 1928 (the current version) and thrives today with live performances

and productions. If you catch a show at the Orpheum, you may want to sit close to seat C-5. It's said the ghost of "Mary" often sits in this seat. She has been witnessed in the venue many times (reportedly, she was even seen by actor Yul Brynner) and is said to wear a white dress and have pigtails. Stories vary as to how she ended up haunting the site—but most believe she was struck out front by a trolley and died after being brought inside for assistance.

Address: 203 South Main Street
Website: www.orpheum-memphis.com
Activity: A, E, T

Memphis Woodruff-Fontaine House

The ghost of Mollie Woodruff is the second most well-known spirit in Memphis (right behind Mary at the Orpheum). She was the daughter of Amos Woodruff, a local carriage maker and politician who built this home in 1870. Mollie was married there in the mansion in 1871 to Egbert Wooldridge and would later suffer the tragic loss of her first born in her old bedroom (due to yellow fever), now called the "Rose Room." Sadly, her husband would also pass away in this same room from pneumonia. Though Mollie remarried and moved away, it's said she returned to this house after she passed away in 1917. Her old bedroom is, reportedly, the hottest spot. Activity includes disembodied voices, visual evidence that Mollie has been sitting/lying on her bed, and, of course, the apparition of Mollie herself. There is also the possibility of a second entity—investigators from Paranormal Inc recorded EVPs of a male apparition in the first-floor parlor—the area where an employee reported having a necklace torn from her neck by unseen hands.

Address: 680Adams Avenue
Website: www.woodruff-fontaine.com
Activity: A, E, T

Mountain City Prospect Hill Bed & Breakfast Inn

This country mansion was erected in 1889 by Major Joseph Wagner, who served in the Union army during the Civil War. The mansion passed through the hands of a couple more families, but eventually ended up as the B&B it is today. Completely renovated and featuring five guest rooms (along with a private cottage), Prospect Hill is close to many varied and interesting attractions—including stock car racing, outdoor sports, and the theater. The paranormal activity in this house is even more varied. Reading some of the accounts, you will come across phantom scents (including baking cookies), strange sounds (footsteps, a baby crying, and slamming doors), and odd occurrences (exploding glasses and photos of spectral fire coming from an unlit fireplace). But most dramatic of all are the sightings of a Civil War era male apparition that's been seen staring out a front widow.

Address: 801 West Main Street
Website: www.prospect-hill.com
Activity: A, E, T, N

Nashville Belmont Mansion

Originally spelled "Belle Mont," this massive estate dates back to 1853. Built for Joseph Alexander Smith Acklen and Adelicia Franklin after they married, it featured an on-site zoo that was open to the public for viewing. Unfortunately, Joseph died in Louisiana during the Civil War, forcing Adelicia to marry a third husband. After she passed away while visiting New York, the house became a women's college and finally a living museum. You can tour this home, as well as attend events there and rent the facilities for private affairs. Perhaps you will also get to visit with Adelicia while you're there. Despite dying in NYC (in a hotel from pneumonia), her spirit is hanging out in her old house. She's usually blamed for motion detectors going off unexpectedly and for moving objects around the house during the evening. Of course, it helps that folks have actually seen her apparition there as well. Workers on the site, security guards, and even visitors to the museum have all reported seeing Adelicia walking her stately manor, dressed in a full-length gown.

Address: 1900 Belmont Boulevard
Website: www.belmontmansion.com
Activity: A, T

Nashville The Hermitage

Caretakers of this wonderful mansion have restored the place to its 1837 appearance and have added a welcome center there that features a café, a mini-theater (where you can watch a brief movie about the property), and a gift shop. The Hermitage was the home of President Andrew Jackson and his wife, Rachel. During his term as president, the house suffered a fire in 1934 that resulted in the home being remodeled to its current look. After Rachel passed away in 1828 and Andrew did the same in 1845, the home was passed down through the family and was eventually taken over by the state government. When you tour this house, consider the history that was created by those who lived there—and also consider that you may run into these people! Caretakers of the mansion have seen and heard President Jackson on the premises (including one occurrence that seemed to sound like him riding a horse up the stairs). Others say he is not alone either. Activity in the kitchen (items moving around, sounds of footsteps, etc.) seems to suggest a former servant may still be there as well.

Address: 4580 Rachel's Lane
Website: www.thehermitage.com
Activity: A, E, T

Glimpses of apparitions, the sounds of disembodied voices, and objects being manipulated by unseen hands top the list of activity at this plush getaway.

Address: 1001 Broadway
Website: www.unionstationhotelnashville.com
Activity: A, R, E, T

Nashville Tennessee State Capitol Building

Built in 1859, this massive structure was modeled after the monument of Lysicrates in Greece by an architect who is buried in the building above the cornerstone (William Strickland). During the Civil War, the area was occupied by Union forces, who renamed the spot Fort Andrew Johnson. The Capitol is still in use by the Tennessee government today—though you can tour the facilities and check out some of their wonderful murals and pieces of art there. If you're lucky, you may even see one of the ghosts there as well. It's rumored that Strickland now roams the building with the spirit of Samuel Morgan (the money man for the project, who is also interred in the Capitol building). Witnesses say the two argue much like they did when they worked together to fund and build the structure.

Address: 400 Charlotte Avenue
Website: www.bonps.org/tour/capitol
Activity: A, E

Nashville Union Station Hotel

Housed within a railroad station that dates back to 1900, this upscale masterpiece is a pleasure to visit. In addition to luxurious rooms and furnishings, the hotel offers the highly touted Prime 108 restaurant right on the premises. The station was built in a unique Gothic design (Richardsonian-Romanesque to be exact) and was later the site of a tragic accident (or at least near to the site). In 1918 two passenger trains collided head-on, killing 101 people and injuring an additional 171. It is because of this horrible loss of life that folks believe the hotel to now be haunted.

Red Boiling Springs Thomas House

News concerning the haunting of this bed and breakfast became nationally known when the television series *Paranormal State* featured the house on one of their episodes. Dating back to 1890, the place was recently renovated after a fire tore through the home (2001). In addition to providing accommodations, the B&B also has a dinner theater program and a Sunday buffet. Information regarding the haunting of the Thomas House is widespread thanks to the televised program and concerns the spirit of a little girl who is thought to have died there. Red Boiling Springs is known for its spa-like waters and was founded when travelers came to partake in these healing properties. The female spirit that walks this house is thought to have come for this reason—but didn't make it through her illness. She has been seen and heard in many areas of the house—but especially in the now-infamous Room 37.

Address: 520 East Main Street
Website: www.thomashousehotel.com
Activity: A, E, T, S

Rugby Newbury House Bed & Breakfast

This area was a popular place for the British to settle in during the 1800s. When Thomas Hughes, an English author, moved in (circa 1880), the town of Rugby was formed. Even today, it's said the town is like an English Victorian village—though not exactly the Utopian-styled colony that Hughes envisioned. The Newbury House was originally constructed as a boardinghouse for the travelers coming in to settle. It pretty much does the same thing today—though the six rooms have been significantly updated since then! As a paranormal enthusiast, you will probably want to rent Room 2. Over the years, there have been significant reports of a male apparition standing in this room (thought to be a Mr. Charles Oldfield, who passed away there of heart failure in the 1880s). Other reported activity includes disembodied voices and doors that open/close by themselves.

Address: 5517 Rugby Highway
Website: www.historicrugby.org
Activity: A, E, T

Sevierville Little Greenbrier Lodge

This country inn is said to be haunted by a previous owner of the property, Margretta Craig. According to the owners of the lodge, they even have a photograph of the ghost—it hangs in the room that shares her name. (This is the area that the spirit is also thought to spend the most time). The lodge first opened in 1939 and is going as strong as ever today. If you visit, you will have a great time exploring the premises, as well as the nearby outdoors. The ghost of Margretta is said to be quite pleasant and is known for closing doors behind people and generally helping out around the house. Rent her room, and perhaps you will get to meet the friendly ghost at Greenbrier.

Address: 3685 Lyon Springs Road
Website: www.innsite.com/inns/A105241
Activity: A, M, E, T

Shiloh Shiloh National Military Park

When this battle took place in April of 1862, it was one of the first major clashes of the Civil War. With over 23,000 casualties, Shiloh would remain a bloody memory for everyone who fought there. Confederate forces would suffer the loss of their commander, General Albert Sidney Johnston, as well as Kentucky governor George W. Johnson. The battle raged for two days and ended with a Union victory that drove southern troops south to Corinth, Mississippi. The park today has many of the major battle points marked, including the Hornet's Nest (where many have reported hearing the ghostly sounds of battle still occurring) and Bloody Pond (where the apparition of a woman, thought to be a nurse who tended the wounded there, has been seen). You can also visit the national cemetery, watch a wonderful film about the battle at the welcome center, and pick up books/videos concerning Shiloh and the Civil War at their gift shop.

Address: 1055 Pittsburg Landing Road
Website: www.nps.gov/shil/
Activity: A, R, E

Smyrna The Sam Davis Home and Museum

This historic house was built in 1810 by Moses Ridley, and was already well-worn before the Davis family purchased the property in 1850. During the Civil War, this household was one of sorrow—Sam Davis was hanged on November 27, 1863, after being convicted of spying on the Union army. Visitors to the museum can see exhibits of the period, as well as items that belonged to the Davis family. Though ghost stories are not part of the tours, you may be able to get a tale or two out of the staff. It was they who reported to the *Murfreesboro Post* that they were experiencing paranormal activity on the property. According to this account, the sounds of a woman weeping have been heard in the museum, and visitors have told of seeing the apparition of a man that resembles Oscar Davis.

Address: 1399 Sam Davis Road
Website: www.samdavishome.org
Activity: A, E

Wartrace Walking Horse Hotel

This historic site was first constructed in 1917 and is said to be the birthplace of the famous Tennessee Walking Horse. There are several paranormal tales concerning this hotel—the first of which involves a Vietnam vet who is said to have killed several people there in the 1970s while experiencing a war-related flashback (the residual sounds of the violence are still said to be heard today). More recently, the new owner, Joe Peters, suffered the loss of his wife, Chais, prior to opening the newly renovated hotel (he named the music hall there for her). Since he has moved in, a female apparition has been witnessed on the property (as well as heard). Hot spots in the Walking Horse include Room 11 and the entire third floor (in the process of being renovated). Paranormal investigators, including Paranormal Inc from Memphis, have investigated this site and confirmed the activity.

Address: 101 Spring Street
Website: www.walkinghorsehotel.com
Activity: A, E, T, O, C

TEXAS

Abilene Fort Phantom Hill

Originally named Post on the Clear Fork of the Brazos, this fort was established in 1851 by the U.S. Army to guard frontiersmen pushing west. And though the military moved on in 1854 (and a fire took out most of the area), the place remains as one of the most pristine historic sites in the state. You can visit the original stone guardhouse, powder magazine, and commissary on the post, as well as see a great example of early life in Texas. If you're lucky, you may even see a ghost! Going back to the early soldiers who occupied the fort, sightings of spectral Indians on the grounds occurred often (and is said to be the reason the fort was renamed its current moniker). There is also a female apparition that's said to roam the nearby lake who's been dubbed the "Lady of the Lake." But the most commonly reported activity is the appearance of misty apparitions in the old powder magazine building.

Address: FM Road 600
Website: www.fortphantom.org
Activity: A, R, M

Abilene The Grace Museum

Once known as the Grace Hotel, this building now hosts three separate museums. In addition to that, the facility also holds special events in their elegantly restored ballroom. There's definitely plenty to do here: the History Museum features a restored boot shop, the Art Museum contains five galleries, and the Children's Museum has a miniature version of the Paramount Theater! The hotel itself dates back to 1909 and is listed on the National Register of Historic Places—and it is considered to be haunted. Sightings of apparitions and the sounds of voices/footsteps have been heard on the premises since it was a hotel in the 1970s. Most of the activity is said to happen in the ballroom and on the third floor where the History Museum resides.

Address: 102 Cypress Street
Website: www.thegracemuseum.org
Activity: A, E, T

Austin Inn at Pearl Street

Located on historic Judge's Hill, this circa 1896 home was the residence of Judge Charles A. Wilcox and his wife Stella. They raised five children in the house and would eventually move on to other climes, leaving the property to sit. In 1993, the house was purchased and renovated into a magnificent bed and breakfast that serves as a local favorite spot for weddings. The inn is also noted for its persistent residual haunting. According to several witnesses, the apparition of Stella Wilcox can be seen walking from the Gothic Suite down the hall and into the French Room. Others have seen the apparition of Stella gently holding a small child in a rocking chair located in the French Room. It's known that Stella lost two of her children (both at the age of two) while living in the home, so the context of this tragic site is appropriate.

Address: 1809 Pearl Street
Website: www.innpearl.com
Activity: R, A, T

Austin The Tavern Restaurant & Bar

When this location was first built as a grocery store in 1916, this area of Austin was the outskirts of town. Now it's in the heart of a bustling downtown neighborhood. Of course, it isn't a grocery store any more either. The Tavern with its "air conditioned" bar is a favorite hangout for twenty-somethings in the capital city. The business sprung into existence right after the repeal of prohibition—though rumors point

to the place operating as an illegal speakeasy for some time prior. And this takes us to the ghost dubbed "Emily" by the staff. she is thought to be a prostitute who worked there during the speakeasy years. She has been seen staring out of second-floor windows after closing and is usually the scapegoat for strange happenings in the restaurant, such as dishes moving around and televisions turning on/off.

Address: 922 West 12th Street
Website: www.austintavern.com
Activity: A, T

Austin Texas Governor's Mansion

Dating back to 1856, this mansion served as the home of the state governor, starting with Elisha Marshall Pease. The entire estate was recently renovated to the tune of $4 million and is now decked out with authentic nineteenth-century American furniture, including an original writing desk that belonged to Stephen F. Austin. Over the years, locals in Austin have spun quite a few tales about the mansion. According to various reports, up to four ghosts may inhabit the premises. The first is said to be a maid that worked there—she is supposed to be seen standing outside the home. Then there's the ghost of Pendleton Murrah, a governor who supported the Confederacy and fled to Mexico, and the spirit of Sam Houston, who likes to hang out around his old bed. But the most commonly told tale is that of Pendleton Murrah's nephew, who reportedly shot himself in an upstairs bedroom and is now seen and heard moaning there.

Address: 1010 Colorado Street
Website: www.txfgm.org
Activity: A, E

Corpus Christi Blackbeard's on the Beach

The kitchen of this ocean side restaurant was once the original bar there. Owners of the property added on to the structure, making the place not only the oldest bar on the beach, but one of the best. Known to locals as a fun rock-'n-roll bar, Blackbeard's is a favorite haunt with the locals. It's also popular with a prankster spirit that's said to reside in the restaurant. Patrons have witnessed salt shakers jumping around on a table, chairs moving by themselves, and doors opening on their own. The spirit is thought to be a man who was killed on the property while fighting another over a red-haired girl. Since there's no history to confirm this murder, though, the ghost remains a point of controversy.

Address: 3117 North Surfside
Website: http://blackbeardsrestaurant.net
Activity: T

Corpus Christi USS Lexington Museum on the Bay

Commissioned in 1943 for World War II, the USS Lexington is an Essex-class aircraft carrier. It operated until 1991 when it was decommissioned and docked permanently in Corpus Christi. The ship was involved with almost every major campaign of the war and was responsible for destroying over 800 aircraft and sinking 300,000 tons of enemy cargo. With this much action, it seems little wonder that the ship would be haunted. According to the tour guides who walk this ship (as well as visitors over the years), the spirit of an engine-room operator called "Charly" has been seen in his old work area. A second apparition has been seen on the deck of the ship as well. It's said this sailor was killed when a Japanese plane crashed there. Visit the Lexington and tour the ship for yourself—even without the ghosts, the history makes this living museum a worthy trip.

Address: 2914 North Shoreline Boulevard
Website: www.usslexington.com
Activity: A, E, T

Dallas The Adolphus

This legendary hotel has had its fair share of ghost stories spun about it. St. Louis beer baron Adolphus Busch built the hotel when he found that Dallas didn't have any plush accommodations to fit his needs. It was constructed in 1912 and was an immediate success. Dignitaries and celebrities alike have made the Adolphus their home away from home while visiting the city. The story of the "Lady in White" at this hotel is a well-known urban legend in Dallas—though paranormal activity suggests that something is awry there. For years, employees have reported receiving phone calls from guests complaining about people running through the halls and playing loud old-time music. As for the famous ghost, she's said to be a bride who was left at the altar during her wedding at the hotel. Once she realized her fiancé was a no-show, she went to her room on the nineteenth floor and committed suicide. Her apparition is now witnessed in this area—or at least a female apparition of some kind is seen.

Address: 1321 Commerce Street
Website: www.hoteladolphus.com
Activity: A, E, R

Dallas Hotel Lawrence

This circa 1925 hotel is decorated to resemble the European "boutique" style accommodations that are so popular overseas. Even the on-site restaurant, Founders Grill, seems to take you back to simpler times. It was built to service travelers passing through the nearby Union Station, and if you are to believe the numerous stories concerning this haunted hotel, many have decided to stick around. The tenth floor is said to be haunted by a woman who fell to her death at the hotel in the 1940s (Room 1009 is said to be the most haunted), and the second floor (once an on-site casino) is said to be the stomping grounds for a male spirit that's been seen. But the most well-known story involves Room 807. A ghost nicknamed "Smiley" haunts this area and is known for blocking the door from opening and, at one time, grabbing a guest by the neck.

Address: 302 South Houston Street
Website: www.hotellawrencedallas.com
Activity: A, E, T

Dallas Snuffer's Restaurant & Bar

This is the original restaurant of this name (Snuffer's is a local chain has several locations in Texas) and it was first opened in 1978 by entrepreneur Pat Snuffer. The eatery could only hold 55 customers (a number that has now grown to 350) and was known even then for awesome cheddar fries. In addition to the great menu, Snuffer's is known today for their ghost as well. During the early years of operations, a young woman was reportedly killed in a restroom. Most believe the pale, misty apparition that's seen walking between the old and new sections of the restaurant is her. She's usually blamed for other activity on the premises as well—things like lights swinging on their own, sudden cold spots, and chairs moving by themselves.

Address: 3526 Greenville Avenue
Website: www.snuffers.com
Activity: A, M, T, C

El Paso Camino Real

Visitors to this circa 1912 hotel are treated to a number of amenities. There's the Azulejos restaurant, the Dome restaurant (and bar) and a number of plush suites in the heart of downtown El Paso. History is evident in this old building when you see their crystal chandeliers and Tiffany-designed dome ceiling. This hotel did not skimp on the details when it was renovated by the Camino Real chain. The haunting on the other hand, is lacking quite a few details. What is known is that a female spirit dubbed the "Lady in White" has been seen quite a few times in the building (usually in the basement, but reports have come from the common areas as well). However, there's no name to attach to the entity or any details concerning why she is there. She simply is.

Address: 101 South El Paso Street
Website: www.caminoreal.com
Activity: A

Fort Davis Fort Davis National Historic Site

Visitors to this historic location are treated to one of the finest examples of an Indian Wars–era fort. It was occupied between 1854 and 1891 by American troops whose primary mission was to protect supplies and mail moving west. The site today has a visitor's center, five fully restored buildings, and numerous other ruins. It will take you an entire day to tour the whole fort—especially if you want to spend some time in their haunted areas. The old hospital on the property is said to be a vortex of sorts: visitors have experienced visions of the past, seen apparitions, and felt cold spots. There is also residual activity on the grounds as visitors have reported hearing the sounds of horses and soldiers there.

Address: 101 Lt. Henry Flipper Drive
Website: www.nps.gov/FODA/
Activity: R, A, C

Fort Worth Miss Molly's Hotel

Talk about a good place going bad! This location started out as a family boardinghouse, but would end up servicing the local male population as a bordello. It was built in 1910 and is located in the famous Fort Worth's Stockyards. Though it has "hotel" in the name, the place is really more of a bed and breakfast. They feature seven guest rooms decked out in period furnishings and about the same number of spirits as well. The ghosts are said to be "working girls" of the bordello days, and they like to hang out in the Cowboys and Cattlemen's rooms. The spirit of a little girl has also been seen on the property who's thought to date back to the boarding house days. Activity in the hotel includes apparitions, objects moving of their own accord and disembodied voices. Regardless of their shady past, this B&B is a welcome and luxurious getaway.

Address: 109 West Exchange Avenue
Website: www.missmollyshotel.com
Activity: A, E, T

Fort Worth The Texas White House Bed and Breakfast

This circa 1910 house was the home of the Newkirk family. The last member of the family passed away in 1967 and the property was converted into several businesses before becoming a bed and breakfast. Visitors to the B&B receive personal attention in this five-room guesthouse that features on-site spa services (such as massages and facials) and a full gourmet breakfast. And for female guests, this property can make for an interesting paranormal evening. It's said that women who sleep in the Lone Star Room often feel the strange sensation of someone getting into bed with them. One guest even reported feeling someone sleeping back-to-back with them, felt them get up and then witnessed the light in the room switching on by itself! The ghost is harmless, though, and thought to be Mr. Newkirk, who passed away in his old home.

Address: 1417 Eighth Avenue
Website: www.texaswhitehouse.com
Activity: E, T

Fort Worth Thistle Hill House Museum

Owned and operated by Historic Fort Worth, Inc., this 1904 estate house was built by A. B. Wharton for his wife, Electra Waggoner. They would sell the property in 1911 to Winfield Scott, who would pass away while renovations he ordered were still unfinished. (He converted the home from a Colonial-style dwelling to a Greek Revival style). The current owners offer tours of the premises (check their website for more info) and even allow people to rent out the property for private events. If you visit the mansion, keep an eye out for the "Lady in White" that appears on the grand staircase (thought to be Electra). Additional activity includes spectral music that's heard in the ballroom and the occasional ghostly voice.

Address: 1509 Pennsylvania Avenue
Website: www.historicfortworth.org
Activity: A, R, E

Galveston 1859 Ashton Villa

This home was one of Galveston's first Broadway mansions. It dates back to the year in its name and was built by James Brown to be a place of opulence. It would take four years to complete—pretty much existing in a constant state of renovation during the Civil War despite being used as a Confederate hospital for a time. It now belongs to the Galveston Historical Foundation and is available for rent. (It's quite popular for weddings considering the famous Gold Room and the magnificent ballroom). The resident spirit of the mansion is said to be Bettie Brown, who has been seen walking up the stairway and standing on the second-floor landing. Others have reported strange activity in the Gold Room (also attributed to Bettie), which includes furniture moving by itself and feeling the sensation of someone standing alongside you.

Address: 2328 Broadway Street
Website: www.galvestonhistory.com
Activity: A, T

Galveston Hotel Galvez

After a massive storm took out most of the beachfront property on this island in 1900, it was decided the city needed an upscale getaway. The Hotel Galvez was constructed on the site of the old Beach Hotel and opened its doors to much acclaim in 1911. Though there have been numerous famous guests at this hotel (including Dwight D. Eisenhower, Frank Sinatra, and Howard Hughes), none are as famous as the ghost that haunts this place. According to the tale, a young woman was staying at the hotel while waiting for her beau to return from sea. She would climb to the top of the turrets and watch for his ship. When she heard it sunk, she committed suicide right there on the property. She is now said to haunt Room 500, where guests have reported seeing her apparition and hearing her voice. Other hot spots include the ladies restroom (where stalls have been shook by invisible hands), the back stairway (the site of a "presence"), and Room 505 (haunted by a dark entity that smells of gardenias).

Address: 2024 Seawall Boulevard
Website: www.wyndham.com
Activity: A, E, T, N

Goliad Presidio La Bahia

Haunted locations don't get much more historic than this circa 1721 fortress. It was built on the ruins of the doomed Fort St. Louis, but due to trouble with the local Native Americans, the structure would move twice! The post would endure multiple attacks from the French, the Texas Revolution, and a horrible event that occurred in 1836. It's now known as the Goliad Massacre and it involved the execution of 342 men (more than twice the number of deaths at the Alamo and San Jacinto combined) by Mexican soldiers. When you tour this site, you will want to pay the most attention to the area around the old chapel and the living quarters. The apparition of a woman has been seen in the chapel, while the spirit of a priest hangs around the front door there. The old barracks is the site of cold spots and the sounds of disembodied voices.

Address: U.S. Highway 183 7A
Website: www.presidiolabahia.org
Activity: A, E, C

Grand Prairie Ripley's Believe it or Not!

Believe it or not, this place is haunted. At least the Louis Tussaud's Palace of Wax section of the museum is. Can there possibly be any place creepier than a haunted wax museum? Activity in the building is blamed on a fire that's said to have broken out there in 1988 that almost completely destroyed the place (though I could find no information regarding any deaths in said fire). Ghostly happenings usually include motion detectors going off for no reason, problems with the electricity in this section, and the sounds of a person screaming in agony.

Address: 601 Palace Parkway
Website: www.grandprairie.ripleys.com
Activity: E, T

Gruene Adobe Verde

This Tex-Mex restaurant is a favorite with the locals in Gruene. With great food and even better happy hour prices, it's no wonder the place is almost always busy. When you visit, take a look around. This place used to be one of the first-ever electric cotton gins in the area (dating back to the 1920s). Local legend says that a worker named "Frank" once came to work at the gin in a despondent mood. It seemed his lady had left him, so Frank decided to hang himself right there. Employees of the Adobe Verde blame most strange happenings around the restaurant on Frank, who is said to now be a prankster in the afterlife. Activity in the restaurant includes items moving around in the dining room, the sounds of footsteps, and the occasional light turning itself on or off.

Address: 1724 Hunter Road
Website: www.adobeverde.com
Activity: E, T

Hillsboro 1895 Tarlton House B&B

Sometimes a story is just so tragic that it haunts a place forever. Some say this is true of the haunting of this bed and breakfast. Greene Duke Tarlton built this home for his new bride, Sarah Elizabeth, in 1895. They lived a happy existence there until poor Sarah passed away in 1907. He would mourn and remarry another Elizabeth (Millard) in 1910. When she, too, passed away in 1931, Greene lasted only one day before he joined her. The official cause of death for him was "influenza," but there's a darker version of the story. Some say he couldn't take losing another wife, so he hanged himself in the home. Either way, visitors who stay on the third floor have reported hearing phantom footsteps and feeling a cool breeze brush their face. At least one person actually saw the apparition of Mr. Tarlton as well. Get more info when you visit this B&B. They have ghost tours and even keep a journal of their haunted happenings.

Address: 211 North Pleasant Street
Website: www.1895tarltonhouse.com
Activity: A, C, E

Houston La Carafe Wine Bar

This location is in the oldest commercial building still in use in Houston (it's listed as such on the National Register of Historic Places)—and the bar itself is believed to be the oldest drinking establishment in the city. Situated in the heart of what used to be the Old Market Square, it's a popular place for those who want a stellar wine list and great music. The haunting of this bar is said to be (in part) caused by a brothel that existed on the square. The madame, Pamelia Mann, is now said to be seen in La Carafe—along with several other entities (to possibly include Sam Houston). But, perhaps, the most commonly seen spirits are those of John Kennedy, the former owner of the building who once ran a bakery there, and "Carl," who's said to be a former bartender.

Address: 813 Congress Avenue
Website: www.owlnet.rice.edu/~hans320/
    projects/lacarafe/
Activity: A, S, E, T

Jefferson Cavalier House Bed & Breakfast

Originally built as a tavern, this house has stood the test of time since 1850. It's now a B&B that features three guest rooms, a gentlemen's parlor, and a massive front veranda. Thanks to an article written about the haunting of this house in the magazine *Haunted Times*, the ghosts at the Cavalier are quite a local draw. Most believe the haunting to be of a residual nature, since a lot of the sounds experienced seem to date back to the tavern (such as the sounds of boots walking around the room, music, voices, etc.). However, others believe there is an intelligent spirit on the premises as well. You should probably visit and decide for yourself—you'll have a great time exploring all the haunts of Jefferson, Texas.

Address: 202 East Dixon Street
Website: www.jeffersoncavalierhouse.com
Activity: R, E, T

Jefferson The Grove

You know you're in for a great paranormal getaway when the place is owned by the author of several books on hauntings! Such is the case with the Grove. Built in 1861 by Frank and Minerva Stilley, this tour home features a formal parlor, the original dining room set (dating back to 1885), and a garden that's featured in the local Butterfly Garden Tour. The house also plays host to three spirits: a man in a black suit (who's been seen in the garden), an elderly gentleman (seen in the home), and the infamous "Lady in White." She has been witnessed many times over the years by people in the neighborhood—both inside and outside the home. She's thought to be simply going out to the porch to survey the neighborhood. Check out the Grove's website to find out what's going on.

Address: 405 Moseley Street
Website: www.thegrove-jefferson.com
Activity: A, T, S, E, N

Jefferson The Jefferson Hotel

This set of historic lodgings began as a massive warehouse for storing cotton. At the turn of the century, though, it was converted into a hotel. During the 1920s, the property was known as the Crystal Palace and was a local hangout for those who wanted to enjoy some ragtime music and do some dancing. These days, it's a quaint hotel that oozes history—and features a fantastic restaurant called Lamache's. As for the ghosts, you can read about them on the hotel's website. Almost every area of the hotel is considered to be haunted and guests have had quite a few encounters with the spectral residents. Activity on the premises includes disembodied voices (sometimes children), the sounds of residual music, and apparitions. There's the ghost of a man in black who visits people in Room 5, a young woman who hangs out in Room 14, and Room 24 is haunted by a small woman who's said to touch people with icy fingers.

Address: 124 West Austin Street
Website: www.historicjeffersonhotel.com
Activity: A, R, E, T, M

Laredo La Posada Hotel

This set of upscale accommodations was built upon the foundations of the city's first government, the Casa Judicial. It was constructed in 1916 as a Spanish Colonial convent and serviced the area as a school. The site was converted into a hotel in 1961 by a local businessman—though the original structures still stand on the property. The San Agustin Convent is now the San Agustin Ballroom and the George Washington's Birthday Association Museum. There is also the former A. M. Bruni residence (a Victorian home) that now houses the Tack Room Bar & Grill. For paranormal tourists, this hotel provides yet another historic exhibit—the spirit of an early-twentieth-century nun. She's been seen in the ballroom and is known for appearing with an intense cold spot.

Address: 1000 Zaragoza Street
Website: www.laposadahotel.com
Activity: A, C, E, T

Laredo Rio Grande Plaza

How often do you get to check out paranormal activity at a three-star hotel? The Rio Grande Plaza is a 15-story tall, 205-room getaway that features a pool and fitness center. It's a rather modern affair and would seem to be the farthest thing from being haunted. According to employees and guests, though, the place does have some activity. It's said to stem from a local tragedy at the nearby Rio Grande River. A woman

named "Maria" is said to have pushed her three children off a cliff, killing them. She then returned to the same spot the next day and leaped from the precipice, killing herself. Because of these acts, spirits are now said to roam the area around the hotel. Go for a late-night stroll and see if you can find Maria. She's said to approach those she sees with her arms reaching out—like she's trying to grab one of her children.

Address: 1 South Main Avenue
Website: www.venturastreet.com/
  RioGrandePlaza/
Activity: A

Liberty The Haunted Historic Ott Hotel

With the word "haunted" right in its name, you know there are paranormal things happening at this hotel! The property dates back to 1928 and was originally owned by Joshua and Sallie Ott. They built the place to capitalize on the sudden influx of people to the area that came because of the oil boom. It was also stationed close to the railway and provided overnight accommodations for visitors traveling through. This hotel is quite liberal toward ghost hunters these days; basically, if you rent the rooms for your investigators to stay in, they get to investigate! This is good news when you consider the tale of their two ghosts. According to the story, a girl named Lucy was meeting her lover at the hotel for a rendezvous when her husband came knocking at the door. They started arguing and two shots were heard. When folks rushed over to see what happened, Lucy and her husband lay dead. It's a mystery who actually shot them, but both of them are now said to haunt the Ott Hotel.

Address: 305 Travis Street
Website: www.hauntedotthotel.com
Activity: A, E, R

Mineral Wells The Crazy Water Hotel

This hotel was constructed on the site of the city's third well (circa 1927)—and earned a unique name by doing so. The story goes that a local insane woman would visit the well there and drink on a daily basis. After doing this for a while, the townsfolk noticed she became much better—some say she was even completely cured. It wasn't long before the Crazy Well became the Crazy Pavilion and then grew into the Crazy Hotel. The place is now a long-term rental establishment with an assisted living option, so you will have to settle for simply touring the building (unless you move to Mineral Wells). Ghost tales include the spirit of a young girl who's been seen and heard crying in the basement and the apparition of a man in a coat and hat has been witnessed in the kitchen.

Address: 401 North Oak Avenue
Website: www.hauntedotthotel.com
Activity: A, E

Nacogdoches Sterne Hoya House Museum and Library

This living museum was once the home of Adolphus Sterne and was built in 1830 before Texas was even a republic! It was visited by several key figures in Texas' history, including Sam Houston and Davy Crockett, and even provided lodging for a group of New Orleans Greys on their way to fight at the Alamo. Tours are offered (check their website for hours), so you will be able to check out this historic home to see if it is haunted for yourself. The ghost story about this home is a strange one: Employees working on the property have reported encountering an entity on the second floor that likes to touch people. On at least one occasion, the touchee was said to suddenly feel dizzy and felt the need to exit the area. But isn't this how most people feel when a ghost touches them?

Address: 211 South Lanana
Website: www.ci.nacogdoches.tx.us
Activity: T

New Braunfels The Faust Hotel

The Traveler's Hotel first opened its doors to the public in 1929 and it was a warm welcome for those returning from World War I. It was built by Walter Faust and it managed to just get rolling when the Great Depression hit. That, coupled with a boll weevil blight, brought the hotel to its knees, but it did not close. These days, the hotel is thriving with an on-site microbrewery (The Faust Brewing Company), a lounge, and a scenic courtyard. The Faust also has a few ghosts as well. A male apparition dressed in old-fashioned clothes is seen, sometimes accompanied by a female apparition holding a child. The usual paranormal report, though, concerns the spirit of a little girl who plays in the hallways of the hotel.

Address: 240 South Seguin Avenue
Website: www.fausthotel.com
Activity: A, E, T

Port Aransas The Tarpon Inn

Built in 1886 using the lumber from an old set of Civil War barracks, the Tarpon Inn was created as temporary housing for people working on the Mansfield Jetty. The building was rebuilt in 1919 after enduring a fire, a hurricane, and a tidal wave (the current version of the inn today) and it recently underwent a renovation. The property features 24 guest rooms that all open onto the building's massive porch, a swimming pool, and the new Palapa Room. According to several sources, there is a unique haunted location at the Tarpon—a bathroom, that's said to sometimes glow with an eerie spectral light and to be filled with disembodied voices. Check in with the staff of the inn to get more info about the privy and to book your stay.

Address: 200 East Cotton Avenue
Website: www.thetarponinn.com
Activity: O, E

San Antonio The Church at King William

This location is mostly known to paranormal enthusiasts by its former name, the Alamo Street Restaurant and Theatre. Located in a former church, this location is one of the city's few operating dinner theatres. Where else are you going to get a good meal as well as get a little art in your life? Like most theatres, there are several ghost stories about this site. The first concerns the spirit of a former actress named Margaret Gething, who's been seen in the old choir loft. Then there's the ghost that's been named "Eddie" by the staff. He's said to be a prankster and that he likes to play with silverware and dishes on the tables, as well as move things around in the kitchen.

Address: 1150 South Alamo Street
Website: www.churchbistroandtheatre.com
Activity: A, T

San Antonio Emily Morgan Hotel

The Emily Morgan may only date back to 1984, but the building it resides in was constructed in 1924. Originally known as the Medical Arts Building, it functioned as such until 1976. It was then converted into an office building, then this hotel. Emily's features a unique on-site library, welcomes pets, and has one of the best cocktail lounges in the city (called Oro Restaurant & Bar). Of course, with a past that includes patients and doctors, it would figure that the hotel would be haunted. Little things happen all over the hotel: doors slamming, cold spots, lights switching on/off, etc. Employees say that the seventh, ninth, and twelfth floors are the most active—with the exception of the basement.

This area was used as a morgue and is said to have apparitions that frequent it.

Address: 705 East Houston Street
Website: www.emilymorganhotel.com
Activity: A, T, C

San Antonio Menger Hotel

William A. Menger built this hotel in 1859 close to the Alamo, and it was a popular destination for politicians in its heyday. People like Theodore Roosevelt, Ulysses S. Grant, and Robert E. Lee stayed at the hotel and enjoyed the amenities. You can do the same—although the amenities are quite updated these days (such as the restaurant, fitness center, and pool). It's believed that the Menger hosts upward of 30 ghosts—there's enough haunted tales about the hotel to fill a book by itself. The spirits there are said to include Teddy Roosevelt (in the lobby bar), Captain Richard King (said to haunt the suite that bears his name), and a frumpy woman who's seen in the lobby. But the most well-known ghost story is that of Sallie White. She was an employee at the hotel who was beaten to death by her husband after he found out she cheated on him. The Menger paid for her funeral and now her apparition is seen in the Victorian Wing of the hotel.

Address: 204 Alamo Plaza
Website: www.mengerhotel.com
Activity: A, E, T, C, S

San Antonio Mission San Jose

This is one of four mission-style communities included in the San Antonio Missions National Historic Park. They were all constructed in the 1700s in order to spread Catholicism in the area, as well as to stem the tide of foreign expansion. The church at Mission San Jose y San Miguel de Aguayo was built between 1762 and 1782. It's known as the Queen of the Missions and has its own legendary love story. It's said that one of the workers who was building the church fell in love with a female caretaker on the premises. The woman died while the church was still under construction, so they added a "Rose window" in her honor. The apparition of said woman is, reportedly, seen staring from this window. Urban legend or truth? Go find out.

Address: 6701 San Jose Drive
Website: www.nps.gov/saan/
Activity: A

San Antonio Sheraton Gunter Hotel

Built as a luxury getaway in 1909, the Gunter is a San Antonio landmark. Now owned by the Sheraton chain, this hotel features Barron's Restaurant and a bakery that's been operating for over a hundred years. With the Majestic Theatre located just across the street, the Gunter has been a celebrity hangout over the years as well, hosting guests like Roy Rogers and John Wayne. The haunting of the hotel is said to stem from a crime that happened in 1965. A man checked in with a false name (Albert Knox) along with a blonde girlfriend. Three days later, a maid entered Room 636 to find "Mr. Knox" standing beside a bloody body. He fled the crime scene but was tracked down at the nearby St. Anthony Hotel where he shot himself to avoid capture. Since these incidents occurred, Room 636 has been haunted. Guests have reported seeing a female apparition walking toward them with her arms outstretched.

Address: 205 East Houston Street
Website: www.gunterhotel.com
Activity: A, E

Spring Wunsche Brothers Café

If you're looking for one of the best cheeseburgers you've ever eaten while you're looking for ghosts, then this café should be your first stop. The property dates back to 1902 when it was known as the Wunsche Brothers Hotel & Saloon (and some say it was known as a brothel as well). It closed down during prohibition, but would reappear as the Spring Café in 1949. The last member of the family to have worked in the old hotel was Willie Wunsche, who died on the property when he was in his 90s. It is Willie that's also said to still be hanging around the café. The sounds of footsteps and things moving around on the upper floor of the building are commonplace at the eatery and most are comforted by the thought that old Willie is still looking over the business.

Address: 103 Midway Street
Website: www.wunschebroscafe.com
Activity: E, T

Waxahachie Catfish Plantation Restaurant

This Victorian manor was built in 1895 by the Anderson family. It remained a family home for decades until it was transformed into a marvelous Cajun restaurant (though it did sit empty for some time). Once renovations on the restaurant were finished, the owners of the eatery (as well as patrons) started noticing some strange things were afoot. Dishes would be found stacked up, ghostly blue lights would be seen in empty rooms, and the apparition of a woman was witnessed staring out a front window. The haunting of this location has been featured in books and on several television programs, and it is always the subject of conversation when folks eat there. Feel free to get current ghost info while you enjoy a good southern meal.

Address: 814 Water Street
Website: www.catfishplantation.com
Activity: A, O, T, E

Yorktown Yorktown Memorial Hospital Site

This former hospital is now an official ghost-hunting property. It was operated between 1950 and the late 1980s by the Felician Sisters of the Roman Catholic Church and is said to be quite haunted. Typical experiences here include disembodied voices, shadowy apparitions, and the sounds of footsteps. The building can be rented for your group to investigate (just visit their website for more information regarding dates and pricing) or you can visit for a tour (this must be set up in advance). The property is associated with another nearby haunted site—Victoria's Black Swan Inn—so it is also possible to make this paranormal trip a two-for-one investigation and set up an advance price for both places.

Address: 728 West Main Street
Website: www.yorktownhospital.com
Activity: S, E, T, O

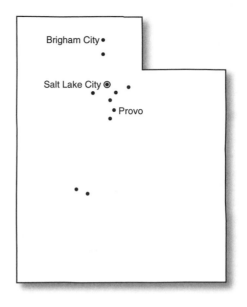

UTAH

Brigham City Golden Spike Historic Site

This national park commemorates the day (May 10, 1869) that the Central and Pacific Railroads connected their tracks to form one of the first transcontinental systems. If you tour this site, you can actually drive on a portion of those original tracks—as well as catch a ride on a locomotive. When the famous "golden spike" was pounded in the ground back then, though, there was a group of people there who were not so celebratory. They were the Chinese immigrants who toiled daily laying down the track. The activity in this area is a residual haunting that reminds us of this. Visitors to the park have reported hearing disembodied voices and cries along the original tracks, and have seen ghostly blobs of light bobbing along. Like most haunted railroads, locals will say these are the phantom lights of past trains, but it's more likely that these are simply "ghost lights" or orbs of spirits who crossed over there.

Address: Highway 83 West of the City
Website: www.nps.gov/gosp/
Activity: R, E, O

Brigham City Idle Isle Café

This local favorite is perhaps more known for their homemade candies than for the café—though this can be the reason for a visit as well. Another great excuse for swinging by Idle Isle would be to catch a glimpse of the Native American apparition that's been witnessed there! This location (along with several neighboring businesses) have all experienced paranormal activity—all thought to stem from this same spirit. Workers in the café have seen the male ghost standing near the soda fountain, and once downstairs in the candy-making area. This spirit is also known to move items in the shop. If this isn't enough to pique your interest, there's also the possibility of a second entity—that of a female dressed in mid-1900s attire. Both are reportedly part of old Main Street's past and like to visit the buildings in the area.

Address: 24 South Main Street
Website: www.idleisle.com
Activity: A, E, T

Brigham City Union Pacific Depot/ Railroad Museum

This depot opened in 1907 and was constructed to provide the Union Pacific railroad access to the Pacific Northwest. The line was instrumental in shuttling passengers in and out of the city, as well as bringing in supplies and food for the local community (not to mention the mail). During World War II, the use of this depot increased as soldiers traveled by rail to their areas of deployment. Today, the depot belongs to the Golden Spike Association of Box Elder County and it functions as a museum. Not long after beginning renovations to get the place ready to open to the public, volunteers started noticing strange things were afoot. A shadowy apparition was spotted several times, and the sounds of a disembodied voice/footsteps were heard. A local paranormal group was called in, and they captured evidence of the haunting. Visit this museum to capture your own.

Address: 800 West Forest Street
Website: www.brighamcity.utah.gov
Activity: A, S, E

Brighton Silver Fork Lodge

During the 1850s, a great portion of this building was used as a general store for miners working in the area. Today it is a classic ski lodge–style bed and breakfast that will place you in the vicinity of some of the state's best winter sports attractions. For many years now, employees of the Silver Fork have been talking about the ghostly happenings at this vacation spot—activity that almost seems "poltergeist" in nature. Numerous eyewitness accounts of items moving by themselves and appliances switching on/off have occurred there. Throw in a couple apparition sightings and the sounds of deep moans heard in various parts of the B&B and you have one interesting haunting. If you plan to visit this site, though, pay attention to the "high seasons" of skiing and snowboarding, as you may have to book well in advance to get rooms during these periods.

Address: 11332 East Big Cottonwood Canyon
Website: www.silverforklodge.com
Activity: A, E, T

Cove Fort Cove Fort Historic Site

In 1867, Mormon leader Brigham Young directed Ira Hinckley to build a fort to protect travelers journeying between Saint George and Salt Lake City. The fort was constructed on the remains of a former post (Fort Walden) and was built using volcanic rock found west of the property. This place is the last remaining Mormon fortress built during their travels west and it has endured many a hardship, as well as attacks from neighboring Native Americans. Employees at Cove Fort have been seeing strange things there for years—especially in the former Hinckley home. Sightings of an apparition—sometimes accompanied by a disembodied voice—have occurred in this area along with the overwhelming feeling of being watched. Check out the kitchen and "family rooms," as they are the hot spots for paranormal activity.

Address: Interstate 15 at Interstate 70
Website: www.covefort.com
Activity: A, E

Marysvale Moore's Old Pine Inn

Once known as the Pines Hotel, this location was first built in 1882, and it is the oldest running hotel in the state of Utah. Butch Cassidy was a regular visitor—and according to the inn's website, author Zane Grey wrote his novel *Riders of the Purple Sage* while staying there. Today, the inn likes to keep its Old West atmosphere, so you won't find any televisions in the rooms and much of the antique furnishings from the place's early days are still stationed throughout the property. There's also another remnant from the hotel's past that's still present: the ghosts of an elderly woman and two small children! These apparitions have been seen by several guests who have stayed there, and are a commonly discussed subject with the owners of the inn. So get a room at the Old Pine, check in with the innkeepers about current activity, and enjoy your stay in this historic hotel.

Address: 60 South State Street
Website: www.oldpineinn.com
Activity: A, E

Ogden Ben Lomond Historic Suites

This location was originally known as the Bigelow Hotel and it was constructed in 1927 in a rare Italian Renaissance Revival style. The place was built on the site of a former inn called the Reed Hotel, and was considered one of three "grand hotels" in Utah. Of the three, the Ben Lomond is the last to still provide accommodations. In 1933, Marriner S. Eccles bought the hotel and renamed it what it is today. As for the ghosts there—well, rumors starting circulating about the place being haunted in the 1960s. If you ask the employees there about the activity, you're most likely to hear the two following stories: During World War II, a woman checked into the hotel to await word concerning the welfare of her son who had been injured. When she found out he died, she checked out and disappeared (in another version, she kills herself). Now she is known for haunting Room 1106 where she has been seen, heard, and makes calls down to the front desk. The second tale involves a bride who drowned in a bathtub in Room 1102. She is thought to haunt this room, along with the spirit of her son who roams next door in Room 1101. When his mother drowned, he came to the hotel to get her belongings. He became so depressed and distraught at her death, that he committed suicide so he could join her.

Address: 2510 Washington Boulevard
Website: www.benlomondsuites.com
Activity: A, E, T, C

Ogden Gray Cliff Lodge Restaurant

This Craftsman-styled lodge is known for miles around for their Sunday brunch—as well as their home-cooked meals the other six days of the week. The paranormal activity at this restaurant is a mixture of past area inhabitants and a residual haunting that predates the coming of the "white man." Those who work at the Gray Cliff have had reports over the years from guests who have seen a shadowy apparition of a man in old-time clothes. He's thought to be a frontiersman who perhaps resided in the vicinity at some point. Along with this spirit, there are also sightings of Native American ghosts seen wandering outside the property and the phantom sounds of children playing in the halls of the lodge.

Address: 508 Ogden Canyon
Website: www.graycliffledge.com
Activity: A, R, E

Ogden Ogden Union Station

This historic station stands as a living monument and museum of Ogden's railroading history. The first version of this structure was completed in 1889 and was intended to serve the Union Pacific and Central Pacific railroads (which had recently joined their tracks). The station burned down in 1923 and was immediately replaced with the current version—a Spanish Colonial Revival masterpiece that was built over the basement of the first station. At one time, Ogden was considered a very rough town—and was once even dubbed the murder capital of the West! The nearby Ben Lomond Hotel was said to have had tunnels that ran under the city, and one of them supposedly connected to this station. The tunnels were used to ferry drugs, prostitutes, etc. With these types of goings-on, it's no wonder the station is haunted. Apparitions and disembodied voices are reported on a regular basis, and if you query the museum employees, you will get an earful.

Address: 2501 Wall Avenue
Website: www.theunionstation.org
Activity: A, E, S

Park City Snowed Inn Sleigh Company

Before visiting this location, be sure to check out their website for their current operating schedule, as they only offer sleigh rides during the snow season. This unique restaurant offers packages that include a meal with your sleigh ride (though both are available à la carte as well). According to locals familiar with the haunting tale of Snowed Inn, the structure was built to resemble a relative's home—the original owner's grandmother's house. This same grandma later passed away in this house and now walks the place in the afterlife. Her apparition has been seen in the restaurant, usually accompanied by the sounds of footsteps and her voice. Additional activity includes items moving on the tables and a strange mist that's been seen on the stairs leading to the second floor.

Address: 3770 North Highway 224
Website: www.snowedinnsleigh.com
Activity: A, M, E, T

Pleasant Grove The Grove Theatre

This theatre was one of the first silent movie venues in the area, and was originally known as the Alhambra. It was built by Albert Vanwagoner and his brothers and opened in 1926 to host a local Republican convention. The site was purchased in 1942 by John H. Miller, who changed the name to its current moniker. He owned the property for over 30 years before new owners took over the place in 1978, 1982, 1999, and 2003. Now the Grove is an event center that's available to the public for rent. Ghostly activity in the theatre was first noticed during a renovation prior to the 1999 opening. Employees were there working late at night when they heard voices, footsteps, and the sound of doors opening/closing coming from the upstairs area. There was nobody up there, so the sounds were unexpected. Shadow shapes and disembodied voices have also been witnessed in the front lobby of the theatre.

Address: 20 South Main Street
Website: www.groveeventcenter.com
Activity: S, E

Salt Lake City The Armstrong Mansion Bed and Breakfast

This Queen Anne home was completed in 1893 as a wedding gift from Francis Armstrong to his new bride, Isabel. They both lived and died while residing here (Francis died at the age of 59, but Isabel lived on until 1930). After that, the place went through a series of owners and vocations until a group of investors purchased the house and completely renovated it. Today it is a B&B that you can also rent for special events. The mansion is reputedly haunted by a past resident, Florence Armstrong, who is known for spooking guests and employees on the property. Maids have seen her spirit—and a guest even identified Florence from a picture that hangs there. This entity is said to visit folks who stay overnight as well. One couple was sleeping upstairs when they heard the sound of their closet door's handle jiggling during the night, and another reported seeing a female staring at them from their room's window as they were leaving for the evening.

Address: 667 East 100 South
Website: www.armstrongmansion.com
Activity: A, T

Salt Lake City Brigham Young Farm House/This is the Place Heritage Park

This house was the original home of Brigham Young, the infamous Mormon leader, and was built in 1863. It was used for experimental agriculture projects and was managed by several of Young's wives (at his peak, he had 56 of them!). During the 1970s, the farmhouse was moved into This is the Place Heritage Park, along with several other historic structures. Visitors have reported seeing the spectral image of a woman within the place—a woman that seems to resemble Ann Eliza Webb Dee Young, one of Brigham's wives who divorced him and then went on to denounce Mormonism. Her apparition is often accompanied by the sounds of footsteps and the smell of cooking that comes from the kitchen.

Address: 2601 East Sunnyside Avenue
Website: www.thisistheplace.org
Activity: A, E, N

Salt Lake City Deveraux Mansion Heritage Gardens

This location's past is as fascinating as it is eclectic. It first functioned as a private home when it was erected in 1857, but since then it has been an administrative office, a restaurant, and even a local haunted house—probably the most appropriate role for this historic house. This "for rent" mansion (events, meetings, ghost hunts, etc.) is thought to be haunted by the spirit of a young girl. Locals will regale you with tales concerning the young ghost and how she is known to appear with a sudden cold spot and has been seen peering from the second-floor windows. Owners over the years have reported phenomena as well—the sounds of the girl's voice has been heard coming from the upper level (laughing, singing, crying, etc.) and the entity has also thrown items, including the occasional slamming door.

Address: 340 West South Temple
Website: www.saltlakecity.com
Activity: A, E, T

Salt Lake City Fort Douglas Military Museum

Camp Douglas, predecessor to the fort, was established in 1862 to facilitate the delivery of local mail and to oversee the Mormon population (mainly to make sure they did not rebel against the government). The post saw minor action against local Native American tribes, but escaped the Civil War pretty much unharmed. When the war was over, it became an area logistics center until it was needed to house prisoners of war during both World Wars. It closed house in 1991 and is now a historic site and museum. The fort is well known for its ghosts, and tales concerning the haunting there are quite common—just ask employees on the site! Their most famous ghost is "Clem" who is said to be a Civil War-era soldier that likes to hang out in the museum. Then there is a female spirit who's been seen in Carlson Hall, and a young girl whose disembodied head has been witnessed floating in the Humanities House.

Address: 32 Potter Street
Website: www.fortdouglas.org
Activity: A, E, T

Salt Lake City McCune Mansion

This home was built by mining entrepreneur Alfred McCune and his wife, Elizabeth in 1900. They lived in the house until 1920. At that point, their child had reached adulthood, so they donated the place to the Mormon Church and moved away. The church transformed the mansion into the McCune School of Music, and then it became an events center, and then a dance school, and then ... finally ... a place for local receptions, parties, and events (as it remains today). As is usual with most historic houses, paranormal activity got kicked up when the furnishings were made-over. Voices, spectral music, and sudden cold spots top the list—though glimpses of two pale apparitions (thought to possibly be Alfred and a young girl who attended the music school) have also taken place.

Address: 200 North Main Street
Website: www.mccunemansion.com
Activity: A, E, R, T, C

Salt Lake City Shilo Inn Suites Hotel

The haunting of this chain hotel is quite a disturbing tale. It's said that in the 1970s, an insane mother came to the place with her children and then decided she would murder the kids and then commit suicide. She did this by throwing the children off a balcony and then leaping to her own death (in another version of this story, the father murdered all of them). Now, in the afterlife, they are all said to still roam the grounds—especially around the indoor pool. People have seen the apparitions of a woman along with a young girl and have heard female voices/laughter around the pool. The entities are also said to haunt the maintenance area of the hotel, but this section is off limits. Check in with the staff at this hotel to get recommendations and current paranormal sightings. Clearly, though, you will want a room by the pool.

Address: 206 South West Temple
Website: www.shiloinns.com
Activity: A, E

Santaquin Leslie's Family Tree Restaurant

This eatery is a local favorite for home-cooked food and is as well known for their hospitality as they are for their ghost. When the place first opened, folks who were there preparing for the day's business started seeing strange things around the building. Things like pots and pans being moved during the night, the doorbell ringing on its own, and the apparition of a woman who was seen in the backroom area. Though the identity of this female spirit is unknown, it's thought perhaps it has something to do with a local boy who drowned at the rear of the property in a canal. Or maybe not. Either way, the ghostly happenings continue at this restaurant and you can visit for your chance to see the apparition and to have a good meal.

Address: 77 West Main Street
Website: www.santaquin.org
Activity: A, E, T

Tooele The Kirk Hotel

This hotel dates back to 1928 and it has been continuously serving the Tooele community ever since. Most of the rooms have been completely renovated and the lodging is relatively close to most of the area sights. As for the haunting there ... well, there's not much information. The ghost stories have circulated for some time about the Kirk, but nobody has ever placed a name to the ghost, or even a gender for that matter. What is known is that hotel employees and guests have seen pale, barely visible apparitions (more like full-bodied mists, really) in various locations—including several guest rooms. Other activity includes items that are found moved during the night and the sounds of whispered voices. Check in with the hotel staff to get current paranormal info and for room suggestions. They should know where the action is happening.

Address: 57 West Vine Street
Website: www.kirkhotel.com
Activity: A, M, E, T

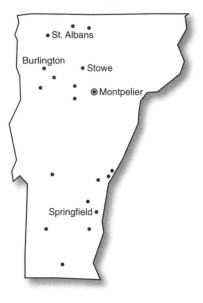

VERMONT

Burlington American Flatbread

Formerly known to paranormal investigators as the Carburs Restaurant, this eatery cooks up unique flatbread sandwiches and even brews its own beer. Haunted tales concerning the property began just after an employee of Carburs committed suicide in the basement. It's said that you can see the hole in the wall where the bullet landed—after it passed through the employee's skull. This has resulted in almost constant activity in the basement, which is a problem because it is also where kegs of beer and other restaurant items are stored. In particular, female employees don't like to venture into that area because the occurrences seem to happen more often when a woman is present. Though the majority of the tales at this restaurant involve the basement, the occasional event

does make its way to the dining room. Things like barware/diningware moving on the tables, doors slamming shut, and sudden drops in temperature that seem to indicate that diners aren't quite alone.

Address: 115 St. Paul Street
Website: www.americanflatbread.com
Activity: E, T, C

Enosburg Falls Enosburg Falls Opera House

This theater sprung into existence when a local medicine magnate, Dr. B. J. Kendall, donated this building to the city in 1892. Noted for its outstanding acoustics, the opera house played host to a number of musical composers and musicians over the years (including John Philip Sousa). In 1975, the Enosburg Opera House Association was formed and the declining property was renovated—a process that's still ongoing with the Friends of the Opera House today. To visit the theater, check out their calendar of community events. As for the ghost at this site, employees have decided he is Willy, the son of a laborer who fell to his death while doing repairs. Though he has never actually been seen, plenty of folks there have heard his voice/footsteps and found many a prop moved by unseen hands.

Address: 99 Depot Street
Website: www.enosburgoperahouse.org
Activity: E, T

Manchester Village The Equinox Resort

This phenomenal location makes for one of the best trips in the state of Vermont—for both the paranormal and the normal, tourist. Its history dates back to 1769 and includes the property operating as Marsh Tavern, Thaddeus Munson's New Inn, Widow Black's Inn, Vanderslip's Hotel, and several other names to boot. It became the Equinox House in 1853, and it has used this name ever since. There are a couple of reasons why this upscale resort is so popular with ghost hunters. The first is the infamous Room 346, where a male apparition is said to be seen and is known for taking guests' personal belongings and stacking them. Then there's the mother and child spirits that have been witnessed in the third-floor hallways. Interestingly, many believe the female entity to be Mary Todd Lincoln, who spent two summers staying at the Equinox.

Address: 3567 Main Street Route 7A
Website: www.equinoxresort.com
Activity: A, E, T

Montgomery The Montgomery House Bed and Breakfast

This restored stagecoach stop used to be known as the Black Lantern Inn. It was a regular stop for paranormal tourists in the area—even those who live in Canada, as the place is only 15 miles or so from the border. They offer a comfy stay with ten rooms, five suites, and a spacious outdoor hot tub. Tales concerning the haunting of the B&B, again, date back to the Black Lantern—though there's no reason the place wouldn't still be haunted. It's been reported by investigators that

Room 3 is occupied by a male apparition that's known for messing with guests' items and playing with the shower in this room. It's unknown whether or not an actual apparition has been seen, but at least one witness reported hearing a male voice there. The spirit is harmless, though, and most likely is just wanting to be noticed. Stop by and say hello.

Address: 2057 North Main Street
Website: www.montgomeryhouseinn.com
Activity: E, T

Moretown The Belding House Bed & Breakfast

This historic farmhouse was built by David and Florinda Belding in 1810 and is a Federal Colonial styled home. It makes for a great headquarters for exploring the Mad River Valley, as well as the nearby towns of Sugarbush and Stowe. Tales concerning the place being haunted date back to a previous business in the property, the Caravan B&B. Folks who stayed there would report encountering a female apparition on the second and third floors—one that suspiciously looked like Florinda herself. The Belding family cemetery is on the property (with eight family members buried there) to add to the spooky atmosphere of this location (though to go inside, you'd never consider the place scary). Florinda has also been witnessed by passersby peering from an upstairs window, looking out toward the family plot. Additional paranormal activity includes the sounds of footsteps and small electric appliances going awry.

Address: 746 Route 100
Website: www.beldinghouse.com
Activity: A, E, T

Norwich The Norwich Inn

Though this property dates back to 1890, there has been an inn located at this spot since 1797. The original version was built by Colonel Jasper Murdock, and it played host to famous visitors like President James Monroe before it burned down in 1889. When you stay at this luxury resort, you don't just get a nice room—you also get a pub (Jasper Murdock's Alehouse) that serves up great microbrewed beer and one of the area's best wine collections. For the paranormal traveler, you will want to stay in Room 20 at the Norwich. This area is thought to be haunted by a past innkeeper, Mary Walker. She has been seen in this room, and is known for turning on the water faucet in the bathroom and using the rocking chair. On occasion, she has also been witnessed walking into the dining room wearing a long black formal gown.

Address: 325 Main Street
Website: www.norwichinn.com
Activity: A, E, T

Proctorsville Golden Stage Inn

This haunted bed and breakfast is older than the state it is located in! It offers year-round service in eight guest rooms and is minutes away from winter sports facilities and the towns of Weston and Woodstock. The owners and innkeepers of this inn refer to their on-site entity as "George," and it's thought that he dates back to the early 1800s when travelers would often rest and recuperate at the inn. He has been seen in various areas and is dressed in a long cloak and hat. Visitors to the inn say the spirit is of a friendly nature, so there's no fear involved with encountering him. Check in with the innkeepers there to get current information regarding their haunting, as well as to get one of the more active guest rooms.

Address: 399 Depot Street
Website: www.goldenstageinn.com
Activity: A, E

Quechee The Quechee Inn at Marshland Farm

Originally known as Marshland Farm, this house was constructed in 1793 by Colonel Joseph Marsh and his wife Dorothy. Marsh was instrumental in establishing Vermont, and was the state's first lieutenant governor. The home remained in their family for several generations before transferring to John and Jane Porter, who lived there until the early 1900s. Today, you can experience the history of this house whether you're staying there in one of their rooms, having an enjoyable meal at their restaurant, or even hosting your event on the property. As for the paranormal activity, it's thought that the estate is now home to two spirits: Jane Porter and Patrick Marsh. Jane is said to roam Rooms 1–6 (an area that once held her study) and the dining room (where she has been seen walking). Patrick has been known to visit Room 9 and is usually blamed for sudden cold spots and objects that have been moved during the night.

Address: 1119 Main Street
Website: www.quecheeinn.com
Activity: A, E, T, C, S

Saxtons River Saxtons River Inn

This location is known for its unique history, as well as its outstanding on-site restaurant. During the anti-Masonic craze of the early 1800s, the local fraternity was forced to suspend meetings that were held regularly at this property since it had been erected in 1817 (it would take 30 years before the Masons would be accepted in the community again). The original inn would eventually be torn down and replaced with a more modern version in 1903 (the current version that exists today)—though a remnant of the earlier hotel would stick around. It seems that at least two female spirits now walk the inn. One entity is thought to be from the 1800s and is seen in various areas in and around Room 3 (she was, reportedly, seen sitting on the bed and speaking to a guest staying there). The second apparition is often seen in the ballroom and common areas. She is a more modern spirit (witnesses say she looks like she's wearing clothes from the 1970s) and likes to spend her time staring out a dining-room window.

Address: 27 Main Street
Website: www.innsaxtonsriver.com
Activity: A, E, S

Shelburne Shelburne Museum

This museum was founded in 1947 by Electra Havemeyer Webb, a collector of American folk art. When it became apparent that one structure would not be able to contain the bulk of the museum's art pieces, she had the idea of relocating historic properties to Shelburne to hold the exhibits. To this effect, 20 buildings (including several houses, a jail, and a schoolhouse) were brought in. For those interested in the paranormal, one structure is of the most interest—the Dutton House. This particular home was first located in Cavendish, Vermont and was built in 1782. It was added to the museum in 1950—and it wasn't long before employees started noticing strange things there. The most common occurrence was the sound of a young girl crying, which would be heard in several rooms on the second floor. Then there's the apparition of the man. He appears as a grizzled old man dressed in a white shirt and slacks. He's been seen on the top floor, crouched beneath the slant of the roof.

Address: 5555 Shelburne Road
Website: www.shelburnemuseum.org
Activity: A, E, T

Springfield Hartness House Inn

James Hartness built this luxurious mansion in 1904 and resided there until his death in 1934. He was so desirous of privacy that he actually constructed an apartment and study under the front lawn of the house in 1912. He spent a great deal of his time down there perfecting his telescope and other projects away from the interruptions of daily life. Today, you can stay at the home in the main house, the Victorian wing, or the old carriage house. For a ghostly experience, though, you will have to stay in the main area. For years, housekeepers have reported odd events at the house, including finding objects in strange locations throughout the property (like somebody moved or hid them) and the persistent feeling of being watched. Most say the first floor of the mansion (along with the basement) is the most active, but since these are mostly common areas, it won't matter which room you stay in.

Address: 30 Orchard Street
Website: www.hartnesshouse.com
Activity: T, S

St. Albans Back Inn Time

Victor Atwood built this house in 1860 and it is the picture perfect early Victorian domicile. Amazingly, there were only three previous owners before the current innkeepers took possession. Another interesting fact about this inn is that the subject of ghosts is openly discussed (and is even mentioned on their website). There are two spirits on the property, a male and a female, and both are pretty much harmless—though they do like to make themselves known. The first ghost is thought to be Lora Weaver, a previous owner. She's often seen in the room that's named for her, though she has been spotted on occasion in other areas as well. The male entity has been witnessed roaming the downstairs parlor. Nobody has placed a name to this ghost, though he, too, is presumed to be an early resident of the property. Be sure to mention you're into the paranormal when you stay at the inn; the owners will regale you with the sightings and eyewitness accounts of past guests.

Address: 68 Fairfield Street
Website: www.backinntime.us
Activity: A, E, S

St. Albans Welden Theatre

Paranormal activity has been happening in this theatre since it first opened in the 1940s. It was constructed over the basement of a former jail (you can actually still see some of the cells) and most of the activity is attributed to this fact. Workers who venture into this area often hear voices and, on occasion, see the apparition of an older man (thought to be a homeless person who passed away there). Strange things do happen in other parts of the theatre as well—the projection booth is said to be particularly plagued by projectors starting on their own and the sounds of whispers. Catch a movie at the Welden and hopefully you will see a ghost there, too, as a shadowy entity is often noticed darting through the seating area.

Address: 104 North Main Street
Website: www.weldentheatre.com
Activity: A, S, E, T

Stone The Green Mountain Inn

This inn was once the private residence of Peter C. Lovejoy and was built in 1833. It was later traded to Stillman Churchill, who added two new wings to the structure and dubbed the place the "Mansfield House." The inn has changed names, as well as owners, several times over the years before it was purchased by the current occupants in 1983. As for the ghost, it's thought that the spirit is a tap dancer by the name of Boots Berry. He was born in Room 302 of the inn—and, supposedly, died in the place after he saved a young girl from the roof of the inn during a snowstorm. Boots has been seen and heard in his old room, and is even known to move items around in there (such as the rocking chair). Sounds in this area usually include a mumbling voice, footsteps, and the sounds of someone tap dancing.

Address: 18 Main Street
Website: www.greenmountaininn.com
Activity: A, E, T

Stowe The Gold Brook Bridge

Though almost every state has a "haunted bridge," most of these locations can be ruled out almost immediately as simple urban legend. This bridge (known to locals as Emily's Bridge), though, has to be included in these listings if for no other reason than the overwhelming amount of personal experiences that have happened there. The bridge dates back to 1844 and was built using a Howe Truss by architect

John W. Smith. "Emily" is said to have been dumped by a lover in the 1800s, and, finding herself pregnant, she decided to hang herself on the bridge. For more than a hundred years, locals in Stowe have reported seeing the apparition of a young woman on this bridge, as well as walking the road. If you search online for tales about Emily, you will find all kinds of bizarre stories—including her attacking cars. These of course, fall into the "legend" category and resemble nothing like the actual haunting of this bridge.

Address: On Gold Brook Road
Website: www.gostowe.com
Activity: A, E, O

Waterbury The Old Stagecoach Inn

This bed and breakfast was once a prominent stagecoach stop and tavern (circa 1826) for travelers swinging through old Waterbury Village. It was built by the city's first lawyer, Dan Carpenter, and served as the local Masonic meeting place (for the King David Lodge) in addition to serving as accommodations. Today, there are eight rooms and three suites on the property—all of which are nice and include one of the area's best breakfasts. It's said that Room 2 of this inn is haunted by a previous owner/resident named Margaret Spencer. She died on the property at the ripe old age of 98 in the aforementioned room and is now known to appear before startled guests. Witnesses say she is bent over and wearing a shawl when she appears. Though you may try to speak to her, it's reported that she simply looks at you, and then disappears.

Address: 18 North Main Street
Website: www.oldstagecoach.com
Activity: A

White River Junction Comfort Inn

This 93-room chain hotel has had its fair share of haunted happenings—all associated with the woman that's thought to haunt Room 112. According to local legend, a distraught woman checked in to the inn and committed suicide there. Not much can be found concerning this reputed death (mainly because most newspapers will not cover suicides in hotels for fear of "copycat" deaths), but even employees of the Comfort Inn tell the stories concerning this room. Guests who have stayed there report lamps moving during the night, hearing the sounds of someone breathing heavily, and experiencing the constant sensation of being watched in the room.

Address: 56 Ralph Lehman Drive
Website: www.comfortinn.com
Activity: E, T

Williston Catamount's Bed and Breakfast

This B&B is part of the Catamount Outdoor Family Center—a local park environment filled with trails and outdoor activities. It was originally a home that was built in 1796 for Giles Chittendon by his brother Thomas (the first governor of Vermont). It served as his family home for some time before becoming a prominent area dairy farm. Take a look at all the historic belongings as you walk through the property—and keep an eye out for their resident ghosts. Glimpses of male and female apparitions on the property, as well as the sounds of children heard on the second floor, top the list of paranormal happenings here. And if you visit during the Halloween season, you will also be treated to the "Haunted Forest" attraction that they host every year.

Address: 592 Governor Chittenden Road
Website: www.catamountoutdoor.com
Activity: A, E

Wilmington Averill Stand B&B

Though they are mostly known for their luxurious accommodations, this location has also gained notoriety for their same-sex civil unions (they offer a package deal for the affair). Of course, there's lots more to this place—including a history that dates back to the 1700s and the Averill family. The property served as a family home, a stagecoach stop, and a tavern over the years, and all of this history has left a permanent impression on the premises. It's said by local paranormal investigators that this B&B has one of the state's best and most persistent residual hauntings. The sounds of horses and carriages are often heard outside the home, and the apparition of a woman is often seen walking the same path (she's thought to be the wife of a local lumber baron named Martin Brown—though she is also attributed to the haunting of the next location listed here as well). On the intelligent-haunt side, activity in the home includes utensils moving by themselves in the kitchen and sightings of a female apparition who is assumed to be Lavina Field Averill. Lavina died in the home and is buried in the family cemetery outside.

Address: 236 Route 9 East
Website: www.averillstand.com
Activity: A, R, E, T

Wilmington White House Inn

As mentioned in the previous listing, this home-turned-inn is reportedly haunted by the ghost of Mrs. Martin Brown. Built in 1915, it was originally called the House at Beaver Brook Farm. After Martin passed away, the place was converted into a country inn in 1965. Though the property pretty much looks the way it did back in the day, modern amenities (such as an indoor pool and sauna) have been added, making this a top-notch paranormal getaway. Sightings of Mrs. Brown walking the property—coupled with the sounds of her speaking and her footsteps—have occurred enough over the years to actually encourage the owners of the place to start marketing the haunting. They host a haunted evening at the mansion every Halloween that includes a Victorian-era styled séance. According to one couple that attended the séance there, strange things happened during the session—things that were not part of the program or their special effects.

Address: 178 Route 9 East
Website: www.whitehouseinn.com
Activity: A, C, E, T

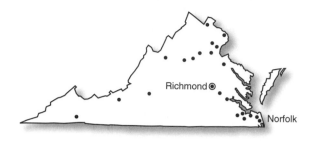

VIRGINIA

nition. The Union soldiers got wind of this and visited the site. Two rebels were killed in the commotion and are now said to walk the area. Many believe the founder of the theatre, Robert Porterfield, joins them in the afterlife as well.

Address: 127 West Main Street
Website: www.bartertheatre.com
Activity: A, E, T

Abingdon Barter Theatre

This theatre started with a unique idea—let patrons pay to see productions with food and produce. Of course, this was in 1933—the heart of the Great Depression. It was because of this practice, though, that the venue was called the "Barter." The actual building that houses the theatre dates back to 1833 and was originally called the Sinking Springs Presbyterian Church. It would go on to be the city hall, and even the firehouse, before becoming a theatre. The two spirits that haunt this historic site are shared by another neighboring, haunted site—the Martha Washington Inn (see the next entry). During the Civil War, the inn was used as a Confederate hospital. To capitalize on the "no aggression zone" of the hospital, the troops dug a tunnel to the Barter Theatre building to store ammu-

Abingdon The Martha Washington Hotel & Spa

Built as a home for General Francis Preston (with his wife, Sarah, and their nine children) in 1832, much of this inn originates from those days. Just check out the lobby—it's the original living room of the house! The home would go on to become a women's college and even function as a training ground and hospital during the Civil War. It closed briefly because of the Depression, but reopened as a hotel. When you stay at this historic location, you may want to get Room 403. It's said that this is the site of a romantic, but tragic ghost story. According to the tale, a Union officer named Captain John Stoves lay dying in this room and a young nurse—a student of the school—tended to him.

She would play the violin as he slowly grew worse and eventually died. Her name was Beth and she is said to now haunt this room, where she has been seen and heard. There is also the spirit of a Confederate soldier that's been seen around the area where he was shot. In addition, there are reputedly ghosts in the tunnels.

Address: 150 West Main Street
Website: www.marthawashingtoninn.com
Activity: A, E

Abingdon The Tavern Restaurant

Dating back to 1779, this stagecoach route tavern and boardinghouse has hosted such guests as Henry Clay, Andrew Jackson, and the King of France. Over the years, it has also functioned as the neighborhood post office, a bank, and a hospital for wounded soldiers during the Civil War. If you visit this restaurant today for their wonderful menu and wine collection, be sure to ask your server about their ghost stories. There are several of them. The first concerns the ghost of a prostitute called the "Tavern Tart," who is often seen in the dining room. Then there's the spirit of a Confederate soldier that's been seen in several areas of the eatery. But the most well known entity in the tavern is that of the "Lady in White" or often called the "Lady of the Tavern." She has been seen and heard in the kitchen and dining room of the place.

Address: 222 East Main Street
Website: www.abingdontavern.com
Activity: A, E, T

Alexandria Gadsby's Tavern

Originally consisting of a tavern and hotel, this site has serviced the seaport community of Alexandria since 1785. It's named after John Gadsby, an innkeeper who ran the property from 1796 to 1808. Many historic people have visited and stayed at the tavern since its inception—including George Washington, Thomas Jefferson, and John Adams—though they will treat you just the same. They are open for lunch and dinner, and even offer a Sunday brunch menu. If you ask about the ghost at this restaurant, you're bound to hear an interesting tale. According to local legend, a woman visiting the tavern in the early 1800s fell ill and died before anyone could even learn her name. She was buried in an anonymous grave (said to be located there in town), but her spirit decided to stick around. A female apparition has been seen roaming the old tavern and an old lantern is said to light with a spectral flame in the room where she died.

Address: 138 North Royal Street
Website: www.gadsbystavernrestaurant.com
Activity: A

Alexandria Woodlawn

This 128-acre estate was originally part of George Washington's famous Mount Vernon property. The main house was built in 1805 and served as a home for Major Lawrence Lewis and his wife, Eleanor. Lewis was Washington's nephew, and he owned the plantation until 1846. At that point, it became a "free labor colony" and was raided several times during the Civil War. Of course, you can learn this history and more if you visit the house. It is open for exhibits and is available for private tea parties—and if you visit during the Halloween season, you may be able to take a haunted tour of the premises. Ghostly activity on the property includes shadowy apparitions, disembodied voices/footsteps, and the spectral sight of Washington himself on horseback.

Address: 9000 Richmond Highway
Website: www.woodlawn1805.org
Activity: A, S, E, T

of a death then). Either way, employees and patrons alike have witnessed shadowy apparitions shooting across the stage and heard the sounds of disembodied voices in the old theatre.

Address: 135 College Avenue
Website: www.thelyric.com
Activity: S, E, T

Champlain Linden House Plantation

This planters-style home was built in the 1750s for a man named Lewis Browne. It remained in his family for several generations before transferring to a series of different owners (and eventually becoming a bed and breakfast). When you visit, you can stay in one of the four rooms in the main house (one of which is a suite) or in the carriage house (where there are three additional rooms). If you want to experience the paranormal, though, you should stay in the manor. Tales from those who have stayed in the B&B include the sounds of disembodied voices (male and female) and a weird light that's said to occasionally appear as an apparition. Most of the activity happens on the second floor of the estate, but you may want to check with the owners concerning the most current goings-on. They are quite open about their haunting and have had their own experiences in the home.

Address: 11770 Tidewater Trail
Website: www.lindenplantation.com
Activity: A, E, O, M

Bedford Avenel

Located in the heart of Bedford, this historic home has been one of the social centers of the area since 1838. It was built for William and Frances Burwell, though it's mostly known for J. W. Ballard and family who purchased the property in 1906. The Ballards would keep the home until 1985, at which point it was sold to the Avenel Foundation and transformed into the living museum it is today. You can visit Avenel during one of their hosted evenings—or even rent the place for your own event. This house has had a haunted reputation for some time. Workers on the property, as well as an area paranormal group, have witnessed a "Lady in White" who walks the property. Most believe the spirit is that of Letitia Burwell, one of the daughters of the original owners.

Address: 413 Avenel Avenue
Website: www.historicavenel.com
Activity: A, E, T

Blacksburg The Lyric Theatre

This venue first opened to the public on April 17, 1930. It was built in a combination of the Art Deco and Spanish Colonial Revival styles, but this is the third incarnation of the theatre (the first two being built in 1909 and the 1920s). Today, the theatre screens art-house movies and features live music—though you will probably be visiting for the ghost that resides there. Most believe the spirit is that of a construction worker who died while working there in 1929. Of course, this could also just be the product of urban legend as well (since there's no record

Charles City Edgewood Plantation

Dating back to 1849, this bed and breakfast's haunting made national news when it was featured on the television series *Ghost Hunters*. Following the airing of the episode, the home offered ghost tours and more info about their resident spirit, Lizzie Rowland. It's said that Lizzie died of a broken heart while waiting for her lover to return from the Civil War and that she's now seen in her old room (called Lizzie's Room at the B&B), as well as on the staircase leading to the second floor. As was also revealed on the television program, the cottage beside the house seems to be haunted—at least one guest staying there in Dolly's Room reported having a conversation with Civil War–era soldiers.

Address: 4800 John Tyler Memorial Highway
Website: www.edgewoodplantation.com
Activity: A, E

Charles City Shirley Plantation

This massive estate was Virginia's first plantation (circa 1613) and is North America's oldest family-run business (dating back to 1638). It survived Bacon's Rebellion, the Revolutionary War, and the Civil War. You can soak in all this history when you visit this living museum and gift shop. You can also soak in the haunted history of the plantation if you visit during Halloween—the staff hosts regular ghost tours this time of year. They will tell you the story of Aunt Pratt, the Shirley family ghost. Martha Hill Pratt was the daughter of Edward Hill III, an early resident of the house. After she passed away, it seemed she wanted a portrait of her to be hung in the home. At night, those in the mansion would hear the sounds of something moving around in the attic. Once they figured out it was the painting, it was hung once again in the home—though it's said Aunt Pratt will still make a racket if her painting is moved.

Address: 501 Shirley Plantation Road
Website: www.shirleyplantation.com
Activity: E, T

Charlottesville Monticello

Though construction on this house began in 1769, improvements and additions would continue until 1809. The house belonged to President Thomas Jefferson, and it was the center of plantation life there during his residence. After Jefferson passed away, the home (along with almost all of his belongings/furnishings) was sold to help pay off the $107,000 worth of debt that was left behind. Today, visitors to Monticello are treated to a top-notch museum, a gift shop, and an on-site café. As for ghostly activity, visitors have reported hearing the phantom sounds of whistling (thought to be Jefferson surveying his property) and seeing the apparition of a young boy on the second floor. The child entity is said to be wearing Colonial-era clothing, including a tricorn hat.

Address: 931 Thomas Jefferson Parkway
Website: www.monticello.org
Activity: A, E

Fredericksburg Historic Kenmore

This home was built by the sister of George Washington, Betty Washington Lewis, and her husband, Fielding. It was constructed in a Georgian style and sat square in the middle of almost 1,300 acres of land. A staunch patriot, Fielding sold off most of his assets in order to finance the building of an arms plant to support the war against England. He would die in 1781—mere weeks after Cornwallis surrendered to Washington. Today, the home is a living museum that you can tour, along with Ferry Farm (the boyhood home of George Washington). If you're lucky, maybe you'll even see Colonel Lewis there as well. Employees and guests at the mansion have, reportedly, seen the apparition of Fielding in the upstairs area of the house that used to be his study. Other activity includes the sounds of heavy footsteps and the occasional door that opens/closes on its own.

Address: 1201 Washington Avenue
Website: www.kenmore.org
Activity: A, E, T

Gordonsville Civil War Museum at the Exchange Hotel

This museum focuses on the history of the town of Gordonsville, as well as the effects of the railroad industry and the Civil War on said area. It is housed within the historic Exchange Hotel—a structure that dates back to 1860. It was built to accommodate folks traveling along the railway, but was transformed into a "receiving hospital" during the Civil War. This means they received the wounded directly from the battlefield, making it the site of untold death and agony. It is because of this that the place is now haunted. Numerous visitors (as well as employees) have felt something touching them when nobody was around, heard voices, and seen whispy figures darting down hallways/ through rooms. Local paranormal investigators checked out this location and obtained some interesting evidence that supports the haunting there. But don't take their word for it—visit the museum and check out the ghosts for yourself.

Address: 400 South Main Street
Website: www.hgiexchange.org
Activity: A, E, T, C, O

Hampton The Chamberlin

Though this historic hotel is now an adult-living community, it is open to the public for special events and dining. The hotel was built over the burnt remains of the original hotel of this name in 1928. It's told locally that, during the fire, a young woman was burned to death on the eighth floor of the original hotel. Her name was Ezmerelda and she is said to haunt this same floor in today's version of the place. It's thought she was waiting for her father to return from sea when the fire hit the building. Many sightings of her apparition have occurred in this area of the Chamberlin over the years. The building is located on old Fort Monroe (a location that has its own ghost stories), so plan ahead when visiting. There are two dining areas you can eat at—the Chesapeake Dining Room and the Channel Bistro—though you may want to reserve your appetite for their legendary brunch menu.

Address: 2 Fenwick Road
Website: www.historicchamberlin.com
Activity: A, E

Leesburg Oatlands Historic House and Gardens

While this plantation dates back to 1798, the house was built in 1804 by George Carter. He added a greenhouse (one of the oldest in the country and still standing), a smokehouse, and a massive barn. George passed away prior to the Civil War, leaving his wife (Elizabeth Grayson Carter) to manage the property during the conflict. After the war, the lack of slave labor took the family and the property through some hard times—though you'd never know it to look at the place today. Visit the main house, the gift shop, and the wonderful gardens on this property during your visit—and keep an eye out for spectral guests. So who haunts Oatlands? There are different opinions concerning this, including the possibility of past family members being there and spirits from the nearby Battle of Ball's Bluff. Either way, glimpses of apparitions and the sounds of footsteps/voices are said to occur at this location. Visit them for a haunted tour during the fall, or query the tour guide when you visit the estate for more information.

Address: 20850 Oatlands Plantation Lane
Website: www.oatlands.org
Activity: A, E

Manassas Manassas National Battlefield Park

Two battles were fought on the site of this military park. The first battle took place in 1861 and pitted Union General McDowell against southern Generals Beauregard, Jackson, and Johnson. The day ended with a Confederate victory. The second clash took place a year later and lasted three days. This battle was a massive victory for the Confederacy, as the combined might of General Lee and General Jackson drove Union troops under General Pope's command back to Washington, D.C. The combined battles resulted in almost 12,000 deaths in this area, so it's no wonder the place is haunted. Sightings of a spectral Union soldier are often reported in the Deep Cut part of the park, a ghostly Zouave-styled Union soldier walks by the old railroad embankment and the old stone house located on Sudley Road is thought to be inhabited by a shadowy apparition that's been termed a "negative entity."

Address: 6511 Sudley Road
Website: www.nps.gov/mana/
Activity: A, R, S, E, T

Middletown Wayside Inn

The tradition of offering guests quality room and board at this inn dates back to 1797. Back then it was known as Wilkenson's Tavern, and the place was a popular stagecoach stop for those traveling through the Shenandoah Valley. With 22 guest rooms and an on-site restaurant/bar, the Wayside is still quite the popular stop. The Wayside also has a unique tradition—listening for the ghostly moan that occurs every night at 11:30. Folks will tell you that the sound comes from the oldest part of the inn (a small loft that dates back to 1742) and that the source of the moans is the spirit of Lord Fairfax, but this is unlikely. Tales have also circulated concerning the sightings of several apparitions that appear to be soldiers from the Civil War era—but you may want to check with the innkeepers for the most accurate information, and to get a room close to the nightly concert.

Address: 7783 Main Street
Website: www.alongthewayside.com
Activity: A, E

Newport News The Boxwood Inn

This bed and breakfast was established in 1896 as the home of Simon and Nannie Curtis. The couple ran a general store out of their house and, for a while, the place was even the site of the local post office. The B&B features four exquisite rooms and offers a unique form of fun they term "dinnertainment" (check out their website for more info). The house is so nice that folks never want to leave—a tradition that seems to date back to one of the original owners, Nannie Curtis. She is said to now haunt the inn. The spirit is known for knocking on people's doors early in the morning (consider it a unique wake-up call) and for opening/closing doors throughout the house. The inn also has a second entity—during a reenactment on the property, several visitors witnessed the apparition of an older man in the front parlor.

Address: 10 Elmhurst Street
Website: www.boxwood-inn.com
Activity: A, E, T

Norfolk Page House Inn

Located close to many of the area sights, such as the Chrysler Museum of Art and the Nauticus Maritime Center, this bed and breakfast makes for handy and comfortable accommodations. They feature four rooms, three suites, and a fitness center—as well as one of the best breakfasts in the area. The inn is also the site of a rather benign haunting. According to several sources, the house is haunted by a woman named Jean Martino—the mother of one of the inn's owners. It's said that, on occasion, Jean will unlock and open a china cabinet. Jean passed away about a year before the B&B was opened, and she was quite proud of her china.

Address: 323 Fairfax Avenue
Website: www.pagehouseinn.com
Activity: T

Occoquan Occoquan Inn

It's said that the entire city of Occoquan is a massive haunted location. It was first settled in the early 1700s and was named by the Dogue Indians. (The name means "at the end of the water.") The inn dates back to 1810 and was built to service folks traveling by water and road. If you travel there, you will be greeted by a wonderful restaurant that serves contemporary, upscale cuisine. Along with your meal, you may even be graced by the presence of the ghost. According to local legend, the last Dogue Indian used to visit this inn quite often—mostly because he was having an affair with the owner's wife! One night, he was sneaking down the staircase to leave the inn when the owner saw him and shot him dead. Guests have reported seeing the apparition of the Indian in the ladies restroom mirror and even glimpsing him through the smoke that emanates from the downstairs fireplace.

Address: 301 Mill Street
Website: www.occoquaninn.com
Activity: A

Orange Mayhurst Inn

If you are interested in visiting a beautiful inn with a mysterious ghost story, the Mayhurst just may be up your alley. The structure dates back to 1859 and is a rare example of Italianate architecture in the area. It's in the proximity of three presidential mansions, six battlefields, and many of the state's best wineries. During the Civil War, Generals Lee, Jackson, and Hill visited the manor house—and, today, you can visit as well. The inn features seven unique guest rooms—and one unknown ghost. The spirit at this historic site is, indeed, a mystery. Not much is known about the entity—other than the occasional guest report of haunting happenings. The stories usually include hearing voices, the feeling of someone watching them, or a window that's said to open by itself (in the Madison Room). The owners have reported experiencing almost nothing in the old home, but maybe you should spend the night and see what you experience!

Address: 12460 Mayhurst Lane
Website: www.mayhurstinn.com
Activity: E, T

Portsmouth The Glencoe Inn

This bed and breakfast features a wonderful view of the Elizabeth River and four rooms that feature antique furniture. It was built in 1890, and was the Victorian home of two Scottish immigrants who dubbed the house "Glen Coe." Visitors to the inn often speak of the wonderful gardens on the property—an area that's also reportedly popular with their resident spirit. It's said that the apparition of an elderly woman has been seen walking the garden, as well as roaming throughout the house. Most believe the woman is a former owner who became displeased when her rose garden was destroyed during renovations. According to witnesses, the ghost often appears with the strong scent of roses. Check in with the innkeepers for current sightings and room recommendations.

Address: 222 North Street
Website: www.glencoeinn.com
Activity: A, N

Richmond The Museum of the Confederacy

Containing three floors of galleries featuring artifacts from the Civil War, this museum is a holy pilgrimage for those interested in the War Between the States. Exhibits include Robert E. Lee's field tent, General J. E. B. Stuart's pistol, and the structure that once functioned as the White House of the Confederacy. This is the area that is, reportedly, haunted as well. During Jefferson Davis' tenure at the historic home, one of his sons (Joseph Evan Davis) tragically died after falling from a second-story window. This was in 1864, and the boy was only five years old. According to several sources, the home is now haunted by this young spirit. He has been seen and heard on the property. But whether you see the ghost or not, the Museum of the Confederacy is a great stop in a great town.

Address: 1201 East Clay Street
Website: www.moc.org
Activity: A, E

Richmond The Poe Museum

Housed in "the Old Stone House," this museum opened in 1922 and is only a few blocks away from Edgar Allan Poe's first home in Richmond, as well as the site of his first employment there, the Southern Literary Messenger. The museum features exhibits of Poe's furniture, his works, and an "Enchanted Garden" that was created as a shrine to the author. All of this, in itself, is worth making a visit there—but when you add in the ghost stories, it becomes a must-see site. There are several spirits reported at the museum—the first of which being a pair of children that often appear in photographs taken in the courtyard. Then there's the shadowy apparition that has been spotted on the property and iss usually blamed for moving items around. Many believe this entity to be Poe himself sticking around to guard his old belongings.

Address: 1914 East Main Street
Website: www.poemuseum.org
Activity: A, T, S, E

Richmond Tuckahoe Plantation

This property was founded by the Randolph family in 1733. They added on to the home in 1740 and created one of the most complete eighteenth-century plantations in the country. William Randolph built this home on land his father (dubbed "Thomas of Tuckahoe") had procured in 1714. But the estate is mostly known for being the childhood home of Thomas Jefferson. The Jeffersons moved into the home and cared for the Randolph children after their parents died prematurely. Of course, Mary Randolph is said to still walk the grounds at her old house. Her apparition has been witnessed walking a path on the estate that's named "the Ghost Walk." But don't pass up on the tour of the house that's offered at this living museum—there are said to be ghosts inside as well. The sounds of disembodied voices and glimpses of shadowy spirits have been experienced within the mansion.

Address: 12601 River Road
Website: www.tuckahoeplantation.com
Activity: A, S, E, T

Staunton The Belle Grae Inn

This historic Victorian home (circa 1873) shares the property with three other sets of lodgings—though you will want to stay in the main house if you want to visit with "Mrs. Bagsby," the resident ghost. It's reported that she lived in the house in the late 1800s and raised her family there. After she passed away, people started seeing her apparition hanging out in a second-floor room, staring out the window into the city. After renovations were made on the property, the only way to get into this area became a small "portal" door that leads from Room 7—a door that's said to be opened on a regular basis by Mrs. Bagsby. The spirit is also known for moving around guests' items during the night and playing the occasional prank. Get a room in this wonderful inn and have a great time checking out the antique furnishings, as well as chasing down Mrs. Bagsby.

Address: 515 West Frederick Street
Website: www.bellegrae.com
Activity: A, T

Virginia Beach Adam Thoroughgood House

When Adam Thoroughgood moved to Virginia in 1621, he was an indentured servant. He would be granted a land parcel in 1636—though the current residence you can visit dates back to somewhere between 1680 and 1720. This is the first of two properties associated with Thoroughgood that's reputedly haunted (see the Ferry Plantation House below). At one point, the house was falling into disrepair as the cities of Norfolk and Virginia Beach fought over who owned the place (neither wanted to take care of the property). Maybe this was the catalyst that caused two spirits from the past to once again take up residence in the home. Visitors to the historic site have witnessed apparitions (a spectral woman has been seen peering from a window and the spirit of a man in a suit is there as well), heard ghostly voices, and seen objects moving by themselves.

Address: 1636 Parish Road
Website: www.virginiabeachhistory.org/
   thoroughgoodhouse
Activity: A, E, T

Virginia Beach The Cavalier Hotel

Standing as a landmark on the beach since 1927, the Cavalier has played host to such distinguished guests as Dwight D. Eisenhower and Richard Nixon (in fact, seven U.S. presidents have stayed at the hotel). They offer two separate lodgings, Cavalier on the Hill (the original) and Cavalier Oceanfront. For a paranormal experience, you will want to stay in the original building. There are several tales concerning the place, including the apparition of a man who is known for walking through the Pocahontas Room, the spirits of a woman and dog that have been seen in the lobby, and numerous experiences in the actual guest rooms there (including objects being manipulated, towels mysteriously changing locations, etc.). Perhaps the most intriguing story is that of the ghost of Adolph Coors, the beer magnate. He died at the hotel after a fall in 1929—and many believe it was a suicide (Coors' business was in decline at the time thanks to prohibition). The sixth floor of the hotel is said to be haunted by Coors—people have felt cold spots, heard a male voice, and felt the sensation of being watched.

Address: 4201 Atlantic Avenue
Website: www.cavalierhotel.com
Activity: A, E, T, C

Virginia Beach Ferry Plantation House

This three-story Federal-style mansion dates back to 1830, though its name was derived from the fact that a ferry service once ran at this spot (circa 1642). Adam Thoroughgood commissioned the ferryman Saville Gaskin, who operated the service for many years. In addition to the main house, there is also the Old Donation Church on the property. It was built on the site of a former courthouse where Grace Sherwood was convicted of witchcraft and imprisoned— and is now said to be haunted by her. Dubbed the "Witch of Pungo," her apparition has been witnessed on the premises many times. There are additional ghost stories concerning the area, as well as the plantation house, but you should learn these while visiting there (especially during Halloween). Check their website for dates and hours for tours and other events.

Address: 4136 Cheswick Lane
Website: www.ferryplantation.org
Activity: A, E, T

Williamsburg Kings Arms Tavern

This eatery was first opened in 1772 by Jane Vobe, who ran one of the area's most social atmospheres. The tavern was known for miles around as the place for gentlemen to converse about their affairs, as well as to grab a drink and a meal. And after more than 200 years, nothing much has changed! The food is still excellent and it's a great place to take a break while touring Colonial Williamsburg. While you enjoy your visit, keep an eye out for Irma, the tavern's resident ghost. She's said to be a past worker who passed away on the property during a fire (reputedly from a dropped candle, though some tales also say Irma died of a heart attack). Irma likes to look over the guests at the restaurant and is said to often be heard talking and moving around items in the dining room.

Address: 416 East Duke of Gloucester Street
Website: www.history.org/visit/
    diningexperience/kingsarms/
Activity: E, T

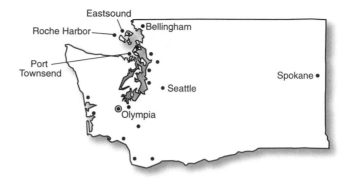

WASHINGTON

Bellingham Mt. Baker Theatre

Constructing this theatre was a Herculean effort that required 80 master craftsmen (mostly masons and carpenters) working on the site constantly to get it finished. The doors opened on April 29, 1927, and almost immediately employees saw strange things were afoot. When the city determined they would build a theatre, a local home was razed to make way. This was Judy's home, and it seems she was not too happy with this—because her spirit now roams this location. It's said that when the place is closing up after a show a blast of cold air, sometimes accompanied by a strange mist or the sound of clothes rustling, will suddenly appear. Judy has also been seen as a glowing ball of light that bobs along the stage. This ghost is well known among those who work at this theatre—her story is even on their website. They even have a photograph that they say is the misty version of Judy.

Address: 104 North Commercial Street
Website: www.mountbakertheatre.com
Activity: M, O, C, E

Carson Carson Mineral Hot Springs Spa

This stretch of hot springs was first discovered in 1876 by Isadore St. Martin. When his wife, Margaret, suddenly felt the healing properties of the water there (she suffered from neuralgia), he decided to build a hotel. It was finished in 1901 and was called the Hotel St. Martin. The current version of this resort is, of course, more upscale and offers many more amenities, including a restaurant, a golf course, and an on-site spa. The accommodations are now said to be haunted due to a tragic tale. In 1910, Isadore had a heated argument with a local man named Robert Brown. While Isadore was "escorting" Brown off the property, Brown stabbed Isadore. Sadly, he died in his room there a short while later. Margaret was heartsick and passed away, too, quite soon. It is Margaret who is now seen and heard on the property—especially in the front lobby and in the second-floor hallways.

Address: 372 St. Martin's Road
Website: www.carsonhotspringresort.com
Activity: A, E

Coupeville Captain Whidbey Inn

This circa 1907 rustic inn features accommodations in the main house, a lagoon-side lodge, and individual cabins. It's located along Whidbey Island's Penn Cove and is considered one of the state's most romantic getaways. It's also quite good for paranormal tourists. A female apparition is said to hang out in the main inn area, as well as walk the paths toward the cabins—locations where startled guests have bumped into the spirit. Employees on the site have had their experiences as well—they have reportedly found made up beds marked with the imprints of a ghostly body that has lain on them, as well as found objects moved from their usual spot. Additional activity includes cold spots that have appeared along with the sensation of someone standing near.

Address: 2072 West Captain Whidbey Inn Road
Website: www.captainwhidbey.com
Activity: A, T, C

Eastsound Rosario Resort & Spa

Robert Moran, a local shipbuilder who would later become the mayor of Seattle, built this luxury resort between the years of 1906 and 1909. It originally served as his mansion home, and he lived there until 1938 when he sold the property. The actual mansion is now a living museum that offers live music performances (often on the 1913 Aeolian pipe organ or the resort's 1900 Steinway grand piano). This is also the area that's considered haunted on this property. The ghost is said to be Alice Rheems, a member of the family that purchased the house from Moran. Her apparition has been seen in and around her old room in the mansion. It's rumored that Alice was a sort of "wild child" of the day—she would wear flamboyant clothes and spend a lot of time drinking and carousing in town—all of which contributed to her death, resulting from alcoholism, there in the home.

Address: 1400 Rosario Road
Website: www.rosarioresort.com
Activity: A, E, T

Edmonds The Edmonds Theater

Originally called the Edmonds Princess Theater, this location dates back to 1927. It was a family-run business that functioned until the 1960s when it was sold to a local dentist. These days, the place has undergone a massive renovation (mostly to the seats and sound system), but has retained its original balcony. It's one of the state's last single-screen theaters, and you can watch a movie there today. If you're lucky, it will be a double feature: the film and, of course, a ghost. Locals say the theater is haunted by a strange, glowing apparition that has been seen wandering about the seats. It is strange in that the spirit itself is seen as a massive shadow shape, but a glowing aura seems to surround the entity.

Address: 415 Main Street
Website: http://theater.jminsight.com/
Activity: A

Fort Lewis The Fort Lewis Military Museum

In order to visit this museum, you have to enter the Fort Lewis military post (which means you must check in at the front gate for a visitor's pass). At last check, the museum was undergoing renovations, but it should reopen sometime in 2010 or 2011, so check out their website and hours before driving there! Housed within the historic Red Shield Inn (built circa 1918 by the Salvation Army to house World War I soldiers), this location is said to be haunted by past soldiers and even the Native American spirits of those who perished in the area. Many also believe the ghostly happenings are attached to the relics of past wars that are on display in the museum. Either way, people have reported seeing a ghostly face peering from a third-story window and employees claim to have heard strange sounds and found objects in the building moved during the night.

Address: Building 4320 Main Street
Website: www.lewis.army.mil
Activity: A, E, T

Hoquiam The Polson Museum

There are several unique and interesting sights to see at this location, including the circa 1924 Arnold Polson mansion. Then there's the railroad camp, the museum store, and the neighboring Hoquiam River. The house itself is the museum—and the location you will want to visit for a possible paranormal experience. Several sources (including local paranormal investigators) have claimed that this place is haunted by two spirits. There's the spectral woman, who has been seen in various rooms (sometimes referred to as the "Lady in White"), and then there's the spirit of a child, who has been witnessed in the old nursery area. If you don't manage to catch a glimpse of these ghosts, you can at least enjoy yourself by checking out the wonderful exhibits at this museum!

Address: 1611 Riverside Avenue
Website: www.polsonmuseum.org
Activity: A

Kelso The Kelso Theater Pub

This unique movie venue offers customers the chance to sit on a couch, to order from a full menu of food and drinks, and to enjoy a film with a ghost. The Kelso Theater Pub opened in 1997 in a circa 1937 theater (some say the building is as old as 1910) that was reputedly built on the grounds of an old funeral home. Sightings of a female apparition have occurred on the site—

mostly in the balconies and the restrooms—and a local paranormal group has claimed to have evidence of a male entity there as well. The spirits are harmless and seem to like playing pranks on the employees. Workers have reported hearing the sounds of a woman laughing and repeatedly finding the curtains over one of the exits opened. More often than not, though, the paranormal activity on this site involves seeing a shadowy torso of an apparition moving through the balcony.

Address: 214 South Pacific Avenue
Website: www.ktpub.com
Activity: A, S, E, T

Lakewood Thornewood Castle Inn and Gardens

This massive bed and breakfast offers a lot for the discriminating tourist. Upscale accommodations, a great location near a lot of local attractions, and an on-site "mystery theater" top the list. The mansion was finished in 1911 to the exact specifications of its owner, Mr. Chester Thorne. He lived in the home until his death in 1927, and the property would remain in the family until 1959. If you stay in the castle, you will want to rent either "Chester's" room or "Anna's Suite." Each is said to be haunted by their namesake (Anna was Chester's wife). According to several sources, there is also the possibility of a third spirit in the house—the spirit of a young boy (thought to have drowned in the nearby lake) who has been seen on the ground floor, as well as by the lake. If you want to see more of this gothic masterpiece, check out the Stephen King miniseries Rose Red—the Thornewood has a starring role in the production.

Address: 8601 North Thorne Lane Southwest
Website: www.thornewoodcastle.com
Activity: A, E, T

Morton St. Helen's Manorhouse

This bed and breakfast is housed within a circa 1910 home. They offer three guest accommodations (called the Blue, Green, and Pink rooms) and feature a wonderful meal to start your day. Since the current owner of the B&B purchased the place, she has noticed strange things going on, including a door that likes to shut by itself every night at 4:20 a.m. A psychic has indicated that there are two female spirits in the house—but this, of course, must be taken with a grain of salt. What is known for sure, though, is that guests often report feeling a presence in the room with them and smelling the phantom scent of perfume.

Address: 7476 Highway 12
Website: www.sthelensmanorhousebab.com
Activity: E, T, N

Olympia The Governor's Mansion

A nonprofit named the Governor's Mansion Foundation maintains and operates this historic location. They offer tours of the property that seem to transport you back in time to the days when this Georgian-styled mansion was home to the state's top official. It was designed in 1908, and the first people to live there were Marion E. Hay and his wife, Lizzie. After several attempts by politicians to remove this site, it was finally awarded with the funding needed to restore the place and transform it into what it is today. As for the ghost here, there's really not much information. Several sources report that the estate is haunted by a young, male apparition who is seen wearing a blue sailor's uniform. He has reputedly been witnessed in the lobby and in the area that used to be the first family's bedrooms.

Address: 14th and Capitol Way Street
Website: www.wagovmansion.org
Activity: A

Port Townsend Manresa Castle

This unique set of accommodations includes an on-site restaurant and lounge, as well as a spectacular view of the neighboring Cascade and Olympia Mountains. The mansion was originally constructed in 1892 as the home for Charles and Kate Eisenbeis, and was made to look like the Prussian castles of Charles' youth. He passed away in 1902 and Kate remarried and moved away, leaving the estate empty for almost 20 years (except for a caretaker who was stationed there for upkeep). It ended up being purchased for use as a Jesuit school and was named Manresa Hall. When they left in 1968, the place was converted into a hotel. Most of the third floor of the castle is considered to be haunted—though Room 306 is said to be the center of it all. According to the legend, a girl leaped from a window to her death and now haunts this room. A second ghost is said to be in the tower and is thought to be a Jesuit priest that hanged himself there.

Address: 7th and Sheridan Street
Website: www.manresacastle.com
Activity: A, E, T

Roche Harbor Hotel de Haro

This hotel is part of a larger complex that's known as the Roche Harbor Resort. The resort itself stemmed from a small company town that was established by the Tacoma and Roche Harbor Lime Company in 1886, along with the construction of this hotel. Famous guests over the years include Theodore Roosevelt and John Wayne (just check out the antique guest registry in the lobby)—though you may be interested in a permanent guest that has less celebrity. The ghosts at this hotel are thought to be members of the McMillin family (past on-site residents) and their secretary, Ada Beane. Several pale apparitions have been seen in the common areas of the hotel that resemble the McMillins, and the gift shop has been the site of multiple Ada Beane sightings. This area was once Ada's private lodgings.

Address: 248 Reuben Memorial Drive
Website: www.rocheharbor.com
Activity: A, E

Roslyn The Brick Saloon

Also known simply as "The Brick," this bar was featured in the television series *Northern Exposure* (the entire town of Roslyn and nearby Cle Elum was used during the shooting of the show). It was built in 1889 by John Buffo and Peter Giovanni to serve up cold drinks for area miners and has been continuously running since (the second longest in the state). Interestingly, the saloon is also known for having a makeshift prison in the basement that was built to either house naughty miners or was constructed for the film *The Runner Stumbles* (stories vary). The ghost story would point to the cells dating back to the old days, though; employees who work at the Brick have reportedly heard ghostly sounds in the basement, as well as seeing the apparition of a miner there.

Address: 100 West Pennsylvania Avenue
Website: www.myspace.com/thebricksaloon
Activity: A, E

Seattle The Baltic Room

This stylish dance bar was designed to look like the classic music venues of the 1940s. If you plan to visit, be sure to check out the events schedule (via their website), as their dress code varies based on the evening's happenings. Of course, you may only be interested in one happening: witnessing the pair of ghosts that are said to roam this property. The first apparition that's been seen appears to be a woman from the 1930s, and she usually hangs out on the balcony level of the club. The second spirit is that of a man from

the same era, who is seen wearing a dark suit and hat, that's been witnessed roaming the ground level. They both appear dressed for a good time (the female is seen wearing a ball gown), so it looks like they've picked the right place to haunt!

Address: 1207 Pine Street
Website: www.thebalticroom.net
Activity: A

Seattle Central Saloon

Known until recently as the Central Tavern, this building was constructed in 1892—one of the first businesses of this kind to open following the devastating fire of 1889. It was known as the Watson Bros. Famous Restaurant, and then later on as the Seattle Bar. During the heyday of grunge music, this venue was a regular for bands like Mother Love Bone and Nirvana, and it gained a reputation for its outstanding musical acts. It also gained an altogether different reputation. Employees at the Central would report seeing and hearing strange things in the building after closing. Reports of hearing voices and glimpses of apparitions (usually a shadowy male entity or a pale woman dressed in 1800s clothing) are now almost commonplace.

Address: 207 1st Avenue South
Website: www.centralsaloon.com
Activity: A, S, E, T

Seattle The College Inn

This location was built in 1909 for the Alaska-Yukon Exposition. It contains a hotel (with extremely reasonable rates), a café, and a convenience store. But perhaps the most interesting place to visit is the on-site pub. It's a favorite with students at the nearby University of Washington, and it has a couple different ghostly tales. The first concerns the possibility of a male apparition that's been seen in the pub—and according to one report—heard. A waitress is rumored to have heard a phantom voice shout, "Ten feet beyond the wall!" Local legend states that this man was murdered there while visiting the university campus. Another story tells of a spirit that likes to play the piano. The sounds of said instrument have been heard in the place with nobody there to do the playing!

Address: 4000 University Way Northeast
Website: www.collegeinnseattle.com
Activity: A, E

Seattle Hotel Andra

This modern masterpiece is housed within a completely renovated historic hotel that dates back to 1926. The Hotel Andra offers modest, but upscale, accommodations with a Scandinavian flair and two restaurants: Lola and the Assaggio Ristorante. For paranormal investigators familiar with this area, the place is more well known by a past name—the Claremont Hotel. Ghost hunters would travel to this location to experience one of the state's most persistent residual haunts. It's reported that the hotel is still experiencing the sights and sounds of the Roaring 20s—guests will check in and hear the sounds of old jazz and voices in the middle of the night. There is also the spirit of a young woman that has been seen on the premises. She is thought to be there after falling to her death from one of the upper stories. So, does the haunting continue at the Hotel Andra? You might want to check that out for yourself…

Address: 2000 Fourth Avenue
Website: www.hotelandra.com
Activity: A, R, E

Seattle Mayflower Park Hotel

Originally named the Bergonian Hotel, this location first opened in 1927 and it hasn't closed since. They have a lounge in the building called Oliver's (that actually started out as a Bartell Drug Store because the hotel opened during prohibition) that's known for their top-notch mixologists and a restaurant called Andaluca. They are also known (especially among the employees) as a haunted hotel. It's thought that the ghost is an elderly male that, perhaps, lived on the sixth floor in one of the hotel's apartments. His apparition has been seen on that floor several times, and is known for walking straight through doors and walls right before the astonished eyes of witnesses!

Address: 405 Olive Way
Website: www.mayflowerpark.com
Activity: A

Seattle The Moore Theatre

This theatre was featured on the television show *Ghost Hunters*. It was built in 1907 and is named for its first owner, James A. Moore. It opened to a locally produced musical titled *The Alaskan*, and over 2,500 locals came out for that show. Today, the theatre is as strong as ever with regular shows and tours of the establishment. The spirits in the Moore are a well-discussed subject (especially since appearing on television). There is a spirit of a woman in a ball gown who has been seen on the stage, the apparition of a young boy who is known for wandering the backstage area, and strange voices and noises that seem to emanate from around patrons who sit in the balcony.

Address: 1932 Second Avenue
Website: www.stgpresents.org
Activity: A, E, T

Snohomish The Oxford Saloon & Eatery

Established in 1910, this classic Old West tavern is in a building that dates back to 1889 (when it was called Blackman's Dry Goods). It was recently completely restored, but it still contains many of their oldest artifacts (including a bar that came from the Seattle Hotel in 1890). The basement area of the saloon is known as the Ole Time Pub and the upper floor is called the Red Door Salon—though they are mostly just separate dining areas from the main bar. It's been guessed that the Oxford has as many as 18 ghosts, but most visitors are interested in their two main spirits: Kathleen and Henry. Kathleen wears an 1800's style gown and is usually seen on the second floor (she's said to hang out in Room 5 of the old brothel area). Henry was a police officer who was killed in a knife fight on the stairs that lead from the main floor to the basement area. His spirit has been seen in almost every section of the building and is known for calling out people by name and playing with barware.

Address: 913 1st Street
Website: www.theoxfordsaloon.com
Activity: A, E, T

Spokane The Davenport Hotel and Tower

When this hotel first opened in 1914, it was the first in the area to have air conditioning and a central vacuuming system. It also hosted the first radio station to broadcast in Spokane and quite a few celebrities of the day (including nearly every American president). Unfortunately, the Davenport started to decline in the 1940s, and by the 1980s, it was slated for demolition. But new owners swooped in, purchased the whole city block, and renovated the hotel to the tune of $38 million. Believe it or not, though, the ghost at this hotel is not the product of renovation (like so many are). The spirit was seen in the building long before the new owners took over. Witnesses say the entity is a female dressed in 1920's attire and she's often seen watching over the lobby. Many believe the woman is Ellen McNamara, who died after she fell through the hotel's lobby skylights. Ac-

cording to a newspaper report, her last words to her attending physician were, "Where did I go?"

Address: 10 South Post Street
Website: www.thedavenporthotel.com
Activity: A

Tokeland Tokeland Hotel & Restaurant

Every once in a while you come across a haunted spot that is proud of their spectral guests. This is the case with the Tokeland Hotel (they have a sign that warns people not to disturb their ghost). Dating back to 1885, the building was once the home and business of William S. Kindred. It was an inn that served passengers coming in from the nearby Toke's Point port for many years. Perhaps their ghost was once one of these folks (many believe the spirit was a Chinese worker who died after arriving). Investigators aren't really sure who haunts the hotel—but they're sure at least one entity is, indeed, there. EVPs have been recorded, interesting data has been collected, and many dramatic personal experiences have occurred there. If you visit, maybe you'll get to hang out with "Charlie" (the name they've given the ghost) as well.

Address: 100 Hotel Road
Website: www.tokelandhotel.com
Activity: A, E, T

Vancouver Fort Vancouver National Historic Site

The Hudson Bay Company established this post sometime around 1825 to protect the local fur trade and to look over their business investments in the area. In 1849, the U.S. Army built a fort of their own directly across from the original version. Later on, the military would pretty much take over the entire complex. There are reputedly several haunted locations on this site: Officer's Row (where several different homes have this reputation), the Grant House (which is haunted by a ghost called "Sully"), and the veteran's hospital (where residual screams, etc., are often documented). You can visit the Grant House (which is now a café), as well as take a long walk down Officer's Row—many believe this entire area is haunted (including outside) because the houses were actually built on the gravesites of the early colonials who were buried there.

Address: 1501 East Evergreen Boulevard
Website: www.nps.gov/fova/
Activity: A, R, E

Charleston

Lewisburg

Harpers Ferry

WEST VIRGINIA

Ansted Hawks Nest State Park

So you like the paranormal and you like the outdoors. What better way to spend the day than exploring this state park? On the outdoors side, you have boating, hiking, and swimming (though you may want to take a break and visit the restaurant and gift shop at some point). On the paranormal side... well, there are a few stories concerning this location. The first is the tragedy that constantly surrounds the "Lover's Leap" there—it's reported that several people have committed suicide from this spot (possibly dating all the way back to Native Americans who lived there). Then there's the infamous "Death Tunnel" that was built to funnel off water (it resulted in hundreds of deaths caused by silicosis) and the explosion that occurred at the Bachman Mine that killed several folks. It all adds up to one haunted area. Activity includes sightings of misty apparitions, disembodied voices, and glowing balls of light that roam the cliffs.

Address: 49 Hawks Nest Park Road
Website: www.hawksnestsp.com
Activity: A, M, O, E

Beckley Soldiers Memorial Theatre and Arts Center

Currently the center of community events for the town of Beckley, this former theatre offers classes to the public (on such varied subjects as belly dancing and karate) and live concert events. It was first dedicated on Memorial Day in 1932 and was constructed to honor the memories of those who served during World War I. There are several different stories circulating concerning the haunting of this theatre. Some suppose the apparition of an elderly man that's seen there was a fatality during construction. Others tell of the disembodied voices, cold spots, and shadowy shapes that occur there and how they may be a product of the Civil War (the building is rumored to have been built on a former veteran's cemetery). But most witnesses to the activity there have simply experienced the sounds of children playing and laughing.

Address: 200 South Kanawha Street
Website: www.myspace.com/smt_arts_centre
Activity: A, R, E, C, S

Ceredo Z. D. Ramsdell House

This living museum was built in 1858 by its namesake, a man who journeyed into the area after his friend, Eli Thayer, founded the town of Ceredo a year before. Both men were strong abolitionists, and it's rumored that the basement of the house was used as a stop along the Underground Railroad. The home remained in the Ramsdell family until 1977, and then it became a historic site owned by the city (which you can now visit). A couple of different paranormal groups have investigated this site, and there are tales that involve the staff and visitors—tales that support the idea the house is haunted. Reported activity includes apparitions of former soldiers and slaves (sometimes even seen walking outside the home), doors/lights manipulating themselves, and disembodied voices that are heard coming from the basement.

Address: 1106 B Street
Website: www.museumsusa.org/museums/
    info/1164651
Activity: A, E, T

Charleston Capitol Plaza Theatre

Owned and operated by the West Virginia State University, this theatre first opened in 1912. It was remodeled in 1921 to become one of the area's premiere vaudeville venues. This success would not last long, though. The place suffered a fire, only to rebuild and begin a slow decline in patronage. In 1982, the theatre closed down. But not for long... It was reopened, redecorated,

and soon new owners—the university. As for the ghosts, they are the product of a house that was torn down before the theatre was built. It was known as the Welch mansion, and it had stood at this location since 1798. Two family members from this period, John Welch and his daughter Molly, are now said to haunt the theatre. John likes to move props around and appear with a massive cold spot. Molly, who died at a young age from pneumonia, is often seen sitting in the front row seats.

Address: 123 Summers Street
Website: www.capcenter.wvstateu.edu
Activity: A, E, C

Charleston The Empty Glass

Known as the one of the area's preeminent music venues, the Empty Glass is a local hangout for those interested in catching a live show and some pub grub. It's located under a three-story house and it's the site of a tragic story/haunting. It's said that after a bartender who worked there was killed in an automobile accident, strange things started happening at the bar. Primarily, the jukebox would kick on all by itself and start playing songs that were of particular interest to the deceased employee. According to one account, a worker even witnessed a shadowy shape pass in front of the jukebox when this act occurred. There is the possibility of additional entities on the premises as well—the second floor is said to be plagued by voices and objects moving by themselves. It's thought that this may be the product of previous tenants of the building and house.

Address: 410 Elizabeth Street
Website: www.myspace.com/theemptyglass
Activity: S, E, T

Charleston State Capitol Building

This massive structure was actually built in three stages: the west wing was finished in 1925, the east wing in 1927, and the rotunda in 1932. It was dedicated to the public on June 20, 1932 (the 69th anniversary of West Virginia's statehood), by Governor William G. Conley. So how does a place like a public building become haunted? Well, there are two stories concerning ghosts at the Capitol. The first involves a maintenance worker who is said to have died from a heart attack there. His spirit has been seen walking the hallways, along with the apparition of a woman. Employees aren't really sure who she could be, though she is mostly known for walking through the rotunda section of the building and ignoring those around her.

Address: 1900 Kanawha Boulevard East
Website: www.wvculture.org/agency/capitol
Activity: A

Elkins Graceland Inn & Conference Center

Dating back to 1893, this mansion-turned-inn was once the summer home of Henry Gassaway Davis (a U.S. senator). It's built in a Queen Anne–style of architecture and was originally called Mingo Moor by locals—though Davis would refer to the home as "Graceland," named for his youngest daughter. The house remained in the family until it was sold in 1939. Today, much of this tradition is still evident in the inn—there is the Mingo Room restaurant and many of the guest rooms are named after the original family of the house. If you visit, you will want to stay in either Grace's Suite or the Nursery Room. These are said to be the hottest of spots. The entire third floor of the house is, reportedly, the stomping grounds for the apparition of "Miss Grace," who has been seen there many times. She has also been witnessed in the room that bears her name (usually standing by the bed), and the Nursery Room has been the location of disembodied voices that sound like children at play.

Address: 100 Campus Drive
Website: www.gracelandinn.com
Activity: A, S, E, T

Glen Farris Glen Farris Inn

This inn was established in 1839 by Aaron Stockton who built the site by adding on to an existing house that was there. He constructed the place to service stagecoach travelers passing through the area—and the inn served soldiers from both sides of the conflict during the Civil War (and possibly even functioned briefly as a hospital). With fifteen rooms and three suites, the business is still serving the public much as it did back then. The service there is so good, it seems that a past visitor has decided to stick around. According to at least one paranormal group in the area, the apparition of a Confederate officer is often seen (sometimes only from the waist up) hanging around the kitchen there. He has been dubbed "the Colonel" by those who frequent the inn, and he is said to also manipulate the doors in the building and move the occasional object.

Address: U.S. Route 60
Website: www.glenferrisinn.com
Activity: A, T

Harper's Ferry Harper's Ferry National Historic Park

This state site actually occupies two other states as well: Virginia and Maryland. It has been a historically significant city throughout the years—though it's most noted for the activities that occurred there prior to, and during, the Civil War. Bloody clashes, including the takedown of John Brown and his abolitionists, were commonplace at this crossroads location. Because of this, many say the entire area is haunted. Visitors have experienced the residual sights and sounds of battles past—and the guest house located within the park is said to be haunted by the spirits of what seems to be an entire family. The apparition of a man in a top hat and cane has been witnessed several times in the house, as well as a young woman and boy.

Address: 485 Filmore Street
Website: www.nps.gov/archive/hafe/
Activity: R, A, E

Hillsboro Droop Mountain Battlefield State Park

This park marks the site of West Virginia's last significant battle of the Civil War. It offers trails for hiking and is a part of the Civil War Discovery Trail (a series of more than 300 war locations that you can visit and explore). The battle took place on November 6, 1863, and ended with the Union army pretty much controlling the entire state. Like many other Civil War sites (just check out nearby Gettysburg in Pennsylvania), Droop Mountain experiences the backlash of the traumatic events that took place there in the form of a residual haunting. Visitors to the park have reported seeing phantom soldiers, horses, etc., and hearing the sounds of battle.

Address: HC 64 Box 189
Website: www.droopmountainbattlefield.com
Activity: R, A, E

Huntington Colonial Lanes

This bowling alley—in addition to having an on-site bar called Rebels and Redcoats Taproom—is also known locally for its paranormal activity. The establishment dates back to 1959, and features 34 wooden lanes. But don't look for their resident spirit while you're bowling—you won't see or hear him in this area. It's in the taproom where most people hear the sounds of disembodied voices and footsteps and see doors open/close. One theory for the haunting of this location involves a past owner, Mr. Frankel. Employees say it wasn't long after his death that folks starting noticing strange things there. People would hear a whispering voice speak to them and suddenly smell the scent of tobacco. The haunting is said to continue, so you may want to rent some shoes and hit the lanes.

Address: 626 West 5th Street
Website: www.coloniallaneswv.com
Activity: E, T, N

Huttonsville Hutton House Bed & Breakfast

This Queen Anne–style house was built in 1898 by Eugene Hutton, and the site had been in the family dating back to 1805. There had previously been a log cabin home, but this was burned in 1861 by Union soldiers who were angry at the family for supporting the Confederacy. Visitors today are less surly—probably because of the luxurious guest rooms (they have six of them) and great breakfast. As for the ghost … well, the haunting of this B&B is definitely a subtle affair. According to one source, a guest who stayed at the Hutton House found that a large desk in his room moved during the night, and people smell the phantom scents of food being cooked downstairs, even when nobody is in that area (much less cooking). Check in with the owners for more information regarding this haunt.

Address: Route 219 at Union Street
Website: www.wvonline.com
Activity: E, N

Kingwood Kingwood Public Library

Though this library is pretty much a modern affair, with all the most up-to-date resources available to the local community (including free Internet access), the site it is located on is quite historical. The city, founded in 1815, was a rough-and-tumble place back in the day. Back then, the location the library now resides on was a prison that housed some of the most notorious criminals. So when workers at the library began reporting that books were seen moving by themselves and that ghostly footsteps were being heard in the basement, it seemed only natural that the spirit would be a now-deceased prisoner. Locals say that the ghost is that of a man who hanged himself in this area to avoid a lifetime of imprisonment. If you don't see any ghosts when you visit this library, maybe some more research is in order.

Address: 205 West Main Street
Website: www.kingwood.lib.wv.us
Activity: E, T

Lesage The Jenkins Plantation Museum

Currently being renovated by the U.S. Army Corps of Engineers, this plantation house dates back to 1835. It was the home and property of the Jenkins family—most notably of which was General Albert Gallatin Jenkins. Jenkins was torn by his loyalties during the Civil War as he has served in Congress, but owned slaves. In the end, he decided to fight for the Confederate States of America, so he formed and led a unit of border rangers that often made raids into neighboring Ohio. Unfortunately, he was later wounded and captured at the Battle of Cloyd's

Mountain—a wound that resulted in his death 12 days later. Visitors to the museum now say you can see and hear General Jenkins there in his old home. Sightings of a misty apparition and the sounds of heavy boots walking have been experienced multiple times in the place, as well as the strange sight of a bearded face peering from a front window.

Address: 8814 Ohio River Road
Website: www.wvculture.org
Activity: A, M, E

Lewisburg The General Lewis Inn & Restaurant

This inn, as well as the city it's located in, is named after General Andrew Lewis, a Revolutionary War hero. It was built around a historic house that dated back to 1834 (the Withrow House) and was first opened to the public in 1929. These days, you can take in all of this history, as well as a great meal, when you stay at the inn. Talk around the table concerning the paranormal at this site is quite common—the innkeepers even keep a log book of the ghostly happenings. It's said there are three ghosts (at least) on the property. The first is a former slave that hangs out in the dining room and is known for moving the cutlery and napkins. The second is that of a little girl, who has been witnessed in Room 202 and 206 (usually seen standing by the bed). The last spirit is probably the most famous. Known as the "Lady in White," she is usually spotted in Room 208. Witnesses say she wears a long gown from the Civil War era.

Address: 301 East Washington Street
Website: www.generallewisinn.com
Activity: A, E, T

Martinsburg Poorhouse Farm Park

This historic property dates back to 1766 and a land grant from Lord Fairfax. It was passed down through several owners before becoming a county "poor farm" in 1850. It operated as such for many years until the two main lodgings on the premises were converted into a private home and part of the Eastern Panhandle Mental Health system. The county took over the entire property in 1994 and kept the bigger of the two structures intact, along with a barn that's now available for rent to the public. Locals in Martinsburg have told ghost stories about this old house for a long time. According to eyewitness accounts, the apparition of a Civil War-era soldier has been seen in and outside the stone house and there are also sounds of a whispery voice/heavy breathing.

Address: Poorhouse Farm Road
Website: www.mbcparks-rec.org/fac_phfb
Activity: A, E

Moundsville West Virginia Penitentiary

This Gothic-styled prison needs no introduction with paranormal enthusiasts. It's an eventual pilgrimage that must be made at some point. Dating back to 1876, prisoners were kept at this institution all the way until 1995. During operations, 94 men were executed at the penitentiary (the vast majority by hanging). You can visit this prison today and take a tour, or tag along on one of their ghost hunt events. Hot spots in the building include the basement (where the ghost of a maintenance man is said to hang out), the old gallows (haunted by several spirits, including a past inmate named Arvil Paul Adkins), and the "Sugar Shack" section (known for its particularly gruesome violence). Of course, most of this location is considered haunted. Remember that as you tour the cell

blocks—and keep an eye out for "Inmate Roberts," who's been seen in this area many times.

Address: 818 Jefferson Avenue
Website: www.wvpentours.com
Activity: A, R, S, E, T

Parkersburg The Blennerhassett Hotel

This hotel was built in 1889 by Parkersburg local, William Chancellor. It was the gem of the city and one of the state's most upscale accommodations at the time. Today, the high level of service and amenities that made it so popular in those days still exists. So does William Chancellor. According to employees and guests alike, the spirit of the man has been seen many times walking the hallways, looking over his hotel. Eyewitnesses say he appears with the scent of tobacco smoke, and he is sometimes blamed for strange activities that happen on the premises during the night. It's said that at 4 a.m. each day, a series of four quick knocks are heard—the catch is, they don't always occur at the same spot! You may want to put out the Do Not Disturb sign when you visit...

Address: 320 Market Street
Website: www.theblennerhassett.com
Activity: A, E, T

Parkersburg Parkersburg Art Center

The city of Parkersburg has a reputation for being haunted—just ask any paranormal enthusiast in the area. This is mostly due to its sordid past. During the Civil War, this area was a popular place for soldiers to take their leave and was well known for their abundance of taverns and brothels. Perhaps the paranormal activity on this property is a result of these happenings. More likely, though, it has something to do with the Camden Theater. It was the original structure on this site and was built in the 1890s. A massive fire destroyed the theater in 1927. Either way, visitors to this location have reported seeing objects being moved by unseen hands and have felt the presence of the otherworldly within the center.

Address: 725 Market Street
Website: www.parkersburgartcenter.org
Activity: T

Parkersburg Smoot Theatre

In 1989, this theatre was saved from demolition by a volunteer group who purchased the place along with the land it was on. It was originally constructed in 1926 as a vaudeville theatre, but was later purchased by Warner Brothers (circa 1930) to screen their films to the public. If you visit, you can catch a play, musical, or live performance at the Smoot these days. As for the ghost there—well, there's not much info. Even the staff disagrees as to whether the place is haunted. According to locals, though, there are simply too many tales concerning shadowy apparitions in the backstage area, as well as other activity that includes cold spots, whispering disembodied voices, and the occasional prop that's moved.

Address: 213 Fifth Street
Website: www.smoot-theatre.com
Activity: S, E, T, C

Point Pleasant The Historic Lowe Hotel

Originally known as the Spencer Hotel, this Point Pleasant landmark was built in 1901. It was the talk of the town and the center for social affairs in the area until the stock market crashed in 1929. At that point, the place was sold to Homer D. Lowe who promptly changed the name and put an end to the shady goings-on that were happening there (mostly gambling, but prostitution was probably occurring as well). When you stay at this hotel, be sure to visit the Red Parrot Café, the on-site restaurant, which is renowned for their food and service. There are also quite a few paranormal hot spots you will want to visit in the hotel. First, there's the second-floor mezzanine where the spirit of a young girl has been seen (many believe she is

Juliette Smith, the daughter of Homer Smith, one of the original owners of the hotel). The second floor is also haunted by the ghost of a small child who's seen and heard there. On the third floor, there are three ghosts (a former maid, a male spirit dubbed "Captain Jim," and a man from the 1930s) that tend to hang around Rooms 314 and 316. Last, but not least, hit the ballroom where spectral music is often heard.

Address: 401 Main Street
Website: www.thelowehotel.com
Activity: A, R, E, T, C, N

Romney Old Hampshire County Jail

If you want to tour this historical site, you will need to visit their website (below) and set up an appointment—or you can visit during their annual Heritage Days festival when they host an open house for the public. It's thought that this prison dates back to the 1700s, and it housed prisoners all the way until the year 2000. Though there are no prisoners in the jail today, the place is the headquarters for the local sheriff's office. The spirit that's rumored to roam this prison is also a sheriff. According to legend, a small group of men broke into the jail to rescue one of the prisoners there and shot an officer during the process. The poor man fell down the stairs to his death as they got away. It's said you can still hear the residual sounds of this horrible act.

Address: 66 North High Street
Website: www.hampshirecountysheriffwv.com/
old_jail
Activity: R

Sistersville The Wells Inn

This hotel first opened to the public in 1895 and was founded by Ephraim Wells. It was built to service those who worked in the local oil industry and to handle the sudden influx of entrepreneurs to the area. Over the years since then, the inn has had many owners and suffered many hard times, but things are looking up at this location. Visitors now get comfy rooms at a reasonable price in a historic hotel. And if you're lucky, you'll get more than that. Maybe you'll get a visit from their resident ghost, old Ephraim himself! He gets blamed for most of the paranormal activity—including doors slamming shut, objects turning up missing, and the sounds of phantom footsteps. Hot spots at this location include the area of his old office and Room 324, where maids often have problems with the doors magically locking and closing.

Address: 316 Charles Street
Website: www.hotelwells.com
Activity: A, E, T

Weston Trans Allegheny Asylum

This is the second of West Virginia's must-see haunted locations (the first being the penitentiary in Moundsville). It was constructed between 1858 and 1881 and is the second largest hand-cut stone building in the world (the Kremlin being the largest). It served the mentally ill until 1994, when it closed down and crushed the local economy. During the Civil War, when the asylum was used for Union soldiers and was briefly called Camp Tyler, the northern army robbed the place of food, clothing, and many thousands of dollars (which were held at the bank). Catch a tour or ghost hunt at the asylum (both are offered), and you'll learn more about their history and the fascinating (but sometimes horrible) treatment for insanity in those days. Sightings of apparitions and shadow shapes—as well as the usual sounds of disembodied voices, etc., are heard here on a daily basis.

Address: 71 Asylum Drive
Website: www.trans-alleghenylunaticasylum
    .com
Activity: A, S, E, T, C

White Sulfur Springs The Greenbrier Hotel

This resort goes all the way back to 1778 when visitors would travel to the "White Sulfur Springs" to drink the healing waters there. After a stagecoach line was established, a hotel was erected called the Grand Central Hotel. It functioned until the Civil War swept through (both sides would occupy the area at some point). In 1913, the Greenbrier would be built to service workers and travelers of the C&O Railroad. Curiously, the U.S. Army would use the hotel as a hospital during World War II and would eventually build a massive underground bunker there (closed today), but the hotel would survive. It is the picture of opulence today, with several cafés, bars, and restaurants on the premises. As for the ghost, locals say the place is haunted—and employees agree (for the most part), but specifics are few and far between. What better place to solve a mystery? Start by talking to the staff and visiting the Virginia Room where folks have spotted an apparition.

Address: 300 West Main Street
Website: www.greenbrier.com
Activity: A, E

WISCONSIN

Appleton Hearthstone Historic House
Museum

This location has the distinction of being the world's first house to be solely powered by hydroelectricity. The system was designed by Thomas Edison, and it began operation in the home in 1882. The structure itself was designed by William Waters, a prominent architect of the day, and it remained a family home all the way into the 1930s when it became the "Hearthstone," a local restaurant. Today, the place is a living museum where you can still see the elements of early era electricity, as well as furnishings of the day. One of the exhibits that's not advertised in the brochure, though, is the spirit of A. W. Priest. He was a former resident of the house prior to its conversion into an eatery. Activity in the museum includes a disembodied voice (that's often heard sneezing) and a sudden, overwhelming sensation of someone standing beside you.

Address: 625 West Prospect
Website: www.focol.org/hearthstone/
Activity: E

Chippewa Falls The James Sheeley House Restaurant and Saloon

This location was first constructed prior to the Civil War as a boardinghouse for local workers of the lumber trade and people traveling along the railroad. In 1884, the owner of another boardinghouse, John B. Paul, purchased the property and turned it into "the Paul House." It featured a saloon, Paul's lodging, and a place for boarders to sleep on the upper floor. James Sheeley stayed at the house while working on the railroad and fell in love with it, so he purchased the place in 1905. Though you can't stay overnight in the house these days, you can still visit for great food and live music. The stairs are known for almost constant ghostly activity—the loud sounds of heavy boots stomping up and down the steps have been experienced on an almost nightly basis for years. The spirit is also known for playfully moving things around and even locking or unlocking doors when you least expect it. The employees like to think the spirit is that of Anna Sheeley, but more investigation is warranted to prove or disprove this.

Address: 236 West River Street
Website: www.jamessheeleyhouse.com
Activity: E, T

Eau Claire The Stones Throw

This restaurant, bar, and live music venue is currently undergoing an ownership/management change, so be sure to check out their website prior to traveling there. Once they reopen, you can experience many of the same things that locals have been treated to over the years—including, of course, their ghost! The active spirit that roams this restaurant is known for hurling bottles and dishes across the dining room and slamming doors at all hours of the day. Local tradition tells of a bartender that became fed up with the behavior, so he yelled at the entity to get out of the restaurant. Much to his amazement, a male apparition rose up from one of the dining room tables and exited the room! Sightings of this spirit have happened with guests and employees of the bar, so you may want to add the Stones Throw to your travel itinerary (once it reopens).

Address: 304 Eau Claire Street
Website: www.thestonesthrow.com
Activity: A, E, T

Ferryville Swing Inn

This rustic tavern has functioned in Ferryville for a very long time—though nobody can place the exact date it was built. In the early 1900s, this site was the center of activity—mostly because of their ladies of the night that serviced the patrons there. Though that "amenity" isn't exactly available to the customers these days, you can still get good food and drink at this location. You might also be able to coax out a few tales from your waiter concerning their ghost. The employees call the spirit "Blue Moon" and say that she was a prostitute during the heyday of the tavern. Try to visit during typical slow periods of dining—when the restaurant is quiet, it's said that you can hear the footsteps and, sometimes, even the voice of the female spirit.

Address: 106 Main Street
Website: www.visitferryville.com
Activity: E

Fond du Lac The Historic 1856 Octagon House

Interestingly, this house was built as an Indian fort in 1856, but is more well known for the role it played prior to and during the Civil War. There are nine passageways in the house (and even an underground tunnel) that were used to smuggle and hide runaway slaves. For most of them, this was the last stop before reaching freedom in neighboring Canada. The place is a sort of "private museum" today that you can visit by appointment or during one of their special events (such as the Halloween party they host most years). According to locals, this house is haunted by the spirit of a young boy. He has been seen in the house (as an apparition and a shadowy figure) and is known for playing with various displays there.

Address: 276 Linden Street
Website: www.marlenesheirlooms.com/octagon
Activity: A, S, T

Fond du Lac Historic Galloway House and Village

This Victorian mansion has 30 rooms, four fireplaces, and is surrounded by 25 buildings that pretty much date back to the same era. You will feel like you've stepped into a time machine as you walk through this village—and as you check out all the historic furnishing in the Galloway home. With the environment so much to their liking, it isn't surprising that a historical spirit might choose to stay around! The actual Galloway House is thought to be the stomping grounds of a past member of the family. Voices (sometimes laughter) have been heard in the second-floor rooms and items in the kitchen have been known to be moved during the night. Though the activity at this location is sporadic, reports do still trickle out—sometimes from employees, sometimes from tourists.

Address: 336 Old Pioneer Road
Website: www.fdlhistory.com
Activity: E, T

Genoa Big River Inn

This hotel and restaurant looks like something out of an Old West movie. It was built in 1879 and originally functioned as a local tavern for folks who worked in the area (the fur trading industry was huge at that time). At last look, the restaurant in this inn was up for sale—though still functioning—and the hotel side was still in operation. So get a room here (they are quite affordable and well apportioned), and take a trip to the restaurant. It's here that the spirit of an ex-employee still roams. Reputedly, the ghost is that of a man named "Kenny," who used to work at the restaurant. When things of a paranormal nature starting happening in the eatery, regulars and employees noticed the activity seemed quite Kenny-ish. Things like the television constantly changing to his favorite channel and coffee mugs (representing his favorite drink) turning up missing from the kitchen.

Address: 200 Beaver Street
Website: www.bigriverinnwi.com
Activity: E, T

Green Bay Brewbaker's Pub

Not much is known about this restaurant and pub, except that it's a local favorite spot for watching the Green Bay Packers play—and that it has a reputation for being haunted. The stories involving the paranormal at Brewbaker's originated when employees began relating tales of closing up and seeing/hearing strange goings-on. They would check to make sure everybody was gone for the night, switch off the lights, and then hear the sounds of voices and footsteps coming from the upstairs area. At other times, they would come to the pub to open for the day and find that the lights would already be turned on or things would be moved behind the bar. So who is perpetrating all the ghostly happenings at this pub? Nobody knows.

You may have to become a temporary "Cheese Head" and find out for yourself.

Address: 209 North Washington Street
Website: www.myspace.com/brewbakerspub
Activity: E, T

Keshena Menominee Casino Bingo and Hotel

This location claims to be the first Las Vegas-style casino in the state of Wisconsin. It opened in 1987, but the building itself served as a bingo hall before that. The business is operated by the Menominee Indians and even employs over 300 members of the tribe. As for the haunting there... well, it sounds more like an urban legend than an actual event. Local paranormal groups back the story up, though, and insist that the tale is true. Supposedly, guests in the casino were complaining about some children who were being too loud, so two security guards went to check it out. One guard went to the site; one guard went to the security station to watch for them on the monitors. The guard on location could find no evidence of any children bothering anybody, but the officer watching the surveillance monitor could see three phantom kids running to and fro around the other guard.

Address: Highway 47 at Duquaine Road
Website: www.menomineecasinoresort.com
Activity: A, E

Kewaunee Kewaunee Inn

Because of its natural harbor, the city of Kewaunee became the trading center of this area in 1836. A trading post was opened and commerce grew to the point that, by 1858, the city needed a hotel, so local entrepreneur Charles Brandes built a boarding facility by the name of the Steamboat House. William Karsten purchased the property in 1911, but it soon burned down and another was built (this time with bricks). It was originally called Hotel Karsten, but for paranormal investigators, the place will always be known by its later name, the Karsten Inn. According to this hotel's website, three spirits now make the place their home: William Karsten, Billy Karsten, and the housekeeper, Agatha. William is often seen sitting in the bar area and is usually accompanied by an unpleasant smell. Billy passed away at the age of five, and it's said that his little feet can be heard pattering down the second-floor hallways—along with the sounds of a child's laughter. Agatha has been seen and heard in her old residence, Room 310. She's said to dislike men and has been known to shove male employees walking the stairs!

Address: 122 Ellis Street
Website: www.kewauneeinn.com
Activity: A, E, T, C, M

Kohler The American Club

Of all the haunted locations in the state of Wisconsin, none get more upscale than this hotel and spa. It was awarded AAA's five-star rating (the only hotel in the area with this distinction), and it offers accommodations in the main hotel and in the neighboring carriage house. There are several haunted tales concerning the American Club—and all them involve the main hotel (so you will want to stay there). The first story involves a female apparition that's said to hang out around and in Room 209 (several people have seen her there by the fireplace). Some say she committed suicide in this room after her significant other passed away. Witnesses say she will approach you, and then simply fade away. There is also the spirit of a man that's often seen walking out of Room 315, but he seems more residual in nature, as he is said to ignore those around him. At least one guest said to have attempted to speak to this apparition (thinking he was alive), but blinked in amazement when he vanished. This was all reputedly caught on the hotel's security camera, sans ghost.

Address: 419 Highland Drive
Website: www.destinationkohler.com
Activity: A, E

Madison Capone's Bar Next Door

During the years of prohibition, Chicago mobsters decided to open an illegal drinking establishment in Madison. They called the place the Wonder Bar, and it was the center of a whole slew of illegal operations in the area. The gangsters built the bar to be bulletproof and bombproof and even dug out an escape tunnel under the premises. Today, you can legally drink all the beer you want at the bar, though you may have to share the space with the undead. Guests have witnessed a male apparition in the main area of the bar that seems to be dressed in 1930's attire. This entity is also sometimes seen as a shadow mass that likes to hover around the dark corners of the turret areas. Other activity in the bar includes disembodied voices, footsteps, and the odor of "body funk" that seems to appear, intensify, and then suddenly evaporate.

Address: 222 East Olin Avenue
Website: www.thecoliseumbar.com
Activity: A, S, E, T, N

Menomonie Mabel Tainter Theatre

This Victorian-era theatre was constructed in 1889 as a tribute to Mabel Tainter, a local musician who died at an early age. It was commissioned by her father, Captain Andrew Tainter, and was designed by renowned architect Harvey Ellis. The venue functioned then much like it does today—with year-round performances and productions, it is still one of the area's biggest attractions. If you visit this theatre, you will want to check out the Reading Room, which contains information and artifacts related to Laura Ingalls Wilder. Though this building was erected four years after her death, it's thought that Mabel Tainter now haunts this theatre. A female apparition has been seen on the second floor of the venue, as well as in the first-floor bathrooms—and many say the glowing ball of light that's been seen in the Reading Room is also Mabel.

Address: 205 Main Street
Website: www.mabeltainter.com
Activity: A, O

Milwaukee The Brumder Mansion

For the paranormal tourist, choosing between a massive hotel and an intimate bed and breakfast is a no-brainer—nothing beats the charm and intimacy of staying in a historic home. This B&B was built in 1910 by George Brumder for his son of the same name. George Jr. lived in this house with his wife, Harriet, and their eleven children for about ten years until Harriet passed away. They then sold the place, triggering a string of unique and different owners over the years. The place functioned as a speakeasy, a boardinghouse, and even a church annex for a spell. These days, the owners just concentrate on providing top-notch accommodations for visitors. As for the ghosts, well, there are three of them at this location. There's a female entity that hangs out in the Gold Room, a young female apparition that likes to visit with folks in Marion's Room and Emma's Room, and then there's a male spirit that's often encountered in George's Suite and the downstairs parlor.

Address: 3046 West Wisconsin Avenue
Website: www.milwaukeebedbreakfast.com
Activity: A, E, T, C

Milwaukee The Pfister Hotel

When this upscale Victorian masterpiece opened in 1893, it was the most ornate hotel of the day. Guido Pfister and his son, Charles, operated the place and made sure that every want and need of their guests were satisfied—this meant decking out the place with every modern amenity of the time (including electricity and thermostats in every room). This high level of customer care still takes place at the hotel today from both the staff and the spirit of Charles Pfister. Employees and guests have both seen the apparition of Pfister on the ninth floor of the hotel, as well as on the grand staircase. Those who have witnessed the ghostly activity say that the spirit will simply stop and smile when he is noticed. While you stay at the hotel, be sure to check out the ballroom—the upper area/balcony of this room is said to be Charles' favorite hangout.

Address: 424 East Wisconsin Avenue
Website: www.thepfisterhotel.com
Activity: A

Oshkosh Grand Opera House

Architect William Waters began designing this theater in 1882, and the doors opened just a year later with a production of *The Bohemian Girl.* It was designed with a Victorian flair and could seat over a thousand people (making it quite a large venue for its day). The opera house continues operations these days much like it did in the 1800s by featuring live performances and theater productions. During the 1980s, the place underwent a massive renovation—one that apparently kicked up some paranormal activity (as these makeovers tend to do). Sightings of a male apparition began to occur along with the sounds of phantom footsteps and a disembodied voice. Most believe the spirit is a past manager of the theater, Percy Keene. Activity continues to this day, so add a little culture to your trip and catch a performance at the opera house.

Address: 222 Pearl Avenue
Website: www.grandoperahouse.org
Activity: A, E, S, T, C

Superior Fairlawn Mansion & Museum

Built as a place of residence for Martin and Grace Pattison in 1891, this living museum displays artifacts and furnishings of the era. It is also one of the area's best examples of Queen Anne architecture (just check out the massive turret section running along one corner of the house). Since the home was opened to the public for tours and private events, there have been several ghost occurrences. Tour guides began to sporadically run into a hazy female apparition in the house (thought to be a former maid) and, later on, visitors began asking who the two "small girls" were that they saw running through the basement. Before being purchased by the city in 1963, the house was used as the Superior Children's Home, so it makes sense that a couple younger spirits would be having fun in the place.

Address: 906 East Second Street
Website: www.superiorpublicmuseums.org
Activity: A, E

Townsend Hillcrest Lodge

After World War II, folks in Wisconsin started paying more attention to the simpler things in life—such as taking a nice vacation out in the country. Capitalizing on this sentiment, this lodge was created in 1946 to offer such visitors a place to have a great meal and wet their whistle. To visit with the resident spirit of the place, "Dr. Fred," you simply have to go for a nice meal (locals swear by the weekly Friday Fish Fry they offer). It's said that the ghost likes to hang out in the main area of the lodge, and on occasion, the third floor, where he lived for some time prior to his accident (he was hit by a car while walking the road adjacent to the lodge). Dr. Fred makes his presence known by generally moving things such as doors, light switches, and various objects within the place. The employees are quite familiar with their ghost (they even mention him on their website), so feel free to question them about current activity.

Address: 16704 Nicolet Road
Website: www.hillcrest-lodge.com
Activity: T, E

Wisconsin Dells Captain Brady's Showboat Saloon

This location always has been—and probably always will be—a saloon. Known for miles around as the best place to grab some good food and have a few drinks (along with live music on certain nights), this location makes for a fun paranormal trip. The place was originally constructed in 1907 by William and Minnie Stanton, and they pretty much ran the business the same as it operates today (with the exception of the Prohibition era when they had to sell candy for a while …). As for their ghost … well, the employees just call her "Molly." She's said to hang out around the bar and the stage where she is often seen and heard. They say you can tell when Molly is around because you will feel a strong cold spot sweep over you, followed by a feeling of nausea. So you may want to allow a little time for Molly to show up before you have a meal there.

Address: 24 Broadway Street
Website: www.showboatsaloon.com
Activity: A, E, C, T

Wisconsin Rapids Hotel Mead

This mostly modern hotel has a sort of dated feel to it—not exactly old, not exactly new. The rooms are great for the price and you are treated to two restaurants (the Grand Avenue Grill and Café Mulino), as well as the Grand Avenue Tavern. Finding out about the paranormal activity in this hotel makes for an interesting conversation with the employees, as the story varies quite a bit from person to person. Mostly, it goes like this: During the 1950s, there was a bar in the hotel basement called the Shanghai Room that may or may not have had gambling there. A young female server sadly was caught in the middle of an altercation there and was stabbed to death. Now she roams the hotel. Of course, under scrutiny, the tale doesn't hold much water as there's no record of this death. But the ghostly happenings on the site point to at least one spirit actually being there. Employees have heard a female disembodied voice in the basement, as well as seen a female apparition on the stairs. Darker reports say you can even smell blood when the entity appears …

Address: 451 East Grand Avenue
Website: www.hotelmead.com
Activity: A, E, N

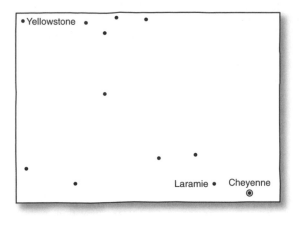

WYOMING

Casper Ivy House Inn

This circa-1916 home was the property of Frank and Rhea White for many years. After Frank passed away, Rhea lived in the house with her cats until she passed away at the age of 93 in the home in 1995. A year later, the current owners purchased the place and opened this bed and breakfast. Being located in a town called Casper, it's probably no big surprise that this place is haunted! Rhea, a controlling woman when she was alive, is now said to still be roaming the halls of her old home. She has been seen and heard in several rooms by various customers and the owners as well. Interestingly, there are also reports of strange, small shadowy shapes darting about the place that are assumed to be the spirits of her two Siamese cats she loved so much. But it doesn't end there. Sightings of a shadowy appari-

tion in the parking lot have happened as well—and this spirit has even set off car alarms!

Address: 815 South Ash Street
Website: www.ivyhouseinn.com
Activity: A, S, E, T

Cheyenne Atlas Theatre

This location began its career as a tea room in 1888, but was converted into a theatre in 1908 by architect William Dubois. Traveling vaudeville troops would often perform at the Atlas and even stay in the boardinghouse that was located upstairs in the building. When the theatre shut down in 1929, the venue was used as a movie theater and a nightclub. The resident production company today, Cheyenne Little Theatre Players, took over the theatre in 1966 and gave it back its original name. The haunting of this location is thought to be the product of the boardinghouse upstairs. Dark stories concerning possible murders and suicides abound, but the deaths were most likely of a mundane nature, since most people who lived there were destitute. Whatever the circumstances, employees and guests have experienced objects moving, dark shadow shapes moving across the stage, and disembodied voices in the backstage area.

Address: 211 West 16th Street
Website: www.cheyennelittletheatre.org
Activity: S, E, T

Cheyenne The Plains Hotel

This hotel first opened in 1911 as the premier accommodations for the city of Cheyenne. Because of their massive banquet rooms and the Wigwam Lounge, visitors would travel great distances to stay in the place. These days, this reputation is still in effect thanks to amenities like an on-site spa, the Capitol Grille, and 30 suites in the hotel. There are several tales of murder/death involving this hotel that are said to be the source of the haunting. First, there is the story of a murder involving someone being shoved out an upper-story window onto the ground below. Then there's the story of "Rosie." It's said that Rosie caught her husband leaving the Wigwam Lounge with a prostitute, so she followed them, killed them, and then turned the gun on herself right there on the premises. Sightings of a man in early 1900's clothing have since been seen throughout the hotel, but especially on the fourth floor. Interestingly, the two women are now hanging out together in the afterlife, as they are both usually seen and heard on the second floor.

Address: 1600 Central Avenue
Website: www.theplainshotel.com
Activity: A, E, T

Cody Buffalo Bill's Irma Hotel

William F. Cody was one of the cofounders of this town that bears his name in 1895, and it was where he built his ranch. Later, in 1902, he financed construction of the Irma Hotel from the money he made with his Wild West show. He kept two suites in the hotel for himself, as well as an office, and was known to stay in the place quite often when it filled up with folks traveling along the Burlington Railroad. Today, the business still retains much of the charm of a historic hotel, while supplying travelers with an upscale room to sleep in. The resident spirits of the hotel include the daughter of Buffalo Bill (Irma herself) and the apparition of a Civil War-era soldier. Room 16 is said to once have been Irma's room and she now visits people who stay there (she likes to use the rocking chair in the room). Room 35 is the stomping grounds of the Confederate soldier who likes to appear before astonished visitors.

Address: 1192 Sheridan Avenue
Website: www.irmahotel.com
Activity: A, E, T

Green River Sweetwater County Library

It sounds like something straight out of a horror movie: This library was built on top of a graveyard! When the city needed a location for their library, they decided that a circa 1860s graveyard was sitting in the best place, so they moved it—the graveyard that is. The problem is that there were a lot of unmarked graves. After the library was in place and operational, the occasional grave was still being found—all the way up until the 1980s. As a result, the library has had an uncanny amount of paranormal activity, including balls of light seen shooting through the building, the sounds of voices and flapping noises, and the apparition of what appears to possibly be a female. Eyewitnesses who have seen the spirit say she stares at you until you approach her, then she shoots into the ceiling with a loud "popping" or "flapping" sound. Activity is pretty regular in this place, and if you question a librarian, you'll probably get an earful of stories—but, hey, that's their job.

Address: 300 North 1st Street
Website: www.sweetwaterlibraries.com
Activity: A, S, E, O, T

Kemmerer Fossil Country Pioneer Museum

This museum and gift shop features exhibits that illustrate the natural and cultural histories of the area, as well as offer a great place you can rent for special events (a ghost hunt maybe?). The building is also the location of a rather mild haunting—at least that seems to be the case. According to the accounts that have been related concerning the activity here, a friendly entity walks this museum. It's said that after closing, the strange sounds of constant footsteps are heard, as well as the odd knocks and bangs that are usually associated with hauntings. Though this sounds like something a local would have just "made up," local paranormal groups confirm the story is true and say the place is, indeed, haunted.

Address: 400 Pine Avenue
Website: www.hamsfork.net/~museum/
Activity: E

Laramie Fort Laramie National Historic Site

This historic fort began as a private venture to handle fur trading in the area. It was established in 1834 and was originally known as Fort John before the government purchased the property in 1849 and gave it its current name. The primary focus of the post during operations was to protect the Oregon Trail from the constant harassment of the Plains Indian tribes—and this is what it did until it shut down in 1890. Like most military parks, the area is said to have a residual haunting that people have experienced there (the sounds of guns, etc.). But there are also two good ghost stories. The first involves the daughter of the head agent of the American Fur Company, who turned up missing from Fort John. She was never found, but her apparition is said to roam the area outside the fort and along the trail. The second tale concerns the Captain's Quarters (a building that still stands today) and a ghost the park personnel call "George." George is known for roaming the building as a glowing ball of light. There are more tales concerning the post as well, such as the ghostly cavalry officer in the "Old Bedlam" building and spectral soldiers seen wandering the grounds around the old barracks.

Address: 965 Gray Rocks Road
Website: www.nps.gov/fola/
Activity: R, A, E, O, T

Laramie Wyoming Territorial Prison State Historic Site

This location is one haunted place you will have to visit in the spring, summer, or fall months as they close for most of the long Wyoming winter. Much like the other haunted prison (see the Rawlins listing), this property is a nationally recognized historic site and was primarily used to hold criminals from the frontier days. It was established in 1872 and it locked up notable criminals like Butch Cassidy. When the prison in Rawlins was opened, this site was converted into an agricultural office. If you tour the prison today, you'll get to see the cell areas, the warden's house, and the barn/stables. While in the actual prison, keep an eye out for the ghost there. This area is reportedly haunted by the spirit of one Julius Greenwelch. This particular criminal died in the prison of natural causes after being sentenced there for life for killing his wife (he found her working in a local bordello). Activity includes the smell of cigar smoke (he made cigars for the prison), the sounds of his voice talking in his cell, and even the appearance of his full-bodied apparition that never fails to scare the tourists.

Address: 975 Snowy Range Road
Website: www.wyomingtourism.org
Activity: A, E, N

Lovell Shoshone Bar

Strange tales have circulated about this bar for decades. With over 60 years of operation as a tavern, you can imagine the sheer amount of weird characters and incidents that have occurred on this site! Perhaps the strangest is the story of Ted Louie. It's said that he was a local salesman who visited the tavern quite often in the 1940s. One night, he complained to the barkeep that he wasn't feeling well, so he was transported to his hotel. Later, it became apparent that Louie had disappeared. He never made it to his hotel room and he was never seen again. His night in the tavern was his last—and it would continue forever as Louie now haunts the Shoshone Bar. He's blamed for most of the activity in the place, including items magically moving on the bar, the sounds of a male disembodied voice, and the appearance of an apparition in the main area.

Address: 159 East Main Street
Website: www.myspace.com/467402838
Activity: A, S, E, T

Medicine Bow Virginian Hotel

Since 1911, the Virginian has been the stop of choice for the weary traveler in southern Wyoming. This was mostly because it was located in the most populated area between the cities of Denver and Salt Lake City, so stopping to sleep overnight in this hotel was a no-brainer. In addition to standard rooms and suites in the hotel, you can also choose to stay in one of the hotel's sixteen antique rooms or four antique suites to experience life in the early 1900s. Much like other hotels of the day, the Virginian was often the last stop for many people in their lives. Whether it's the product of wrongdoing or just the aftermath of natural deaths that have occurred there, the hotel is thought to be haunted. It is, in fact, quite a popular spot for paranormal groups in the area. Sightings in the hotel usually involve apparitions that seem to flicker in and out and are accompanied by the sounds of music (residual maybe?) or involve items being moved within the guest rooms.

Address: 404 Lincoln Highway
Website: www.historicvirginianhotel.net
Activity: A, R, E, T

Rawlins Wyoming Frontier Prison Museum

This prison was used for 80 years before shutting down in 1981. Visitors who tour the grounds get to see the cells where frontier outlaws were held and often killed by other inmates, the Death House where criminals were executed, and the cafeteria where they ate (sort of anti-climactic). With horrible contraptions like the "Julian Gallows" on the property (a type of "automatic" hanging), it's no wonder that some of the prisoners would still haunt this place. Over the years, there were many deaths in the prison—including several guards and many of the inmates, who died either by execution, murdering each other, or because of the horrible living conditions. Tour guides have seen the entire gamut of paranormal activity on these grounds, including shadowy apparitions in the cell block, the crazed apparition of a man in "the hole," and muttering disembodied voices/moans in the Death House.

Address: 500 West Walnut Street
Website: www.wyomingfrontierprison.org
Activity: A, S, E, C, T

Riverton Acme Theatre

This historic theatre was built in 1920 by local businesswoman Belle Mote and opened to much fanfare in the area. It was the social center of the city of Riverton throughout the first half of the 1900s and was eventually purchased by Tom Knight in the 1950s. Today it is part of the Gabel Theatres chain and features movies in a grand atmosphere. For many people who visit the theatre for a late-night movie, they get a bonus attraction:—a ghost! Sightings of a male apparition wearing a 1920's hat and suit have been occurring for decades. The spirit is usually seen in the upper balcony during the wee hours of the night (so you might want to catch the late show) and is thought to be associated with the early days of venue.

Address: 312 East Main
Website: www.gabletheaters.com/acme
Activity: A

Sheridan Kendrick Mansion/Trail End State Historic Site

It's said that this mansion museum is the largest, and most authentic, of its kind in the state of Wyoming. Nearly everything in the home is original to the Kendrick family who lived in the house or is authentic to the era. The Kendricks built the mansion in 1913 beside a small carriage house that was already on the property (it dates back to 1910) and lived there for many years. John B. Kendrick, a Texas rancher and politician, spared no expense in the home—something that's still evident when you tour the place. Whether or not this location is actually haunted may be something you have to discover for yourself. The locals staunchly defend the stories concerning ghosts there, but the facts point to the tale being more urban legend than fact. According to the story, the local police department has been called onto the property several times because of surveillance picking up a man walking through the home after hours. When the police get there, there is (of course) nobody in the house. Could it be a Kendrick family member back from the grave? Could be. You may have to visit this place to get the real story.

Address: 400 Clarendon Avenue
Website: www.trailend.org
Activity: A

Sheridan The Sheridan Inn

While this inn is currently undergoing a serious renovation project, it is still open to the public to tour and for dining at the wonderful 1893 Grille & Spirits (a coy hint at the ghost on the property?). The hotel was first opened in 1893 and was, for a time, home for Buffalo Bill Cody. But the place is more known for quite another resident of the hotel, Catherine Arnold, who is known to employees of the Sheridan as "Miss Kate." Catherine lived and worked in the hotel between 1901 and 1965 (when the place shut down business). When re-opening the hotel was discussed, Catherine was right in the middle of the talks. Miss Kate died in 1968 and it's said she requested that her ashes be buried in the hotel within a wall. Whether or not this happened you may have to find out for yourself when you visit. Regardless, the spirit of Miss Kate now walks the hotel, and it's rumored that you can actually follow her spirit by listening to her footsteps or even feeling a strange cold spot that seems to wander.

Address: 856 Broadway Street
Website: www.sheridaninn.com
Activity: E, T, C

Yellowstone Old Faithful Inn

This place is actually two hotels in one—the original part of the lodge dates back to 1904 and is known as the Old House. The newer sections/wings were added in the 1910s and 1920s (though almost every room and area has undergone restoration at some point over the last hundred years). Being in the close proximity of Old Faithful, there's plenty for you to do outside around here. Within the inn, though, you can occupy your time visiting the on-site dining room or the Bear Paw Deli. Of course, you could also spend some of your time ghost hunting. There are said to be two spirits in the inn: a man who is seen wearing a dark frontiersman's hat and a female who's been seen ... well ... part of her is seen ... on the second floor. The hotel staff is quite used to discussing their spectral residents, so feel free to question them about current sightings and hot spots.

Address: Within Yellowstone National Park
Website: www.travelyellowstone.com
Activity: A, S, T, R

SOURCES

As mentioned in the introduction, I have verified each of the haunted locations listed in this book through at least two different sources (oftentimes many more than that). Doing this has helped me to eliminate many sites that turned out to be only local legends rather than actual haunted places. It has also helped me to rule out false or incorrect information presented on many websites and in certain books. My primary source of information for this book has been the actual occupants of the haunted locations—whether this is a manager, an innkeeper or current occupant/employee of the place (when they would discuss their ghost).

My secondary sources for the book include the numerous websites and local paranormal groups scattered all across the United States that feature local and national listings of haunted places. Here, I list the websites that I used while writing this book. The sources are arranged by state, as well as include the more "nationwide" sites. Using regional books about haunted spots would have been nice, but the cost of buying so many books is simply not very cost-effective (one of the reasons I decided to write this volume).

The practice of documenting a tale through at least two sources is a good one for you to utilize as well. Quite often, separating the legend of a place from the real history can be the most challenging aspect of investigating the paranormal—but also the most rewarding. Mostly because the old saying is true: Truth is often stranger than fiction!

On a final note, I also want to mention that all these ghost stories belong to nobody and everyone. Over the years, I've seen many paranormal groups/investigators get angry when a location they frequent is investigated by somebody else—especially if they make new discoveries or gather great evidence there. This should not be the case. Think of a haunting as just another news story; it's great if you break it first, but in the end it is news that everyone can share and retell. Just as you enjoy reading about a haunting that others have experienced, be glad that others are reading about your investigations as well.

Be respectful of these locations and your fellow ghost hunters. Happy investigating!

Alabama

www.unsolvedmysteries.com
www.historichotels.org
www.pubcrawler.com
www.ghosttn.com

Alaska

www.freewebs.com/iopialaska/

Arizona

www.sgha.net

Arkansas

www.arkansas.com
www.oldhardytown.net

California

www.hauntedtravels.com
www.iloveinns.com
www.bedandbreakfast.com

Colorado

www.rockymountainparanormal.com
www.candcparanormal.com
www.hauntedcolorado.net

Connecticut

www.cpeargroup.com
www.shekinahparanormal.com
www.sageamerican.com
www.nearhome.com

Delaware

www.m-and-m-investigators.com
www.delawareghosthunters.com
www.mlparanormal.com
www.destateparks.com
www.delawarebeautiful.com

District of Columbia

www.dchauntings.com

Florida

www.hauntedflorida.com
www.floridaghostteam.com
www.floridastateparks.com
www.visitflorida.com

Georgia

www.roswellparanormal.com
www.southernghosthunters.com

Idaho

www.idahoparanormal.com
www.idahospiritseekers.com
www.idahohauntings.com
www.idahohistory.net
www.thingsthatgoboo.com

Illinois

www.illinoishauntings.com

Indiana

www.indianaparanormal.com
www.indianaspi.com
www.hauntedindiana..com

Iowa

www.diepart.com
www.carrollareaparanormalteam.com
www.chronicletimes.com

Kansas

www.kansascityparanormalinvestigations.com
www.darkkansas.com
www.coffeyville.edu
www.kansastravel.org

Kentucky

www.nkyparanormalgroup.com
www.louisvilleghs.com
www.bbonline.com
www.myoldkentuckyghost.com
www.innsite.com

Louisiana

www.laspirits.com
www.hauntla.com
www.hauntedneworleanstours.com

Maine

http://southernmaineparanormalsociety.com
www.hauntspot.com
www.maineparanormal.org
www.mainetoday.com

Maryland

www.phprs.org
www.baltimoresun.com
www.iamhaunted.com
www.thecabinet.com
www.chesapeakelifemag.com
www.fredericknewspost.com

Massachusetts

www.masscrossroads.com
www.praofb.org
www.berkshireparanormal.com
www.worcesterparanormal.com

Michigan

www.michigansotherside.com
www.miparahaunt.com
www.sempsi.com
http://ghostwatchers.org/
www.paranormalmichigan.com
www.michiganparanormalencounters.com
www.connectmidmichigan.com
www.michigan.org
www.articlesbase.com

Minnesota

www.minnesotaghosts.com
www.kstp.com
www.unexplainedresearch.com

Mississippi

www.theellisvillemississippiparanormalsociety
   .com
www.mississippi-spi.com
www.meridianstar.com
www.mississippiheritage.com
www.columbus-ms.info

Missouri

www.millersparanormalresearch.com
www.missourighosts.net
www.missouriparanormal.com
www.spookstalker.com
www.paranormaltaskforce.com
www.mo-river.net
www.visitkc.com
www.mostateparks.com
www.bistateparanormal.com

Montana

www.tsimt.net
www.montanaparanormal.com
www.mtprs.org
www.distinctlymontana.com
www.unexplainable.net

Nebraska

www.doyouseedeadpeople.org
www.nebraskahistory.org
www.dreadcentral.com

Nevada

www.hauntednevada.com
www.visitrenotahoe.com
www.visitvirginiacitynv.com

New Hampshire

www.newhampshire.com
www.visit-newhampshire.com
www.nhghosts.com
www.ghostquest.org

New Jersey

www.sjpr.org
www.nnjpr.org
www.southjerseyghostresearch.org
www.atlanticcityweddings.com
www.paranormalvisions.com

New Mexico

www.sgha.net
www.lostdestinations.com

New York

www.lispr.com
www.isisinvestigations.com
www.capitalnews9.com
www.deadframe.com
www.ghostmag.com
www.roadsidehorrors.com
www.gothicghoststories.com
www.ghostofcooperstown.com
www.spectralreview.com
www.epicparanormal.com
www.paranormal-nyc.com
www.wnyparanormal.org
www.liparanormalinvestigators.com

North Carolina

www.hauntednc.com
www.easternparanormal.com
www.ashevilleparanormalsociety.com
www.ncparanormal.com
www.myreporter.com

North Dakota

www.unearthlyrealms.com

Ohio

www.deadohio.com
www.forgottenoh.com
www.ohorgparanormalstudies.com
www.graveaddiction.com
www.hauntedhocking.com
www.spookymarion.com

Oklahoma

www.ghouli.org
www.okpri.com
www.centraloklahomaparanormalstudies.com
www.soonerparanormalofok.com
www.pittok.com
www.eerieok.com
www.ghostgadgets.com

Oregon

www.nwpprs.com

Pennsylvania

www.delcoghosts.com
www.sepps.org
www.neppi.info
www.groupspectre.com
www.ghosttheory.com
www.peergb.com
www.horror-hill.net
www.nepaparanormal.com
www.nbcphiladelphia.com

Rhode Island

www.the-atlantic-paranormal-society.com
www.riparks.com

South Carolina

www.scprai.org

South Dakota

www.sdgfp.com
www.midlandsd.com
www.rapidcityjournal.com

Tennessee

www.paranormalincorporated.com
www.tnghosthunters.com
www.clarksvilleghosthunters.com
www.johnnorrisbrown.com
www.appalachianghostwalks.com
www.hauntmastersclub.com

Texas

www.lonestarspirits.org
www.texashauntsociety.com
www.yourghoststories.com
www.texasghosthunters.com
www.everydayparanormal.com
www.austinparanormal.com
www.spiritquestsghostquest.com

Utah

www.utahghost.org
www.uropa.org

Vermont

www.vtliving.com
www.oddinns.com
www.vermonter.com
www.vermontbridges.com

Virginia

www.vampinvestigations.com
www.ghostec.us
www.virginia.org
www.valleyghosthunters.com
www.virginiabeachhistory.org

Washington

www.washingtonstateghostsociety.com
www.swpr.org
www.paranormalunderground.net
www.evergreenparanormal.com

West Virginia

www.hauntedparkersburg.com
www.westvirginiaghosthunters.com
www.huntingtonparanormal.com
www.wvghosts.com

Wisconsin

www.paranormalresearchgroup.com
www.ghosteyes.com

Wyoming

http://wyparanormalinvestigators.com
www.wyomingtourism.org

U.S./National Sites

www.prairieghosts.com
www.hauntedhouses.com
www.hauntedtraveler.com
www.ghosttraveller.com
www.carpenoctem.tv
www.shadowlands.com
www.ghostvillage.com
www.hollowhill.com
www.lostdestinations.com
www.ghostinmysuitcase.com
www.haunted-places.com
www.hauntspot.com
www.paranormalknowledge.com
www.legendsofamerica.com
www.hauntedtravels.com
www.ghostsandcritters.com
www.paranormalunderground.com
www.associatedcontent.com
www.allstays.com
www.usatoday.com
www.examiner.com
www.strangeusa.com
www.waymarking.com

PHOTO CREDITS

Alabama

Fort Gaines. Public domain photo by Altairisfar. Courtesy of Wikimedia Commons.

King House, Montevallo University. Public domain photo by Alarob. Courtesy of Wikimedia Commons.

Sloss Furnaces. Photo by Timjarrett. Courtesy of Wikimedia Commons. Licensed under the Creative Commons Attribution ShareAlike 3.0 License.

USS Alabama. Photo by Ben Jacobson. Courtesy of Wikimedia Commons. Licensed under the GNU Free Documentation License.

Alaska

The Alaskan Hotel. Public domain photo courtesy of the Alaskan Hotel.

Golden North Hotel. Public domain photo from the United States government. Courtesy of Wikimedia Commons.

Kennecott Mines. Photo by Sewtex. Courtesy of Wikimedia Commons. Licensed under the GNU Free Documentation License.

Red Onion Saloon. Photo by Meredith Peruzzi. Courtesy of Wikimedia Commons. Licensed under the GNU Free Documentation License.

Arizona

Birdcage Theatre. Public domain photo from the United States government.

El Tovar Hotel. Public domain photo from the United States government.

Hotel San Carlos. Photo courtesy of Georgene Coffman. Used with permission.

Red Garter B&B Inn. Photo courtesy of the Red Garter and the Longino Mora Family. Used with permission.

Arkansas

The 1886 Crescent Hotel and Spa. Photo by Rich Newman.

Elkhorn Tavern, Circa 1880. Public domain photo from the United States government.

Magnolia Hill Bed and Breakfast. Photo by Rich Newman.

California

Alcatraz. Public domain photo by Edward Z. Yang. Courtesy of Wikimedia Commons.

Black Diamond Mines. Photo by Sanfranman59. Courtesy of Wikimedia Commons. Licensed under the GNU Free Documentation License.

Murphy's Hotel, Circa 1860s. Public domain photo from the United States government. Courtesy of Wikimedia Commons.

The Presidio. Public domain photo by Jon Sullivan. Courtesy of Wikimedia Commons.

Queen Mary. Photo by Sfoskett. Courtesy of Wikimedia Commons. Licensed under the GNU Free Documentation License.

The Stagecoach Inn Museum. Photo by Los Angeles. Courtesy of Wikimedia Commons. Licensed under the GNU Free Documentation License.

Possible Spirit on the USS Hornet. Photo by Heidi C. Schave. Used with permission.

Colorado

Beaumont Hotel & Spa. Public domain photo from the Denver Public Library. Courtesy of Wikimedia Commons.

Hotel Jerome. Photo courtesy of the Hotel Jerome. Used with permission.

Historic Spruce Lodge. Photo by Dee Plucinski. Used with permission.

Connecticut

Statue at Fort Nathan Hale. Public domain photo by 2112guy. Courtesy of Wikimedia Commons.

New London Ledge Lighthouse. Public domain photo. Courtesy of Wikimedia Commons.

Noah Webster House. Public domain photo by Robert Fulton III. Courtesy of Wikimedia Commons.

Old State House. Public domain photo from the United States government. Courtesy of Wikimedia Commons.

Delaware

The Deer Park Tavern. Public domain photo. Courtesy of Wikimedia Commons.

Fort Delaware. Photo by Worldislandinfo. Courtesy of Wikimedia Commons. Licensed under the Creative Commons Attribution 2.0 License.

District of Columbia

Decatur House on Lafayette Square. Public domain photo by John O. Brostrup. Courtesy of Wikimedia Commons.

Possible Ghost at Ford's Theatre. Public domain photo by Matthew Brady. Courtesy of Wikimedia Commons.

The White House. Public domain photo courtesy of the Library of Congress and Wikimedia Commons.

Florida

Cuban Club. Photo by Ebyabe. Courtesy of Wikimedia Commons. Licensed under the GNU Free Documentation License.

Herlong Mansion Bed and Breakfast. Photo by Ebyabe. Courtesy of Wikimedia Commons. Licensed under the GNU Free Documentation License.

Seven Sisters Inn. Photo by Ebyabe. Courtesy of Wikimedia Commons. Licensed under the GNU Free Documentation License.

St. Francis Inn. Photo by Ebyabe. Courtesy of Wikimedia Commons. Licensed under the GNU Free Documentation License.

Stranahan House. Public domain photo courtesy of the Florida Memory Project and Wikimedia Commons.

Georgia

Forsyth Park. Photo by Daniel Mayer. Courtesy of Wikimedia Commons. Licensed under the GNU Free Documentation License.

Georgia Aquarium. Photo courtesy of the Georgia Aquarium. Used with permission.

Holliday Dorsey Fife House Museum. Photo courtesy of the Holliday-Dorsey-Fife House Museum. Used with permission.

Kennesaw Mountain, Circa 1864. Public domain photo from the United States government. Courtesy of Wikimedia Commons.

Windsor Hotel. Public domain photo by Eoghanacht. Courtesy of Wikimedia Commons.

Hawaii

Hulihe'e Palace. Public domain photo by Calbear22. Courtesy of Wikimedia Commons.

Iolani Palace. Public domain photo by Jiang. Courtesy of Wikimedia Commons.

Idaho

Craters of the Moon National Monument. Public domain photo from the United States government. Courtesy of Wikimedia Commons.

Egyptian Theatre. Public domain photo from the United States government. Courtesy of Wikimedia Commons.

Illinois

Cave In Rock State Park. Photo by Rich Newman.

Historic Hotel Baker. Photo by G. LeTourneau. Courtesy of Wikimedia Commons. Licensed under the GNU Free Documentation License.

Original Springs Mineral Spa & Hotel. Photo by Rich Newman.

Reubel Hotel. Photo by Rich Newman.

Indiana

Hannah House. Photo courtesy of Eerie Radio. Used with permission.

Ivy House Bed & Breakfast. Photo courtesy of the Ivy House. Used with permission.

Slippery Noodle Inn. Photo by Hal Yeagy. Used with permission.

Willard Library. Photo courtesy of the Willard Library. Used with permission.

Iowa

The Grand Opera House. Photo by Mike Willis.

Historic Dodge House. Public domain photo by Kathy Kahue. Courtesy of Wikimedia Commons.

Mason House Inn & Caboose Cottage. Photo by Joy Hanson. Used with permission.

Pottawattamie County Jail. Public domain photo from the United States government. Courtesy of Wikimedia Commons.

Kansas

Eldridge Hotel. Public domain photo by Quasselkasper. Courtesy of Wikimedia Commons.

Fort Scott National Historic Site. Photo by Nationalparks. Courtesy of Wikimedia Commons. Licensed under the Creative Commons Attribute ShareAlike 2.5 License.

Hollenberg Pony Express Station. Public domain photo from the United States government. Courtesy of Wikimedia Commons.

Kentucky

Bobby Mackey's Music World. Photo by R. J. Seifert. Used with permission.

Gratz Park Inn. Courtesy of the Gratz Park Inn. Used with permission.

Liberty Hall Historic Site. Public domain photo by William Gus Johnson. Courtesy of Wikimedia Commons.

The Octagon Hall Museum. Photo by Rich Newman.

The Old Talbott Tavern. Photo by Rich Newman.

Louisiana

Canal Street Postcard/Hotel Monteleone. Public domain photo courtesy of Wikimedia Commons.

Destrehan Plantation. Photo by Michael Overton. Courtesy of Wikimedia Commons. Licensed under the Creative Commons Attribute ShareAlike 2.5 License.

Oak Alley Plantation. Photo by Zeb Mayhew. Used with permission.

Old Louisiana State Capitol. Public domain photo from the United Sates government. Courtesy of Wikimedia Commons.

Maine

The Berry Manor Inn. Photo courtesy of the Berry Manor Inn. Used with permission.

The Greenville Inn. Photo by Terry Johannemann. Used with permission.

Limerock Inn. Photo by P. J. Walter. Used with permission.

Maryland

The Admiral Fell Inn. Photo courtesy of the Admiral Fell Inn. Used with permission.

Beall Dawson House. Photo by Aude. Courtesy of Wikimedia Commons. Licensed under the Creative Commons Attribute ShareAlike 2.5 License.

The Hager House. Photo by Acroterion. Courtesy of Wikimedia Commons. Licensed under the GNU Free Documentation License.

Schifferstadt Architectural Museum. Photo by Acroterion. Courtesy of Wikimedia Commons. Licensed under the GNU Free Documentation License.

USS Constellation. Courtesy of Historic Ships in Baltimore. Used with permission.

Massachusetts

The Colonial House Inn. Photo by Malcolm J. Perna. Used with permission.

Lizzie Borden. Public domain photo. Courtesy of Wikimedia Commons.

The Mount Estate & Gardens. Photo by Midnightdreary. Courtesy of Wikimedia Commons. Licensed under the GNU Free Documentation License.

Nathaniel Hawthorne. Public domain photo by Daderot. Courtesy of Wikimedia Commons.

Longfellow's Wayside Inn. Photo by Dudesleeper. Courtesy of Wikimedia Commons. Licensed under the GNU Free Documentation License.

Michigan

Bowers Harbor Inn's Genevive Stickney. Photo courtesy of Steve Thrall. Used with permission.

The Historic Holly Hotel. Photo by Chrissy Haas Kutlenios. Used with permission.

Michigan Firehouse Museum. Photo by Chris Christner. Courtesy of Wikimedia Commons. Licensed under the Creative Commons Attribute ShareAlike 2.0 License.

Doubletree Guest Suites Fort Shelby. Photo by Mike Russell. Courtesy of Wikimedia Commons. Licensed under the GNU Free Documentation License.

The Landmark Inn. Photo by Daniele Carol. Used with permission.

Old Presque Isle Lighthouse. Public domain photo from the United States government. Courtesy of Wikimedia Commons.

Minnesota

Minneapolis Municipal Building Commission. Public domain photo from the United States government. Courtesy of Wikimedia Commons.

Palmer House Hotel, Restaurant and Pub. Photo by Martin Bydalek. Used with permission.

Wardens House Museum. Photo by Kirsta Benson. Used with permission.

Mississippi

Anchuca Historic Mansion and Inn. Public domain photo by James Butters. Courtesy of Wikimedia Commons.

Linden Bed and Breakfast. Photo courtesy of NatchezMS.com. Used with permission.

Old State Capitol Building. Public domain photo by Lester Jones. Courtesy of Wikimedia Commons.

Missouri

Historic Photo of Nurses at Glore Psychiatric. Photo courtesy of the Glore Psychiatric Museum. Used with permission.

1859 Jail, Marshal's House & Museum. Public domain photo by Ecjmartin1. Courtesy of Wikimedia Commons.

The Lehmann House Bed & Breakfast. Photo by Rich Newman.

The Lemp Mansion Restaurant & Inn. Photo by Rich Newman.

The Parlor Bed and Breakfast. Photo by Rich Newman.

Possible Ghost Photo Taken at Prosperity Bed & Breakfast. Photo by Brandi Beam. Used with permission.

Pythian Castle. Photo by Tamara Finocchiaro. Used with permission.

Montana

Chico Hot Springs Resort & Day Spa. Photo courtesy of Chico Hot Springs. Used with permission.

Custer and Wife. Public domain photo by Mathew Brady. Courtesy of Wikimedia Commons.

Ghost Rails Inn. Photo by Thom Garrett. Used with permission.

Old Montana Prison Museum. Photo courtesy of the Old Montana Prison. Used with permission.

Nebraska

Fort Sidney Museum. Photo by Rich Newman.

Nebraska State Capitol Building. Photo by Mawhamba. Courtesy of Wikimedia Commons. Licensed under the Creative Commons Attribute ShareAlike 2.0 License.

Nevada

Boulder Dam Hotel. Photo by Sarah Nichols. Courtesy of Wikimedia Commons. Licensed under the Creative Commons Attribute ShareAlike 2.0 License.

Piper's Opera House. Public domain photo from the United States government. Courtesy of Wikimedia Commons.

Silver Queen Hotel. Public domain photo by Epukas. Courtesy of Wikimedia Commons.

Thunderbird Lodge Historical Site. Photo by Vance Fox. Used with permission.

New Hampshire

The 1875 Inn at Tilton. Public domain photo by SayCheeeeeese. Courtesy of Wikimedia Commons.

Eagle Mountain House. Courtesy of the Eagle Mountain House. Used with permission.

Mount Washington Resort. Photo by John Sinal. Used with permission.

Portsmouth Harbor Lighthouse. Photo by Jeremy D'Entremont. Used with permission.

New Jersey

Burlington County Prison Museum. Public domain photo by Nathaniel R. Ewan. Courtesy of Wikimedia Commons.

The Proprietary House. Public domain photo from the United States government. Courtesy of Wikimedia Commons.

The Red Mill Museum. Photo by Ddogas. Courtesy of Wikimedia Commons. Licensed under the GNU Free Documentation License.

Van Winkle House. Photo by Richard Arthur Norton. Courtesy of Wikimedia Commons. Licensed under the Creative Commons Attribute ShareAlike 2.5 License.

New Mexico

Church Street Café. Courtesy of Marie Coleman. Used with permission.

El Rancho Hotel. Photo by Richie Diesterheft. Courtesy of Wikimedia Commons. Licensed under the Creative Commons Attribute ShareAlike 2.0 License.

The Lodge Resort and Spa. Photo courtesy of the Lodge Resort & Spa. Used with permission.

The Mine Shaft Tavern. Photo by Melinda Bon'ewell. Used with permission.

Historic Plaza Hotel. Photo courtesy of the Plaza Hotel. Used with permission.

New York

Belhurst Castle. Public domain photo by Rochester, NY. Courtesy of Wikimedia Commons.

Buffalo Central Terminal. Photo by Paranormal Skeptic. Courtesy of Wikimedia Commons. Licensed under the GNU Free Documentation License.

Fire Island Lighthouse. Public domain photo from the United States government. Courtesy of Wikimedia Commons.

Garibaldi Meucci Museum. Photo by Rolfmueller. Courtesy of Wikimedia Commons. Licensed under the GNU Free Documentation License.

The Iron Island Museum. Photo by Linda J. Hastreiter. Used with permission.

Merchant's House Museum. Photo by Madeleine Doering. Used with permission.

Mohonk Mountain House. Photo by Mwanner. Courtesy of Wikimedia Commons. Licensed under the GNU Free Documentation License.

North Carolina

Fort Fisher. Public domain photo from the United States government. Courtesy of Wikimedia Commons.

Fort Raleigh National Historic Site. Public domain photo from the United States government. Courtesy of Wikimedia Commons.

Historic Latta Plantation. Courtesy of the Historic Latta Plantation. Used with permission.

Battleship North Carolina. Public domain photo from the United States government. Courtesy of Wikimedia Commons.

North Dakota

Custer House, Ft. Abraham Lincoln. Photo by MatthewUND. Courtesy of Wikimedia Commons. Licensed under the GNU Free Documentation License.

Ohio

Bear's Mill, Charlie Andrews and Duke. Courtesy of Bear's Mill. Used with permission.

Fairport Harbor Lighthouse. Photo by Laszlo Ilyes. Courtesy of Wikimedia Commons. Licensed under the Creative Commons Attribute ShareAlike 2.0 License.

The Historic Loveland Castle. Public domain photo by ConlonTT. Courtesy of Wikimedia Commons.

The Red Brick Tavern. Public domain photo from the United States government. Courtesy of Wikimedia Commons.

Snow Hill Country Club. Courtesy of Snow Hill Country Club. Used with permission.

Squire's Castle. Photo by Yu-Hong Yen. Courtesy of Wikimedia Commons. Licensed under the Creative Commons Attribute ShareAlike 2.0 License.

Thurber House. Courtesy of the Thurber House. Used with permission.

Oklahoma

Cain's Ballroom. Photo by MNajdan. Courtesy of Wikimedia Commons. Licensed under the GNU Free Documentation License.

Fort Gibson. Public domain photo by Fred Q. Casler. Courtesy of Wikimedia Commons.

Oregon

Geiser Grand Hotel. Photo by Cacophony. Courtesy of Wikimedia Commons. Licensed under the GNU Free Documentation License.

The Grand Lodge. Photo by Liz Devine of McMenamins. Used with permission.

Heceta Head Lighthouse. Public domain photo by HISE Studios. Courtesy of Wikimedia Commons.

Mission Mill Museum. Public domain photo by Aboutmovies. Courtesy of Wikimedia Commons.

Pennsylvania

Betsy Ross House. Public domain photo courtesy of Wikimedia Commons.

Fort Mifflin. Photo by Joe Minardi. Courtesy of Wikimedia Commons. Licensed under the GNU Free Documentation License.

Gettysburg Battlefield. Public domain photo from the United States government. Courtesy of Wikimedia Commons.

Independence Hall. Photo by Dan Smith. Courtesy of Wikimedia Commons. Licensed under the Creative Commons Attribute ShareAlike 2.0 License.

Jean Bonnet Tavern. Courtesy of the Jean Bonnet Tavern. Used with permission.

The Old Jail Museum. Photo courtesy of Betty Lou McBride. Used with permission.

The Railroad House Inn. Photo by Ross Kribbs. Used with permission.

Railroaders Memorial Museum. Courtesy of the Railroaders Memorial Museum. Used with permission.

Rhode Island

Hotel Viking. Photo by Sammy Dyess, Courtesy of the Hotel Viking. Used with permission.

Slater Mill. Public domain photo by Marcbela. Courtesy of Wikimedia Commons.

The White Horse Tavern. Photo by Swampyank. Courtesy of Wikimedia Commons. Licensed under the Creative Commons Attribute ShareAlike 2.0 License.

South Carolina

The Abbeville Opera House. Public domain photo by K. Armstrong. Courtesy of Wikimedia Commons.

Fort Sumter. Public domain photo courtesy of Wikimedia Commons.

South Dakota

Bullock Hotel. Photo by Puroticorico. Courtesy of Wikimedia Commons. Licensed under the Creative Commons Attribute ShareAlike 2.0 License.

Hotel Alex Johnson. Photo by Ono-sendai. Courtesy of Wikimedia Commons. Licensed under the Creative Commons Attribute ShareAlike 2.0 License.

Tennessee

Carter House. Photo by Rich Newman.

Magnolia Manor Bed & Breakfast. Photo by Rich Newman.

Shiloh National Military Park. Photo by Rich Newman.

Tennessee State Capitol Building. Public domain photo by Kaldari. Courtesy of Wikimedia Commons.

Walking Horse Hotel. Photo by Rich Newman.

Woodruff Fontaine House Museum. Photo by Rich Newman.

Texas

Camino Real. Courtesy of the Camino Real Hotel. Used with permission.

The Grove. Photo courtesy of Mitchel Whitington. Used with permission.

Hotel Galvez, Circa 1911. Public domain Photo by H. H. Morris. Courtesy of Wikimedia Commons.

Mission San Jose. Photo by Zereshk. Courtesy of Wikimedia Commons. Licensed under the GNU Free Documentation License.

Presidio La Bahia. Public domain photo from the United States government. Courtesy of Wikimedia Commons.

The Tarpon Inn. Photo by Larry D. Moore. Courtesy of Wikimedia Commons. Licensed under the GNU Free Documentation License.

The Texas White House Bed and Breakfast. Photo by Jennie Crust. Used with permission.

USS Lexington. Photo by Cliff. Courtesy of Wikimedia Commons. Licensed under the Creative Commons Attribute ShareAlike 2.0 License.

Utah

Golden Spike Historic Site, Circa 1869.
Public domain photo by Andrew J. Russell.
Courtesy of Wikimedia Commons.

Moore's Old Pine Inn. Courtesy of the Old
Pine Inn. Used with permission.

Vermont

Enosburg Falls Opera House. Photo by
Suzanne Hull-Parent. Used with permission.

The Equinox Resort. Courtesy of the Equinox
Resort. Used with permission.

Virginia

Avenel. Photo by Sue Sereno. Used with
permission.

Barter Theatre. Courtesy of Barter Theatre.
Used with permission.

The Glencoe Inn. Photo by Andrea McGlynn.
Used with permission.

Monticello. Public domain photo from the
United States government. Courtesy of
Wikimedia Commons.

Oatlands Historic House and Gardens. Photo
by Acroterion. Courtesy of Wikimedia
Commons. Licensed under the GNU Free
Documentation License.

The Museum of the Confederacy, Circa 1865.
Public domain photo by Mathew Brady.
Courtesy of Wikimedia Commons.

Washington

Fort Vancouver National Historic Site. Photo
by Glenn Scofield Williams. Courtesy of
Wikimedia Commons. Licensed under the
Creative Commons Attribute ShareAlike 2.0
License.

The Governor's Mansion. Photo by Tradnor.
Courtesy of Wikimedia Commons. Licensed
under the GNU Free Documentation
License.

Hotel Andra. Photo by Joe Mabel. Courtesy of
Wikimedia Commons. Licensed under the
GNU Free Documentation License.

Rosario Resort. Photo by Joe Mabel. Courtesy
of Wikimedia Commons. Licensed under
the GNU Free Documentation License.

West Virginia

State Capitol Building. Photo courtesy of
Wikimedia Commons. Licensed under the
GNU Free Documentation License.

The Greenbrier Hotel. Photo by Bobak Ha'Eri.
Courtesy of Wikimedia Commons. Licensed
under the GNU Free Documentation
License.

Harpers Ferry, Circa 1865. Public domain
photo from the United States government.
Courtesy of Wikimedia Commons.

West Virginia Penitentiary. Photo by Tim Kiser.
Courtesy of Wikimedia Commons. Licensed
under the Creative Commons Attribute
ShareAlike 2.0 License.

Wisconsin

The Brumder Mansion. Photo by Tom Carr.
Used with permission.

Fairlawn Mansion. Photo by Bobak Ha'Eri.
Courtesy of Wikimedia Commons. Licensed
under the GNU Free Documentation
License.

Hearthstone Historic House Museum. Photo
by the Hearthstone House. Courtesy of
Wikimedia Commons.

The Stones Throw. Photo by Todd Pernsteiner.
Used with permission. Licensed under the
Creative Commons Attribute ShareAlike 2.0
License.

Wyoming

Atlus Theatre. Public domain photo by Jack
Boucher. Courtesy of Wikimedia Commons.

Buffalo Bill's Irma Hotel. Photo by
Acroterion. Licensed under the GNU Free
Documentation License.

The Sheridan Inn. Public domain photo from
the United States government. Courtesy of
Wikimedia Commons.

INDEX

THE SALLIE HOUSE HAUNTING
A True Story
DEBRA PICKMAN

Who knew that our experience would push us over the edge of disbelief and through the door of certain terror?

Debra Pickman had always wanted a ghost of her own. She never expected her wish to come horrifically true when she, her husband, and their newborn son moved into a century-old home in Atchison, Kansas, that—to their shock—is also occupied by a fire-starting spirit child named Sallie … and darker, aggressive forces.

Gradually, Debra becomes attached to Sallie and adjusts to her ghostly mischief—toys turning on by themselves, knick-knacks moving, and electrical disruptions. But serious problems arise when she can't control Sallie's habit of lighting fires. What's worse, her husband Tony becomes the victim of scratches, bites, and terrifying ghostly attacks that are clearly the work of other menacing entities. Discover how the ongoing terror takes its toll on their nerves, sanity, and marriage, and what finally forces the Pickmans to flee the infamous Sallie House.

978-0-7387-2128-6
288 pp., 6 x 9 $16.95

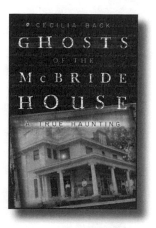

GHOSTS OF THE McBRIDE HOUSE
A True Haunting
CECILIA BACK

It took Cecilia Back only a few weeks to confirm that her new home—a Victorian mansion just across the street from a historic military fort—was haunted. But instead of fleeing, the Back family stayed put and gradually got to know their "spirited" residents over the next twenty-five years.

Meet Dr. McBride, the original owner who loves scaring away construction crews and the author's ghost-phobic mother. Try to catch sight of the two spirit children who play with Back's son and daughter and loud, electronic toys in the middle of the night. Each ghost has a personality of its own, including one transient entity whose antics are downright terrifying.

Despite mischievous pranks, such as raucous ghost parties at two a.m., the Back family have come to accept—and occasionally welcome—these unique encounters with the dead.

978-0-7387-1505-6
216 pp., 5³⁄₁₆ x 8 $14.95

True Ghosts 2
More Haunting Tales from the Vaults of FATE Magazine
Edited by David Godwin

A young man falls victim to faeries. A newborn baby brings "friends" from the Other Side. A beloved Siamese cat miraculously returns to her owner after death.

Since 1948, *FATE* magazine has documented the strange, otherworldly, and truly bizarre. This new thrilling collection of true stories—visits from family spirits, bouts with poltergeists, encounters with life-saving angels—offers another compelling glimpse into the paranormal. From terrifying haunted houses to loving spirit animals to shocking out-of-body experiences, these eyewitness accounts will provoke chills, tears, and laughter—and bring poignancy to the vast wonders that fill our lives.

978-0-7387-2294-8
288 pp., 5³⁄₁₆ x 8 $15.95